Windows Vista™
ALL-IN-ONE DESK REFERENCE
FOR
DUMMIES®

by Woody Leonhard

Wiley Publishing, Inc.

Windows Vista™ All-in-One Desk Reference For Dummies®

Published by
Wiley Publishing, Inc.
111 River Street
Hoboken, NJ 07030-5774
www.wiley.com

Copyright © 2007 by Wiley Publishing, Inc., Indianapolis, Indiana

Published by Wiley Publishing, Inc., Indianapolis, Indiana

Published simultaneously in Canada

For general information on our other products and services, please contact our Customer Care Department within the U.S. at 800-762-2974, outside the U.S. at 317-572-3993, or fax 317-572-4002.

For technical support, please visit www.wiley.com/techsupport.

Wiley also publishes its books in a variety of electronic formats. Some content that appears in print may not be available in electronic books.

Library of Congress Control Number: 2006934840

ISBN-13: 978-0-471-74941-7

ISBN-10: 0-471-74941-9

Manufactured in the United States of America

10 9 8 7 6 5

1O/RV/QX/QY/IN

WILEY

About the Author

Curmudgeon, critic, and self-described "Windows Victim," **Woody Leonhard** runs www.AskWoody.com, the Web's single best source of up-to-the-nanosecond news about Windows and Office — warts and all. Check it out for answers to your most pressing questions, no-bull analysis of Microsoft's latest gaffes, and all sorts of information that you can't find anywhere else.

With several dozen computer books under his belt, Woody knows where the bodies are buried. He was one of the first Microsoft Consulting Partners and a charter member of the Microsoft Solutions Provider organization. He's a one-man, major Microsoft beta testing site and delights in being a constant thorn in Microsoft's side. Along with several coauthors and editors, he's won an unprecedented six Computer Press Association Awards and two American Business Press Awards.

Woody; his long-time girlfriend, Duangkhae Tongthueng (better known as "Add"); and twelve talented Thai staff run Khun Woody's Bakery and its sister operation, the Sandwich Shoppe, in Patong, Phuket, Thailand. Woody moved to Phuket in late 2000, where he now lives with Add; his father, George; his teenage son, Justin; and their all-American beagle, Chronos.

Most mornings you can see him jogging on Patong Beach with the dogs and then downing a latte and New Yawk bagel-n-Philly at the Shoppe. Feel free to drop by and say, "Sawadee krap!" Microsoft hit squads, please take a number and form a queue at the rear of the building.

Dedication

To Dad, who's always been there for me.

And to Add, who's helped me in more ways than I ever thought possible.

Author's Acknowledgments

Many thanks to Becky Huehls, who's slaving away at this very moment trying to get this tome whipped into shape. Best of luck with your latest, uh, endeavor, Becky! To the entire editorial crew at Wiley, the ones who righted my wrongs and slapped my scratchings into something legible, and especially to Melody Layne, head editorial honcho on this project. To the folks at Snagit who kept their screen grab utility working all the way through the Vista beta versions. (Whew!) And particular thanks, as always, to Claudette Moore and Ann Jaroncyk at Moore Literary Agency.

Publisher's Acknowledgments

We're proud of this book; please send us your comments through our online registration form located at www.dummies.com/register/.

Some of the people who helped bring this book to market include the following:

Acquisitions, Editorial, and Media Development

Project Editor: Rebecca Huehls

Senior Acquisitions Editor: Melody Layne

Copy Editor: John Edwards

Technical Editor: Lee Musick

Editorial Manager: Leah P. Cameron

Media Development Manager:
Laura VanWinkle

Editorial Assistant: Amanda Foxworth

Sr. Editorial Assistant: Cherie Case

Cartoons: Rich Tennant
(www.the5thwave.com)

Composition Services

Project Coordinator: Erin Smith

Layout and Graphics: Claudia Bell, Jonelle Burns, Denny Hager, Stephanie D. Jumper Barbara Moore, Barry Offrings, Heather Ryan

Proofreaders: Laura Albert, John Greenough, Christine Pingleton, Christine Sabooni

Indexer: Techbooks

Anniversary Logo Design: Richard Pacifico

Special Help Mary Lagu, Rebecca Senninger

Publishing and Editorial for Technology Dummies

 Richard Swadley, Vice President and Executive Group Publisher

 Andy Cummings, Vice President and Publisher

 Mary Bednarek, Executive Acquisitions Director

 Mary C. Corder, Editorial Director

Publishing for Consumer Dummies

 Diane Graves Steele, Vice President and Publisher

 Joyce Pepple, Acquisitions Director

Composition Services

 Gerry Fahey, Vice President of Production Services

 Debbie Stailey, Director of Composition Services

Contents at a Glance

Introduction *1*

Book 1: A Vista Orientation *9*

Chapter 1: Windows 4 N00bs 11
Chapter 2: Vista versus the WinXPerienced 27
Chapter 3: Choosing a Version 35
Chapter 4: Upgrades and Clean Installs 43

Book 11: Vista Boot Camp *59*

Chapter 1: Running Vista from Start to Finish 61
Chapter 2: Controlling Users 97
Chapter 3: Maintaining Your System 113
Chapter 4: Getting the Basic Stuff Done 147
Chapter 5: Getting Help with Vista 171

Book 111: Securing Vista *187*

Chapter 1: Lock Down: Spies, Spams, Scams, and Slams 189
Chapter 2: Security Center Overview 217
Chapter 3: Windows Firewall Backward and Forward 225
Chapter 4: Patching and Plugging 249
Chapter 5: Virus Protection and the Big Defender 263

Book 1V: Customizing Vista *281*

Chapter 1: Personalizing Your Desktop 283
Chapter 2: Organizing Your Vista Interface 303
Chapter 3: Searching on Your Desktop 321
Chapter 4: Beating and Cheating Vista's Games 333

Book V: Vista on the Internet *345*

Chapter 1: Getting the Most from the Internet 347
Chapter 2: Finding Your Way around Internet Explorer (And Firefox) ...363
Chapter 3: Making Internet Explorer Your Own 387
Chapter 4: Windows Mail and the Alternatives 399
Chapter 5: Working Together — IM OK, You're OK 413
Chapter 6: Searching on the Internet 425

Book VI: Adding Cool Hardware 437

Chapter 1: Finding and Installing the Hardware You Want 439

Chapter 2: iPimping iPods and iTunes.. 465

Chapter 3: Adding a Second (Or Third) Hard Drive................................ 485

Chapter 4: Picking Printers and Printer/Scanner/Faxers 493

Book VII: Joining the Multimedia Mix 511

Chapter 1: Jammin' with Windows Media Player 513

Chapter 2: Podcasting.. 553

Chapter 3: Discovering Digital Cameras 563

Chapter 4: Mugging in the Photo Gallery 581

Chapter 5: Lights! Action! Windows Movie Maker 595

Book VIII: Vista Video 617

Chapter 1: Preparing a Media Center PC 619

Chapter 2: Starting Media Center 631

Chapter 3: Turning On the Tube... 641

Chapter 4: Beyond the Media Center Basics 651

Book IX: Setting Up a Vista Network 667

Chapter 1: Those Pesky Network Things You Need to Know 669

Chapter 2: Building Your Network... 683

Chapter 3: Putting the Why in Wi-Fi 705

Index 721

Table of Contents

Introduction *1*

About This Book 2
Conventions 3
What You Don't Have to Read 3
Foolish Assumptions 4
Organization 4
Icons 6
Where to Go from Here 7

Book 1: A Vista Orientation *9*

Chapter 1: Windows 4 N00bs **11**

Hardware and Software 12
Why Do PCs Have to Run Windows? 14
Buying a Computer 14
 Inside the big box 15
 Screening 17
 Managing disks and drives 18
 Making PC connections 20
 Futzing with sound 22
A Terminology Survival Kit 23

Chapter 2: Vista versus the WinXPerienced **27**

What You See 27
 The Glass UX 27
 Improved video effects 27
 Sidebar: A truly active desktop 29
What You Get 30
What Stands in the Way 31
Do You Need Windows Vista? 32

Chapter 3: Choosing a Version **35**

The Eightfold Path 35
Versions to Ignore 37
The Final Four 38
 Home Basic: Thumbs down 39
 Business Edition: Maybe 39

Home Premium: Usually the sweet spot............................41
The Ultimate...41
Windows Live OneCare 41

Chapter 4: Upgrades and Clean Installs 43

Can Your Computer Handle Vista?..43
Performing a Clean Install...45
Working through the Welcome Center 48
Using Easy Transfer 51
What will transfer 52
Making the transfer 52
Product Activation 54
What If the Wheels Fall Off? 58

Book II: Vista Boot Camp 59

Chapter 1: Running Vista from Start to Finish 61

A Few Quick Steps to Make the Desktop Your Own................61
Disabling the Welcome Center..63
Changing the background 64
Enabling the Sidebar 65
Cleaning up useless icons and programs 65
Making the taskbar taller...66
Mousing with Your Mouse 66
Working with Files and Folders 67
Showing filename extensions 69
Sharing folders 71
Recycling 79
Starting with the Start Button 81
Getting Around 84
Using Windows Explorer 84
Working with the Windows taskbar 90
Creating shortcuts...92
Sleep: Perchance to Dream 94

Chapter 2: Controlling Users 97

Logging On 98
Choosing Account Types 99
Using standard accounts 100
Using administrator accounts 100
Working with User Account Control 101
Disabling User Account Control 104
Adding Users..105

Enabling the Guest Account 107
Changing Accounts 107
    Changing other users' settings 108
    Changing your own settings..110
Switching Users 111

Chapter 3: Maintaining Your System 113

Using the Control Panel..113
Removing and Changing Programs..116
Removing Windows Patches...118
Making Backups 118
    Using shadow copies/previous versions.............................120
    Creating data backups 122
    Restoring backed-up data 127
    Ghosting with CompletePC backups..................................130
Maintaining Drives 131
    Running an error check 132
    Scheduling cleanups 134
    Defragmenting a drive 134
Scheduling the Task Scheduler 134
Zipping and Compressing 139
    Compressing with NTFS 141
    Zipping the easy way with Compressed (zipped) Folders...........142
Creating Checkpoints and Using System Restore 143

Chapter 4: Getting the Basic Stuff Done 147

Burning CDs and DVDs...147
    Understanding -R and -RW 148
    What to burn 149
    Mastered or Live File System? 150
    Burning with Vista 152
Improving Your Experience Index..158
Getting Word Processing — Free 160
    Running Notepad...160
    Writing with WordPad...162
    Taming the Character Map..164
Calculating — Free..165
Painting..166
Using Sneaky Key Commands..167
    Conjuring up the Task Manager..167
    Switching coolly 169

Chapter 5: Getting Help with Vista 171

Meeting Windows Help and Support 171
How to Really Get Help...174

Connecting to Remote Assistance 176
  Understanding the interaction 176
  Limiting an invitation 177
  Troubleshooting Remote Assistance 178
  Making the connection 178
Getting the Most from Vista Help 184
  Ensuring that you get all the Help 184
  Working through the index 185
Getting Help on the Web 186

Book III: Securing Vista *187*

Chapter 1: Lock Down: Spies, Spams, Scams, and Slams **189**
Understanding the Hazards 189
  Zombies and botnets 191
  Phishing 193
  0day exploits 195
Staying Informed 196
Getting Protected 198
  Viruses, viruses everywhere 198
  Credit card fraud 200
  Defending your privacy 202
  Keeping cookies at bay 203
  Reducing spam 207
Recovering from an Attack 209
Don't Become Part of the Problem 209
Using Parental Controls 211

Chapter 2: Security Center Overview **217**
Entering the Security Center 217
Working with the Security Center 219
Scanning for Rootkits 220

Chapter 3: Windows Firewall Backward and Forward **225**
Comparing Firewalls 225
Understanding Vista Firewall's Basic Features 227
Speaking Your Firewall's Lingo 229
Peeking into Your Firewall 230
Using Public and Private Networks 231
  Establishing a network type 232
  Changing network types 233
  Changing individual network settings 235
Starting, Stopping, and Goosing Inbound WF 237

Making Inbound Exceptions 238
  Adding a program..240
  Adding a port 241
Coping with Vista's Outbound Firewall 243

Chapter 4: Patching and Plugging **249**

Patching Woes 250
Choosing an Update Level 252
Setting Your Update Level..253
Selectively Patching (A Panacea for Those Woes) 255
  Applying patches from Windows Update........................256
  MS-DEFCON 258
  Getting what you need from a Security Bulletin............259

Chapter 5: Virus Protection and the Big Defender **263**

Understanding Antivirus Software...263
  The challenges for antivirus software 265
  What's a false positive? 266
Live OneCare and the Safety Center 267
Caring for Your Antivirus Program 270
Downloading and Installing AVG Free.....................................272
Making Windows Acknowledge Your AV Program 274
Dealing with Spyware 276

Book 1V: Customizing Vista *281*

Chapter 1: Personalizing Your Desktop **283**

Recognizing Desktop Levels 283
Setting Colors in Vista 286
Picking a Background 288
Energizing the Sidebar..289
  Changing Sidebar settings..290
  Playing with the gadgets 291
Controlling Icons...292
Changing Mouse Pointers 294
Selecting Screen Savers 295
  Changing the screen saver 296
  Setting up a Super Boss Key 297
Using Desktop Themes..301

Chapter 2: Organizing Your Vista Interface **303**

Customizing the Start Menu 303
  Genesis of the Start menu 304
  Pinning to the Start menu 305

Reclaiming most recently used programs....................................309
Changing the All Programs menu..311
Showing recent items..314
Making minor tweaks to the Start menu 315
Using the Quick Launch Toolbar...317
Performing a Custom Startup...318

Chapter 3: Searching on Your Desktop **321**

A Brief History of Finds 321
Scanning versus indexing...322
Desktop search 322
Wither, er, whither WinFS 323
Searching Basics...324
Saving and Reusing Searches 330

Chapter 4: Beating and Cheating Vista's Games **333**

Solitaire..334
Standard scoring 335
Vegas scoring 336
FreeCell...337
Spider Solitaire 339
Minesweeper...340
The Other Games 343

Book V: Vista on the Internet *345*

Chapter 1: Getting the Most from the Internet **347**

What Is the Internet? 348
Getting Inside the Internet 349
What Is the World Wide Web?..350
Who Pays for All This Stuff?...351
Connecting through Dialup or Broadband Services............................353
The last mile...354
Uses and excuses for broadband 355
Setting Up an Internet Connection...357
Finding Internet Reference Tools 359
DSLReports..359
DNSStuff 359
The Wayback Machine...360

Chapter 2: Finding Your Way around Internet Explorer (And Firefox) 363

Exploring Internet Explorer Alternatives 363
Ready, Set, Browse! 365
    Changing the default home page 366
    Switching the default search service 367
Taking a Walk around the IE Window 367
Surfing with Style 370
Pick a Tab, Any Tab 371
Thwarting Phishers 372
    The consequences of anti-phishing .375
    Using the Internet Explorer filter 375
    Fighting phishing with Firefox 378
Doing Stuff with Web Pages 379
    Saving Web pages 379
    Printing Web pages 381
Playing Favorites 382
    Adding Favorites of your own 383
    Organizing your favorites 384

Chapter 3: Making Internet Explorer Your Own 387

Getting the Most from Internet Explorer (And Firefox) 387
Making IE Run Faster 389
Using Links 391
Dealing with Cookies 393
Blogging with Internet Explorer 393
Working with RSS Feeds 395

Chapter 4: Windows Mail and the Alternatives 399

Choosing an E-Mail Program 399
Getting Started with Windows Mail 402
Conversing with E-Mail 404
    Setting up mail accounts 404
    Retrieving messages and attachments 405
    Creating a message 409
    Sending a message 412

Chapter 5: Working Together — IM OK, You're OK 413

Exploring the Alternatives 413
Making Windows Live Messenger Work 416
Tweaking Settings in Windows Live Messenger 421
Sharing Folders 422

Chapter 6: Searching on the Internet **425**

Choosing a Search Engine 425
Changing Search Engines — the Advanced Course..............................430
Googling Tricks 433

Book VI: Adding Cool Hardware *437*

Chapter 1: Finding and Installing the Hardware You Want **439**

Understanding Hardware Types...439
Juggling internal and external devices 440
Choosing an interface 440
Internal interfaces 440
External interfaces 442
Upgrading the Basic Stuff...443
Choosing a new monitor..444
Picking a video adapter 450
Upgrading keyboards..451
Choosing a mouse — or alternatives....................................452
Key Drives, SuperFetch, and ReadyBoost...454
USB Hubs...457
Installing New Hardware 458
Have the store do it 458
Do it yourself...459
Installing USB hardware...463

Chapter 2: iPimping iPods and iTunes **465**

What You Can't Do 466
iPod the Apple Way..467
Bringing everything up to date...467
Getting iTunes ready to feed your iPod................................470
Moving music to your iPod 476
Synching 479
Copying Songs to Your PC..481
The iPod Ecosystem 483

Chapter 3: Adding a Second (Or Third) Hard Drive **485**

Choosing a Second Hard Drive..485
Interfaces for Disk Drives...486
Installing a New SATA Drive 488

Chapter 4: Picking Printers and Printer/Scanner/Faxers **493**

Evaluating Printers...493
Printing photos 494
Considering multifunction devices 494

Exploring exotic features...495
Making a final decision 496
Installing a Printer...496
Attaching a local printer...497
Connecting a network printer.....................................501
Using the Print Queue...503
Displaying a print queue 504
Pausing and resuming a print queue 505
Pausing, restarting, and resuming a document............506
Canceling a document 506
Troubleshooting..507

Book VII: Joining the Multimedia Mix 511

Chapter 1: Jammin' with Windows Media Player 513

What You Need to Know about C.R.A.P. 514
Adjusting WMP Privacy Settings 515
Setting options when you install WMP 516
Tweaking options after installation.............................519
Playing with Now Playing..521
Playback buttons...522
Playing a CD 522
Copying from a CD (Also Known as Ripping) 524
Organizing Your Library..527
Where the Library comes from.....................................527
Leafing through the WMP Library 530
Finding the tracks you want...531
Playing tracks in the Library.......................................534
Nailing Track 6, Unknown Artist, Unknown Album.......535
Managing playlists...536
Deleting tracks from the Library 539
Burning CDs 540
Burning an audio CD 541
Burning data CDs and DVDs with Media Player 544
Syncing with a Portable Player..545
Moving tracks to the player 545
Moving tracks from the player to your PC....................547
Deleting tracks from your player 548
Choosing a Skin 549
Switching skin modes 549
More skins! 550
Customizing WMP 551

Chapter 2: Podcasting 553

Understanding Podcasting..553
Finding and Playing Podcasts..555
Publishing Your Own Podcasts 559

Chapter 3: Discovering Digital Cameras 563

Choosing a Camera..564
Understanding digital cameras...566
Using conventional cameras...570
Plugging webcams...570
Panning camcorders...571
How to Buy a Camera/Camcorder 572
Moving Images to Your Computer 574
Sharing Your Pictures on the Web 578

Chapter 4: Mugging in the Photo Gallery .581

Leafing through the Gallery..582
Adding Photos to the Photo Gallery...583
Using Vista's Picture and Video Import program.....................584
Copying to the Pictures folder...584
Adding photos from a different folder 585
Finding Pictures..586
Looking by location..586
Skipping through tags...587
Touching Up Pictures 590

Chapter 5: Lights! Action! Windows Movie Maker 595

Introducing Windows Movie Maker..596
Gathering Clips..598
Assembling a Movie...599
Creating a project 599
Playing a clip or a movie 601
Viewing the storyboard and timeline 602
Trimming a clip..603
Making transitions and adding effects.......................................604
Splitting and combining clips 605
Typing titles 606
Using sound clips..608
Importing clips from other sources 610
Publishing the Movie...611

Book VIII: Vista Video 617

Chapter 1: Preparing a Media Center PC 619
Do You Need Media Center? 619
Organizing the Normandy Invasion 622
    Gathering the tools for an easier setup 622
    Working with Media Center's shortcomings 623
Getting Windows in Gear....................................624
    Making your video card acquiesce 624
    Setting sound straight.............................627

Chapter 2: Starting Media Center 631
Altering Vista 631
Setting Up Media Player 632
Setting Up Photo Gallery...................................634
Setting Up Media Center — At Last 634

Chapter 3: Turning On the Tube 641
Setting Up Your TV..641
Getting the Guide 646
Editing TV Stations in the Guide 648

Chapter 4: Beyond the Media Center Basics 651
Recording TV 652
    Setting the settings................................652
    Selecting a show to record 656
Using the Mini Guide......................................656
Playing Recorded TV Shows 659
Burning DVDs 660
Getting the Most out of Other Media.........................664
Tweaking Till the Cows Come Home 665

Book IX: Setting Up a Vista Network 667

Chapter 1: Those Pesky Network Things You Need to Know 669
Understanding Networks 669
    What a network can do for you 670
    How a network networks............................671
Organizing Networks 672
    Understanding servers and serfs 672
    Introducing client/server networks 673

Introducing peer-to-peer networks 675
Comparing the p-pros and c-cons 677
Cutting through the Terminology 678
Making Computers Talk...679
Understanding Ethernet 680
Adding wireless 682

Chapter 2: Building Your Network **683**

Planning Your Network...683
Using a wired network 684
Blocking out the major parts 684
Knowing what you (probably) can't network....................................688
Hooking up to the Internet..688
Selecting a hub/router 693
Selecting cables 694
Scoping out the installation 695
Installing Your Network...695
Troubleshooting...701
Two Mother Hens fighting..701
Internet Explorer doesn't work with Internet
Connection Sharing 702
Networking on the road..703

Chapter 3: Putting the Why in Wi-Fi **705**

802.11g..705
Installing a Wireless System 707
Wireless cards..707
Location, location, location 708
Setting Up a Secure Wireless Network 709

Index..*721*

Introduction

*W*elcome to *Windows Vista All-In-One Desk Reference For Dummies* —
the no-bull, one-stop Vista reference for the rest of us. Microsoft
spent almost five years putting Vista together, and it shows. From a fervent
(and frequently irritating) devotion to security at all costs, to a new user
interface crackling with Hollywood glitter, to enormous strides in the parts
of Windows that folks use most, Vista rates as a landmark achievement in
the history of computing.

At the same time, Windows still throws conniption fits like an ornery little
cuss, with pitfalls and pratfalls and utterly inscrutable shenanigans galore.
If you think using Vista is easy, you haven't tried hard enough.

If some of this sounds vaguely familiar, it should. Microsoft has touted
"security" among the number-one reasons for upgrading Windows in each
version over the past decade. User interface improvements have played a
crucial role in selling Windows to the unwashed masses since the days
when "overlapping windows" — the ability to put one window on top of
another — counted as a major achievement.

But this version of Windows is different. No, really. Security improvements
go down deep; they aren't plastered in a thin layer over the top, as has been
the case so many times before. The new Aero Glass interface qualifies as a
"glittergrade" — a term of derision among propellerheads — to be sure,
but being able to peek through the edges of your windows also helps you
find the programs and data you want faster, easier, and more accurately.
The Sidebar may bear more than a passing resemblance to Konfabulator
(now known as Yahoo! Widgets) and a nearly identical Mac OS/X rip-off, er,
feature, but Vista's Sidebar beats the living daylights out of Windows XP's
Active Desktop, which never worked worth the powder to blow it to
Redmond.

When it comes to music and movies and photos, Vista has run out far, far
ahead of the parade, at least on the PC. If you do anything with any kind of
media — which is to say, if you have a life — Vista rules.

Microsoft continues its wayward ways, keeping legions of lawyers lapping at the trough, bobbing and weaving in court, dragging its heels when caught with its collective hand in the cookie jar. There's little to like about the company, its reputation, or its culture. But, oh!, its software. Vista harbors legions of problems. But I, for one, wouldn't hesitate to rank Windows Vista as one of the great engineering feats in human history. No gush. Just fact.

We're all in this big, leaky boat together. Sobering thought, that.

About This Book

Windows Vista All-in-One Desk Reference For Dummies takes you through the Land of the Dummies — with introductory material and stuff your grand-mother could (and should!) understand — and then continues the journey into more advanced areas, where you can really put Windows to work every day. I don't dwell on technical mumbo-jumbo, and I keep the baffling jargon to a minimum. At the same time, though, I tackle the tough problems you're likely to encounter, show you the major road signs, and give you a lot of help where you'll need it the most.

Whether you want to set up a quick, easy, reliable network in your home office or publish provocative photos of your Boykin Spaniel on the Web, this is your book. Er, I should say *nine* books. I've broken the topics out into nine different minibooks, so you'll find it easy to hop around to a topic — and a level of coverage — that feels comfortable.

I didn't design this book to be read from front to back. It's a reference. Each chapter and each section is meant to focus on solving a particular problem or describing a specific technique.

Windows Vista All-in-One Desk Reference For Dummies should be your refer-ence of first resort, even before you consult Windows Help and Support. There's a big reason why: Windows Help was written by hundreds of people over the course of many, many years. Some of the material was written ages ago, and it's confusing as all get-out, but it's still in Windows Help for folks who are tackling tough "legacy" problems. Some of the terminology in the Help files is inconsistent and downright misleading, largely because the technology has changed so much since some of the articles were written. The proverbial bottom line: I don't duplicate the material in Vista's Help and Support, but I will point to it if I figure it'll help you.

Conventions

I try to keep the typographical conventions to a minimum:

✦ The first time a buzzword appears in text, I *italicize* it and define it immediately. That makes it easier for you to glance back and re-read the definition.

✦ When I want you to type something, I put the letters or words in bold. For example: "Type **William Gates** in the Name text box." If you need to press more than one key on the keyboard at a time, I add a plus sign between the keys' names. For example, "Press Ctrl+Alt+Delete to initiate a Vulcan Mind Meld."

✦ I set off Web addresses and e-mail addresses in monospace. For example, my e-mail address is `woody@AskWoody.com` (true fact), and my Web site is at `www.AskWoody.com` (another true fact).

There's one other convention, though, that I use all the time. I always, absolutely, adamantly include the filename extension — the period and (usually) three letters at the end of a filename, such as `.doc` or `.vbs` or `.exe` — when talking about a file. Yeah, I know Windows Vista hides filename extensions by default, but you can and should go in and change that. Yeah, I know that Bill G. hisself made the decision to hide them, and he won't back off. (At least, that's the rumor.)

I also know that hundreds — probably thousands — of *Microsoft employees* passed along the ILOVEYOU virus, primarily because they couldn't see the filename extension that would've warned them that the file was a virus. Uh, bad decision, Bill.

(If you haven't yet told Vista to show you filename extensions, click the Start icon — that circle in the bottom-left corner of the screen — and pick Documents. Press the Alt key on your keyboard. Click Tools ➪Folder Options; then click the View tab. At the bottom of the Advanced Settings box, uncheck the line marked Hide Extensions for Known File Types. Click OK, then "X" out of the Documents folder. For full details, take a gander at Book II, Chapter 1.)

What You Don't Have to Read

Throughout this book, I've gone to great lengths to separate out the "optional" reading from the "required" reading. If you want to find out more about a topic or solve a specific problem, follow along in the main part of the text. You can skip the icons and sidebars as you go, unless one happens to catch your eye.

On the other hand, if you know a topic pretty well but want to make sure you've caught all the high points, read the paragraphs marked with icons and make sure that information registers. If it doesn't, glance at the surrounding text.

Sidebars stand as "graduate courses" for those who are curious about a specific topic — or stand knee-deep in muck, searching for a way out.

Foolish Assumptions

I don't make many assumptions about you, dear reader, except for the fact that you're obviously intelligent, well-informed, discerning, and of impeccable taste. That's why you chose this book, eh?

Okay, okay. Least I can do is butter you up a bit. Here's the straight scoop. If you've never used Windows before, bribe your neighbor (or, better, your neighbor's kids) to teach you how to do three things:

✦ Play Solitaire

✦ Get on the Web

✦ Shut down Windows and turn off the computer

That covers it. If you can play Solitaire, you know how to turn on your computer, use the Start button, click, drag, and double-click. After you're on the Web, well, heaven help us all. And if you know that you need to click the Start icon in order to Stop, you're well on your way to achieving Dummy Enlightenment.

And *that* begins with Book I, Chapter 1.

Organization

Windows Vista All-in-One Desk Reference For Dummies contains nine minibooks, each of which gives a thorough airing of a specific topic. If you're looking for information on a specific Windows topic, check the headings in the Table of Contents or refer to the Index.

By design, this book enables you to get as much (or as little) information as you need at any particular moment. Want to know how to jimmy your Minesweeper score to amaze your boss and confound your co-workers?

Look at Book IV, Chapter 4. Want to activate Vista's outbound firewall? Try Book III, Chapter 3. Also by design, *Windows Vista All-in-One Desk Reference For Dummies* is a reference that you reach for again and again whenever some new question about Vista comes up.

Here are the nine minibooks, and what they contain:

Book I: A Vista Orientation: What Windows can and can't do. What's inside a PC, and how Windows controls it. Do you really need Vista? Which of the eight (!) versions is right for you? How do you upgrade?

Book II: Vista Boot Camp: How to get Vista working right. Adding users — with a particular nod to security. Manipulating files. Using the Windows taskbar and shortcuts. Getting help. The care and feeding of hard drives. Using the built-in applications for word processing and image manipulation.

Book III: Securing Vista: A look at the Security Center. Windows Firewall. Using the Microsoft Management Console snap-in to monitor outbound traffic. Automatic Updating and when to avoid it. Virus Protection — free. What the bad guys already know, and what you can do about it.

Book IV: Customizing Vista: Cranking up the Sidebar and getting gadgets. Glass. Personalizing the desktop with themes, colors, backgrounds, and the like. Mouse Pointers. Screen Savers. Changing the Start menu. Using the Quick Launch toolbar. Beating Vista's games, the sneaky way.

Book V: Vista on the Internet: Why you really need broadband. Logging into your computer from the Internet. Internet Explorer. RSS feeds. Dealing with popups. Blogging for fun and prophet. Managing passwords. Windows Mail, Windows Live Mail, and more. Working the newsgroups. Messaging outside the Microsoft sphere.

Book VI: Adding Cool Hardware: The iPod vs. Vista — and better alternatives elsewhere. Cameras, scanners, printers, audio, memory, USB key drives, monitors, and more. Choosing the right products and getting them to work.

Book VII: Joining the Multimedia Mix: Podcasting tricks and traps. Windows Media Player. Plays for sure (yeah, sure). Ripping from audio CDs. Burning your own CDs and DVDs. Capturing Windows Media streams. Digital licensing and what you can do to thwart Microsoft's encroaching lockdowns. Windows Movie Maker, digital cameras, camcorders, and other video devices. "Unshaking" your movies. Printing and sharing pictures. Converting file formats. Photo Gallery.

Book VIII: Vista Video: Do you have what it takes? How to pick a good Media Center PC. Installation and set up. Running Media Center for you and me. Burning video DVDs — and the traps.

Book IX: Setting Up a Vista Network: Concepts behind peer-to-peer and client/server networking. How to build your own network quickly, easily, and reliably. Wi-Fi and other ethereal wireless topics. Protecting your network and your privacy.

Icons

Some of the points in *Windows Vista All-in-One Desk Reference For Dummies* merit your special attention. I set those points off with icons.

When I'm jumping up and down on one foot with an idea so absolutely cool I can't stand it anymore, that's when I stick a Tip icon in the margin. You can browse through any chapter and hit the very highest points by jumping from Tip to Tip.

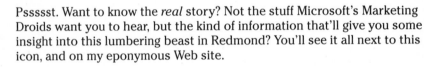

Pssssst. Want to know the *real* story? Not the stuff Microsoft's Marketing Droids want you to hear, but the kind of information that'll give you some insight into this lumbering beast in Redmond? You'll see it all next to this icon, and on my eponymous Web site.

You don't need to memorize the stuff marked with this icon, but you should try to remember that there's something special lurking about.

Achtung! Cuidado! Thar be tygers here! Any place you see a Warning icon, you can be sure that I've been burnt — badly — in the past. Mind your fingers. These are really, really mean suckers.

Okay, so I'm a geek. I admit it. Sure, I love to poke fun at geeks. But I'm a modern, new-age sensitive guy, in touch with my inner geekiness. Sometimes I just can't help but let it out, ya know? That's where the Technical Stuff icon comes in. If you get all tied up in knots about techie stuff, pass these by. (For the record, I managed to write this whole book without telling you that an IP Address consists of a unique 32-bit combination of network ID and host ID, expressed as a set of four decimal numbers with each octet separated by periods. See? I *can* restrain myself sometimes.)

There are also voluminous diversities in the various versions of Vista. (Say that ten times really fast.) When a particular feature appears in, say Vista Home Premium Edition, but it doesn't appear in Vista Home Basic, I won't tag the difference with an icon, but I will mention that fact loud and clear. If you find a feature that you can't wait to try, make sure your version of Vista supports it before you get too carried away.

Where to Go from Here

That's about it. Time for you to crack the book open and have at it.

Don't forget to bookmark my Web site, www.AskWoody.com. It'll keep you up to date on all the Windows Vista news you need to know — including notes about this book, the latest Windows bugs and gaffes, patches that are worse than the problems they're supposed to fix, and much more — and you can submit your most pressing questions, for free consultation from The Woodmeister hisself.

See ya! woody@AskWoody.com

Book I

A Vista Orientation

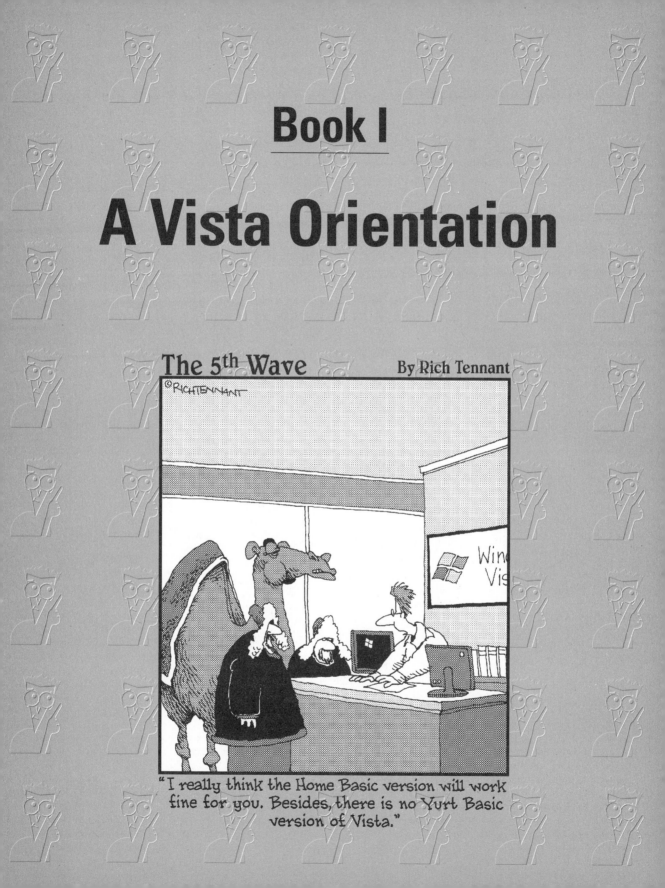

The 5th Wave   By Rich Tennant

"I really think the Home Basic version will work fine for you. Besides, there is no Yurt Basic version of Vista."

Contents at a Glance

Chapter 1: Windows 4 N00bs 11

Chapter 2: Vista versus the WinXPerienced 27

Chapter 3: Choosing a Version 35

Chapter 4: Upgrades and Clean Installs...43

Chapter 1: Windows 4 N00bs

In This Chapter

✔ A newbie's quick guide

✔ Why hardware's hard . . . and software's hard, too

✔ Windows' place in the grand scheme of things

✔ Those computer words all the grade-schoolers understand

✔ Buying a Vista computer

Don't sweat it. We all started out as N00bs ("newbies").

All those high-fallutin' technical words you have to memorize, eh?

So you're sitting in front of your computer, and this thing called Windows Vista is staring at you. The screen you see — the one with the people's names on it — is called a Welcome screen, but it doesn't say "Welcome" or "Howdy" or even "Sit down and get to work, bucko." It only has names and pictures for people who can use the computer. Why do you have to click your name? What if your name isn't there? And why in the %$#@! can't you bypass all this garbage, log on, and get your e-mail?

Good for you. That's the right attitude.

Windows Vista ranks as the most sophisticated computer program ever made. It cost more money to develop and took more people to build than any previous computer program, ever. So why is it so blasted hard to use? Why doesn't it do what you want it to do the first time? For that matter, why do you need it at all?

Someday, I swear, you'll be able to pull a PC out of the box, plug it into the wall, turn it on, and get your e-mail — bang, bang, bang, just like that, in ten seconds flat. In the meantime, those of us who are stuck in the early 21st century have to make do with PCs that grow obsolete before you can unpack them, software that's so ornery you find yourself arguing with it, and Internet connections that surely involve turtles carrying bits on their backs.

If you aren't comfortable working with Windows, and still worry that you might break something if you click the wrong button, welcome to the club! In this chapter, I try to present a concise school-of-hard-knocks overview of how all this hangs together, and what to look for when buying a Vista PC. It may help you understand why and how Windows has limitations. It also may help you communicate with the geeky rescue team that tries to bail you out, whether you rely on the store that sold you the PC, the smelly guy in the apartment downstairs, or your eight-year-old daughter's nerdy classmate.

Hardware and Software

At the most fundamental level, all computer stuff comes in one of two flavors: hardware or software. *Hardware* is anything you can touch — a computer screen, a mouse, a CD. *Software* is everything else: e-mail messages, that letter to your Aunt Martha, pictures of your last vacation, programs like Microsoft Office. If you have a roll of film developed and put on a CD, the shiny, round CD is hardware — you can touch it — but the pictures themselves are software. Get the difference?

Windows Vista is software. You can't touch it. Your PC, on the other hand, is hardware. Kick the computer screen and your toe hurts. Drop the big box on the floor and it smashes into a gazillion pieces. That's hardware.

Chances are very good that one of the major PC manufacturers — Dell, HP/Compaq, IBM/Lenovo, Acer, Gateway, Toshiba, and so on — made your hardware. Microsoft, and Microsoft alone, makes Windows Vista. The PC manufacturers don't make Windows. Microsoft doesn't make PCs, although it does make other kinds of hardware — video game boxes, keyboards, mice, and a few other odds and ends.

When you bought your computer, you paid for a license to use one copy of Windows on the PC that you bought. The PC manufacturer paid Microsoft a royalty so that it could sell you Windows along with your PC. You may think that you got Windows from, say, Dell — indeed, you may have to contact Dell for technical support on Windows questions — but, in fact, Windows came from Microsoft.

When you first set up your PC, Windows had you click "I accept" to a licensing agreement that's long enough to wrap around the Empire State Building. If you're curious about what you accepted, a printed copy of the End User License Agreement (EULA) is in the box that your PC came in or in the CD packaging, if you bought Windows Vista separately from your computer.

If you can't find your copy of the EULA, here's how to retrieve it (and, at the same time, get some experience using the instructions in this book as well as finding your way around Vista's Help system, which I talk about in Book II Chapter 5):

1. **Click the big round button in the lower-left corner of your screen.**

   I call that button the "Start" button because in Windows XP, it bore the word *Start*. If you hover your mouse above the circle, a little box appears that says *Start,* too.

2. **On the right, at the bottom, click Help and Support.**

   The Windows Help and Support center springs into view.

3. **Type** eula **in the Search text box and press Enter.**

   Windows shows you one or more results for your inquiry (see Figure 1-1).

4. **Click the Read the Microsoft Software License Terms link.**

   Windows brings up the EULA that you agreed to, back in your younger and more naïve days.

Now you know who to blame, for sure.

Book I
Chapter 1

Windows 4 N00bs

Type the term for which you need help

Figure 1-1:
Recall what you agreed to in the End User License Agreement.

Start button

Chase down the article here

Why Do PCs Have to Run Windows?

Here's the short answer: You *don't* have to run Windows on your PC.

The PC you have is a dumb box. (You needed me to tell you that, eh?) To get the dumb box to do anything worthwhile, you need a computer program that takes control of the PC and makes it do things such as show Web pages on the screen, respond to mouse clicks, or print résumés. An *operating system* controls the dumb box and makes it do worthwhile things, in ways that mere humans can understand.

Without an operating system, the computer can sit in a corner and count to itself, or put profound messages on the screen, such as `Non-system disk or disk error. Insert system disk and press any key when ready`. If you want your computer to do more than that, though, you need an operating system.

Windows is not the only operating system in town. The single largest competitor to Windows is an operating system called Linux (pronounced *LIN-uchs*). Some people (I'm told) actually prefer Linux to Windows, and the debates between pro-Windows and pro-Linux camps can become rather heated. The Mac operating system can run on PCs, but only on a special kind of PC. Suffice it to say that, oh, 99 percent of all normal PC users stick with Windows. You probably will, too.

Buying a Computer

Here's how it usually goes. You figure you need to buy a new PC. So you spend a couple of weeks brushing up on the details — bits and bytes and kilobytes and megabytes and gigabytes — and comparison shopping. You end up at your local Computers Were Us shop, and this guy behind the counter convinces you that the absolutely best bargain you'll ever see is sitting right here, right now, and you'd better take it quick before somebody else nabs it.

Your eyes glaze over as you look at yet another spec sheet and try to figure out one last time whether a RAM is a ROM, how fast hard-drive platters spin, and whether you need an ATA, SATA, SATA I, or SATA II. In the end, you figure the guy behind the counter must know what he's doing, so you plunk down your plastic and pray you got a good deal.

The next Sunday morning you look in the paper and discover you could've bought twice as much machine for half as much money. The only thing you know for sure is that your PC is hopelessly out of date, and the next time you'll be smarter about the whole process.

If that describes your experiences, relax. It happens to everybody. Take solace in the fact that you bought twice as much machine for the same amount of money as the poor schmuck who went through the same process last month.

Here's everything you really need to know about buying a Vista PC:

✦ Buy at least 1GB of memory; 2GB is better.

✦ You need a powerful video card with at least 128MB of memory, but 256MB (or more) is better.

✦ If you want to record TV shows on your PC, you need Vista Home Premium or Ultimate (see Book I, Chapter 2), and a video input card that's Vista certified, and a Media Center compatible remote control.

✦ Get a high-quality monitor, a solid keyboard, and a mouse that feels comfortable. (I don't like cordless mice, but I'm kinda crotchety anyway.)

✦ Everything else they try to sell ya pales in comparison.

In this section, I try to give you just enough information about the inner workings of your PC so that you can figure out what you have to do with Windows. The details can change from week to week. But these are the basics.

Inside the big box

The big box that your computer lives in is sometimes called a *CPU,* meaning Central Processing Unit (see Figure 1-2). Right off the bat, you're bound to get confused, unless somebody clues you in on one important detail: The main computer chip inside that big box is *also* called a CPU. I prefer to call the big box "the PC" because of the naming ambiguity, but you have probably thought of a few better names.

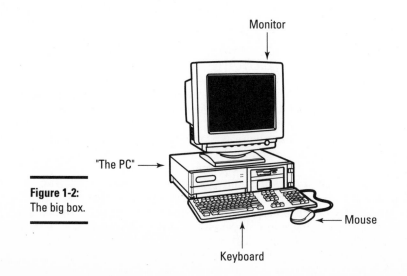

Figure 1-2:
The big box.

Monitor

"The PC" →

Mouse

Keyboard

The big box contains many parts and pieces (and no small amount of dust and dirt), but the crucial, central element inside every PC is the *motherboard* (see Figure 1-3). Attached to the motherboard you find the following items:

✦ **The *processor* or CPU:** This gizmo does the main computing. It's probably from Intel or AMD or one of their competitors. Processors are typically rated by speed, measured in MHz (megahertz) or GHz (gigahertz, 1 GHz = 1,024 MHz). Vista runs like a slug on anything slower than 1 GHz.

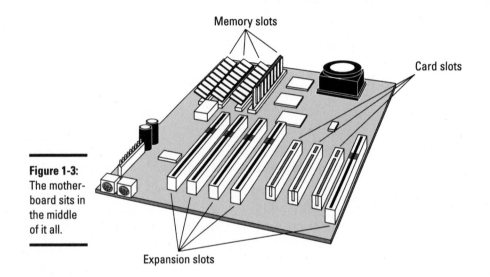

Figure 1-3:
The motherboard sits in the middle of it all.

Memory slots

Card slots

Expansion slots

If you're buying a new computer, the speed really doesn't mean much, unless you're designing airplane wings or reshooting *Jurassic Park,* or unless you play a lot of games on your PC. Ignore the salesperson. If you want to improve Vista performance, your money should go to more memory (see the next item), a better video card, or a fast Internet connection.

✦ **Memory chips and places to put them:** Memory is measured in megabytes (1MB = 1,024KB = 1,048,576 characters) and gigabytes (1GB = 1,024 MB). Windows Vista can run on a machine with 256MB — I've done it — but Microsoft recommends a minimum of 512MB (see www.microsoft.com/technet/windowsvista/evaluate/hardware/vistapc.mspx). Unless you have an exciting cornfield to watch grow while Vista saunters along, aim for 1GB or more. Most computers allow you to add more memory to them, and boosting your computer's memory to 2GB from 1GB makes the machine much snappier, especially if you run memory hogs such as Office, PageMaker, or Photoshop. If you leave Outlook open and work with it all day, and run almost any other major program at the same time, 1GB is a must, and 2GB isn't overkill.

✦ **Card slots (also known as expansion slots):** Modern slots come in three flavors: PCI, AGP, and PCI Express. Don't get too hung up on the alphabet soup, but if you can get a few PCI Express slots, do so. Vista makes video cards work hard, and PCI Express video cards generally give you the best bang for the buck. Or ruble.

✦ **Lots of other stuff:** You'll never have to play with this other stuff, unless you're very unlucky.

Here are a few upgrade dos and don'ts:

✦ **Don't** let a salesperson talk you into eviscerating your PC and upgrading the CPU: A 3.0 GHz PC doesn't run a whole lot faster than a 2.4 GHz PC.

✦ When you hit 2GB in main memory, **don't** expect big performance improvements by adding more memory.

✦ On the other hand, if you have an older video card, **do** consider upgrading it to a faster card, or one with 128MB or more memory. Vista will soak it up.

✦ Instead of nickel-and-diming yourself to death on little upgrades, **wait** until you can afford a new PC, and give away your old one.

If you decide to get more memory, have the company that sells you the memory install it. The process is simple, quick, and easy — if you know what you're doing. Having the dealer install the memory also puts the monkey on his back if a memory chip doesn't work or a bracket gets snapped.

Screening

The *computer monitor* or *screen* — you may think of it as a hoity-toity TV — uses technology that's quite different from old-fashioned television circuitry. A traditional TV scans lines across the screen from left to right, with hundreds of them stacked on top of each other. Colors on each individual line vary all over the place. The near-infinitely variable color on a TV combined with a comparatively small number of lines makes for pleasant, but fuzzy, pictures.

By contrast (pun absolutely intended, of course), computer monitors, and plasma and LCD TVs, work with dots of light, called *pixels*. Each pixel can have a different color, created by tiny colored gizmos sitting next to each other. As a result, computer monitors (and plasma and LCD TVs) are much sharper than conventional TV tubes.

Most people set up Windows Vista to run at a resolution of 1280 x 1024 pixels — that is, their monitors show 1280 pixels across the screen, with 1024 running up and down. (Widescreen owners may try 1920 x 1200.) You may have an older, smaller, or fuzzier monitor that can't handle 1280 x 1024 — or you may have eyes that can't take it. That's okay: Vista looks pretty good at 1024 x 768.

The more pixels you can cram on a screen — that is, the higher the *screen resolution* — the more information you can pack on the screen. That's important if you commonly have more than one word-processing document open at a time, for example. At a resolution of 800 x 600, two open Word documents placed side by side look big but fuzzy, like caterpillars viewed through a dirty magnifying glass. At 1280 x 1024, those same two documents look sharp, but the text may be so small that you have to squint to read it.

A special-purpose computer called a *graphics processor* or GPU, stuck on your video card, creates everything that's shown on your computer's screen. The GPU has to juggle all the pixels and all the colors — so if you're a gaming fan, the speed of the GPU's chip (and, to a lesser extent, the speed of the monitor) can make the difference between a zapped alien and a lost energy shield. If you want to experience Vista in all its glory, particularly the see-through "glass interface," you need a fast GPU with at least 128MB — and preferably 256MB — of its own memory.

Computer monitors are sold by size, measured diagonally, like TV sets. Just like TV sets, the only way to pick a good computer screen over a run-of-the-mill one is to compare them side by side or to follow the recommendation of someone who has.

Managing disks and drives

Your PC's memory chips hold information only temporarily: Turn off the electricity, and the contents of main memory go bye-bye. If you want to reuse your work, keeping it around after the plug has been pulled, you have to save it, typically on a disk. The following are the most common types of disks and drives:

✦ **Floppies:** The 1.44MB floppy disk drives that were ubiquitous on PCs for many years have bit the dust. There's very little reason to buy one nowadays. But . . .

✦ **SD/xD/CF card memory:** Even now, long after the demise of floppy disks, many computer cases have drive bays built for floppies. Why not use the open spot for a multifunction card reader? That way you can slip a memory card out of your digital camera (or Dick Tracy wristwatch for that matter) and transfer files at will. SD cards, xD, CompactFlash, memory stick — whatever you have — the multifunction readers cost a pittance and read almost everything. Including minds.

✦ **Hard drives:** Get the biggest, cheapest one(s) you can. Electronic pictures swallow up an enormous amount of space, and the average teenager's music collection could easily consume as much storage as the first mission to the moon. Although it's generally true that more expensive hard drives are more reliable than cheaper ones, objective numbers are hard to come by, and individual results can vary.

Speed doesn't matter much unless you're transferring enormous amounts of data. That said, you should still consider shelling out a few extra shekels for the newer SATA II hard drive technology. For a whole host of reasons, SATA II is rapidly replacing the older IDE (also called, confusingly, ATA) approach, with the old clunky IDE ribbon cables giving way to sleek, thin, flexible SATA II ones.

Don't be afraid to stick a hard drive in a box, and plug the box into your computer via a USB cable. External hard drives run almost as fast as internal hard drives, they can be picked up and moved on a whim — and they don't contribute to your computer's heating problems.

If you buy a new hard drive, have the dealer install it. You have to worry about lots of permutations and combinations, and it simply isn't worth the effort. Life's too short.

✦ **CD, DVD, and Blu-ray drives:** Of course, these drives work with CDs, DVDs, and Sony's Blu-ray discs, which can be filled with data or contain music or movies. CDs hold about 700 MB of data; DVDs hold 4GB, or six times as much as a CD. Dual-layer DVDs (which use two separate layers on the top of the disc) hold about 8GB, and Blu-ray discs hold 50 GB, or six times as much as a dual-layer DVD.

Windows Vista Service Pack 1 includes extensive support for Blu-ray devices. If you're having trouble getting a Blu-ray drive to work on your Vista PC, make sure you have Service Pack 1 installed (see Book I, Chapter 3).

Unless you want to stick a high-definition movie on a single disc or play Blu-ray discs that you buy or rent in your local video store, 50GB of data on a single disc is overkill. Some day the price of Blu-ray drives and discs will come down out of the stratosphere, but at least for now, most Vista users will do quite well with a dual-layer DVD-RW drive. You can always use a dual-layer drive to record regular (single-layer) DVDs or CDs. If you're nervous about installing a new drive, get an external USB version: Vista loves external DVD drives, and it tolerates external Blu-ray drives.

Many older audio CD players — like the one you may have in your car or your home stereo — can play only CDs that are burned once. If you reburn the CD, it won't play, so for those machines, stick to CD-Rs instead of reburnable CD-RWs.

If you intend to burn CDs or DVDs on a new computer and play them on a CD or DVD player that you already own, it would behoove you to test-burn a CD or DVD before you buy the computer. Many cheap DVD players can handle a whole disc of MP3 files (that's, oh, 50 to 100 *hours* of music) with aplomb. Others — even expensive players — can't see past the first file. The only way to know for sure is to give it a whirl.

✦ **USB flash drives:** Treat them like lollipops. Half the size of a pack of gum, and able to hold an entire PowerPoint presentation or two or six, flash memory should be your first choice for external storage space or for copying files between computers. Pop one of these guys in a USB slot (see the next section in this chapter), and suddenly Windows Vista knows it has another drive — except this one's fast, portable, and incredibly easy to use. Go for the cheapest flash drives you can find: Most of the "features" on fancy key drives are just, uh, Windows dressing.

This list is by no means definitive: You can buy Jaz disks, Zip drives, and recordable media that sing till the cows come home.

Making PC connections

Your PC connects to the outside world using a bewildering variety of cables and connectors. The most common are as follows:

✦ **USB (Universal Serial Bus) cables:** These cables have a flat connector that plugs into your PC. The other end is usually shaped like a *D,* but different pieces of hardware have different *terminators.* ("I'll be back . . . Hasta la vista, baby . . .") USB is the connector of choice for just about any kind of hardware — printers, scanners, MP3 players, Palm/pocket computers, portable hard drives, and even mice. If you run out of USB connections on the back of your PC, get a USB hub with a separate power supply and plug away.

✦ **LAN cables (also known as CAT-5, CAT-6, and/or RJ-45 cables):** These are the most common kind of network connectors. They look like overweight telephone plugs (see Figure 1-4). One end plugs into your PC, typically into a *NIC* (Network Interface Card, pronounced *nick*), a network connector on the motherboard, or a network connector on a card that slides into a port (a so-called "PC card" or "PCMCIA card"). The other end plugs into your network's hub (see Figure 1-5), switch, or possibly into a cable modem, DSL box, router, or other Internet connection–sharing device.

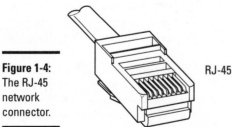

Figure 1-4:
The RJ-45
network
connector.

RJ-45

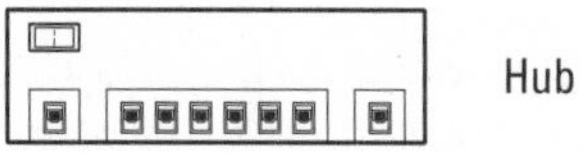

Figure 1-5:
A network
hub.

Hub

✦ **PS/2 or mini-DIN connectors:** These are round connectors with six pins and a plastic hump that prevents you from getting the connector twisted around in the wrong direction (see Figure 1-6). Commonly found on keyboards and mice, it's ancient technology that works great.

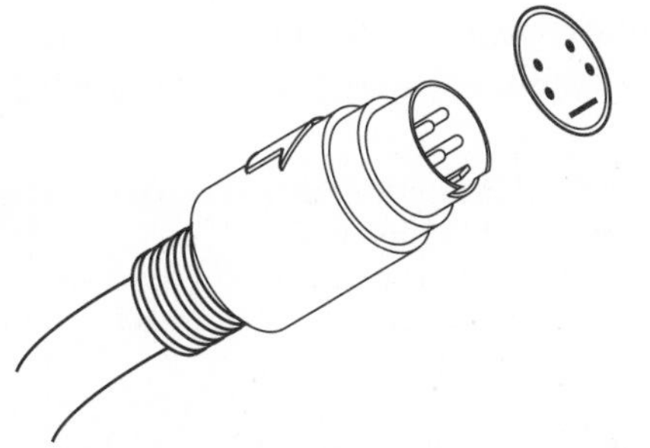

Figure 1-6:
A PS/2 or
mini-DIN
connector.

If you have a mouse and a keyboard, both with PS/2 connectors, but your PC sports only one PS/2 slot, not to worry! Most cable manufacturers have Y connectors that allow you to attach two PS/2 devices to a single port. Surprisingly, both the mouse and the keyboard can coexist with nary a hiccup. Visit www.cablestogo.com.

More and more mice and keyboards are coming with USB connectors. That's too bad, really, because most computers don't have enough places to plug in USB connectors, and it's a waste to take up USB slots with the mouse and keyboard. You can solve the problem by buying USB-to-PS/2 adapters, and plugging both mouse and keyboard into the respective PS/2 slots on the computer.

✦ **Parallel and serial ports:** These are the long (parallel, 25-pin, with 13 pins on top and 12 on the bottom) and short (serial, 9-pin, 5 on top and 4 on the bottom) connections on the back of your computer. The serial port is notoriously slow, and both kinds sometimes fall apart — which is particularly disconcerting when you unscrew a connector and a nut falls off inside your computer. If you have a choice, choose USB.

Futzing with sound

Chances are pretty good that you are running Vista on a PC with at least a little oomph in the audio department. In the simplest case, you have to be concerned about four specific sound jacks (or groups of sound jacks) because each one does something different. Your machine may not have all four (are you feeling inadequate yet?), or it may look like a patch board at a Korn concert, but the basics are still the same.

Here's how the four key jacks are usually marked, although sometimes you have to root around in the documentation to find the details:

✦ **Line in:** A stereo input jack. Feeds a stereo audio signal into the PC. Use this jack to get audio output from a cable box, TV set, radio, CD player, cassette player, electric guitar, or some other audio-generating box into your computer.

✦ **Mike in:** If you use a cheap microphone for Skype or some other VoIP service that lets you talk long distance for free (see Book IV, Chapter 5), plug in the microphone here. In a pinch, you can plug any of the "Line in" devices into the "Mike in" jack — but you'll probably only get mono sound, not stereo.

✦ **Line out:** A stereo output jack that, in the simplest case, bypasses the computer's internal amplifier. If you don't have fancy output jacks, this is the source for the highest-quality sound your computer can produce.

✦ **Headphone or speaker out:** Goes through the internal amplifier. Use this jack for headphones or speakers, but avoid it in all other situations.

Fancy sound cards can have full Dolby DTS or THX 5.1 output (that's left front, center front, right front, left surround, right surround, and a subwoofer). The 6.1 configuration adds a back-surround jack, and 7.1 uses two back surrounds. Front panel output — where your sound card connects to jacks on the front of your PC, possibly a panel in a hard drive bay — makes connections easy. With a sufficiently bottomless budget, you can make your living room sound precisely like the 07L runway at LAX.

PC manufacturers love to extol the virtues of their advanced sound systems, but the simple fact is that you can hook up a rather plain-vanilla PC to a home stereo and get great sound. Just connect the "Line out" jack on the back of your PC to the "Aux in" jack on your home stereo or entertainment center. *Voilà!*

Wireless keyboards and mice?

No thank you. I've been trying to wean myself off of keyboard and mouse cables for many years, with little luck. Wireless contraptions skip and drop with alarming frequency — too much for me to handle. When I press a key, I expect a letter to appear; when I move my mouse, the cursor better march in locked time. The signal-strength-detecting and calibrating software offered with newer keyboards and mice doesn't overcome wireless congenital defects, for me at least. If you prefer cables too, hey, don't feel like a Luddite.

A Terminology Survival Kit

Some terms pop up so frequently that you'll find it worthwhile to memorize them, or at least understand where they come from. That way, you won't be caught flatfooted when your first-grader comes home and asks whether he can download a program from the Internet.

If you really want to drive your techie friends nuts, the next time you have a problem with your computer, tell them that the hassles occur when you're "running Microsoft." They won't have any idea whether you mean Windows, Word, Outlook, Live Messenger, Windows Live Search, Defender, Media Center, or any of a gazillion other programs.

A *program* is *software* (see the first section in this chapter) that works on a computer. Windows, the *operating system* (see the second section), is a program. So are computer games, Microsoft Office, Microsoft Word (which is the word processor part of Office), Internet Explorer (the Web browser in Windows), Windows Media Player, those nasty viruses you've heard about, that screen saver with the oh-too-perfect fish bubbling and bumbling about, and so on.

A special kind of program called a *driver* makes specific pieces of hardware work with the operating system. For example, your computer's printer has a driver, your monitor has a driver, your mouse has a driver, and Tiger Woods has a driver (several, actually, and he makes a living with them). Would that we were all so talented.

Sticking a program on your computer, and setting it up so that it works, is called *installing* the program.

When you crank up a program — that is, get it going on your computer — you can say you *started* it, *launched* it, *ran* it, or *executed* it. They all mean the same thing. (Book II, Chapter 1 has more details.)

If the program quits the way it's supposed to, you can say it *stopped, finished, ended, exited,* or *terminated.* Again, all these terms mean the same thing. If the program stops with some sort of weird error message, you can say it *crashed, died, cratered, croaked, went belly up,* or *GPFed* (tech-speak for "generated a General Protection Fault" — don't ask), or employ any of a dozen colorful but unprintable epithets. If the program just sits there and you can't get it to do anything, you can say the program *froze, hung, stopped responding,* or *went into a loop.*

And then you have *wizards.* Windows comes with lots of 'em. They guide you through complex procedures, moving one step at a time. Typically, wizards have three directional buttons on each screen: Back, Next (or Finish), and Cancel (see Figure 1-7). Wizards remember what you've chosen as you go from step to step, making it easy to experiment a bit, change your mind, back up, and try a different setting, without getting all the check boxes confused.

Move back to change a setting

Figure 1-7:
The Windows Back Up Files Wizard guides you through setting up automatic backups.

Go to the next step

Quit without changing anything

A *bug* is something that doesn't work right. (A bug is not a *virus!* Viruses work right far too often.) Admiral Grace Hopper often repeated the story of a moth being found in a relay of an ancient Mark II computer. The moth was taped into the technician's logbook on September 9, 1947, with the annotation "1545 Relay #70 Panel F (moth) in relay. First actual case of bug being found."

The people who invented all this terminology think of the Internet as being some great blob in the sky — it's *up*, as in "up in the sky." So if you send something from your computer to the Internet, you're *uploading*. If you take something off the Internet and put it on your computer, you're *downloading*.

When you put computers together, you *network* them, and if your network doesn't use wires, it's *wireless*. At the heart of a network sits a box, commonly called a *hub* or a *router*, that computers can plug into. If the hub has rabbit ears on top, for wireless connections, it's usually called a *wireless router*. Yes, there are fine lines of distinction among all these terms. No, you don't need to worry about them. Book IX is your guide to networking.

If you hear your computer connect to the Internet with a ping-ping-ping sound, like that on a fax machine, you have a *dial-up connection*, and the box that connects to the phone lines is a *modem*. Anybody with a connection considerably faster than yours has *broadband* access, which may run via *DSL* or *ADSL* over the phone lines, via *cable* (as in cable TV) or via *satellite*. The DSL, cable, or satellite box is commonly called a modem, too, although it's really a router. In Book V, you find out more about going online with Vista.

Turning to the dark side of the force, Luke, the distinctions among *viruses*, *worms*, and *Trojans* grow more blurry every day. In general, they're programs that replicate and can be harmful, and the worst ones blend different approaches. *Spyware* gathers information about you and then phones home with all the juicy details. *Adware* gets in yer face, frequently installing itself on your computer without your knowledge or consent. I tend to lump the two together and call them *scumware* or something a bit more descriptive and less printable.

If a bad guy (and they're almost always *guys*) manages to take over your computer without your knowledge, turning it into a zombie that spews spam via remote control, you're in a *botnet*. (And, yes, the term *spam* comes from the immortal Monty Python routine set in a café serving Hormel's SPAM luncheon meat, the chorus bellowing, "lovely Spam, wonderful Spam.") Check out Book III for details about preventing scumware and the like from messing with you.

The most successful botnets employ rootkits — programs that run "underneath" Windows, evading detection because normal programs, such as your antivirus program or Windows Defender, can't see them. Rootkits rate as the wave of the future because they're hard to find, hard to remove, and the person controlling a rootkit-based botnet can charge ungodly amounts of money to people who want to use the services of the botnet to distribute spam, collect data, ping the living daylights out of a Web site, or distribute even more malware.

Although it's true that some rootkits run on Vista PCs, the majority by far subvert Windows XP machines. It's considerably more difficult for a bad guy to get a rootkit installed on a Vista machine than on one running XP, and keeping the program's activities in the dark rates as a first-class pain. If you have Vista, you need to be cautious about rootkits (see Book III), but there's no need to be overly paranoid. Yet.

That should cover about 90 percent of the buzzwords you hear in common parlance. If you get stuck at a party where the bafflegab's flowing freely, don't hesitate to invent your own words. Nobody will ever know the difference.

Chapter 2: Vista versus the WinXPerienced

In This Chapter

✓ **What every experienced Windows XP user should know about Vista**

✓ **New eye candy . . .**

✓ **. . . but the changes go deeper**

✓ **Do you really need Vista?**

If you're among the billion-or-so souls on the planet who've been around the block with Windows XP, you're in for a shock. In many ways, Vista looks like XP with a bit of gussying-up around the edges. Many of the pieces of Vista work much like their XP counterparts. But underneath the surface, much has changed.

Here's a quick guide to what's new — and what's still the same — with some down 'n' dirty help for deciding whether you really need Vista.

What You See

If you didn't get suckered into buying Vista Home Basic Edition (see Book I, Chapter 3), and your video card packs some oomph, Vista's Aero Glass interface (see Figure 2-1) rates as a significant improvement over Windows XP's boxy, now-antiquated look.

The Glass UX

Microsoft's marketeers insist on calling Aero Glass a "UX" (for "User Experience"). I guess they have a point — particularly if you can't get the %$#@#! thing to work. What an experience.

You can call Aero Glass a UX if you like — heck, you can call it a Lifestyle Enhancement Package and tout its medicinal and neuro-linguistic benefits. Under that pretty face, Aero Glass embodies a completely new way of making windows float and interact on the screen.

Windows Media Player works better

Sidebar holds
all sorts of suprises

See-through band around
each window lets you peek

Close button
lights up

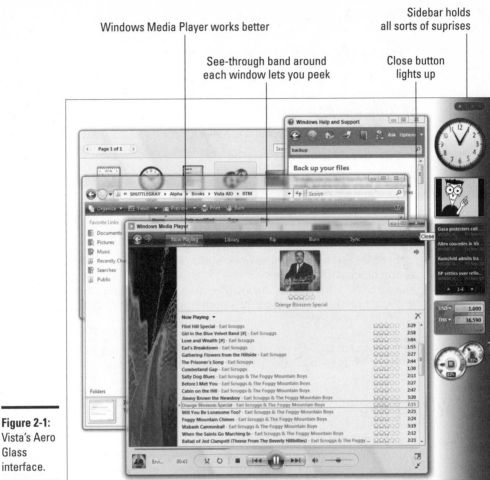

Figure 2-1:
Vista's Aero
Glass
interface.

Aero Glass qualifies as much more than YAMG — Yet Another Microsoft
Glittergrade — of which you have endured many over the years. Use it for a
few hours, and you'll find that

✦ You can frequently locate the specific window that you want faster,
easier, and more accurately.

✦ Organizing windows by stacking them on the desktop works better.

✦ Switching among windows feels less like a black art than it did in every
previous version of Windows.

Improved video effects

Under the hood, Vista intervenes between programs and the screen, adding an extra layer of processing called the Desktop Window Manager. Historically, extra processing layers have really gummed up Windows — DirectX was invented specifically to bypass all the Windows overhead. Now, thanks to powerful processors on video cards, and more than a little bit of programming savvy, Vista can intercede without bringing your computer to a grinding halt.

You see the effects the Desktop Window Manager in Vista's omniscient handling of all video. One example is the aforementioned glass effects — windows peeking out from under other windows, fast shading, transitional effects that smoothly roll a window onto the screen, making the "X" exit button glow when the mouse goes over the button. You'll also see two new features that make scanning your open windows and finding the one you want much easier:

✦ Vista shows you thumbnails of running programs when you hover your mouse over a running program on the taskbar (see Figure 2-2).

Figure 2-2:
A live
window
preview.

✦ The Windows Flip feature, which is activated by holding down the Windows key and repeatedly pressing Tab (or by clicking the Switch Between Windows icon, to the right of the Start button) lets you leaf through running programs much like riffling a deck of cards (see Figure 2-3).

Sidebar: A truly active desktop

Microsoft has tried to put "active" items on the Windows desktop for nearly a decade. Finally, with Vista's Sidebar (see the right side of Figure 2-1), success seems within grasp. Stability problems that dogged previous versions aren't as readily apparent — which is to say, Sidebar doesn't crash nearly as often as, say, Active Desktop in Windows XP — and the items it offers actually help.

The items in the Sidebar, termed *Gadgets,* can interact with you, with Windows, with files and folders, with your network, and with other Gadgets. Vista ships with a handful of moderately interesting Gadgets — a clock (you can put more than one clock on your desktop, each set to a different time zone), an RSS reader, an application launcher, and others.

Gadgets start on the Sidebar, but they don't have to stay there. Simply click and drag a Gadget anyplace you like.

Figure 2-3:
Windows
Flip lets you
riffle through
running
programs.

Gadget creation has blossomed into a cottage industry. To add more, hover your mouse over the Sidebar, click the plus sign (+) at the top of the Sidebar, or run a Google search on "Vista Gadgets."

What You Get

The old Windows XP Media Center Edition was billed — and sold — as a separate operating system, almost exclusively available on new PCs. That always struck me as odd because Media Center is an application that runs on top of Windows just like, oh, Internet Explorer or the Windows Media Player.

In Vista, if you buy the right version (Home Premium or Ultimate; see Book I, Chapter 3), Media Center comes along for the ride. Remarkably, if Media Center isn't included in your version of Vista, Microsoft allows you to upgrade to Media Center–savvy versions without much fanfare: All you need is a credit card.

Many other features — less sexy but every bit as useful — put Vista head and shoulders above XP. The standout features include the following:

✦ Improved backup (although Home Basic Edition won't let you back up automatically, or onto network drives).

✦ Photo management (via PhotoGallery).

✦ Second monitor support (not in Home Basic — do you detect a pattern here?).

✦ Easy wireless networking.

✦ Desktop search gets built into the operating system itself, instead of tagging along like a hungry puppy.

✦ Vista also helps you burn DVDs from your home movies with a very rudimentary DVD burning program.

What Stands in the Way

Security is A Good Thing. No, really.

Vista's security settings can drive you nuts, and make you click and click and click again. In Jefferson's day, the price of freedom was eternal vigilance. Today, the price of security is infernal clicking.

Progress.

Vista includes built-in defenses against many kinds of malware, spyware, and phishing attempts. The "Standard" user security level settings (see Book II, Chapter 2) aren't as powerful as those in WinXP. That means you, or a rogue program trying to pretend it's you, can't clobber the system as easily as if you had the power to change anything and everything on your PC. Conversely, if a Standard user wants to make significant changes to her PC, she should expect some delay, inconvenience, and the occasional utterly inscrutable message — lots of reasons to keep this book at hand.

Perhaps surprisingly, Vista's outbound firewall — the piece of software that monitors information going out of your PC — lacks a decent user interface. If you want to keep track of the data leaving your machine, expect lots of, uh, challenges (see Book III, Chapter 3).

Many of Vista's new security features feel like they were bolted onto the old Windows XP framework — and, truth be told, some of them were. The most important security improvements, however, lie deep within Vista itself. See `www.microsoft.com/technet/windowsvista/evaluate/feat/` `secfeat.mspx` for a detailed explanation.

Do You Need Windows Vista?

Probably not.

If you have a PC with Windows XP installed, and it works well enough for what you want to do, leave it alone. Ain't broke. Don't fix. Keep your Windows XP machine updated with the latest security patches, as soon as they're tested and found to be reliable (see `www.AskWoody.com`). But don't throw it in the trash heap yet.

Some programs that Microsoft created for Vista run just fine on Windows XP. Windows Defender, the antispyware product, works on XP. Vista's initial version of Windows Media Player, WMP 11, runs rings around its earlier incarnation, as does Internet Explorer 7 — but you can run both on Windows XP. Don't pay for Vista if you have an XP system and you only want the latest versions of Defender, WMP, or IE. You have better ways to throw away your greenbacks.

More than that, if the computer you have only supports Vista Home Basic (probably because of an older video card), don't bother with Vista; stick with Windows XP. You won't see much benefit — literally and figuratively.

On the other hand, if you want to take advantage of the many, manifest, and truly compelling goodies in Vista, you could consider upgrading in the following cases:

✦ If you own a fairly modern PC (say, an Intel Pentium 4 running at 1.8 GHz or so, or an AMD Opteron 144 or higher), with several hundred megabytes of free disk space.

✦ If you have 1GB of memory or you're willing to shell out the grub to get it.

✦ If your video card can handle the load. Many laptops simply can't run Vista, and video upgrades rate as too expensive — or just plain impossible.

I don't recommend that you try to upgrade to Vista unless you have enough video power to drive the Aero Glass interface. For most Windows XP users, that's the crucial upgrade decision point: The video card represents the biggest — and costliest — hurdle.

Most (but not all!) video cards that run Aero Glass use chipsets from the Big Five video chip manufacturers. For the latest info on Vista video vicissitudes, see the sites listed in Table 2-1.

Want to know which video card inhabits your PC? Click Start, right-click Computer, choose Properties. In the ensuing dialog box, click the Device Manager link at the top. If you have an Administrator account, click Continue to get through the blasted User Account Control warning. (If you don't have an Administrator account, you have to beg, borrow or steal an Administrator ID and password.) Double-click the line that says Display Adapters. *Violá.*

Table 2-1	Manufacturers' Vista Sites
Manufacturer	*Web Site*
NVidia	www.nvidia.com/page/technology_vista_home.html
ATI	www.ati.com/technology/windowsvista/index.html
S3	www.s3graphics.com/en/products/vista/index.jsp
VIA	www.via.com.tw/en/products/vista/platform.jsp
Intel	www.intel.com/support/graphics/sb/CS-023621.htm

Technically, at a minimum, the graphics card must have "DirectX 9" and "Windows Display Driver Model" (WDDM) support, but it's easier to let the chipset manufacturers guide your decision than to wade through detailed spec sheets, doncha think?

Here's the bottom line: You probably will be more productive with Vista, and if your machine (particularly your graphics card) can handle the load, I recommend that you upgrade. It isn't easy. But, in my experience at least, it's well worth the effort.

Chapter 3: Choosing a Version

In This Chapter

✔ The eight flavors of Vista

✔ Versions you don't want — and features that you do want

✔ Choosing the right version for you

✔ Considering Windows Live OneCare

*I*f you haven't yet bought a copy of Vista, you could save yourself some headaches and more than a few bucks by getting the right version the first time. And if you're thinking about paying for Windows Live OneCare, hey, put that money back in your pocket.

It's hard to keep track of all the various Vista versions without a scorecard. That's where this chapter comes in.

The Eightfold Path

Windows Vista appears in eight — count 'em *eight* — different versions. Fortunately, most people only need to concern themselves with four, and you can probably winnow the list down to two or three pretty quickly.

Microsoft chose the feature sets assigned to specific Vista versions with one specific goal in mind: maximizing Microsoft profits. That's why you'll find plenty of upgrade routes and plenty of opportunity to spend more money through the Windows Anytime Upgrade program (see Figure 3-1), which lets you upgrade from Home Basic Edition to Home Premium, Home Basic to Ultimate, Home Premium to Ultimate, or Business Edition to Ultimate. That's also why it's important for your financial health to get the right version the first time.

Windows Anytime Upgrades count as pure gravy for Microsoft: Log on to the Internet or call a Microsoft "partner," hand over your credit card number, and upgrade on the spot. You don't get a new box or a new CD. All you get is a new product key and the instructions for installing the software from media that's already in your possession — plus or minus a few big downloads. Pure profit for the folks in Redmond. Smart.

In a nutshell, Vista's eight versions (and targeted customer bases) look like this:

✦ **Windows Starter 2007** (Microsoft won't even call it "Vista"), a severely stunted version. Starter's only available in specific developing countries, where the price of Vista generally exceeds the average monthly income.

✦ **Vista Home Basic Edition,** directed at first-time home computer users who are looking for a bargain. Cheap, in all senses of the word.

✦ **Vista Home N** matches Home Basic, except Windows Media Player has been removed. It's a goofy version mandated by Microsoft's losses in court.

✦ **Vista Home Premium Edition** has all the features home users want and need, as well as many features that appeal to folks with small businesses.

✦ **Vista Business Edition** aims for small-business users — those who work for companies without computer departments — who have no interest in the fun side of PCs. Really.

✦ **Vista Business N** includes everything in the Business Edition, except for Windows Media Player. Goofy with a tie.

✦ **Vista Enterprise Edition** has all the extra bells and whistles needed to attach the PC to a large corporate network, plus several enhanced security features.

✦ **Vista Ultimate** includes everything in the Home Premium and Enterprise Editions, plus the promise that Microsoft may dribble out extra goodies. Microsoft has shown almost no interest in providing free goodies, and Vista Service Pack 1 has significantly toned down the "Extras" hype.

Figure 3-1:
Windows
Anytime
Upgrade.

The subscription model

Microsoft is trying valiantly to move from a "purchase" sales model to a "subscription" model: Instead of selling you a shrink-wrapped box with Windows inside, or bundling a fully functional copy of Windows with new PCs, Microsoft wants to keep you going back to the trough, dropping a few bucks here and a few bucks there.

Many large companies now rent their copies of Windows and Office, using one of several Microsoft volume licensing plans. The companies benefit by being able to upgrade to the latest and greatest new versions with no additional charge. Microsoft benefits by sucking in cash year after year. The overlying question, obviously, is whether the companies are paying too much.

There aren't any plans, as yet, to move consumers like you and me over to the pay-and-pay-and-pay-as-you-go approach. (Microsoft tried the subscription model for Office consumers in Australia several years ago, and it failed miserably. A pilot program for Vista is ongoing in developing countries, but it hasn't drawn much interest.) Instead, in Vista, you'll find persistent attempts to get you to upgrade — a harbinger of marketing approaches to come.

Before you tear your hair out trying to determine whether you bought the right version, or which edition you should buy your Great Aunt Ethel, rest assured that choosing the right version is much simpler than it first appears.

Versions to Ignore

Of the eight versions listed in the preceding section, you can immediately ignore four of them:

+ Even if Windows Starter 2007 is available where you live, you don't want it. Microsoft hobbles it severely — it's limited to 1024 x 768 screens, has no networking, has no Aero Glass, offers a maximum of three simultaneous open windows, and on and on — and generally locks Starter in with a non-English interface.

+ Forget about the "N" versions, too. The "N" stands for "No Windows Media Player," and these versions exist solely to placate European regulators whose court battles resulted in victory long after the cows had left the barn. Of course, if you don't like WMP (and I make alternate recommendations several places in this book), you're under no requirement to *use* WMP: Simply ignore it and WMP pretty much goes away. I can't imagine why anybody would buy an "N" Vista.

+ Microsoft makes Windows Vista Enterprise Edition available solely as part of a volume licensing plan — in other words, you can't buy it. You can only rent it, and you have to rent at least five copies at a time. If your company gives you a copy of Enterprise Edition, take it, but realize that you won't be able to burn video DVDs and you won't get any of the Media Center goodies. On the other hand, you have everything you need to hook up to your company's big network and keep your PC secure to corporate standards, which may or may not suit your tastes.

The Final Four

The final four Vista versions — Home Basic, Home Premium, Business, and Ultimate — include your most likely choices. See Table 3-1 for an overview of the key features in Home Basic, Home Premium, and Business. Vista Ultimate, of course, has everything.

Table 3-1	Vista Versions and Key Features		
Feature	*Home Basic*	*Home Premium*	*Business*
Aero Glass interface	No	Yes	Yes
Media Center	No	Yes	No
Burn DVD videos	No	Yes	No
Remote Desktop "host"	No	No	Yes
MeetingSpace for ad-hoc networking	No	Yes	Yes
Automated and network backups	No	Yes	Yes
Auto-backups (ShadowCopy)	No	No	Yes
Parental controls	Yes	Yes	No
BitLocker drive encryption	No	No	Yes

As I explain in Book I, Chapter 2, the Aero Glass really works only if you have a sufficiently powerful graphics card. If you're wondering what some of this other stuff is, let the following points be your guide:

✦ Remote Desktop is a program that lets someone control your PC or vice versa, with the computer owner's permission. If you work in an office at a medium-to-large corporation, some IT employee has probably used it to help you fix a problem on your PC. If you're interested in running your PC from another PC, perhaps to retrieve your e-mail or grab a forgotten file while you're traveling, look at less-problematic programs like LogMeIn. See Book V Chapter 1 for details.

✦ If your hard drive has ever crashed or your computer has otherwise gone berserk, you know the value of a backup, whether you had one at the time or not. All Vista versions include the ability to manually run a backup and store the backup on your PC. Home Premium and Business add both the ability to back up to networked drives (hard drives inside other computers on your network) and the ability to run scheduled backups (so the backups happen automatically and you don't have to think about it).

✦ Some folks need an extra layer of security — especially if they work with spreadsheets of employees' personal data or other confidential information. BitLocker encrypts an entire hard drive, so even if the drive (or your computer) is stolen, the bad guys will have a very hard time recovering any data on it.

Home Basic: Thumbs down

Vista Bait 'n' Switch, er, Home Basic Edition comes preinstalled on cheap PCs (literally and figuratively).

Microsoft released this version for two good reasons:

✦ Installing Home Basic on consumer PCs keeps the initial purchase price for some new PCs at a deceptively low level.

✦ Home Basic gives you the, uh, opportunity to buy an upgrade to Home Premium — the version you should've bought in the first place.

Golly. Leave it to Microsoft to find yet another way to milk that old cash cow.

Home Basic doesn't support the Aero Glass interface (see Book I, Chapter 2). No Media Center. No high-definition video editing. No DVD video burning. No Tablet PC support. You can't back up to a networked drive or have your computer backed up automatically in the middle of the night. You can watch a MeetingSpace presentation (an ad-hoc collaboration of PCs that are near each other), but you can't give one. In short, many of the reasons why most people like Vista in the first place just don't appear in Home Basic.

If you took the bait and bought Home Basic, fish out your credit card and follow the Windows Anytime Upgrade instructions that came with your PC to hook up with Premium — or even tackle Vista Ultimate.

Business Edition: Maybe

Vista Business Edition aims for the small business user, but most people can find good business reasons to buy either Home Premium or Ultimate.

Pick the Business Edition over the Home Premium version of Vista for any of the following reasons:

✦ You have a computer that contains two physically separate CPU sockets or a 64-bit system with more than 128GB of memory. Would that we were all so lucky.

✦ You want ShadowCopy to automatically make backup copies of all your files whenever you change them, or you want to be able to make full "ghost" copies of an entire hard drive.

Many applications, including all the Microsoft Office applications, can make backup copies automatically every time you open them.

✦ You need added security, as in the Encrypting File System (see the sidebar), you want control over the installation of drivers, or you use logon validation with, say, smart cards. (But if you want BitLocker, you have to get the Enterprise Edition — which is only available for licensees — or Ultimate.)

✦ You might plug your computer into a "domain" client/server network. In that case, you need the Business Edition's software to connect to the server and access the network. Moreover, Windows Rights Management System (RMS) may rear its ugly head in a domain, and Business Edition includes the program you need to get to RMS-blocked documents.

✦ You want to use your computer as a Remote Desktop host, turning your computer into a long-distance puppet. Any authorized Windows computer connected to the Internet can control the Remote Desktop host, but you must have Vista Business Edition or Ultimate to allow it to be controlled.

Many businesspeople find that LogMeIn, a free alternative to Remote Desktop, does everything they need, and that Remote Desktop amounts to overkill.

While the Business Edition does support Aero Glass, it doesn't include Media Center, Windows Movie Maker, or DVD video burning — all of which should prove worthwhile for many businesspeople.

The Encrypting File System and BitLocker

The Encrypting File System (EFS) encrypts designated files or folders on a hard drive. EFS does a good job of locking down data, but it can be compromised if a bad guy can get to your computer. Widely available tools can crack EFS if the cracker can reboot the, uh, crackee's computer. Thus, for example, EFS can't protect the hard drive on a stolen laptop.

That's why you may want Microsoft's BitLocker, which is only available in Vista's Business Enterprise and Ultimate versions. If you want to protect your data from being viewed by anyone who steals your hard drive, you need BitLocker. You may also decide that hardware-level encryption isn't worth the expense or effort, because many applications provide competent (but not unbreakable) encryption for individual files.

Home Premium: Usually the sweet spot

For almost everyone, Home Premium rates as the sweet spot among the eight versions. You get all the features that most people want in the Ultimate Edition except the following:

✦ Remote Desktop host. A good free alternative, LogMeIn, is discussed in the preceding section.

✦ Windows Web Server and Fax Client, which you probably don't want anyway.

✦ A handful of obscure capabilities, including a UNIX subsystem, a single-session Virtual PC, the Multi-Language User Interface (which lets one copy of Vista show interfaces in different languages), and Secure Startup. If you need any of those, you already know it.

The Ultimate

Microsoft may find some compelling additions to make the Ultimate Edition worthwhile — the list, no doubt, will change from time to time. But most folks who shell out the extra bucks aren't as concerned about saving money as they are in having all the bells and whistles. Serious bragging rights, too.

Sure, it's a cool toy, but you can live without it. Unless you absolutely *have* to get Hold em Poker.

Windows Live OneCare

Microsoft tries, in many ways, to get you to sign up for Windows Live OneCare, the 'Softie's fledgling attempt to make money by plugging the holes in its own product.

Here's what $50 per year buys, for up to three computers in a single household:

✦ **An antivirus program:** AVG Free (see Book III, Chapter 5) does a great job, and it's free for individual use.

✦ **An antispyware program:** Windows Defender (see Book III, Chapter 5) is a very good program, although it has flaws, both by commission and omission. Still, it's free and already built into Vista. You don't need to pay for it.

✦ **A firewall:** But you already have a good one, with a lousy interface (see Book III, Chapter 3).

✦ **A bunch of little guys:** A backup program (you already have one; see Book II, Chapter 3), a Windows patching program (see Book III, Chapter 4), a program that defrags your hard drive (see Book II, Chapter 3) . . . well, you get the picture.

Wonder what's really happening? See the sidebar "The subscription model," earlier in this chapter.

 Find a non-Microsoft alternative to Windows Live OneCare, or go with the free products discussed in this book. Save your money for something worthwhile and, by doing so, encourage Microsoft to fix its products free of charge. The nerve.

Surviving Service Packs

Microsoft releases security patches for Windows Vista every month, with various non-security patches appearing sporadically. Once in a blue moon — say, every year or so — the Softies aggregate all the security patches, toss in some miscellaneous fixes and updates, and unleash a granddaddy of an update called a *Service Pack*.

Don't read anything into the terminology: At various times, in different contexts, Microsoft has labeled these granddaddy updates *patch roll-ups, Service Releases,* and *Service Packs.* One Service Pack, Windows XP Service Pack 2, incorporated so many key changes and improvements that it could've been billed as a whole new operating system. Most other roll-ups, releases, and packs pale in comparison. And that brings me to Windows Vista Service Pack 1.

Vista SP1 (as it's known to the cognoscenti) rolls up the security patches; fixes several confounding flaws (including Vista's leisurely approach to shut down and its voracious appetite for network bandwidth when looking at networked files); adds support for some new technology (such as Extensible Firmware Interface, which is slowly replacing BIOS); and improves the way Vista plays with other software. All in all, it's pretty ho-hum.

Microsoft's primary impetus for releasing SP1? Major changes in the way Vista interacts with servers in Big Corporate Networks. Vista plumbing had to be fixed in anticipation of Windows Server 2008.

That said, every Vista owner should take an hour or so (depending on your Internet speed) to install Vista Service Pack 1. To see if you already have SP1, click Start, right-click Computer, and choose Properties. The box that says Windows Edition mentions Service Pack 1 if your machine has already swallowed the SP1 pill. To get SP1, should you need it, choose Start ➪ Programs and at the top of the list choose Windows Update. Follow the instructions and you get SP1 with a minimum of fuss.

Chapter 4: Upgrades and Clean Installs

In This Chapter

✔ **What's a clean install?**

✔ **Performing an upgrade or a clean install**

✔ **Getting your files and settings transferred from another computer**

✔ **Activating Vista**

✔ **Did Vista die? Don't panic**

*I*f your current machine runs Windows XP, you can upgrade to Windows Vista by simply starting Windows, inserting the Vista CD into the CD drive, and following the instructions.

Before you do, though, take a few minutes to read this chapter. It may save you hours, days, or even months of headaches.

And if you ever get the urge to throw in the towel, wipe out your hard drive and install Vista all over again, follow the nostrums here to minimize the chances of complete disaster.

Can Your Computer Handle Vista?

Before you install Vista on a PC, it would behoove you to find out exactly what you're going to get. The primary question isn't whether Vista can run on your PC — requirements for Vista's minimal existence are surprisingly Spartan. What you really need to know is whether your computer can handle the "Glass" interface — or whether Vista will automatically turn off Glass. The answer to that question is by no means certain.

Here's what Microsoft says:

✦ You can run Vista on almost any modern computer (800-MHz processor or faster) with a fair amount of main memory (512MB) and a plain-vanilla video card (800 x 600 SVGA). You also need a DVD player because Vista ships on a DVD, but the DVD player can be a portable player, connected via a USB port.

Just because you *can* run Vista doesn't mean you really want to — or that you'll be able to live with yourself or your computer if you try. In my experience, Vista runs like a slug on a 1-GHz (1,000-MHz) processor with 512MB.

✦ If you want the Glass experience, you'll need a 1-GHz computer with 1GB of memory, plus a fairly powerful graphics card with at least 128MB of its own memory, capable of running Microsoft's DirectX 9 or WDDM (Windows Display Driver Model) software.

Every video card chip manufacturer says that all its recent chipsets can handle Glass — but what would you expect them to say? The single greatest bottleneck most people will have in upgrading to Vista lies in the video card. If you're stuck with an on-board video card (many laptops can't be upgraded), think long and hard about moving from Windows 2000 or XP to Vista.

Before you upgrade an existing PC to Vista, you should check the machine to make sure that there are no known problems and that you have enough hardware to run the parts of Vista that appeal to you. One way to do this is to use a program Microsoft distributes called the Windows Vista Upgrade Advisor. To reach into the innermost parts of your PC with this program, follow these steps:

1. **Download the Advisor from `www.microsoft.com/windowsvista/getready/upgradeadvisor/default.mspx`. You may also find a copy on a free CD at your friendly local computer shop.**

Before you can run the Windows Vista Upgrade Advisor on a Windows XP computer, you have to install a big, bloated, buggy set of programs called the .NET Framework. If you expect that you'll be wiping out your XP computer and installing Vista anyway, there's no harm in succumbing to the .NET siren call. But if you might not be upgrading to Vista, think twice about installing the .NET can of worms.

2. **Run through the installation wizard.**

3. **Follow the prompts as the Advisor asks you to choose which features you want in Vista (for example, controlling a TV or connecting to a corporate network).**

The Advisor then recommends a version of Vista that meets your requirements and adjusts its scan accordingly. You'll see its reports on potential problems with the upgrade, hardware deficiencies (see Figure 4-1), drivers that may require manual installation (see Figure 4-2), and incompatible software.

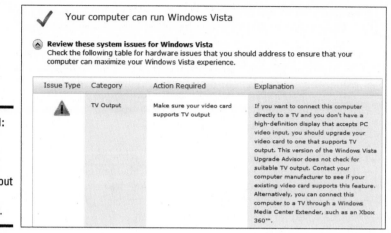

Figure 4-1:
The Vista
Upgrade
Advisor
warns about
missing
hardware.

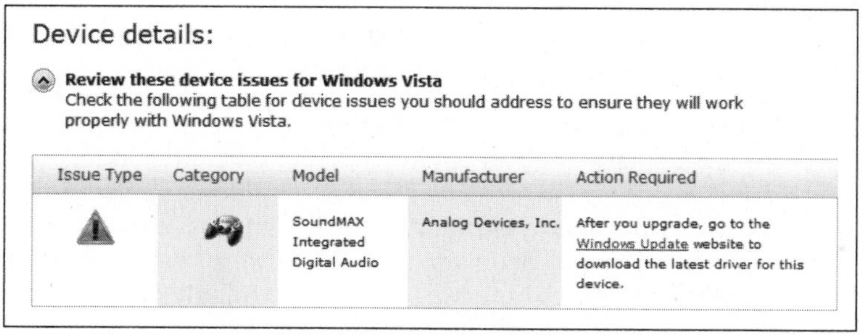

Figure 4-2:
The Upgrade
Advisor also
checks for
all neces-
sary drivers,
warning if
you have to
go looking
for them.

You can find a tremendous, unbiased list of Vista compatibility problem reports covering every imaginable piece of hardware and software available at www.ntcompatible.com/compatibility.html. In spite of its name, the NT Compatible Web site deals with Windows NT, 2000, XP, and Vista.

Performing a Clean Install

Windows Vista is an enormously complex program. In the best of all possible worlds, if you upgrade from your current version of Windows XP, the upgrade routines successfully grab all your old settings, get rid of the extraneous garbage that's floating around on your old machine, and install a stable, pristine copy of Windows Vista, ready for you to take around the block.

Unfortunately, the world is not always a pretty place, and your hard drive probably looks like a bit-strewn sewer. Historically, Windows has been considerably less stable for upgraders than for those who perform a *clean install* — wiping out the contents of the hard drive and starting over again. All the flotsam and jetsam left from an old version of Windows invariably mucks up the works with the new version.

A clean install is not for the faint of heart. No matter how hard you try, you will lose data, somewhere, somehow — it always happens, even to those of us masochists who have been running clean installs for a decade. If you value everything on your computer, go for the simple upgrade. If you want your PC to run more smoothly, think about a clean install.

The following is my general procedure for a clean install on computers that can boot from the CD drive, in very broad terms:

1. **Download and install Revelation from SnadBoy software at www.snadboy.com (see Figure 4-3).**

   Revelation lets you look "underneath" the ***** blocked-out passwords in almost all Windows applications. In particular, it lets you retrieve the passwords that you use in Outlook, Outlook Express, and/or Windows Mail to download your mail. Easy Transfer (see the next section in this chapter) is supposed to pick up e-mail settings, but it would behoove you to keep track of those passwords and any others you come across.

2. **Use Revelation for a few days (or weeks!) to grab any passwords that you may have stashed away. Just click the icon, drag it over the password you want to see, and jot down the password that appears. (See Figure 4-3.)**

   Revelation can't pick up passwords on Web pages, but it does a very credible job of revealing passwords for almost everything else.

3. **If you use Roboform (see Book V, Chapter 3) to keep track of your Web passwords, transfer your password file to a key disk and use that disk for a while to ensure that you have everything.**

   Take your time and get all your passwords. They may be very difficult to retrieve or re-create after a clean install.

Click this icon   Read the password here

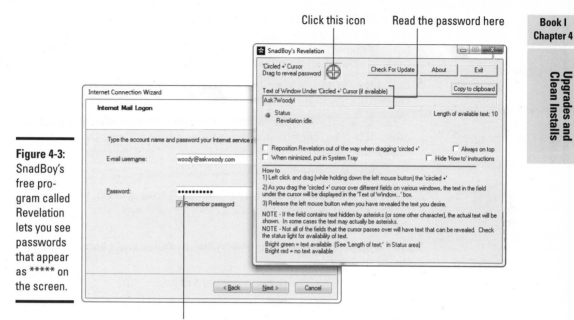

Figure 4-3:
SnadBoy's
free pro-
gram called
Revelation
lets you see
passwords
that appear
as ***** on
the screen.

Drag icon over a password

4. Make sure that you have current CDs for all the software that you nor-mally use.

If the programs require installation keys (sometimes called the product key, CD key, or activation code, among others), you need those keys, too. You can see the installation keys for Windows and Office by running Nir Sofer's free ProduKey, available at `www.nirsoft.net/utils/product_cd_key_viewer.html`.

If you're using Windows XP and plan to perform a clean install of Vista on the same machine, take a minute to make sure that you still have your old Windows XP product key — that 25-character monstrosity printed on a yellow tag on the CD jewel case or on a label on your computer case. That way, if Vista goes to Hades in a handbasket, at least you can reinstall Windows XP. Can't find the jewel case? ProduKey can tell you the key.

5. Back up everything. Twice.

If you have a Windows Vista computer handy, and you can attach it to the PC that you're upgrading through a network or a direct-connect cable, you may want to try a Vulcan Mind Meld, er, a before-and-after Windows Vista Easy Transfer. First, use Easy Transfer (see the "Using Easy Transfer" section, later in this chapter) to transfer all your files and settings from the computer you'll be upgrading to the interim PC, temporarily. Then upgrade your PC. Finally, follow the instructions again to move the files and settings from the interim PC back to your (freshly upgraded) original PC.

6. Insert the Windows Vista installation disc in the CD drive, and then choose Start⇨Shut Down to go through a full shut down.

Windows Vista may offer to install itself while you're trying to shut down. If it does, click the Cancel button. Power off the PC and wait at least a full minute.

7. Turn the power on.

8. If the PC is capable of starting ("booting") from the CD, you see text on the screen that says something like `Press any key to boot from CD`. Press Enter.

9. Go through the steps indicated by the installer and choose to format the hard drive.

That wipes out all the data on the hard drive.

10. Pick up your jaw from the floor, kick yourself twice for being so obstinate, pat yourself on the back for starting out fresh, and follow through with the rest of the installation.

Windows Vista does a good job of taking you through the steps. The only really tricky part of the installation: Windows Vista has to restart your PC once in the installation process. When that happens, you'll probably get that `Press any key to boot from the CD` message again. This time — the second time you see the message — ignore it. Let Windows Vista start itself from the hard drive.

11. Continue with the steps in this chapter to work with the Welcome Center.

If you started a Vulcan Mind Meld in Step 4, your old PC's identity is waiting for you on an interim PC. Use Windows Easy Transfer to bring it back.

Clean installs rate right up there with root canals. Nobody in his right mind will try one, unless he really wants to make sure that Windows will run smoothly. That said, I try to perform a clean install on all my systems at least once a year. It can make a big performance difference.

Working through the Welcome Center

Immediately after you turn on your new computer, or upgrade to Vista, Windows greets you with the "welcome to your computer" screen shown in Figure 4-4.

Figure 4-4:
Vista's
Welcome
Center.

Take a few minutes to step through the following Get Started with Windows topics:

1. **If you can see it, click the Set Up Devices link. (If you can't see a Set Up Devices link, breathe a sigh of relief and go to Step 2!)**

If Vista had a hard time installing a device driver during the initial setup, you have a chance to reprimand it here. Sound cards frequently appear on the list. It doesn't make much sense, but Vista has an easier time installing device drivers when it's already up and running. If you need to install additional drivers, click the Set Up Devices option and follow the instructions.

2. **If more than one person will be using the computer, and you haven't already set up an account for each of them, click the Add New Users option.**

Follow the steps indicated to add new accounts. It's easy, although choosing between account types — Standard or Administrator — can be tough (see Book II, Chapter 2).

3. **Click the View Computer Details option, and then click Show More Details (near the top).**

This is the place to fume over the fact that your computer's Windows Experience Index isn't anywhere close to what you thought it would be (see Figure 4-5).

Microsoft doesn't release much information about the methods it uses to calculate the Experience Index. If you try a Google search on "Vista Experience Index" or "Vista Performance Rating," you find an enormous collection of speculation and rumor, but precious little fact. Suffice it to say that a PC with a rating of 4 generally runs faster than one rated a 3 but not by enough to worry about. The difference between a 5 and a 2, though, can knock your socks off. See Technique 1 in my *Vista Timesaving Techniques For Dummies* (also from Wiley) for a thorough explanation.

4. **To see details about your computer's performance, and to run through recommendations that Microsoft makes to improve performance on your machine, click the Performance link in the lower-left corner.**

5. **Back in the View Basic Information panel, click the Change Settings link to bring up the System Properties dialog box (you may have to click Continue to get through the User Account Control warning), and then click the Change button.**

This is the easiest place in all of Vista to change the name of your computer, or to tell Vista the name of your "workgroup" network.

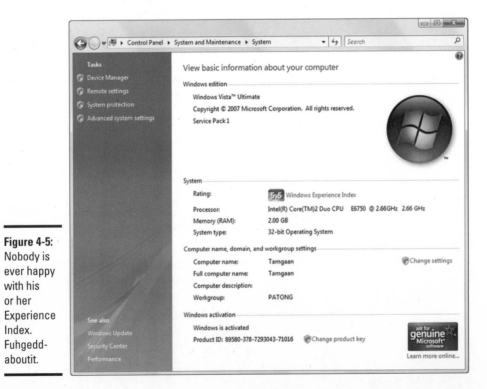

Figure 4-5: Nobody is ever happy with his or her Experience Index. Fuhgedd-aboutit.

6. **To hook your computer into your workgroup, type its name in the bottom box, marked Workgroup, and then click the OK button twice.**

   You'll have to restart your computer, but when it comes up for air, it'll be attached to the workgroup you designated.

7. **If you want to move files and settings from another computer to this one, back at the Welcome screen (refer to Figure 4-4), click the Transfer Files and Settings link . . .**

   . . . and continue with Windows Easy Transfer in the next section.

Using Easy Transfer

Windows Vista's Easy Transfer feature makes transferring certain kinds of settings and data files between two computers comparatively easy. It sounds great and works well, as long as you don't expect too much. You need to be aware of the following limitations:

+ **It's best if the two PCs are connected.** The PC you're transferring files and settings *to* must be running Windows Vista. If at all possible, it should be connected to the PC that you're transferring settings *from*. The *from* PC can be running Windows 2000, XP, or Vista.

   Easy Transfer can send a humongous amount of data from one PC to another. You can schlep a key disk from one machine to another, if you have a few spare hours (or days). Far better, though, is if you can get both PCs talking to each other on a network. Failing that, you can connect the PCs with a USB cable, use an external hard drive, or even burn and then read CDs or DVDs. Easy Transfer can work with any of 'em.

+ **Easy Transfer can't install your old programs on your new PC.** You have to do that yourself, manually, one at a time, generally from the original CDs that the programs came on.

   If you use Easy Transfer but you don't install all your old programs on your new PC, weird things may happen on the new PC. You may double-click a file in Vista, for example, and have Windows say that it can't find the program associated with the file. Outlook may have trouble displaying a file attached to a message. Nothing earth-shattering will happen, mind you, but it can be annoying.

+ **Easy Transfer only picks up data files, some settings, and Windows Registry entries (see the next section).** That means you can't expect it to pull across all your passwords, and some copy-protection schemes (on games, for example) may go haywire.

On the plus side, though, Easy Transfer doesn't pick up much of the garbage that seems to accumulate in every Windows PC, such as vestiges of long-forgotten programs and Registry entries that lead nowhere, which means you can use it without gumming up your new computer. Too much.

Vista's Windows Easy Transfer takes advantage of technology developed by an innovative Hawaii-based company called Alohabob. Microsoft bought Alohabob late in Vista's development cycle, so the very early copies of Vista didn't include the Alohabob transfer goodies. As long as you've updated your copy of Vista (using Windows Update or Microsoft Update; see Book III, Chapter 4), you have all of the Alohabob improvements at your disposal. All in all, Windows Easy Transfer works very well indeed.

What will transfer

Here are the kinds of things Easy Transfer should pick up in a transfer:

+ **Data files:** If you're transferring *from* Windows XP or 2000, expect to see files from your Windows desktop, the My Documents folder (including My Pictures and My Music, if you have those in the My Documents folder), and the Shared Desktop and Documents folders. If you're transferring from another Vista machine, the folder names are different (for example, Documents instead of My Documents), but the usual suspects remain the same.

+ **Other files scattered around your hard drive(s),** as long as Windows recognizes them as common data files.

Easy Transfer generally chooses which files to transfer based on the filename extension. It looks for filename extensions that are commonly associated with data files, such as .doc or .jpg. See the section on showing filename extensions in Book II, Chapter 1 for a lengthy tirade on this topic.

+ **Settings for Windows (desktop, screen savers, taskbar options, and so on), Windows Explorer, Internet Explorer (including your list of Favorites), and Outlook Express:** If your *from* machine runs Vista, you'll get the settings for Windows Mail.

+ **All your Microsoft Office settings,** plus many of the Registry-based settings for other programs.

Making the transfer

To use Easy Transfer, follow these steps:

1. **Make sure that Windows Vista is up and running on the *to* PC.**

Get your hardware installed, go through the Welcome Center (see the section "Working through the Welcome Center," earlier in this chapter), and run Windows Vista long enough to be familiar with it.

2. **Log on to the *to* PC as the user who's supposed to receive all the files and settings from the *from* PC.**

   If both the *to* and *from* PCs are connected to your network, choose Start⇨Network Places or Start⇨Computer to make sure that the network connection is up and kicking. If they aren't connected to the same network, get a USB cable and attach it to the USB ports on both PCs, or get that big stack of CDs ready.

3. **Choose Start⇨Windows Easy Transfer, if it's on the Start menu.**

   If it isn't on the Start menu, choose Start⇨All Programs⇨Accessories⇨System Tools⇨Windows Easy Transfer.

4. **Follow the steps on the screen (see Figure 4-6).**

   The exact steps vary depending on the method you're using to transfer the data. If you have many large documents or picture files, set aside a few hours to work through the whole process.

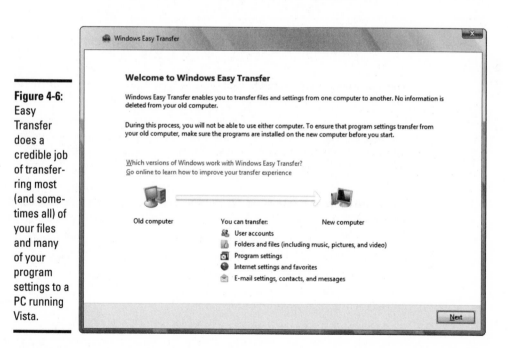

Figure 4-6: Easy Transfer does a credible job of transferring most (and sometimes all) of your files and many of your program settings to a PC running Vista.

Product Activation

When you buy a copy of Windows Vista in a shrink-wrapped box, you're allowed to install it on one — and only one — PC.

When you buy a new PC with Windows Vista preinstalled, Windows stays with the PC. You can't transfer Windows Vista from the original, bundled machine to a different machine. Microsoft uses a technique called *BIOS locking* to make sure that the copy of Windows Vista that ships with a PC stays tied to that specific PC, forever and ever.

Some ifs, ands, and buts are floating around (for example, what if you upgrade to Windows Vista and the next day your PC suddenly dies?), but in general, you can't copy Windows Vista and pass around pirate CDs to your buddies or install a single copy on all the machines in your home. If you have three PCs, and you want to run Windows Vista on all of them, you have to buy three copies of Windows Vista, either in shrink-wrapped boxes or preinstalled on new machines.

Corporate licenses are a little different. I talk about them at the end of this section.

Windows Vista enforces this one-Windows-one-PC licensing requirement with a technique called *Windows Product Activation,* or WPA. Here's how WPA works:

1. **The Windows Vista installer asks you to type the unique 25-character code that's printed on the case of your Windows Vista CD.**

Later, the Product Activation program looks at various serial numbers inside your PC — the processor, network card, and disk drives, among others — mixes them together, and produces a second 25-character code that identifies your PC. Those 50 characters, taken together, are called the *Installation ID.*

2. **When you *activate* Windows Vista, you give Microsoft that 50-character Installation ID.**

If you bought a new PC with Vista installed, it's already been activated.

If you installed Vista from a CD, you probably told Vista to activate itself as soon as it was online (see Figure 4-7). Passing Windows Activation automatically approves you for the Windows Genuine Advantage program (see the nearby sidebar for details).

If you haven't activated your copy of Vista, a not-so-subtle "bubble" reminder near the system clock tells you how many days remain before you must activate.

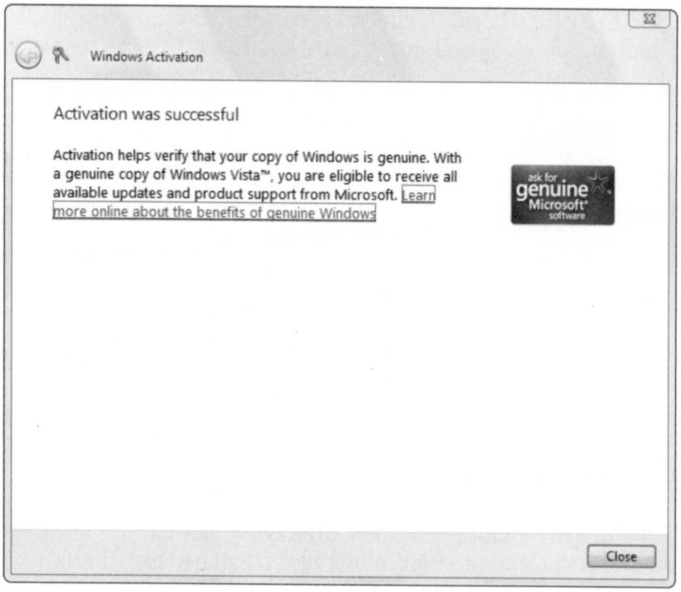

Figure 4-7:
The
Windows
Activation
window.

> Windows Activation
>
> Activation was successful
>
> Activation helps verify that your copy of Windows is genuine. With
> a genuine copy of Windows Vista™, you are eligible to receive all
> available updates and product support from Microsoft. Learn
> more online about the benefits of genuine Windows
>
> ask for
> **genuine**
> Microsoft®
> software
>
> Close

When you or your computer attempt to activate Vista over the Internet, Microsoft checks to see whether anybody else has submitted the 25-character code from the case of the Windows Vista CD.

- If nobody else has activated that 25-character code from the CD case, or if the 25-character code has been activated with that specific Installation ID (which means you activated this particular copy of Windows Vista from the same PC twice), Microsoft sends back a 42-character *Confirmation ID.* Both the Installation ID and the Confirmation ID are stored on your PC.

- If that 25-character code has already been used on a different PC, though, you get a polite message on your machine saying, `According to our records, the number of times that you can activate Windows with this product key has been exceeded. Please enter a different product key, and then click Retry.` You're given further instructions for contacting Microsoft, if you feel the need.

3. **Every couple of weeks or so, when Windows Vista starts, it recalculates the 25-character code that's based on the various serial numbers inside your PC.**

   If the code matches the one that's stored on your PC, and the Confirmation ID is good, Windows takes off.

4. On the other hand, if the recalculated 25-character code doesn't match your original code, pandemonium breaks loose.

Your hard drives start spinning at twice their normal speed, your keyboard gets short-circuited with your PC's power supply, and the local constabulary receives an urgent fax from Redmond with a preapproved no-knock search warrant. Okay, okay. I'm exaggerating a little bit. Here's what really happens:

- If Windows decides that you've only made a few changes to your PC — replaced a hard drive, say, or even changed the motherboard — it lets you start Windows anyway.

- On the other hand, if Windows determines that you've made too many changes, it refuses to start and insists that you contact Microsoft for a new Confirmation ID. That starts the activation cycle all over again. Microsoft has full details at `www.microsoft.com/piracy/basics/activation`.

When you install Vista, you have 30 days to activate it. Windows tries to get you to activate it while you're installing. Failing that, it continues to remind you, relentlessly, as the 30 days tick away. Reinstalling Vista doesn't bypass the activation requirement.

Activating via the Internet makes the whole process of generating, sending, and receiving ID codes invisible: All you know is that the process worked, and you can continue to use the software you bought. If you activate by telephone, though, you have to be sitting at your computer with your Windows Vista installation CD handy. You get to read a bunch of numbers to the rep on the other end of the phone line, and she reads a bunch of numbers back to you so that you can type them into the WPA Wizard.

The original version of Vista would go into an extreme "reduced functionality" mode if you tried to use it after the activation period expired: Basically, you could get at the data (via Safe Mode) and use Internet Explorer for an hour, but that's about it. Vista Service Pack 1 (see Book I, Chapter 3) isn't so draconian. If you've installed SP1, but your copy of Vista fails activation, every hour Vista changes your computer's background to solid black and nags that "this copy of Windows is not genuine," but you can continue to use your computer normally. You can even change the background back to its original state, if you feel so inclined.

Activation is not the same as registration. When you activate Windows Vista, your computer sends Microsoft a 50-character Installation ID — *and nothing else.* When you register Windows Vista (see Figure 4-8), you set up a Windows Live ID (formerly called a Microsoft Passport) and send Microsoft your name, address, telephone number, and any other information that the screens can extract from you.

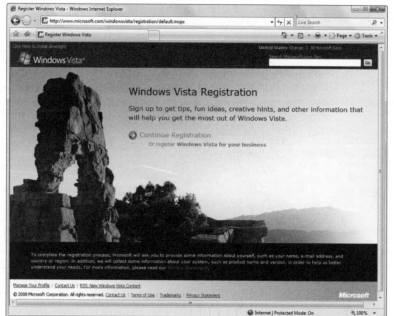

Figure 4-8:
Activation is
mandatory.
Registration
is optional.
There's
absolutely
no reason to
register
Vista.

Activation is a given: You have to activate Vista or it dies. Registration, on the other hand, is entirely optional — and basically useless for pretty much everyone, everywhere. (What? You think Microsoft wants your mailing address to send you a product recall? A birthday card? Sheeesh.) You have no reason in the world to register Windows Vista. Don't do it.

An activation bypass

Big companies with big bucks don't have to put up with Windows Product Activation. (One guess why.) Any company that buys Windows Vista via a site license — that is, buys many copies at a time — gets a special version that doesn't require activation.

If you hear rumors on the Internet about a key that magically bypasses Windows Product Activation, it's probably a jimmied corporate key that somebody is passing around the Net. Microsoft's Windows Genuine Advantage program sniffs out the most widely available and well-known pirated keys, sticks embarrassing notes on your desktop if your copy of Vista doesn't pass muster, and blocks access to all sorts of goodies. (Don't confuse these ham-fisted, widely disseminated pirate keys with the results of "keygen" programs, which produce unique, untraceable, fully functional keys. Big difference.)

Cracking Windows Vista is illegal, immoral, and fattening. Don't do it.

What If the Wheels Fall Off?

So what should you do if Windows Vista dies? Check out the following options:

✦ If you got Windows Vista bundled with a new PC, scream bloody murder at the vendor who sold you the %$#@! thing. Don't put up with any talk about "It's a software problem; Microsoft is at fault." If you bought Vista with a new PC, the company that sold you the machine has full responsibility for making it work right.

✦ If you upgraded from Windows XP or 2000 to Vista, you can always uninstall Vista and go back to your old operating system, as unpalatable as that may seem.

✦ If you upgraded from Windows XP or 2000 and you didn't go through a clean install, try that. You don't have much to lose, eh? Follow the instructions in the section "Performing a Clean Install," earlier in this chapter.

✦ If you've done a clean install and Vista still falls over and plays dead, man, you have my sympathies. Check with your hardware manufacturer and make sure that you have the latest BIOS version installed. (Make sure that you get an instruction book; changing the BIOS is remarkably easy, if you follow the instructions.) Visit the online newsgroups or drop by my lounge, www.askwoody.com/askforhelp.php, to see whether anybody there can lend a hand. If all else fails, admit defeat and reinstall your old operating system.

Life's too short.

Book II

Vista Boot Camp

The 5th Wave   By Rich Tennant

UBER-USER DWAYNE GRANTZ CHALKS UP BEFORE PUTTING WINDOWS VISTA THROUGH ITS PACES.

Contents at a Glance

Chapter 1: Running Vista from Start to Finish 61

Chapter 2: Controlling Users...97

Chapter 3: Maintaining Your System 113

Chapter 4: Getting the Basic Stuff Done 147

Chapter 5: Getting Help with Vista...171

Chapter 1: Running Vista from Start to Finish

In This Chapter

✔ Moving around the desktop

✔ Working with windows (that's "windows" with a wittle *w*)

✔ Showing filename extensions

✔ Taking control of your files

✔ Getting to know a button named Start

✔ Logging off

This chapter explains how to find your way around the Windows windows. If you're an old hand at Windows, you know most of this stuff — such as mousing and interacting with dialog boxes — but I bet some of it will come as a surprise.

Most of all, you need to understand that you don't have to accept all the defaults. Vista was designed to sell more copies of Vista. A lot of that folderol just gets in the way. What's best for Microsoft isn't necessarily best for you, and a few quick clicks can help make your PC more usable, and more . . . *yours.*

User Account Control — the abominable Vista "feature" that halts your computer, demands a response, and flashes the screen like a firefly in heat — falls under the general rubric of "security." I talk about UAC (and how to disable it!) in Book II, Chapter 2. Windows Automatic Update leaves the door open for Microsoft to install anything it likes on your computer. I tell you how to receive notification of impending patches — but keep the 'Softies' mitts off — in Book III, Chapter 4.

A Few Quick Steps to Make the Desktop Your Own

As soon as you *log on* to the computer (that's what it's called when you click your name), you're greeted with an enormous expanse of near-nothingness, cleverly painted with a pretty picture. Your computer manufacturer may have chosen the picture for you, or you might've chosen one yourself during installation.

Vista also shows you the Welcome Center, which you'll probably want to clobber as soon as you can.

Your Windows destiny, such as it is, unfolds on the computer's screen. The screen that Windows shows you every time you start is called the *desktop,* although it doesn't bear much resemblance to a real desktop. Try putting a pencil on it.

I talk about changing and organizing your desktop in Book IV, Chapter 2, but every new Vista user will want to make a few quick changes. In the end, your desktop should look something like Figure 1-1.

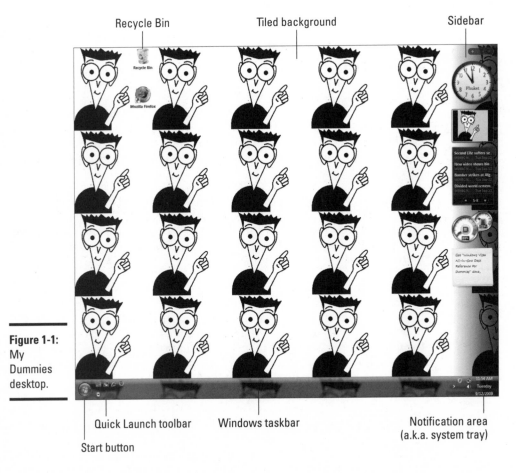

Figure 1-1: My Dummies desktop.

Recycle Bin   Tiled background   Sidebar

Quick Launch toolbar   Windows taskbar   Notification area (a.k.a. system tray)

Start button

The Windows desktop looks simple enough, but don't fool yourself: Underneath that calm exterior sits the most sophisticated computer program ever created. Hundreds of millions of dollars went into creating the illusion of simplicity — something to remember the next time you feel like kicking your computer and screaming at the Vista gods.

Disabling the Welcome Center

First, disable the Welcome Center by following these steps:

1. **Use the Welcome Center (Figure 1-2) once, by all means, to get your computer set up.**

I have a few pointers in Book I, Chapter 4, but keep in mind that your PC's manufacturer probably put a lot of junk in the Welcome Center to keep you coming back to buy more and more.

2. **When you're done with the Welcome Center, deselect the Run at Startup check box in the lower left.**

3. **Click the *X* in the upper-right corner to permanently get rid of the Welcome Center.**

**Book II
Chapter 1**

**Running Vista from
Start to Finish**

Figure 1-2:
Welcome
to the
Welcome
Center.

If you ever have the uncontrollable urge to bring the Welcome Center back, you can always choose Start⇨Control Panel⇨Get Started with Windows (which is under the heading System and Maintenance). The Welcome Center springs back to life, like an Anne Rice character.

Changing the background

Second, change the wallpaper (er, the "desktop background"). If you bought a new computer with Vista installed, your background probably says "Dell" or "Vaio" or "Billy Joe Bob's Computer Emporium / Dial 555-3765 for a good time." Bah. Change your wallpaper by following these steps:

1. Right-click on an empty part of the desktop and choose Personalize.

Vista hops to the Control Panel's Personalization pane.

2. Click the Desktop Background link.

You see the Choose a Desktop Background dialog box shown in Figure 1-3.

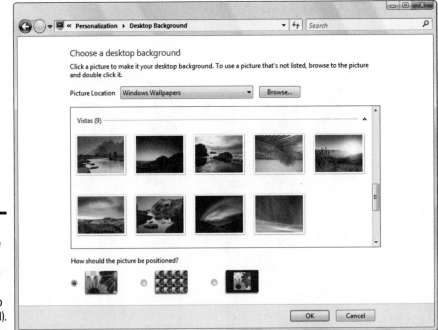

Figure 1-3: Change the Vista wallpaper (also known as the desktop background).

3. **Click a picture, click the down arrow to choose from different groups of pictures, or click the Browse button and select a picture to use as the wallpaper.**

   If you click the down arrow and choose Solid Colors, Vista provides choices of solid-color wallpaper, using the background color indicated at the bottom of the dialog box.

4. **At the bottom of the dialog box, choose how you'd like to position the picture, if you chose one: Stretched to fill the screen, centered in the middle of the desktop, or tiled over the desktop.**

5. **Click the OK button and then the red *X* to exit the Control Panel's Personalization pane.**

   Your new wallpaper settings take effect.

Enabling the Sidebar

Third, almost everyone should enable the Sidebar, if you can't see it already. You might want to avoid the Sidebar if you've had problems with it crashing, or if your computer isn't very fast, but it's well worth the effort if your machine can handle it (for details, see Book IV, Chapter 1). To get it working, choose Start➪All Programs➪Accessories➪Windows Sidebar.

Cleaning up useless icons and programs

Fourth, get rid of the useless icons and obnoxious programs that your PC vendor probably stuck on your machine.

If you bought a new computer with Windows XP preinstalled, the manufacturer probably sold some desktop real estate to a software company or an Internet Service Provider (ISP). (Oh yeah, the AOLs and Nortons of the world compensate the Dells and HPs for services, and space, rendered.) You might want to keep offerings from companies like Google, which bring a great deal of power to the table. But the last thing you need is yet another come-on to sign up for AOL, or an antivirus program that begs you for money every week.

You can get rid of most icons by simply right-clicking them and choosing Delete. But to get rid of the program behind the icon, as well as the icon itself, choose Start➪Control Panel➪Uninstall a Program (which appears in the Programs section). When the Uninstall or Change a Program dialog box opens, double-click a program to remove it.

Making the taskbar taller

If you want to make the Windows taskbar taller so that you can see the date in the lower-right corner, make sure that the taskbar isn't locked (right-click an empty spot on the taskbar and make sure that the Lock the Taskbar check box is deselected). Then move your mouse cursor over the top of the taskbar until it turns into a two-headed arrow. Click and drag the edge of the taskbar up.

Mousing with Your Mouse

Your computer's mouse serves as the primary way of interacting with Windows, but you already knew that. You can click the left mouse button or the right mouse button, or you can roll the wheel in the middle (if you have one), and the mouse will do different things, depending on where you click or roll. But you already knew that, too.

If you're left-handed, you can interchange the actions of the left and right mouse buttons — that is, you can tell Windows Vista that it should treat the left mouse button as if it were the right button, and the right button as if it were the left. The swap comes in handy for some left-handers, but most southpaws I know (including my son) prefer to keep the buttons as is, because it's easier to use other computers if your fingers are trained for the "normal" setting. To switch left and right mouse buttons, follow these steps:

1. **Choose Start⇨Control Panel⇨Mouse (which is in the Hardware and Sound section).**

2. **Click the Buttons tab.**

3. **Select the Switch Primary and Secondary Buttons check box.**

4. **Click the OK button, and then click the red *X* to exit the Control Panel.**

Windows has a feature called ClickLock that can come in handy if you have trouble holding down the left mouse button and moving the mouse at the same time — a common problem for laptop users who have fewer than three hands. When Windows uses ClickLock, you hold down the mouse button for a while (you can tell Windows exactly how long) and Windows "locks" the mouse button so that you can concentrate on moving the mouse without having to hold down the button. To turn on ClickLock, follow these steps:

1. **Choose Start⇨Control Panel⇨Mouse (which is in the Hardware and Sound section).**

2. **On the Buttons tab, select the Turn on ClickLock check box.**

3. **Immediately click the Settings button and adjust the length of time you need to hold down the mouse button for ClickLock to kick in.**

4. **Click the OK button twice, and then click the red *X* to exit the Control Panel.**

The best way to get the feel for a new mouse? Play one of the games that ships with Windows. Choose Start➪Games and take it away. I recommend Minesweeper, Chess Titans, and Solitaire for mouse orienteering. Try clicking in unlikely places, double-clicking, or right-clicking in new and different ways. Bet you'll discover several wrinkles, even if you're an old hand at the games. (See Book IV, Chapter 4 for more on Windows games.)

Inside the computer, programmers measure the movement of mice in units called *mickeys*. Nope, I'm not making this up. Move your mouse a short distance and it has traveled a few mickeys. Move it to Anaheim, and it's put on a lot of mickeys.

Working with Files and Folders

"What's a file?" Man, I wish I had a nickel for every time I've been asked that question.

A file is a, uh, thing. Yeah, that's it. A thing. A thing that has stuff inside it. Why don't you ask me an easier question, like "What is a paragraph?" or "What is the meaning of life, the universe, and everything?"

A *file* is a fundamental chunk of stuff. Like most fundamental chunks of stuff (say, protons, Congressional districts, or earwax), any attempt at a definitive definition gets in the way of understanding the thing itself. Suffice it to say that a Word document is a file. An Excel workbook is a file. That photograph your cousin e-mailed you the other day is a file. Every track on Nine Inch Nails' latest CD is a file, but so is every track on every audio CD ever made. Trent Reznor isn't *that* special.

Filenames and folder names can be very long, but they can't contain the following characters:

```
/ \ : * ? " < > |
```

Files can be huge. They can be tiny. They can even be empty, but don't short-circuit any gray cells on that observation.

Folders hold files and other folders. Folders can be empty. A single folder can hold millions — yes, quite literally *millions* — of files and other folders.

Keeping folders organized

If you set them up right, folders can help you keep track of things. If you toss your files around higgledy-piggledy, no system of folders in the world can help. Unfortunately, there's a fundamental problem with folders. Permit me to illustrate.

Say you own a sandwich shop. You take a photograph of the shop. Where do you stick the photo? Which folder should you use? The answer: There's no good answer. You could put the photo in with all your other "shop" stuff — documents and invoices and payroll records and menus. You could stick the photo in the Pictures folder, which Vista automatically provides. You could put it in the Public or Public Documents or Public Pictures folder so that other people using your PC, or other folks connected to your network, can see the photo of the shop. You could create a folder called Photos and file the picture away chronologically (that's what I do), or you can even create a folder called Shop inside the Photos folder and stick the picture in \Photos\Shop.

In the end, you have to go with what feels right for you. The important thing isn't so much the location as the consistency: As long as you know that all your shop photos are in one place, you won't have any problem finding them.

This where-to-file-it/where-to-find-it conundrum stands as one of the hairiest problems in all of Windows, and Microsoft hasn't done much to help. (In fact, given all the different ways of storing Office documents over the years — don't get me started on Binders — Microsoft has gone out of its way to make the problem worse.) Vista has "search folders" (also known as "stored searches," "saved searches," and "virtual folders," among others); I talk about them in Book IV, Chapter 3. Search folders can help, but they require a great deal of care and feeding — and they don't always turn up what you want.

Someday we'll see technology that will bring database storage and retrieval capabilities to the Windows file system so that you don't have to remember every picayune detail. (Microsoft had such a system, called WinFS, that was supposed to become part of Vista, but they cancelled the project as Vista went into widespread testing.) Until that day comes, the best you can hope for is the old housekeeper's adage: A place for everything, and everything in its place.

To look at the files and folders on your machine that you're most likely to bump into, choose Start⇨Documents. You see something like the list shown in Figure 1-4.

The picture of Documents that you see in Figure 1-4 comes from a part of Vista called *Windows Explorer,* which can help keep your files and folders organized. See the section "Using Windows Explorer," later in this chapter.

If you're looking at Documents on your computer, and you can't see the period and three-letter suffixes of the filenames (such as .doc and .xls) that are visible in Figure 1-4, don't panic! You need to tell Windows to show them — electronically knock Windows upside the head, if you will. See the next section.

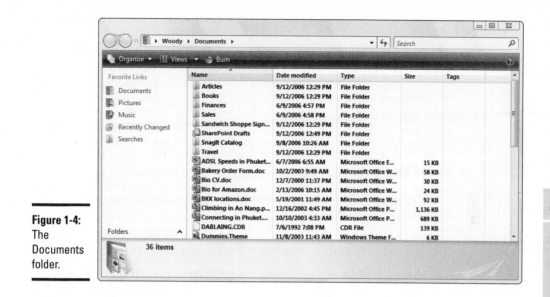

Figure 1-4:
The
Documents
folder.

Showing filename extensions

In my opinion, every single Vista user should force Windows to show full filenames, including the (usually three-letter) "extension" at the end of the name.

I've been fighting Microsoft on this topic for many years. Forgive me if I get a little, uh, steamed — yeah, that's the polite way to put it — in the retelling.

Every file has a name. Almost every file has a name that looks more or less like this: `Some Name or Another.ext`.

The part to the left of the period — `Some Name or Another`, in this example — generally tells you something about the file, although it can be quite nonsensical or utterly inscrutable, depending on who named the file. The part to the right of the period — `ext`, in this case — is called a *filename extension,* the subject of my diatribe.

Filename extensions have been around since the first PC emerged from the primordial ooze. They were a part of the PC's legacy before anybody ever talked about "legacy." Somebody, somewhere decided that Windows wasn't going to show filename extensions any more. (My guess is that Bill Gates himself made the decision, about ten years ago, but it's only a guess.) Filename extensions were considered dangerous: too complicated for the typical user, a bit of technical arcana that novices shouldn't have to sweat.

Garbage. Pure, unadulterated garbage.

The fact is that nearly all files have names like `Letter to Mom.doc`, `Financial Projections.xls`, or `ILOVEYOU.vbs`. But Windows, in its infinite wisdom, shows you only the first part of the filename. It cuts off the filename extension. So you see `Letter to Mom`, without the `.doc` (which brands the file as a Word document), `Financial Projections` without the `.xls` (a dead giveaway for an Excel spreadsheet), and `ILOVEYOU` without the `.vbs` (which is the filename extension for Visual Basic programs).

I really hate it when Windows hides filename extensions, for four big reasons:

✦ If you can see the filename extension, you can usually figure out what kind of file you have at hand.

✦ It's almost impossible to get Windows to change filename extensions if you can't see them.

✦ Microsoft Outlook forbids you from sending or receiving specific kinds of files, based solely on the filename extension. (You can find a list of 72 dangerous filename extensions at `http://office.microsoft.com/en-us/assistance/HA011402971033.aspx`.)

✦ You bump into filename extensions anyway. No matter how hard Microsoft wants to hide filename extensions, they show up everywhere — from the `Readme.txt` files mentioned repeatedly in Microsoft's official documentation to discussions of `.jpg` file sizes on Web pages, and a gazillion places in between.

Take off the training wheels, okay? To make Windows show you filename extensions, follow these steps:

1. **Open Windows Explorer (by, say, choosing Start⇨Documents).**

2. **Press Alt to show the menu; then choose Tools⇨Folder Options and click the View tab.**

You see the Folder View's Advanced Settings dialog box, as shown in Figure 1-5.

3. **Deselect the Hide Extensions for Known File Types check box.**

4. **Click the OK button.**

While you're here, you may want to change two other settings if you can avoid the temptation to delete or rename files that you don't understand. Select the Show Hidden Files and Folders option button if you want Windows to show you all the files that are on your computer. Also consider deselecting the Hide Protected Operating System Files (Recommended) check box. Sometimes you really need to see all your files, even if Windows wants to hide them from you.

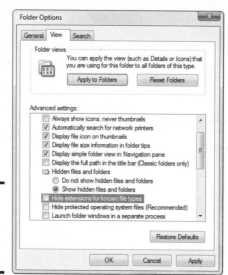

Figure 1-5:
Make Vista
show you
filename
extensions.

Sharing folders

Sharing is good, right? Your mom taught you to share, didn't she? Everything you need to know about sharing you learned in kindergarten — like how you can share your favorite crayon with your best friend and get back a gnarled blob of stunted wax, covered in mysterious goo.

Vista supports two very different ways for sharing files and folders:

✦ **You can move the files or folders that you want to share into the Public folder.** The \Public folder is kind of a big cookie jar for everybody who uses your PC: Put a file or folder in the \Public folder, and all the other people who use your computer can get at it. You can make the \Public folder available to other people on your network, if you have one, but if you do so, you have little control over who, specifically, can get at the files and folders. See the next section in this chapter for details.

✦ **You can share individual files or folders, without moving them anywhere.** When you share a file or folder, you can tell Vista exactly who can get at the file or folder, and whether they can just look at it or if they can change or delete it. I talk about the details in the section "Sharing and permissions," later in this chapter.

Making the Public folder public

You might think that simply moving a file or folder to the \Public folder would make it, well, public. You'd be wrong, of course. Or perhaps *Public* means different things to different people.

Any file or folder that you put in the \Public folder, or any folder inside the \Public folder, can be viewed, changed, or deleted by anybody who's using your computer, regardless of what kind of account they may have and whether they're required to log on to your computer. \Public is (if you'll pardon a rather stretched analogy) a big cookie jar, open to everybody who is in the kitchen.

Follow these easy steps to put a file or folder in one of the \Public folders:

1. **Use Windows Explorer (by choosing, say, Start⇨Documents or Start⇨ Pictures) to navigate to the file or folder that you want to move into the Public folder.**

   In Figure 1-6, I chose Start⇨Pictures.

Figure 1-6: Moving a folder to \Public is easy if you know the trick.

2. **Right-click the folder that you want to move and choose Cut.**

   In Figure 1-6, I right-click Leonhard Family Photos.

3. **On the left, click the up arrow next to the word *Folders*.**

   You see the Folders list shown on the lower left of Figure 1-6.

4. **Right-click the \Public folder (or subfolder) where you would like to locate the shared folder, and choose Paste.**

   In Figure 1-6, I move the Leonhard Family Photos folder to the \Public\ Pictures folder.

Do you have a network? Unless you explicitly tell Vista that you want to let other people on your network into the \Public folder, the contents of that folder are completely, utterly, totally inaccessible to others on your network. You have to tell Vista to let other people into the, er, kitchen.

Here's how to open the \Public folder so others can get to it:

1. **Choose Start⇨Control Panel⇨Network and Internet⇨Network and Sharing Center.**

   Vista brings up the Network and Sharing Center panel shown in Figure 1-7. Permit me to give you my recommendations for all of these settings. Your mileage may vary, of course.

   User Account Control kicks in when you attempt to change any of these settings. Don't be intimidated. Click Continue and ignore it. Maybe it'll go away.

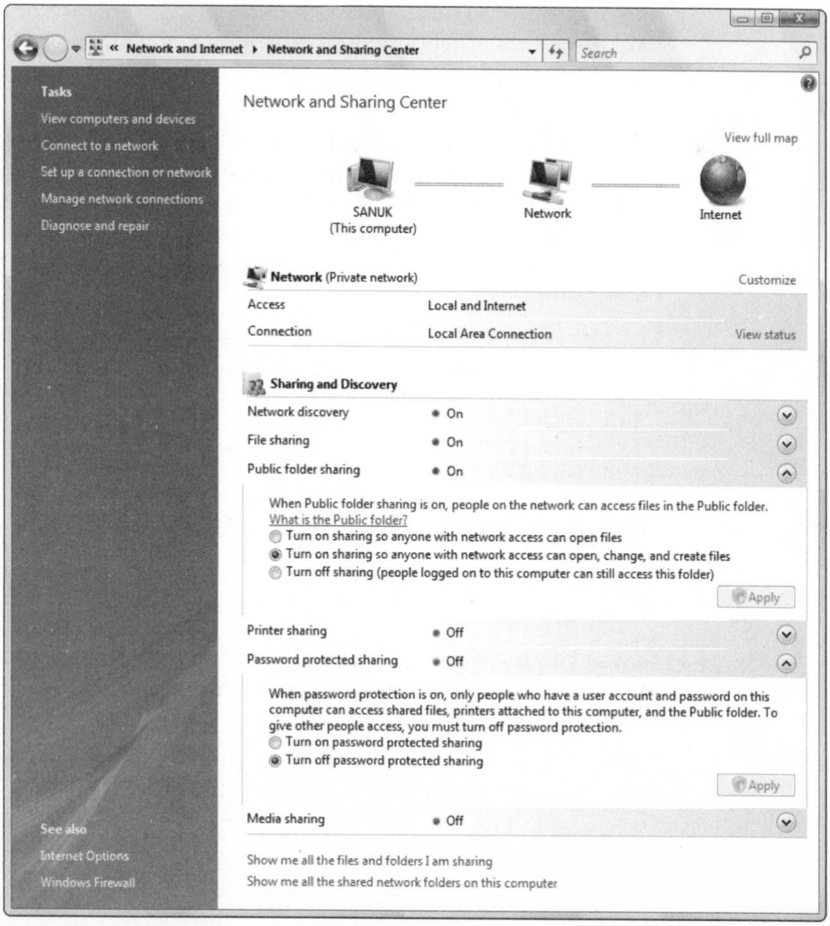

Figure 1-7:
You must tell Vista whether you want to make the \Public folders public.

Network and Sharing Center

Tasks
View computers and devices
Connect to a network
Set up a connection or network
Manage network connections
Diagnose and repair

SANUK
(This computer)

Network

Internet

View full map

Network (Private network)   Customize

Access   Local and Internet
Connection   Local Area Connection   View status

Sharing and Discovery

Network discovery   ● On
File sharing   ● On
Public folder sharing   ● On

When Public folder sharing is on, people on the network can access files in the Public folder.
What is the Public folder?
○ Turn on sharing so anyone with network access can open files
● Turn on sharing so anyone with network access can open, change, and create files
○ Turn off sharing (people logged on to this computer can still access this folder)
Apply

Printer sharing   ● Off
Password protected sharing ● Off

When password protection is on, only people who have a user account and password on this computer can access shared files, printers attached to this computer, and the Public folder. To give other people access, you must turn off password protection.
○ Turn on password protected sharing
● Turn off password protected sharing
Apply

Media sharing   ● Off

See also
Internet Options
Windows Firewall

Show me all the files and folders I am sharing
Show me all the shared network folders on this computer

2. **If you have a computer that's commonly connected to a network you trust, turn on Network Discovery. (Click the down arrow to the right of Network Discovery, select the button marked Turn on Network Discovery, and click Apply.) On the other hand, if you don't have a network, keep Network Discovery and all of the other settings in Figure 1-7 turned Off.**

   If you ever connect your computer to a "public" network — like in a coffee shop or an airport — Vista gives you the opportunity to turn Network Discovery off.

3. **If you have a computer that's commonly connected to a network you trust, turn on File Sharing. (Click the down arrow to the right of File Sharing, select the button marked Turn on File Sharing, and click Apply.) On the other hand, as I mentioned in the preceding step, if you don't have a network, keep File Sharing and all of the other settings in Figure 1-7 turned Off.**

   In rare instances, if you have ultra-confidential files on a computer that you don't want to be shared with other computers on a network, you can turn File Sharing off. But in most cases, if you have a network, you want to share the files in your \Public folder. In order to do that, you have to turn File Sharing on.

4. **Consider whether you want to give people on your network access to the \Public folders. If so, think about whether they should only be able to see the files in those folders, or whether they should also be able to add, change, or delete them. Click the down arrow next to Public Folder Sharing and make your choice (see Figure 1-7), then click Apply.**

   In most cases, you want to let other people on your network look at the \Public folders. That's why they're public, eh? Whether you want them to be able to add files to those folders, or change or delete files — that's up to you.

   If someone gets into your \Public folder, or a folder hanging under the \Public folder, and deletes a file, it's gone. Nope, you won't find it in the Recycle Bin. If you own Vista Ultimate Edition, you might be able to retrieve a shadow copy (see Book II Chapter 3 for details), but otherwise you're basically outta luck. Think twice before you allow others to delete files in \Public folders.

5. **Unless you have a very bizarre reason for preventing other people on your network from sharing any printer you may install now or in the future, turn on Printer sharing.**

   If it isn't on already, click the down arrow to the right of Printer Sharing, select Turn on Printer Sharing, and click Apply.

6. **Consider whether you want to restrict access to your** \Public **folder (and printers and other shared folders) so only people who have a user ID and password** *on your computer* **can get in. If you want to let anybody on your network get into your** \Public **folders (or use your printer or get into other shared folders), turn Password protected sharing off. On the other hand, if you want to block the unwashed masses, so they have to answer a dialog box like the one in Figure 1-8 before they're allowed to use anything on this computer, turn Password protected sharing on.**

This setting is more than a little confusing because it operates independently of File sharing, Public folder sharing, and Printer sharing. Think of this setting as the guard dog for your computer. You can either tell Masher (good dog, down boy) to let anybody in. Or you can tell Masher that he's only to admit people with user IDs and passwords that are currently valid on this computer.

Vista allows you to restrict \Public folder access (and printer and shared folder access) to those who know a username and password on your computer in no small part because that automatically keeps out worms that travel from other computers to your computer. Unfortunately, if you block the worms, you also make it more difficult for people on other computers to get to your \Public folders — and, not so coincidentally, to use printers on your computer, too.

**Book II
Chapter 1**

**Running Vista from
Start to Finish**

Figure 1-8:
The challenge that faces people on your network if you turn on Password protected sharing.

If you log on to the network with a username and password that matches the username and password on this computer, Vista lets you go straight through, without a "challenge." It doesn't matter if Password protected file sharing is on or off.

Personally, I don't require other people on my network to sign in to my computer before they can get at \Public folders, printers, or other shared folders. So I turn Password protected sharing off. But that's just me, OK? I'm a trusting kind of guy — and I have a lot of safeguards in place to prevent worms from entering the network on any computer. In other words, my guard dogs cover all the entries to the network, so I figure that I don't have to get Masher worked up on my computer.

To change your Password Protected Sharing setting, click the down arrow to the right of Password Protected Sharing, select the option you like, and click Apply.

7. **If you have a network, turn on Media sharing. (What, you don't want to share your music and videos with other Vista PCs running Media Center?) To do so, click the down arrow next to Media sharing, click Change, check the box marked Share My Media, and click OK. When the Media Sharing dialog comes back, click Allow, then click OK.**

And I bet you thought using the \Public folder would be easy, huh?

Sharing and permissions

Using the \Public folder, as described in the preceding section, constitutes a quick 'n' dirty approach to sharing: Everybody using your computer gets full access to all the \Public files, and people coming in from the network either get in or they don't. You have a little bit of fine control over who gets in and what they can do, but by and large, \Public's a blunt object.

This is far finer: Vista's ability to establish sharing *permissions* for individual files and folders on your PC. You can assign fine-grained permissions for individual users or groups of users using Vista's built-in permission levels, which come in four flavors, described in Table 1-1.

Table 1-1		Vista's Built-in Folder Permissions		
Permission Level	Open, Copy Files	Add New Files, Change or Delete Files That the User Added	Change or Delete Any Files	Set Permissions for Others
Reader	Yes	No	No	No
Contributor	Yes	Yes	No	No
Co-owner	Yes	Yes	Yes	No
Owner	Yes	Yes	Yes	Yes

This kind of fine-grained sharing is a minefield that you should not undertake unless you're willing to keep permissions updated. You should also be tolerant of many potential problems, because I guarantee you'll bump into them. Instead of assigning detailed sharing permissions to a file or folder, you might find it smarter (and much easier) to put the files you want to share in `\Public`, and use read-only or read/write passwords to control access to the data in those files. All the Office applications, and many others, have heavy-duty password protection available.

If you're convinced that using user-level folder permissions is the way to go, here's how to set up fine-grained sharing for a folder that's not in the `\Public` folder:

1. **Navigate to the folder you want to share.**

Try choosing Start⇨Documents or Start⇨Computer.

2. **Click the folder once.**

If you're the designated owner of the folder, a Share button appears at the top of the Windows Explorer window.

3. **Click the Share button.**

Vista opens the File Sharing dialog box shown in Figure 1-9.

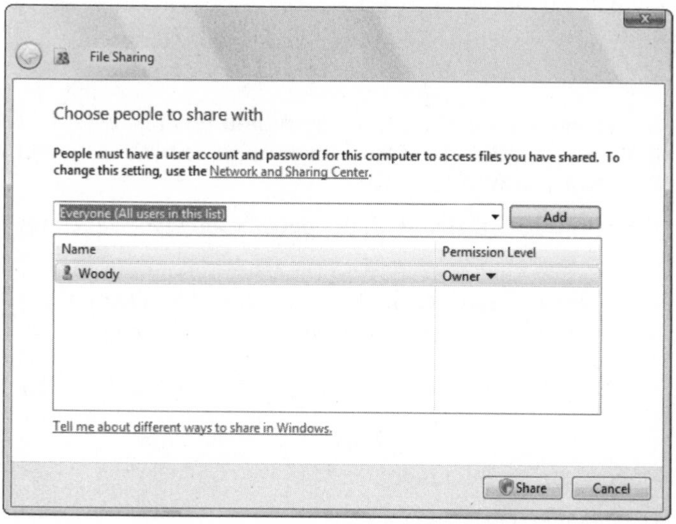

Figure 1-9:
Set folder-
sharing
permissions
in the File
Sharing
dialog box.

4. **Choose the user that should have permission to get into the folder. If you want to give everyone on your computer (or anyone who can answer the challenge dialog box shown in Figure 1-8) permission to get into the folder, choose Everyone. Then click the Add button.**

Vista adds the person (or Everyone) to the list of folks who have permission, as shown in Figure 1-10.

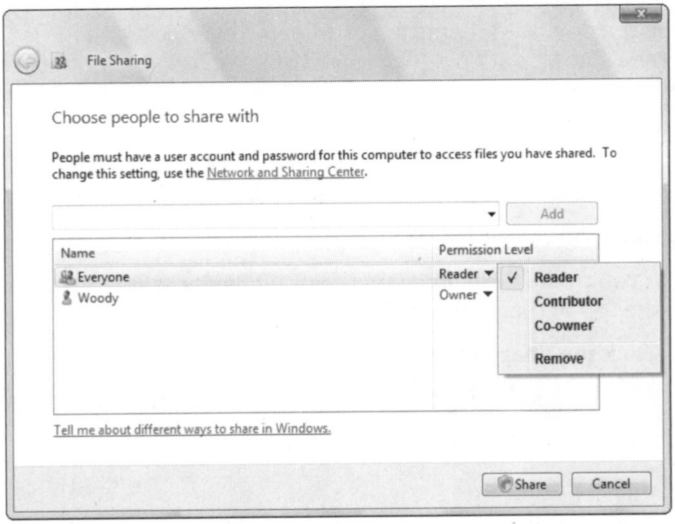

Figure 1-10: New users are given Reader permission automatically.

File Sharing

Choose people to share with

People must have a user account and password for this computer to access files you have shared. To change this setting, use the Network and Sharing Center.

[▾] [Add]

Name	Permission Level
🔲 Everyone	Reader ▾
👤 Woody	Owner ▾

✓ Reader
Contributor
Co-owner

Remove

Tell me about different ways to share in Windows.

[🛡 Share] [Cancel]

5. **If you want to increase the permission level (see Table 1-1) for a particular user, click the down arrow next to his or her name and select the level you think is right.**

6. **When you're satisfied with the permission levels, click the Share button.**

You have to click Continue on the User Account Control dialog. Vista responds with a confirmation dialog box, telling you that the folder is shared. Click the Done button and you're, uh, done.

Vista makes it easy to see all the folders that you have shared. Follow these steps:

1. **Choose Start➪Documents.**

Windows Explorer opens.

2. **At the bottom, click the up arrow next to the Folders line.**

You see a list of folders.

3. Scroll down the list of folders and choose Searches.

Vista shows you all your custom (saved) searches as well as the built-in ones, as shown in Figure 1-11.

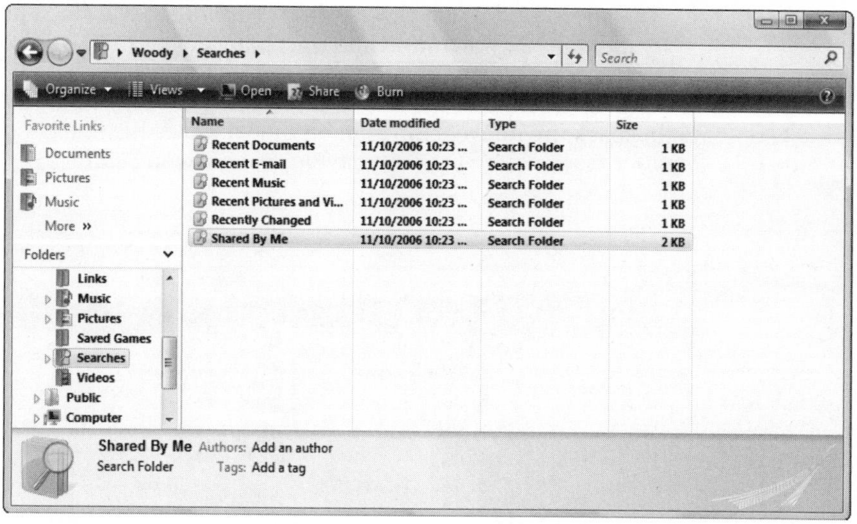

Figure 1-11:
Vista
conveniently
saves a
search that
includes all
your shared
folders.

Book II
Chapter 1

Running Vista from
Start to Finish

4. On the right, in the Name column, double-click Shared by Me.

Vista shows you all the folders (and files) that you have shared.

Recycling

When you delete a file, it doesn't go to that Big Bit Bucket in the Sky. An intermediate step exists between deletion and the Big Bit Bucket. It's called *purgatory* — oops. Wait a sec. Wrong book. (*Existentialism For Dummies,* anybody?) Let me try that again. Ahem.

The step between deletion and the Big Bit Bucket is called the *Recycle Bin.*

When you delete a file or folder from your hard drive — whether by selecting the file or folder in Windows Explorer and pressing Delete or by right-clicking and choosing Delete — Windows doesn't actually delete anything. It marks the file or folder as being deleted but, other than that, doesn't touch it.

Files and folders on floppy drives, key drives, and network drives really *are* deleted when you delete them. The Recycle Bin doesn't work on floppies, key drives, or drives attached to other computers on your network.

That's a good news/bad news state of affairs:

+ **The good news:** If you ever accidentally delete a file or a folder, you can easily recover the "deleted" file from the Recycle Bin.

+ **The bad news:** All those deleted files take up space on your hard drive. The space isn't reclaimed until you go through the steps necessary to empty the Recycle Bin — and thus truly delete the files.

To rummage around in the Recycle Bin, and possibly bring a file back to life, double-click the Recycle Bin icon on the Windows desktop. Windows Explorer takes you to the Recycle Bin, as shown in Figure 1-12.

Figure 1-12:
Restore files one at a time, or *en masse.*

To restore a file or folder (sometimes Windows calls it *undeleting*), click the file or folder and then click Restore This Item in the Recycle Bin Tasks box in the upper-left corner. You can select a bunch of files or folders by holding down Ctrl as you click.

To reclaim the space that the files and folders in the Recycle Bin are using, click the Empty the Recycle Bin link. Windows asks whether you really, really want to get rid of those files permanently. If you say yes, they're gone.

Okay, I lied. After you empty the Recycle Bin, the emptied files and folders are still on the disk; they're just significantly harder to get to. When you delete files from a floppy, key drive, network drive — or even your digital camera — you might be able to recover them, if you act quickly. Check out Active@ Undelete from LSoft, www.active-undelete.com. A free demo version can undelete files up to 64KB in size. The paid version ($39.95) can handle any size.

The lowdown on fonts

Nowadays everybody takes fonts for granted. If you want to see a list of fonts on your computer, choose Start➪Control Panel➪Appearance and Personalization➪Fonts. If you want to install a font file, double-click it. Easy. But Vista's slick handling of fonts belies a tortuous history, and if you go looking for fonts in all the wrong places, some of the old demons may jump up and bite you.

I'll never forget the first time I bought a font. I paid Adobe $119 for a copy of the Tekton font. Just couldn't live without it. Nowadays, of course, you can buy a font very close to Tekton for less than a buck. In fact, you can buy a hundred fonts for less than a buck and download thousands more for free. Well-constructed classic fonts, like classic wine and classic episodes of South Park, command a premium. Whether they're worth the money depends largely on your tastes and expectations, and

whether you can see the difference: What you see is, most definitely, what you get.

Technologically, the original Windows fonts proved crude. In the early Windows years, Adobe started shaking up the market with its development of the PostScript and Type 1 font. Microsoft then licensed TrueType from Apple, putting the squeeze on Adobe. When the license began to chafe, Microsoft developed its own technology, joining with ex-foe Adobe in 1996 to announce the OpenType specification, and tried to drive Apple out of the business. Apple responded with yet another format, which hasn't caught on.

Most fonts available nowadays appear in either .TTF (TrueType) or .OTF (OpenType) format. Most font folk find OTF fundamentally superior; if you're given the choice, it's wise to stick to OTF.

Starting with the Start Button

Vista orientation rightfully starts in the lower-left corner of the screen with the button that shows the Windows logo — the "Start" button, if you will.

Microsoft's subverting the Rolling Stones classic "Start Me Up" for Windows 95 advertising may be ancient history by now, but the royal road to Vista still starts at the Start button. Click the Start button and you get the Start menu, which looks something like the one shown in Figure 1-13.

The Start menu looks like it's etched in granite, but it isn't. You have the following options:

✦ To change the name or picture of the current user, see Book II, Chapter 2.

✦ To remove a program from the "pinned" programs list (upper left) or the recently used programs list (lower left), right-click it and choose Remove from This List.

✦ To add a program to the "pinned" programs list, navigate to the program (by choosing, say, Start➪All Programs), right-click the program, and choose Pin to Start Menu. Book IV, Chapter 2 has more details on pinning.

Current user's name and picture

Pinned programs

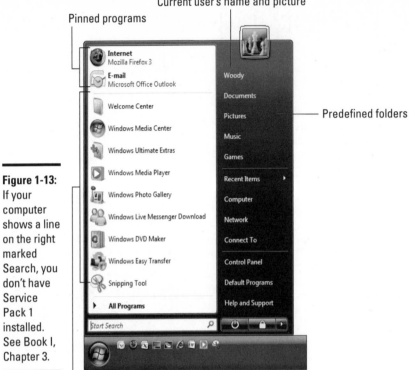

Predefined folders

Figure 1-13:
If your
computer
shows a line
on the right
marked
Search, you
don't have
Service
Pack 1
installed.
See Book I,
Chapter 3.

Recently used programs, sorta

If you bought a new computer with Vista preinstalled, the people who make
the computer may have sold one of the spots on the Start menu. Think of it
as an electronic billboard on your desktop. Nope, I'm not exaggerating. I keep
expecting to bump into a Windows machine with fly-out Start menu entries
that read, oh, "Surveys have shown⇨Near and far⇨That people who drive
like crazy⇨Use⇨Burma Shave." You can always delete those pesky Start
menu billboards by right-clicking them and choosing Remove from This List.

I explain many hints for making the Start menu work better in *Windows Vista
Timesaving Techniques For Dummies* (published by Wiley).

The right side of the Start menu contains an odd mélange of items:

✦ Shortcuts to many of Vista's predefined folders.

✦ Quick access to features, such as Connect To, which launches the
Connect to a Network Wizard.

✦ Entrée to the Control Panel, which I discuss in Book II, Chapter 3, and the Help and Support Center, which I discuss in Book II, Chapter 5.

✦ The means for putting your computer to sleep, locking it, restarting it, or shutting it off. For details, see "Sleep: Perchance to Dream" in this chapter.

You can modify most of the right side of the Start menu by using the Customize Start Menu dialog box (see Figure 1-14).

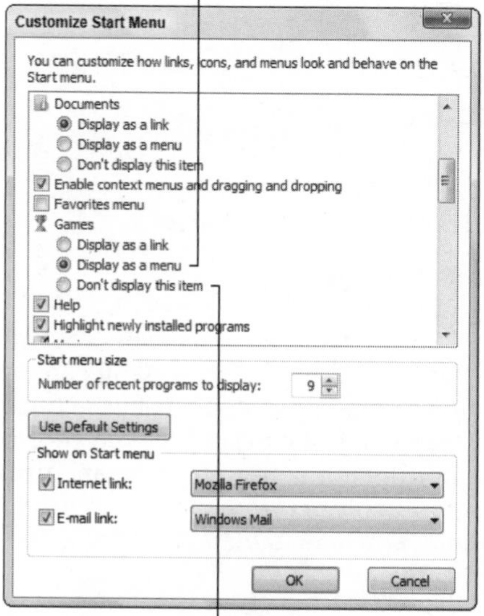

Click here to make games
a fly-out menu, as in Figure 1-15

Figure 1-14:
Control the
behavior of
items on the
right side
of the Start
menu.

Click here and Games doesn't
appear on the Start menu

Here's how to make the Start menu work your way:

1. Right-click the Start button and choose Properties.

The Taskbar and Start Menu Properties dialog box appears.

2. On the Start Menu tab, at the top, click the Customize button.

Vista shows you the Customize Start Menu dialog box shown in Figure 1-14.

3. **Add or remove items, or change the way they behave, by selecting or deselecting the appropriate check boxes.**

The Display as a Menu option button enables a fly-out cascading menu, as shown in Figure 1-15.

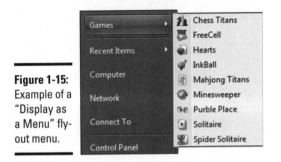

Figure 1-15: Example of a "Display as a Menu" fly-out menu.

4. **When you're done, click the OK button twice.**

Vista makes the changes immediately.

Old-timers used to have a "Run" item on the Start menu that allowed you to type a DOS command and have it executed directly. You can bring back the Run item by selecting the Run Command check box in the Customize Start Menu dialog box. Or (much easier), you can simply type your command in the Start Search box at the bottom of the Search menu and press Enter.

The old Windows key+R shortcut works in Vista, too: Press the two together and the Run dialog box appears.

Getting Around

Your PC is a big place, and you can get lost easily. Microsoft has spent hundreds of millions of dollars to make sure that Vista points you in the right direction and keeps you on track through all sorts of activities.

Amazingly, some of it actually works.

Using Windows Explorer

If you're going to get any work done, you have to interact with Windows. If Windows is going to get any work done, it has to interact with you. Fair 'nuff.

Microsoft refers to the way Vista interacts with people as the *user experience*. Gad. Windows Explorer lies at the center of the, er, user experience. When you want to work with Vista — ask it where it stuck your wedding pictures, show it how to mangle your files, or tell it (literally) where to go — you usually use Windows Explorer.

If you choose Start⇨Documents, Start⇨Pictures, or Start⇨Music or Computer or Network, Windows Explorer jumps to your command like an automated bird dog, pointing at whatever location you selected. When you run a search by choosing Start⇨Search, Windows Explorer takes the reins.

Navigating

Windows Explorer helps you get around in the following ways:

✦ **Click a folder to see the files you want.** On the left of the Windows Explorer window (see Figure 1-16), you can click a real folder (such as Documents or Pictures), a shortcut that you've dragged to the list on the left, or one of Vista's predefined "search" folders such as Recently Changed or Searches.

**Book II
Chapter 1**

Running Vista from
Start to Finish

Click the wedges to
move among folders

Search all currently visible folders

Common actions

Cute icons in Tiles view

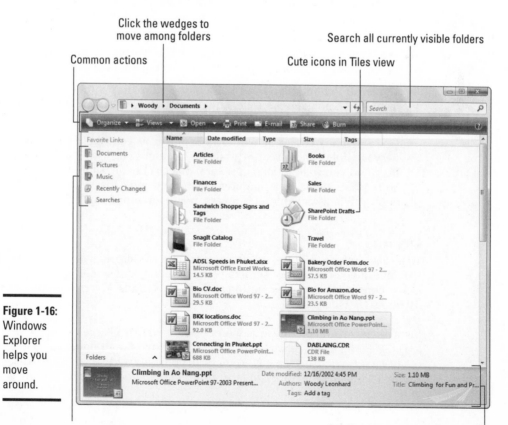

Figure 1-16:
Windows
Explorer
helps you
move
around.

Click a folder to move directly to it

Details about selected file or folder

+ **Use the "cookie crumb" navigation bar to move around.** At the top of the Windows Explorer window (see Figure 1-16), you can click the wedges to select from available folders.

Vista lacks the Up One Level button found in all previous versions of Windows, largely because of security conflicts: With Vista's default security settings, you frequently aren't allowed to move "up one level." For example, in Figure 1-16, I can click Woody (at the top, to the left of Documents) to move up one level. But once I'm in the Woody folder, I can't go "up" any more: The wedge to the left of Woody lets me go to other folders, but not the one above Woody.

+ **Details appear below.** If you click a file or folder once, details for the selected file or folder appear in the details box at the bottom of the Windows Explorer window. If you double-click a folder, it becomes the current folder. If you double-click a document, it opens. (For example, if you double-click a Word document, Windows fires up Word and has it start with that document open and ready for work.)

+ **Many of the actions that you might want to perform on files or folders show up in the command bar at the top.** Most of the other actions you might want to perform are accessible by right-clicking the file or folder.

Within rather strict limits, you can change the actions listed on the command bar by changing a *folder template*. See *Windows Vista Timesaving Techniques For Dummies* for the (rather complex) details.

+ **To see all the options, press Alt.** Windows Explorer shows you an old-fashioned command bar (File, Edit, View, Help, and so on) with dozens of functions tucked away.

+ **Open as many copies of Windows Explorer as you like.** That can be very helpful if you're scatterbrained like I am . . . er, if you like to multi-task, and you want to look in several places at once. Simply choose Start➪Documents (or Computer, whatever), and a totally independent copy of Windows Explorer appears, ready for your finagling.

Viewing

Tiles view (refer to Figure 1-16) is, at once, visually impressive and very cumbersome. If you get tired of scrolling (and scrolling and scrolling) through those icons, click the Views button and choose Details. You get the succinct list shown in Figure 1-17.

Vista offers several picturesque views — dubbed Extra Large Icons, Large Icons, Medium Icons, Small Icons, and Infinitesimal Eyestraining Icons (okay, I got carried away a bit) — that can come in handy if you're looking through a bunch of pictures. In most other cases, though, the icons only get in the way.

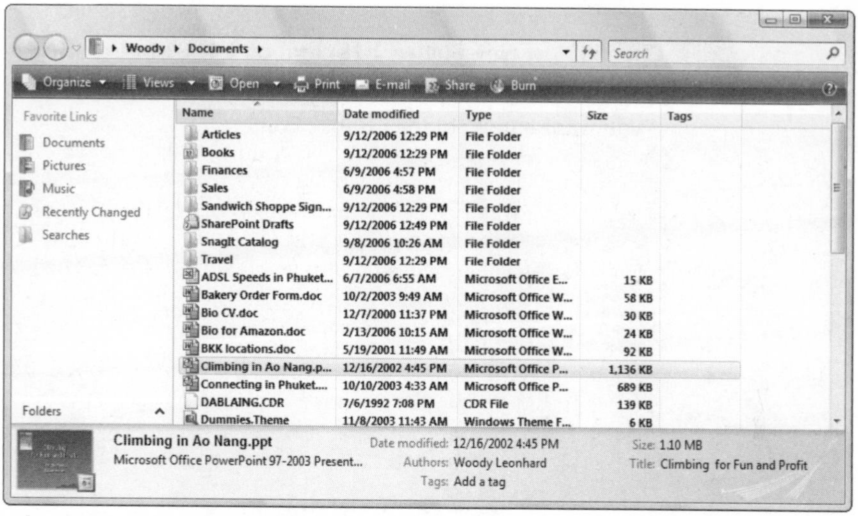

Figure 1-17:
Details
view —
more meat,
less sizzle.

In Details view, you can sort the list of files by clicking one of the column headings — Name, Date Modified, and so on. You can right-click one of the column headings and choose More to change what the view shows (get rid of Type, for example, and replace it with Size).

Creating files and folders

Usually, you create new files and folders when you're using a program. You make new Word documents when you're using Word, say, or come up with a new folder to hold all your offshore banking spreadsheets when you're using Excel. Programs usually have the tools for making new files and folders tucked away in the File⇨Save and File⇨Save As dialog boxes. Click around a bit and you'll find them.

But you can also create a new file or folder directly in Vista's Documents folder quite easily, without going through the hassle of cranking up a 900-pound gorilla of a program. Follow these steps:

1. **Move to the location where you want to put the new file or folder.**

For example, if you want to stick a new folder called Revisionist Techno Grunge in your Music folder, choose Start⇨Music.

2. **Right-click a blank spot in your chosen location.**

By "right-click a blank spot" I mean "don't right-click an existing file or folder," okay? If you want the new folder or file to appear on the desktop, right-click an empty spot on the desktop.

3. **Choose New (see Figure 1-18) and pick the kind of file you want to create.**

   If you want a new folder, choose Folder.

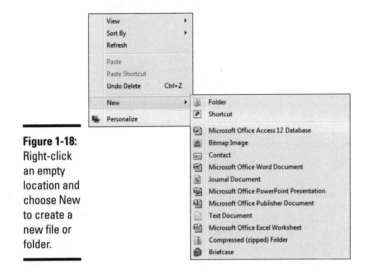

Figure 1-18:
Right-click
an empty
location and
choose New
to create a
new file or
folder.

4. **Windows creates the new file or folder and leaves it with the name highlighted so that you can rename it by simply typing.**

Modifying files and folders

As long as you have permission (see the section "Sharing folders," earlier in this chapter), modifying files and folders is easy — rename, delete, move, or copy them — if you remember the trick: right-click.

To copy or move more than one file (or folder) at a time, select all the files (or folders) before right-clicking. To select more than one file:

✦ Hold down Ctrl while clicking.

✦ Click and drag around the outside of the files and folders to "lasso" them.

✦ Use the Shift key if you want to choose a bunch of contiguous files and folders — ones that are next to each other. Click the first file or folder, hold down Shift, and click the last file or folder.

Saving searches

Windows Vista allows you to set up dynamic, saved searches. The concept is pretty easy: You set up a search criteria, and Vista automatically scans every file, more or less immediately, to look for matches. If you set up a saved search for the word *Office,* for example, the associated saved search keeps track of every document, spreadsheet, e-mail message, program file — almost anything you can think of — with the word *Office* in it.

To set up your own saved search, start by running the search: You can type something into the Search box in the upper-right corner of most Windows Explorer windows, or you can click the Start button and type something in the Search box. When the search is done, click the Save Search button at the top of Windows Explorer, give the search a name, and click the Save button.

To get at the contents of the saved search, open Windows Explorer (by, say, choosing Start⇨Documents or Start⇨Computer). On the left, click the Searches link. Then look through the list of saved searches for the one you created. Double-click it, and Vista presents you with an up-to-the-nanosecond list of all the files that match the search criteria.

Book IV, Chapter 3 covers searching your desktop in greater detail.

Previous versions

If you shelled out the bucks for a copy of Vista Ultimate, one of Ultimate's features may save your tail one day. Vista uses a fancy method to keep track of previous versions of all the files that you open and change. Vista doesn't actually store a snapshot of all states of your lovely files. Instead, it uses a very sophisticated method to keep track of changes to your files. In geek-speak, it "stores the deltas."

If you want to know which versions of a modified (even a deleted!) file exist in Vista's monstrous maw, and bring it back, follow these steps:

1. **Navigate to the munged file or folder — the one you want to bring back from the crypt — and right-click it.**

   If you accidentally deleted the file and can't bring it back from the Recycle Bin (see the section "Recycling," earlier in this chapter), click the folder that used to contain the file.

2. **Choose Restore Previous Versions.**

   This only works in Vista Enterprise (which you probably don't have) and Vista Ultimate (in which case I applaud your bank account). If you don't see a Previous Versions option, you didn't pay for it.

Vista shows you the Properties dialog box for the file or folder you selected, opened to the Previous Versions tab, as shown in Figure 1-19.

3. **Click the Open or Copy button and copy the older version of the file onto your desktop.**

WARNING!

Avoid the temptation to click the Restore button. This button overwrites whatever you may have — a hasty decision, at best, because even the most munged file or folder may have usable bits inside.

4. **Work with the restored version for a while and make sure that it's what you want. When you're happy with the result, copy the file to its original location.**

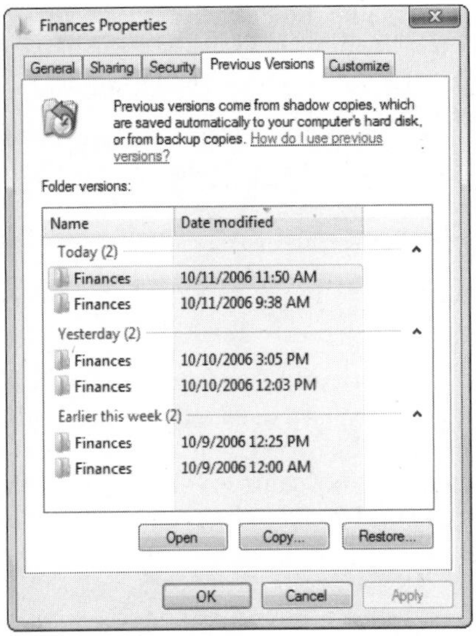

Figure 1-19:
If you have Vista Ultimate, previous versions can save your tail.

Working with the Windows taskbar

If you have more than one program running, the fastest way to switch from one program to another is via the Windows taskbar, as shown in Figure 1-20.

Figure 1-20:
The Windows taskbar makes switching among programs easy.

Word has three documents open

Quick Launch toolbar

Windows explorer is looking at the Documents folder

With a few small exceptions, each running program carves out a chunk of space on the Windows taskbar. If you hover your mouse over one of the taskbar buttons, you see a small thumbnail of the running program. If more than one copy of a program is running (not an unusual state of affairs for Windows Explorer, among others) or if a program has more than one file open (common in Word, for example) and Windows runs low on real estate in the taskbar area, the chunks are grouped together, with the number of open documents in front of the program name.

If you click the button marked 3 Microsoft Word (as shown in Figure 1-20), for example, you see a list of the three documents that Word currently has open. Click one of those documents, and Word comes up with that document loaded forbear.

The Windows taskbar has many tricks up its sleeve, but it has one capability that you're likely to need. *Auto-Hide* lets the taskbar shrink to a thin line until you bump your mouse pointer way down at the bottom of the screen. As soon as your mouse pointer hits bottom, the taskbar pops up. Here's how you teach the taskbar to auto-hide:

1. **Right-click an empty part of the taskbar.**

Usually the area immediately to the right of the Start button is a good place.

2. **Choose Properties.**

The Taskbar tab should be visible.

3. **Select the Auto-Hide the Taskbar check box and then click OK.**

Book II
Chapter 1

Running Vista from
Start to Finish

If you don't want to hunt around for the mouse — or if your mouse has suddenly gone out to lunch — Vista has a feature called Windows Flip that lets you switch among running programs, while (insert your best W.C. Fields impression here) your fingers never leave your hands . . . er, your fingers never leave the keyboard. Wink, wink. Just hold down Alt and press Tab. When you get to the program you want, release Alt. Bam!

If you have enough video card horsepower to run Glass, the fancy see-through Vista interface (and you aren't hobbled with Vista Home Basic, which won't show you Glass at all), hold down the Windows key and press Tab. Alternatively, click the icon marked Switch between Windows to the right of the Start button. You can riffle through your running programs, much like riffling a deck of cards (see Figure 1-21). Microsoft calls that Windows Flip 3D. I call it seriously cool — and surprisingly useful.

If you hold down Ctrl and Windows key together and then press Tab, Vista "locks" into Flip 3D mode. Press the Windows key again to go back to normal.

Figure 1-21:
Windows
Flip 3D
makes it
easier to
sort through
all your
running
programs.

Although the taskbar can get cramped at times, many people are willing to give up a little bit of taskbar room for a fancy one-click program launcher called the Quick Launch toolbar. The Quick Launch toolbar sits next to the Start button (see Figure 1-20), and you can fill it with a handful of little icons that can start your favorite programs. Judicious use of the Quick Launch toolbar can save you gobs of time. I explain everything you need to know about displaying and customizing the Quick Launch toolbar in Book IV, Chapter 2.

Creating shortcuts

Sometimes life's easier with shortcuts. (As long as the shortcuts work, anyway.) So, too, in the realm of Vista, where shortcuts point to things that can be started. You may set up a shortcut to Word and put it on your desktop. Double-click the shortcut, and Word starts, the same way as if you chose Start➪All Programs➪Microsoft Word.

You can set up shortcuts that point to the following items:

✦ Programs, of any kind

✦ Web addresses, such as `www.askwoody.com`

✦ Documents, spreadsheets, databases, PowerPoint presentations, and anything else that can be started in Windows Explorer by double-clicking it

✦ Specific chunks of text inside documents, spreadsheets, databases, presentations, and so on (they're called *scraps*)

✦ Folders (including the weird folders that are inside digital cameras, the Fonts folder, and others that you may not think of)

✦ Drives (hard drives, CD drives, key drives, and so on)

✦ Other computers on your network, and drives and folders on those computers, as long they're shared

✦ Printers (including printers attached to other computers on your network), scanners, cameras, and other pieces of hardware

✦ Dialup network connections

Shortcuts can do many amazing things. For example, you can set up a shortcut to a specific network printer on your desktop. Then, if you want to print a file on that printer, just drag the file onto the shortcut. Windows takes care of all the details.

You have many different ways to create shortcuts.

Say that you use the Windows Calculator all the time, you don't want to use Vista's Sidebar (which has a calculator), and you want to put a shortcut to the Windows Calculator on your desktop. Here's an easy way to do it:

1. **Choose Start⇨All Programs⇨Accessories.**

Vista shows you a list of Windows programs that Microsoft loosely describes as "accessories."

2. **Right-click Calculator, and then choose Send To⇨Desktop (Create Shortcut).**

Windows places an icon of the Windows Calculator on your desktop. The icon has an arrow, a kind of visual hint that the icon exists as a shortcut to the Calculator.

Anytime you double-click the Windows Calculator shortcut on your desktop, the Calculator comes to life.

You can use a similar procedure for setting up shortcuts to any file, folder, program, or document on your computer or any networked computer.

**Book II
Chapter 1**

**Running Vista from
Start to Finish**

Believe it or not, Windows thrives on shortcuts. They're everywhere, lurking just beneath the surface. For example, every single entry on the Start menu is a (cleverly disguised) shortcut. The icons on the Quick Launch toolbar are all shortcuts. Most of Windows Explorer is based on shortcuts — although they're hidden where you can't reach them. So don't be afraid to experiment with shortcuts. In the worst-case scenario, you can always delete them. Doing so gets rid of the shortcut but doesn't touch the original file.

Here's yet another way to create a shortcut. Say you want to put a shortcut to a network printer on your desktop. Follow these steps:

1. **Choose Start⇨Control Panel and click the Printer link (it's listed under Hardware and Sound).**

2. **Right-click the printer that you want to be shortcutted. (Uh, the printer you want the shortcut to go to? The shortcuttee? Somebody run and get me the Funk and Wagnalls.)**

3. **Choose Create Shortcut.**

Windows may display the dialog box shown in Figure 1-22. You'll find that "Create Shortcut" is a common option when right-clicking almost anything in Vista.

4. **Click the Yes button, and the shortcut that you wanted appears on your desktop.**

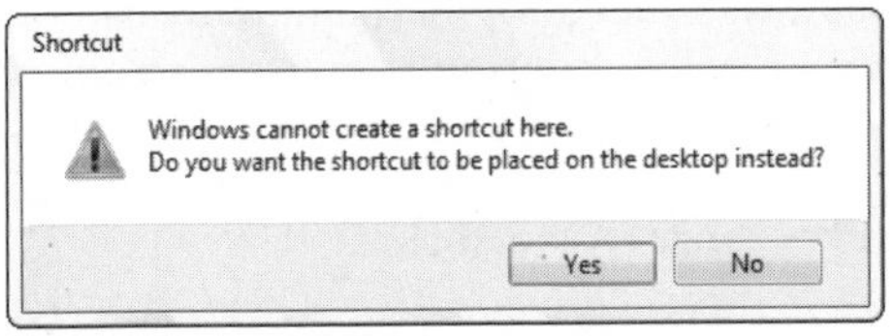

Figure 1-22:
The quick way to add a printer shortcut.

Shortcut

Windows cannot create a shortcut here.
Do you want the shortcut to be placed on the desktop instead?

Yes   No

Sleep: Perchance to Dream

Aye, there's the rub.

A fundamental dichotomy exists in the way computers store information, and the difference dictates how well and how fast a PC can spring back to life.

Main memory is relatively small (you probably have 1 or 2GB), very fast, but "volatile" — if you turn off the juice, everything disappears. Hard drives, on the other hand, are massive (100GB? 500?) and slow, but data that gets written to a hard drive sticks around for years, with no power required.

That's why, when you click the Start button, then the round "Off" button, telling Vista to sleep, you set off a rather complex sequence of events:

1. Vista copies the programs, documents, and anything else that's running from memory to the computer's hard drive.

2. Vista "freezes" the contents of memory, putting a blanket around everything so that it can come back quickly.

3. Vista winds down the hard drive, the monitor, and anything else that drains power, keeping a little trickle going to the memory, to maintain the memory as long as possible.

Think of it as a modern version of two logs crossing. If the, uh, powers that be manage to maintain a constant supply of electricity to the computer, when you start Vista again, it only needs to unwrap the blanket and get your system kick-started. On the other hand, if the juice runs out — whether the batteries run down, the UPS goes belly-up, or the cat finally gnaws all the way through the power cord — Vista can retrieve a snapshot of memory from the hard drive and get going in fairly short order.

Most of the time, "sleep" is good enough. But at least once a week — possibly once a day — you should restart your computer. Why? Vista should have an opportunity, from time to time, to start with a clean slate. Follow these steps to restart your computer:

1. **Click the Start button.**

   In the lower-right corner of the Start menu you see a padlock with a right-wedge next to it.

2. **Click the wedge, and then choose Restart (or Shut Down, if you want to turn off your computer).**

   If other people are using your computer, Vista will warn you, but if not, the computer goes away and then comes back.

Book II
Chapter 1

Running Vista from
Start to Finish

Turn off your computer at night?

Some people believe, strongly, that leaving a computer on overnight wears it down — the hard drive bearings take an unnecessary beating and the fans keep whirring — and leaving a computer on certainly consumes power (perhaps a few watts, if no screen saver is running). Keeping a PC turned off limits potential attacks and so on.

Other people believe, strongly, that turning off a computer wears it down — the self-same bearings grind to a halt and then groan back to life, and the fans wind down and then back up. Leaving a PC on gives antivirus programs a chance to get themselves updated, system maintenance can run, and so on.

Who's right? After years of research and extensive testing, I've come to the inescapable conclusion that both camps are right. Or wrong. Or both. You should do whatever you darn well like and invent any excuse that sounds good.

You should always turn off your computer the "official" way, by following the preceding steps. If you just flip the power switch off, unplug the machine, or press the reset switch, Windows can accidentally zap files and leave them unusable. (Yes, pressing the power switch or reset switch is supposed to initiate the appropriate shutdown sequence inside Vista. No, it doesn't always work the way it's supposed to.) Windows needs time to make sure that everything is in order before turning the lights off. Make sure that it gets the time it needs by choosing Shut Down.

Chapter 2: Controlling Users

In This Chapter

✔ Logging on

✔ Adding users

✔ The (in)security of it all

*T*his chapter explains how to take control of users on a Vista PC. You'd think it would be simple. No way. Like it or not, user control has all sorts of implications for security, sharing, and what you get to do with your PC.

Even if you're the only person who ever uses your PC, you might want to create a second account — another user, as it were — even if the second user is just you. (As Pogo said, "We have met the enemy, and he is us.") Then again, you might not. And therein lies this chapter's story.

If you're running Windows Vista Business, Enterprise, or Ultimate, and your PC is connected to a big corporate network (in the parlance, a *domain*), you have little or no control over who can log on to your computer and what a logged-on user can do after he or she is on the machine. That's a Good Thing, at least in theory — your company's network administrator gets to worry about all the security stuff, relieving you of the hassles of figuring out whether the guy down the hall should be able to look at payroll records or the company Christmas card list. But it can also be a pain in the neck, especially if you have to install a program, like, right now, and you don't have a user account with sufficient capabilities. If you're attached to a domain, your only choice is to convince (or bribe) the network admin to let you in.

The nostrums in this chapter only apply to PCs that are connected to small networks (*workgroups,* in Microsoft-speak) or to stand-alone PCs. If you're on a big network, you must pay homage to the network gods. Pizza, beer, and a smile can help.

Logging On

Vista assumes that, sooner or later, more than one person will want to work on your PC. All sorts of problems crop up when several people share a PC. I get my screen set up just right, with all my icons right where I can find them, and then my son comes along and plasters the desktop with a shot of Alpha Centauri. He puts together a killer teen Media Player playlist and "accidentally" deletes my Grateful Dead playlist in the process.

It's worse than sharing a TV remote.

Windows helps keep peace in the family — and in the office — by requiring people to *log on.* The process of logging on (also called *signing on*) lets Windows keep track of each person's settings: You tell Windows who you are, and Windows lets you play in your own sandbox.

Having personal settings that activate when you log on to Vista isn't heavy-duty security, at least on a stand-alone PC or one connected to a peer-to-peer "workgroup" network. (Big networks — domains — running Active Directory rate as a cabal of the first order.) Unless your Vista PC is a slave to a big Active Directory domain network, your settings can get clobbered, and your files deleted, if someone else with access to your computer or your network tries hard enough. But as long as you're reasonably careful and follow the advice in this chapter, Vista's security works surprisingly well.

If someone else can put his or her hands on your computer, it isn't your computer any more. That can be a real problem if someone swipes your laptop, if the cleaning staff uses your PC after hours, or if a snoop breaks into your study. Unless you use BitLocker (in the Enterprise and Ultimate versions of Vista), anybody who can restart your PC can look at, modify, or delete your files, or stick a virus on the PC. How? In most cases, a miscreant can bypass Windows directly and start your PC with some other operating system. With Vista out of the picture, compromising a PC doesn't take much work.

When it's ready to get started, Vista greets you with a *Welcome screen* — variously called a "Logon screen" or a "Sign-on screen" as well — like the one shown in Figure 2-1. The screen lists all the users who have been signed up to use the computer. It may also show a catch-all user called "Guest." (I guess that sounds better than "Other" or "Hey, you!")

I explain how to set up new users, and optionally the Guest account, in the sections "Adding Users" and "Enabling the Guest Account," later in this chapter.

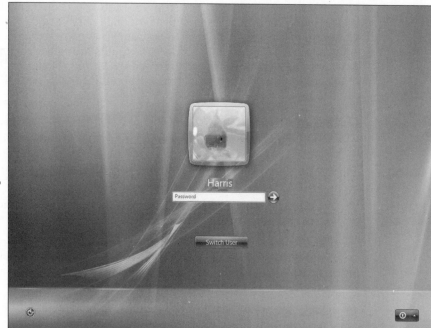

Figure 2-1:
The
Welcome
screen helps
sort out the
settings
attached to
each user
account.

Unless you assign a password to a specific account, nothing prevents
anyone sitting at the computer — friend, foe, or mother-in-law — from
clicking one of the other icons and logging on under an assumed identity:
In general, Vista (unless it's connected to a big corporate network "domain")
relies on the gentlemanly conduct of all participants to keep its settings
straight.

If you can't rely on gentlemanly conduct, you need to set up a password for
your account, although a password probably doesn't give you as much protection as you think. I talk about the vagaries of password-protected
accounts in the section, "Changing other users' settings," later in this chapter.

Choosing Account Types

When dealing with user accounts, you bump into one existential fact of Vista
life, over and over again: The type of account you use puts severe limitations
on what you can do.

Unless you're hooked up to a big corporate network, user accounts can generally be divided into two groups: the haves and the have-nots. (Users attached to corporate domains get assigned accounts that can exist anywhere in the have-to-have-not spectrum.) The have accounts are called *administrator accounts*. The have-nots are called *standard accounts*. That's it. "Standard." Kinda makes your toes curl just to think about it.

Using standard accounts

A person running with a standard account can only do, uh, standard things:

✦ Run programs that are installed on the computer, including programs on key drives (but he or she can't install new programs).

✦ Use hardware that's installed on the computer (but he or she can't install new hardware).

✦ Create, view, and use documents/pictures/sounds in his Documents/ Pictures/Music folders, as well as in the PC's Public folders, providing that the Public folders have been opened by someone with an administrator account (see Book II, Chapter 1).

✦ Change his or her password or switch back and forth between requiring a password for his account and not requiring one.

✦ Change the picture that appears next to his or her name on the Welcome screen and the Start menu, change the desktop wallpaper, resize the Windows toolbar, add items to the Start menu and Quick Launch toolbar, and make other small changes that don't affect other user accounts.

If you're running with a standard account, you can't even change the time on the clock. It's quite limited.

Using administrator accounts

People using administrator accounts can change almost anything, anywhere, at any time. (Certain folders remain off-limits, even to administrator accounts, and you have to jump through some very difficult hoops to get around the restrictions.) People using administrator accounts can even change other user accounts' passwords — a good thing to remember if you ever forget your password.

If you start Vista with a standard account, and you accidentally run a virus or worm or some other piece of bad computer code, the damage is limited: The malware can delete files in your Documents folder, and probably in the Public folders, but that's just about the extent of the damage. In particular, the virus can't install itself into the computer, so it can't run repeatedly, and it may not be able to replicate. Poor virus.

Those with administrator accounts can get into all the files owned by other users: If you thought that attaching a password to your account and putting a top-secret spreadsheet in your Documents folder would keep it away from prying eyes, you're in for a rude surprise. Anybody who can get into your machine with an administrator account can look at it. Standard users, on the other hand, are pretty effectively limited to only looking at their own files.

Working with User Account Control

Administrator accounts and standard accounts aren't set in concrete. In fact, Vista helps you shape-shift between the two as circumstances dictate:

✦ Even if you are using an administrator account, Vista normally runs as if you had a standard account, adding an extra hurdle when you try to run a program that can make substantial changes to your PC — *substantial* being a very subjective term. Before running a program that can make substantial changes, Vista usually requires you to click a security warning box that asks for your permission (see Figure 2-2). You have to clear the same kind of hurdle if you try to get into folders that aren't explicitly shared. That extra hurdle helps prevent destructive programs from sneaking into your computer and running with your administrator account, doing their damage without your knowledge or permission.

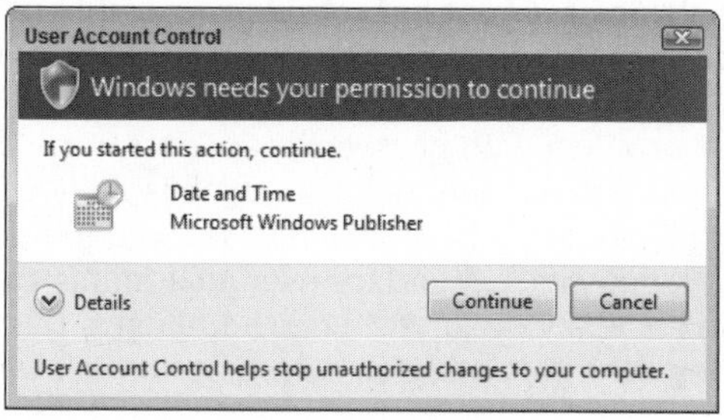

Figure 2-2:
Vista asks
permission
before
performing
administra-
tive actions.

> **User Account Control**
>
> 🛡 Windows needs your permission to continue
>
> If you started this action, continue.
>
> 📅 Date and Time
>   Microsoft Windows Publisher
>
> ⌄ Details   [Continue]   [Cancel]
>
> User Account Control helps stop unauthorized changes to your computer.

✦ Conversely, even if you are using a standard account, Vista gives you an opportunity to run programs that would normally require an administrator account. When you try to run such a program, Vista asks you to provide the password for an administrator account (see Figure 2-3).

If the person using the standard account selects an administrator account without a password, simply clicking the Submit button allows the program to run.

Figure 2-3:
On a standard account, Vista gives you a chance to supply an administrator's credentials.

Most experts recommend that you use a standard account for daily activities and only switch to an administrator account when you need to install software or hardware, or get at files outside the usual shared areas. Most experts ignore their own advice: It's the old do-as-I-say-not-as-I-do syndrome. It's also a bit of a head-in-the-sand approach, because you're given a chance to shoot yourself in the foot (er, run programs that make substantial changes) as if you were using an administrator account, by simply filling in the administrator password and clicking the OK button in the dialog box shown in Figure 2-3. Owning an administrator account but forcing yourself to use a standard account just doesn't make sense. I believe the term is *self-deluding*.

In addition, an inherent problem with passwords appears in spades right here. Those running with a standard account need an administrator username and password to "elevate" their security clearance high enough to make substantial changes to the PC. But if you give a standard user an administrator password, that standard user can basically do anything an administrator can do — including simply logging off and logging on with that administrator account.

After you've given away an administrator password (or created an administrator account without a password), you've given away the keys to the executive washroom. The only way to get them back is to log on with that administrator account and change the password.

Here's the best compromise I've found: Stick with administrator accounts on PCs that will be used by people who are moderately aware of the dangers of running unknown programs, and are sufficiently jaded to question the wisdom of running any program they don't understand. But if you have users who might not be so circumspect — or if folks use your computer who don't have any business digging around in other users' files — give them standard accounts, and lock out any administrator accounts with passwords. Then jealously guard the passwords.

Disabling User Account Control

Does User Account Control (UAC) drive you *nuts?* Have you finally reached the point where you never look at the UAC dialog boxes — whenever your screen goes dark, you just click the Continue button to get the stupid thing out of the way?

Yeah. Me, too. (See the nearby sidebar, "What went wrong with UAC?")

If you're absolutely sure that UAC only gets in your way, and that it doesn't contribute one iota to your system's security, you have several options.

What went wrong with UAC?

Let me tell you how I came to the conclusion that Vista's User Account Control is all wet. I had to change my system clock. I was using my administrator account. I clicked the clock, in the lower-right corner of the screen, clicked Date and Time Settings, and then clicked Change Date and Time. Bang. User Account Control told me that I had to give my permission to continue.

What the $#@! is up with that? I mean, I just clicked *three times,* telling Vista that I wanted to change the clock. Why do I have to click *again* to jump through some security hoop?

User Access Control originated as a cure for a fundamental design decision made by Windows' originators 20 years ago. From the beginning, Windows was designed to let programs pull each others' strings: You could click the clock, then click the Date and Time Settings button, but in a very similar way, a program running on your computer could "click" the clock, then click the Date and Time Settings button. Anything you can do, a program can do: send e-mail, reformat a hard drive, or ping `www.whitehouse.gov`. Twenty years ago, that was cool. Now it's considered dangerous. For good reason.

I believe that Microsoft missed the boat on UAC. By tackling the problem from a programmer's point of view, I fear that Vista's designers didn't look hard enough from the user's point of view.

Vista's designers will tell you that UAC has to verify that you were the one who started the potentially dangerous program. In my example, I clicked the clock, then Date and Time Settings, then Change Date and Time. The Vista folks note, correctly, that a program could've done the same thing. Thus, the UAC dialog box confirms that you were the one who started the program.

As far as I'm concerned, that's a disingenuous and short-sighted approach. Vista has many ways to verify that I was the one who did the clicking: input buffers and counters, screen coordinates, draw commands, and much more. Vista hooks directly into the hardware. If Vista is smart enough to draw the button on the screen, smart enough to know that I clicked the screen, and smart enough to know that the place I clicked was on top of the Change Date and Time button, why isn't Vista smart enough to remember that I was the one who clicked it?

The answer, of course, is that Vista isn't designed to remember such things. The records are there, but they're buried deep, and it would take a major reworking of Windows to make that kind of interface tracking both accessible and secure.

It took Microsoft six years to build Vista. The lapses continue to amaze me.

You can turn off User Account Control completely. The quick way: Click Start and then click your picture at the top of the right column. Click Turn User Account Control On or Off. Deselct the Use User Account Control (UAC) check box to help protect your computer. Click OK and reboot your computer. Unfortunately, that approach turns off UAC for all users. Anyone using your computer with a Standard account won't even be prompted to supply an administrator account and password.

If you have Vista Business, Enterprise, or Ultimate, there's a much better way: You can selectively disable UAC prompts for Administrator accounts only. Unfortunately, this option doesn't exist in Vista Home Basic or Premium; see Scott Dunn's article in PC World, `tinyurl.com/37jn7k`, for some alternatives

1. **In Vista Business, Enterprise, or Ultimate, click the Start button. In the Start Search box, type** secpol.msc **and press Enter.**

You have to click through the User Account Control dialog box, of course, but then you arrive at the Microsoft System Policy Editor, which looks like Figure 2-4.

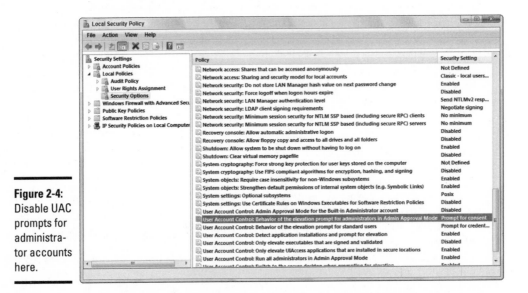

Figure 2-4:
Disable UAC prompts for administrator accounts here.

2. **On the left, double-click Local Policies and then Security Options.**

3. **On the right, double-click the line marked User Account Control: Behavior of the Elevation Prompt for Administrators in Admin Approval Mode.**

Vista shows you the Local Security Setting dialog box shown in Figure 2-5.

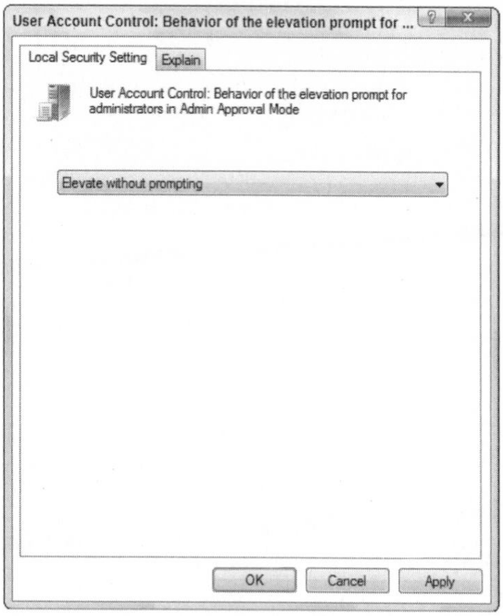

Figure 2-5:
The security setting that enables UAC prompts for administrator accounts.

4. **In the drop-down box, choose Elevate Without Prompting and then click the OK button.**

5. **Click the red *X* to exit the Local Security Setting dialog box, and your change takes effect immediately.**

   Go ahead. Try it. Vista bellyaches and sends up a security notification balloon, but you can ignore it.

Adding Users

After you log on by clicking your name on the Welcome screen, you can add more users quite easily. The Welcome Center (see Book II, Chapter 1) invites you to Add or Remove User Accounts. Even if you've banished the Welcome Center — and you should — adding new users is a snap. Here's how:

1. **Choose Start⇨Control Panel and under the User Accounts and Family Safety heading, click the Add or Remove User Accounts option.**

   After you click through the User Account Control security box, you see the Manage Accounts window, as shown in Figure 2-6.

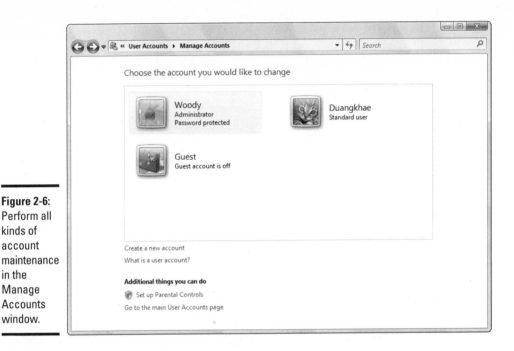

Figure 2-6:
Perform all
kinds of
account
maintenance
in the
Manage
Accounts
window.

2. **Click the Create a New Account option.**

3. **Type a name for the new account.**

You can give a new account just about any name you like: first name, last name, nickname, titles, abbreviations. No sweat, as long as you don't use the characters / \ [ ] " ; : | < > + = , ? or *.

4. **Tell Windows whether you want the account to be a standard user account or an administrator account.**

The choice of standard versus administrator account status isn't nearly as straightforward as Microsoft's description would lead you to believe. See the section, "Choosing Account Types," earlier in this chapter.

5. **Click the Create Account button.**

You're done. Rocket science. The name now appears on the Welcome screen.

This is more than a bit confusing, but you aren't allowed to create a new account called `Administrator`. There's a good reason why Vista prevents you from making a new account with that name: You already have one. Even though Vista goes to great lengths to hide the account called `Administrator`, it's there, and you will bump into it if you ever have to restore your system.

For now, don't worry about the ambiguous name and the ghostly appearance. Just refrain from trying to create a new account called Administrator.

Enabling the Guest Account

The Guest account is a special standard account that comes in handy if many different people need to use a computer, but you don't want any of them to be able to get at important information — or run potentially destructive programs. To make the Guest account available on your computer, follow these steps:

1. **Choose Start➪Control Panel and under the User Accounts and Family Safety heading, click the Add or Remove User Accounts option.**

You see the Manage Accounts dialog box shown in Figure 2-6.

2. **Click the Guest icon.**

Windows asks whether you want to turn on the Guest account.

3. **To enable the Guest account, click the Turn On button.**

From that point, Windows will show "Guest" as an account on the Welcome screen.

If you only have a few people who sporadically use your PC, take the time to set up standard accounts for each of them. That way, your PC can save their settings and make them available the next time each person logs on. But if you have more than a handful of guests, enable the Guest account and have all of them use the Guest account.

Don't enable the Guest account unless you need it. One more account is just one more potential hole for a slobbering cretin virus writer to exploit.

If you ever encounter instructions on the Internet that show you how to get rid of the Guest account, ignore them, okay? The Guest account exists on every Vista PC, and it's used for all sorts of behind-the-scenes stuff. You need the Guest account lurking in the background, even if you don't enable it, and it isn't visible on the Welcome screen — no matter what those self-appointed experts might say.

Changing Accounts

If you have an administrator account, you can reach in and change every detail of every single account on the computer — except one.

Changing other users' settings

If you pick an account from the Manage Accounts screen (see Figure 2-6), which you open by choosing Start➪Control Panel and clicking the Add or Remove User Accounts option (under the User Accounts and Family Safety heading), Windows immediately presents you with several options. (See Figure 2-7.) Click any of these options to begin the chosen task. Here's what the options entail:

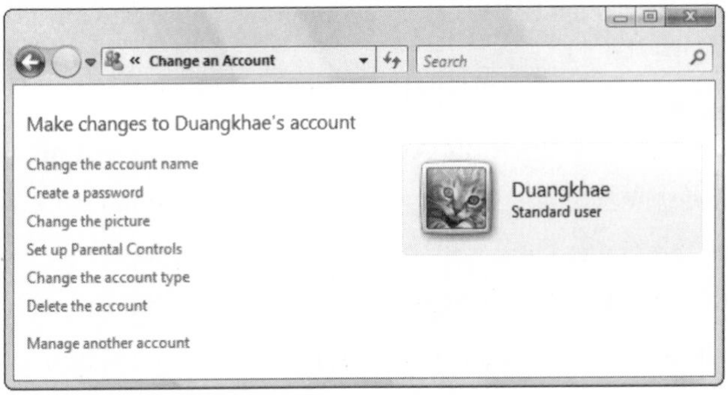

Figure 2-7: Maintain another user's account.

> Make changes to Duangkhae's account
>
> Change the account name
> Create a password
> Change the picture
> Set up Parental Controls
> Change the account type
> Delete the account
>
> Manage another account
>
> Duangkhae
> Standard user

✦ **Change Name:** Modifies the name displayed on the Welcome screen and at the very top of the Start menu, while leaving all other settings intact. Use this option if you want to change the name on the account only — for example, if "Little Bill" wants to be called "Sir William."

✦ **Create/Change/Remove a Password:** If you create a password for the chosen user, Vista requires a password to crank up that user account. You can't get past the Welcome screen (using that account) without it. This is a weird setting because you can change it for other people: You can force "Bill" to use a password when none was required before, you can change Bill's password, or you can even delete the password. Worse yet, you specify the initial password when you create a password, so Bill would have to pry the password out of you before he can log on to his own account.

Passwords are cAse SenSitive — you must enter the password, with uppercase and lowercase letters, precisely the way it was originally typed. If you can't get the computer to recognize your password, make sure that the Caps Lock setting is off. That's the number one source of logon frustration.

If you decide to put a password on another user's account, tell that person to take a couple of minutes to run the Forgotten Password Wizard, as described in the next section.

✦ **Change the Picture:** Changes the picture that appears next to the user's name on the Welcome screen, the Start menu, and in the User Accounts areas. You can choose a picture from any of the common file types: GIF, BMP, JPG, or PNG. Windows offers a couple dozen pictures to choose from, but you can reach out and grab any picture, anywhere. If you pick a big picture, Windows automatically scales it down to size.

✦ **Set Up Parental Controls:** I talk about parental controls in Book III, Chapter 1.

✦ **Change the Account Type:** Lets you change accounts from administrator to standard and back again. The implications are somewhat complex; I talk about them in the section, "Choosing Account Types," earlier in this chapter.

✦ **Delete the Account:** Allows you to deep-six the account, if you're that bold (or mad, in all senses of the term). Windows offers to keep copies of the deleted account's Documents folder and desktop, but warns you quite sternly and correctly that if you snuff the account, you rip out all the e-mail messages, Internet Favorites, and other settings that belong to the user. Definitely not a good way to make friends.

Changing your own settings

Changing your own account is just a little bit different from changing other users' accounts. Follow these steps:

1. **Choose Start⇨Control Panel, click the User Accounts and Family Safety heading, and then click the User Accounts option.**

2. **Click the icon next to your own username.**

You see the Make Changes to Your User Account dialog box, shown in Figure 2-8.

Figure 2-8:
Change
your own
account.

Most of the options for your own account mirror those of other users' accounts, as described in the preceding section.

If you put a password on your own account (or somebody else does it for you), it's important that you click the Create a Password Reset Disk link. That launches the Forgotten Password Wizard, which creates a "password reset disk." This nifty little program creates a file that you can use to unlock your password and get into your account, even if your precocious seven-year-old daughter changes it to MXYPLFTFFT.

Back in the early days of Windows, the reset disk was a floppy disk. Nowadays, though, almost everybody stores his password reset information on a key drive (USB drive). Make sure that you have a key drive handy, and work your way through the wizard.

You have to run the wizard just once. The file it shuffles to your key drive (or floppy disk) can always unlock your account, no matter how many times the password is changed, or by whom.

Deleting yourself

AHA! Compare Figure 2-7 to Figure 2-8. You get bonus Dummies Merit Points if you noticed a subtle difference. (One hundred Dummies Merit Points are redeemable for one Severe Bragging Right at any local Dummies store. Tell 'em Woody sent ya.)

You can't delete your own account.

Windows has to protect itself. Every PC must have at least one user with an administrator account. If Vista lost all its administrators, no one would be around to add new users or change existing ones, much less to install programs or hardware, right?

Although you and I could probably think of a few dozen ways to ensure that a PC always has at least one administrator account, Microsoft has chosen a rather straightforward approach. First, you can't turn yourself into a standard user if only one administrator account is on the computer. Second, you can't delete your own account.

Betwixt the two of those requirements, Vista is assured of always having a minimum of one administrator account available at its beck and call.

Switching Users

Vista allows you to have more than one person logged on to a PC simultaneously. That's very convenient if, say, you're working on the family PC checking Billy's homework when you hear the cat screaming bloody murder in the kitchen, and your wife wants to put digital pictures from the family vacation in the Public Pictures folder while you run off to check the microwave.

The ability to have more than one user logged on to a PC simultaneously is called *Fast User Switching,* and it has advantages and disadvantages:

✦ **On the plus side:** Fast User Switching lets you keep all your programs going while somebody else pops onto the machine for a quick jaunt on the keyboard. When she's done, she can log off, and you can pick up precisely where you left off before you got bumped.

✦ **On the minus side:** All the idle programs left sitting around by the inactive ("bumped") user can bog things down for the active user, although the effect isn't too drastic. You can avoid the overhead by logging off before the new user logs on.

You probably won't be surprised to find that you have to click the Start button to log off or switch users. Simply click the Start button, click the right-wedge to the right of the Lock icon, and then click the Switch User option or the Log Off option.

**Book II
Chapter 2**

Controlling Users

Chapter 3: Maintaining Your System

In This Chapter

✔ Keeping track of the programs installed on your PC

✔ Working with drives

✔ Scheduling boring things so that your computer does them automatically

✔ Storing more and spending less with Zip files

✔ Using backups, checkpoints, and other things you'll wish you would've created

*O*nto every glass window a little rain must fall.

Or something like that.

Windows Vista is a computer program, not a Cracker Jack toy, and it's going to have problems. The trick lies in making sure that you don't have problems, too.

This chapter takes you through all the important tools you have at hand to make Vista do what you need to do, to head off problems, and to solve problems as they (inevitably!) occur.

Windows Update — the big, complicated system that (usually) helps your system reach out to Microsoft's computers, and then retrieve and apply security patches — falls under the Security Center umbrella and, as such, is discussed in Book III, Chapter 2.

Using the Control Panel

The inner workings of Windows Vista reveal themselves inside the mysterious (and somewhat haughtily named) Control Panel. Choose Start➪Control Panel to plug away at the innards (see Figure 3-1).

Figure 3-1:
Vista's
packed
Control
Panel.

I cover various Control Panel components at several points in this book, but the lion's share of the discussion appears in this chapter.

The main categories of the Control Panel span the breadth (and plumb the depth) of Vista-dumb:

✦ **System and Maintenance:** Use an enormous array of tools for trouble-shooting and adjusting your PC, backing up your data, controlling how Windows conducts searches, checking your performance rating, and generally making your PC work when it doesn't want to. Unfortunately, this category also includes all the tools you need to shoot yourself in the foot, consistently and reliably, day in and day out. Use this part of the Control Panel with discretion and respect.

✦ **Security:** Check out the components of Vista's mighty security arsenal, including Windows Firewall (at least, the inbound part of Windows Firewall; see Book III, Chapter 3), Windows Defender (Book III, Chapter 5), and the efficacy of your antivirus software. This is also the place to go to institute parental controls (Book III, Chapter 1) and make changes to Internet Explorer's security settings (Book V, Chapter 3).

✦ **Network and Internet:** Set up a network. Set up Internet connections, particularly if you're sharing an Internet connection across a network, or if you have a cable modem or digital subscriber line (DSL) service. Deal with conflicting wireless networks. Sign in for Windows Collaboration

(Book V, Chapter 5) or configure synchronization between computers. Many security settings in this category duplicate those in the Security category.

✦ **Hardware and Sound:** The "all other" category. Add or remove printers and connect to other printers on your network. Troubleshoot printers. Install, remove, and set the options for scanners and digital cameras, mice, game controllers, joysticks, keyboards, and pen devices. Power settings are here, too.

✦ **Programs:** Add and remove specific features in some programs (most notably Windows Vista and Office). Uninstall programs. Block programs that try to start themselves when you boot Windows, using Windows Defender (Book III, Chapter 5). Change the association between filename extensions (see Book II, Chapter 1) and the programs that run them (so you can, for example, have iTunes play WMA audio files). Microsoft also kindly gives you an easy way to buy new programs online. Gawrsh.

✦ **User Accounts and Family Safety:** Add or remove users from the Windows Welcome screen. Enable the Guest account (see Book II, Chapter 2). Change user account characteristics, including passwords. Set up parental controls (Book III, Chapter 1).

✦ **Appearance and Personalization:** Turn on the Glass effect, and make your windows translucent. Change what your desktop looks like — wallpaper, colors, mouse pointers, screen saver, icon size and spacing, and so on. Set screen resolution (for example, 1280×1024 or 2048×1280) so that you can pack more information onto your screen — assuming that your eyes (and screen) can handle it. Make the Windows taskbar hide when you're not using it, and change the items on your Start menu. Change what Windows Explorer shows when you're looking at folders. Add or remove fonts.

✦ **Clock, Language, and Region:** Set the time and date — although double-clicking the clock on the Windows taskbar is much simpler — or tell Windows to synchronize the clock automatically. Here you can also add support for complex languages (such as Thai) and right-to-left languages, and change how dates, times, currency, and numbers appear.

✦ **Ease of Access:** Change settings to help you see the screen, use the keyboard or mouse, or have Windows flash part of your screen when the speaker would play a sound. Also sets up speech recognition.

Many of the Control Panel settings duplicate options you see elsewhere in Vista, but some capabilities that seem like they should be Control Panel mainstays remain mysteriously absent. You have at least 157 different ways in the Control Panel to turn on Windows automatic updating, for example (OK, so I exaggerated a little bit), but you won't find the controls for adjusting Vista's outbound firewall anywhere in the long Control Panel list.

**Book II
Chapter 3**

Maintaining Your
System

If you want to change a Windows setting, by all means, try the Control Panel, but don't be discouraged if you can't find what you're looking for. Instead, look in this book's Table of Contents or index.

Removing and Changing Programs

Windows only lives to serve — or so I'm told — and, more than anything, Windows serves programs. Most of us spend our time working inside programs, such as Outlook or Word or PageMaker or CorelDRAW. Windows acts as traffic cop and nanny but doesn't do the heavy lifting. Programs rule. Users rely on Windows to keep the programs in line.

Installing programs is easy. When you want to install a program, you typically insert a CD into your CD drive and follow the instructions, or double-click on a downloaded program. You've done that a hundred times.

Removing well-behaved programs is just as easy, if you follow the instructions in this section. Changing programs, on the other hand, is a different kettle of fish, as you will soon discover.

Windows Vista includes a one-stop shopping point for removing and making massive changes to programs. To get to it, choose Start⇨Control Panel, and then under the Programs heading, click the Uninstall a Program link. You see the dialog box shown in Figure 3-2.

Click to start the program's installer

You may have choices to change or repair

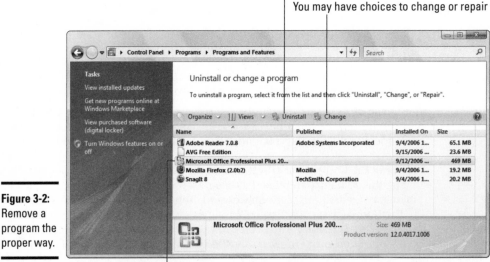

Figure 3-2:
Remove a program the proper way.

Select the program

When Vista talks about changing programs, it isn't talking about making minor twiddles — this isn't the place to go if you want Microsoft Word to stop showing you rulers, for example. The Uninstall or Change a Program dialog box is designed to activate or deactivate big chunks of a program — graft on a new arm or lop off an unused head (of which there are many, particularly in Office). If you look at Figure 3-3, you can see the kind of grand scale I'm talking about: In the Uninstall or Change a Program dialog box for Office 2007, for example, you may tell Excel that you want to use its Analysis ToolPak add-in for financial analysis. Similarly, you may use the Uninstall or Change a Program dialog box to completely obliterate Office's Speech Recognition capabilities. That's the kind of large-scale capability I'm talking about.

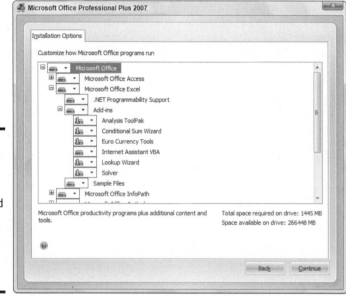

Figure 3-3:
The Office 2007 Setup dialog box, as launched by the Uninstall or Change a Program dialog box.

Yes, it's true. If you want to *install* a big chunk of a program, you have to click the *Un*install a Program link in the Control Panel. The terminology stinks. Vista really should say something like "Bring up a program's installer/uninstaller." But I guess speaking the truth plainly would be too confusing.

Windows Vista itself doesn't do much in the Uninstall or Change a Program dialog box. Vista primarily acts as a gathering point: Well-behaved programs, when they're installed, are supposed to stick their uninstallers where the Uninstall or Change a Program dialog box can find them. That way, you have one centralized place to look in when you want to get rid of a program. Microsoft doesn't write the uninstallers that the Uninstall or Change a Program dialog box runs; if you have a gripe about a program's uninstaller, you need to talk to the company that made the program.

A couple of school-of-hard-knocks comments pertain:

+ You rarely use the Uninstall or Change a Program dialog box to remove parts of a program. Either you try to add features in a program that you forgot to include when you originally installed the program — most commonly with Office — or you want to delete a program entirely, to wipe its sorry tail off your hard drive.

Why sweat the small stuff? When you install a program, install all of it. With large hard drives so cheap they're likely candidates for a landfill, it never pays to cut back on installed features to save a few megabytes. In for a penny, in for a pound.

+ Many uninstallers, for reasons known only to their company's programmers — I won't mention Adobe by name — require you to insert the program's CD into your CD drive before you uninstall the program. That's like requiring you to show your dog's vaccination records before you kick it out of the house.

When you start a program's uninstaller, you're at the mercy of the uninstaller and the programmers who wrote it. Windows doesn't even enter into the picture.

Removing Windows Patches

If you install a Windows patch and discover a minute (or a day or week) later that the patch causes more problems than it solves, you may — *may* — be able to roll back the patch.

To see whether the fix that bedevils you can be exorcised, choose Start⇨ Control Panel⇨Programs and under Programs and Features, click View Installed Updates.

Vista presents you with a list of all the patches that have been applied to your system. Click the one that's the most likely source of your problems, and then click the Remove button. If you're allowed to uninstall the patch, Vista will do it for you.

Making Backups

Of course you make backups. Doesn't everybody?

Seriously, you really should back up your data periodically — and store the major backups *off-site* (that's computer lingo for "anyplace that's far enough away from your computer that a fire won't take out your computer and your backup, unless you live next to Mrs. O'Leary's cow").

Backup to the Internet?

If you have any version of Vista other than Home Basic, a fast Internet connection, and you don't mind storing your data on a gigantic company's computer, consider backing up to Box.net (www.box.net). The free version allows you to store up to 1GB of data with a maximum file size of 10MB. For $19.95 per month, you can get 15GB. Microsoft offers a similar online storage capability called SkyDrive (skydrive.live.com). Bjarke Viksoe offers a free program called GMail Drive that turns your Gmail account into online storage: see www.viksoe.dk/code/gmail.htm. If you'd rather let a separate backup program do the work, look at Mozy (mozy.com). For $4.95 per month, Mozy offers unlimited backup space to home users and the software to go with it.

Vista backups fall into four categories, not all of which are available to all Vista owners:

✦ **Shadow copies** (also called *previous versions* and, confusingly, *backup copies*) of your data files, which Vista keeps for you automatically. Previous versions, er, shadow copies, are only available in the Business, Enterprise, and Ultimate Editions of Vista.

✦ **File backups** are backups of specific kinds of data files in which you use the Backup Files Wizard to make copies of data files on your drive(s). Every version of Vista can run data backups, but if you have Home Basic, you can't set up automatic scheduled data backups (you have to start backups by hand), and you can't use a network drive to store backups.

✦ **System Restore points** back up most of your computer's internal settings, drivers, and certain key system files. Every version of Vista automatically creates a System Restore point daily. Vista also usually creates a restore point prior to installing new software. Restore points are quite different from data backups; I talk about them in their own section at the end of this chapter.

✦ **Complete backups** (also called *CompletePC backups, system backups, image backups, ghosts,* and several other imaginative appellations), where a snapshot of the entire contents of your drive(s) gets copied. Only Business, Enterprise, and Ultimate Editions of Vista have ghosts.

If you have a version of Vista that makes you feel like a second-class WinCitizen, your suspicions may be confirmed by consulting Table 3-1.

Table 3-1	**Your Backup Options**		
Feature	*Home Basic*	*Home Premium*	*Business, Enterprise, or Ultimate*
Create shadow copies (previous versions)	No	No	Automatic
Create data backups	Manual only	Scheduled, manual	Scheduled, manual
Backup to/restore from	DVD, local drive only	DVD, local drive, network	DVD, local drive, network
System Restore points	Automatic	Automatic	Automatic
Complete system image backups	No	No	Yes

Using shadow copies/previous versions

If you have Vista Home or Vista Home Premium, you don't get shadow copies/previous version protection. Skip to the next section to run your own data backups.

Shadow copies live on the same hard drive that contains the original data, so they won't protect you from disasters that take out the drive, like an errant ball bearing rolling to meet its maker or a talented cup of coffee performing a swan dive into your computer's case. Instead, shadow copies exist to help you recover if you accidentally delete or otherwise screw up an important file.

To understand the real-world benefits and shortcomings of shadow copies, it's important to realize that different programs save changes in different ways — and the differences can cost you hours of frustration. For example:

✦ When you're using Microsoft Word and you save a Word document, Word puts the updated information on disk, but it saves all your intermediate steps. As long as you don't close the document, you can undo any mistakes that you've made. If you really mess up a document, and you catch the problem in time, you can click the Undo button and move back to any previous state. After you close the document, though, Word forgets all the undo steps.

✦ By contrast, when you're using Microsoft Excel and you save an Excel spreadsheet, Excel puts the updated information on disk, but it then immediately forgets all your undo steps. If you really mess up an Excel spreadsheet, and discover the error of your ways immediately after you saved, the best that you can hope for (with apologies to Kenny Rogers) is to die in your sleep. To a first approximation, anyway.

Vista makes shadow copies of your data files sporadically. At the very least, you should have an automatically generated shadow copy (er, previous version) of every data file on your main hard drive, and at any given moment, that shadow copy should be no more than 24 hours old.

If you suddenly get that "oooops" feeling and want to recover your data, follow these school-of-hard-knocks steps:

1. **If you're working on a document (spreadsheet, whatever) and you get the sinking feeling that something has gone awry, *don't* panic, *don't* save the document, *don't* close the document, and *don't* shut down the application.**

2. **Click the application's Undo button.**

   Almost all the Office applications, and many other applications, have a drop-down arrow next to the Undo button that lets you group undos and apply many of them at once. See whether you can get the document back to the state you want by undoing.

3. **If you can't undo your way out of the mess, *don't* save or close the screwed-up document.**

   Leave it open, right where it is, in case you can use some of the jumbled mess to make an older version of the document right.

4. **Choose Start⇨Documents and navigate to the document that's causing you problems. Right-sclick the document and choose Restore Previous Versions. (Remember this doesn't work in Vista Home or Home Premium.)**

   Vista shows you the Previous Versions dialog box for the afflicted file (see Figure 3-4).

5. **Click the Copy button (don't click the Open button), and give the copy of the old version of the file a name that you can remember.**

   Clicking Open in the Previous Versions dialog box can cause all sorts of confusion — and you may not know that you have a problem until you try to save or close the recovered file.

   If the Open and Copy buttons are both grayed out, avoid using the Restore button. Instead, click the red *X* to exit the Previous Versions dialog box, go back into the original application, and choose File⇨Save As to save the screwed-up version of the file, giving it a new name. Then repeat Steps 1 to 4, and use the Previous Versions dialog box to open the older version of the file. Yes, it's complicated. A scorecard helps.

6. **Open the (renamed) previous version.**

   You can now copy and paste between the previous version and the screwed-up version of the document. When you're done, close and delete the screwed-up version.

Click the file if you want to restore once

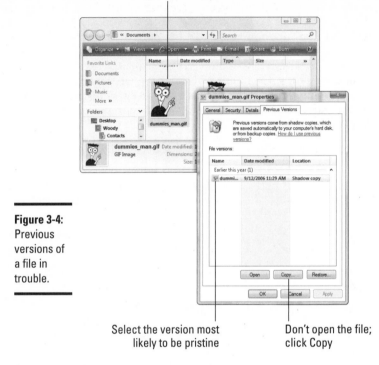

Figure 3-4:
Previous
versions of
a file in
trouble.

Select the version most
likely to be pristine

Don't open the file;
click Copy

Shadow copies can also be useful if you accidentally delete a file — although I recommend that you use the Recycle Bin, if at all possible (double-click the Recycle Bin on the desktop, select the file you wish to restore, and then click the Restore button). The Recycle Bin is much less confusing.

Creating data backups

Every Vista user should take advantage of the Back Up Files Wizard to make copies of his key files — and then ensure that those files are stored off-site, away from the computer from whence they came.

If you own Home Basic, you have to manually run the Back Up Files Wizard every time you want to back up your data. All the other versions of Vista can take your cue and, after being started, automatically run a backup once a week, or according to any schedule you may establish.

Note that Vista's Back Up Files Wizard only backs up *your* data files — more accurately, it only backs up the data files associated with the current user account. If other user accounts are on the computer, the other users have to run the wizard, too.

Vista's backup wizard packs a whole bunch of smarts. Unless you specifically change one of the settings, it performs *incremental backups* — that is, it only backs up files that have changed since the previous backup. It stores the backups as regular, old, everyday Zip files, in locations that you can find, understand, and get to. Recovering backed up files only takes a few clicks. All in all, the wizard's a remarkable achievement, incorporating features that other backup programs have had for, oh, a decade or more.

When it comes to backup, how often is often enough? I dunno. How long is a string? I back up every night, and I let the wizard do the heavy lifting, but then again I don't have to worry about running out of drive space or swapping DVDs. If you have data that changes frequently — in my case, I'm a slave to e-mail — consider backing up nightly, too.

Even if you have the Business, Enterprise, or Ultimate version of Vista, and you feel smug about your fancy automatic shadow copies/previous versions, here are two good reasons for running this more mundane style of backup:

✦ From time to time, you definitely want to store backups someplace other than the drive on which the original data resides. Unless you (or your company's network administrator) have changed things, shadow copies go on the same drive as the original data.

✦ You might not trust Vista's automatic shadow copying to create an automatic copy at the right time. If you run a manual backup, you know darn good and well that the data's backed up.

To use the Back Up Files Wizard and run a manual backup, follow these steps:

1. **Choose Start⇨Control Panel.**

Vista shows you the Control Panel (refer to Figure 3-1).

2. **Under the System and Maintenance heading, click the Back Up Your Computer link.**

Vista shows you the Backup and Restore Center. Depending on which version of Vista you're running, it looks more or less like Figure 3-5.

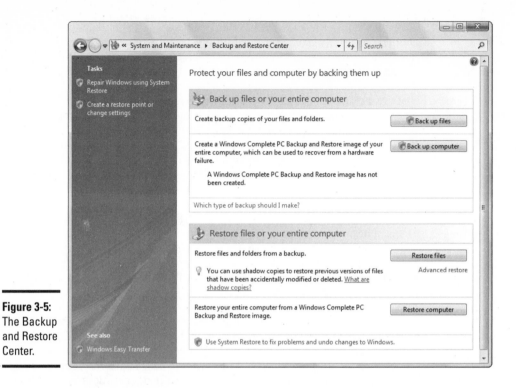

Figure 3-5:
The Backup
and Restore
Center.

3. **In the upper-right corner, click the Back Up Files button under the Back Up Files heading. (If you've already used the program, a line that says Change Settings appears below the Back Up Files button. Click it if you aren't sure whether your settings are good or not.)**

   Click through the User Account Control security warning, and Vista asks where you want to save your backup files (see Figure 3-6).

4. **If at all possible, choose a location other than your main hard drive for your backups. When you find a location you can live with, click the Next button.**

   Depending on your Vista version, you may or may not be allowed to save backups on a network (see Table 3-1).

   If you choose a CD or DVD drive for automatic backups, you need to remember to put a blank CD or DVD in the drive before the backup runs. (In the case of CD-RW or DVD-RW discs, you can keep reusing the same disc, backup after backup.) If your backup doesn't fit on a single CD or DVD, you need to keep feeding the drive blank discs while the backup progresses — that's kinda hard to do if you aren't sitting at the PC when the automatic backup runs.

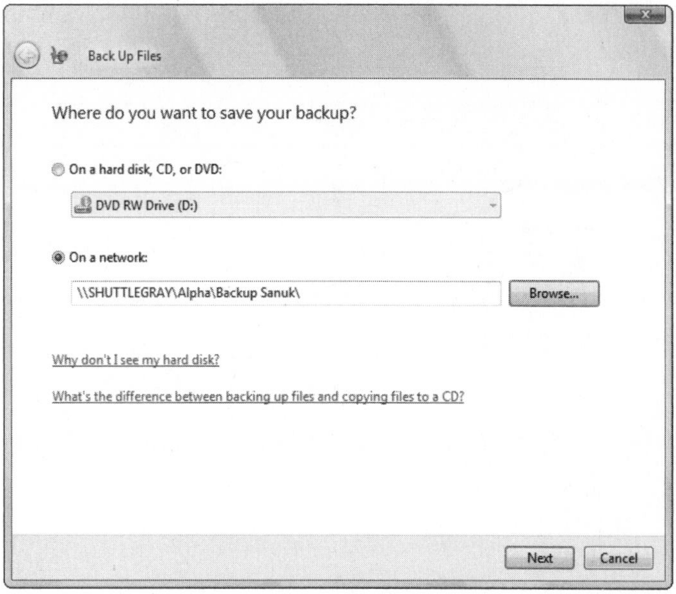

Figure 3-6:
Choose a
location
for your
backup files.

Should you decide to back up to a drive somewhere on your network, you need to provide a computer name, username, and password that can log on to the network (as shown in Figure 3-7). Note that the user-name you provide *must* have a password — the wizard won't let you back up to the network unless you provide a computer name, username, and password that are valid at the time the backup runs.

Figure 3-7:
You must
specify
a user
account with
a password
that works
on the
network and
enter it in
this manner.

The Back Up Files Wizard asks which file types you want to back up (see Figure 3-8).

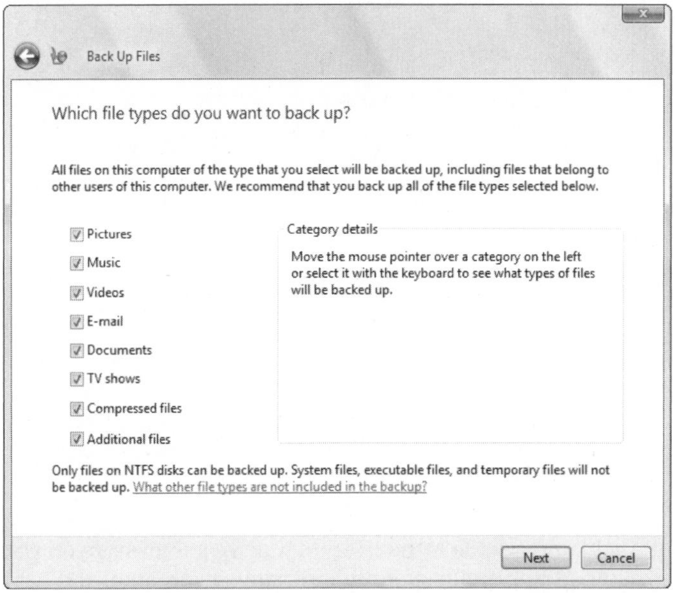

Figure 3-8:
You can save a lot of time and storage space if you don't need to back up specific kinds of files.

5. **If you have a specific reason to ignore certain kinds of files — perhaps all your music files are backed up elsewhere or you've burned all your photos to CD anyway — deselect the types of files that you don't want to back up and then click the Next button.**

How does Vista know what kinds of files you have on your drive? By looking at each file's filename extension, of course. You should be able to see and work with the same filename extensions that Windows uses. If you haven't already, follow the instructions in Book II, Chapter 1 to show filename extensions.

Unless you're using Home Basic, Vista asks how often you want to perform a backup.

6. **Choose how often and when you want to perform backups (see Figure 3-9), and then click the Save Settings and Start Backup button.**

Windows backup warns that it will save your settings and close. Click the Yes button, the backup kicks off (with a potentially long wait formatting a CD-RW or DVD-RW disc), and your new automatic backup settings take effect.

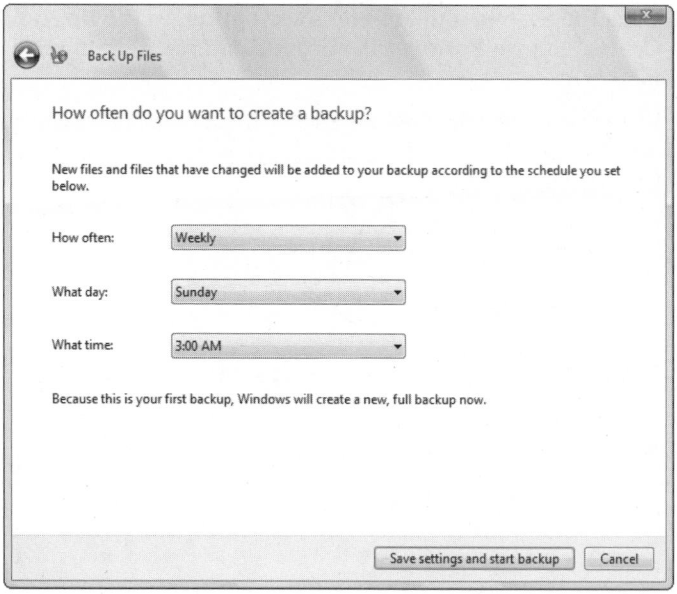

Figure 3-9:
Set the
backup
frequency.

The Back Up Files Wizard warns you that a backup is in progress. Don't yank out the CD or key drive, and don't disconnect your network connection, while the backup is in progress.

Restoring backed-up data

With all that backed-up data floating around on your machine, you might think that restoring a backed-up file would prove daunting, at best. Not so. The Restore Files Wizard makes it surprisingly easy.

To retrieve an older file, follow these steps:

1. **If you've hopelessly screwed up a file,** *don't* **save or close it. See whether you can turn back the clock without resorting to a restore by following Steps 1 through 3 in the section "Using shadow copies/ previous versions," earlier in this chapter.**

Along the same lines, if you delete a file accidentally, don't restore it with the Restore Files Wizard. Go to your desktop, double-click the Recycle Bin, and restore it from there.

2. **If you can't fix things the easy way, choose Start⇨Control Panel.**

Vista shows you the Control Panel (refer to Figure 3-1).

3. **Click the System and Maintenance option. In the Backup and Restore Center, choose Restore Files from Backup and then click the Restore Files button.**

Vista shows you the Restore Files Wizard (see Figure 3-10).

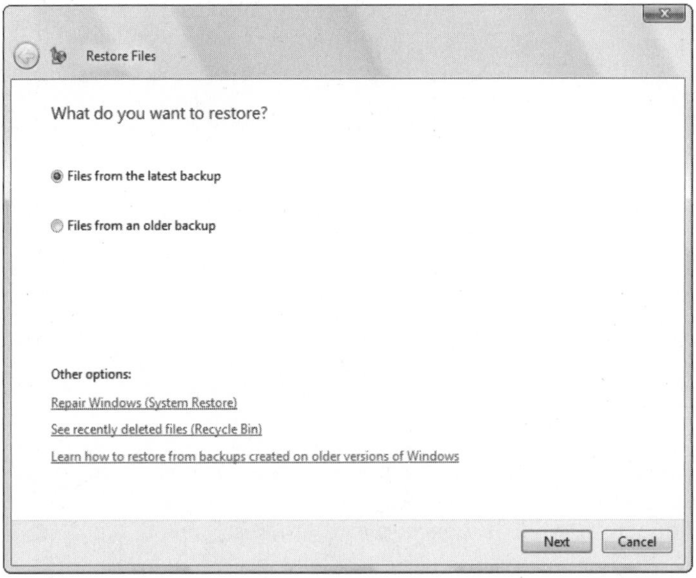

Figure 3-10: The other half of backup and restore.

4. **Unless you have an overwhelming need to go fishing for older versions of a particular file, select the Files from the Latest Backup option and click the Next button.**

Vista asks which files and folders you want to restore.

5. **Click the Add Files button.**

You see the Add Files to Restore dialog box (see Figure 3-11), which looks remarkably similar to a plain, old-fashioned Windows Explorer window. There's one big difference: All the files and folders you see, and all that you can get to from the Favorite Links bar on the left or the File Name search box at the bottom, are backups.

6. **Choose the file or folder(s) that you want to restore and click the Add button.**

The Restore Files Wizard returns to asking you which files and folders you want to restore. If you want to restore more files or folders, click the appropriate Browse button or use Search.

7. **When you're done gathering all the file(s)/folder(s) you need, like roses in May, click the Next button.**

Figure 3-11:
A complete list of all available backups.

The Restore Files Wizard asks where you want to save the recovered files.

8. **Click the In the Following Location option, click the Browse button, and navigate to a neutral place — say, your desktop (see Figure 3-12). Then click the Start Restore button.**

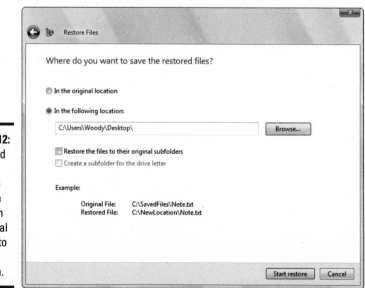

Figure 3-12:
You should always restore to a location other than the original location, to avoid confusion.

By restoring the file to a location other than its original location, you eliminate the possibility (indeed, the likelihood) of shooting yourself in the foot by confusing the restored file(s) with any original files.

The Restore Files Wizard takes a few second (or minutes or weeks) to restore the file(s).

9. **When the wizard presents you with a final dialog box, click the Finish button.**

10. **Immediately open the restored file, and make sure that you got what you thought you were going to get.**

If you got the right file, you can feel comfortable about moving it to its original location, possibly zapping out a screwed-up version.

11. **If you have the wrong file, go back to Step 1 and, in Step 3, select the Files from an Older Backup option.**

Going back more than one generation is a tricky job, fraught with potential errors. Work slowly, and don't overwrite anything until you're sure you have the correct file.

Ghosting with CompletePC backups

CompletePC backups (also called *system backups, image backups, ghosts,* and *system image backups*) take a full snapshot of your system, and store it away so that you can restore your system in the event of a calamitous crash. System image backups are only available to Business, Enterprise, and Ultimate Edition cardholders (see Table 3-1), but if you don't qualify, don't feel left out.

Unlike the other backup methods discussed in this chapter, restoring a system image backup completely obliterates *everything* on your hard drive, replacing the whole works with the saved copy. It's a drastic, scorched-earth approach that most Vista users should only employ in the most dire circumstances — typically when malware has so completely taken over your system that you can't get it to work, and you don't really care whether you have to throw out all the data that you acquired after the last good CompletePC backup.

Yes, in some circumstances, propeller heads need ghosts, er, CompletePC backups: If you're running more than one copy of Windows on the same machine or if you swap out hard drives like burgers at McDonalds, ghosting can save you quite a bit of time. But for the typical user, restoring a full system image rarely cures anything and always obliterates much.

Microsoft recommends that you take a system image backup when you first set up your computer, and update it every six months. I disagree. If you have all your installation CDs (or your computer manufacturer has a recovery disc or drive image stored somewhere), you have everything you need to start all over again. And restoring a gunked-up year-old copy of Vista is *worse* than starting all over again.

If you're convinced that you need to store a system image backup, just in case the sky starts falling, wait until your machine is absolutely, totally stable and clean, with drivers up to date and no viruses in sight. (Hard to believe I'm talking about Windows, eh?) Choose Start➪Control Panel➪ Back Up Your Computer, and then click the Back Up Computer button. CompletePC backup will take you through the motions.

You can create a system image with no ill effects. Just don't *restore* a system image unless you know what you're doing.

Maintaining Drives

E pur, si muove. Even so, it does move.

— Galileo, to his inquisitors, April 30, 1633

Drives (floppies, hard drives, CDs, DVDs, and other types of storage media) seem to cause more computer problems than all other infuriating PC parts combined. Why? They move. And unlike other parts of computers that are designed to move — printer rollers and keyboard springs and mouse balls, for example — they move quickly and with ultra-fine precision, day in and day out.

Like any other moving mechanical contraption, an ounce of drive prevention is worth ten tons of cure. Unlike other moving mechanical contraptions, a good shot of WD-40 usually won't cure the problem.

If you're looking for help installing a new hard drive, you're in the wrong place. I talk about adding new drives and getting Vista to recognize them in Book VI, Chapter 3.

Hard drives die at the worst possible moment. A hard drive that's starting to get flaky can display all sorts of strange symptoms: everything from long, long pauses when you're trying to open a file to completely inexplicable crashes and other errors in Windows itself.

Windows Vista comes with a grab bag of utilities designed to help you keep your hard drives in top shape. One of these utilities runs automatically every time your system shuts down unexpectedly, like when the dog finally chews through the power cord: The next time you start your system, Windows scans your hard drives to see whether any pieces of files were left hanging around.

You can spend a lot of time futzing around with your hard drives and their care and feeding if you want, but as far as I'm concerned, just three utilities suffice: Check Disk, Disk Cleanup, and Disk Defragmenter. You have to be a designated administrator (see the section on using account types in Book II, Chapter 2) to get them to work.

Running an error check

If a drive starts acting weird — for example, you get errors when trying to open a file, or Windows crashes in unpredictable ways — run the Windows error-checking routines.

What is formatting?

If you'll forgive a slightly stretched analogy, the surface of a floppy disk or the surface of the platters inside a hard drive is a lot like a blank audio cassette tape — you know, the kind you can buy for 29 cents at a discount store. The surface of the drive is coated with some sort of magnetic gunk that somehow magically stores electrical impulses, holds onto them, and then spits them back when you want them.

Audio cassette tapes are amazingly forgiving — ever turn one into an accordion with a lousy capstan? — but hard drives generally aren't so forgiving. Drives try to pack a lot of data into a small space, and because of that, they need to be calibrated. That's where *formatting* comes in.

When you format a drive, you calibrate it: You mark it with guideposts that tell the PC where to store data and how to retrieve it. Every floppy disk and every hard drive has to be formatted before it can be used. The manufacturer probably formatted your drive before you got it. That's comforting, because every time a drive gets reformatted, everything on the drive gets tossed out, completely and irretrievably. *Everything.*

You can format or reformat any hard drive other than the one that contains Windows by choosing Start⇨Computer, right-clicking the hard drive, and choosing Format. To format a floppy disk, insert a disk into the floppy drive and then follow the same approach. You can also "format" rewritable CDs, DVDs, USB (key) drives, and SD or other removable memory cards — delete all the data on them — by following the same approach. If you want to reformat the drive that contains Windows, you have to reinstall Windows. See the instructions for a clean Windows install in Book I, Chapter 4.

If you're an old hand at Windows — or an even older hand at DOS — you probably recognize the following steps as the venerable CHKDSK routine, in somewhat fancier clothing.

Follow these steps to run Check Disk:

1. **Choose Start⇨Computer.**

2. **Right-click the drive that's malfunctioning and choose Properties.**

3. **On the Tools tab, click the Check Now button.**

You may have to click through a User Account Control dialog box, but ultimately the Check Disk dialog box appears (see Figure 3-13).

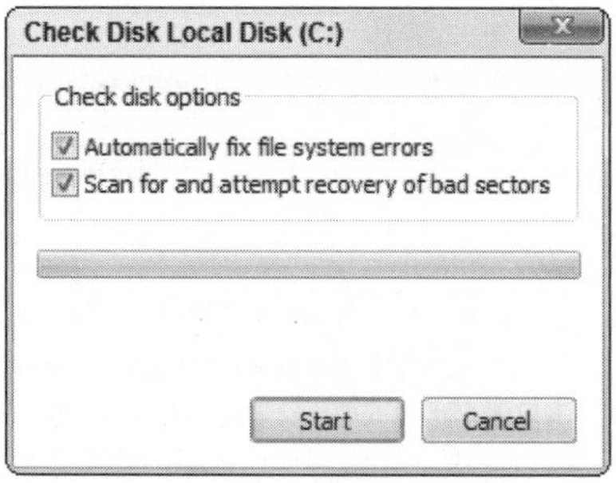

Book II
Chapter 3

Maintaining Your
System

Figure 3-13:
Check Disk
performs a
complete
surface
scan.

Check Disk Local Disk (C:)

Check disk options

☑ Automatically fix file system errors
☑ Scan for and attempt recovery of bad sectors

Start   Cancel

4. **In most circumstances, you want to select the Scan for and Attempt Recovery of Bad Sectors check box, and then click the Start button.**

If you don't want to sit and wait and wait for Windows to finish, you probably want to select the Automatically Fix File System Errors check box, too.

As long as you aren't using any files on the hard drive that Windows is scanning, Windows performs the scan on the spot and reports on what it finds. If you are using files on the hard drive, however — and that always happens if you're scanning the drive that contains Windows itself — Windows asks whether you want to schedule a scan to run the next time you restart your machine. If you say yes, you have to turn the computer off and then turn it back on again before Windows runs the scan. (Note that merely logging off isn't sufficient.)

Scheduling cleanups

In addition to running an error check from time to time, I use the Windows Task Scheduler to periodically go through and remove temporary files that I don't need; I use the utility called Disk Cleanup. I tell you how to do that in the section "Scheduling the Task Scheduler," later in this chapter.

Defragmenting a drive

Once upon a time, *defragmenting* your hard drive — instructing Windows to rearrange files on a hard drive so that the various parts of a file all sit next to one another — rated as a Real Big Deal. Windows didn't help automate running defrags, so few people bothered. As a result, drives started to look like patchwork quilts with pieces of files stored higgledy-piggledy. On the rare occasion that a Windows user ran the defragmenter, bringing all the pieces together could take hours — and the resulting system speed-up rarely raised any eyebrows, much less rocketed Windows fans into hyperthreaded bliss.

Vista changes that by simply and quietly scheduling a disk defragmentation run every week. You don't need to touch a thing.

If you're curious about how your computer's doing in the defrag department, choose Start➪All Programs➪Accessories➪System Tools➪Disk Defragmenter. Click through the User Account Control notices, and Disk Defragmenter gives you a full report, allowing you to make scheduling changes if you so desire. If you have Vista Service Pack 1 installed (see Book I, Chapter 3), you can also choose which drives you want to defrag.

Scheduling the Task Scheduler

Windows Vista has a built-in scheduler that runs just about any program according to any schedule you specify — daily, weekly, monthly, middle of the night, on alternate blue moons.

The scheduler comes in handy in three very different situations:

✦ **When you always want to do something at the same time of day every day, week, or month:** Perhaps you always want to start Outlook at 6:15 every morning so that your machine is connected and your mail's ready by the time you drag your sorry tail into your desk chair. Or maybe you want to run a PowerPoint presentation every morning at 7:30 so that your boss hears the telltale sounds as she walks by your cubicle. (And who said Dummies aren't Devious?)

✦ **When you want to make sure that the computer performs some mundane maintenance job when it won't interfere with your work time:** Thus, you may schedule disk cleanups every weekday at 2:00 in the afternoon because you know you'll always be propped up in the mop closet taking a snooze.

✦ **When you want to do something every time you log on, or when your computer starts:** You can even have the Task Scheduler send an e-mail message to your boss every time you log on. Interesting possibilities there.

Any discussion of scheduled tasks immediately conjures up the old question, "Should I leave my computer running all night, or should I turn it off?" The fact is that nobody knows which is better. You can find plenty of arguments on both sides of the fence. Suffice it to say that your computer has to be on (or suspended) for a scheduled task to run, so you may have to leave your computer on at least one night a week (or a month) to get the maintenance work done.

Unlike previous versions of Windows, Vista's Task Scheduler can readily be told to wake up a PC that's suspended or hibernating, runs the scheduled task, and then puts the PC back to sleep.

You find absolutely no debate about one "should I leave it on" question, though. Everybody in the know agrees that running a full surface scan of your hard drive daily is a bad idea (specifically running Check Disk; see the "Running an error check" section, earlier in this chapter). A full scan simply inflicts too much wear and tear on the hard drive's arms. It's kind of like forcing yourself to fly every morning just to keep your shoulders in shape.

One of the most important uses of the Task Scheduler is driving a Windows file cleanup program called, imaginatively, Disk Cleanup. Here's how to get Disk Cleanup scheduled — and how to use the Task Scheduler in general.

First, you need to set the Disk Cleanup parameters. Because Disk Cleanup can be run many different ways, Vista allows you to store many different sets of parameters, each set identified by a number. In this case, I (completely arbitrarily) call this set of parameters *9.* Follow these steps to set your Disk Cleanup parameters:

1. **Click the Start button. Type** cleanmgr /sageset:9 **in the Start Search box and press Enter.**

   Be sure you put a space before the slash, but don't type spaces anywhere else. This command runs Vista's Disk Cleanup, saving your settings as "number 9." Just like The Beatles' *White Album.*

2. **Click through the User Account Control dialog box, and the Disk Cleanup Settings dialog box appears (see Figure 3-14).**

3. **Select the check boxes that correspond to the types of files that you want Vista to delete.**

Figure 3-14:
Make your
Disk Cleanup
choices
here.

Microsoft Office 2003, bless its pointed little head, has on at least two occasions triggered complex errors if you have the temerity to remove the Office 2003 Setup Files. The errors only crop up later, and in obscure circumstances. If you see an Office Setup Files check box, don't select it.

4. Click the OK button.

Vista saves the Disk Cleanup settings, identifying them as "number 9."

With Disk Cleanup configured properly, you can set it to run every night, by following these steps:

1. Choose Start➪All Programs➪Accessories➪System Tools➪Task Scheduler.

You may have to click the Continue button on one or more User Access Control messages. In the end, the Task Scheduler starts (see Figure 3-15).

2. On the right, click the Create Basic Task option.

The Task Scheduler Wizard appears with a welcome (see Figure 3-16).

3. Type a name for the task, and then click the Next button.

The wizard asks for a trigger — geek-speak for "Under what circumstances do you want the scheduled task to run?"

4. Choose Daily if you want the cleanup to run every day, and then click the Next button.

5. Set the time of day that you want cleanup to run, and click Next.

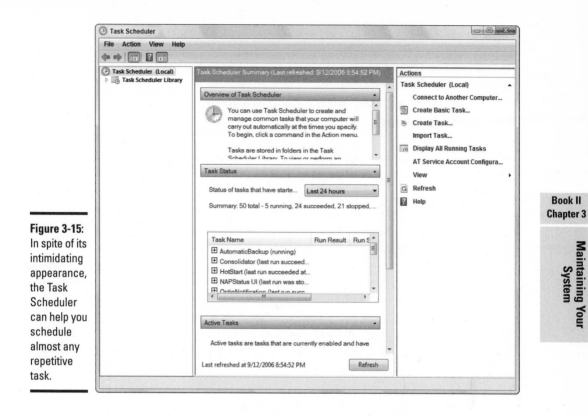

Figure 3-15:
In spite of its intimidating appearance, the Task Scheduler can help you schedule almost any repetitive task.

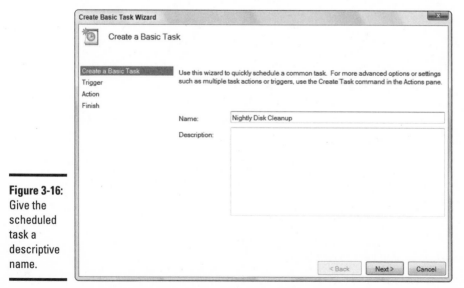

Figure 3-16:
Give the scheduled task a descriptive name.

6. **Choose an action. In this case, click the Start a Program button and then click Next.**

   The Task Scheduler asks you for the program that you want to run (see Figure 3-17).

7. **To run Vista Disk Cleanup, click the Browse button, navigate to** `\Windows\System32\cleanmgr.exe`, **click the program once, and click the Open button.**

   You can similarly run any other program with the Task Scheduler by clicking the Browse button, navigating to the program, and clicking Open.

8. **In the Add Arguments (Optional) box, type** /sagerun:9. **As you probably guessed, this tells Vista Disk Cleanup to use the "number 9" parameters.**

9. **Click Next, check the Open the Properties Dialog for This Task When I Click Finish box, and then click the Finish button.**

   The Task Scheduler Wizard adds your cleanup run to its list of active tasks. You can verify it by clicking the Refresh button at the bottom of the Task Scheduler window and then scrolling through the active tasks.

10. **In the Task Properties box, select the Run Whether User Is Logged On or Not option, then click OK.**

   You have to go through this final step in the Task Properties dialog so the cleanup can run whether you're logged on or not.

Figure 3-17:
Vista
Cleanup
cleverly
disguised as
the program
`cleanmgr`
`.exe`.

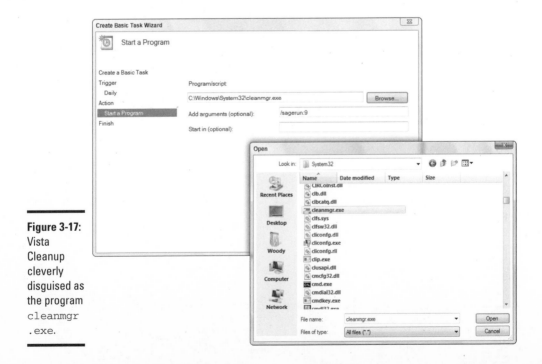

Zipping and Compressing

Windows Vista supports two very different kinds of file compression. The distinction is confusing but important, so bear with me.

File compression reduces the size of a file by cleverly taking out parts of the contents of the file that aren't needed, storing only the minimum amount of information necessary to reconstitute the file — *extract* it — into its full, original form. A certain amount of overhead is involved because the computer has to take the time to squeeze extraneous information out of a file before storing it, and then the computer takes more time to restore the file to its original state when someone needs the file. But compression can reduce file sizes enormously. A compressed file often takes up half its original space — even less, in many cases.

How does compression work? That depends on the compression method you use. In one kind of compression, known as *Huffman encoding,* letters that occur frequently in a file (say, the letter *e* in a word-processing document) are massaged so that they take up only a little bit of room in the file, while letters that occur less frequently (say, *x*) are allowed to occupy lots of space. Instead of allocating eight 1s and 0s for every letter in a document, for example, some letters may take up only two 1s and 0s while others could take up 15. The net result, overall, is a big reduction in file size. It's complicated, and the mathematics involved get quite interesting.

Windows Vista's two file compression techniques are as follows:

✦ Files can be compressed and placed in a "Compressed (zipped) Folder," with an icon to match.

✦ Files, folders, or even entire drives can be compressed using Vista's file system's (NTFS's) built-in compression capabilities.

Here's where things get complicated.

NT File System (NTFS) compression is built into the file system: You can use it only on NTFS drives, and the compression doesn't persist when you move (or copy) the file off the drive. Think of NTFS compression as a capability inherent to the hard drive itself. That isn't really the case — Windows Vista does all the sleight-of-hand behind the scenes — but the concept can help you remember NTFS compression's limitations and quirks.

Although Microsoft would have you believe that "Compressed (zipped) Folder" compression is based on folders, it isn't. A "Compressed (zipped) Folder" is really a file — *not* a folder — but it's a special kind of file called a Zip file. If you've ever encountered Zip files on the Internet (they have a file-name extension of .zip and they're frequently manipulated with programs such as WinZip, www.winzip.com), you know exactly what I'm talking about. Zip files contain one or more compressed files, and they use the most common kind of compression found on the Internet. Think of "Compressed (zipped) Folders" as being Zip files, and if you have even a nodding acquaintance with Zips, you'll immediately understand the limitations and quirks of "Compressed (zipped) Folders." Microsoft calls them "Folders" because that's supposed to be easier for users to understand. You be the judge.

If you have Windows show you filename extensions — see my rant about that topic in the section on showing filename extensions in Book II, Chapter 1 — you see immediately that "Compressed (zipped) Folders" are, in fact, simple Zip files.

Table 3-2 shows a quick comparison of NTFS compression and Zip compression.

Table 3-2	NTFS Compression versus "Compressed (Zipped) Folders" Compression
NTFS	**Zip**
Think of NTFS compression as a feature of the hard drive itself.	Zip technology works on any file, regardless of where it is stored.
The minute you move an NTFS-compressed file off an NTFS drive — by, say, sending a file as an e-mail attachment — the file is uncompressed, automatically, and you can't do anything about it: You'll send a big, uncompressed file.	You can move a "Compressed (zipped) Folder" (actually a Zip file, with a `.zip` filename extension) anywhere, and it stays compressed. If you send a Zip file as an e-mail attachment, it goes over the ether as a compressed file. The person who receives the file can view it directly in Windows Vista, or he can use a product such as WinZip to see it.
A lot of overhead is associated with NTFS compression: Windows has to compress and decompress those files on the fly, and that sucks up processing power.	Very little overhead is associated with Zip files. Many programs (for example, antivirus programs) read Zip files directly.
NTFS compression is great if you're running out of room on an NTFS-formatted drive.	"Compressed (zipped) Folders" (that is to say, Zip files) are in a near-universal form that can be used just about anywhere.
You have to be using an administrator account to use NTFS compression.	You can create, copy, or move Zip files just like any other files, with the same security restrictions.
You can use NTFS compression on entire drives, folders, or single files. They cannot be password protected.	You can Zip files or folders, and they can be password protected.

If you try to compress the drive that contains your Windows folder, you won't be able to compress the files that are currently in use by Windows.

Compressing with NTFS

To use NTFS compression on an entire drive, follow these steps:

1. **Make sure that you are using an administrator account (see Book II, Chapter 2).**

2. **Choose Start⇨Computer and right-click the drive that you want to compress. Choose Properties and then click the General tab (see Figure 3-18).**

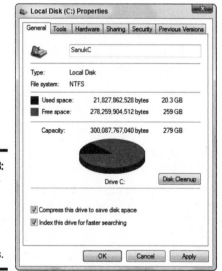

Figure 3-18: NTFS compression is available on most modern hard drives.

3. **Select the Compress This Drive to Save Disk Space check box. Then click the OK button.**

Windows asks you to confirm that you want to compress the entire drive. Windows takes some time to compress the drive — in some cases, the estimated time is measured in days. Good luck.

To use NTFS compression on a folder or single file, follow these steps:

1. **Make sure that you are using a full-fledged administrator account (see Book II, Chapter 2).**

2. **Navigate to the folder or file you want to compress (for example, choose Start➪Documents or Start➪Computer). Right-click the file or folder you want to compress. Choose Properties and click the Advanced button on the General tab.**

   The Advanced Properties dialog box appears.

3. **Select the Compress Contents to Save Disk Space check box and then click the OK button.**

   To uncompress a file or folder, go back into the Advanced Properties dialog box (right-click the file or folder, choose Properties, and then click the Advanced button) and deselect the Compress Contents to Save Disk Space check box.

Zipping the easy way with Compressed (zipped) Folders

The easiest way to create a Zip file, er, a "Compressed (zipped) Folder" is with a simple right-click. Here's how:

1. **Navigate to the file(s) that you want to zip. (For example, choose Start➪Documents or Start➪Computer and go from there.)**

2. **Select the file or files that you want to zip together. (You can Ctrl+click to select individual files or Shift+click to select a bunch.) Right-click any of the selected files and choose Send To➪Compressed (Zipped) Folder.**

   Windows responds by creating a new Zip file, with a `.zip` filename extension, and placing the selected file(s) in the new Zip folder.

   The new file is just like any other file — you can rename it, copy it, move it, delete it, send it as an e-mail attachment, save it on the Internet, or do anything else to it that you can do to a file. (That's because it *is* a file.)

3. **To add another file to your "Compressed (zipped) Folder," simply drag it onto the zipped folder icon.**

4. **To copy a file from your Zip file (uh, folder), double-click the zipped folder icon and treat the file the same way you would treat any "regular" file (see Figure 3-19).**

5. **To copy all the files out of your Zip file (folder), click the Extract All Files button on the command bar.**

   You see the Windows Vista Compressed (zipped) Extract Compressed (Zipped) Folders Wizard, which guides you through the steps.

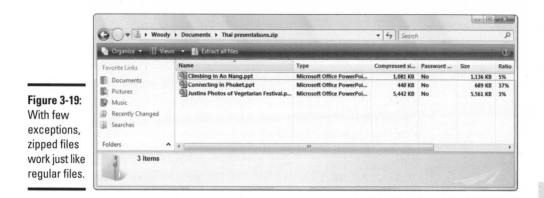

Figure 3-19:
With few
exceptions,
zipped files
work just like
regular files.

 The Compressed (zipped) Folders Extraction Wizard places all the copied files into a new folder with the same name as the Zip file — which confuses the living bewilickers out of everybody. Unless you give the extracted folder a different name from the original "Compressed (zipped) Folder," you end up with two folders with precisely the same name sitting on your desktop. Do yourself a huge favor and feed the wizard a different folder name while you're extracting the files.

Creating Checkpoints and Using System Restore

Ever get the feeling that things were going right?

Moments later, did you get the feeling that something must be wrong *because* things are going right?

Now you understand the gestalt behind System Restore. If you take a snapshot of your PC from time to time, when things are going right, it's relatively easy to go back to that "right" time when the wolves come howling at the, uh, Gates.

Windows Vista automatically takes System Restore snapshots — called *restore points* or *checkpoints* — once a day.

 When Vista can tell that you're going to try to do something complicated, such as install a new network card, it sets a restore point. Unfortunately, Windows can't always tell when you're going to do something drastic — perhaps you have a new CD player and the instructions tell you to turn off your PC and install the player *before* you run the setup program. So it doesn't hurt one little bit to run System Restore from time to time, all by yourself.

Here's how to generate a System Restore checkpoint:

1. **Wait until your PC is running smoothly.**

   No sense in having a checkpoint that propels you out of the frying pan and into the fire, eh?

2. **Make sure that you're using an administrator account (see Book II, Chapter 2).**

3. **Choose Start➪Control Panel. Under the System and Maintenance heading, click the Back Up Your Computer link.**

   Vista shows you the Backup and Restore Center (see Figure 3-5).

4. **On the left, under Tasks, click the Create a Restore Point or Change Settings link.**

   After you clear the User Account Control hurdle, Vista opens the System Properties dialog box, with the System Protection tab showing (see Figure 3-20).

5. **At the bottom, click the Create button.**

   Vista asks you to type a description to help identify the restore point. Choose something that you can remember, such as "Before installing the new DVD-RW drive."

6. **Type a descriptive checkpoint name and click the Create button.**

   Windows automatically brands the checkpoint with the current date and time.

7. **Windows creates a restore point with little fanfare and lets you go on your merry way.**

Figure 3-20: Set a restore point manually in the System Properties dialog box.

If you ever need to restore your computer to a previous state, follow these steps:

1. **Save your work and then close all running programs.**

System Restore doesn't muck with any data files, documents, pictures, or anything like that. It only works on system files. Your data is safe.

2. **Choose Start⇨All Programs⇨Accessories⇨System Tools⇨System Restore.**

Vista opens the System Restore Wizard.

3. **Unless the recommended restore point appeals to you immediately, click the Choose a Different Restore Point option and then click Next.**

The System Restore Wizard shows you a list of available restore points (see Figure 3-21).

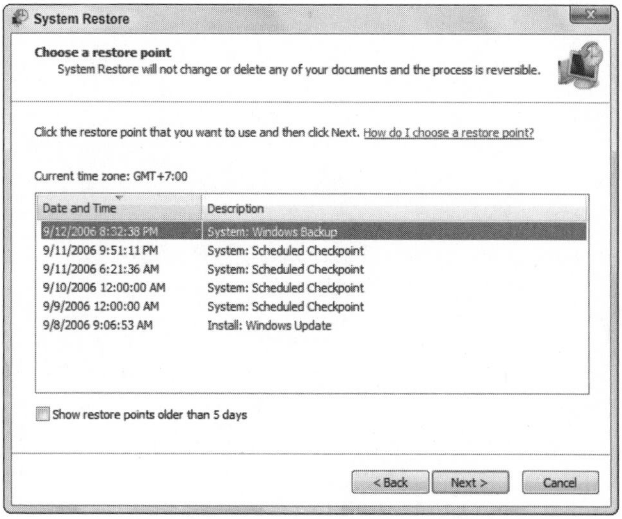

Book II
Chapter 3

Maintaining Your
System

Figure 3-21:
Choose the restore point that you need.

System Restore

Choose a restore point
System Restore will not change or delete any of your documents and the process is reversible.

Click the restore point that you want to use and then click Next. How do I choose a restore point?

Current time zone: GMT+7:00

Date and Time	Description
9/12/2006 8:32:38 PM	System: Windows Backup
9/11/2006 9:51:11 PM	System: Scheduled Checkpoint
9/11/2006 6:21:36 AM	System: Scheduled Checkpoint
9/10/2006 12:00:00 AM	System: Scheduled Checkpoint
9/9/2006 12:00:00 AM	System: Scheduled Checkpoint
9/8/2006 9:06:53 AM	Install: Windows Update

☐ Show restore points older than 5 days

< Back   Next >   Cancel

4. **Select the date and specific restore point that you want to restore to, and then click Next.**

5. **Windows shuts down, restarts, and restores itself to the point you chose.**

System Restore is a nifty feature that works very well.

Chapter 4: Getting the Basic Stuff Done

In This Chapter

✔ Burning CDs and DVDs

✔ Improving your performance rating

✔ Word processing, calculating, painting, and more

✔ Taking control when a program goes haywire

✔ . . . And lots of boring stuff you need to know anyway

You bought your PC to get things done, right? I guess it depends on what you mean by "things." You need know how to write a letter, even if you don't have Microsoft Office installed on your PC. You should figure out how to use the Windows Calculator, even if the thought of employing a $1,000 tool to solve a two-bit problem leaves you feeling a little green.

Hey, I have to talk about that stuff somewhere.

This chapter also digs into the truly cool Windows Vista support for burning CDs and DVDs, and what you can (and can't!) do to improve your performance rating, er, experience index.

You know. Stuff.

Burning CDs and DVDs

Windows Vista includes simple, one-click (or two- or three-click) support for *burning* CDs or DVDs — burning or *writing* being the process of putting stuff on a CD or DVD. You can burn music, video, recorded TV shows, photos, and all kinds of data. Pyromania on a platter.

You need a CD recorder (a CD-RW drive) or DVD recorder (variously, DVD-RW, DVD+RW, DVD+-RW) to make your own CDs or DVDs, of course, but most PCs these days have them built in. If you don't like the optical drive in your PC and buy a cheap dual-layer DVD+-RW drive that attaches to your PC via a USB cable, your most difficult job will be pulling it out of the Styrofoam padding. See Book VI, Chapter 3, for more about installing external devices.

Many people use the software that shipped with their computer (which, in turn, probably came from the company that made the drive) to burn CDs and DVDs. In almost all cases, though, Vista itself does yeoman work, and it doesn't suffer from the Windows compatibility problems that dog other manufacturers' software.

The mother lode of all CD-R information sits on the Web (where else?) in Andy McFadden's CD-R FAQ, www.cdrfaq.org. If you go to that site, Andy has information for downloading and reading the massive tome. For DVD information, check out Jim Taylor's www.dvddemystified.com/dvdfaq.html, an invaluable and authoritative reference. And for ultimate Blu-ray coverage, including a mighty FAQ, see www.blu-ray.com.

Understanding -R and -RW

Sorry, Marshall. When it comes to DVDs, the medium isn't the message. To get a handle on all this CD/DVD/HD-DVD/Blu-Ray bafflegab, it's easiest to start with the disc itself, the silvery piece of coated plastic that's just one short step away from becoming a coffee-table coaster.

Before you burn a CD or DVD, you should understand the fundamental difference between "R" and "RW." Most optical drives these days can burn DVD-Rs and DVD-RWs as well as CD-Rs and CD-RWs: The main question is whether you should spend extra money for more-capable discs. Silver for silver, as it were. You have to choose the kind of disc that suits your situation, as I describe in the following list:

✦ **CD-Recordable (CD-R):** These discs can be played in CD players or read on computers, but the data on them cannot be erased. Although it's physically possible to record on a CD-R disc more than once, the "old" data isn't erased — "new" data gets added to the end of the CD-R.

If you're trying to burn a regular, old, everyday audio CD that can work in most old-fashioned audio players, CD-R is your best (and cheapest!) choice — but if the burn goes awry, you end up with a coaster that can't be fixed.

✦ **CD-Record/Write (CD-RW):** These discs can be erased, and the erased area can be rewritten with new stuff. CD-RW discs do not work in some audio CD players, particularly older ones, but most newer players swallow CD-RW discs with aplomb. You can rewrite CD-RW discs hundreds of times before they wear out.

✦ **DVD-Recordable (DVD-R or DVD+R):** These discs can be played in almost any DVD player, but they cannot be erased. A technical distinction exists between the "+" and the "-" that only enters into the picture if you have an older DVD player. For most purposes, DVD-R, DVD+R, and DVD+-R work the same.

+ **DVD-Record/Write (DVD-RW or DVD+RW):** These discs can work in almost any DVD player, and they can be erased. Again, the distinction between "+" and "-" is largely academic, although some players can get picky. They put up with hundreds of rewrites.

Not surprisingly, CD-R discs cost less than the others, and DVD-RW discs cost the most. CDs can hold about 700MB of data. DVDs go up to 4.7GB — or six and a half times as much.

Confused yet? Allow me to make things worse. *Dual-layer* DVD-RW drives work with special discs that hold up to 8.5GB of data. Before you burn a dual-layer DVD, though, be sure that the disc is destined for another dual-layer drive. You can't play or read a dual-layer DVD in a "normal" DVD drive.

Blu-ray discs hold up to 50GB of data, but both the players and the discs themselves (as of this writing anyway) can send shivers down your pocketbook. If you really want to watch the latest movies in full, glorious high definition — HD files are so big you need a Blu-ray size disc to hold them — buying a Blu-ray player may make some sense. But for day-to-day burning and schlepping, stick to DVD-RW.

What to burn

DVDs and CDs hold bits — 1s and 0s. There's nothing particularly mysterious about it.

Unfortunately, confusingly, the bits can be interpreted in different ways, and the different interpretations can be hard to follow:

+ **Audio tracks** are (by computer standards) an ancient art form. When you buy an audio CD from a music store, the CD (usually) contains audio tracks. Every audio CD player I've ever seen understands standard audio, the progenitor of all CD formats.

To a first approximation, tracks on an audio CD are very similar to WAV files. The main difference is this: Audio tracks have a layer of error-correcting codes on the CD. Regardless of what Windows may tell you, no "files" exist on an audio CD: If your computer shows you `.cda` files on an audio CD, it's acting like a Jedi Knight, creating a beneficent illusion.

The process of converting audio tracks into data files that a computer can handle more readily is called *ripping*. I talk about ripping extensively in Book VII, Chapter 1.

+ **Video tracks** may not be as ancient as audio tracks, but they're certainly growing long in the tooth. When you buy a movie or rent one, the DVD you get contains video tracks. The process of converting video tracks into data files that a computer can handle more readily is called, uh, ripping. Is there an echo in here?

✦ **Data files** can take on any form — literally anything you can put in your computer can go on a CD or DVD. Someday the world will wean itself off audio and video tracks, and we'll only have to deal with data files. But it won't happen any time soon.

When you rip audio tracks and turn them into data files, the resulting files can come in many different flavors — MP3s, WMAs (Microsoft's *proprietary* format), AACs (Apple's proprietary format), OGGs, and many more. Video tracks can turn into WMVs (Microsoft again), M4Vs (playable on iPods, not proprietary), MPGs, AVIs, and many others.

What's a *proprietary* format? It's a method of storing and interpreting bits that's owned lock, stock, and barrel by a company. Microsoft hopes to control the format of our music and video files with its proprietary WMA and WMV formats — and make money by selling licenses to companies that make CD and DVD players, among many others. See my discussion of C.R.A.P. music (a term coined by ZDNet's David Berlind) in Book VII, Chapter 1.

Newer CD players can handle CDs that contain MP3 and WMA files. Some can even handle DVDs with MP3 and WMA files. That's an RBD, er, a Real Big Deal, because Vista makes it surprisingly easy to burn DVDs chock-full of MP3 files. Consider this: A typical audio CD, filled with audio tracks, holds about an hour's worth of music — say, 15 songs. But if you rip the songs and store them as MP3s, then burn the MP3s to a CD, that same size CD can hold, oh, about 100 to 150 songs. A single DVD can hold 1,000 songs. Mind-boggling. For a look at the economics of the situation, see Table 4-1.

Table 4-1			**How Much to Burn a Song?**		
Disc	*Data*	*No. of Songs*	*Media*	*Disc Price*	*Cost per Song*
CD	Audio tracks	15	One-time	$0.30	$0.0200
			Rewritable	$1.00	$0.0670
CD	MP3 files	150	One-time	$0.30	$0.0020
			Rewritable	$1.00	$0.0067
DVD	MP3 files	1,000	One-time	$1.00	$0.0010
			Rewritable	$2.50	$0.0025

Mastered or Live File System?

You have many different ways to arrange data on a CD or DVD, but most folks need only concern themselves with the following two different (sets of) standards:

✦ **Mastered formatting** (sometimes called *ISO*), the older version, works with almost any kind of drive. If you're going to burn a CD or DVD that's going to be used in an older CD or DVD player, you should use Mastered.

When you burn a Mastered disc, you have to choose all the files that you're going to burn, and burn them all at once. Vista goes through a kind of preprocessing step to convert all the files to the ISO format and then writes all the files continuously onto the disc.

✦ **Live File System formatting** (sometimes called, confusingly, *File System* or *UDF*), the new version, is a good choice for discs that are used in computers running Windows XP or Vista. At this writing, few audio CD players or DVD players can accept UDF/Live File System–formatted discs.

When you burn a Live File System disc, Vista writes the data one file at a time, without preprocessing each file. You can burn a few files on the disc today and a few more tomorrow.

Close that session!

Ready for the advanced course? You can write multiple times on a CD-R (or DVD-R) disc. It's confusing. If you've never had to wrangle with multiple CD-R *sessions,* count yourself lucky. (This only applies to CD-R and DVD-R discs; you can write to CD-RW and DVD-RW discs till the cows come home.)

When you burn a CD-R using the Mastered (ISO) format, Windows preprocesses the files you have chosen to burn and then writes them all onto the CD-R (or DVD-R) at once. Invariably, some unused space exists at the end of the CD-R, so you can have Windows gather more files, preprocess them, and burn the next bunch, all at once. Each bunch of files constitutes a *session*.

Here's where the terminology gets confusing — the manufacturers themselves don't completely agree on the names of things, so watch out. You can *close* a session and increase the chances that your CD-R or DVD-R can be read by another computer (see the next paragraph). Vista automatically closes each session after it's written. You can also *finalize* a disc, which not only closes the last session but also marks the CD-R as complete: After you finalize a CD-R or DVD-R, you can't add any more data to it. Ever.

Here are two infuriatingly simple rules for Mastered (ISO) CDs:

✔ A CD-R (or DVD-R) drive that is not an RW drive usually can't read a CD-R (or DVD-R) unless it has been closed. Because audio CD players (and movie DVD players) usually can't record, you almost always have to close a CD-R (or DVD-R) before it can be played in a traditional player (but, again, Vista closes each session for you automatically).

✔ Most audio CD players can only get at the first session on a CD.

CDs burned with the Live File System, uh, File System, er, UDF format, on the other hand, may need to be closed before the CD can work on other computers. You can close the same CD or DVD many times; each clump of data between two "closes" constitutes a session. I cover that procedure in the "Burning with Vista" section in this chapter.

Here's the bottom line: CDs are cheap. Don't try to fool Mother Nature and record multiple sessions on a CD-R that's destined to be played in a "normal" audio CD player. Ditto for DVD. But if you want to experiment, hey, it's a lot of fun getting closer to the hardware.

Vista contains a lot of help documentation (some very confusing!) about making a choice between Mastered/ISO and Live File System/UDF. Until more players can actually use Live File System/UDF, the choice is pretty easy: If you're creating a CD or DVD that will absolutely, positively, only be used on a Windows XP or Vista computer, go ahead and use Live File System/UDF. Otherwise, given a choice, stick with Mastered/ISO.

What's the best way to get a feel for the differences between Mastered and File System formatting? Go through the process of burning CDs in each format, following the steps in the next section.

Burning with Vista

The first time you try to burn a CD (or DVD) with a new CD (or DVD) drive, work with data files instead of music or video. Start out with the easiest possible scenario (simple data files) before you work your way up to the most complex (high-definition video DVDs). That increases your chances of finding and solving problems when they're easiest to tackle. When you have a CD-R, CD-RW, DVD-R, or DVD-RW drive installed and working, transferring your files to CD or DVD couldn't be simpler.

Note: If you want to burn music files, don't follow these instructions. Use Windows Media Player (WMP). I tell you how to use Windows Media Player in Book VII, Chapter 1. WMP has all sorts of bells and whistles that are specific to music, and it does a fine job of burning music CDs with all the ancillary information including playlists.

If you're accustomed to the Windows XP way of burning discs, the Vista method may feel a bit uncomfortable until you get the hang of it. Many folks who grew up with XP tend to choose the files they want to burn first, mark them for burning, insert a blank disc, and then sit back while XP does the dirty deed.

In Vista, you'll find it much easier to work the other way around: Put a blank CD or DVD into the drive *before* you pick your files. By inserting the blank disc up front, Vista can tell how much space is on the disc. It can also ask whether you want to burn in Mastered/ISO or Live File System/UDF format, and prepare the CD or DVD appropriately in response to your choice.

Follow these steps to burn a CD (or DVD) with data files:

1. **Decide whether you want to burn in Live File System/UDF format or Mastered/ISO format.**

See the section "Mastered or Live File System?" earlier in this chapter.

2. **Pick the kind of CD or DVD that you want to use, and stick it in the drive.**

See the section "Understanding -R and -RW," earlier in this chapter, for tips on picking the right disc for the job.

When you put the CD or DVD in the drive, Vista responds with the AutoPlay dialog box shown in Figure 4-1.

Figure 4-1: Insert a blank disc before selecting the files.

Book II
Chapter 4

Getting the Basic
Stuff Done

3. **Click the Burn Files to Disc Using Windows option.**

Vista responds with the Burn a Disc dialog box shown in Figure 4-2.

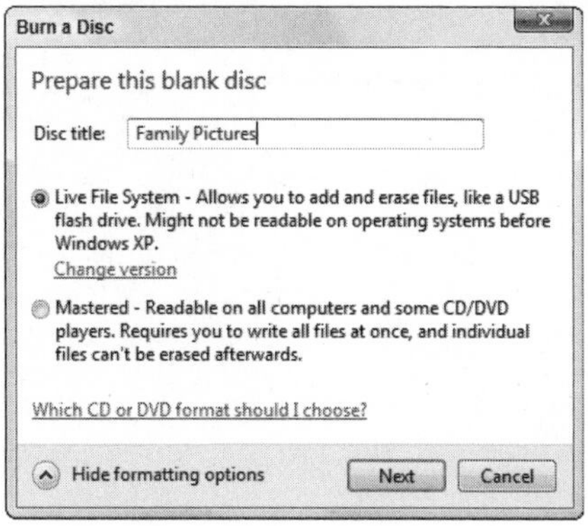

Figure 4-2: Choose between Live File System/ UDF and Mastered/ ISO formats.

4. **Click the down arrow next to Show Formatting Options, and choose Mastered (ISO) or Live File System (UDF) formatting.**

Use the guidelines in the section "Mastered or Live File System?" earlier in this chapter. If you know that the CD or DVD will only be used in Windows XP or Vista computers, Live File System/UDF is a good choice.

In spite of what Figure 4-2 says, recording to a random-access USB flash drive isn't anything at all like burning to a sequential CD. Using Live File System/UDF on a CD is much more like writing to a giant floppy drive or an extremely slow and small hard drive.

5. **Type a label for the disc in the Disc Title box, and then click Next:**

   • **Mastered (ISO):** If you chose the Mastered/ISO format in Step 4, Vista takes a couple of seconds to verify the size of the CD or DVD in the drive and then shows you a Windows Explorer window that says Drag Files to This Folder to Add Them to the Disc, like the "burn" window shown in Figure 4-3.

   • **Live File System (UDF):** If you chose Live File System/UDF in Step 4, Vista formats the CD or DVD by writing guiding marks on the disc. The process can take many minutes, especially if you're using a DVD. When Vista finishes, click OK on the Format Complete message. Vista then presents you with a Windows Explorer window (Figure 4-4) that differs from Figure 4-3 in two important ways: There is no Burn to Disc button, and the CD title already appears on the disc.

The Burn to Disc button appears because ISO CDs must be burned in a separate step

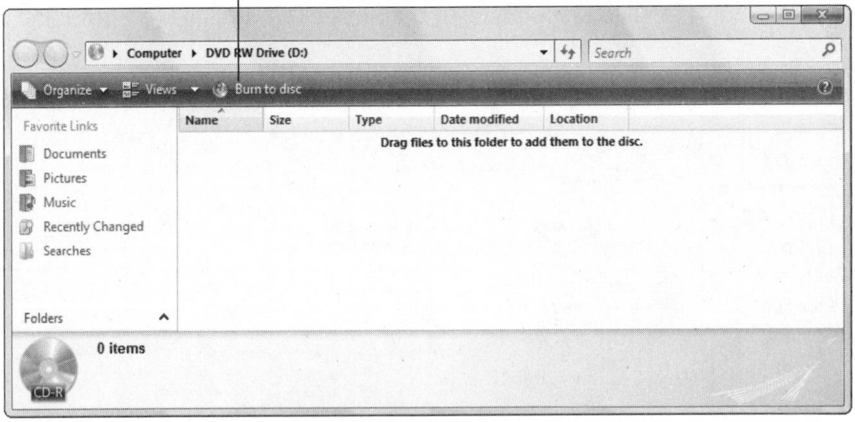

Figure 4-3:
The "burn" Windows Explorer window for a Mastered (ISO) disc.

6. **Navigate to the files you want to copy (for example, choose Start⇨ Pictures or Start⇨Music), click the files, and drag them to the "burn" window.**

   • **Mastered (ISO):** If you chose the Mastered/ISO format in Step 4, Vista copies the files you select into a "holding area" on your hard drive. If you try to drag more files into the holding area than can fit on the disc you're burning, Vista doesn't warn you (see Step 10, when Vista finally gets smart).

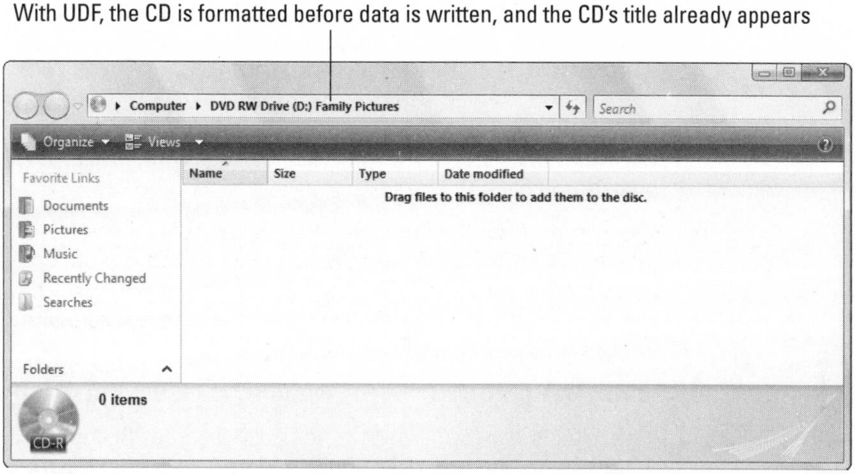

With UDF, the CD is formatted before data is written, and the CD's title already appears

Figure 4-4:
The "burn"
window for
a Live File
System/
UDF disc.

- **Live File System (UDF):** If you chose the Live File System/UDF format in Step 4, Vista copies the files you drag into the folder directly onto the CD (or DVD). If you try to put too much data on the CD (or DVD), Vista warns you that you don't have enough space, per Figure 4-5.

    You can delete files on the CD, or move them off the CD back onto your hard drive, if you need more room on the CD (or DVD). That's true *even with a CD-R disc,* as long as you're using the UDF format.

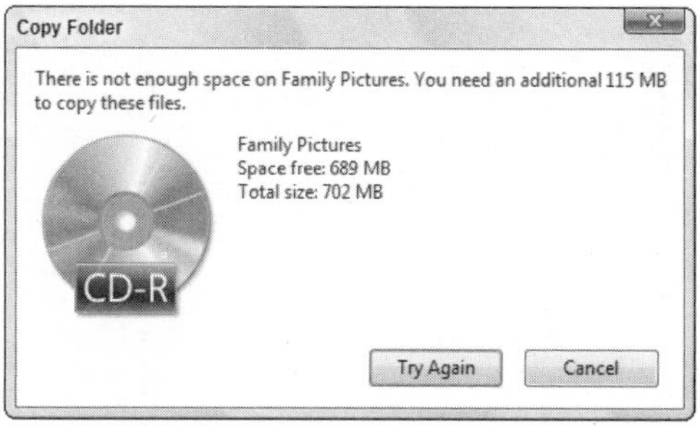

Figure 4-5:
With UDF,
Vista warns
that the CD
has too
much data.

7. **If you're using Live File System/UDF format, you're done. If you're using Mastered/ISO format, you still have to burn the CD — move the data out of the temporary holding area on your hard drive and stick the data on the CD (or DVD) that you inserted in Step 2. Proceed to Step 8.**

When you eject a Live File System/UDF CD or DVD from the drive, by default, Vista closes the session. You see a message in the notification area (next to the clock) that says `Please wait while this session is closed so the disc can be used on other computers`. Closing the session removes 20MB from the amount of free data on the CD, but it also increases the chances that your CD (or DVD) can be read on other drives.

You can remove the Live File System/UDF CD or DVD and store it away, take it to another computer, or use it as a fashionable coaster or even-more-fashionable ear-lobe extender. Anytime you want to add data to it (or delete data, for that matter), slip the disc back into the drive and use Windows Explorer in the usual way.

8. **In the Mastered/ISO "burn" window, click the Burn to Disc button.**

Vista opens the first windows in the Mastered/ISO disc burning wizard, filled in with the title that you typed in Step 5 (see Figure 4-6).

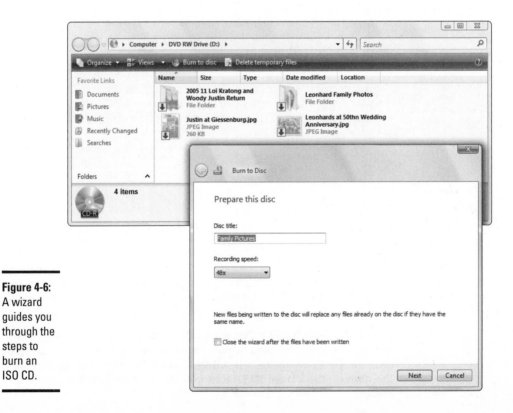

Figure 4-6:
A wizard
guides you
through the
steps to
burn an
ISO CD.

9. **Change the disc title, if you like, and then click the Next button.**

If you dragged too much data into the ISO "burn" window, Vista belly-aches at this point that you need to remove files. Do so.

When you delete temporary files from the CD/DVD writer's holding area, Vista asks "Are you sure you want to move this folder (or file) to the Recycle Bin?" Not to worry. Vista won't delete your original folder or file. It just wants your permission to delete the copy sitting in the holding area.

Vista takes ages to write the data. First, it constructs a "disc image" suitable for burning on the CD and then it transfers the image, thus copying the files that you dragged into the "burn" window onto the CD. Even on a relatively fast CD drive, it can take 15 minutes to burn a full CD.

When Vista finishes, you see the ISO disc burning wizard message shown in Figure 4-7.

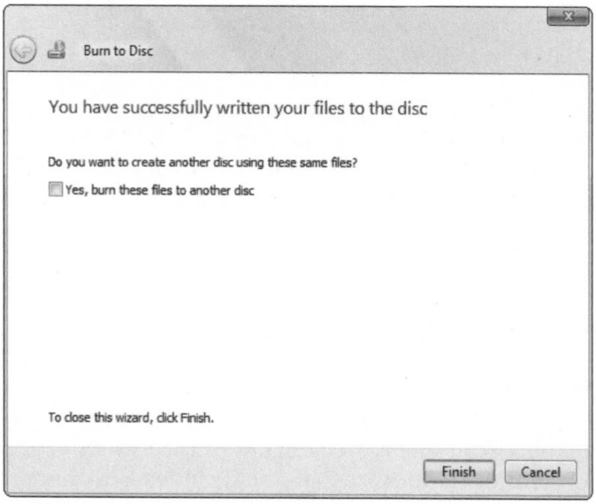

**Book II
Chapter 4**

**Getting the Basic
Stuff Done**

Figure 4-7:
Make sure
that the
burn went
okay before
clicking the
Finish
button.

10. **Don't click the Finish button yet. Take the CD out of the burner, and try to read it on a different machine. If you have no other machine, take it out of the drive and try to read it on the same machine.**

If it looks like all the files were burned correctly, click the Finish button in the Burn to Disc dialog box in Figure 4-7. But if it looks like you have a useless piece of plastic on your hands, select the Yes, Burn These Files to Another Disc check box and then click the Finish button.

You can add files to a Mastered/ISO CD-R (as long as the disc isn't full) by sliding the CD-R into your drive and copying files to the drive using any of Vista's myriad methods (see Figure 4-8).

Figure 4-8:
Adding
more files to
a Mastered/
ISO CD-R is
easy —
drag them to
the drive's
folder and
they appear
with a down
arrow.

The first time you drop a file in the Mastered/ISO "burn" window, Vista asks you what kind of formatting you would like to use, as in Step 4 in the preceding procedure. Gather the files you would like to add to the CD, drag them to the "burn" window, and when you're ready, click the Burn to Disc button. Then follow along from Step 8.

Improving Your Experience Index

Vista's performance rating benchmarks remain clouded in mystery — and controversy. To see how your system stacks up, choose Start➪Control Panel➪System and Maintenance. Then, under the System icon, click the Check Your Computer's Windows Experience Index Base Score option. You should see the Performance Information and Tools dialog box, with a big number for the overall rating and with five smaller numbers delineating Microsoft's take on your computer's performance in five key areas (see Figure 4-9).

If you think that your system hasn't been given a fair shake, click the Update My Score link. Vista runs through all its performance benchmarks, recalculates the component ratings, and comes up with a new number. Unless you've changed hardware lately, the new number is precisely the same as the old number.

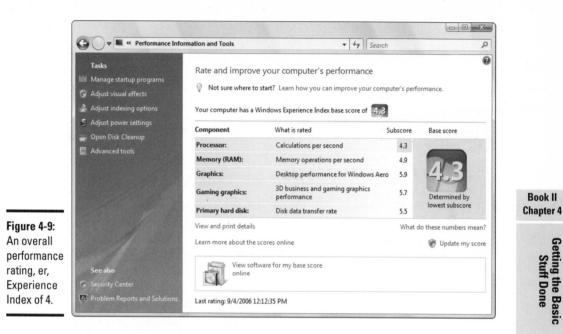

Figure 4-9:
An overall performance rating, er, Experience Index of 4.

There's a good reason why Microsoft doesn't release a lot of details about its performance benchmarks; for decades, computer benchmarking has been a black art. Far too often, benchmark numbers don't say much about how a machine actually performs; frequently large variances in benchmark values have almost no correlation with reality. Hardware manufacturers "build to benchmark," altering designs solely to improve benchmark numbers, regardless of the effect on real performance.

Vista jumps through lots of bizarre hoops to arrive at the Windows Experience Index, and the number probably doesn't mean what you think it does. For all the gory details, see Technique 1 in my *Windows Vista Timesaving Techniques For Dummies.*

See that link near the bottom of Figure 4-9 that says "View software for my base score online?" If you click that link, you're transported to Windows Marketplace, where you can sort through products that are appropriate for your computer's capabilities. Sorta.

Companies pay a great deal of money to Microsoft for the honor of being listed in Windows Marketplace. If you buy anything in Windows Marketplace, Microsoft gets a cut. Of course.

By all means, step through the items in the Performance Information and Tools dialog box, and see whether you can improve your system's performance. But don't knock yourself out. Adding more memory (up to 1GB, and possibly 2GB) and changing to a faster graphics card do more to improve your overall rating than all the little tweaks combined.

Getting a faster Internet connection trumps anything and everything Vista has to offer.

Getting Word Processing — Free

If you're serious about word processing, you undoubtedly have Microsoft Word (and probably even Microsoft Office) installed already. Word is a great program — and one that can serve you well, along with the other useful programs in the Office suite. Personally, I've been swearing at Office for almost a decade — my first four books were about it.

On the other hand, if you only mess around the periphery of word processing, with an occasional letter to Mom or a diatribe to the local newspaper, you'll be relieved to know that Windows Vista includes two programs that you can use for simple word processing. Although WordPad and Notepad are not word processing powerhouses like Word, they can help a little bit — as long as you don't have any great expectations, anyway.

As this book went to press, several new, exciting, online word processing alternatives were starting to take shape. Google, in particular, may make Vista's word processing support utterly obsolete. (I hope so!) Keep on top of the latest developments at my Web site, www.AskWoody.com.

Running Notepad

Reaching back into the primordial WinOoze, Notepad was conceived, designed, and developed by programmers, for programmers — and it shows. Although Notepad has been vastly improved over the years, many of the old limitations pertain. Still, if you want a fast, no-nonsense text editor (certainly nobody would have the temerity to call Notepad a word processor), Notepad's a decent choice.

Notepad understands only plain, simple, unformatted text — basically the stuff you see on your keyboard. It wouldn't understand formatting like **bold** or an embedded picture if you shook it by the shoulders, and heaven help ya if you want it to come up with links to Web pages.

On the other hand, Notepad's shortcomings are, in many ways, its saving graces. You can trust Notepad to show you exactly what's in a file — characters are characters, old chap, and there's none of this frou-frou formatting stuff to mess things up. Notepad saves only plain, simple, unformatted text; if you need a plain, simple, unformatted text document, Notepad's your tool of choice. To top it off, Notepad's fast and reliable. Of all the Windows programs I've ever met, Notepad is the only one I can think of that's never crashed on me.

The following tidbits of advice will be all you'll likely ever need to success-fully get in and around Notepad:

✦ **To start Notepad,** choose Start⇨All Programs⇨Accessories⇨Notepad, or double-click any text (`.txt`) file in Windows Explorer. You see some-thing like the file shown in Figure 4-10.

Figure 4-10:
Notepad
rocks in a
geriatric
sort of way.

Poe.txt - Notepad

File Edit Format View Help

Once upon a midnight dreary...

✦ **Notepad can handle files up to about 48MB in size.** (That's not quite the size of the Encyclopedia Britannica, but it's close.) If you try to open a file that's larger, a dialog box suggests that you open the file with a dif-ferent editor.

✦ **You can change the font, sorta.** When you first start Notepad, it displays a file's contents in the 10-point Lucida Console font. That font was chosen by Notepad's designers because it's relatively easy to see on most com-puter monitors.

Just because the text you see in Notepad is in a specific font, don't assume for a moment that the characters in the file itself are formatted. They aren't. The font you see on the screen is just the one Notepad uses to show the data. The stuff inside the file is plain-Jane, unformatted, everyday text.

If you want to change the font that's displayed on the screen, choose Format⇨Font and pick from the offered list. You don't need to select any text before you choose the font because the font you choose is applied to all the text on the screen — and it doesn't affect the contents of the file.

✦ **You can wrap text, too.** Notepad, being ever-true to the file it's attached to, skips to a new line only when it encounters a line break — usually that means a carriage return (or the Enter key), which typically occurs at the end of every paragraph.

Notepad allows you to wrap text on-screen, if you insist, so that you don't have to go scrolling all the way to the right to read every single paragraph. To have Notepad automatically break lines so that they show up on the screen, choose Format➪Word Wrap.

✦ **And there's a geeky timestamp feature.** Notepad has one little trick that you may find amusing — and possibly worthwhile. If you type **.LOG** as the first line in a file, Notepad sticks a time and date stamp at the end of the file each time it's opened.

Writing with WordPad

If you really want and need formatting — and you're too cheap to buy Microsoft Word — Windows Vista's WordPad will do. If you've been locked out of Word by Microsoft's nefarious Office (De)Activation Wizard, you'll no doubt rely on WordPad to keep limping along until Microsoft can reactivate you.

If you find yourself reading these words because Office has slipped into "reduced functionality mode" (gawd, I love that phrase!), take heart, but be forewarned: If you aren't careful, you can really clobber your Word files by saving them with WordPad. If you have to edit a Word 97, 2000, 2002, 2003, or 2007 document with WordPad, always follow these steps:

1. **Make a copy of the Word document, and open the copy in WordPad.**

Do *not* edit original Word documents with WordPad. You'll break them as soon as you save them. Do *not* open Word documents in WordPad, thinking that you'll use the Save As command and save with a different name. You'll forget.

2. **When you get Word back, open the original document, choose Tools➪ Compare and Merge Documents. Pick the WordPad version of the document, and click the Merge button.**

The resulting merged document probably looks like a mess, but it's a start.

3. **Use the Revisions toolbar (which is showing) to march through your original document and apply the changes you made with WordPad.**

This is the only reliable way I know to ensure that WordPad doesn't accidentally swallow any of your formatting.

WordPad works much the same as any other word processor, only less so. Its feature set reflects its price: You can't expect much from a free word processor — at least, not from Microsoft. That said, WordPad isn't encumbered with many of the confusing doodads that make Word so difficult for the first-time e-typist, and it may be a decent way to start figuring out how simple word processors work.

To get WordPad going, choose Start⇨All Programs⇨Accessories⇨WordPad (see Figure 4-11).

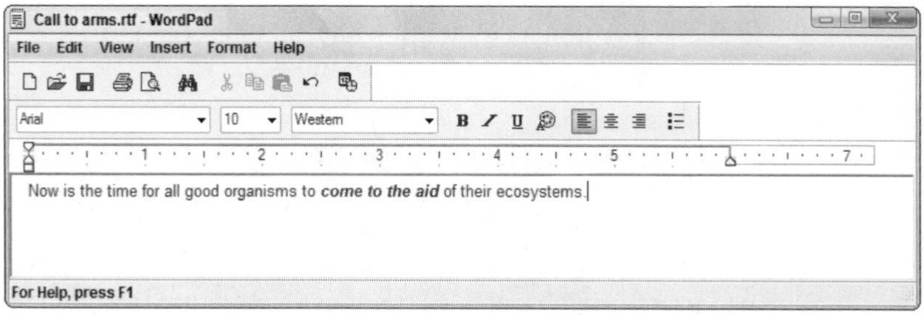

Figure 4-11: WordPad includes rudimentary formatting capabilities, as well as the ability to embed images, free.

Like a Word document or a text file, Rich Text Format (RTF) is another type of file. RTF documents can have some simple formatting, but nothing nearly as complex as Word 97, for example. Many word processing programs from many different manufacturers can read and write RTF files, so RTF is a good choice if you need to create a file that can be moved to a lot of places.

If you're just starting out with word processing, keep these facts in mind:

✦ To format text, select the text you want to format; then click the formatting you want from the toolbar, or choose Format⇨Font.

✦ To format a paragraph, simply click once inside the paragraph and choose the formatting from the toolbar, or choose Format⇨Paragraph. Alternatively, you can select all the text in the paragraph, or in multiple paragraphs, before applying the formatting.

✦ General page layout (such as margins, whether the page is printed vertically or horizontally, and so on) is controlled by settings in the Page Setup dialog box. To get to the Page Setup dialog box, choose File⇨Page Setup.

✦ Tabs are complicated. Every paragraph starts out with tab stops set every half inch. You set additional tab stops by choosing Format➪Tab, but the tab stops you set up work only in individual paragraphs: Select one paragraph and set a tab stop, and it works only in the selected paragraph; select three paragraphs and set the stop, and it works in all three.

WordPad treats tabs like any other character: A tab can be copied, moved, and/or deleted, sometimes with unexpected results. Keep your eyes peeled when using tabs and tab stops. If something goes wrong, choose Edit➪Undo (or press Ctrl+Z) immediately and try again.

WordPad lacks many of the features that you may have come to expect from other word processors: You can't even insert a page break, much less a table. If you spend any time at all writing anything but the most straightforward documents, you'll outgrow WordPad quickly.

Taming the Character Map

Windows Vista includes a utility called the Character Map that may prove a lifesaver if you need to find characters that go beyond the standard keyboard fare — "On Beyond Zebra," as Dr. Seuss once said. Using the Character Map, you can ferret odd characters out of any font, copy them, and then paste them into whatever word processor you may be using (including WordPad).

Windows ships with many fonts — collections of characters — and several of those fonts include many interesting characters that you may want to use. To open the Character Map, choose Start➪All Programs➪Accessories➪System Tools➪Character Map. You see the screen shown in Figure 4-12.

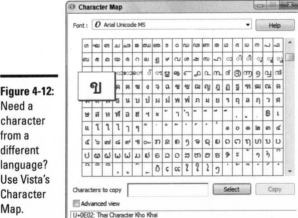

Figure 4-12: Need a character from a different language? Use Vista's Character Map.

You can use many characters as pictures — arrows, check marks, boxes, and so on — in the various Wingdings and Webding fonts. Copy them into your documents, and increase the font size as you like.

Calculating — Free

Windows Vista includes a very capable calculator. Actually, it contains two very capable calculators. Before you run out and spend 20 bucks on a scientific calculator, check out the two you already own!

To run the Calculator, choose Start⇨All Programs⇨Accessories⇨Calculator. You probably see the standard calculator.

To use the Calculator, just type whatever you like on your keyboard and press Enter when you want to carry out the calculation. For example, to calculate 123 times 456, type **123 * 456** and press Enter.

The following are several Calculator tricks:

✦ You can use your mouse to "press" the keys on the Calculator — an approach that's very slow and quite error prone.

✦ Nope, an *X* on the keyboard doesn't translate into the times sign. I don't know why, but computer people have had a hang-up about this for decades. If you want "times," you have to press the asterisk key on the keyboard — the *, or Shift+8.

✦ You can use the number pad, if your keyboard has one, but to make it work you have to get "Num Lock" going. Try typing a few numbers on your number pad. If the Calculator sits there like a dodo and doesn't realize that you're trying to type into it, press the Num Lock key. The Calculator should take the hint.

Of all the applications in Windows, you'd think that the %$#@! Calculator would let you select the number in the read-out window so that you could copy it or paste over it, using any of the Windows-standard methods. Uh-uh. No way. Calculator limits you to copying the entire contents of the read-out (by choosing Edit⇨Copy or pressing Ctrl+C) or overwriting the entire read-out (choose Edit⇨Paste or Ctrl+V). The Calculator doesn't even have the usual File menu, so you can't save anything, print anything (like an audit tape), or even choose File⇨Exit. Ahhhh! Don't get me started.

If you need to do some fancy-shmancy calculatin', choose View⇨Scientific to bring up the scientific version of the Windows Calculator, shown in Figure 4-13. The Scientific Calculator slices and dices and cooks dinner, too. For details on all the options, choose Help⇨Help Topics.

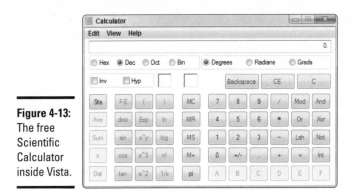

Figure 4-13:
The free
Scientific
Calculator
inside Vista.

Painting

The Windows Paint program has taken a lot of hard knocks for a lot of years, but Paint can actually do a few things that you might need. It's a just-barely-good-enough application for manipulating existing pictures, and it helps you convert among the various picture file formats (JPEG, GIF, and so on), but it's certainly no competition for a real drawing tool like CorelDRAW or Adobe Illustrator, or even a free graphics editor like Irfan View (www.irfanview. com). And if you want to correct red-eye or adjust for a bad exposure, Windows Photo Gallery has tools that you need (see Book VII, Chapter 4).

That said, you can have a lot of fun with Windows Paint. To bring it to life, choose Start➪All Programs➪Accessories➪Paint. You see a screen like the one shown in Figure 4-14.

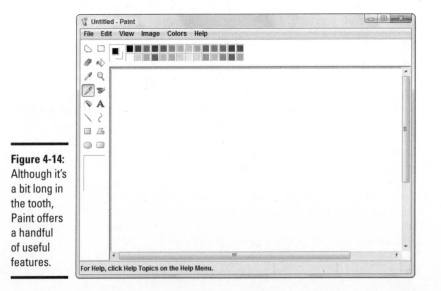

Figure 4-14:
Although it's
a bit long in
the tooth,
Paint offers
a handful
of useful
features.

Opening, saving, and closing pictures in Paint is a snap; it works just like any other Windows program. Scanning pictures into Paint goes like a breeze (choose File⊃From Scanner or Camera). Where you're bound to get in the most trouble is in free-form drawing, which can be mighty inscrutable until you understand the following points:

+ You select a line color (used by all the painting tools as their primary color) by clicking the color on the palette (near the bottom of the window).

+ You select a fill color (used to fill the inside of the solid shapes, such as the rectangle and oval) by right-clicking the color.

+ Many of the painting tools let you choose the thickness of the lines they use — in the case of the spray can, you can choose the heaviness of the spray — in the box that appears after you select the tool.

General rules for editing are a lot like what you see in the rest of Windows — select, copy, paste, delete, and so on. The only odd editing procedure I've found is for the Free-form Selection tool. If you click this tool and draw an area on the picture, Paint responds by selecting the smallest rectangle that encloses the entire line that you've drawn. It's . . . different.

You can specify the exact size of your picture by choosing Image⊃Attributes.

Using Sneaky Key Commands

Windows Vista includes two well-buried key commands that everyone should know about. Neither of the key combinations works if your machine is hopelessly frozen, but in most normal circumstances, they should help a lot, especially if a program isn't behaving the way it should.

Conjuring up the Task Manager

Windows Vista has a secret command post that you can get to if you know the right handshake, uh, key combination. Whatever. The key combination works all the time — unless Windows is seriously out to lunch — as long as you're a designated administrator. (For a discussion of administrators, see the section on using account types in Book II, Chapter 2.)

To open the Task Manager, press Ctrl+Alt+Delete. Vista comes up with a screen that looks suspiciously like the Welcome screen. Click the Start Task Manager link. The Task Manager should appear with a list of all the applications that are currently running (see Figure 4-15).

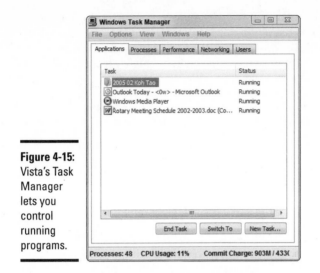

Figure 4-15:
Vista's Task
Manager
lets you
control
running
programs.

With the Task Manager, you can do the following things:

✦ Click an application and then click the End Task button to initiate an orderly shutdown of the application. Windows tries to shut down the application without destroying any data. If it's successful, the application disappears from the list. If it isn't successful, it presents you with the option of summarily zapping the application (called End Now to the less imaginative) or simply ignoring it and allowing it to go its merry way.

✦ Click an application and then click the Switch To button, and Windows brings up the switched-to application. This is very convenient if you find yourself stuck somewhere — in a game, say, that won't "let go" while it's taken control of your system — and you want to jump over to a different application.

The Task Manager goes way beyond application control. For example, if you have a somewhat dominant techie gene (it runs in the family), you may be tickled to watch the progress of your computer on the performance monitor, which is in the Task Manager on the Performance tab (see Figure 4-16).

If the Task Manager's Performance tab gets your juices going, try this. Click the Resource Monitor button. Whoa. The Vista Resource Monitor shows you every imaginable performance detail, in real time. You could spend a lifetime in there.

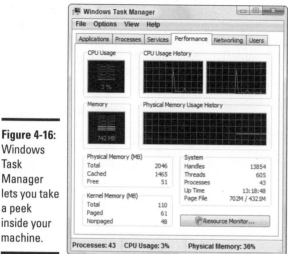

Figure 4-16:
Windows
Task
Manager
lets you take
a peek
inside your
machine.

Switching coolly

Windows includes a quick, easy way to switch among running applications without diving for the mouse to click the Windows taskbar. It's known as the CoolSwitch (yes, that's the technical term for it), and it works on any computer, any time, unless Windows is totally out to lunch. Which happens sometimes.

To use the CoolSwitch, hold down Alt and press Tab. You see something like the screen shown in Figure 4-17.

Figure 4-17:
Vista's
CoolSwitch
lets you leaf
through
running
programs
easily.

As you press Tab repeatedly, Windows cycles through the running programs. When you arrive at the program that you want to run, simply release the Alt key, and the selected program comes to life.

By simply sliding over to the Windows key — the one with the Microsoft Windows logo on it — and repeatedly pressing Tab, you launch Vista into one of its most famous poses, called Flip 3D (see Figure 4-18). You can do the same thing by clicking the Switch Between Windows icon, to the right of the Start button. I'm not sure that Flip 3D works any better than CoolSwitch, but it sure draws a lot of attention. Cool, eh?

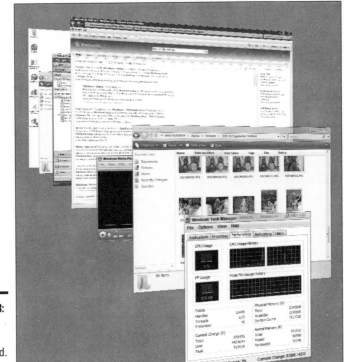

Figure 4-18:
Flip 3D,
Vista's
poster child.

Chapter 5: Getting Help with Vista

In This Chapter

✔ **Windows Vista Help: A resource of first resort**

✔ **Using Remote Assistance**

✔ **Searching for help in all the right places**

✔ **Getting more help when you're ready to give up**

Think of this chapter as help on Help. When you need help, start here.

Windows Vista ships with acres and acres — and layers and layers — of Help. Some of it works well. Some of it *would* work well, if you could figure out how to get to the right help at the right time.

This chapter tells you when and where to look for help. It also tells you when to give up and what to do after you've given up. Yes, destroying your PC is an option. But you may have alternatives. No guarantees, of course.

This chapter also includes detailed, simple, step-by-step instructions for inviting a friend to take over your computer, via the Internet, to see what is going on and lend you a hand *while you watch.* I believe this Remote Assistance capability is the most powerful and useful feature ever built into any version of Windows.

This chapter shows you what you can do when you're ready to tear your hair out.

Meeting Windows Help and Support

When you choose Start➪Help and Support, Vista presents you with a wide array of choices. Many of the top-level choices that you see in Figure 5-1 "drill down" to the same bits of information. By giving you many different ways to get to that information, Microsoft hopes to make finding what you need easier for you, even if you don't know the answer to your question in advance — a common problem in all versions of Windows Help.

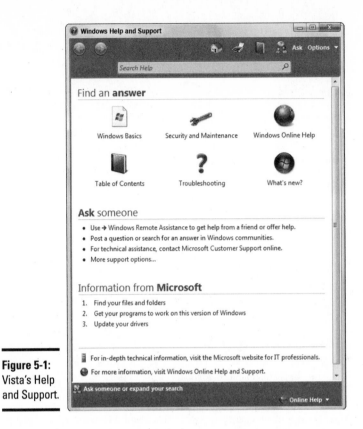

Figure 5-1:
Vista's Help
and Support.

Windows Help and Support only offers the Microsoft Party Line. If a big problem crops up with Vista, you find only a milquetoast report here. If you want searing insight or unbiased evaluations, look elsewhere — like, oh, in this book.

Windows Help morsels fall into the following categories:

✦ **Overviews, articles, and tutorials:** Explanatory pieces aimed at giving you an idea of what is going on, as opposed to solving a specific problem

✦ **Tasks:** Step-by-step procedures for solving a single problem or changing a single setting

✦ **Walk-throughs and guided tours:** Marketing demos . . . uh, multimedia demonstrations of capabilities that tend to be, uh, light on details and heavy on splash

✦ **Troubleshooters:** Take you through a series of (frequently complex) steps to help you identify and resolve problems

If you aren't connected to the Internet when you open Windows Help and Support, Vista falls back to a stunted version of the Help system. If you really need help with almost anything that's fairly complex, you have to be online.

Windows Help and Support exists primarily to reduce Microsoft's support costs, which is both good and bad. Microsoft has tried hard to enable you to solve your own problems, and to help you connect with other people who may be willing to volunteer. That's good. At the same time, Microsoft has made it pretty difficult to figure out how to pick up the phone and chat with somebody in Product Support Services. That's bad. I spill the beans — and give you some much better alternatives — in the next section of this chapter.

Windows Help and Support puts a happy face on an otherwise sobering (and bewildering!) topic. After you click past the sugarcoating, you find the following gotchas that you should know about:

Book II
Chapter 5

Getting Help with Vista

✦ You can't configure the Help and Support search engine. Vista's Help and Support already looks in all the places it can. Your only option is to cut off online searches — which makes about as much sense as cutting off your clicking finger.

✦ Live, one-on-one support from Microsoft is notoriously uneven. One day you get a support rep who can solve your problem in the blink of an eye. The next day you spend hours on hold, only to be told that you need to reformat your hard drive and reinstall Windows. If you get bumped up to "Level 2" live support, you're more likely to find someone who knows what he or she is doing, but you have to persist to "Level 3" before you get to talk to a real, live, breathing guru. Few customers have the patience or the savvy to convince Microsoft product support droids to escalate their problem to Level 3.

✦ When troubleshooters work, they work well, but they cover only the most basic problems and the most direct solutions.

✦ Although Remote Assistance is a great idea, in practice the idea has several problems:

   • Both you and your assistant have to be connected to the Internet (or to the same local network).

   • You should probably establish a telephone connection prior to setting up the session.

   • If firewalls exist between you and your assistant, Remote Assistance might not work.

   See the section "Connecting to Remote Assistance," later in this chapter, for lots of details.

✦ Windows newsgroups ("Windows communities") on the Internet are unmoderated, which means anybody can post anything. Many well-meaning support-group participants dole out utterly execrable advice.

✦ Sometimes Windows Updates are worse than the problem they're supposed to fix. I usually wait for an update to be in general circulation for at least a week before I apply it to my machine. That way, Microsoft has a chance to withdraw or reissue problematic updates (of which there are many). And I wait at least a month to apply hardware driver updates, unless they solve a specific problem that's been killing me.

It never hurts to run a System Restore checkpoint when Windows is firing on all cylinders. The worst possible time to create a checkpoint? When your system has gone to the dogs. Right now, while you're thinking about it and Windows makes you smile from ear to ear, follow the instructions in Book II, Chapter 3 to run a checkpoint. That way, when the inevitable falling out occurs, you'll have something to fall back on.

How to Really Get Help

You use Windows Help and Support when you need help and support, right? Well, yes. Sorta.

In my experience, Help and Support works best in the following situations:

✦ When you want to understand what functions the big pieces of Vista perform, and you aren't overly concerned about solving a specific problem (for example, "What is Windows Photo Gallery?")

✦ When you have a problem that's easy to define ("My printer won't print")

✦ When you have a pretty good idea of what you want to do, but you need a little prodding on the mechanics to get the job done ("How do I change my desktop's picture?")

Help and Support doesn't do much for you if you have only a vague idea of what's ailing your machine, if you want to understand enough details to think your way through a problem, if you're trying to decide on what hardware or software to buy for your computer, or if you want to know where the Vista bodies are buried.

For all that, and much more, you need an independent source of information — like this book, for example.

My Web site, www.AskWoody.com, can come in handy, especially if you're trying to decide whether you should install Microsoft's latest security patch of a patch of a patch. AskWoody.com answers questions, too, with hundreds of volunteers helping thousands of bewildered Vista victims! You'll find more than half a million searchable posts, absolutely free. Drop by from time to time to see what's happening.

If you can't find the help you need in Windows Help and Support or at AskWoody.com, expand your search for enlightenment in this order:

1. Far and away the best way to get help involves simple bribery. Buttonhole a friend who knows about this stuff, and get her to lend you a virtual hand. Promise her a beer, a pizza, a night on the town — whatever it takes. If your friend knows her stuff, it'll be cheaper and faster than the alternatives. If you can cajole your machine into connecting to the Internet — and get your friend to also connect to the Internet — Windows Vista makes it easy for a friend to take over your computer while you watch with a feature called Remote Assistance, which I discuss in the next section of this chapter.

2. If your friend is off getting a tan at Patong Beach, you may be able to find help elsewhere on the Internet. See the section "Getting Help on the Web," later in this chapter.

3. If all else fails, you can try to contact Microsoft by e-mail. You may qualify for free e-mail support using something called Microsoft Online Assisted Support. The best way to find out whether you qualify, and connect with a support droid if you do, is to jump through the following hoops:

    i. **Choose Start⇨Help and Support.**

    ii. **In the upper-right corner, click the Ask button. Then choose Contact Microsoft Customer Support Online.**

    iii. **In the Support box, click the link Contact Microsoft Customer Support online.**

    iv. **You connect to Microsoft's support site on the Internet, and at that point, you have a chance to review what support is available to you and how much it will cost.**

4. As a last resort, you can try to contact Microsoft by telephone. Heaven help ya.

Microsoft offers support by phone — you know, an old-fashioned voice call — but some pundits (including yours truly) have observed that you'll probably have more luck with a psychic hotline. Be that as it may, the telephone number for tech support in the United States is (425) 635-3311; in Canada, it's (905) 568-4494.

**Book II
Chapter 5**

Getting Help with Vista

Connecting to Remote Assistance

Raise your hand if you've heard the following conversation:

Overworked Geek, answering the phone: "Hi, honey. How's it going?"

Geek's Clueless Husband: "Sorry to call you at work, but I'm having trouble with my computer."

OG: "What kind of trouble?"

GCH: "I clicked on the picture and it went into Microsoft, you know, and I tried to look at this report my boss sent me, but the computer said it couldn't."

OG: "Huh?"

GCH: "I'm sure you've seen this a hundred times. I clicked on the picture but the computer said it couldn't. How do I look at the report?"

OG: "Spfffft!"

GCH: "What's wrong? Why don't you say anything? You have time to help the other people in your office. Why can't you make time for me?"

OG wonders, for the tenth time that day, how she ever got into this bloody business.

At one time or another, you may have been on the sending or the receiving end of a similar conversation — probably both, come to think of it. In the final analysis, one thing's clear: When you're trying to solve a computer problem — whether you're the solver or the solvee — being able to look at the screen is worth ten thousand words. Or more.

Understanding the interaction

Windows Vista includes a feature called Remote Assistance that lets you call on a friend to take over your PC. The interaction goes something like this:

1. **You create an invitation for your friend, asking him to take a look at your computer. You put a password on the invitation.**

2. **You send the message to your friend, either by Outlook or Windows Mail e-mail, or by giving your friend a file. You also have to tell your friend the password.**

The file can go any way you can imagine: attach it to an e-mail message, send it via an instant messaging program that allows you to transfer files, put it on a network shared drive, post it on your company's intranet, stick it on a USB key drive, or burn it on a CD. You can even *<gasp!>* stick it on a floppy disk. It's just a text file. Nothing fancy.

3. **Your friend receives the message or file and responds by clicking a specific link and then typing in the password.**

4. **Your PC displays a message saying that your friend wants to look at your computer.**

5. **If you give the go-ahead, your friend can see what you're doing.**

6. **Your friend may ask whether he can take over your computer. If you give your permission, he takes complete control of your machine. You watch as your friend types and clicks, just as you would if you knew what the heck you were doing. Your friend solves the problem as you watch.**

7. **Either of you can break the connection at any time.**

The thought of handing your machine over to somebody on an Internet connection probably gives you the willies. I'm not real keen on it either, but Microsoft has built some industrial-strength controls into Remote Assistance. Your friend must supply a password *that you specify* before he can connect to your computer. He can take control of your computer only if he requests it and you specifically allow it. And you can put a time limit on the invitation: If your friend doesn't respond within an hour, say, the invitation gets canceled.

Limiting an invitation

Unless you change things, an invitation that you send out requesting Remote Assistance expires after six hours. To change the expiration time, follow these steps:

1. **Choose Start⇨Control Panel⇨System and Maintenance.**

2. **Under the System icon, click the Allow Remote Access link.**

   You probably have to click through a User Access Control message.

3. **Make sure that the Remote tab is showing, and in the box marked Remote Assistance, click the Advanced button.**

4. **In the Invitations box, choose the amount of time you want invitations to remain open. Click the OK button twice, and then click the red *X* to exit the Control Panel.**

Troubleshooting Remote Assistance

Plenty of pitfalls lurk around the edges of Remote Assistance, but it mostly rates as an amazingly useful, powerful tool. The following are among the potential problems:

✦ You and your assistant have to be connected to the Internet or to the same local network. If you can't connect to the Internet — especially if that's the problem you're trying to solve — you're outta luck.

✦ If you have a dialup Internet connection, you have to *stay connected* from the time you create the invitation through the time you send the invitation, while your friend responds, and all the way until the time that the Remote Assistance session ends. You can't hop on the Internet, send an invitation, break your Internet connection, and then dial back an hour later to get the Remote Assistance session going.

✦ Both of you have to be running Windows XP, Vista, Windows Server 2003, or some other operating system that supports Remote Assistance.

✦ One of the following must be true so that you can send the invitation and your friend can use the invitation to get connected to your PC:

  • You must be able to send, and your friend must be able to receive, e-mail with an attached file that includes a hot link.

  • You must be able to send a file to your friend — possibly by Instant Messenger, over a network, or by simply handing your friend a key drive or CD.

✦ If a firewall sits between either of you and the Internet, it may interfere with Remote Assistance. Windows Firewall (the firewall that's included in Vista as well as Windows XP Service Pack 2 and later) doesn't intentionally block Remote Assistance, but other firewalls may. If you can't get through, either contact your system administrator or dig into the firewall's documentation and unblock "Port 3389" — that's the communication channel Remote Assistance uses.

You — the person with the PC that's going to be taken over — must initiate the Remote Assistance session. Your friend can't tap you on the shoulder, electronically, and say something like (with apologies to Dire Straits): "You an' me, babe, how 'bout it?"

Making the connection

When you're ready to set up the connection for Remote Assistance, here's what you need to do:

1. **Make sure that your friend is ready.**

Call him or shoot him an e-mail and make sure that he's going to have his PC on, connected to the Internet, and running Vista, Windows XP, or Windows Server 2003. Also, make sure that he will have his Instant Messenger program cranked up, will be checking e-mail frequently, or will be waiting for you to hand him a file or make one available on your network.

Make sure that you can contact your friend using your selected method: If you're using e-mail, make sure that he's in your address book and send him a test message to make sure that you have his e-mail address down pat; if you're going to send a floppy disk by carrier pigeon, make sure that the pigeon knows the route and has had plenty of sleep.

2. **When you contact your friend, make up a password and give it to him.**

   It doesn't have to be fancy — anything six or more characters long is fine — and it shouldn't be a password you use for anything else. It's a one-timer that will be valid only for this single Remote Assistance session.

3. **Start your machine (the PC that your Remote Assistance friend, the Expert, will take over), and make sure that it's connected to the Internet.**

4. **Choose Start➪Help and Support to open Windows Help and Support (refer to Figure 5-1).**

5. **Under the Ask Someone list, click Invite My Worthless Brother-in-Law to Rummage through All My Secret . . . wait a sec . . . click the Use → Remote Assistance to Get Help from a Friend or Offer Help link.**

   The first window of the Windows Remote Assistance Wizard appears (see Figure 5-2).

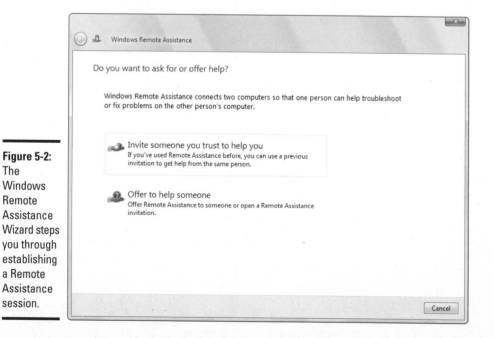

Figure 5-2:
The Windows Remote Assistance Wizard steps you through establishing a Remote Assistance session.

Windows Remote Assistance

Do you want to ask for or offer help?

Windows Remote Assistance connects two computers so that one person can help troubleshoot or fix problems on the other person's computer.

Invite someone you trust to help you
If you've used Remote Assistance before, you can use a previous invitation to get help from the same person.

Offer to help someone
Offer Remote Assistance to someone or open a Remote Assistance invitation.

Cancel

6. **Click the Invite Someone You Trust to Help You link.**

7. **You have two choices for notifying your assistant:**

   - If you're using Outlook or Windows Mail as your e-mail program, and your assistant is waiting for an e-mail message from you, click the Use E-Mail to Send an Invitation option.

     If you choose to use e-mail, Vista simply constructs a message and attaches an invitation file.

   - If your assistant expects to get an invitation file from you, whether it's going to be sent by an Instant Messenger program, attached to an e-mail message you craft yourself, posted on a network shared folder, copied to a USB key drive, or tapped onto a cuneiform tablet (theoretically possible, but a bit cumbersome), click the Save This Invitation as a File option.

   If you choose the second option, the wizard asks you to fill out a few details, as shown in Figure 5-3.

8. **Choose a place to put the invitation file, and type (and retype) a password that you make up. Click the Finish button.**

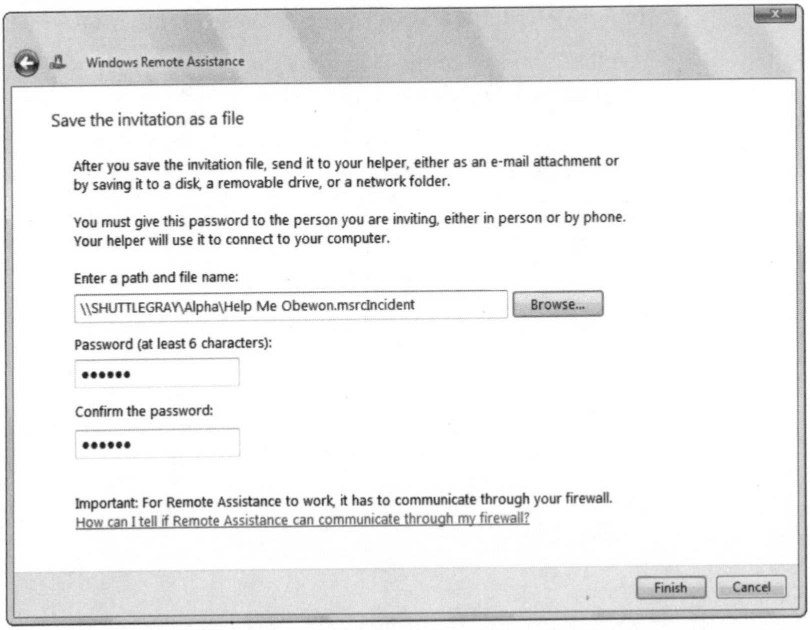

Figure 5-3: The details Vista needs to create an invitation file.

If you think that Vista's Firewall might interfere with your session, or you've had firewall trouble in the past, click the line marked How Can I Tell If Remote Assistance Can Communicate Through My Firewall, and refer to Book III, Chapter 3. Vista Firewall is probably already set up to allow Remote Assistance connections. If you're using a different firewall, you may have to adjust it manually.

Vista creates a Remote Assistance invitation file (with the filename extension .msrcIncident) and saves it in the location you picked. In Figure 5-3, Duangkhae saved the file on a shared drive called Alpha.

Vista puts a Windows Remote Assistance control bar on your desktop (see Figure 5-4) and waits for the Expert to contact you. You can continue to work, swear, play Minesweeper, or do whatever it takes to keep you sane until your friend can connect.

Book II
Chapter 5

Getting Help
with Vista

Figure 5-4:
The control bar on the "puppet" computer.

⚠ Windows Remote Assistance

Waiting for incoming connection...

Cancel   Stop sharing   Pause   Settings   Chat   Send file   Help

9. **Send the invitation file to the Expert.**

10. **Your friend, the Expert, needs to double-click the invitation file to initiate the Remote Assistance session.**

Vista asks for the password that you created and gave to the Expert. He types it in the indicated box and clicks the OK button.

Windows Remote Assistance then asks you whether it's okay to allow the Expert to connect to your computer (see Figure 5-5).

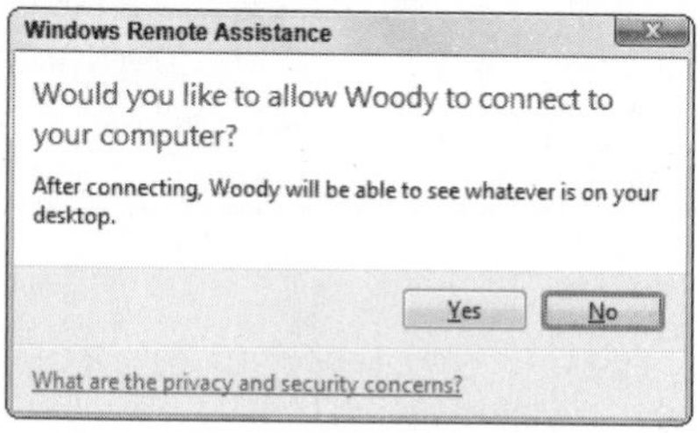

Figure 5-5:
You must give permission to begin.

Windows Remote Assistance

Would you like to allow Woody to connect to your computer?

After connecting, Woody will be able to see whatever is on your desktop.

Yes   No

What are the privacy and security concerns?

11. **Click the Yes button, and two things happen simultaneously.**

First, your computer's Remote Assistance bar shows that you're connected, as shown in Figure 5-6.

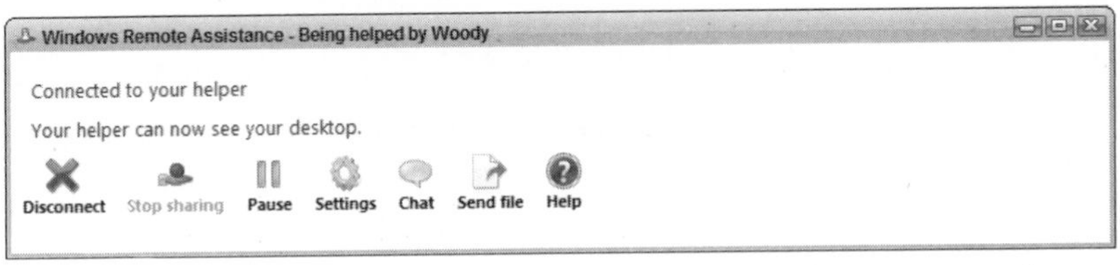

Figure 5-6:
The bar tells
you the
Expert is
watching.

Second, your friend's computer — which is to say, the Expert's computer — receives a Remote Assistance bar that looks a little bit like yours, but it also has an attached viewing box that displays everything on your screen. (See Figure 5-7.)

12. **If your friend wants to take control of your PC, he needs to click the Request Control icon on the Remote Assistance bar.**

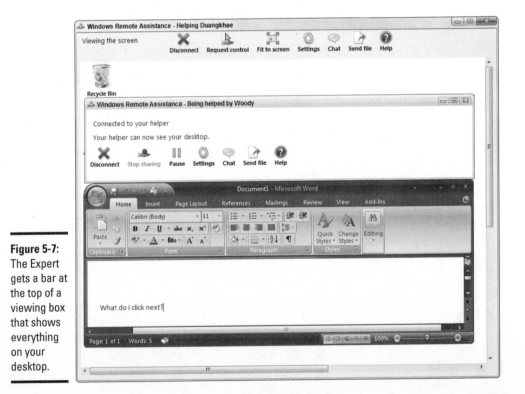

Figure 5-7:
The Expert
gets a bar at
the top of a
viewing box
that shows
everything
on your
desktop.

If he does that, your machine warns you that the Expert is trying to take control, displaying the dialog box shown in Figure 5-8.

If you allow your "Expert" to respond to User Account Control prompts (see the check box in Figure 5-8), he'll have to know an administrator user ID and password that's valid on *your* machine.

13. **The Expert can now control your computer, move the mouse, and type on the keyboard while you watch. Anytime either of you wants to sever the connection, click the Disconnect icon on the Remote Assistance bar.**

    In addition, you — the person who requested the session — can cancel the session at any time by pressing Esc.

After a Remote Assistance session is under way and you've released control to your friend, your friend can do anything to your computer that you can do. Anything at all, except change users. (If either of you log off, the Remote Assistance connection is cancelled.) Both of you have simultaneous control over the mouse pointer. If either or both of you type on the keyboard, the letters appear on-screen. You can stop your friend's control of your computer by pressing Esc.

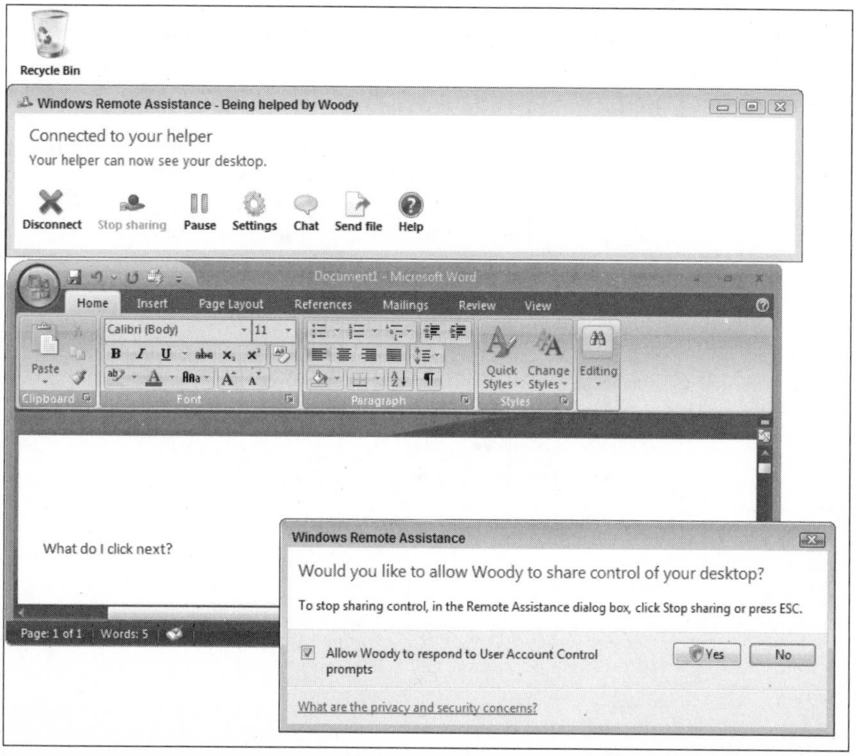

Recycle Bin

Windows Remote Assistance - Being helped by Woody

Connected to your helper
Your helper can now see your desktop.

Disconnect Stop sharing Pause Settings Chat Send file Help

Document1 - Microsoft Word

Home   Insert   Page Layout   References   Mailings   Review   View

Calibri (Body)   11

Paste

Clipboard   Font   Paragraph   Styles   Editing

What do I click next?

Page: 1 of 1   Words: 5

Windows Remote Assistance

Would you like to allow Woody to share control of your desktop?

To stop sharing control, in the Remote Assistance dialog box, click Stop sharing or press ESC.

☑ Allow Woody to respond to User Account Control prompts

Yes   No

What are the privacy and security concerns?

Figure 5-8:
You must give your permission a second time if you want to allow the Expert to take control of your machine.

Your friend can rest assured that this is a one-way connection. He can take control of your computer, but you can't do anything on his computer. He can see everything that you can see on your desktop, but you aren't allowed to look at his desktop. Whoever said life was fair?

Getting the Most from Vista Help

Windows Vista Help has been set up for you to jump in, find an answer to your problem, resolve the problem, and get back to work.

Unfortunately, life is rarely so simple. So, too, with Help. You probably won't dive into Help until you're feeling very lost. And when you're there, well, it's like the old saying, "When you're up to your <insert favorite expletive here> in alligators, it's hard to remember that you need to drain the swamp."

Ensuring that you get all the Help

Vista's Help has very few options that you can set, but you should check one key setting. Follow these steps:

1. Choose Start⇨Help and Support.

Vista shows you the Windows Help and Support main page (refer to Figure 5-1).

2. In the upper-right corner, choose Options⇨Settings.

Vista has just two settings (see Figure 5-9), but one of them is vital.

Figure 5-9:
Make sure that Vista Help looks online.

> **Help Settings**
>
> **Help Settings**
>
> Search results
>
> ☑ **Include Windows Online Help and Support when you search for help**
>
> Get the most up-to-date content from Windows Online Help when you're connected to the Internet.
>
> Help Experience Improvement program
>
> ☐ **Join the Help Experience Improvement program**
>
> By participating you can help us improve the quality and relevance of your Help experience. It is anonymous and we will not collect any contact information.
>
> Read the privacy statement online
>
> OK   Cancel

3. **Ensure that the Include Windows Assistance Online When You Search for Help check box is selected, and then click the OK button.**

   When Help is connected to the Internet, you see the Online Help icon in the lower-right corner of every Help screen.

Working through the index

Just as this book has an index, so, too, does the Windows Help and Support Center. To find the index, click the Browse Help icon, the one in the upper-right corner of the Help and Support main page that looks like a book (refer to Figure 5-1). The index appears, as shown in Figure 5-10.

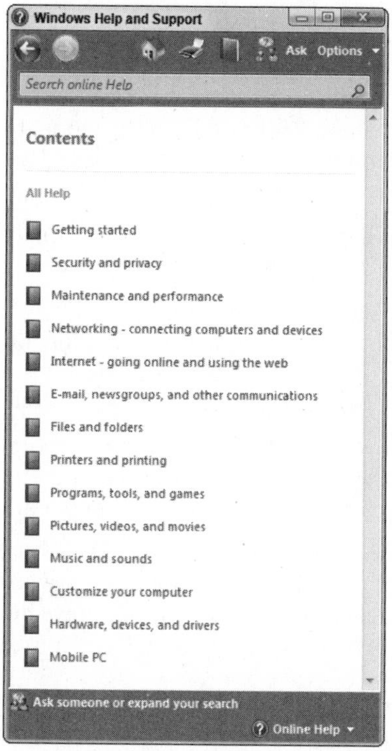

Book II Chapter 5

Getting Help with Vista

Figure 5-10: Help's frequently overlooked index.

The Windows Help index is quite thorough but, like any index, relies heavily on the terminology being used in the Help articles themselves. That leads to frequent chicken-and-egg situations: You can find the answer to your question quite readily if you, uh, know the answer to the question — or if you know the terminology involved (which is nearly the same thing, eh?).

Generally, typing keywords in the Search Help text box is the best way to approach a problem, but the index comes in handy from time to time. Don't hesitate to use it.

Getting Help on the Web

Of course, the single greatest source of information about Windows Vista is the single greatest source of information about *everything* — the Web. Vista's Help and Support weaves in and out of the Web in a multitude of ways. As long as you're connected (see the section "Ensuring that you get all the Help," earlier in this chapter), Vista pulls in information from the Internet with no assistance required on your part.

If Vista's Help doesn't work out, here are the best sources I've found for Windows Help and information:

+ **The Microsoft Knowledge Base:** This is the mother lode, the source of information that all Microsoft tech-support people use. Go to `http://support.microsoft.com` and click the Search Knowledge Base button.

+ **AskWoody.com:** The Knowledge Base shows you Microsoft's Official Party Line. AskWoody.com gives you the rest of the story.

+ **Google:** Type in the keywords of your question, and you can usually find an answer — although you may have to wade through a lot of chaff. As with any search engine, it works better if you already know the answer to your question. Check it out at `www.google.com`.

+ **Windows Help and Support:** The direct-access online version of Vista Help and Support. To get there, choose Start⇨Help and Support, and in the upper-right corner, click the Windows Online Help icon.

+ **Windows newsgroups:** These are a great source of information, but you have to remember that not everybody posting to the newsgroups knows whereof he speaks. The easiest way to use the Windows newsgroups has the advantage of simultaneously scanning *all* the newsgroups: go through Google. Go to `http://groups.google.com` and follow the instructions. Alternatively, you can use the official approach: Choose Start⇨Help and Support and click the Post a Question or Search for an Answer in Windows Communities link.

+ **Product support options:** If you're curious about the tech support available directly from Microsoft, what you qualify for, and how much it will cost, visit `http://support.microsoft.com` and review the Support Options section on the left side of the page.

Book III

Securing Vista

The 5th Wave   By Rich Tennant

"Well, the first level of Windows Vista security seems good–I can't get the shrink-wrapping off."

Contents at a Glance

Chapter 1: Lock Down: Spies, Spams, Scams, and Slams 189

Chapter 2: Security Center Overview 217

Chapter 3: Windows Firewall Backward and Forward 225

Chapter 4: Patching and Plugging 249

Chapter 5: Virus Protection and the Big Defender..263

Chapter 1: Lock Down: Spies, Spams, Scams, and Slams

In This Chapter

✔ Taking responsibility for your computer's security — proactively

✔ Discovering how and why you're vulnerable

✔ Avoiding the best-engineered traps: botnets, keyloggers, and phishing trips

✔ Becoming part of the solution, not part of the problem

✔ Using parental controls

Windows XP had more holes than a prairie-dog field.

Vista is built on top of Windows XP. The holes are hidden better.

The settings in Vista focus on keeping the software itself intact: Firewalls, automatic updates, and user account restrictions — the Windows Security Holy Trinity — are all meant to keep the bad guys out of your computer. Windows Defender, bolted onto the side of Vista, offers some spyware protection, but it's prone to problems of both omission and commission (see Book III, Chapter 5). Microsoft can sell you antivirus protection, but it can't cover 0day assaults (more about this later in the chapter).

Security goes deeper than the Vista applications. Much deeper.

In this chapter, I explain the source of real threats — more details follow in the next few chapters — but I also want to take you outside the box, to see the kinds of problems we all face with our computer systems and to look at a few key solutions.

Understanding the Hazards

Not long ago, most PC viruses planted themselves on floppy disks. People spread infections by passing around infected disks. Machines got infected when they started — booted — with infected disks in the disk drive. Infected machines subsequently put copies of the virus on every disk that had the misfortune of being stuck in the PC's disk drive. Although they had a bit of competition from other types of viruses, so-called Master Boot Record viruses ruled the PC roost for several years. The most famous — er, infamous — boot record virus, Michelangelo, received an enormous amount of media publicity in early 1992. John McAfee became a TV talk-show celebrity, claiming that 5 million machines were infected, and his company made a fortune. If you were around at the time, you may recall that Michelangelo fell far short of the doomsayer's predictions, putting egg on the face of more than a few self-appointed "experts" who predicted the Demise of Computing as We Know It.

You'll find that's a recurring theme.

One day in the summer of 1995, somebody wrote a little virus using WordBasic, the macro programming language that came embedded within Microsoft Word. The virus didn't do much more than show the uninspiring dialog box shown in Figure 1-1. As a matter of fact, it's a wonder it worked at all. But by the end of August 1995, a very large percentage of all the PCs on Microsoft's Redmond campus were infected with the Winword.Concept.A virus. Microsoft called it a "prank macro" at the time and downplayed its significance. Boy howdy, what a prank!

Figure 1-1:
The Concept.A virus didn't work very well.

Winword.Concept.A spawned an entire industry — two of them, in fact: the virus writers (whom I generally call "the guys in black hats" or equivalently, "cretins") and the antivirus software folks ("the guys in white hats"). Nobody knows how much the cretins make, but the antivirus industry hauls in more than $5,000,000,000 per year.

Many of the best-known Internet-borne scares in the past decade — the Bagles, the Netskys, the Melissas, the ILOVEYOUs, the Blasters and Slammers, and their ilk — work by using the programmability built into the computer application itself, just like good ol' Concept.A, or by taking advantage of Windows holes to inject themselves into unprotected machines.

Fast-forward a dozen years and the, uh, concepts have changed. The old threats are still there, but they've taken on a new twist: The scent of money has made cracking far more sophisticated. What started out as a bunch of miscreants playing programmer one-upsmanship at our expense has turned into a profitable — sometimes highly profitable — business enterprise.

Where's the money? At least at this moment — and for the foreseeable future — the greatest profits are made with botnets and phishing attacks. That's where you should expect the most sophisticated, most damnably difficult attacks.

Zombies and botnets

Every month, Microsoft posts a new "malicious software removal tool" that scans PCs for malware and, in many cases, removes it. In a recent study, Microsoft reported that 62% of all the PC systems that were found to have "malicious" software also had backdoors. That's a sobering figure.

A *backdoor* is a program that breaks through Windows' usual security measures and allows a cretin to take control of your computer, effectively turning it into a zombie. The most sophisticated backdoors allow creeps to adapt — upgrade, if you will — the malicious software running on a subverted machine. And they do it by remote control.

Backdoors typically arrive on your PC when you install a program that you want, not realizing that the backdoor came along for the ride.

What's a buffer overflow?

If you've been following the progress of malware in general, and the beatings delivered to Windows in particular, you've no doubt run across the phrase *buffer overflow* or *buffer overrun* — a favorite tool in the arsenal of many virus writers. It may sound mysterious, but at its heart, a buffer overflow is quite simple.

Programmers set aside small areas in their programs to transfer data from one program to another. Those places are called *buffers*. A problem arises when too much data gets put in a buffer (or if you look at it from the other direction, when the buffer is too small to hold all the data that's being put in it). You might think that having ten pounds of offal in a five-pound bag would make the program scream bloody murder, but many programs aren't smart enough to look, much less cry uncle and give up.

When too much data exists in the buffer, some of it can spill out into the program itself. If the cretin who's stuffing too much data into the buffer is very clever, he/she/it may be able to convince the program that the extra data isn't data at all but, instead, is another part of the program, waiting to be run. The worm sticks a lot of data in a small space and makes sure that the piece that flops out will perform whatever malicious deed the worm's creator wants. When the offal hits the fan, the program finds itself executing data that was stuffed into the buffer — running a program that was written by the worm's creator. That's how a buffer overrun can take control of your computer.

Every worm that uses a buffer-overrun security hole in Windows takes advantage of a stupid programming error inside Windows. Programs inside Vista should be checking their buffers all the time. Sorry, Microsoft, but that's a stone-cold fact, even if it means that Vista runs slower.

Less commonly, PCs acquire backdoors when they come down with some sort of infection: The Sobig and Mydoom worms installed backdoors. Many of the infections occur on PCs that haven't been kept up to date with Microsoft's security patches (see Book II, Chapter 4), *buffer overflows* being a favorite delivery mechanism (see the nearby sidebar). Looking into the future, it's likely that 0day ("zero day") exploits (see the section "0day exploits," later in this chapter) will evolve into the delivery mechanism of choice.

A cretin who controls one machine via a backdoor can't claim much street cred. But someone who's put together a *botnet* — a collection of hundreds or thousands of PCs — can take their zombies to the bank:

✦ A botnet running *keyloggers* — programs that watch what you type, sporadically sending the data to the botnet's controller — can gather all sorts of valuable information. The single biggest problem facing those who gather and disseminate keylogger information? Bulk. The sheer volume of stolen information. How do you scan millions of characters of logged data and retrieve a bank account number or a password?

✦ Unscrupulous businesses hire botnet controllers to disseminate spam, "harvest" e-mail addresses, even direct coordinated *Distributed Denial of Service (DDoS)* attacks against rivals' Web sites. (A DDoS attack guides thousands of PCs to go to a particular Web site simultaneously, blocking legitimate use.)

There's a fortune to be made in botnets.

The most successful botnets run as rootkits. A *rootkit* is a collection of programs that operate deep inside Windows, concealing files and making it very difficult to detect their presence.

You probably first heard about rootkits back in late 2005, when a couple of security researchers discovered that certain CDs from Sony BMG surreptitiously installed rootkits on computers: If you merely played the CD on your computer, the rootkit took hold. Several lawsuits later, Sony finally saw the error of its ways and vowed to stop distributing rootkits with its CDs. Nice guys. (The researchers, Mark Russinovich and Bryce Cogswell, were later hired by Microsoft.)

A very thorough, eye-opening white paper about botnets is from Paul Barford and Vinod Yegneswaran at the University of Wisconsin at www.cs.wisc.edu/ ~pb/botnets_final.pdf. They talk specifically about the structure of Agobot, SDBot, SpyBot, and GT Bot, the most widespread bots currently on the Net. If you're curious about the inner workings of the infernal beasts, that's a great place to start.

As far as I'm concerned, you can call a rootkit a backdoor, you can call a backdoor a botnet, and you can call a botnet a three-toed tree sloth. You can even call me late for dinner. But please, please don't call any of these ornery critters *bugs*. Viruses, worms, Trojans, rootkits — none of them are bugs. A *bug* is a mistake in a program. Many viruses and worms have bugs — the cretins who write them aren't always the brightest lights on the tree, know what I mean? — but that doesn't mean that they *are* bugs. Got it?

Phishing

Think that message from Wells Fargo (or eBay, PayPal, Citibank, a smaller regional bank, Visa, MasterCard, whatever) asking to verify your account password (social security number, account number, address, telephone number, mother's maiden name, whatever) looks official? Think again.

Phishing — sending e-mail that attempts to extract personal information from you, usually through a bogus Web site — has in many cases reached levels of sophistication that exceed the standards of the financial institutions themselves. Some phishing messages, such as the completely bogus message in Figure 1-2, warn you about the evils of phishing, in an attempt to get you to send your account number and password to some scammer in Kazbukistan (or New York).

Figure 1-2:
If you click the link, you arrive at a page that looks very much like PayPal's, and any information you enter is sent to a scammer.

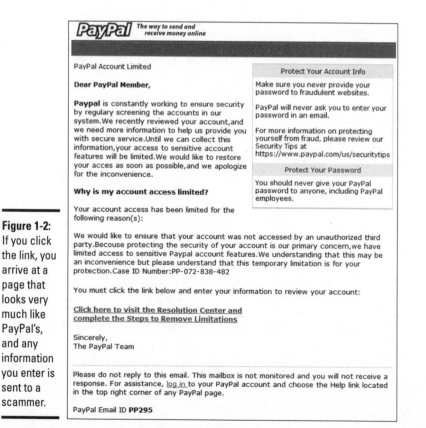

**Book III
Chapter 1**

Lock Down:
Spies, Spams,
Scams, and Slams

Here's how it works:

1. Some scammer, often using a fake name and a stolen credit card, sets up a Web site. Usually it's a very professional-looking Web site — in some cases, indistinguishable from the "real" site.

   The Web site asks for personal information — most commonly your account number and password, or the PIN for your ATM card.

2. The scammer turns spammer and sends out hundreds of thousands of bogus messages. The messages include a clickable link to the fake Web site and a plausible story about how you must go to the Web site, log on, and do something to avoid dire consequences. The "from" address on the messages is *spoofed* so that the message appears to come from the company in question. The message usually includes official logos — many even include links to the "real" Web site, even though they encourage you to click through to the fake site.

3. A small percentage of the recipients of the spam e-mail actually open it and click through the fake site. If they enter their information, it's sent directly to the scammer.

4. The scammer watches incoming traffic from the fake Web site, gathers the information typed by gullible people, and uses it quickly — typically by logging on to the bank's Web site and attempting a transfer, or by burning a fake ATM card and using the PIN. Within a day or two — sometimes just hours — the Web site is shut down, and everything disappears into thin ether.

Phishing has become so popular because of the sheer numbers involved. Say a scammer sends out 1 million e-mail messages advising Wells Fargo customers to log on to their accounts. Only a small fraction of all the people who receive the phishing message will be Wells Fargo customers, but if the hit rate is just 1 percent, that's 10,000 customers.

Most of the Wells Fargo customers who receive the message will be smart enough to ignore it. But a sizable percentage — maybe 10 percent, maybe just 1 percent — will click through. That's somewhere between 100 and 1,000 suckers, er, customers.

If half of the people who click through provide their account details, the scammer gets 50 to 500 account numbers and passwords. If most of those arrive within a day of sending out the phishing message, the scammer stands to make a pretty penny indeed — and he or she can disappear with hardly a trace.

Note that I'm *not* talking about using your credit card online. Online credit card transactions are as safe as they are face to face — more so, actually, because if you use a U.S.-based credit card, you aren't liable for any loss due to somebody snatching your card information or any other form of fraud. I use my credit cards online all the time. You should, too.

Fight against phishing in these ways:

✦ If you get an e-mail message that contains any links to the Web, don't click the links. Nowadays, almost all messages with links to commercial sites are phishing come-ons. Financial institutions, in particular, don't send out messages with links anymore — and few other companies would dare. If you feel motivated to check out a dire message, go into Internet Explorer and type the address of the company by hand.

✦ Don't ever include personal information in an e-mail message and send it. Don't give out any of your personal information unless you've manually logged on to the company's Web site.

✦ If you get a phishing message that may be new or different, check www.millersmiles.co.uk to see whether it's a well-known, uh, phish. If you don't see your phish listed, forward a copy of the mail to the FBI's Internet Fraud Complaint Center (www1.ifccfbi.gov/cf1.asp). If eBay or PayPal is involved, forward a copy of the message to spoof@ebay.com or spoof@paypal.com. Then log on to the MillerSmiles Web site (www.millersmiles.co.uk/identitytheft/report-form.html) and submit a report. Hold onto the mail for a while to see whether the authorities need a copy of the message header: If so, they'll send you instructions.

MillerSmiles has a wealth of information on phishing, including an invaluable description of the steps you should take if you accidentally gave your personal information to a phisher. See www.millersmiles.co.uk/idntitytheft/oah-6.htm.

0day exploits

What do you do when you discover a brand-new security hole in Windows, Office, or some other Microsoft product? Why, you sell it, of course.

At one point, a security company called iDefense offered a $10,000 bounty to anyone who found a sufficiently important security hole in a Microsoft product. iDefense "buys" the security hole, works with Microsoft on a solution, and at the same time protects its customers from the threat, even before

**Book III
Chapter 1**

**Lock Down:
Spies, Spams,
Scams, and Slams**

Microsoft releases the fix. (Details may change by the time you read this. Got a hole to sell? See `http://labs.idefense.com/vcp.php`.) The data network company 3Com offers a similar bounty, as do others. One enterprising bug catcher offered up his hole for sale to the highest bidder on eBay.

Rumor has it that several less-than-scrupulous sites arrange for the buying and selling of new security holes. Apparently the Russian hacker group that discovered a vulnerability in the way Windows handles WMF graphics files sold its new hole for $4,000, not realizing that it could've made much more (see `http://eweek.com/article2/0,1895,1918198,00.asp`).

When a person writes a malicious program that takes advantage of a newly discovered security hole — a hole that even the manufacturer (in this case Microsoft) doesn't know about — that malicious program is called a *0day exploit*. (Fuddy-duddies call it a *zero day exploit*. The hopelessly hip call it a *sploit*.)

How do you protect yourself from 0day exploits? In some ways, you can't: By definition, nobody sees a 0day coming, although most antivirus products employ some sort of *heuristic detection* that tries to clamp down on exploits based solely on the behavior of the offensive program. Mostly, you have to rely on the common-sense protection that I describe in the section "Getting Protected," later in this chapter. It's also important that you stay informed, which I talk about in the next section.

Staying Informed

Botnets and sploits and phishing holes, oh my!

If you rely on the evening news to keep yourself informed about the latest threats to your computer's well-being, you'll quickly discover that the mainstream press frequently doesn't get the details right. Hey, if you were a newswriter with a deadline ten minutes away, and you had to figure out how the new Bandersnatch 0day exploit shreds through a Windows Vista TCP/IP stack buffer — and you had to explain your discoveries to a TV audience, at a presumed 6th-grade intelligence level — what would you do?

Fortunately, some very reliable sources of information exist on the Internet. It would behoove you to check them out from time to time, particularly when you hear about a new computer security hole, real or imagined:

✦ **The Microsoft Security Response Center (MSRC) blog** (`http://blogs.technet.com/msrc/default.aspx`) presents thoroughly researched analyses of outstanding threats.

Two problems exist:

- The MSRC postings tend to lag other sources: It appears as if the information presented goes through many levels of internal review and approval prior to posting, which can take quite a while.

- The information you see on the MSRC blog is 100% Microsoft Party Line — so there's a tendency to add more than a little "spin control" to the announcements.

That said, Microsoft has the most, best resources to analyze and solve Windows problems, and the MSRC blog frequently has inside information that you can't find anywhere else.

✦ **The SANS Internet Storm Center (ISC)** (`http://isc.sans.org`) pools observations and analysis from thousands of active security researchers. You can generally get the news first — accurately — from the ISC.

✦ **The Windows Secrets newsletter** (`www.windowssecrets.com`), distributed twice a month, contains excellent recaps of all the latest problems. Also, my site, AskWoody.com, strives to present the latest security information in a way that doesn't require a Ph.D. in computer science.

Take a moment right now to look up those sites and add them to your Internet browser's Favorites (or Bookmarks) list.

Microsoft releases security patches frequently (once a month, as of this writing). You can get advance notice about upcoming patches on the MSRC blog. When the patches become available, they're described and presented in *Security Bulletins* bearing sequential numbers such as MS07-001, MS07-002, and so on (the *07* means they have a license to kill, Moneypenny). The patches themselves are attached to Microsoft Knowledge Base (KB) articles with numbers resembling *KB 912345*. Microsoft keeps the bulletins separate from the patching programs because a single Security Bulletin may have many associated patches.

It's hard to keep all the patches straight without a scorecard. I maintain an exhaustive list of patches, their known problems, and Microsoft's patches of the patches (of the patches) on my Microsoft Patch Reliability Ratings page at AskWoody.com.

**Book III
Chapter 1**

**Lock Down:
Spies, Spams,
Scams, and Slams**

Getting Protected

The Internet is wild and woolly and wonderful — and, by and large, it's unregulated, in a Wild West sort of way. Some would say it's unregulatable, and I'd have to agree. Although some central bodies control basic Internet coordination questions — how the computers talk to each other, who doles out domain names such as dummies.com, and what a Web browser should do when it encounters a particular piece of HyperText Markup Language (HTML) — no central authority or Web Fashion Police exists.

In spite of its Wild West lineage and complete lack of couth, the Internet doesn't need to be a scary place. If you follow a handful of simple, common-sense rules, you'll go a long way toward making your Internet travels more like Happy Trails and less like Doom III.

Viruses, viruses everywhere

"Everybody" knows that the Internet breeds viruses. "Everybody" knows that really bad viruses can drain your bank account, break your hard drive, and give you terminal halitosis — just by looking at an e-mail message with "Good Times" in the Subject line. Right.

In fact, botnets and keyloggers can hurt you, but hoaxes and lousy advice abound. Every Vista user should take these seven steps:

1. **Use a firewall.**

Vista's Firewall works well on incoming traffic, but it's impossible to use in the outbound direction. If there's any chance that your computer's been turned into a zombie or that a keylogger might be phoning home, get a decent two-way firewall like ZoneAlarm (free at www.zonelabs.com).

2. **Don't install programs that look fishy. For example, install Tiki Trouble, shown in Figure 1-3, and you get "Zango and the Zango Search Assistant . . . [which] occasionally deliver comparison websites relevant to your online searching and shopping."**

Unless the downloadable software comes from a reputable manufacturer whom you trust, and you know precisely *why* you need it, you probably don't want it.

You may think that you absolutely have to synchronize the Windows clock (which Vista does amazingly well, no extra program needed), tune up your computer (gimme a break), use those cute little smiley icons (gimme a bigger break), install a pop-up blocker (both Internet Explorer and Firefox already do that well), or get an automatic e-mail signer (your e-mail program already can — read the manual, pilgrim!). What you end up with is an unending barrage of hassles and hustles.

Figure 1-3:
Avoid
downloading
programs
that look
fishy.

3. **Buy, install, update, and religiously use one of the major antivirus software packages and one of the major antispyware packages.**

It doesn't matter which AV package you use — all of them are good. See Book III, Chapter 5 for more on antivirus and antispyware software.

In spite of the name, antivirus software frequently looks for more than just viruses. Many 0day exploits can be nipped in the bud, shortly after their appearance, by a recently updated antivirus scan.

4. **Never, ever open a file attached to an e-mail message until you do the following:**

- Contact the person who sent you the file and verify that he or she did, in fact, send you the file intentionally.

- After you contact the person who sent you the file, don't open the file directly. Save it to your hard drive and run your antivirus software on it before you open it.

5. **Follow the instructions in Book II, Chapter 1 to force Vista to show you the full name of all the files that are on your computer.**

That way, if you see a file called `something.cpl` or `iloveyou.vbs`, you stand a fighting chance of understanding that it could be an infectious program waiting for your itchy finger.

6. **Don't trust e-mail.**

Every single part of an e-mail message can be faked, easily. The return address can be spoofed. Even the header information — which you don't normally see — can be pure fiction. Links inside e-mail messages may not point where you think they point. Anything you put in a message can be viewed by anybody with even a nodding interest — to use the old analogy, sending unencrypted e-mail is a lot like sending a postcard.

7. **Check your accounts.**

Look at your credit card and bank statements, and if you see a charge you don't understand, question it. Log on to all your financial Web sites frequently, and if somebody changed your password, scream bloody murder.

You have to be careful. But your uncle's sister-in-law's roommate's hair-dresser's soon-to-be-ex-boyfriend, who's a really smart computer guy (but kinda smelly), may not be the best source of unbiased information.

Credit card fraud

A very large percentage of people who use the Web refuse to order anything online because they're afraid that their credit card number will be stolen and they'll be liable for enormous bills. Or they think that the products will never arrive, and they won't get their money back.

If your credit card was issued in the United States and you're ordering from a U.S. company, that's simply not the case. Here's why:

✦ The Fair Credit Billing Act protects you from being charged by a company for an item you don't receive. It's the same law that governs orders placed over the telephone or by mail. A vendor generally has 30 days to send the merchandise, or it has to give you a formal, written chance to cancel your order. For details, go to the Federal Trade Commission's Web site, `www.ftc.gov/bcp/conline/pubs/buying/mail.htm`.

✦ Your maximum liability for charges fraudulently made on the card is $50 per card. The minute you notify the credit card company that somebody else is using your card, you have no further liability. If you have any questions, the Federal Trade Commission can help. See `www.ftc.gov/bcp/conline/pubs/credit/cards.htm`.

Some online vendors, such as Amazon.com, absolutely guarantee that your shopping will be safe. The Fair Credit Billing Act protects any charges fraudulently made in excess of $50. Amazon says it reimburses any fraudulent charges *under* $50 that occurred as a result of using its Web site. Many credit card companies now offer similar assurances.

That said, you should still take a few simple precautions to make sure that you aren't giving away your credit card information:

✦ When you place an order online, make sure that you're dealing with a company you know. In particular, *don't* click a link in an e-mail message and expect that you'll go to the company's Web site. Type the company's address into Internet Explorer or Firefox, or use a link that you stored in IE's Favorites list.

✦ Only type your credit card number when you're sure that you've arrived at the company's site and when the site is using a secure Web page. The easy way to tell whether a Web page is secure is to look at the address and look for the lock icon to the right of the address (see Figure 1-4). Secure Web sites scramble data so that anything that you type on the Web page is encrypted before it's sent to the vendor's computer.

Beware of the fact that crafty Web programmers can fake the lock icon and show an `https://` address to try to lull you into thinking that you're on a secure Web page. To be safe, make sure that you're using a reputable company's Web site — and the only way to do that is to type the address into Internet Explorer's address bar or use a Favorites link that you've set up.

Figure 1-4:
Security pages, such as bank logon pages, are always secure pages and should show the "lock" icon in the lower-right corner.

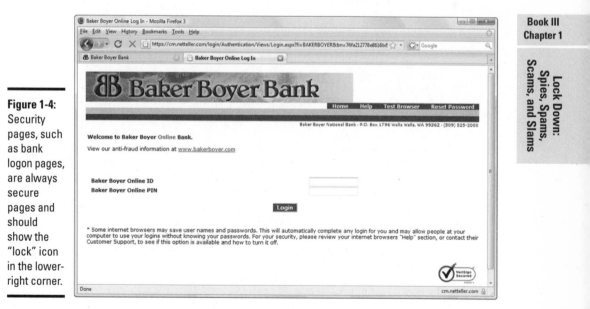

✦ Don't send your credit card number in an ordinary e-mail message. E-mail is just too easy to intercept. And for heaven's sake, don't give out any personal information when you're chatting online.

✦ If you receive an e-mail message requesting credit card information that seems to be from your bank, credit card company, Internet Service Provider, or even your sainted Aunt Martha, don't send sensitive information back via e-mail. Insist on using a secure Web site and type the company's address into Internet Explorer.

The rules are different if you're not dealing with a U.S. company and using a U.S. credit card. For example, if you buy something in an online auction from an individual, you don't have the same level of protection. Make sure that you understand the rules before you hand out credit card information.

Identity theft continues to be a problem all over the world. Widespread availability of personal information online only adds fuel to the flame. If you think someone may be posing as you — to run up debts in your name, for example — see the U.S. government's main Web site on the topic at www.consumer.gov/idtheft.

Defending your privacy

"You have zero privacy anyway. Get over it."

That's what Scott McNealy, CEO of Sun Microsystems, said to a group of reporters on January 25, 1999. He was exaggerating — Scott's been known to make provocative statements for dramatic effect — but the exaggeration comes awfully close to reality. (Actually, if Scott told me the sky was blue, I'd run outside and check. But I digress.)

I continue to be amazed at Windows users' odd attitudes toward privacy. People who wouldn't dream of giving a stranger their telephone numbers fill out their mailing addresses for online service profiles. People who are scared to death at the thought of using their credit cards online to place an order with a major retailer (a very safe procedure, by the way) dutifully type in their Social Security numbers on Web-based forms.

Vista — particularly through Microsoft's online "Live" services — gives you unprecedented convenience. That convenience comes at a price, though: Everything you do with Windows Live Mail, Messenger, Safety Center, Defender, OneCare, Urge — or just about any commercial site on the Web, for that matter — ends up stored away in a database somewhere. And as the technology gets more and more refined, your privacy gets squeezed.

I suggest you follow these few important privacy points:

+ **Use work systems only for work.** Why use your company e-mail ID for personal messages? C'mon. Drop by www.yahoo.com or www.gmail.com or any of dozens of other Web sites for a free e-mail ID.

  In the United States, with very few exceptions, anything you do on a company PC at work can be monitored and examined by your employer. E-mail, Web-site history files, even stored documents and settings are all fair game. At work, you have zero privacy anyway. Get over it.

+ **Clear your cache.** Internet Explorer saves copies (in a *cache*) of Web pages that you've accessed, to make things faster if you look at the same page again. IE also maintains 20 days' worth of history, listing the sites you've visited. Clear them both by starting Internet Explorer (choose Start⇨Internet Explorer), pressing Alt, choosing Tools⇨Internet Options, and choosing the appropriate buttons under the General tab.

+ **Surf the Web anonymously.** It's easy. Check out www.anonymizer.com for a free anonymizer toolbar. Be aware of the fact, though, that surfing anonymously still leaves a trail on your PC. To get rid of the trail, follow the instructions in the previous paragraph to clear the history and cache.

+ **Send e-mail anonymously, too** — nobody can trace it back to its source. You can sign up for a free e-mail account at Gmail, Yahoo!, or Hotmail, and provide fanciful personal information. Or you can send it directly: Look at www.gilc.org/speech/anonymous/remailer.html. It's particularly valuable for journalists. Whistle-blowing friends of mine inside a, uh, certain company in Redmond use it all the time.

Keep your head low and your powder dry!

Keeping cookies at bay

So what's a cookie, anyway?

A *cookie* is a text file that a Web site stores on your computer. Why would a Web site want to store a file on your computer? To identify you when you come back. It's really that simple.

Consider the case of D. Dummy, D. Dummy's computer, and a Web site that D. Dummy visits — say my hometown newspaper's site, www.phuketgazette.net. The *Phuket* (say *poo-KET) Gazette* uses cookies to keep track of when readers last visited its Web site so that readers can click a button and see what's happened since the last time they looked at the site. Nifty feature.

Here's how cookies come into the picture:

1. D. Dummy decides that he wants to look at the *Phuket Gazette*'s site, so he types **www.phuketgazette.net** in Internet Explorer and presses Enter.

2. D. Dummy's computer starts talking to the Web site. "Howdy y'all!" (Did I mention that D. Dummy's computer comes from Texas? Details, details.) "I'm D. Dummy and I'd like to take a look at your main page."

3. The *Phuket Gazette* site, www.phuketgazette.net, starts talking back to D. Dummy's computer. "Hey, D. Dummy! Have you been here before?" (Actually, the *Phuket Gazette*'s site is a whole lot more polite than that, but you get the idea.)

4. D. Dummy's computer runs out to its hard drive real fast and looks for a text file called — bear with me here — DDummy@www.phuketgazette. txt. It doesn't find a file, so D. Dummy's computer says to the Web site, "Nope. I don't have any cookies here from y'all."

5. The *Phuket Gazette* site pulls off its shoes and socks, starts counting fingers and toes, and then says to D. Dummy's computer, "Fair enough. I figure you're user number 1578462. Store that number away, wouldja, so that I can identify you the next time you come back here. And while you're at it, could you also remember that you were last here at 11:36 a.m. on December 14?"

6. D. Dummy's computer runs out, creates a new file called DDummy@ www.phuketgazette.txt, and puts the values 1578462 and 11:36 a.m. on December 14 in it.

The *Phuket Gazette* site's main page starts to come up on the screen. D. Dummy scans the headlines, and then heads off to do some shopping. Two hours (or days or weeks or months) later, dear old D. Dummy goes back to www.phuketgazette.net. Here's what happens:

1. D. Dummy types **www.phuketgazette.net** in Internet Explorer and presses Enter.

2. D. Dummy's computer starts talking to the Web site. "Howdy y'all! I'm D. Dummy and I'd like to take a look at your main page." Texans.

3. The *Phuket Gazette* site, www.phuketgazette.net, says to D. Dummy's computer, "Hey, D. Dummy! Have you been here before?"

4. This time, D. Dummy's computer runs out to its hard drive and finds a file called DDummy@www.phuketgazette.txt. D. Dummy's computer says to the Web site, "Gee willickers. I have a cookie from you guys. It says that I'm user number 1578462 and I was last here at 11:36 a.m. on December 14."

5. That's all the *Phuket Gazette* Web site needs to know. It flashes a big banner that says "Welcome back D. Dummy!" and it puts together a button that says "Click here to see everything that's happened since 11:36 a.m. on December 14."

Note that the *Phuket Gazette* site could also keep track of user 1578462 — stick an entry in a database somewhere — and accumulate information about that user. (The site doesn't, but it could.)

No doubt you've been told that cookies are horrible, evil programs lurking in the bowels of Windows that can divulge your credit card number to a pimply teenager in Gazukistan and then slice and dice the data on your hard drive, shortly before handing you over, screaming, to the Feds. In fact, your uncle's sister-in-law's roommate's hairdresser's . . . and so on probably told you so himself. Well, guess what? A cookie is just a text file, placed on your hard drive by a Web page. Nothing sinister about it.

The Doubleclick shtick

A Web site plants a cookie on your computer. Only that Web site can retrieve the cookie. The information is shielded from other Web sites. ZDNet.com (the *PC Magazine* Web site) can figure out that I have been reading reviews of digital cameras. Dealtime.com knows that I buy shoes. But a cookie from ZDNet can't be read by Dealtime, and vice versa. So what's the big deal?

Enter Doubleclick.net, which was recently bought by Google. For the better part of a decade, both ZDNet.com and Dealtime.com include ads from a company called Doubleclick.net. Don't believe it? Use Internet Explorer to go to each of the sites, press Alt, and choose View⇨Web Page Privacy Policy. Unless ZDNet or Dealtime has changed advertisers, you see Doubleclick.net featured prominently in each site's privacy report.

Here's the trick. You surf to a ZDNet Web page that contains a Doubleclick.net ad. Doublelick kicks in and plants a cookie on your PC that says you were looking at a specific page on ZDNet. Two hours (or days or weeks) later, you surf to a Dealtime page that also contains a Doubleclick.net ad — a different ad, no doubt — but one distributed by Doubleclick. Doubleclick kicks in again and discovers that you were looking at that specific ZDNet page two hours (or days or weeks) earlier.

Multiply that little example by ten, a hundred, or a hundred thousand, and you begin to see how cookies can be used to collect a whole lot of information about you and your surfing habits. There's nothing illegal or immoral about it. Just realize that Big Brother Doubleclick may be watching, no matter where you go online.

Why spam filters get ulcers

There are 1,300,925,111,156,286,160,896 ways to spell *Viagra*. No, really. If you use all the tricks that spammers use — from simple swaps such as using the letter "l" instead of "i" or inserting e x t r a s p a c e s in the word, to tricky ones like substituting accented characters — you have more than one sextillion different ways to spell Viagra.

Hard to believe? See `http://cockeyed.com/lessons/viagra/viagra.html` for an eye-opening analysis.

Spam scanners look at e-mail messages and try to determine whether the contents of the potentially offensive message match certain criteria. Details vary depending on the type of spam scanner you (or your Internet Service Provider) use, but in general, the scanner has to match the contents of the message with certain words and phrases stored in its database. If you've seen a lot of messages with odd spellings come through your spam scanner, you know how hard it is to see through all those sextillion variations.

A cookie can be retrieved only by the same site that sent it out in the first place. So the *Phuket Gazette* can put cookies on my hard drive, but only the *Phuket Gazette* can read its cookies. There's a trick, though. See the sidebar "The Doubleclick shtick" for details.

To understand how cookies can pose problems, you have to take a look at the kind of information that can be collected about you, as an individual, and how big a squeeze that puts on your privacy.

When you visit a Web site, the site can automatically collect a small amount of information about you. It can collect the following bits and pieces:

✦ Your computer's address (actually, the IP address, which identifies your computer on the Internet). If you use a dialup Internet connection, the computer's address changes every time you dial up. But if you have a permanent Internet connection — with a DSL or cable modem — your address probably doesn't change. That means a sufficiently persistent data-mining program can (at least in theory) track your activities over long periods of time.

✦ The name of the browser that you're using, its version number, and the name of your operating system — in other words, the Web site will know that you're using Internet Explorer 7 and Vista. No biggie.

✦ The address of the Web page that you just came from.

That isn't a whole lot of information, but it comes along for the ride every time you visit a Web site. You can't do anything about it. When you're on a site, of course, the site can keep track of which pages you look at, how long you stay at each one, what buttons you click, and so on.

In addition, the site you're visiting can ask you for, quite literally, anything: the size of your monthly paycheck, your mother's maiden name, telephone numbers, credit card numbers, Social Security numbers, driver's license numbers, shoe sizes, and your dowdy Aunt Martha's IQ. If you're game to type the information, the Web site can collect it and store it.

That's where things start getting dicey. Suppose that you go to one Web site and enter your e-mail ID and credit card number and then go to another Web site and enter your e-mail ID and telephone number. If those two sites share their information — perhaps through a third party — it's suddenly possible to match your credit card number and telephone number. See the sidebar, "The Doubleclick shtick," to see where this is all headed.

Microsoft, of course, gathers an enormous amount of information about you in its Windows registration database, its Live ID database, the Windows Update database, and on and on. As of this writing, it doesn't appear that Microsoft has attempted to correlate the data in those databases. Yet.

For in-depth, knowledgeable updates on cookie shenanigans, drop by www.cookiecentral.com.

Reducing spam

Everybody hates spam.

Nobody has any idea how to stop it. Not the government. Not Bill Gates. Not your sainted aunt's podiatrist's second cousin.

You think legislation can reduce the amount of spam? Since the U.S. CAN-SPAM act (www.spamlaws.com/federal/108s877.html) was enacted on January 7, 2003, has the volume of spam you've received increased or decreased?

Heck, I've had more spam from politicians lately than almost any other group. The very people who are supposed to be enforcing the antispam laws seem to be spewing out spam overtime.

By and large, Windows is only tangentially involved in the spam game — it's the messenger, as it were. But every Windows user I know receives e-mail. And every e-mail user I know gets spam. Lots of it.

Spam is an intractable problem, but you can do certain things to minimize your exposure:

✦ Don't encourage 'em. Don't buy anything that's offered via spam (or any other e-mail that you didn't specifically request). Don't click through to the Web site. Simply delete the message. If you see something that might be interesting, use Google or some other Web browser to look for other companies that sell the same thing.

✦ Only "opt out" of the mailings if you know and trust the company that's sending you messages. If you're on the Costco mailing list and you're not interested in its e-mail anymore, click the Opt Out button at the bottom of the page. But don't "opt out" with a company you don't trust: It may just be trying to verify your e-mail address.

✦ Never post your e-mail address on a Web site or in a newsgroup. Spammers have spiders that devour Web pages by the gazillion. If you post something in a newsgroup and want to let people respond, use a name that's hard for spiders to swallow: woody (at) ask woody (dot) com, for example.

✦ Never open an attachment to an e-mail message. Unless you know the person who sent it to you, you've verified with her that she intended to send you the attachment, and you trust the sender to be running an up-to-date antivirus package, it's not wise to open that attachment.

✦ Never trust a Web site that you arrive at by "clicking through" a hot link in an e-mail message. Be cautious about Web sites that you get to from other Web sites. If you don't personally type the address in Internet Explorer's address bar, you might not be in Kansas anymore.

✦ If your e-mail program allows it, block automatic downloading of pictures inside e-mail messages. That reduces the sender's ability to verify your e-mail address using a method called Web beacons. Web beacons are tiny pictures (or other components of a message) that "phone home" when you view the message. Some e-mail programs allow you to sever the link by not downloading pictures unless you specifically, manually request them.

Yes, the rumors you've heard are true. Microsoft used to put Web beacons in its newsletters — another one of those dirty facts the Redmondians would rather sweep under the table.

Ultimately, the only long-lasting solution to spam is to change your e-mail address and only give out your address to close friends and business associates. Even *that* won't solve the problem, but it should reduce the level of spam significantly. Heckuva note, ain't it?

Recovering from an Attack

Every day I get e-mail messages from people who are convinced that their PC has been clobbered by a virus. Most of the time, the problems have nothing to do with viruses — intermittently bad hardware, an aberrant program, or maybe a flaky Internet connection can cause all sorts of grief, and malware has nothing to do with it.

If you think a virus or worm has hit you, you should do three things immediately. Actually, there is one thing you *shouldn't* do, and two things you should do:

+ **DON'T REBOOT YOUR COMPUTER.** This is particularly important advice with Vista because of the way it takes snapshots of "last known good" system configurations. If you get infected, reboot, and Vista mistakenly thinks your infected system is "good," it may update the "last known good" configuration information incorrectly. Resist the urge to press the Reset button until you exhaust all possibilities.

+ Follow your antivirus software manufacturer's instructions. If you threw away your copy of the manual, beg, borrow, or steal another PC and log on to the manufacturer's Web site. All the major antivirus software manufacturers have detailed steps on their Web sites to take you through the scary parts.

+ If you aren't running antivirus software, kick yourself. No, kick yourself twice. Then look in Book III, Chapter 5 and install the free-for-personal-use AVG Free antivirus package.

The days of self-diagnosing and manually removing viruses and other malware have long passed. Nowadays that's akin to do-it-yourself brain surgery. Rely on the professionals. Get help.

Don't Become Part of the Problem

Well-intentioned people want to warn their friends, neighbors, coworkers, and barbecue-station design consultants about all the latest threats. Unfortunately, they frequently compound the problem, adding to the unnecessary fear, uncertainty, and doubt that confronts every computer user.

Tell me whether you've heard any of these:

✦ A virus will hit your computer if you read any message that includes the phrase "Good Times" in the subject (that was a biggie in late 1994). Ditto for any of the following messages: "It Takes Guts to Say 'Jesus'," "Win a Holiday," "Help a poor dog win a holiday," "Join the Crew," "pool party," "A Moment of Silence," "an Internet flower for you," "a virtual card for you," "Valentine's Greetings," and so on.

✦ A deadly virus is on the Microsoft [or put your favorite company name here] home page. Don't go there or your system will die.

✦ If you have a file called [put a filename here] on your PC, it contains a virus. Delete it immediately!

They're all hoaxes — not a breath of truth in any of them.

The hoaxes hurt. Sometimes when real worms hit, so much e-mail traffic is generated from warning people to avoid the worm that the well-intentioned watchdogs do more damage than the worm itself! Strange but true.

Do yourself a favor. (Me, too.) If somebody sends you a message that sounds like the following examples, just delete it, eh?

✦ A horrible virus is on the loose that's going to bring down the Internet.

✦ Send a copy of this message to ten of your best friends, and for every copy that's forwarded, Bill Gates will give [pick your favorite charity] $10.

✦ Forward a copy of this message to ten of your friends, and put your name at the bottom of the list. In [pick a random amount of time] you will receive $10,000 in the mail, or your luck will change for the better. Your eyelids will fall off if you don't forward this message.

✦ Microsoft (Intel, McAfee, Norton, Compaq, whatever) says you need to download something, not download something, go to a specific place, avoid a specific place, and on and on.

If you think you've stumbled on the world's most important virus alert, via your uncle's sister-in-law's roommate's hairdresser's soon-to-be-ex-boyfriend (remember, he's the one who's a *really smart* computer guy, but kind of smelly?), count to ten twice and keep these three important points in mind:

✦ Chances are very good — I'd say, oh, 99.9999 percent or more — that you're looking at a half-baked hoax that's documented on Symantec's hoax page (www.symantec.com/avcenter/hoax.html) or McAfee's hoax page (http://vil.mcafee.com/hoax.asp). Check it out before you click the Forward button.

✦ If it's a real virus, all the major news agencies will carry reports that (even if they're inaccurate!) are far, far more reliable than anything you get through e-mail. Check out www.cnn.com, www.cnet.com, or your favorite news site before you go way off the deep end.

✦ If the Internet world is about to collapse, clogged with gazillions of e-mail worms, the worst possible way to notify friends and family is via e-mail. D'oh! Pick up the phone, walk over to the water cooler, or send out a carrier pigeon, and give your intended recipients a reliable Web address to check for updates. Betcha they've already heard about it anyway.

Try hard to be part of the solution, not part of the problem, okay? And if a friend forwards you a virus warning in an e-mail, do all of us a big favor. Shoot him a copy of the preceding bullet points, ask him to tape it to the side of his computer, and beg him to refer to it the next time he gets the forwarding urge.

Using Parental Controls

As a parent, I'll readily admit that I'm not a big fan of parental controls. Why? They don't work. Never have.

Yes, we all feel the need to protect our kids from inappropriate material on the Internet. No, we don't have the tools. We can log, we can snoop and spy, we can bob and weave, and maybe censor a little here and there. But protect? Don't fool yourself.

Microsoft would have you believe that Vista takes automated parental controls to a new level, but the reality falls far short. You set restrictions for an individual user account — presumably a standard account (see Book II, Chapter 2). Your child must log on with that account for the controls to take effect. Thus, at a minimum, all the other accounts on your computer must be password protected.

To set controls for a specific account, follow these steps:

1. **Choose Start⇨Control Panel.**

2. **Under the User Accounts and Family Safety icon, click the Set Up Parental Controls For Any User link.**

   Vista presents you with a list of all the accounts on the computer, (see Figure 1-5), warning you if any local administrator accounts don't have passwords, or if the master Administrator account (the one you typed when you first set up the computer — it's only used in emergencies) doesn't have a password.

3. **Set a password on all your administrator accounts, if need be, then click the account that you wish to restrict.**

   Vista responds with the User Controls dialog box shown in Figure 1-6.

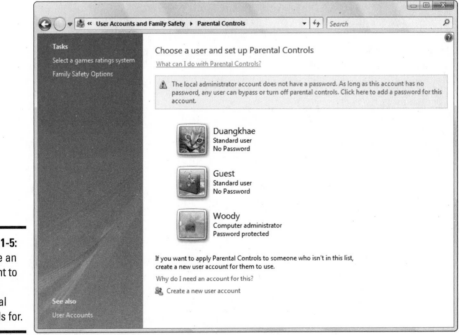

Figure 1-5:
Choose an account to set up parental controls for.

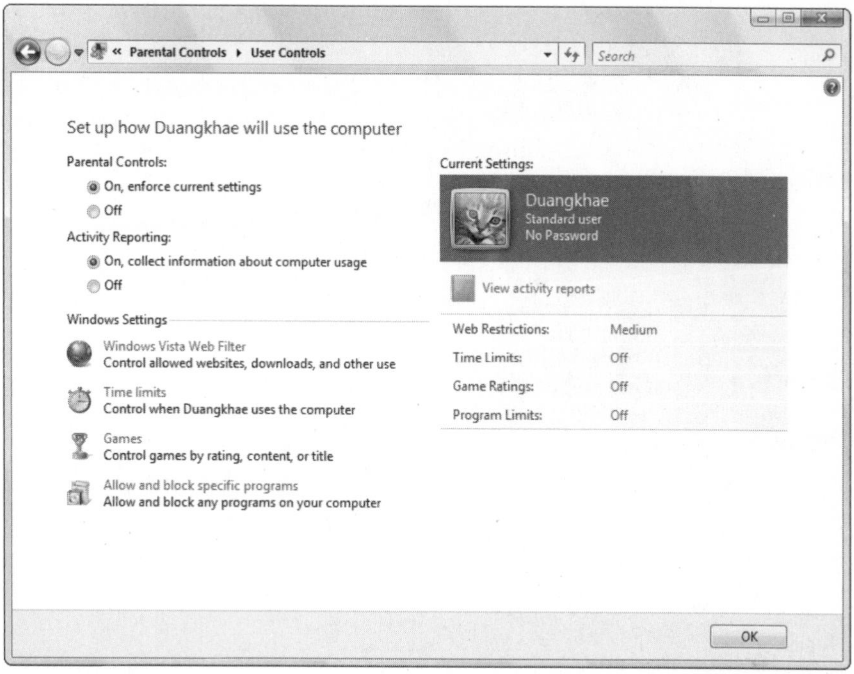

Figure 1-6:
Parental controls can be applied from this dialog box.

4. **If you wish to establish parental controls, start by clicking the On, Enforce Current Settings option.**

5. **To keep track of the account's activities, click the On, Collect Information about Computer Usage option.**

   With this option selected, Vista builds a detailed dossier on the account's usage, which you can view by clicking the View Activity Reports link (see Figure 1-7).

6. **To create white lists (or black lists) of sites the account can (or cannot) access, click the Windows Vista Web Filter link (see Figure 1-6).**

   This is where you can block all downloads.

   Be aware that this kind of blacklisting/whitelisting doesn't work well. Black lists — specifying which sites your child may *not* visit — can't cover more than a tiny fraction of all the objectionable sites on the Internet. White lists — where you choose which sites your child may visit — might be useful with very young children.

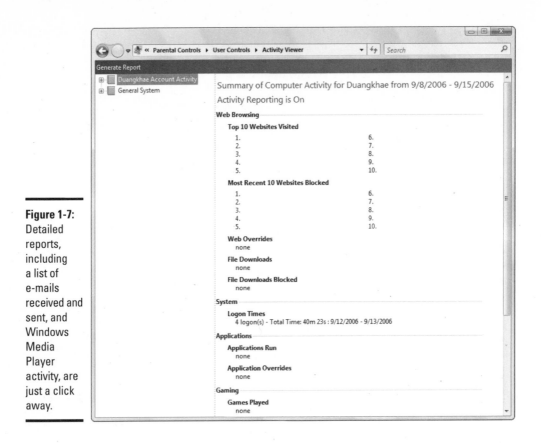

Figure 1-7:
Detailed reports, including a list of e-mails received and sent, and Windows Media Player activity, are just a click away.

7. **To control when your child can (and cannot) use the computer, click the Time Limits link.**

   Vista allows you to set the times that the account can be logged on to the computer (see Figure 1-8).

8. **To control access to certain games, click the Games icon.**

   Note that Vista can only control access to games that appear in the Start➪Games list.

9. **To allow or block certain programs of your choice, click the Allow and Block Specific Programs icon.**

   Vista scans your computer for all executable files in the `\Program Files` folder and disgorges them in a rather unintelligible, unintelligent heap, asking you to pick and choose the good ones — or the bad ones.

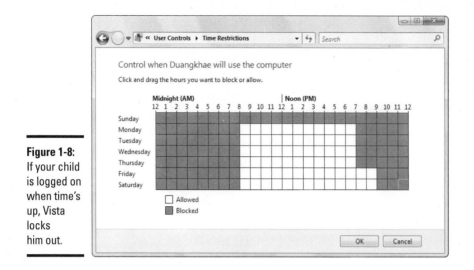

Figure 1-8:
If your child
is logged on
when time's
up, Vista
locks
him out.

So many holes exist in the way Vista "controls" user accounts that your child will, no doubt, find a way around the restrictions in no time — with two exceptions: Because your child has a standard account, it's very difficult for him to install new programs on your computer (a function of User Account Control, not parental controls; see Book III, Chapter 2). And, if you enable spying, er, activity reporting, you can produce a very detailed list of all his activities.

**Book III
Chapter 1**

**Lock Down:
Spies, Spams,
Scams, and Slams**

Chapter 2: Security Center Overview

In This Chapter

✔ **Navigating the Security Center**

✔ **Keeping the bad guys out**

✔ **Running a rootkit scan independently of the Security Center**

✔ **Knowing whether you really need Windows Live OneCare**

In theory, Vista's Security Center offers one-stop shopping for all your security needs. In practice, it's a short stop indeed — and taking control of security settings that aren't accessible through the Security Center can be quite a headache.

In this chapter, I take you through a brief overview of the Windows Security Center — more details follow in the next few chapters.

I also show you how to run a free rootkit scanner. Rootkits don't get the attention they deserve in the Security Center spotlight. You should go the extra mile and make sure your PC hasn't been subverted.

Entering the Security Center

If you go out looking for it, Vista's Security Center sits buried in an obscure corner of the Windows infrastructure. But the Security "shield" sits up front and center. The easiest way to get to it: click the wedge next to the clock in the lower-right corner of the screen. If you see an icon that looks like a shield, that's the Security Center's avatar.

The color of the icon reflects the current status of the Security Center:

✦ **Green** means that you conform to Microsoft's expectations — and that's not necessarily a good thing. See Book III, Chapter 4 for my take on why you should never allow Microsoft to automatically update your computer, and why you should therefore never allow your shield to go green.

✦ **Yellow** means that the Security Center wants your attention. If the shield is yellow only because you've turned off automatic updates, or because you refuse to download and install a security patch that's known to have problems, good for you. Wear the yellow shield like a badge of courage. If it's yellow because you messed up some other setting, you should take a look.

✦ **Red** means that something is wrong, and you need to check it quickly.

If the Security Center shield icon appears down near the Vista clock, you can open the Security Center by double-clicking the icon. If you can't see or find the shield, here's how to make the Security Center show itself:

1. **Choose Start➪Control Panel.**

2. **Click the Security icon — the one shaped like a big shield.**

3. **At the top, click the Security Center shield once again.**

The Windows Security Center appears (see Figure 2-1).

Figure 2-1:
Vista's Security Center gives you a snapshot of your system's protection settings, seen through Microsoft's rosy glasses.

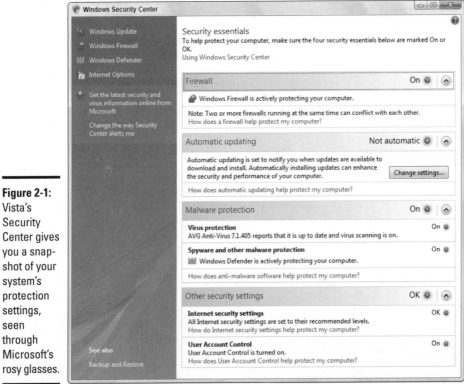

Working with the Security Center

The Security Center itself (see Figure 2-1) consolidates a wide range of settings from many different parts of Windows — indeed, from places outside of Windows — all in one place:

✦ **Firewall:** Blocks access to your computer from the Internet, and vice versa. I talk about Windows Firewall at length in Book III, Chapter 3.

A *firewall* is a program that insulates your PC (or network) from the Internet. At its heart, Vista's *inbound firewall* keeps track of requests that originate on your PC or network. When data from the Internet tries to make its way into your PC or network, the firewall checks to make sure that one of your programs requested the data. Unsolicited data gets dropped. Requested data comes through. That way, rogues on the Internet can't break in.

Vista also has an *outbound firewall,* which is buried so deep that you won't be able to find it without a guidebook. (See Book III, Chapter 3 for details.) The outbound firewall tells you when your computer sends out suspicious data, whether that data comes from a keylogger running on your machine or a naughty piece of Microsoft software surreptitiously phoning home. (Don't get me started about Microsoft's Windows Genuine Advantage spyware.) The Firewall line in the Security Center will say "On" and glow green even if you don't have outbound firewall protection.

For most individual users, Vista's outbound firewall rates as utterly useless. If you need notification about outbound traffic, use ZoneAlarm (free from www.zonelabs.com).

✦ **Automatic updating:** Allows Windows to phone home and check for patches and patches to patches of patches. If you trust Microsoft (heh heh heh), you can even allow Windows to patch itself. Kinda like getting a license for self-administered lobotomies. See Book III, Chapter 4 for more about Automatic Updates.

Fair warning: I firmly believe that automatic updating is for chumps. Read all about it in Book III, Chapter 4.

✦ **Malware protection** comes in two very different parts:

  • **Virus protection** is supposed to tell you whether you have a functional antivirus (AV) program, such as AVG Free, Norton, McAfee, Trend Micro PC-Cillin, and so on. Unfortunately, this notification doesn't work all the time. See Book III, Chapter 5 for more about virus protection.

- **Spyware and other malware protection** similarly looks at your computer and tries to determine whether you have spyware/scumware detection and blocking in force. Of course, Microsoft's Windows Defender appears here — it's built into Vista itself. But you may find Defender's blind spots infuriating. See Book III, Chapter 5 for details.

✦ **Other security settings** are also very Microsoft-centric:

- **Internet security settings** only refer to your security settings in Internet Explorer. As of this writing, at any rate, the Windows Security Center doesn't tell you squat about any other browsers.

- **User Account Control** refers to the $#@! tendency on Vista's part to put dialog boxes like the one shown in Figure 2-2 on the screen. I explain how to cut UAC off at the knees at the end of Book II, Chapter 2.

Figure 2-2:
User
Account
Control
pesters
you with
questions
like this.

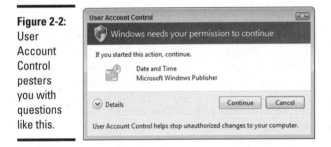

All four of these major settings (and two minor ones) focus on preventing bad stuff outside your PC from getting inside — a noble goal, to be sure, but the baddies that lurk outside of your box are only part of the problem. The other part? You.

To get — and keep — your security and sanity in Vista, you must understand how your PC can be attacked, and what you can do to forestall those attacks, both from a computer point of view and by thinking "outside the box." (That's the theme of Book III, Chapter 1.)

Scanning for Rootkits

Rootkits represent the way of the future for malware: there's a lot of money to be made subverting PCs and turning them into botnets (see Book III, Chapter 1). That's why, in addition to working with the Vista Security

You should make sure that your PC hasn't been subverted already, that you haven't accidentally been turned into a zombie, and that you aren't surreptitiously sending confidential data to that odd-but-nice fellow with a funny accent in Kazbukistan.

The world of rootkits changes by the hour, so any recommendation I make now will be obsolete by the time the ink dries on this book. I suggest that you use Google to search for "free rootkit detection" and download and install a free rootkit detector from a company whose name you recognize.

At this moment, my favorite rootkit detector comes from the antivirus software manufacturer F-Secure. I used to recommend AVG Anti-Rootkit Free, except it, uh, isn't free any more.

Rootkits constitute a major threat to Windows XP users. (In fact, they're probably the greatest single threat to typical WinXP folks.) They're becoming more popular on Vista, but the percentage of Vista machines subverted by rootkits is far, far smaller than their WinXP brethren. Why? It's comparatively much simpler to write and maintain rootkits that target Windows XP. Rootkit writers are in the game for the bucks. It's much easier to pluck off the low-hanging Windows XP fruit. Some day that will change, but for now, Vista users should run an anti-rootkit scan every month or so. Don't lose any sleep over it.

Here's how to run the beta test version of F-Secure BlackLight:

1. **Start your favorite Web browser and go to `www.f-secure.com/security_center`.**

   F-Secure's Security Center lists several scanners, news reports, and the like.

2. **At the bottom of the page, under downloads, click BlackLight.**

   Your browser offers to save a file called `FSBL.EXE`.

3. **Save the F-Secure BlackLight file `FSBL.EXE` on your desktop or someplace where you can find it easily.**

   BlackLight is a simple executable program. It doesn't install anything or hook into your system. It doesn't appear on your Start menu or in the Quick Launch Toolbar, so you want it to be close at hand.

4. **Double-click the `FSBL.EXE` icon.**

   After you click through the inevitable User Account Control dialog box, you see the License Terms box, as in Figure 2-3.

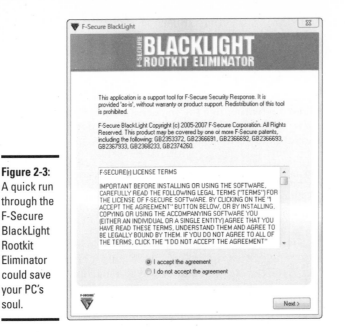

Figure 2-3:
A quick run
through the
F-Secure
BlackLight
Rootkit
Eliminator
could save
your PC's
soul.

5. **Select the I Accept the Agreement radio. Then click Next.**

BlackLight offers to scan your computer, as in Figure 2-4.

Do you need Windows Live OneCare?

"Help get confidence and peace of mind with round-the-clock protection and maintenance — virus scanning, firewalls, tune-ups, file backups, the whole nine yards." That's what the Windows Live OneCare come-on page says.

Wait a sec. Vista *has* a firewall — a two-way firewall (inbound and outbound), if you know where to look. Several great, free-for-private-use antivirus programs are available, including AVG Free (which I discuss in Book III, Chapter 5). Vista already has a backup system — one that's quite capable, as long as you didn't get stuck with Vista Home Basic. Tune-ups? Show me one that delivers speed gains I can feel. Ha. Not sure where I can buy a whole nine yards, but maybe eBay could help. . . .

So what do you get for $49.95? (That's the price for one year of OneCare, working up to three computers.) Do you get faster fixes for bugs in Vista or Office? Nope. If Microsoft started shuffling out fixes faster than the other antivirus companies, the antitrust lawyers would have a field day. Do you get a direct line to a tech-support rep who can help you when Vista freezes? Yeah, right. Maybe a fashionable multicolored key ring?

I, for one, resent the idea that Microsoft charges to fix flaws in its own products. And I find it even more infuriating that Microsoft would charge for features that should be completely functional in Vista anyway. Chutzpah, pure and simple. Tell Live OneCare to take a hike.

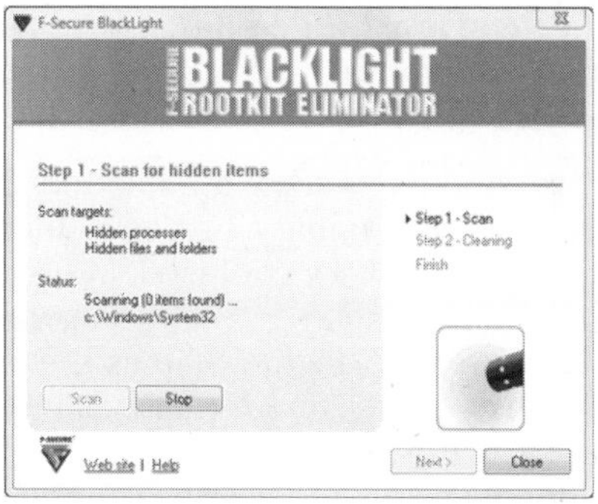

Figure 2-4:
F-Secure
BlackLight
has
essentially
no options.

6. **Click the Scan button.**

F-Secure BlackLight uses a very sophisticated (and closely guarded!) method to scan your computer and see whether there are discrepancies between the programs that say they are running and what's actually happening on your PC.

The scan can take several minutes. When it's done, BlackLight tells you if it has found any hidden items.

7. **If BlackLight reports No Hidden Items Found, click Close.**

You're done.

8. **If BlackLight reports that it has found hidden items, click Next.**

BlackLight shows you a list of hidden items and allows you to rename them. (Figure 2-5 is an example from the F-Secure site.)

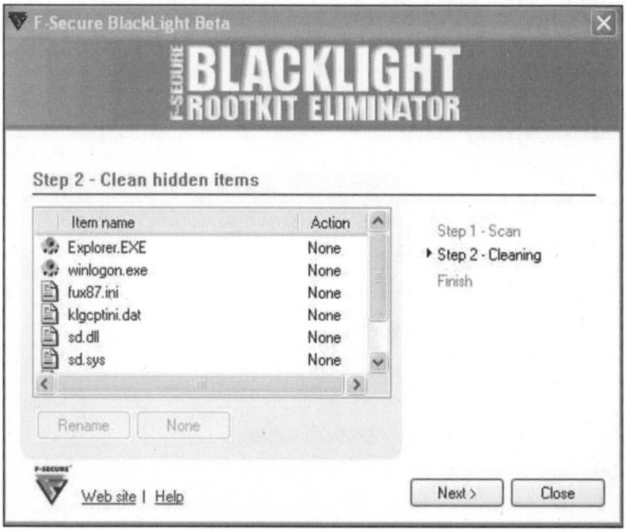

Figure 2-5:
F-Secure
BlackLight
cleans
hidden
items by
renaming
them and
making
them visible.

9. **Before you start trying to clean any hidden items — potential rootkits — make sure you read and understand the instructions at** `www.f-secure.com/security_center/blacklight_help.html`.

   Not all hidden programs are rootkits — some applications hide specific programs for very good reasons. Renaming a benign hidden process can make the offending application very, very confused. More than that, if you rename a key system file (such as `explorer.exe`), Vista itself can get very, very confused. F-Secure BlackLight renames the programs so they won't be loaded when Vista starts, and it renames files and folders so the rootkit can't find them. If the programs aren't loaded, they aren't "cloaked" and you will suddenly be able to see the programs, files and folders.

   In the example in Figure 2-5, a rootkit is hiding two bonafide Windows files, `explorer.exe` and `winlogon.exe`. You want to expose the rootkit, not crash the system. Renaming either of those files could have disastrous effect on your PC's health.

10. **If you aren't sure whether you should rename a specific program, folder, or file, locate your FSBL log file. It's in the same folder as the FSBL.EXE program, with a name like fsblxxxxxxxx.log; see Figure 2-6. Go to the Public Security Newsgroup,** `groups.google.com/ group/microsoft.public.security.virus/topics`, **and see if someone on the group can help.**

    Note that F-Secure does not provide technical support.

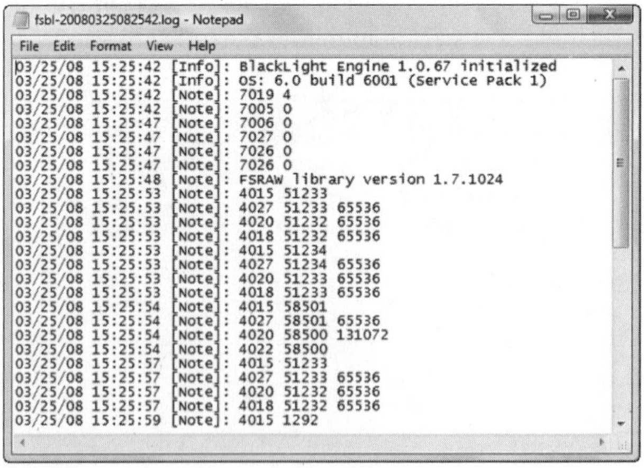

Figure 2-6: An F-Secure BlackLight log file.

Chapter 3: Windows Firewall Backward and Forward

In This Chapter

✔ Discovering what Windows Firewall can — and can't — do

✔ Knowing when Windows Firewall causes problems — and how to get around them

✔ Struggling with the bare-bones outbound Windows Firewall

✔ Making Windows Firewall work the way you want

A *firewall* is a program that sits between your computer and the Internet, protecting you from the big, mean, nasty gorillas riding around on the Information Highway. An *inbound* firewall acts like a traffic cop that, in the best of all possible worlds, only allows "good" stuff into your computer and keeps all the "bad" stuff out on the Internet where it belongs. An *outbound* firewall prevents your computer from sending bad stuff to the Internet, like when your computer gets infected with a virus or has another security problem.

Vista includes a usable (if not fancy) inbound firewall. It also includes a snarly, hard-to-configure, rudimentary outbound firewall, which has all the social graces of a junkyard dog. Unless you know the magic incantations, you'll never even see the outbound firewall — it's completely muzzled until you dig into the Vista doghouse and teach it some tricks.

Everybody needs an inbound firewall, without any doubt. Outbound firewalls are useful, but they can be very hard to understand and maintain. If you figure that you need an outbound firewall, try to use Vista's and when you (inevitably) throw your hands up in disgust, take a look at Microsoft's competitors. This chapter should help you through the minefield.

Comparing Firewalls

Vista's inbound firewall works reasonably well. It lacks many of the fancy features that you can find in competing firewalls, but for most folks, it's good enough.

On the other hand, Vista's outbound firewall doesn't hold a candle to any of the commercially available firewalls. These points explain why:

✦ Competitive firewalls come with a built-in passel of outbound default settings that help you get started without being tripped up by the most common outbound traffic. By contrast, Vista's outbound firewall has exactly zero built-in settings.

✦ You can "train" competitive firewalls by having them watch outbound traffic and then ask you to block or allow specific programs. The firewall remembers your responses and, over time, reduces its level of intrusiveness. Vista's outbound firewall, on the other hand, doesn't ask, doesn't learn, and doesn't care. If you've told Vista to block something in particular, it won't get out of your PC; if you haven't told Vista to block something, it goes through.

✦ Competitors attempt to put a decent interface on their firewalls: The buttons and menus may be overly cute or convoluted, but at least they try to organize the outbound settings in a reasonable fashion. As you can see in the section "Coping with Vista's Outbound Firewall" later in this chapter, Microsoft has done almost nothing to make Vista's outbound firewall easy to use. Quite the contrary. The inbound and outbound firewalls look like they came from two different planets. Which they did.

Microsoft says it disabled Vista's outbound firewall because corporate customers demanded it. That seems mighty disingenuous to me because companies running Active Directory pull all the strings on their users' desktops anyway. I think Microsoft had many reasons for making the outbound firewall so infernally hard to use, not the least of which is the fact that enforcing almost any kind of outbound firewall would've driven Microsoft's support demands through the roof.

Hardware firewalls

Most modern routers and wireless access points include significant firewalling capability. If you have a choice between connecting your computer directly to a "cable modem" (typically via a USB port) and going through a router (typically using a local-area network [LAN] connection or a wireless connection), choose the latter.

Routers and wireless access points add an extra step between your computer and the Internet. That extra jump — called Network Address Translation — combined with innate intelligence on the router's part can provide an extra layer of protection that works independently from, but in conjunction with, the firewall running on your PC.

If you find yourself spending too much time fighting Vista's firewall, consider shelling out the bucks for a top-notch firewall such as ZoneAlarm (www.zonelabs.com), Norton Personal Firewall (www.symantec.com), Trend Micro's PC-cillin Internet Security (www.trendmicro.com), and so on. Run a Google search on "firewall reviews" for the latest features and price comparisons.

Understanding Vista Firewall's Basic Features

All versions of Vista ship with a decent, capable — but not foolproof — stateful firewall called *Windows Firewall (WF)* (see the nearby sidebar, "What's a stateful firewall?"). WF's basic characteristics are as follows:

✦ **WF's inbound firewall is on by default.**

✦ **Unless you change something, Windows Firewall is turned on for all the connections on your PC.** So, for example, if you have a LAN network cable, a wireless networking card, and a modem on a specific PC, WF is turned on for all of them. The only way Windows Firewall gets turned off is if you deliberately turn it off, or if the network administrator on your Big Corporate Network decides to disable it by remote control, or install Windows service packs with Windows Firewall turned off (which may be a good choice, in some cases).

✦ **WF settings for inbound protection can be changed relatively easily.** When you make changes, they apply to all the connections on your PC.

✦ **On the other hand, WF settings for outbound protection make the rules of cricket look like child's play.**

✦ **WF kicks in before the computer is connected to the network.** Back in the not-so-good old days, a lot of PCs got infected between the time they were connected and when the firewall came up.

✦ **WF has an inbound "lockdown" mode.** By selecting one fairly easy-to-find Block All Incoming Connections check box (see Figure 3-1), you can lock down your computer so that it only accepts incoming data that has been explicitly requested by programs running on your computer. Any attempt by outside programs to communicate with your computer gets rebuffed. (I show you how to find this check box in the section, "Starting, Stopping, and Goosing Inbound WF," later in this chapter.)

In practice, that means you can use Internet Explorer to look at Web sites, and you can send and receive e-mail and use instant messengers, as well as using printers and folders on your local network if you have one, but most other online functions are locked out. For example, if you use the Internet to play games with other folks who are online, or if you connect to your computer at work, locking down your PC prevents you from connecting. A lockdown even shuts down any connection to other computers or printers (or other shared devices) on the network. That's great if you're connecting in an airport and don't want other travelers to get at your Shared Documents folder. But it's a real pain in the neck in your home or office.

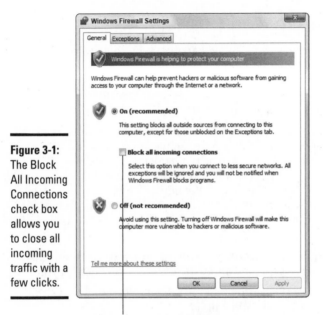

Figure 3-1:
The Block All Incoming Connections check box allows you to close all incoming traffic with a few clicks.

Check this box and click OK
to shut down all incoming traffic

If you hear about a new worm making the rounds, you can easily lock down your computer for a day or two and then go back to normal operation when the worm stops ping-ponging over the Internet. You might need to deselect the Block All Incoming Connections check box long enough to print on a shared printer or to get at some data on your network, but you'll be essentially impenetrable whenever the Block All Incoming Connections check box is selected. If you're connecting to a strange network (say, using a wireless connection at a coffee shop or in a hotel), you can lock down while logged on and sip your latte with confidence.

What's a stateful firewall?

At the risk of oversimplifying a bit, a *stateful firewall* refers to an inbound firewall that remembers. A stateful firewall keeps track of packets of information coming out of your computer and where they're headed. When a packet arrives and tries to get in, the inbound firewall matches the originating address of the incoming packet against the log of addresses of the outgoing packets to make sure that any packet allowed through the firewall comes from an expected location.

Stateful packet filtering isn't 100 percent foolproof. And you must have some exceptions so that unexpected packets can come through for reasons discussed elsewhere in this chapter. But it's a very fast, reliable way to minimize your exposure to potentially destructive packets.

Speaking Your Firewall's Lingo

At this point, I need to inundate you with a bunch of jargon so that you can take control of Windows Firewall. Hold your nose and dive in. The concepts aren't that difficult, although the lousy terminology sounds like it was invented by a first-year advertising student. Refer to this section if you get bewildered when wading through the WF dialog boxes.

As you no doubt realize, the amount of data that can be sent from one computer to another over a network can be tiny or it can be huge. Computers communicate with each other by breaking the data into *packets* — small chunks of data with a wrapper that identifies where the data came from and where it's going.

On the Internet, packets can be sent two different ways:

✦ **UDP** (User Datagram Protocol) is fast and sloppy. The computer sending the packets doesn't keep track of which packets were sent, and the computer receiving the packets doesn't make any attempt to get the sender to resend packets that vanish mysteriously into the bowels of the Internet. UDP is the kind of *protocol* (transmission method) that can work with live broadcasts, where short gaps wouldn't be nearly as disruptive as long pauses, while the computers wait to resend a dropped packet.

✦ **TCP** (Transmission Control Protocol) is methodical and complete. The sending computer keeps track of which packets it's sent. If the receiving computer doesn't get a packet, it notifies the sending computer, which resends the packet. Almost all communication over the Internet these days goes via TCP.

Book III
Chapter 3

Windows Firewall Backward and Forward

Every computer on a network has an *IP address*. The IP address is a collection of four sets of numbers, each between 0 and 255. For example, 192.168.1.2 is a common IP address for computers connected to a local network; the computer that handles the Dummies.com Web site is at 208.215.179.139. I tend to think of the IP address as analogous to a telephone number.

Peeking into Your Firewall

When you add a firewall — and you should — you change the way your computer communicates with other computers on the Internet. This section explains what Windows Firewall is doing behind the scenes so that when it gets in the way, you understand how to tweak it. (You find the ins and outs of working around the firewall in the section, "Making Inbound Exceptions," later in this chapter.)

When two computers communicate, they not only need each other's IP address but they also need a specific entry point called a *port* — I think of it as a telephone extension number — to talk to each other. For example, most Web sites respond to requests sent to port 80. There's nothing magical about the number 80: It's just the port number that people have agreed to use when trying to get onto a Web site's computer. If your Web browser wants to look at the Dummies.com Web site, it'll send a packet to 208.215.179.139, port 80.

Windows Firewall works by handling all these duties simultaneously:

✦ It keeps track of outgoing packets and allows incoming packets to go through the firewall if they can be matched with an outgoing packet. (In other words, WF works as a stateful inbound firewall.)

✦ If your computer is attached to a "private" network, Windows Firewall allows packets to come and go on ports 139 and 445, but only if they came from another computer on your local network and only if they're using TCP. Windows Firewall needs to open those ports for file and printer sharing. (See the next section of this chapter for the details about different network types.)

✦ Similarly, if you're attached to a "private" network, Windows Firewall automatically opens ports 137 and 138 for UDP, but only for packets that originate on your local network.

✦ If you've specifically told Windows Firewall that you want it to allow packets to come in on a specific port and the Block All Incoming Connections check box isn't selected, WF follows your orders. You might need to open a port in this way for online gaming, for example.

✦ Windows Firewall allows packets to come into your computer if they're sent to the Remote Assistance program (unless the Block All Incoming Connections check box is selected), providing that you created a Remote Assistance request on this PC and told Vista to open your firewall (see Book II, Chapter 5). Remote Assistance allows other users to take control of your PC, but it has its own security settings and strong password protection. Still, it's a known security hole that's enabled when you create a request.

✦ You can tell Windows Firewall to accept packets that are directed at specific programs. Usually, any company that makes a program designed to listen for incoming Internet traffic (Skype being a prime example, as are any instant messaging programs) adds its program to the list of designated exceptions when the program gets installed.

✦ Unless an inbound packet meets one of the preceding criteria, it's simply ignored. Windows Firewall swallows it without a peep. Conversely, unless you've changed something, any and all outbound traffic goes through unobstructed.

Using Public and Private Networks

Vista helps simplify things a bit by providing three different collections of security settings — actually, inbound Windows Firewall settings — each identified with a prototypical type of network:

✦ **Private networks** include peer-to-peer "workgroup" networks that are under your control, such as the kind you might set up following the instructions in Book IX, Chapter 2. You can let your hair down a little bit when you're on a private network. When you connect to a new network, if you tell Vista that it's a private network, Vista opens your computer so that others on the network can see it.

✦ **Public networks** include networks that you don't control — airports, Internet cafes, hotels — where a very real chance exists that somebody else connected to the network could go snooping, or may try to shove infected files into your Public folder. When you connect to a new network, if you tell Vista that it's a private network, Vista knows that it shouldn't make your PC visible on the network.

✦ **Domain networks** are Big Corporate Networks — client/server "domains." If you take your laptop to the office and plug it in to a Big Corporate Network, Vista recognizes the fact and automatically puts in place all the security that comes along for the ride. Unlike private and public networks, you don't get to tell Vista which kind of network you're using when you connect into a domain.

**Book III
Chapter 3**

**Windows Firewall
Backward and
Forward**

Establishing a network type

Each connection that you make gets associated with one of the three kinds of network: private, public, or domain. Say you have a laptop with a wireless connection. You follow the instructions in Book IX, Chapter 3 to set up a network at home called SeaBreeze. You also schlep the laptop to your friendly local Sandwich Shoppe and the Microsoft Bob Memorial Airport, and you take it to work. Vista identifies each of those four connections as public, private, or a domain network. Here's how:

✦ When you first make a connection to your home network, Vista asks you what kind of network SeaBreeze might be. You tell Vista that SeaBreeze is a private network in your Home (see Figure 3-2). That way, Vista allows other computers on the network to "see" your computer.

✦ You take your laptop to the Sandwich Shoppe and connect to the wireless network there. Vista asks whether this is a private or public network, and you respond by saying "Public."

✦ Similarly, you take the laptop to Patong Airport and connect to the network there. Vista asks whether this is a private or public network, and you respond by saying "Public."

✦ Then you take your laptop to work and connect to your company's Big Corporate Network. This time, you may not have to tell Vista anything — it knows that you're on a domain, and all the security settings that the network admin has established get pushed onto the PC. If there's any doubt, Vista asks, and you tell it you're at Work.

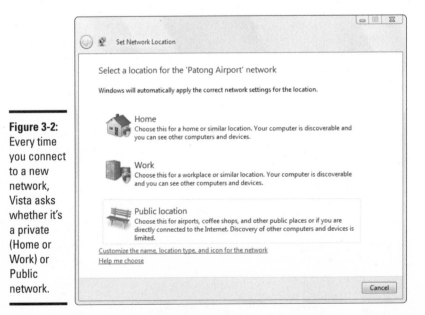

Figure 3-2: Every time you connect to a new network, Vista asks whether it's a private (Home or Work) or Public network.

Each connection has its own Windows Firewall settings. By telling Vista whether a connection is private or public, you're actually telling Vista which bunch of Firewall settings to use initially.

When you first tell Vista that a wireless network is private, it applies the "private" firewall settings to the connection. When you tell Vista that a network is public, it applies the "public" settings. After those initial settings are in place, you can modify specific Windows Firewall settings for that connection.

Changing network types

You can change a network from public to private, or vice versa. To do so, follow these steps:

1. **Connect to the network that you want to change.**

For example, if you want to change your laptop's connection on your home SeaBreeze network from private to public, run back home and connect to the SeaBreeze network.

2. **Choose Start⇨Control Panel. Under the Network and Internet heading, click the View Network Status and Tasks link.**

Vista opens the Network and Sharing Center shown in Figure 3-3.

**Book III
Chapter 3**

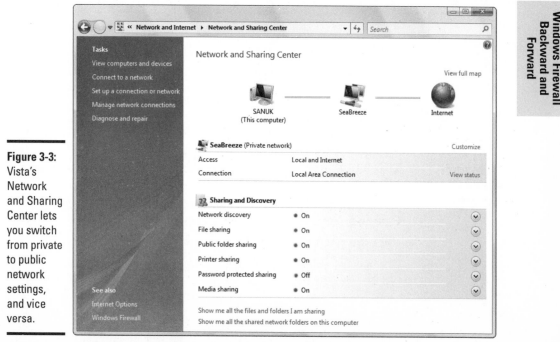

Figure 3-3: Vista's Network and Sharing Center lets you switch from private to public network settings, and vice versa.

**Windows Firewall
Backward and
Forward**

3. **If you want to change a private network to a public network (in other words, if you want to apply the more-stringent "public" firewall settings to this connection), click the Customize link to the right of the Private Network line.**

Vista opens the Personalize Settings for Network dialog box shown in Figure 3-4.

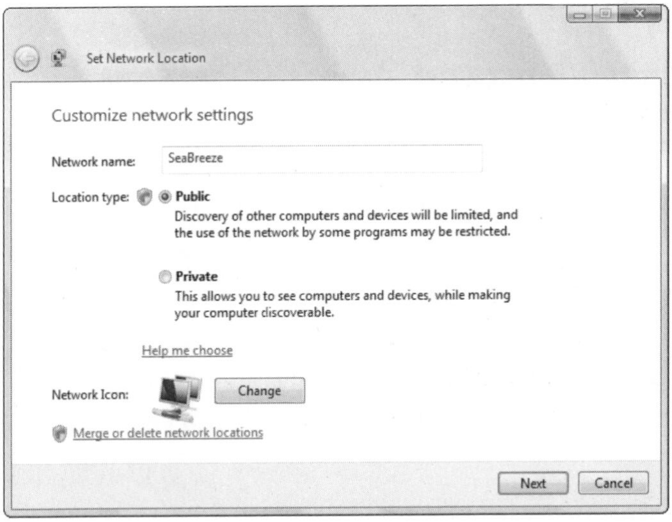

Figure 3-4: Make the switch to public here.

Set Network Location

Customize network settings

Network name: SeaBreeze

Location type: ● **Public**
Discovery of other computers and devices will be limited, and the use of the network by some programs may be restricted.

○ **Private**
This allows you to see computers and devices, while making your computer discoverable.

Help me choose

Network Icon: Change

Merge or delete network locations

Next   Cancel

4. **Choose either Public or Private.**

Remember that Public is more restricted than Private. The terminology can be a bit confusing.

5. **Click OK.**

You may have to click through a User Access Control security dialog box, but in the end, Vista changes the category to Public.

Vista advises you that it has successfully set your network settings. Click Close.

You see the new Network and Sharing Center settings, as shown in Figure 3-5. Note how Network Discovery, in particular, has been turned off.

6. **Click the red *X* to exit the Network and Sharing Center.**

The new firewall settings take effect immediately.

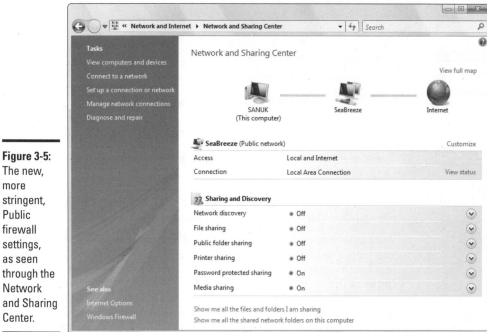

Figure 3-5:
The new,
more
stringent,
Public
firewall
settings,
as seen
through the
Network
and Sharing
Center.

Changing individual network settings

You can modify Windows Firewall settings for each connection by using the Network and Sharing Center.

I step through my recommended settings in Book II, Chapter 1, but you can modify how much you want to share at any point.

Say, for example, that you want to allow people on your network to open files in your Public folder, providing that they can supply a user ID and password on your PC. Follow these steps to do that:

1. **Connect to the network that you want to change.**

2. **Choose Start⇨Control Panel. Under the Network and Internet heading, click the View Network Status and Tasks link.**

   Vista shows you the Network and Sharing Center (refer to Figure 3-5).

3. **To the right of the Public Folder Sharing line, click the down arrow.**

   Vista expands the Sharing and Discovery pane to show you the Public Folder options (see Figure 3-6).

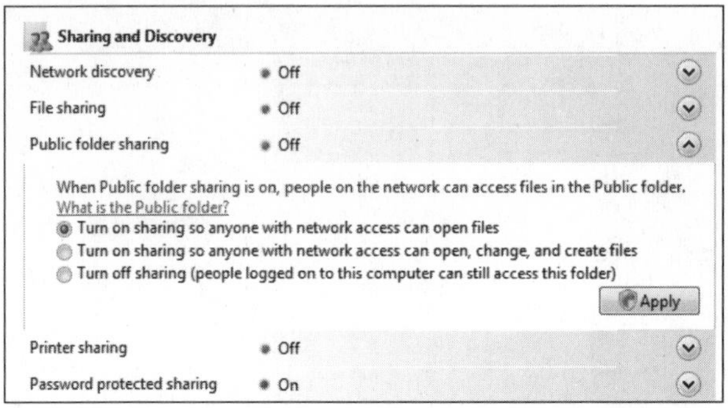

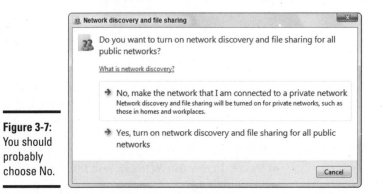

Figure 3-6: Allow read-only access to the Public folder with this setting.

4. **Click the Turn On Sharing so Anyone with Network Access Can Open Files option. Then click the Apply button.**

   Vista makes you click through a security dialog box and then presents you with a difficult choice (see Figure 3-7). Sharing the Public folder requires Vista to make the computer available on the network — so Network Discovery has to be turned on. But in this case, you're working with a public connection, and public connections don't do Discovery. So you have to decide whether you want to change the Public firewall settings so that *every* public connection allows Discovery and Sharing, or whether you want to change this particular connection into a private connection, which would automatically enable Discovery and Sharing on this connection? You probably want the latter.

Figure 3-7: You should probably choose No.

5. **Click the No, Make the Network That I Am Connected to a Private Network link. Then click the red *X* to exit the Network Discovery and File Sharing dialog box.**

   The changes take place immediately.

Starting, Stopping, and Goosing Inbound WF

You may want to twiddle Windows Firewall on, off, or otherwise for any number of reasons. The inbound Windows Firewall is on by default, but if it gets turned off, the little Windows Security Alert icon in the System Notification area (next to the clock in the lower-right corner of your screen) should start pestering you relentlessly with "Windows Firewall is turned off" warnings.

It doesn't hurt to periodically check and be sure that your firewall is working by following these steps:

1. **Choose Start⇨Control Panel⇨Security, and under the Security Center icon, click the Check Firewall Status link.**

You have to click through a security dialog box. Then the Windows Firewall Settings dialog box appears with the General tab showing (refer to Figure 3-1).

2. **Following the recommendations in Table 3-1, choose the setting you need.**

3. **Click OK, and then click the red *X* to exit the Security Center window.**

When you change the type of network from public to private and back, using the method in the preceding section, Vista changes entries in the Exceptions table. It does not, in effect, select the Block All Incoming Connections check box, because even with a public network, some firewalled communication usually takes place. If you want to lock down your inbound firewall and cut off *all* traffic through the firewall, you have to open the Windows Firewall Settings dialog box and select the Block All Incoming Connections check box.

**Book III
Chapter 3**

**Windows Firewall
Backward and
Forward**

Table 3-1	Windows Firewall General Settings	
Setting	*Means*	*Recommendation*
On (Recommended)	Allow incoming packets that conform to the "stateful" criteria, plus any specified on the Exceptions tab.	Use this setting except when you're very concerned about locking down your machine.
Block All Incoming Connections	Only allow packets that conform to the "stateful" criteria.	Use this setting to lock down your connection. Other people on the network can't get into your machine, but you can't use printers or shared files on the "foreign" network, either.
Off (Not Recommended)	Allow all incoming packets.	If you absolutely have to get your computer talking to another computer, you may be forced to use this setting. But if you do, be very mindful of the fact that you've let your guard down completely — and turn Windows Firewall back on the moment you can.

When you install a third-party firewall, it usually asks for permission to disable the Windows Firewall. Running two firewalls at once is very tricky. I suggest you choose just one firewall and stick with it.

Making Inbound Exceptions

Firewalls can be absolutely infuriating. You may have a program that's worked for a hundred years on all sorts of computers, but the minute you install it on a Vista machine with Windows Firewall in action, it just stops working, for absolutely no apparent reason.

You can get mad at Microsoft and scream at Windows Firewall, but when you do, realize that at least part of the problem lies in the way the firewall *has* to work. (See the section "Peeking into Your Firewall," earlier in this chapter, for an explanation of what your firewall does behind the scenes.) It has to block packets that are trying to get in, unless you explicitly tell the firewall to allow them to get in. And — perhaps most infuriatingly — WF has to block those packets by simply swallowing them, not notifying the computer that sent the packet. Windows Firewall has to remain "stealthy" because if it sends back a packet that says, "Hey, I got your packet but I can't let it through," the bad guys get an acknowledgment that your computer exists, they probably can figure out which firewall you're using, and they may be able to combine these two pieces of information to give you a headache. It's far better for Windows Firewall to act like a black hole.

How do you know when you need a port?

Most first-time firewallers are overwhelmed by the idea of opening a port. Although you need to treat ports with care — an open port is a security threat, no matter how you look at it — sometimes you really need to open one. How do you know when you absolutely have to open a port? Usually, you get a phone call like this:

"Dude. My game won't hook up with your game. You got a firewall or somethin'?"

"Uh, yeah. I'm running Windows Firewall."

"Pshaw, man. You want to play Frumious Bandersnatch, you gotta open ports 418, 419, 420, an' 421."

"Does Frumious use UDP or TCP?"

"What's TeeCeePee, some kinda disease? I dunno, man. I just read in the instruction book that ya gotta have 418, 419, 420, an' 421 open. Doncha ever read the manual, dude?"

At that point, you guess that Frumious Bandersnatch uses TCP (that's the most common choice), you run through the Security Center to liberate the four ports, and you have the game working in 30 seconds flat.

You can tell WF to let packets through according to three separate criteria (see Figure 3-8):

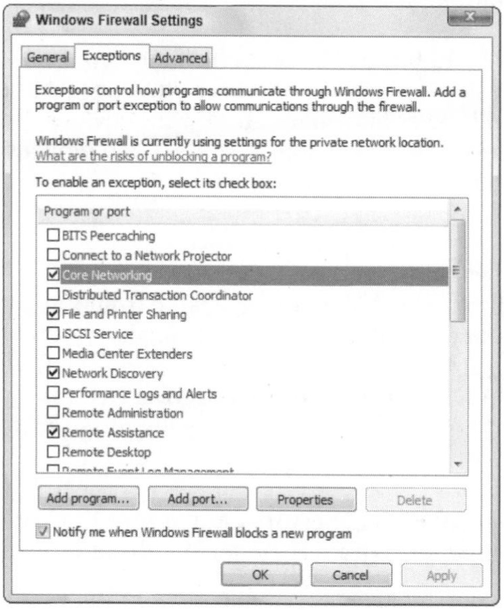

Figure 3-8:
Tell
Windows
Firewall to
allow spe-
cific kinds of
packets into
your PC by
using the
Exceptions
tab.

- ✦ You'll find a list of more than a dozen predefined "services" that you can allow or disallow — for example, File and Printer Sharing, Remote Assistance, Remote Desktop, and the UPnP Framework. Many of these check boxes are selected automatically when you need them — for example, Vista selects the Remote Assistance check box when you create an Assistance request (see Book II, Chapter 5). You can manually select the corresponding check box on the Exceptions tab to allow a service.

- ✦ You can tell WF to let through any TCP or UDP packets on a specific port by clicking the Add Port button (see the "Adding a port" section, later in this chapter). You type the port number, tell WF whether you want to allow TCP or UDP, and click OK, and Windows Firewall adds the port to the exceptions list.

- ✦ You can tell WF to let through any packet that's destined to a specific program by clicking the Add Program button (see the next section in this chapter). You pick the program and tell WF whether you want to allow communication from any address on the Internet, from specific addresses on the Internet, or only from your local network. Click OK, and the firewall allows packets destined for that specific program.

File and printer sharing works by opening ports 139 and 445 for TCP over the local network and by opening ports 137 and 138 for UDP on the local network. (See the section "Speaking Your Firewall's Lingo," earlier in this chapter, for an explanation of TCP and UDP.)

If you deselect the File and Printer Sharing check box on the Exceptions tab (refer to Figure 3-8), you keep other computers on your local network from getting at your shared folders and shared hardware devices. But you also keep your computer from getting at shared folders and devices on the network.

Adding a program

Some programs need to "listen" to incoming traffic from the Internet; they wait until they're contacted and then respond. Usually, you'll know whether you have such a program because the installer tells you that you need to tell your firewall to back off. If you want to tell Windows Firewall that it should let packets through if they're destined for a specific program, follow these steps:

1. **Choose Start⇨Control Panel⇨Security, and under the Windows Firewall icon, click the Allow a Program through Windows Firewall link.**

Click through a security box and you see the Windows Firewall Settings Exceptions tab (refer to Figure 3-8).

2. **Click the Add Program button.**

Windows Firewall displays the Add a Program dialog box, as shown in Figure 3-9.

Figure 3-9:
Choose the program that's the designated receiver for inbound packets.

> **Add a Program**
>
> Select the program you want to add, or click Browse to find one that is not listed, and then click OK.
>
> Programs:
>
> - InkBall
> - Internet Explorer
> - Mahjong Titans
> - Minesweeper
> - Mozilla Firefox
> - Problem Reports and Solutions
> - Purble Place
> - SnagIt 8
> - Solitaire
> - Spider Solitaire
> - Windows Calendar
>
> Path: C:\Windows\system32\wercon.exe   Browse...
>
> Change scope...   OK   Cancel

WARNING!

3. **Pick the program that's designated to receive unsolicited packets from the Internet.**

Realize that you're opening a potential, albeit small, security hole. The program you choose better be quite capable of handling packets from unknown sources.

4. **Click OK twice to go back to the Security window.**

Adding a port

Adding a port to the exceptions list is inherently less secure than adding a program. Why? Because the bad guys have a hard time guessing which programs you've left open — they have a whole lot of programs to choose from — but probing all the ports on a machine to see whether any of them let packets go through is comparatively easy.

Still, you may need to open a port to enable a specific application. When you select the check box to allow Remote Desktop, for example, you're opening port 3389. That's the security price you pay for enabling programs to talk to each other.

Follow these steps to open a port:

1. **Choose Start➪Control Panel➪Security, and under the Windows Firewall icon, click the Allow a Program through Windows Firewall link.**

You get yet another security box. Click the Continue button, and you see the Windows Firewall Settings Exceptions tab (refer to Figure 3-8).

2. **Click the Add Port button.**

Windows Firewall displays the Add a Port dialog box, as shown in Figure 3-10.

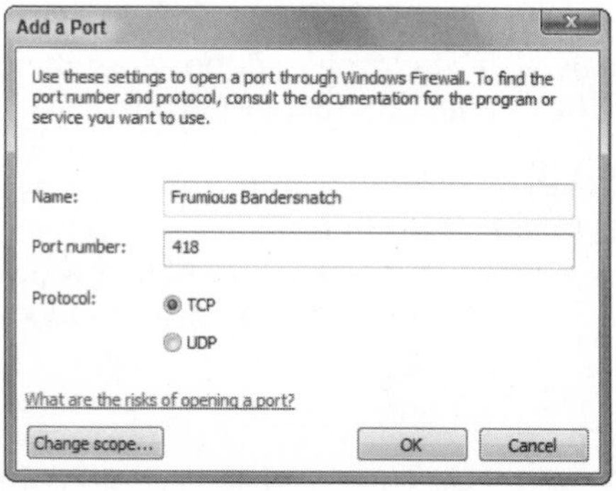

Figure 3-10: To open a port for any packet that tries to use it, type in a port number and specify whether it's TCP or UDP.

Add a Port

Use these settings to open a port through Windows Firewall. To find the port number and protocol, consult the documentation for the program or service you want to use.

Name: Frumious Bandersnatch

Port number: 418

Protocol: ● TCP

◯ UDP

What are the risks of opening a port?

[Change scope...]   [OK]   [Cancel]

3. **Type the port number that you want to open. Select TCP or UDP as the protocol (if in doubt, stick with TCP), give the exception a name, and click OK.**

See the section, "Speaking Your Firewall's Lingo," earlier in this chapter, for a description of TCP and UDP.

The Windows Firewall dialog box gets a new exception entry for the port you just entered (see Figure 3-11).

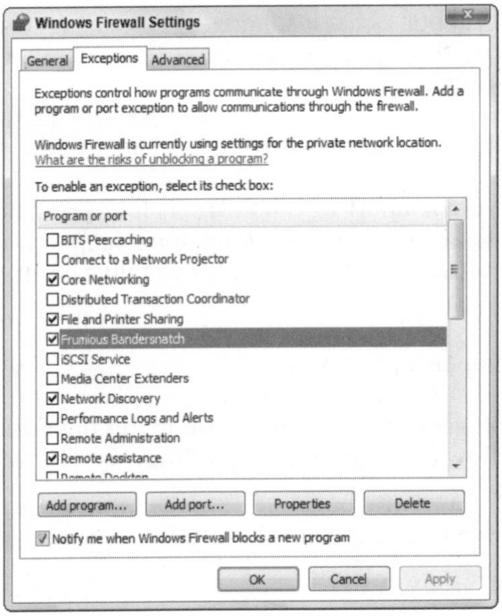

Figure 3-11: Individual ports that you add manually appear as check boxes on the Exceptions tab.

> **Windows Firewall Settings**
>
> General | Exceptions | Advanced
>
> Exceptions control how programs communicate through Windows Firewall. Add a program or port exception to allow communications through the firewall.
>
> Windows Firewall is currently using settings for the private network location. What are the risks of unblocking a program?
>
> To enable an exception, select its check box:
>
> Program or port
> - ☐ BITS Peercaching
> - ☐ Connect to a Network Projector
> - ☑ Core Networking
> - ☐ Distributed Transaction Coordinator
> - ☑ File and Printer Sharing
> - ☑ Frumious Bandersnatch
> - ☐ iSCSI Service
> - ☐ Media Center Extenders
> - ☑ Network Discovery
> - ☐ Performance Logs and Alerts
> - ☐ Remote Administration
> - ☑ Remote Assistance
> - ☐ Remote Desktop
>
> Add program... | Add port... | Properties | Delete
>
> ☑ Notify me when Windows Firewall blocks a new program
>
> OK | Cancel | Apply

4. **Click OK to go back to the Security Center window.**

Every port that you open to the outside world is a potential location for an attack. Open ports sparingly, and when you're done, close them by deselecting the appropriate check box in the Program or Port list.

You can add only one port at a time. If you need to add ports 418, 419, 420, and 421, you have to click the Add Port button four separate times, type the pertinent information four separate times, and select four separate check boxes in the Program and Port list every time you want to block or unblock the ports. Dude.

If you have a hardware firewall (and if you use a router of almost any description, you no doubt have one going full-time), you probably need to open the same port on the hardware firewall, too. You can find an enormous amount of detailed information for poking through every imaginable router at www.portforward.com/routers.htm.

Coping with Vista's Outbound Firewall

Vista's outbound firewall doesn't work, look, or behave anything like the inbound firewall. Basically, it's there and it's on, but it doesn't block a thing unless you tell it to. Whereas the inbound firewall offers the different levels of settings and enables you to further tweak those settings, the outbound firewall has only two basic functions: blocking a program (or port, or something else) you select and unblocking a program you've previously blocked.

To show you how the outbound firewall works, permit me to step you through an example. Consider that (yet another) security hole has been discovered in Internet Explorer (IE) and that you want to ensure that IE isn't allowed to connect to the Internet. Perhaps you use Firefox, and you want to make sure that Vista (or Windows Media Player or Outlook or Windows Update . . .) doesn't surreptitiously crank up IE and turn it loose on the Web.

In firewall terminology, I want to block IE from making any outbound connection. Here's how to do it:

1. Click the Start button. Immediately type mmc **and press Enter.**

After you click through a security dialog box, the Microsoft Management Console appears (see Figure 3-12).

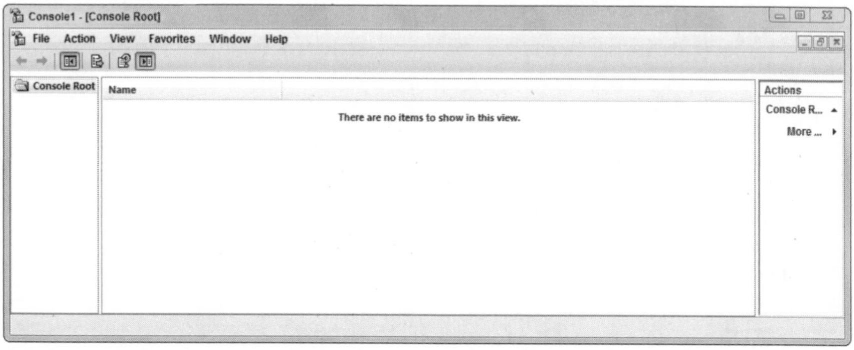

Figure 3-12:
You have to use the Microsoft Management Console to make changes to Vista's outbound firewall.

Console1 - [Console Root]
File   Action   View   Favorites   Window   Help

Console Root   Name

There are no items to show in this view.

Actions
Console R... ▲
More ... ▶

2. **Choose File⇨Add/Remove Snap-in. Scroll way down to the bottom of the Available Snap-ins list, choose Windows Firewall with Advanced Security, and click the Add button.**

MMC responds with the Select Computer dialog box (see Figure 3-13).

3. **Make sure that the Local Computer option button is selected, and click the Finish button. Then click OK in the Add or Remove Snap-ins dialog box.**

Windows Firewall with Advanced Security appears in the Microsoft Management Console dialog box.

4. **Double-click either of the two Windows Firewall with Advanced Security lines.**

The Windows Firewall with Advanced Security (WFWAS) dialog box appears (see Figure 3-14). Note how the WFWAS snap-in maintains three separate profiles, one each for public networks, private networks, and domain networks (see the section "Establishing a network type," earlier in this chapter).

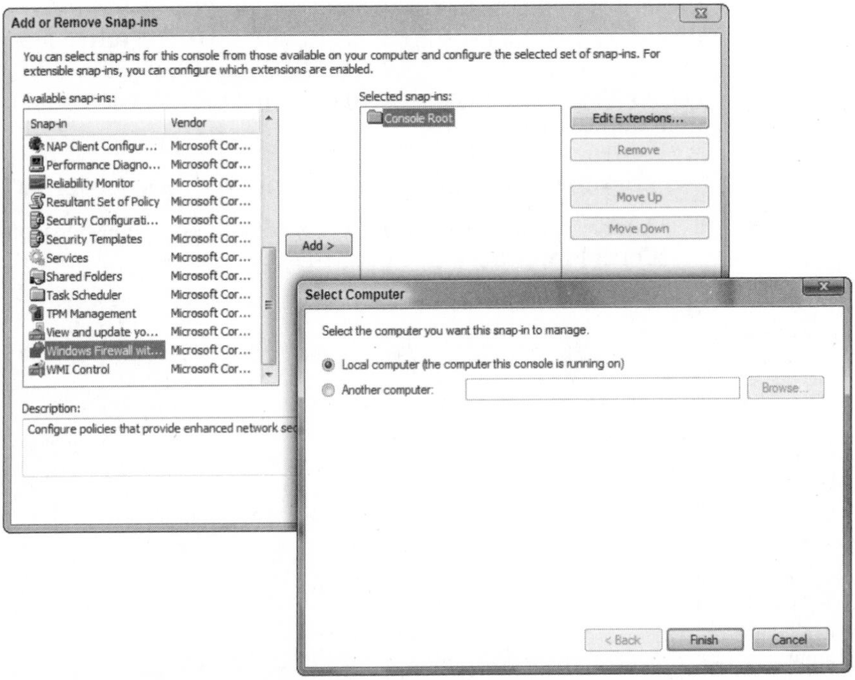

Figure 3-13:
Add the Windows Firewall with Advanced Security snap-in, and enable it for the local computer.

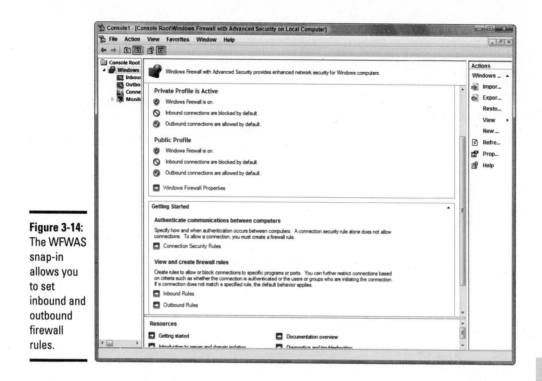

Figure 3-14:
The WFWAS snap-in allows you to set inbound and outbound firewall rules.

5. In the Getting Started box, under View and Create Firewall Rules, click the Outbound Rules link.

WFWAS responds with a list of all the predefined rules known to Vista — and many of them exist (see Figure 3-15).

Don't mess with these rules. One mistake can lead to Dante's Seventh Ring. Trust me on this.

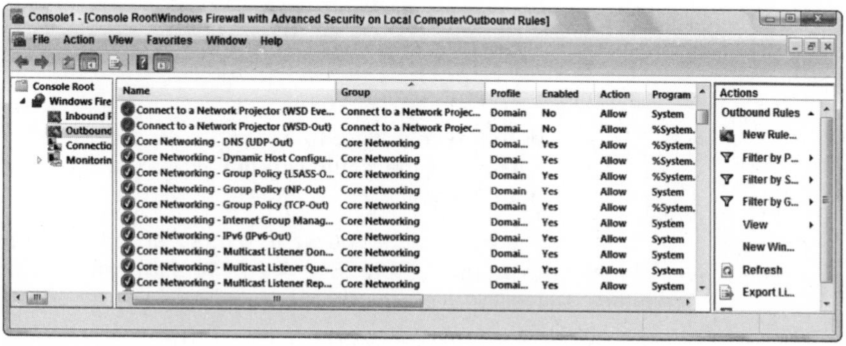

Figure 3-15:
WFWAS lists all the available firewall rules.

6. On the right, under Actions/Outbound, choose New Rule.

WFWAS responds with the first pane of the New Outbound Rule Wizard (see Figure 3-16).

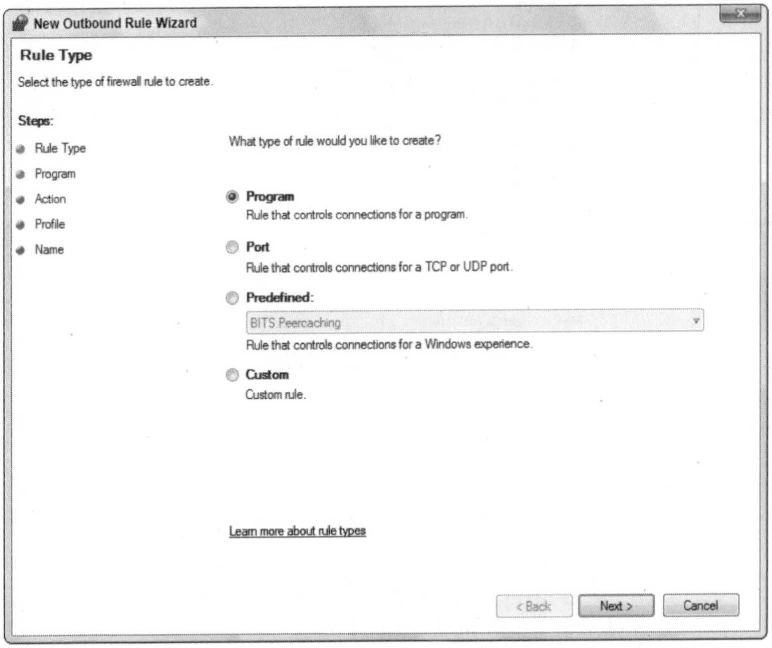

Figure 3-16:
A wizard helps guide you through the creation of an outbound firewall rule.

7. For this example, I want to block a program, Internet Explorer, so I make sure that the Program option is selected and then click Next.

The wizard asks whether you want the rule to apply to all programs or to a specific program.

8. Select the This Program Patch line, and click the Browse button.

The wizard wants you to pick the program that's going to be blocked by this rule.

9. In the Look In box, navigate to `c:\Program Files\Internet Explorer`. **Then, in the Name column, click** `iexplorer.exe` **and click the Open button.**

That tells the wizard that you want to block Internet Explorer (which is really the program `iexplore.exe`). Your wizard should look like Figure 3-17.

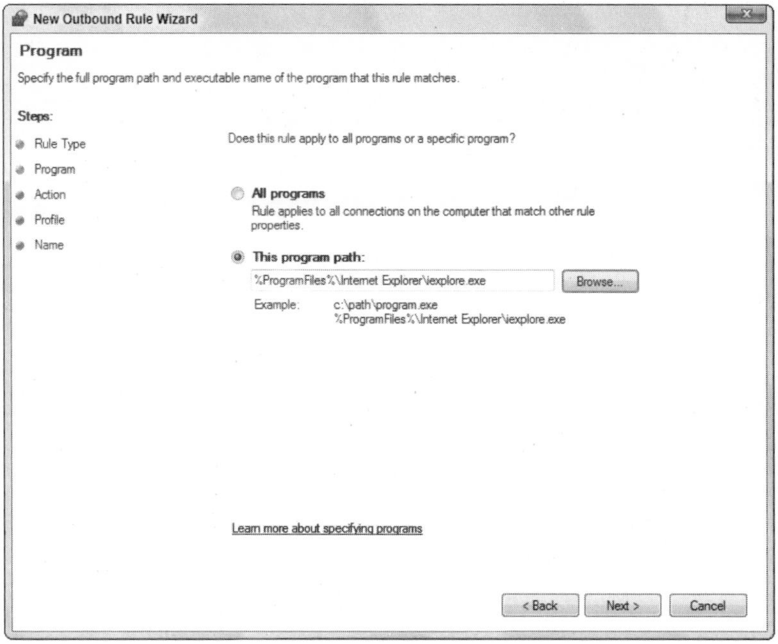

Figure 3-17:
You must choose the specific program that you want to block.

10. Click Next.

The wizard asks whether you want to allow the program to go through the firewall, whether you want to allow it if it obeys something called an IPsec rule, or whether you want to prohibit the program from getting out.

11. Click the Block the Connection button, and click Next.

The wizard wants to know whether this rule applies to private networks, public networks, and/or domain networks (see the section "Establishing a network type," earlier in this chapter).

12. If you want to block IE from going out over a private connection, select the appropriate check box. Similarly, to keep IE from going out over a public network connection, select that check box. Then click Next.

The last step of the wizard asks you for a name for the rule and gives you space to type a description.

13. In the Name box, type something descriptive like Block IE. **Type a description if you like, and then click Finish.**

WFWAS puts your new rule at the top of the list (see Figure 3-18). The new block takes effect immediately.

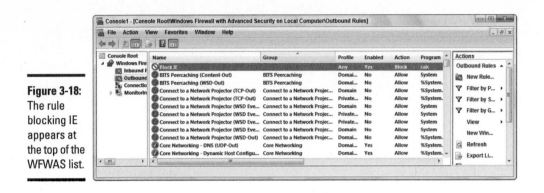

Figure 3-18:
The rule
blocking IE
appears at
the top of the
WFWAS list.

14. **Go ahead and try it. Try to get Internet Explorer to work. I dare ya.**

No way. IE gives you the notice "Internet Explorer cannot display the webpage." Heh heh heh.

15. **To get rid of the rule, right-click it and choose Delete. When WFWAS asks whether you are sure that you want to delete the rule, click Yes.**

Try Internet Explorer again, and it works like a champ.

Imagine setting up rules like that, manually, for every program that you want to block from going out on the Internet. Now you know why I say that Vista's outbound firewall is an ornery, snarly piece of software.

Individual program blocking's only part of the story, of course. If you set the outbound firewall to trap everything headed out of your machine, you'd probably spend most of your waking hours for the next ten years writing exceptions similar to this one, to allow "good" programs to get out.

Decent commercial firewalls have a long list of "good" programs. If they detect the presence of a "good" program, they poke a hole through the firewall for you. You're left with a brief (but intense) training period, where you have to approve each new, unidentified program that's trying to get out — and where you have to track down every outbound request that looks suspicious. It isn't easy, but it is tractable.

Vista's firewall doesn't work that way. You get to do all of the heavy lifting. And you get to perform that work with a user interface — the Microsoft Management Console — that has been known to bring accomplished system administrators to tears.

If you have a specific program that you want to block, Windows Firewall can do the job. But for anything other than blocking the outbound actions of a small number of targeted programs, Vista's outbound firewall rates as a marketing point ("Yes, Vista has an outbound firewall!") and little more.

Chapter 4: Patching and Plugging

In This Chapter

✔ **Getting the whole story about Windows Update**

✔ **Deciding what level of Automatic Update (if any!) is right for you**

✔ **Making Windows Update work the way you want**

*W*indows Automatic Update is for chumps.

I've taken a lot of flak over the years for advising people to turn off automatic updating. I think you should tell Vista to advise you when patches are available, but wait and see if the patches do more harm than good before applying them to your PC.

Let's face it. You *have* to patch, sooner or later. Patching isn't like brushing your teeth, where you can ignore it for a year or two, and things turn smelly then gradually rot and fall out. If you don't patch today, by next month your computer can look and act and feel like toast. The bad guys know what's been patched. They prey on people who don't get their updates.

On the other hand, you don't need to follow Microsoft's dictates and apply patches the moment they're "pushed." More than a few Dummies have seen their computers melt down because of a bad patch that's been force-fed to them via Microsoft's Automatic Update mechanism.

Almost everyone — certainly, anyone reading this book — needs to check out Microsoft's latest missives before applying them. Blindly updating Windows can lead to all sorts of problems.

Windows Update stinks. Massively. Permit me to elaborate.

Both the security patches that Microsoft dribbles out to users *and* the method by which Microsoft delivers those patches to users stinks. Massively.

But you can still keep your system patched while working around the worst these patches and Windows Update have to offer. I explain it all (more or less) in this chapter.

Patching Woes

Microsoft periodically releases security and "high priority" patches for Windows. Anyone with a recent copy of Windows (including Vista and Windows XP) who's chosen "Automatic Updates" gets those patches pushed, automatically, onto their machines, as soon as the PC gets connected to the Internet. You don't need to lift a finger: with automatic updating turned on, you come in one morning and your PC has been patched, and you never hear a word about it.

You can also download and install patches manually, any time they become available, by choosing Start➪All Programs➪Windows Update. The Windows Update Web site will inspect your computer and recommend that you install whatever patches are on offer (see the section, "Applying Patches from Windows Update" later in this chapter).

Most of the time, on most machines, the patches perform as advertised — they fix a defect in the product. Fair enough. Beats a product recall, I guess.

Sometimes, though, the patches don't work right or offer bonus features users neither asked for nor want. A few of my favorites are as follows:

✦ **The pretax predicament:** On April 11, 2006, a Tuesday, Microsoft released the "Windows Explorer VERCLSID" patch, known cryptically as MS06-015 (for a description of the "MS06-*XXX*" patch numbers, see the section "Decoding a Security Bulletin," later in this chapter). Most Windows users in the United States didn't get the patch until Saturday or Sunday. Federal Income Tax returns were due on Monday, April 17. On the weekend before tax returns were due, thousands (possibly tens of thousands) of Windows consumers found themselves unable to navigate to their Documents folder, couldn't open or save files, found that they had to type `http://` into Internet Explorer to keep it from freezing, and on and on. We consumers ultimately discovered that this patch messed up any machine with an older HP scanner program called Share-to-Web, and any machine with an older nVidia video driver.

✦ **The infamous UPnP patch debacle:** In November 2001, Microsoft patched (MS01-059), repatched, and re-repatched a hole in the part of Windows that listens for new items as they're attached to a network. The FBI's National Infrastructure Protection Center (NIPC) followed along after Microsoft like a kid cleaning up after his dog: The NIPC issued a warning about the security hole, an update, another update, and ultimately an advisory that Microsoft had finally solved the problem.

✦ **The ghost in Windows 2000:** In April 2004, Microsoft released a slew of patches, one of which (MS04-014) locked up some Windows 2000 machines tighter than a drum. If you installed the patch on a Windows 2000 machine, and you were unlucky, you couldn't boot the machine. The only solution was to haul out your installation CD and perform major brain surgery.

✦ **Windows Genuine Spyware:** In early 2006, Microsoft started using the Windows Automatic Update mechanism to "push" software that has absolutely nothing to do with security. Most notably, on April 24, 2006 — a day that will live in Windows infamy — Microsoft "pushed" a new version of the Windows Genuine Advantage program onto millions of PCs worldwide. Anyone foolish enough to have Windows Automatic Update enabled woke up one morning with a new piece of scumware, installed by Microsoft without their knowledge or consent.

That version of Windows Genuine Advantage — distributed as a "priority update" — included a component, called WGA Validation, that brands certain PCs with a notification that the PC is running a pirate copy of Windows. ("You may be a victim of software counterfeiting. This copy of Windows is not genuine and is not eligible to receive all updates and product support from Microsoft. Click Get Genuine now to get more information and resolve this issue.") A few days later, we discovered that a second component, called WGA Notification, "phones home" to Microsoft whenever the PC is rebooted or (apparently) once a day, whichever comes first. Of course, WGA couldn't be removed. After you got it, you got it.

Instead of confessing its sins and rectifying the problem, Microsoft continued to distribute the spyware, in some cases refusing to install other Windows updates unless a Windows customer consented to having the WGA scum installed on their machines. Lawsuits ensued. Those of us who have been watching the Automatic Update debacle for years just shook our heads.

Book III
Chapter 4

Patching and Plugging

Almost every batch of patches Microsoft releases these days contains at least one stinker — a patch that, on a certain percentage of PCs, makes things much worse. It's like the cure is worse than the disease.

I've been at this business for a long time — been using Windows since the days of Windows 286, which shipped on a single floppy disk, and I wrangled with DOS long before that. Of all the Microsoft features that I don't trust — and there are many — Windows Automatic Update rates as the single Microsoft feature that I trust the least. Microsoft has gone to extraordinary lengths over the past half-decade to reinforce my distrust and to demonstrate plainly and unambiguously that when it comes to updating Windows, Microsoft doesn't have a clue.

Choosing an Update Level

Windows Automatic Update lets you choose from four different levels of control so that you have some choice over what it does — or doesn't do — to your system. It's worth taking a few minutes to peruse Table 4-1, think through what Windows has to offer, and decide which approach works best for you.

Table 4-1	Choosing a Windows Update Option	
Option	*What It Does*	*Recommended For . . .*
Update Automatically	Lets Windows determine when new updates are available, download them, and install them automatically for you — typically in the middle of the night.	People who get easily confused by the process of telling Windows that it's okay to install new updates. It's also a good option if you don't have the time or inclination to look online to see whether a specific update has major problems.
Download, Don't Install	Lets Windows determine when new updates are available, download them, and then ask your permission to install them.	Those who are a bit more cautious. This is a perfectly reasonable approach, but I think the next one is better.
Notify, Don't Download	Lets Windows determine when new updates are available and then notify you.	Folks who are willing to wait a day or two to install a new patch, and check online to see whether a patch is causing more harm than good.
Never Check for Updates	Turns off Windows Automatic Update.	Hardly anyone. It's hard to imagine any situation where this makes sense.

If you decide that Update Automatically really is the path for you, you just need to check your settings and let Windows Update run in the background. At the same time, though, it leaves your PC vulnerable to Microsoft's spotty patch record. In the worst case, you may come in one morning, turn on your PC, and not be able to use it. Microsoft recommends this setting for all PC users. I only recommend it for people who are too intimidated to take control of their computer's fate. For example, if your Great Aunt Mildred frets about breaking her computer if she plays a round of solitaire, she's a good candidate for automatic updating. Go ahead and set it up for her — but as you do so, recognize your technological co-dependence.

I like the Notify, Don't Download option because it gives me two separate chances to nix a specific patch. First, I scan the list of patches on offer and see whether I want any (or all) of them. Then, later, I have an opportunity to change my mind about a patch before installing it. If you're worried about waiting too long to install a patch, you have reason to be concerned, but the patch ratings at AskWoody.com can help (see the "MS-DEFCON" section, later in this chapter). While the gestation period for new worms is shrinking — the bad guys are picking up on Microsoft's security patches and figuring out how to exploit the holes shortly after the patches are announced — it's rare that a freshly patched security hole turns into an active exploit in a few days. And generally, word of botched security patches surfaces within a few days.

When Windows Update reaches into your computer to see what you have installed, which patches have been applied, and so on, it doesn't retrieve any personally identifiable information. It doesn't even retrieve your activation key. As far as I've been able to tell, Microsoft doesn't attempt to spy on your machine via the Automatic Update program. So don't turn it off entirely unless you're really, really paranoid.

Setting Your Update Level

After you decide on an update approach, as outlined in the preceding section, you have to wade through Windows' jury-rigged interface to make your decision take effect. Here's how to do that:

1. **Choose Start⇨Control Panel⇨Security, and then click the Windows Update icon.**

Vista opens a Windows Update status page, as shown in Figure 4-1.

**Book III
Chapter 4**

Patching and Plugging

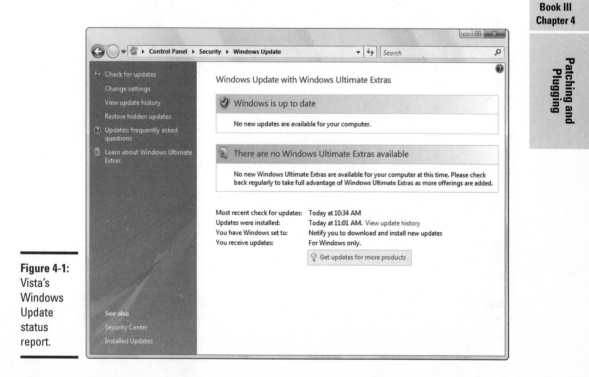

Figure 4-1:
Vista's
Windows
Update
status
report.

2. **On the left side of this screen, click the Change Settings link.**

Vista lets you change your Automatic Update settings (see Figure 4-2).

3. **Follow the discussion in the preceding section to choose an Automatic Update setting. Select the appropriate radio button, and click the OK button.**

If you choose the Update Automatically option, you can also specify whether you want Windows Update to check every day or once a week for updates. If you decide to let Microsoft update your machine without your knowledge or consent, I strongly recommend that you have Windows check for updates every day. Going a full week without an update can leave your system exposed for far too long.

I check the box marked Recommended Updates because I want to see updates that Microsoft doesn't consider "high priority." While I rarely install any of them — in particular, I avoid new video drivers like the plague — occasionally an update appears that proves useful. Because I have Vista check for updates instead of downloading or installing them, it's usually painless to scan the list of every patch that's available — "high priority" or not — and choose the ones I like.

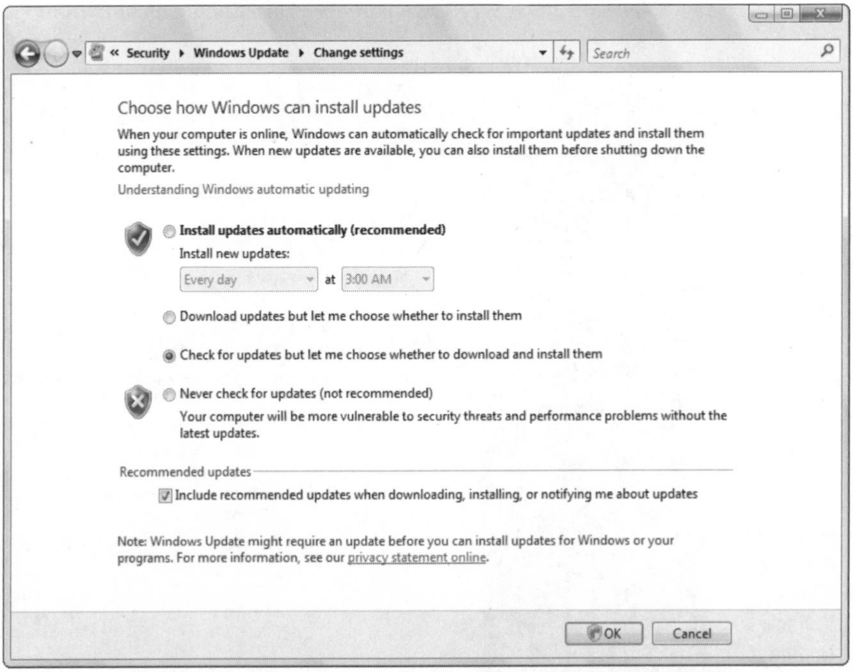

Figure 4-2:
I recommend that you tell Vista to check for updates but not download them.

Security ▸ Windows Update ▸ Change settings | Search

Choose how Windows can install updates

When your computer is online, Windows can automatically check for important updates and install them using these settings. When new updates are available, you can also install them before shutting down the computer.

Understanding Windows automatic updating

○ **Install updates automatically (recommended)**
  Install new updates:
  [Every day ▾] at [3:00 AM ▾]

○ Download updates but let me choose whether to install them

◉ Check for updates but let me choose whether to download and install them

○ Never check for updates (not recommended)
  Your computer will be more vulnerable to security threats and performance problems without the latest updates.

Recommended updates
  ☑ Include recommended updates when downloading, installing, or notifying me about updates

Note: Windows Update might require an update before you can install updates for Windows or your programs. For more information, see our privacy statement online.

[OK]   [Cancel]

I also check the box marked Use Microsoft Update. That way, I see patches for Microsoft Office as well as Vista.

The cryptic note at the bottom of the dialog box refers to the fact that Windows Update — the program that identifies, downloads and on some machines *<shudder!>* installs the patches must, itself, be updated. (In fact, it's a standing joke that the Windows updater gets patched more often than any other piece of Windows software.) The note here warns you that the physician must heal itself, er, the updater must update itself automatically in order to do its job.

When you click OK, Vista responds with one of those pesky User Account Control dialog boxes.

4. **Click the Continue button, and then click the red *X* to exit the Windows update status report.**

   Your new settings take effect immediately.

If you ever want to see which updates have been applied on your PC, choose Start➪Control Panel➪Security, and under the Windows Update icon, click the View Installed Updates link. If you see a warning on the Internet that a particular Vista security patch is causing problems, this is the place to look.

Selectively Patching (A Panacea for Those Woes)

Microsoft really, really wants you to allow Vista to automatically update itself. Unless you have much more faith in Microsoft than I, you should seriously consider defying the Party Line and decide for yourself when (and whether!) patches should be applied. The Windows Genuine Spyware debacle (see the section "Patching Woes," earlier in this chapter) alone amply demonstrates that Microsoft's automatic updating can't be trusted.

Let Microsoft notify you when it wants to install something on your computer, but don't blindly allow the 'Softies to install whatever they want. Wait until millions and millions of hapless Vista customers unknowingly run Microsoft's patch beta tests and then install the patch after the cannon fodder has raised the alarm.

In the following sections, you find out how to steer through the sea of updates to get only what you need, and nothing more.

Applying patches from Windows Update

In the best of all possible worlds, patching Vista isn't a difficult process. It takes a little bit of time, but in the end, your computer's worth it, yes?

Here's how I patch. You can do it, too, with a little help from your friends. Follow these steps:

1. **Make sure you've followed the steps in the section "Choosing an Update Level" earlier in this chapter, so the Vista updater notifies you when a patch is available, but doesn't download or install it.**

   That's easy.

2. **When a patch (or, more likely a slew of patches) becomes available, you see a balloon in the notification area, near the clock, that says something like, "Updates are ready for your computer. Click here to download updates." When you have a few spare minutes, click the balloon.**

   The exact terminology may change, but you see a notification that updates are ready. Don't worry if you can't get to the updates right away. If the balloon disappears, you can bring it back by clicking on the Security Center shield down in the notification area. (See Book III, Chapter 1 if you can't find it.)

   When you click on the balloon, the Vista updater shows you a notification box like the one in Figure 4-3.

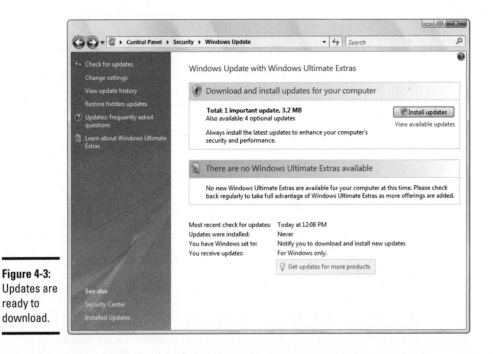

Figure 4-3: Updates are ready to download.

3. **Don't click the button marked Install Updates. Instead, click the link underneath that says View Available Updates.**

   Vista shows you the updates currently on offer, as in Figure 4-4.

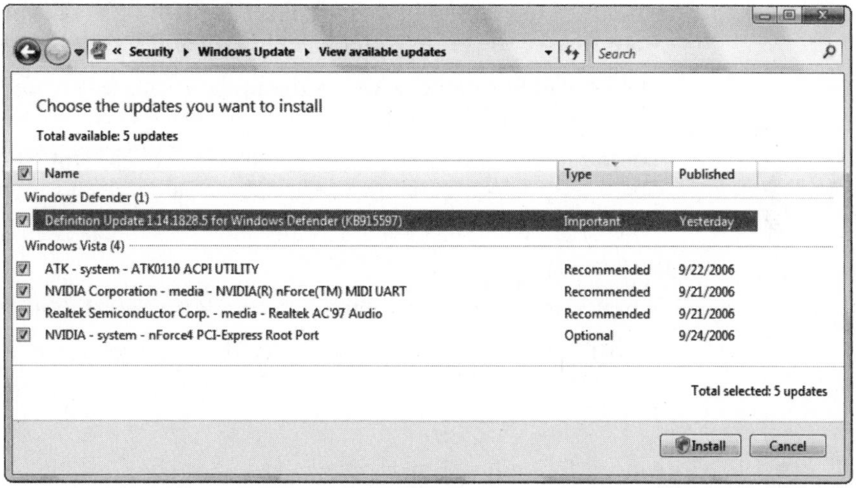

Figure 4-4:
Details
about each
update.

4. **One by one, check each update.**

   You can click on any links in the update list, refer to the appropriate Security Bulletin or Knowledge Base article (see the section "Getting what you need from a Security Bulletin" in this chapter), check my MS-DEFCON status (see "MS-DEFCON" in this chapter), look at your favorite security Web site, or consult that really wired astrologer who hangs out in the park. Bring your own tea leaves.

5. **Wait. Click Cancel to get out of the detailed list, then "X" out of the Windows Update box.**

   The world may be jumping up and down. Heck, the U.S. Department of Homeland Security once issued an emergency bulletin recommending immediate installation of a Microsoft security patch — a patch that turned into a dud. Keep your head while those about you are losing theirs.

6. **Watch.**

   Within a few days, problems with new patches appear — sometimes with disastrous vigor. The mainstream press frequently carries distorted, sensationalized reports either (a) warning you to patch immediately because the sky is falling (I call these "Chicken Littles") or (b) describing disasters that didn't really occur (I call these "he-said-she-said rumors" — or something distinctly less printable).

   Rely on a source you trust. I list the sources I trust in the section about staying informed in Book III, Chapter 1.

**Book III
Chapter 4**

**Patching and
Plugging**

Vista will continue to pester you, mercilessly, with that same balloon warning that "Updates are ready for your computer." That's good. You need to hear the geese cackling.

7. **When you're convinced that patching will cause more good than harm, click on that infernal balloon (or click on the Security Center shield), bring up the update details (Figure 4-6), make sure that you want to take the plunge, and click the Install button.**

Vista's update routine retrieves the updates and asks you for permission to install them. Go ahead and follow the prompts.

There's no need to create a System Restore checkpoint (see Book II, Chapter 3) before installing the updates. Vista does it for you.

Downloading and installing updates can take anywhere from a few minutes to a few hours.

8. **When Vista finishes installing the updates, re-start your computer.**

Even if Vista doesn't require a re-boot, it's a very good idea. Keep your eyes open for any problems and if you hit something, check www.AskWoody. com and run a Google search to get to the bottom of it.

Once more, for emphasis: *you have to keep Vista patched.* But you don't have to do it on Microsoft's terms. Take the bull by the horns, be mindful about the potential problems, and go out and do it your way.

MS-DEFCON

Big companies hire people — sometimes groups of people — to check the latest Microsoft patches, verify that they don't break anything, and then deploy the patches, slowly, throughout the corporate network.

If you can afford to hire a patch-busting team, my hat's off to you. But what are you — a typical Vista user — to do? Where can you turn for understandable, unbiased reporting on Windows flaws and fixes — and flaws in the fixes?

I have a rating system on my Web site, www.AskWoody.com, that lets individual Microsoft consumers know when it's safe to install patches (see Figure 4-5). I call it the Microsoft Patch Defense Condition Level, or MS-DEFCON for short. It's modeled after the U.S. Armed Forces DEFCON system, with the following levels:

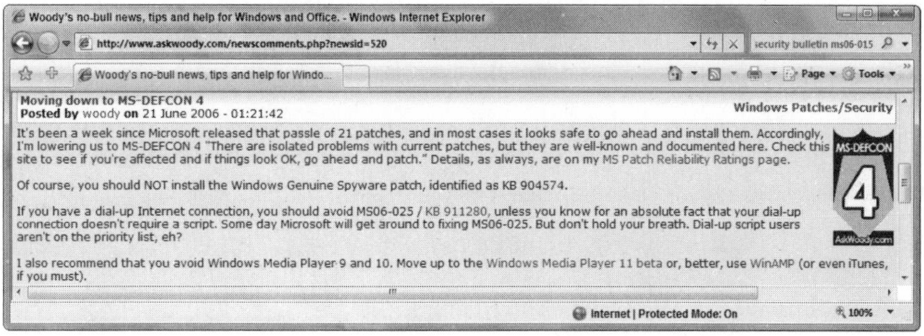

Figure 4-5:
The MS-
DEFCON
level advises
you when
it's safe to
install
patches.

✦ **MS-DEFCON 1:** Current Microsoft patches are causing havoc. Don't patch.

✦ **MS-DEFCON 2:** Patch reliability is unclear. Unless you have an immediate, pressing need to install a specific patch, don't do it.

✦ **MS-DEFCON 3:** Patch reliability is unclear, but widespread attacks make patching prudent. Go ahead and patch, but watch out for potential problems.

✦ **MS-DEFCON 4:** Isolated problems exist with current patches, but they are well known and documented on AskWoody.com. Check the site's Windows Patch Reliability page to see whether you're affected, and if things look okay, go ahead and patch.

✦ **MS-DEFCON 5:** All's clear. Patch while it's safe.

Watch the MS-DEFCON level for an independent, somewhat jaundiced analysis of threats, both from hackers and from Microsoft.

Getting what you need from a Security Bulletin

When Microsoft patches a security hole in Windows, it issues a Security Bulletin (see Figure 4-6). A Security Bulletin gives you some brief information about a particular patch (or patches) and offers a way to download patches without Windows Update. Security Bulletins contain official notice from Microsoft about things that go bump in the night. They're frequently laden with so much jargon that the interpreters need interpreters to translate them into plain English.

To find the latest Security Bulletins, check the Microsoft Security Response Team blog, `http://blogs.technet.com/msrc/default.aspx`. Notice of new or revised Security Bulletins frequently appears on the MSRC blog long before any of the other Microsoft delivery mechanisms get the word out.

Date published and last date revised   Bulletin number and patch description

Knowledge Base article with details

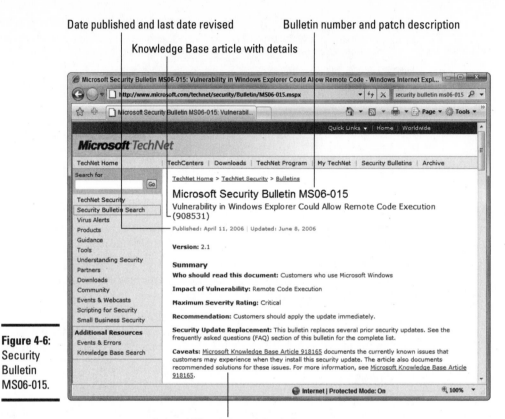

Figure 4-6:
Security
Bulletin
MS06-015.

Second KB article explains bugs

Decoding a Security Bulletin

When you open a Security Bulletin, here are a few helpful pointers on interpreting what Microsoft has to say:

✦ **Security Bulletins get sequential numbers,** such as MS06-015, denoting the 15th Security Bulletin issued in 2006.

You might think that Bulletin MS06-015 would talk about the 15th security patch in 2006, but you'd be wrong. Microsoft bunches up security patches, sometimes releasing several completely unrelated patches in one Security Bulletin. Why? Because Microsoft knows that the world at large correlates the number of Security Bulletins with the relative "holiness" of its software. If Windows releases only 30 patches in a year, and Linux releases 48, which operating system sounds more secure?

✦ **Security Bulletins are dated.** Usually they get revision numbers, too, but revision numbering seems to be, uh, subject to revision, if you know what I mean. If you see a Security Bulletin that's been updated recently, there's a reason why — usually something's gone wrong. If you see a Security Bulletin with a revision number like 2.3 or 4.2, you know that problems bedevil the patch(es), and Microsoft has had to revise and re-revise (and re-re-revise) its explanations.

✦ **Each Security Bulletin refers to one or more Knowledge Base (KB) articles,** which give further details about the patch. The six-digit KB article number appears at the end of the description of the patch (see Figure 4-6, which refers to Knowledge Base article 908531).

✦ **The Knowledge Base article number is important if you need to remove a patch.** Frequently this number is the only way you have to identify the patch. If you need to remove the patch because, say, it clobbers an important part of Windows, you'll need the KB article number.

To remove a Vista patch, choose Start⇨Control Panel⇨Security Center. Under the heading Windows Update, click the link View Installed Updates. Windows patches *that can be uninstalled* appear listed by Knowledge Base number. To remove a patch, click on it and then click Uninstall.

Note that some Vista patches *cannot* be uninstalled — once you got 'em, you got 'em, and no amount of wailing or gnashing of teeth will tear them out of Vista.

✦ **Many patches have a second Knowledge Base article,** referenced in the Caveats section, which exists solely to track the (acknowledged) bugs in the patch. In Figure 4-6, Knowledge Base article 918165 contains a list of the bugs, updated as they are identified.

Getting patches through a Security Bulletin

While you can use Windows Update to identify patches that your computer requires, download the patches, and even install them, you can download a patch manually and run it without Windows Update's interference, er, assistance. That can come in handy if you need to apply the same patch to many PCs, or if you want to download the patch when your Internet connection is not busy but wait to install the patch later.

To download and install a Security Bulletin patch manually, click the Download the Update link for Windows Vista in the Security Bulletin and then follow the instructions to download the patch.

What's a "critical" update?

Microsoft has very strict definitions for its various levels of security patches. The official "severity level system" defines these levels of security holes as follows:

- A *critical* security hole is "a vulnerability whose exploitation could allow the propagation of an Internet worm without user action."

- An *important* hole is "a vulnerability whose exploitation could result in compromise of the confidentiality, integrity, or availability of users' data, or of the integrity or availability of processing resources."

- A *moderate* security rating signifies that "exploitability is mitigated to a significant degree by factors such as default configuration, auditing, or difficulty of exploitation."

- And a *low* hole is "a vulnerability whose exploitation is extremely difficult, or whose impact is minimal."

Lest you really believe that you should install critical updates before you install important updates — or that you can, say, ignore moderate updates — you need to realize that Microsoft's use of the terms is, in fact, quite arbitrary and at times highly debatable. Many "critical" patches don't address unassisted worm propagation. In at least one instance, the severity level of a security hole was changed after enough people complained. One "critical update" removed a symbol from one font in Office 2003. Windows Genuine Spyware, uh, Advantage went out as a "priority update." The assignment of a security level seems to reflect internal Microsoft politics more than anything else. So take the severity level rating with a grain of salt, okay?

Generally, it's much simpler to have Windows keep track of which patches are required and to download them automatically through Windows Update, but if you need to apply the same patch to multiple machines, a manual download can save hours of trouble.

Chapter 5: Virus Protection and the Big Defender

In This Chapter

✔ Understanding how antivirus products work with Windows

✔ Using Windows Live OneCare — and a free alternative *from Microsoft*

✔ Caring for your antivirus program

✔ Downloading and installing AVG Free, a free-for-personal-use antivirus program

✔ Reigning in programs that start automatically whenever you start Vista

✔ Using Windows Defender — and better alternatives

*E*very single Windows user should install, update, and religiously use an antivirus program. No exceptions, no excuses.

One question I hear all the time is, "Which antivirus program is the best?" My answer: They all work great. Pick one of the major packages and *just do it.* While you're worrying about whether this package scans better or that package blocks better, or that another package costs a few bucks more or less, your system is at risk. Flip a coin if you have to. But get your computer protected.

Now, with the advent of a product called AVG Free, first-class antivirus software is available at no cost for personal use. You don't have an excuse anymore. I show you how to install and use AVG Free in this chapter.

You also need an antispyware program. Microsoft's Windows Defender comes along free with Vista, but there are very good reasons why you might not trust Microsoft's product. Good alternatives exist. Check them out at the end of this chapter.

Understanding Antivirus Software

Antivirus software protects your computer from viruses, right? Well, yes and no.

Most antivirus software packages these days work in two very different ways:

✦ **Signature matching:** The antivirus software looks inside files to see whether any portion of the file matches a big database of known "bad" snippets of data. When a new virus or worm is discovered, characteristic parts of the infecting program are added to the signature database. Signature matching still forms the backbone of the antivirus industry, but the black-hat cretins are getting better at writing malware that modifies itself, rendering signatures useless.

Some industry pundits (rightly) observe that a steady flow of updated signature files drives revenue for the antivirus industry: If you drop your subscription, you don't get any new signatures. The antivirus software industry has one of the few software products that becomes nearly obsolete every few days. Powerful economic incentives exist to stick with the signature-matching model — which, by its very nature, only works *after* a new virus has been identified.

✦ **Heuristic analysis:** The antivirus software relies on the behavior (or the expected behavior) of a program to catch the destructive software before it has a chance to run. Although an enormous amount of research has gone into heuristic analysis, a black box that takes a file and determines whether it's going to mess up a PC is still a long way off. In fact, there are sound theoretical reasons why a perfect black box of that ilk can never exist.

When a bad piece of software is identified, the antivirus (AV) program offers to remove the infection. When viruses are attached to other files, in most cases, the offensive program can be removed without destroying the "host" file. Some AV packages have the ability to shut down a PC's links to the outside world if a particularly virulent worm is detected.

Antivirus software typically watches for infections (through signature matching or heuristic analysis) in one of three ways, and each of the ways hooks into Windows in a different manner:

✦ **A complete scan:** Typically, you schedule full scans of all your files in the middle of the night, or shortly after you download a new signature file. The antivirus program runs a full scan as soon as it's up-to-date.

✦ **On the fly:** When you open a file or run a program, Windows alerts your antivirus software, and the AV software kicks in to scan the file before it gets run or opened. Similarly, if you download a program from the Internet, or run a program on a Web page, Windows has your AV software check before you have a chance to shoot yourself in the foot.

✦ **Lurking:** Good antivirus software runs in the background, looking for specific events that may be indicative of an infection. Some AV packages include firewalls, spam blockers, and other components that take lurking to a higher level, but almost all AV software watches while you work, running as a separate Windows task in the background.

In addition, all AV software scans e-mail messages and attachments for infected files. Some scan before the mail gets to the e-mail program; others scan as attachments are opened.

The challenges for antivirus software

Antivirus software manufacturers face many pressures, but aside from detecting all known viruses (and trying to catch some that aren't yet known), one of the top priorities is performance. It takes time to scan a file, and computer folks, being impatient by nature, don't like the idea of waiting while the AV software does its thing. The next time your computer goes out to lunch while you're trying to open a file, take heart. The PC you save may be your own.

Another problem facing antivirus software and its creators is the ever-changing nature of the game. Virus and worm writers can go to great lengths to hide their malicious creations. The *polymorphic* virus illustrates the point. A polymorphic virus changes every time it infects, so signature matching doesn't work very well, if at all. One favored method for making a virus polymorphic: Encrypt it using a key that changes every time the virus infects. When the virus runs, its first job is to decrypt the main part of the virus. After it's decrypted, the main part goes out and infects, but the malicious code it passes on is encrypted with a different password. Thus, no two copies of the virus look the same, and signature-matching on anything but the (typically very small) decrypting part of the virus doesn't work.

Heuristic analysis of files to try to detect malware suffers from one near-fatal flaw. By its nature, heuristic analysis looks at a program's behavior or expected behavior and draws conclusions about the program based on what it looks like it'll do. There's no black-and-white, no signature-matching "AHA! I got a real one!" finality to the analysis. Instead, heuristic programs live in a world of shades of gray, where there's a 60 percent chance this type of behavior is worm-like and a 78 percent chance that behavior is worm-like. Antivirus software analysts have to turn that kind of soft data into an up-or-down "This is a virus" or "That isn't a virus" result. Frequently, the analysts (or, more correctly, their programs) don't guess right.

What's a false positive?

The bane of antivirus software's existence, a *false positive,* occurs when a perfectly good file is identified as infected. Most frequently, simply by chance, part of an uninfected file may contain the same sequence of characters as a virus, which triggers a signature match.

This all sounds like a gentlemanly mix-up, old chap, stiff upper lip and all that, until you come across a file that appears to be infected, but really isn't. One major antivirus package recently flagged a perfectly valid Windows file as infected — and of course, it wasn't. The vendor fixed the screwy signature file immediately, as you might imagine, but not before thousands of people dutifully deleted the Windows system file.

Ground zero

Most Windows worm outbreaks — including the Slammer worm, which infected at least 75,000 computers within 10 minutes of its release in January 2003 — rely on a known, already-patched security hole in Windows. Systems that get infected are only vulnerable because the people who run the systems didn't apply a patch that was readily available from Microsoft. (I discuss patching in Book III, Chapter 4.) The cretins who write worms watch Microsoft's patches closely and try to create programs that exploit the patched holes, knowing full well that a large percentage of all the systems connected to the Internet aren't updated very often.

Some day soon, that will change — and not for the better.

A so-called "0day" worm (also known as "zero day" or "ground zero") would use a previously unknown, and therefore unpatched, hole in Windows. If the really clever guys in black hats ever get smart enough to find a wide-open hole in Windows (and, particularly, Windows Firewall) before Microsoft patches it, we're all in a world of hurt. We've already seen several 0day attacks, primarily based on Microsoft Excel, Word, and PowerPoint. But the first big 0day worm that goes for Windows will wreak havoc.

A precedent exists. Way back in November 1988, Robert Morris, Jr., a grad student at MIT, released a worm that brought down 6,000 UNIX machines — a very large percentage of all the computers connected to the Internet, such as it was. By all accounts, Morris wasn't trying to hurt anything. He only wanted to see what would happen if a program could move from machine to machine. The "version 1.0" worm that got out had mistakes in it — programming bugs — that made it clog up every infected machine, and the rest is history. The Computer Emergency Response Team, CERT, was created in response to Morris's worm.

Every antivirus software manufacturer now tries to protect against 0day attacks, primarily using heuristic analysis. The state of the art is, uh, evolving. Right now your best protection is to stay patched (see Book III, Chapter 4), and to keep your antivirus software up-to-date.

Oh yeah. It happens all the time, with all sorts of files.

Be aware of the fact that antivirus software isn't absolutely foolproof. Sometimes the identified bogeymen only exist as a figment of some pattern-matching program's imagination. Although you should take your antivirus program's recommendation as highly indicative of problems, remember that nothing's infallible. So if you see a virus warning that doesn't make sense, quarantine the problematic file (don't delete it) and contact the company that created the file, to see if something's run afoul of an errant antivirus program.

Live OneCare and the Safety Center

When Microsoft first announced Windows Live OneCare (see Figure 5-1), I was floored. It takes a lot of *cojones* to charge consumers for protection against flaws in your own products. John Dvorak, over at *PC Magazine,* hit it right on the head: "Does the existence of this not constitute an incredible conflict of interest? Why improve the base code when you can sell 'protection'? Is Frank Nitti the new CEO?"

Book III Chapter 5

Virus Protection and the Big Defender

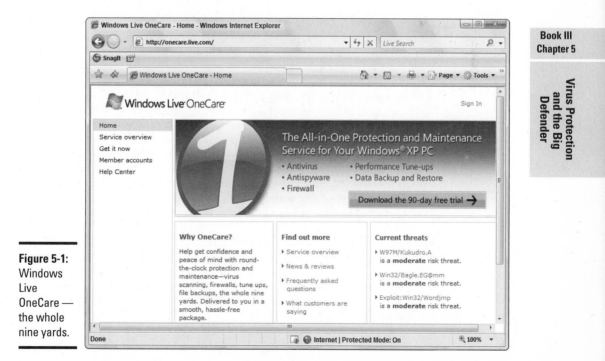

Figure 5-1:
Windows Live OneCare — the whole nine yards.

Microsoft charges $49.95 for one year of Windows Live OneCare, and you pay once to cover up to three computers. Compared to more expensive antivirus programs, that's a deal. Compared to highly capable free packages . . . you do the math.

What is Windows Live OneCare? Microsoft describes it as "round-the-clock protection and maintenance — virus scanning, firewalls, tune-ups, file back-ups, the whole nine yards." Of course, Vista ships with a firewall and decent backup (unless you got conned with Vista Home Basic). You can get very high quality virus scanning for free. It's hard to say whether tune-ups are worth the effort. Not sure where you can buy a whole nine yards. Not even sure where to buy half, for that matter.

I won't pay Microsoft to fix or protect its own products, and I urge you to do the same. Heaven knows we've paid enough already. Instead, Microsoft offers a *free* product that warrants your attention. It has an odd provenance.

In the first month that Windows Live OneCare became available, Microsoft was faced with two real, in-the-wild, 0day attacks, first in Word and then in Excel. (See the sidebar "Ground zero" for a brief explanation of 0day attacks.)

Back in the days before OneCare went live, Microsoft's duty was clear: If a previously unknown way exists to attack a Microsoft product that raises its ugly head, Microsoft unleashes a whole army of programmers and gives them the tools necessary to solve the problem. Then Microsoft notifies all the antivirus software manufacturers, more or less in tandem, giving them details about the problem and potential solutions.

But what happens when Microsoft, too, sells antivirus software?

In the case of these two 0day exploits, Microsoft found itself in a bind with "monopoly" written all over it. If the 'Softies offered a fix via Windows Live OneCare — that is, if the company offered to solve the problem for a fee, prior to the fix becoming widely available to all its competitors, the antivirus manufacturers would have good reason to scream bloody murder.

At the same time, Microsoft was sitting on a solution, and it had an obligation to customers to fix their problems before they got out of hand. It would be unconscionable for the 'Softies to offer protection to those willing to pony up fifty bucks, while those of us unwilling to pay the piper would be left exposed until Microsoft released a security bulletin and patch, weeks or months later.

The solution? Microsoft established the Windows Live OneCare safety scanner (www.safety.live.com, see Figure 5-2), a free alternative to the paid scanner in Windows Live OneCare. For both the Word exploit and a separate Excel zero day hack, Microsoft's fix appeared first in the Windows Live OneCare safety scanner. At least, that's what the Microsoft Security Response Center claims.

The Windows Live OneCare safety scanner Web site goes down frequently. You can't use it with Firefox. It's packed with advertisements for Live OneCare. The content of the site looks like it was thrown together over a long weekend, and crucial information is missing. The site doesn't even tell you which threats are trapped by the program. The scan is so slow I would only run it overnight — and on a big system, overnight might not be long enough.

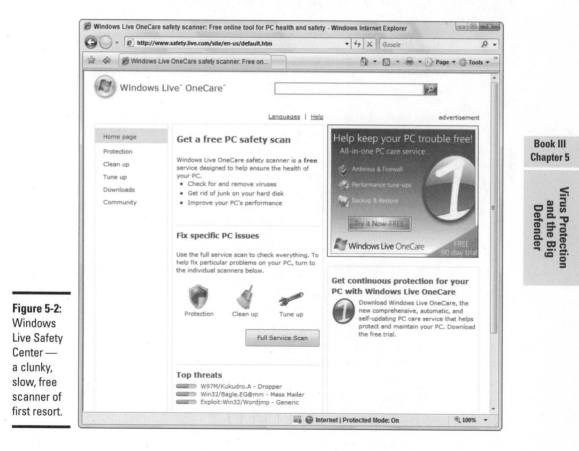

Figure 5-2: Windows Live Safety Center — a clunky, slow, free scanner of first resort.

Book III Chapter 5

Virus Protection and the Big Defender

Hey, Microsoft doesn't make any money off of it. Whaddya expect?

But Microsoft puts its fixes there first, before Windows Live OneCare itself, and sometimes before competing antivirus companies post their updates. The free Windows Live OneCare safety scanner now rates as the resource of first resort — especially for those of us who refuse to pay Microsoft $50 to fix its own products.

The next time you're worried about a problem that's suddenly appeared out of nowhere, go to the Live OneCare safety scanner, click the Full Service Scan button, and run a scan overnight. You might be surprised.

Caring for Your Antivirus Program

McAfee calls them "DAT files." Symantec (Norton) calls them "Virus Definitions" as does Microsoft. F-Secure and Kaspersky both use the term "Antivirus Database," while Grisoft (AVG) goes the other way, with "Virus Database." Trend Micro (PC-cillin) says "Pattern File." Panda uses "Signature Files," and CA has "Virus Signatures." For Sophos, they're "IDEs."

No matter what you call them, the signature-matching database file lies at the center of every antivirus product's capabilities.

In normal use, you should update your antivirus software's signature file daily. I suggest you do it in the morning, just before you start to work. I know that some manufacturers suggest you only update once a week, but I think that's shortsighted, particularly given the current level of malware activity. Here's the security schedule I recommend for most Vista users:

✦ **Keep an eye on Microsoft's updates to Vista, but don't install them automatically.** (See Book III, Chapter 4.) Instead, wait until the other pioneers have arrows in *their* backs, and then make sure that your system won't end up in worse condition after the patch. Check the MS-DEFCON level on www.AskWoody.com for help.

✦ **Download antivirus signature files daily.** Your first job each morning should be to verify that your AV software has been updated properly and that the program's icon is visible in your system tray, next to the clock.

✦ **Check for massive new outbreaks daily.** Most AV software companies have e-mail newsletters that can warn you of major new problems. Checking your AV software manufacturer's home page every day to see whether any news is breaking is also worthwhile. Just keep in mind that your AV manufacturer has a vested interest in getting you to buy more software. Of course, AskWoody.com can give you the straight scoop, round the clock.

Be leery of mainstream press reports of new, pending, or possible infections. The folks who write those breathless newspaper articles frequently don't know what they're talking about — they get the details wrong and hype nonexistent problems. It's far better to rely on more, uh, trustworthy news sources.

✦ **If you think you have a virus, report it to your antivirus software manufacturer.** See the nearby sidebar "How to report a virus" for instructions.

✦ **If a major outbreak occurs, don't — I repeat, *don't* — send e-mails to all your friends.** That only makes the problem worse. Pick up the phone and call anyone who needs to know. Don't worry. If it's a big virus outbreak, they'll probably know already.

✦ **Use your antivirus program to run a complete scan of your system once a month.** If you have your signatures updated and your antivirus software is working properly, you don't need to do a full scan very often.

How to report a virus

Antivirus software manufacturers are constantly looking for new viruses, worms, Trojans, and other forms of malware.

Unfortunately, at least 90 percent (and probably more like 99 percent) of what they receive is junk — requests for technical support, old hoaxes, viruses that have been around for a hundred years, and stuff that doesn't bear any resemblance to real, infectious programs.

If you have a new virus, your AV software manufacturer wants to hear from you. The instructions vary depending on the manufacturer (see the following list), but if you're sure you've found a new creepy-crawly, by all means submit it.

You don't need to submit a new virus to more than one manufacturer. They all talk to each other, regularly, vociferously, and new viruses make their way rapidly from company to company. It's a credit to the AV industry that the lines of communication have been kept open, even among fierce competitors, and that samples of "real" viruses are made available to

legitimate researchers, usually within hours of being identified.

Check your antivirus software manufacturer's site frequently. In fact, while you're thinking about it, bookmark it or add the site to your Web browser's Favorites list.

✔ F-Secure: `http://support.f-secure.com/enu/home/virus problem/sample`

✔ Frisk F-PROT: `www.f-prot.com/virus info/submission_form.html`

✔ Kaspersky: `www.kaspersky.com/support.asp?chapter=26`

✔ McAfee: `http://vil.nai.com/vil/submit-sample.aspx`

✔ Microsoft: E-mail to `avsubmit@submit.microsoft.com`

✔ Symantec (Norton): `www.symantec.com/avcenter/submit.html`

Antivirus software manufacturers create new versions of their programs from time to time and, of course, they'll try to sell you the latest and greatest. In my experience, "old" AV programs with properly updated signature files are still effective six months or even a year after the "new" version comes out. You may get zapped by a completely new piece of malware, but then again, you might get zapped even if you're running the absolutely latest version of the antivirus software with up-to-the-second signature files.

Downloading and Installing AVG Free

What? You don't have an antivirus program? Are you tired of the Windows Security Center icon telling you "Your computer might be at risk/Antivirus software might not be installed"?

Hey, if it takes some nagging to get you with the program, so be it.

If you want a full-featured antivirus package, run down to your nearest software shop (or hit one of the AV software sites on the Internet) and get one of the packages. They all work well. The top-rated package this week will probably be different from the top-rated package next week. Flip a coin, read a review, and dive in.

Or if you're very cheap, like I am, you can download and install a perfectly usable free-for-personal-use antivirus program — AVG Free from Grisoft. It goes in like a champ and coexists peacefully with Windows, and you can't beat the price: free for a home user.

Here's how to download and install AVG Free:

1. **Go to Grisoft's AVG-Free Web site,** `http://free.grisoft.com.`

    The main page should look something like Figure 5-3.

2. **Click the AVG Anti-Virus Free link on the left side of the page.**

3. **At the bottom of the AVG Anti-Virus Free page, click the Download Free Version button.**

    AVG takes you to an advisor page.

4. **Click the file link to download the AVG-Free** `.exe` **file.**

5. **Follow the instructions to download the software. When the download finishes, run the file and click the Setup button.**

    AVG Free steps you through downloading the latest virus signature file (Figure 5-4), creating an emergency boot disk, and running a full scan of your computer.

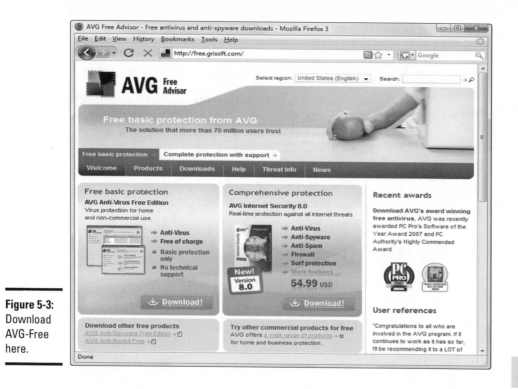

Figure 5-3:
Download
AVG-Free
here.

Figure 5-4:
AVG Free
steps you
through the
process of
installing
and bringing
itself up
to date.

If you're connected to the Internet, the First Run Wizard downloads and updates the signature file. The First Run Wizard takes you through a complete scan of your system.

Sit back and relax. It'll take a while.

6. **When the wizard's done, follow the instructions and re-start your computer. Congratulations. Your system's protected. And you won't see nag screens every day asking you to pony up $30 or $40 to keep your signature files updated.**

If you like AVG Free, tell your friends! Grisoft makes its money by selling the regular version, which includes many more features and a less-congested signature-file download site.

Making Windows Acknowledge Your AV Program

The Windows Security Center has an infuriating habit of not properly identifying installed software. In the specific case of AVG Free, Windows may or may not realize that it's running properly.

If the Windows Security Center icon in the system tray, next to the clock, continues to incorrectly tell you "Your computer might be at risk/Antivirus software might not be installed," even after your AV program is up and running, you can tell Windows to put a cork in it. Follow these steps:

1. **Choose Start⇨Control Panel⇨Security. Then click the Security Center icon.**

   Windows shows you the Security Center. In Figure 5-5, the Security Center tells me that virus protection is not found, even though I know dern good and well that AVG Free is working fine.

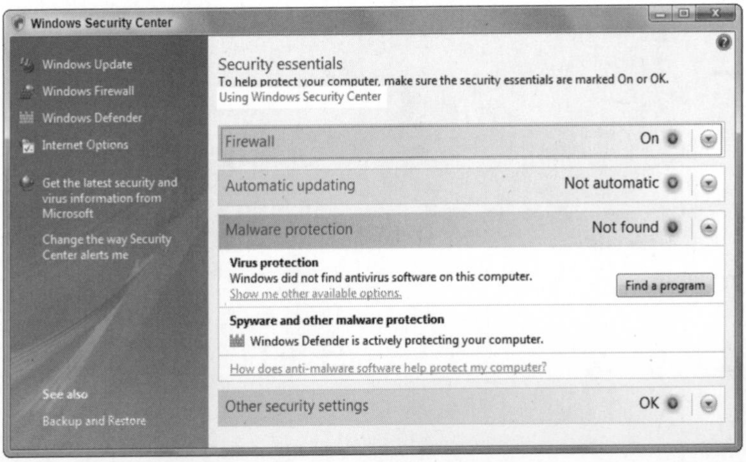

Figure 5-5:
The Security Center can't connect to my antivirus program.

2. **Click the Show Me Other Available Options link.**

   Windows opens the Choose an Antivirus Option dialog box, as shown in Figure 5-6.

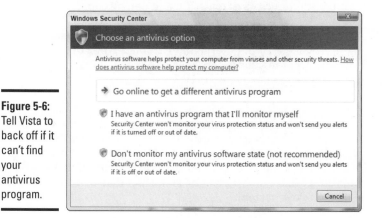

Figure 5-6:
Tell Vista to back off if it can't find your antivirus program.

3. **Click the I Have an Antivirus Program That I'll Monitor Myself option, and then click the Continue button on the inevitable User Access Control warning.**

   Windows obliges by showing the virus protection note shown in Figure 5-7.

   At least Windows stops showing those obnoxious little boxes.

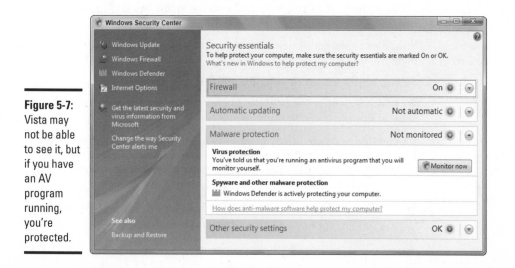

Figure 5-7:
Vista may not be able to see it, but if you have an AV program running, you're protected.

Dealing with Spyware

Windows Vista ships with Microsoft's antispyware program, Windows Defender. Although Windows Defender has many fine attributes, it has come under fire both for errors of omission and commission.

At the heart of the problem: What, precisely, is spyware? Microsoft has published a lengthy, detailed list of criteria that it applies when determining whether a specific program falls in the "spyware" category. You can see it at www.microsoft.com/athome/security/spyware/software/msft/analysis.mspx.

Whether Windows Defender follows those guidelines is the subject of heated debate. For example, Larry Seltzer at *eWeek* claims, "The security business is not like most of the software categories in which Microsoft participates. People care about reputations. Users have to trust the product. And you just can't trust a product that tells you to ignore the fact that Claria's GAIN software is installed on your system."

It's true. Windows Defender recommends that you "ignore" GAIN software as well as software from such industry, uh, luminaries as WhenU, eZula TopText, and New.net.

Here's the bottom line: Go ahead and use Windows Defender (it's already set up to run automatically every day), but don't rely on Microsoft to eliminate all programs that a reasonable person might find scummy.

To take a quick tour of Windows Defender, follow these steps:

1. **Choose Start➪All Programs and choose Windows Defender from the list.**

   Windows Defender appears, showing the results of the last scan (see Figure 5-8).

2. **To run a quick scan of your PC, click the Scan icon.**

   Windows Defender looks in the places that are most likely to harbor spyware and reports on its findings.

   If Defender finds any dicey programs, it shows you a list of the offenders by alert level: Severe/High or Medium/Low. Windows Defender tells you where the spyware appeared and gives you the option to ignore, quarantine, remove, or always allow that item.

3. **To see the results of your most recent scans, click the History icon.**

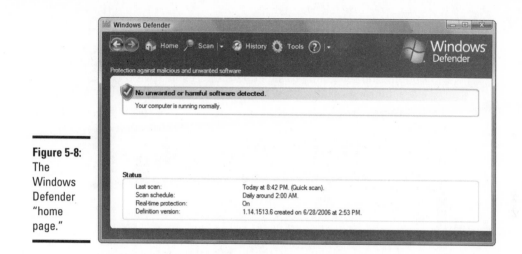

Figure 5-8:
The
Windows
Defender
"home
page."

Windows Defender picks up many strange things — it even flags AVG Free anti-virus as exhibiting "potentially unwanted behavior" (see Figure 5-9).

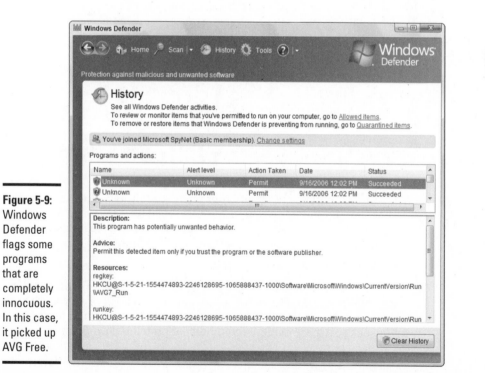

Figure 5-9:
Windows
Defender
flags some
programs
that are
completely
innocuous.
In this case,
it picked up
AVG Free.

4. Click the Tools icon.

Defender shows you the Tools and Settings pane (see Figure 5-10). This is where Defender hides all its settings, including scheduling options and the ability to sign up for Microsoft SpyNet (which sends extra information about any discovered bad program to Microsoft).

Figure 5-10: Windows Defender hides its settings under the Tools icon.

If you accidentally put a bad program in the "always allow" category, click the Allowed Items link to see a list of all the "always allow" items. Click the program that you want to have Windows Defender start looking at again, and then click the Remove from List button.

5. Click the Software Explorer link.

Defender brings up a list of programs, each with considerable detail in the right pane (see Figure 5-11). You can look at a list of all your Startup programs, currently running programs, network-connected programs, or Winsock service providers (communication-related programs).

This is by far the easiest place to identify, and potentially squelch, most of the programs that run automatically whenever you start Vista. (I say "most of the programs" because some programs, particularly rootkits, are smart enough to dodge this list. See Book III, Chapter 2 to scan for rootkits.)

Reigning in startup programs can be very easy — if you see a program on this list that you don't want to start automatically, click on the program, and click the Disable button. Unfortunately, it can also be difficult, or even dangerous, if you don't know what the program you're about to throttle is supposed to do. Don't disable (and for heaven's sake don't remove) a startup program unless you know what the program does.

I talk about using Software Explorer to streamline Vista startup in *Windows Vista Timesaving Techniques For Dummies* (also published by Wiley).

6. **Click the red *X* to exit Windows Defender.**

**Book III
Chapter 5**

**Virus Protection
and the Big
Defender**

Figure 5-11: Windows Defender gives you a great deal of information about many different key programs.

Windows Defender

Home | Scan | History | Tools | ?

Windows Defender

Protection against malicious and unwanted software

Software Explorer

View or manage important security-related areas of the computer. Using Software Explorer

Category: Startup Programs

Name	Classification
Adobe Systems Incorporated	
Adobe Acrobat	Permitted
Microsoft Corporation	
Microsoft Media Center Tra...	Permitted
Microsoft Userinit Logon A...	Permitted
Microsoft Windows Explorer	Permitted
Microsoft Windows Media ...	Permitted
Microsoft Windows Sidebar	Permitted
Windows Defender	Permitted
GRISOFT, s.r.o.	
AVG Anti-Virus System	Not yet classifi...

Adobe Acrobat

File Name: reader_sl.exe
Display Name: Adobe Acrobat
Description: Adobe Acrobat SpeedLauncher
Publisher: Adobe Systems Incorporated
Digitally Signed By: NOT SIGNED
File Type: Application
File Path: C:\Program Files\Adobe\Acrobat 7.0\Reader\reader_sl.ex
File Size: 29696
File Version: 7.0.5.2005092300
Date Installed: 9/23/2005 10:05:26 PM
Startup Type: All Users Startup Folder
Location: C:\ProgramData\Microsoft\Windows\Start Menu\Programs
Classification: Permitted
Ships with Operating System: No
SpyNet Voting: Not applicable

Refresh | Show for all users | Remove | Disable | Enable

Don't rely on Windows Defender alone to protect your computer from scummy programs. Microsoft has shown an alarming, shall we say, flexibility in the way it makes recommendations about quarantining or ignoring specific pieces of junkware.

As of this writing, the best second antispyware program I've found is Webroot SpySweeper (www.webroot.com), which costs $30 for one year or $40 for two years. It's thorough, capable, and unobtrusive; it can work side by side with Windows Defender; and the manufacturer has a long, strong record of protecting consumers from big, rich, powerful scum companies.

Book IV

Customizing Vista

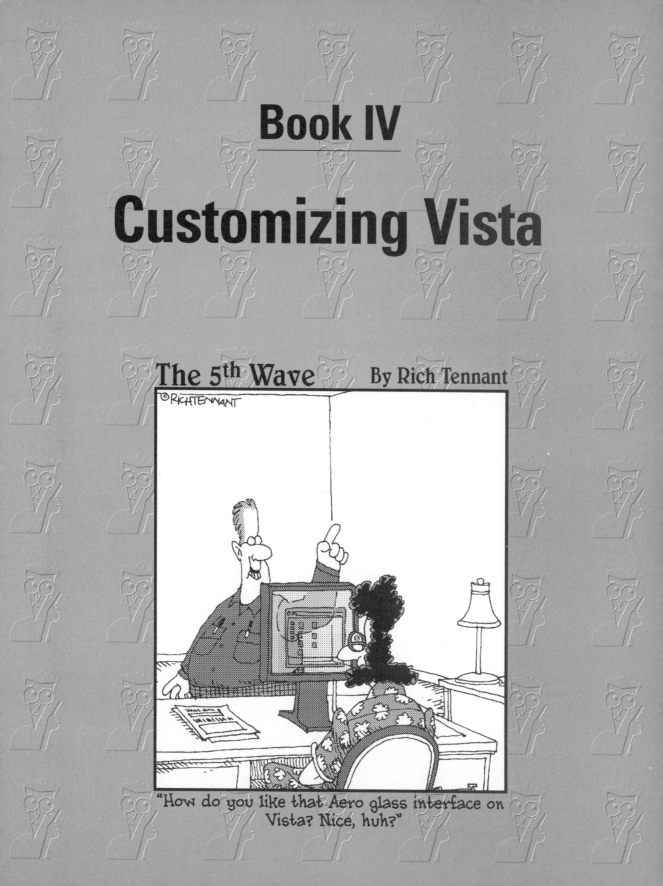

"How do you like that Aero glass interface on Vista? Nice, huh?"

Contents at a Glance

Chapter 1: Personalizing Your Desktop 283

Chapter 2: Organizing Your Vista Interface..303

Chapter 3: Searching on Your Desktop 321

Chapter 4: Beating and Cheating Vista's Games 333

Chapter 1: Personalizing Your Desktop

In This Chapter

✔ Finding the real story on how Windows puts together your desktop

✔ Taking control of each desktop level

✔ Getting the most out of your Vista Sidebar

✔ Starting a screen saver in a flash

✔ Making your folders stand out

*1*t's your desktop. Do with it what you will.

You may think it'd be easy for a computer to slap windows on the screen, but it isn't. In fact, Vista uses six separate layers to produce that Vista, er, vista — and you can take control of every layer. I show you how in this chapter.

I also include a discussion of Desktop Themes, backgrounds in Windows Explorer, and the deservedly famous (but oh so derivative) Vista Sidebar. Pretty cool stuff.

Most importantly, I include instructions for creating a Super Boss Key in the section "Selecting Screen Savers." When you press a key combination that you choose — say Alt+F10 — a Vista screen saver immediately springs into action. If you've ever been surprised when the boss walked in as you were dusting off your résumé, day trading, or playing a mean game of Minesweeper, you now know how to cover your tracks. You're welcome.

Recognizing Desktop Levels

The Vista desktop — that is, the stuff you see on your computer screen — consists of six layers (see Figure 1-1).

Background (formerly known as Wallpaper)

Base color   Icon   Sidebar gadget

Figure 1-1:
The Vista
desktop.

A working window

For a quick change of pace, Desktop Themes change five of the six layers, all at once. I talk about Desktop Themes in the section "Using Desktop Themes," later in this chapter.

Here are the six layers that control how Windows dishes up your desktop:

✦ **Level 1:** At the very bottom, the Vista desktop has a *base color,* which is a solid color that you see only if you don't have a desktop background picture or if your chosen background doesn't fill the entire screen. Most people never see their Windows base color because the background usually covers it up. I tell you how to set the base color and all the other Windows colors — for dialog boxes, the taskbar, the works — in the next section of this chapter.

✦ **Level 2:** Above the base color lives the Windows *desktop background.* (Microsoft used to call it *wallpaper,* and you'll see that name frequently.)

The people who sold you your computer may have placed some sort of dorky ad on the desktop. I tell you how to get rid of the ad and replace it with a picture you want in the section "Picking a Background," later in this chapter.

✦ **Level 3:** Windows puts all its desktop icons on top of the background layer, and underneath everything else. Bone-stock Vista includes only one icon — the Recycle Bin. If you bought a PC with Vista preinstalled, the manufacturer probably put lots of additional icons on the desktop, and you can easily get rid of them. I tell you how in the section "Controlling Icons," later in this chapter.

✦ **Level 4:** Above the icons you (finally!) find the program windows — the ones that actually do work. You know, little things like Word, Excel, and the Media Player. Vista ships with a specific program window style called "Aero" and, if your graphics card is sufficiently capable, the edges of the Aero windows are translucent — the so-called "Glass" effect. That's the origin of the term *Aero Glass.* For more information and many non-Aero non-Glass options, see the next section in this chapter. (See Book I, Chapter 2 to find out more about graphics cards and Vista.)

Program windows share the same layer with Sidebar gadgets — those incredibly useful little tools such as clocks, currency converters, calculators, performance monitors, and slide shows — that everybody and his brother seem to produce nowadays. You can slide a gadget on top of a program window, or you can slide a program window on top of a gadget. I show you how to get the most out of your gadgets in the section "Energizing the Sidebar," later in this chapter.

✦ **Level 5:** Then you have the mouse, which lives in the layer above the program windows. If you want to change the picture used for the pointer, I talk about fancy mouse pointers in the section "Changing Mouse Pointers," later in this chapter.

✦ **Level 6:** At the very top of the desktop food chain sits the screen saver. The screen saver kicks in only if you tell Windows that you want it to appear when your computer sits idle for a spell. I talk about that beast in the section "Selecting Screen Savers," later in this chapter.

If you have more than one user on your PC, each user can customize every single part of the six layers to suit his or her tastes, and Vista remembers every setting, bringing it back when the user logs on. Much better than getting a life, isn't it?

Setting Colors in Vista

Vista ships with eight prebuilt designer color schemes, with Aero being the scheme of choice. You can change to a different designer scheme or invent one all your own. To change color schemes, follow these steps:

1. **Right-click any empty part of the Windows desktop and choose Personalize.**

The Personalize Appearance and Sounds dialog box appears.

2. **Click the Window Color and Appearance icon.**

Vista opens the Window Color and Appearance dialog box (see Figure 1-2).

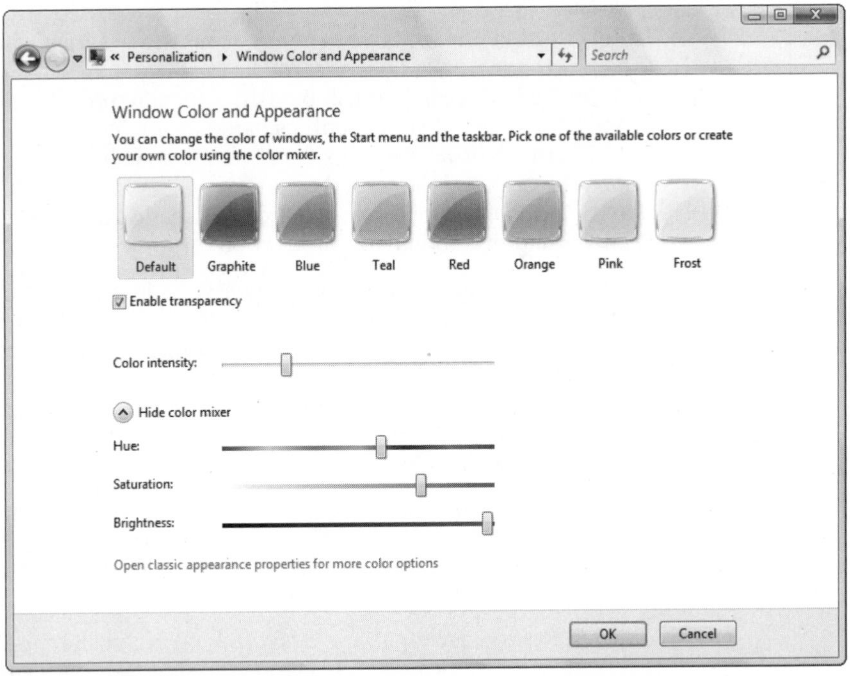

Figure 1-2:
The eight designer color schemes — and a nearly infinite array of alternatives — appear here.

3. **If you want to speed up the display on your computer (but zap one of Vista's coolest features), you can deselect the Enable Transparency check box.**

If the Enable Transparency check box is grayed out, you either don't have a powerful enough video card to run the so-called "Glass" interface, or you got conned into buying the Vista Home Basic edition. See Book I, Chapter 3 for the maddening details.

4. **Make sure that you click the Show Color Mixer down arrow, and then in the Pick a Color box, click the Default, Graphic, Blue, or Teal icon, or whichever color scheme appeals to you.**

You see the Hue, Saturation, Brightness, and Transparency sliders move when you click new color schemes. The eight designer color schemes are just recommendations for specific Transparency, Hue, Saturation, and Brightness settings.

5. **Choose one of the prebuilt color schemes, or mix and match your own by moving the Transparency, Hue, Saturation, and Brightness sliders. When you're done, click the OK button.**

Your chosen color scheme takes effect immediately.

If you want to make Vista look a little bit like the older versions of Windows, you can click the Open Classic Appearance Properties for More Color Options link. That opens the old-fashioned Appearance Settings dialog box (see Figure 1-3), which hasn't changed much since the days of Windows 95.

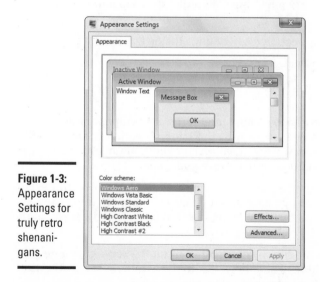

Figure 1-3: Appearance Settings for truly retro shenanigans.

Book IV Chapter 1

Personalizing Your Desktop

And if you're feeling nostalgic about detailed appearance settings for old-fashioned programs and a few backwater Windows utilities, you can click the Advanced button in the Appearance Settings dialog box. The Advanced settings there haven't changed much since Windows 3.1. (Yes, the same old bugs are still there.) Vista doesn't warn you about one key feature of these advanced settings: Everything here is virtually obsolete. You can make changes till you're blue in the face, but you will see very little effect in Vista itself. Buggy-whip stuff.

Picking a Background

If you installed Vista from a CD, you had a chance to choose your initial wallpaper, er, desktop background.

If you bought a PC with Vista preinstalled, the manufacturer chose your background — maybe the manufacturer's own logo or something a bit more subtle, like "Buy Wheaties." Don't laugh. The background is up for sale. PC manufacturers can include whatever they like. You probably have an AOL icon on your desktop. Same thing. Guess who bought and paid for that?

There's nothing particularly magical about the desktop background. In fact, Vista can put *any* picture on your desktop — big one, little one, ugly one, even a picture stolen straight off the Web. Here's how to personalize your desktop:

1. **Right-click any empty part of the Windows desktop and choose Personalize.**

   The Personalize Appearance and Sounds dialog box appears.

2. **Click the Desktop Background icon.**

   Vista shows you the Choose a Desktop Background dialog box, as shown in Figure 1-4.

3. **Click the slider to choose from many different wallpapers that ship with Vista, click down arrow next to Picture Location to choose solid colors or pictures in various locations on your computer, or click the Browse button to choose any picture you want.**

   The Solid Colors category actually changes the base color of the desktop (see the section "Recognizing Desktop Levels," earlier in this chapter) — the color that shows through if your desktop background doesn't fit the whole screen.

4. **If your picture is too big or too small to fit on the screen, you need to tell Windows how to shoehorn it into the available space. Use the three buttons at the bottom to make your selection.**

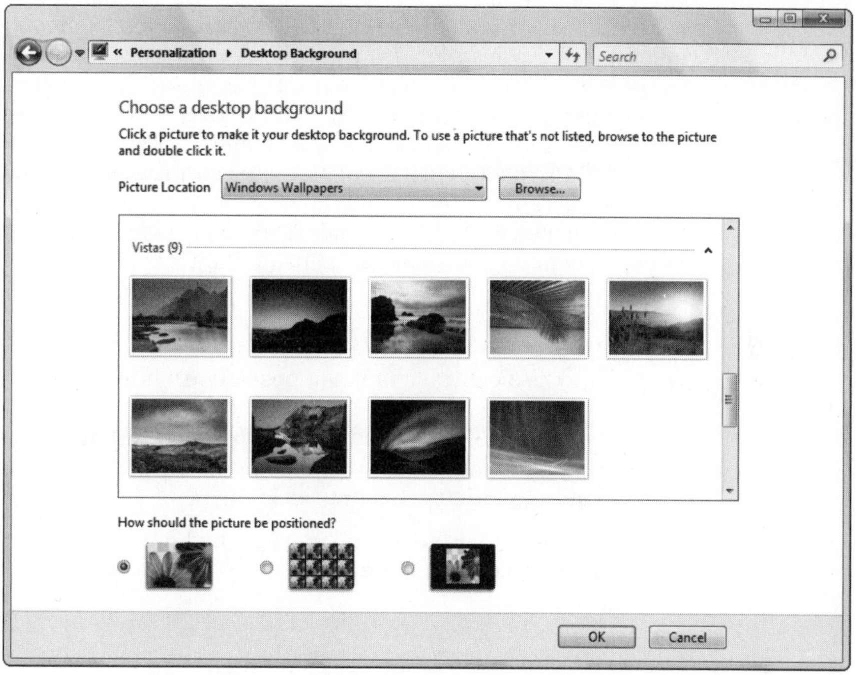

Figure 1-4:
Pick a
wallpaper.

5. Click the OK button and then the red *X* button to exit the Personalize Appearance and Sounds dialog box.

Vista lets you right-click a picture — a JPG or GIF file, regardless of whether you're using Windows Explorer or Internet Explorer — and choose Set as Desktop Background (in Windows Explorer) or Use as Background (in Internet Explorer). When you do so, Vista makes a copy of the picture and puts it in the `C:\Users\`*username*`\AppData\Roaming\Microsoft` folder and then sets the picture as your background.

Energizing the Sidebar

The Vista Sidebar teems with *gadgets,* those little things that float around on your desktop and tell you the time, show pictures, convert money, feed you the news, or do a hundred other important things. If you don't see the Vista Sidebar — and you don't have little gadgets on your screen — you're in for a treat. If you can find the Sidebar icon in the system tray (next to the clock), right-click it and choose Open. If you can't find the Sidebar icon, choose Start➪All Programs➪Accessories➪Windows Sidebar.

**Book IV
Chapter 1**

**Personalizing Your
Desktop**

As you'll discover shortly, after playing with the Sidebar, those little gadgets can be dragged onto your desktop and treated much like regular Windows windows.

You may also discover the dark underbelly of the Sidebar and gadgets: They're definitely "version 1.0" features, and sometimes they don't work quite right. Microsoft had a lot of stability problems with the Sidebar before it shipped Vista, and you might find your machine locking up unexpectedly when it's showing. If you think that the Sidebar may be gumming up your computer, right-click a blank place inside the Sidebar and choose Exit.

Changing Sidebar settings

The Sidebar has a central command post. Here's how to use it:

1. **Right-click the Sidebar and choose Properties. Equivalently, choose Start➪Control Panel➪Appearance and Personalization, and then click the Windows Sidebar Properties icon.**

    No matter how you get there, you see the Windows Sidebar Properties dialog box shown in Figure 1-5.

Figure 1-5:
Control
overall Vista
Sidebar
options here.

Windows Sidebar Properties

Sidebar

☑ Start Sidebar when Windows starts

Arrangement

☐ Sidebar is always on top of other windows

Display Sidebar on this side of screen:
◉ Right
○ Left

Display Sidebar on monitor: 1 ▾

Maintenance

    View list of running gadgets

    Restore gadgets installed with Windows

How do I customize Windows Sidebar?

    OK   Cancel   Apply

2. **You probably want to use the Sidebar (unless it's been destabilizing your computer), so select the Start Sidebar When Windows Starts check box.**

3. **Chances are also good that you don't want the Sidebar "Always on Top," but it doesn't hurt to try. Select the Sidebar Is Always on Top of Other Windows check box, and then click the Apply button.**

   See whether you prefer having the Sidebar stay on top. If not (and I don't), deselect the check box.

4. **Change the location of the Sidebar, if you wish, and when you're happy with your settings, click the OK button.**

   Vista Sidebar changes immediately.

Playing with the gadgets

Each gadget is crafted individually, and very little commonality exists in the way they all work. The following list indicates what the gadgets *do* have in common:

✦ **To add a new gadget,** right-click a blank spot on the Sidebar and choose Add Gadgets. If you don't see a gadget you like, click the Get More Gadgets Online link — or go to Google and search for "Vista sidebar gadgets."

   We commonly cover the coolest new gadgets at www.AskWoody.com.

✦ **To change the way a gadget behaves,** you have to figure out how to get into the gadget's settings. In some cases, you can click once on the Gadget, a small icon that looks like a wrench appears, and then you click on the wrench. In the case of the currency converter gadget (see Figure 1-6), click the down arrow next to the name of the currency and pick whichever currency interests you.

Figure 1-6:
The currency converter gadget.

Konfabulator

Sidebar gadgets bear more than a passing resemblance to a program once called Konfabulator and now known as Yahoo! Widget Engine (find out more about its origins and history at www.konfabulator.com/cartoon/partOne.htm). I guess it's hard to keep a good idea down. Victims of earlier versions of Windows might recall a feature called Active Desktop, a buggy, sloppy, poorly conceived Microsoft product that debuted in Internet Explorer 4, and never went anywhere except down — crashing every version of Windows in sight. Vista Sidebar finally replaces Active Desktop and does it right. We should all bow to Arlo Rose, Perry Clarke, and Ed Voas — the originators of Konfabulator — daily. We're not worthy!

You'll find *lots* of gadgets, and more are coming every day. Microsoft has made sure that gadgets are reasonably easy to program, and it has opened the floodgates for developers to try their hands.

Controlling Icons

Straight out of the box, Vista ships with exactly one icon: the Recycle Bin. Microsoft found that most people appreciate a clean desktop, devoid of icons — but it also found that hiding the Recycle Bin confused the living daylights out of all its guinea pigs (uh, Usability Lab Test Subjects). So Microsoft compromised by making the desktop squeaky-clean, except for the Recycle Bin: Aero Glass and a Recycle Bin. Who could ask for more?

If you bought a PC with Vista preloaded, you probably have so many icons on the desktop that you can't see straight. That desktop real estate is expensive, and the manufacturers get a pretty penny for dangling the right icons in your face. Know what? You can delete all of them, without feeling the least bit guilty. The worst you'll do is delete some shortcut to a manufacturer's tech support software, and if you really need to get to the program, the tech support rep can tell you how to find it from the Start menu.

Vista gives you several simple tools for arranging icons on your desktop. If you right-click any empty part of the desktop, you see that you can do the following:

✦ Choose Sort By and sort icons by name, size, type (folders, documents, shortcuts, and so on), or the date that the icon was last modified.

✦ Choose View and auto-arrange icons — that is, have Vista keep them arranged in an orderly fashion, with the first icon in the upper-left corner, the second one directly below the first one, the third below it, and so on.

✦ Choose View, and if you don't want to have icons arranged automatically, at least you can have Windows *Align to Grid* so that you can see all the icons without one appearing directly on top of the other.

✦ You can even choose View and then deselect the Show Desktop Icons check box. Your icons disappear — but that kinda defeats the purpose of icons, doesn't it?

In general, you can remove an icon from the Windows desktop by right-clicking it and choosing Delete, or by clicking it once and pressing Delete.

Some icons are hard-wired: If you put a Word document on your desktop, for example, the document inherits the icon — the picture — of its associated application, Word. The same goes for Excel worksheets, text documents, and recorded audio files.

Icons for shortcuts, however, can be changed at will. (I talk about shortcuts in Book II, Chapter 1.) Follow these steps to change an icon — that is, the picture — on a shortcut:

1. **Right-click the shortcut.**

2. **Choose Properties.**

3. **In the Properties dialog box, click the Change Icon button.**

4. **Pick an icon from the offered list, or click the Browse button and go looking for icons.**

   Windows abounds with icons. See Table 1-1 for some likely hunting grounds.

5. **Click the OK button twice, and the icon is changed.**

Table 1-1	Places to Look for Icons
Contents	*File*
Everything	`C:\Windows\System32\shell32.dll`
Computers	`C:\Windows\explorer.exe`
Communication	`C:\Windows\System32\hticons.dll`
Household	`C:\Windows\System32\pifmgr.dll`
Folders	`C:\Windows\System32\syncui.dll`
Old programs	`C:\Windows\System32\moricons.dll`

**Book IV
Chapter 1**

**Personalizing Your
Desktop**

Lots and lots of icons are available on the Internet. Use your favorite search engine, and search for "free Windows icons."

Changing Mouse Pointers

Believe it or not, Microsoft has spent many thousands of person-hours honing its mouse pointers. The pointers you see in a standard Vista installation have been selected to give you the best visual "clues" possible, without being overly distracting.

What? You think they're boring? Yeah, me too.

You can control your mouse pointer destiny in three different ways:

✦ By choosing a new Desktop Theme, which replaces all your pointers, along with the background, screen saver, and virtually everything else that can be customized. I talk about Desktop Themes in the section "Using Desktop Themes," later in this chapter.

✦ By selecting and changing individual pointers — so that you can turn, say, the Windows "I'm busy but not completely tied up" mouse pointer (which Windows calls Working in Background) into, oh, a dinosaur.

✦ By changing all your pointers, wholesale, according to schemes that Microsoft has constructed.

To change individual pointers or to select from the prefab pointer schemes, follow these steps:

1. **Choose Start⇨Control Panel⇨Appearances and Personalization⇨ Personalization⇨Mouse Pointers. (Alternatively, right-click any empty part of the desktop and choose Personalize⇨Mouse Pointers.)**

   The Mouse Properties dialog box appears, with the Pointers tab showing (see Figure 1-7).

2. **Modify your pointers in any of the following ways:**

   • **To change all the pointers at the same time,** pick a new pointer scheme from the Scheme drop-down list.

   • **To change an individual pointer,** click the pointer in the Customize box and then click the Browse button.

   Windows shows you all the available pointers — which number in the hundreds. Choose the pointer you want, and click the Open button.

   • **To bring back the original scheme,** choose Windows Aero (System Scheme), which is probably the one you started with.

- **To change an individual pointer back to the original pointer for the particular scheme that you have chosen,** click the pointer in the Customize box and then click the Use Default button.

3. **When you settle on a set of pointers that appeal to you, click the Save As button and give your new, custom scheme a name so that you can retrieve it at any time.**

4. **Click the OK button.**

   Windows starts using the pointers you've chosen.

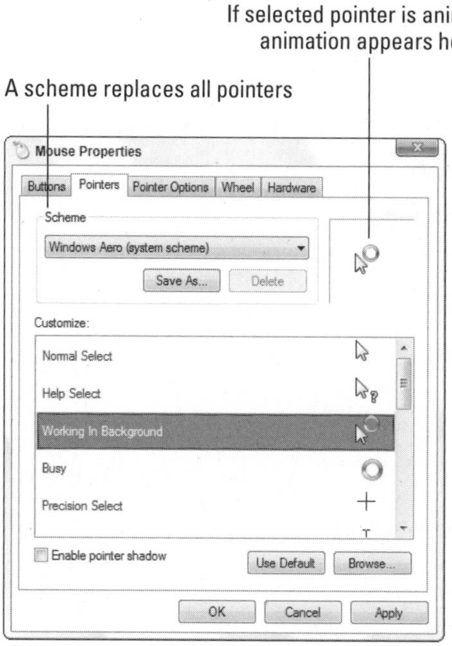

If selected pointer is animated,
animation appears here

A scheme replaces all pointers

Figure 1-7:
Mouse
pointers can
be changed
individually,
or *en masse*.

Selecting Screen Savers

Book IV
Chapter 1

Personalizing Your
Desktop

Windows screen savers are absolutely, totally, utterly, 100 percent for fun. Ten or 15 years ago, screen savers served a real purpose — they kept monitors from "burning in" the phosphors in frequently used parts of the screen. Nowadays, monitors aren't nearly as prone to burn-in (or burnout — as can be the case with humans!), and saving screens rates right up there with manufacturing buggy whips on the obsolescence scale. Flat-panel LCD monitors (such as a laptop's screen) don't have phosphors, so there's nothing to burn.

Still, screen savers are amusing, and if you follow the tricks in the following sections, they serve one truly important function: A screen saver makes an excellent front for a "Super Boss Key" — a key that you can press whenever Da Boss makes an unexpected, unwanted appearance.

Changing the screen saver

Follow these steps to select a screen saver:

1. **Right-click any empty part of the desktop and choose Personalize⇨Screen Saver.**

   Vista shows you the Screen Saver tab (Figure 1-8).

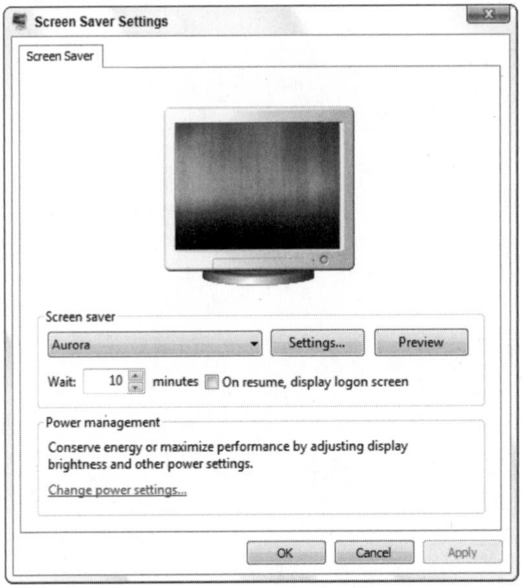

Figure 1-8: Choose a screen saver here.

2. **Choose a screen saver from the Screen Saver drop-down box. Click the Settings button and take the screen saver for a test drive. Don't like it? Pick another one.**

3. **Select or deselect the On Resume, Display Logon Screen check box.**

   This setting can be a bit confusing. Basically, it controls what happens when the computer "wakes up" after the screen saver has kicked in:

   • If the On Resume, Display Logon Screen check box is selected, when the computer wakes up, it shows the Windows logon screen. If the user who was logged on has an account that requires a password, she will have to reenter the password to get back into Windows. (I talk about passwords in the section on changing user settings in Book II, Chapter 2.)

- If the On Resume, Display Logon Screen check box is deselected, when the computer wakes up, it returns to the state it was in when the screen saver started. The user who was logged on remains logged on.

4. **When you're happy with your screen saver settings, click the OK button.**

If you want to get rid of your current screen saver, right-click an empty spot on the desktop, choose Personalize➪Screen Saver, and select None in the Screen Saver drop-down list. Click the OK button, and your screen will never be saved again.

If you want to download screen savers from the Internet, be aware of one painful fact: The overwhelming majority of "free" screen savers you find on the Web carry spyware, adware, and various kinds of scumware, which get installed when you install the screen saver. To minimize the chances of hauling dreck into your computer, install McAfee's free SiteAdvisor (www.SiteAdvisor.com) and use it in your search engine. If SiteAdvisor gives a "free screen saver" Web site a clean bill of health (signified with a green check mark), you can feel reasonably confident that downloads from the site won't include scum.

Setting up a Super Boss Key

Here's the trick you've been waiting for — the reason why you read this chapter in the first place. You can use screen savers to create a Super Boss Key — a key combination, such as Alt+F10, that you can press to make the PC immediately switch over to running the screen saver. The Super Boss Key runs independently of the usual Windows screen saver stuff: The Super Boss Key doesn't affect the screen saver you set up to run on your computer when it's idle. The screen saver is just a handy program that won't look the least bit suspicious if your boss glances at your PC's monitor.

Setting up the Super Boss Key is really quite simple, after you figure out how to get Vista's search engine to work, as I describe in the following steps:

1. **Make sure that Windows is showing filename extensions.**

   I rant about that in the section on showing filename extensions in Book II, Chapter 1. You need to see filename extensions to find your screen saver programs.

**Book IV
Chapter 1**

Personalizing Your Desktop

2. Choose Start⇨Computer. Then press Alt.

Vista opens Windows Explorer, pointing it at the entire computer, and then shows you the traditional menu bar (with the File, Edit, View, and other menus), as shown in Figure 1-9.

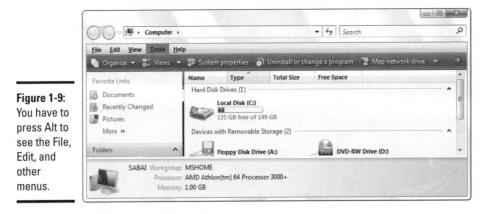

Figure 1-9:
You have to press Alt to see the File, Edit, and other menus.

3. Choose Tools⇨Folder Options, and then click the Search tab.

Vista opens the Folder Options dialog box with the Search tab showing (see Figure 1-10).

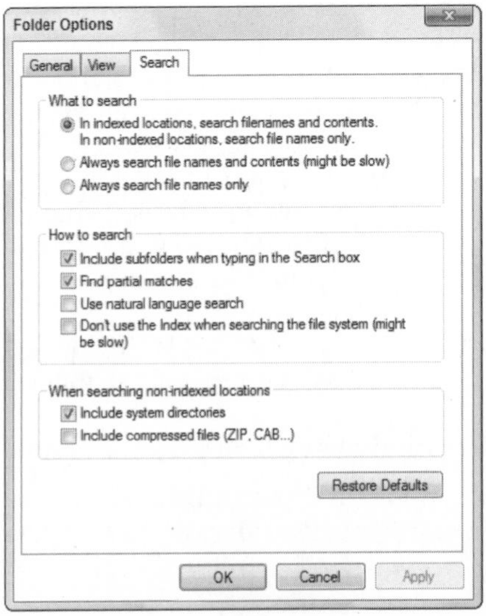

Figure 1-10:
Believe it or not, this is where you set search options.

4. **Select the Include System Directories check box, and click the OK button.**

"Include System Directories" means that Vista Search should look inside system folders. The Windows screen savers are all in system folders (although any screen savers you've downloaded and installed may also be located in other places).

5. **Back in Windows Explorer (Figure 1-9), click the Views button and select Details. Then type scr in the Search box.**

Vista warns you that the search may take a long time. And, man alive, it certainly can!

A few minutes (or decades) later, Vista comes up with, among other things, a list of files whose names contain the characters scr.

6. **Click the Type column heading and scroll down so that you can see all the files of "type" Screen Saver.**

If you open the Screen Saver Settings dialog box, you'll immediately see a correlation between .scr files and the screen savers available in the Screen Saver drop-down list. Refer to Figure 1-11 and Table 1-2.

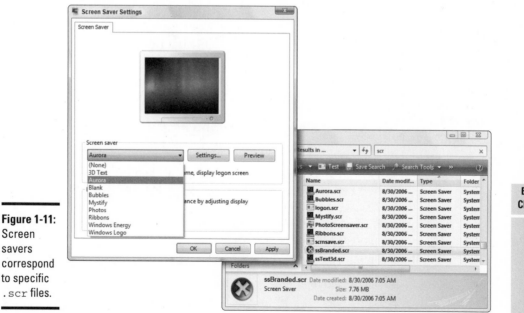

Figure 1-11:
Screen savers correspond to specific .scr files.

7. **Pick a screen saver file that you want to use for the Super Boss Key (perhaps using the Screen Saver Settings dialog box as an aid). Right-click the appropriate file and choose Send To⇨Desktop (Create Shortcut).**

A shortcut to the corresponding .scr file appears on your desktop.

8. **On the desktop, right-click the new shortcut and choose Properties.**

The Shortcut Properties dialog box appears, as shown in Figure 1-12.

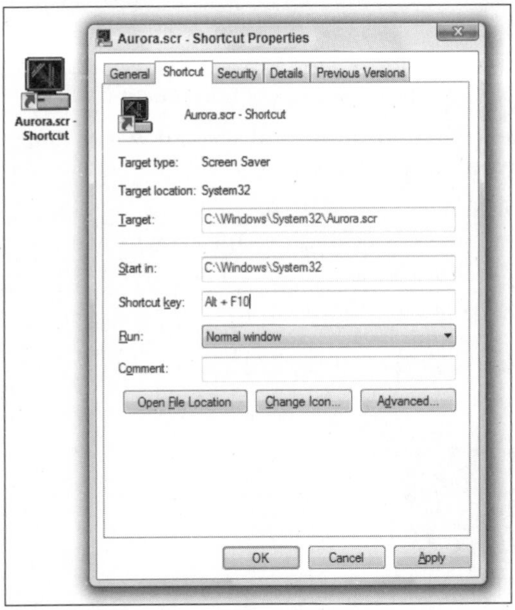

Figure 1-12:
Set the shortcut key in the Shortcut Properties dialog box.

9. **Click once in the Shortcut Key field, and then press the key combination you want to use to activate the Super Boss Key, uh, screen saver.**

In Figure 1-12, I choose Alt+F10 (that is, you hold down the Alt key and then press F10).

10. **Click the OK button, and your Super Boss Key is complete.**

Go ahead and test it — press the key combination that you chose.

Table 1-2	Screen Savers and Their Program Files
Screen Saver	*File*
3D Text	`ssText3d.scr`
Aurora	`Aurora.scr`
Blank	`scrnsave.scr`
Bubbles	`Bubbles.scr`
Mystify	`ssmyst.scr`
Photos	`PhotoScreensaver.scr`
Ribbons	`Ribbons.scr`
Windows Energy	`ssBranded.scr`
Windows Logo	`logon.scr`

A few programs "swallow" certain odd key combinations — if such a program is running, it grabs the key combinations and doesn't hand them over to Windows, so Windows won't know that you want to run your Super Boss Key screen saver. I haven't found many programs that swallow Alt+F10, but some undoubtedly exist. So test your Super Boss Key in all your favorite clandestine situations before you really need to use it, okay? If you find that your chosen key combination doesn't work with an important program (the worst offenders are games), try different key combinations until you find one that makes the Super Boss Key work.

If you want to gussy up your Super Boss Key screen saver, right-click the shortcut and choose Configure. You can change all the screen saver's settings.

Using Desktop Themes

Vista Desktop Themes incorporate many settings in one easy-to-choose package. The themes revolve around specific topics that frequently (and refreshingly) have nothing to do with Windows — say, cars with carapaces, cavorting carnivores, or carnal caruncles. A theme includes five of the six desktop levels I discuss in this chapter plus a few extra goodies — a base color for the desktop, background, settings for fonts and colors of the working windows, pictures for the reserved Windows icons (Recycle Bin, Documents, and so on), a set of mouse pointers, and a screen saver. A theme also includes a set of custom sounds that are associated with various Windows events.

To bring in a new theme, follow these steps:

1. **Right-click any open spot on the desktop and choose Personalize.**

2. **Click the Themes icon.**

3. **Choose a theme from the Themes drop-down list.**

When you bring in a theme, it replaces five of the six desktop levels I discuss in this chapter, plus the sound scheme you may have had in place. The old background, icon pictures, mouse pointers, and screen savers all remain on your PC — the theme doesn't delete them — but if you want to get any of them back, you have to go through the customization steps you used earlier.

From time to time, Microsoft releases various packages that include new Vista themes. If you want to spend your money that way, by all means help yourself. But be aware of the fact that there are zillions of Windows desktop themes available on the Web, many of them quite good, and most of them can work with Vista. Simply instruct any half-sentient Web search engine to find "Windows desktop theme" or visit www.themeworld.com for thousands of free themes.

Chapter 2: Organizing Your Vista Interface

In This Chapter

✔ **Harnessing the power of the Vista Start menu**

✔ **Getting at your most recently used documents quickly**

✔ **Starting your favorite programs with just a click**

✔ **Making workhorse programs start automatically**

*V*ista contains an enormous variety of self-help tools that can make your working (and playing!) days go faster. As you get more comfortable with the Windows inner world, you will find shortcuts and simplifications that really do make a difference.

This chapter shows you how to take off the training wheels.

Customizing the Start Menu

I gave you a brief overview of the Start menu in Book II, Chapter 1. In this chapter, I take a look at the beast in far greater detail by explaining what makes it tick and how you can use this newfound information to practice a little Start-menu mind control so that the menu reflects the way you use your PC.

The tricks you find in this section should appeal especially to those of you who bought your PC with Vista preinstalled, because the PC manufacturer probably stuck some programs on the Start menu that didn't originate with Microsoft. If you want to take control of your Start menu, follow the steps in this chapter to get rid of the stuff you don't want or need. It's your Start menu. You can't break anything. Take the, uh, bull by the horns.

To change the Start menu for everyone who uses your computer, you need to be a designated administrator. Find out more about becoming an administrator in the section on using account types in Book II, Chapter 2.

Genesis of the Start menu

Although the Start menu looks like it sprang fully formed from the head of some malevolent Windows god, in fact Windows creates much of the Start menu on the fly, every time you click the Start button. That's why your computer takes a little while between the time you click the Start button and the time you see the Start menu on the screen.

Here's where the various pieces come from, looking from top to bottom (see Figure 2-1):

✦ The name and picture in the upper-right corner are taken from the Windows sign-on screen. You can change them by following the procedure described in the section on changing user settings in Book II, Chapter 2.

✦ You can *pin* a program or shortcut to the upper-left corner of the Start menu. After being pinned, it stays there until you remove it. I go into pinning details in the next section of this chapter.

✦ The *recently used programs list* maintained by Windows goes on the left side of the Start menu, at the bottom. Although you have a little bit of control over this list, Windows (or your PC manufacturer) may stack the deck, loading favored programs first, whether you use them or not. Most of the time, you'll probably let Windows take control of the list — after you've figured out how to unstack the deck. I talk about the way Windows maintains this list in the section "Reclaiming most recently used programs," later in this chapter.

✦ Down at the bottom, *All Programs* actually connects to folders on your hard drive. This is the part of the Start menu that was designed by Microsoft to be easy to modify. You can add submenus and change or delete items to your heart's content — all of which is really pretty easy. I talk about these features in the section "Changing the All Programs menu," later in this chapter.

Although you can make many little changes to the items on the right side of the Start menu (see the section "Making minor tweaks to the Start menu," later in this chapter) — you should definitely spend a few minutes deciding whether any of the changes are worthwhile for you. The one big change on the right side is the inclusion of a Recent Items list. Some people love it. Some people hate it. Read the "Showing recent items" section, later in this chapter, and decide for yourself.

Recently used programs list

Pin a program here

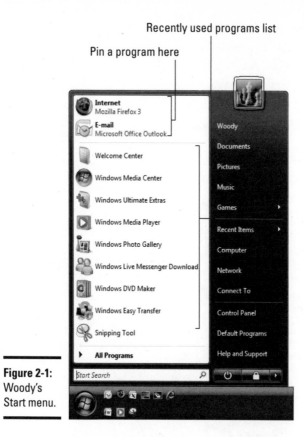

Figure 2-1:
Woody's
Start menu.

Pinning to the Start menu

Do you have one or two programs that run your life? Yeah. Me, too: Word and Outlook. I use them day in and day out. I dream in Word. Sad, but true.

If you have Microsoft Office installed on your computer, the Office installer probably pinned Outlook on your Start menu as your e-mail program. Vista enables you to easily put other programs of your choice way up at the top, in the upper-left corner of the Start menu. That's the high-rent district, the place my mouse gravitates to every time I click Start.

I don't know why, but Microsoft calls this *pinning* — kind of a wimpy name for the most powerful feature on the Start menu, eh?

**Book IV
Chapter 2**

Organizing Your
Vista Interface

Beginning adventures in pinning

When you're ready to start pinning away, here are some handy things to know about customizing this area of the Start menu:

+ **The easiest place to pin from is the All Programs menu.** Choose Start⇨ All Programs; then right-click the program and choose Pin to Start Menu.

   In Figure 2-2, I chose to pin Word 2007.

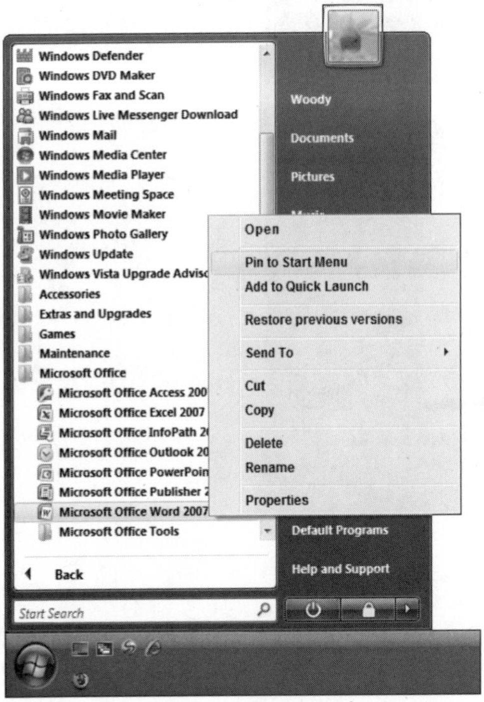

Figure 2-2:
Right-click any program anywhere on the Start menu and pin it in the upper-left corner — the high-rent district.

+ **If the program you want to pin isn't already on the All Programs menu, you can use Windows Explorer or Search to find it.** After you find the program file, simply right-click it and choose Pin to Start Menu. But of course, finding a program isn't always as easy as it sounds because many program filenames don't bear much resemblance to the program itself. For example, you can easily find `Outlook.exe`, Outlook's program file, with a standard Windows Search (see the next chapter), but you may be hard-pressed to identify `Winword.exe` as the progenitor of Word. You can find many program filenames by choosing Start⇨ Computer, double-clicking the main hard drive, and digging into the Program Files folder.

✦ **Pinning a program doesn't move it from its original location.** If you pin a program on the Start menu by right-clicking it and choosing Pin to Start Menu, Windows creates a second entry in the Start menu for the pinned copy. Your original — the program you right-clicked — stays where it was.

✦ **You can also drag and drop a program, file, or folder from anywhere in Windows onto the pinned list.** The program, file, or folder isn't moved anywhere: Vista is smart enough to put a shortcut to the item on the Start menu.

✦ **You can put pinned programs in any order you like.** When the program, file, or folder gets pinned, it appears at the bottom of the pinned pile — which is to say, below your Web browser and e-mail program. To change all that, just click the program and drag it to any other spot in the pinned list.

✦ **If you like, give your pinned programs names that you can live with.** Right-click the program and choose Rename. Figure 2-3 shows Word at the top of the pinned list, with the name shortened from Microsoft Office Word 2007 to plain ol' Word 2007.

If you pin a program on the Start menu by right-clicking it and choosing Pin to Start Menu, both the original Start menu entry and the new pinned entry are linked. If you change the name on one (right-click and choose Rename), the other copy is changed as well.

Figure 2-3:
Word, renamed the way I want, appears at the top.

Removing an item pinned to the Start menu

You can remove any program in the pinned part of the Start menu. If you right-click either of the built-in pinned programs (marked Internet and E-mail) and choose Remove from This List, the program disappears from the pinned programs area. If you right-click any other pinned programs (presumably ones that you put up in the high-rent district, or ones that your computer's manufacturer so graciously added to the list), choose Unpin from Start Menu and the item goes away.

Note that unpinning a program removes it only from the pinned list in the upper-left corner of the Start menu. The program itself stays right where it is. So do any other shortcuts to the program, whether they're elsewhere on the Start menu or somewhere else in your computer, such as on your desktop. Unpin with impunity, sez I.

Changing the pinned Internet and e-mail programs

You can change the Internet and e-mail programs listed at the beginning of the pinned list if you have more than one Web browser or e-mail program installed. (You probably do because Vista installs both Windows Mail and a link to Hotmail, er, Windows Live Mail for e-mail programs, and Office installs Outlook as well.) To change the Internet or e-mail program, follow these steps:

1. **Right-click the Start button and choose Properties.**

   The Taskbar and Start Menu Properties dialog box appears.

2. **On the Start Menu tab, make sure that the Start Menu check box is selected, and then click the Customize button.**

   You see the Customize Start Menu dialog box.

3. **At the bottom, choose your favorite Web browser and/or e-mail program from the drop-down lists.**

4. **Click the OK button twice, and your choices appear on the pinned list.**

I don't know about you, but I hate looking at the name "Microsoft Office Outlook" all the time. I'd much rather have the e-mail link on my pinned list say "Outlook 2007," "M$ Outlook," or something totally obscene. While you can't rename the Internet or E-mail entries on the pinned menu by right-clicking and choosing Properties (as you would with any other entry), it's easy to create a new entry and get rid of the stodgy old one. Here's how to do it with Outlook 2007:

1. **Pin a shortcut to Outlook on the Start menu by choosing Start➪ All Programs➪Microsoft Office.**

2. **Right-click Microsoft Office Outlook 2007 and choose Pin to Start Menu.**

   A big, ugly icon appears near the top of the Start menu that says "Microsoft Office Outlook 2007."

3. **Click the Start button again. Right-click the ugly "Microsoft Office Outlook 2007" icon and choose Rename.**

4. **Type whatever name you like and press Enter.**

You have to jump through one or two User Access Control dialog boxes that mean nothing. In the end, the ugly icon takes on the clever and witty name you typed. (Okay, so I typed **Outlook 2007**. Imaginative, eh?)

5. **Move the newly renamed icon anywhere you like. Then right-click the old icon that says "E-mail / Microsoft Office Outlook" or some such and choose Remove from This List.**

In the end, your Start menu looks something like the one in Figure 2-4.

Figure 2-4:
Outlook
renamed
the way I
want it.

- Word 2007
- Outlook 2007
- Internet
  Mozilla Firefox

Woody

Documents

Pictures

Reclaiming most recently used programs

Directly above the Start button, in the lower-left corner of the Start menu, you find a list of the programs that you've used most recently. This list can be handy: It is updated dynamically as you use programs, so you have a decent chance to see the program you need right there on the list.

When you run a program that's pinned to the upper-left corner of the Start menu (see the preceding section), it doesn't count: The most recently used list includes only programs that aren't up at the top of the Start menu.

At least, that's the theory. In fact, the most recently used programs list — like so many things in Vista — does a little bit more (or less?) than first meets the eye. Unless your hardware manufacturer has jiggered things, the first time you start Vista, you see these programs in the most recently used area:

- ✦ Welcome Center
- ✦ Windows Media Center
- ✦ Windows Media Player
- ✦ Windows Photo Gallery
- ✦ Windows DVD Maker
- ✦ Windows Calendar
- ✦ Windows Meeting Space
- ✦ Windows Easy Transfer

That's an extraordinarily weird arrangement of most recently used programs, until you realize that the Welcome Center is designed to keep you from calling Microsoft for tech support; Windows Media Player gives you, uh, lots of opportunities to purchase goodies from Microsoft; the Media Center ties you in to the Media Player, and from there to (*ka-ching!*) Urge; and so on. Nearly all the "most recently used" programs either save money for Microsoft or make money for Microsoft. Make sense now? (Your most recently used list may be stacked by your PC manufacturer, who simply sells slots to the highest bidder.)

In fact, the most recently used counter that controls what shows up in the most recently used programs box isn't quite kosher. If you play with the list for a while, you discover that the programs higher up on the list tend to stay on the list longer — whether you've used them or not. So Windows Media Player and Media Center tend to hang around a whole lot longer than Easy Transfer (which you would expect) and many programs that you happen to run (which you probably wouldn't expect). I had to run one program a dozen times before it bumped the Media Player off the top of the list.

There's no reason on earth why you should keep Microsoft's advertising (or your PC manufacturer's either, for that matter, if your list varies from the standard one) on your Start menu. Fortunately, you can easily get rid of all the built-in most recently used programs and start out with a clean slate. Just follow these steps:

1. **Right-click the Start button and choose Properties.**

Vista opens the Taskbar and Start Menu Properties dialog box, as shown in Figure 2-5.

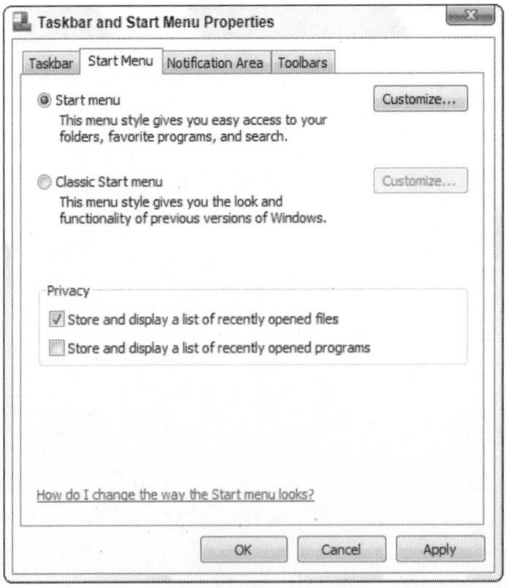

Figure 2-5:
Clear the
most
recently
used
programs
list here.

2. **Deselect the Store and Display a List of Recently Opened Programs check box. Then click the Apply button.**

   That clears the list.

3. **Now select the Store and Display a List of Recently Opened Programs check box. Then click the OK button.**

   By clearing the list and then telling Vista to start showing it again, you get rid of all the bad karma, er, salted programs, and Vista starts keeping track of the programs you really use.

Sometimes Vista doesn't quite keep up with the programs that you open. If you don't see your most recently used list updating properly, try logging off (click the Start button, click the right-facing arrow next to the picture of the lock, and choose Log Off) and logging back on again.

Windows maintains the most recently used program list on its own: You cannot drag and drop items on the list. You can, however, remove programs from the list. Just right-click an offending program and choose Remove from This List.

Changing the All Programs menu

When you choose Start➪All Programs, Windows assembles the list of "all" programs by combining these two separate folders on your hard drive:

✦ The `Start Menu\Programs` folder for you (which is in the `C:\Users\`
   `<your name>\AppData\Roaming\Microsoft\Windows` folder)

✦ The `Start Menu\Programs` folder for Windows itself (which is in the
   `C:\ProgramData\Microsoft\Windows` folder)

If you can't see the AppData folder, you haven't told Vista to show you hidden and system folders. Follow the instructions in Book II, Chapter 1, to get Vista to show you all your data.

If you look at Figure 2-6, you see how the two folders get melded into the All Programs list: Windows' `Start Menu\Programs` folder is on the top; my `Start Menu\Programs` folder is on the bottom. Folders inside the `Start Menu\Programs` folders turn into folders on the All Programs list. Files inside the folders turn into menu entries. Some folders appear on both lists: When that happens, the contents of both folders go on the All Programs menu.

Everything on the All Programs menu comes from one or the other of the two `Start Menu\Programs` folders (or much less commonly from one or the other of the two parent Start Menu folders). To see the contents of your `Start Menu\Programs` folder, right-click the Start button and then choose Explore. To see the Windows `Start Menu\Programs` folder, right-click the Start button and then choose Explore All Users.

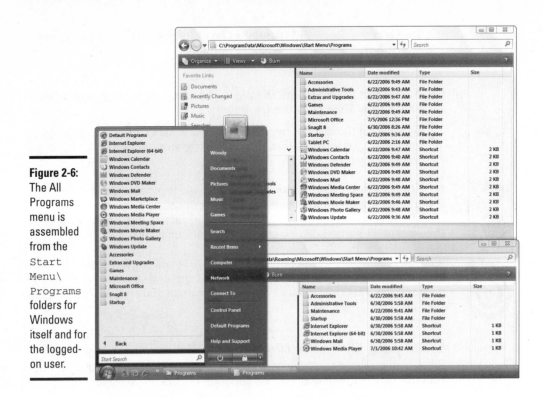

Figure 2-6:
The All Programs menu is assembled from the `Start Menu\ Programs` folders for Windows itself and for the logged-on user.

You can perform plenty of prestidigitation with the All Programs programs (say that ten times really fast) without digging into the folders that spawn the entries. For example, you can do the following:

✦ Right-click a program, folder, or file and drag it to the All Programs list. (You have to "hover" the mouse over the Start button and then hover over All Programs.) When you release the mouse button, choose Create Shortcut Here, and the program, folder, or file will always appear on your All Programs list.

✦ Right-click a program, folder, or file and choose Rename to change the name that appears on the list.

✦ Right-click a program, folder, or file and choose Delete to remove the item from the list.

If you right-click a program, folder, or file and drag it to the All Programs list, Vista puts a shortcut to the program (folder, or file) in your `Start Menu\Programs` folder. That means the shortcut only appears on your All Programs list — other folks using your computer won't be able to see it. If you want to make a shortcut available to everybody on your computer, you need to move it to the Windows `Start Menu\Programs` folder. Here's an easy way to make a shortcut available to everyone on your computer:

1. **Put the shortcut to the program that should be available to everybody on your All Programs list. (Usually you right-click a program, folder, or file and drag it to the All Programs list, choosing Create Shortcut Here.)**

2. **Right-click the Start button and choose Explore All Users. When Windows Explorer opens, double-click the Programs folder.**

   That puts you in the Windows `Start Menu\Programs` folder (see the top part of Figure 2-7).

Figure 2-7: To make a program (folder, or file) on your All Programs list accessible to everyone on your PC, drag it to the Windows `Start Menu\ Programs` folder.

3. **Right-click the Start button and choose Explore. When Windows Explorer opens, double-click the Programs folder.**

   That puts you in your `Start Menu\Programs` folder, and you should see the shortcut to the program (folder, or file) that should be available to everybody (see the bottom part of Figure 2-7).

4. **Right-click the shortcut in question and drag it from the lower window to the upper one. Release the mouse button and choose Move Here.**

   After you clear a couple of security dialog boxes, Vista dutifully moves the shortcut from your `Start Menu\Programs` folder to the Windows `Start Menu\Programs` folder.

5. **Click the red *X* to exit both Windows Explorer windows.**

   If you check, you can see that all the users on your machine now have the shortcut on their All Programs lists.

Showing recent items

In most normal circumstances — with well-behaved programs that don't crash — Windows keeps track of which documents you've opened, and shows them to you when you choose Start⇨Recent Items.

The Recent Items list is far from infallible. Even Word and Excel sometimes "forget" to add a document to the list, on occasion, and other applications range from reliable to very spotty.

Some people love the Recent Items list. Many people hate it. Folks who like the feature appreciate being able to retrieve documents quickly and easily, without spelunking for the program that created them: Click a Word document on the Recent Items list, and Word comes to life, with the document open and ready to rumble.

Folks who hate the feature would just as soon open the application and use the application's most recently opened file list (typically on the File menu) to retrieve their documents. Some of the curmudgeons — present company definitely included — don't particularly want to leave (yet another) record of what they've been doing lying around for prying eyes or snooping programs.

You can remove individual files from the Recent Items list. Just right-click the item and choose Delete.

To remove recent items from your Start menu or to clear the Recent Items list, follow these steps:

1. **Right-click the Start button and choose Properties.**

2. **Deselect the Store and Display a List of Recently Opened Files check box.**

3. **To remove the recent items list from you Start menu, click the OK button.**

   That clears the Recent Items list and takes recent items off the Start menu.

4. **On the other hand, if you only want to clear the Recent Items list, but leave the line on the Start menu, click the Apply button, reselect the Store and Display a List of Recently Opened Files check box, and then click the OK button.**

Note that you can return to this location anytime to clear the Recent Items list. But clearing the list here does *not* clear similar lists in your applications, such as Word or Internet Explorer. For those, you have to refer to the application itself.

Making minor tweaks to the Start menu

You can make a number of additional changes to the Start menu. Some of them are actually useful, particularly if you go into your computer fairly frequently to jiggle things. To tweak, follow these steps:

1. **Right-click the Start button and choose Properties.**

2. **On the Start Menu tab, make sure that the Start Menu check box is selected and then click the Customize button.**

   Vista shows you the Customize Start Menu dialog box shown in Figure 2-8.

Figure 2-8:
Change the behavior of the right side of the Start menu here.

3. **Select or deselect the features you want to enable or disable, based on the following list.**

The following Start menu items can be turned into fly-out menus:

- **Computer:** This item can have its own fly-out menu listing your drives. Enable the fly-out menu by selecting the Display as a Menu option on the Start Menu Items list.

- **Control Panel:** This item can show all the "classic applets" (read "all the individual Control Panel applications") in a fly-out menu. That's the Display as a Menu option in the Start Menu Items list.

- **Favorites menu:** This item creates a Start menu item that appears below Games, with your Internet Explorer Favorites listed on a fly-out menu. To show Favorites, select the Favorites check box on the Start Menu Items list.

- **Documents, Games, Music, your Personal folder, and Pictures:** These items can all have their own fly-out menus, listing files and folders in each. Select the Display as a Menu option on the relevant Start Menu Items list.

If you're an inveterate twiddler (or twiddler-in-training), on the Start Menu Items list, select the System Administrative Tools/Display on the All Programs Menu check box. The programs there will keep you occupied for years.

4. **Click the OK button twice when you're done.**

Do you install new programs rather frequently? Do you get really tired of Windows popping up its little yellow boxes, informing you that you've just installed a new program, when you know darn good and well that you just installed a new program? Here's a way to turn off the little yellow nag boxes:

1. **Right-click the Start button and choose Properties.**

2. **On the Start Menu tab, make sure that the Start Menu check box is selected and then click the Customize button.**

3. **Click the Advanced tab and deselect the Highlight Newly Installed Programs check box. Click the OK button twice.**

I call it the D'oh! switch.

Using the Quick Launch Toolbar

Vista's Quick Launch toolbar is a little tray of icons that sits next to the Start button. Here, you can stick shortcuts to start all your favorite programs, folders, Web favorites, or anything else you can create a shortcut to (see Figure 2-9). It's one of the handiest features in Windows.

Figure 2-9:
The Quick
Launch
toolbar.

Unless you or your evil-but-oh-so-cute twin turned it off, your Quick Launch toolbar appears immediately to the right of the Start button: If you see tiny icons to the right of the Start button, Quick Launch is on duty.

If you can't see the Quick Launch toolbar, you need it quick. Here's how to get it back: Right-click any open spot on the Windows taskbar and choose Toolbars⇔Quick Launch.

Many gadgets for the Vista Sidebar take on the functions of the Vista Quick Launch toolbar. If you prefer the bright lights of a quick-launch gadget, by all means go ahead and give the standard Vista Quick Launch the heave-ho. But remember that those big, beautiful gadget icons take up a lot of screen real estate.

Adding your own icons to the Quick Launch toolbar is very simple, too, but you immediately run into problems trying to squeeze more icons into that teensy-tiny space. Here's how to avoid the problem in the first place:

1. **Make sure that the Quick Launch toolbar is showing (right-click any open spot on the Windows taskbar and choose Toolbars⇔Quick Launch).**

2. **Unlock the taskbar so that you can increase the size of the Quick Launch toolbar. To do so, right-click any open spot on the Windows taskbar and deselect the Lock the Taskbar option.**

Windows shows two small drag handles, one to the left and one to the right of the Quick Launch toolbar.

3. Grab the drag handle on the right and stretch it out (to the right) a bit.

4. Find a program that you want to put on the Quick Launch toolbar.

For example, if you have Microsoft Office installed and you want to put Word down there, choose Start⇨All Programs and look for Microsoft Word.

5. Right-click the program and drag it down to the Quick Launch toolbar. When you release the icon, choose Copy Here.

You see a big, black I-beam on the Quick Launch toolbar that indicates where the icon will go.

When you drag icons to the Quick Launch toolbar, right-click and choose Copy Here so that the original program shortcut stays intact. If you click (or right-click and choose Move Here), the shortcut gets moved.

6. Drag as many icons to the Quick Launch toolbar as you like. When you're done, butt the right drag handle up against the rightmost icon and then right-click the Windows taskbar and choose Lock the Taskbar.

You have more "play" with the Quick Launch toolbar's resizing drag handles than you think. Try squishing the Quick Launch toolbar by setting the right drag handle on top of the rightmost icon and then lock the taskbar. When you right-click the taskbar and choose Lock the Taskbar, all the icons will probably appear anyway. It never hurts to tighten things a bit so that Windows can use as much of the taskbar as possible.

Performing a Custom Startup

Do you start a specific program just about every time you crank up Windows? Maybe you want to get Windows Media Player going every time Windows wakes up. A friend of mine always starts the Windows Calculator. Of course, he's a hopeless drudge, so don't let him influence you.

You can easily tell Vista that you want to run a specific program every time Windows starts. You just have to put the program in the Startup folder.

Say you want to start the Windows Calculator every time anybody logs on to Windows. You can make that happen if you put a shortcut to the Calculator in the Windows `Start Menu\Programs\Startup` folder, like this:

1. Put a shortcut to the Calculator on your desktop by choosing Start⇨ All Programs⇨Accessories, right-clicking Calculator, and choosing Send To⇨Desktop (Create Shortcut).

You should see a shortcut to the Calculator sitting on your desktop.

2. **Right-click the Start button and choose Explore All Users.**

3. **Double-click the Programs folder and then double-click the Startup folder.**

4. **On your desktop, click the shortcut to the Calculator, drag it into the Windows** `Start Menu\Programs\Startup` **folder, and release the mouse button.**

   Vista moves the shortcut into the Startup folder.

5. **Click the red *X* to exit the Startup folder.**

   You're done. The next time anyone logs on to Windows, the Calculator will start.

If you get tired of the Calculator starting every time you start Vista, you can always delete the shortcut from the Startup folder. Better, if you want to block Calculator (or any other program or shortcut in Startup) from starting, use Windows Defender's Software Explorer. I talk about Software Explorer in Book III, Chapter 5.

If you want the Calculator to start for just one user, you need to put a shortcut to the Calculator in that user's Startup folder. Here's the easy way to do that: Have that user log on, right-click the Start button, and choose Explore. Then follow Steps 2 through 4 in the preceding list.

Chapter 3: Searching on Your Desktop

In This Chapter

✔ Sorting through the search maze

✔ Understanding why search is so weird

✔ Using Search settings

✔ Saving and reusing searches

Computers store lots and lots of stuff. As long as you're churning out the stuff, life goes along pretty easily. Sooner or later, though, the time comes when you have to find some stuff — the right stuff — and that's when the stuff hits the fan.

Vista includes a powerful Search feature — actually, several search features — that make it reasonably easy and fast to find stuff stored on your computer.

This chapter explains how to use Vista's search features in ways that won't leave you scratching your head. Or other parts of your anatomy.

If you want to understand how Windows performs searches, you have to be able to see filename extensions — the short (usually three-letter) suffix of each file's name that identifies the file's type, such as .doc and .jpg. Vista does not show you filename extensions unless you specifically tell it to. To make heads or tails out of anything in this chapter, make Windows show you filename extensions by following the steps I outline in Book II, Chapter 1.

A Brief History of Finds

Searching stands as one of the weakest spots in the annals of Windows. Since the very first versions of Windows, Microsoft has given search short shrift, and the effects of more than a decade of neglect will drive you nuts, even today. Especially today.

Scanning versus indexing

There are two fundamentally different ways of looking for things on a computer, scanning and indexing:

✦ *Scanning* involves going through each file, one by one, trying to find what you're looking for. Think of Diogenes walking through the marketplace of Athens, in broad daylight, with a lantern, seeking an honest man. Sometimes Vista stumbles upon the things you seek. Sometimes it doesn't. Every time, it takes forever.

✦ *Indexing* involves digesting the contents of your computer and maintaining a list, not unlike the index in the back of this book. When you have to find an honest man, you needn't walk through the marketplace. You just look under *H* in the Athens Yellow Pages, eh?

In principle, indexing's pretty simple: The computer waits until you aren't doing anything; then it starts looking, methodically, at every file on your hard drive(s). Say the computer's looking at a file called Woody da Dummy.doc. Inside the file, the computer discovers the words "jumping jack flash." It builds an index entry that says, among other things, "the word *jumping* is in Woody da Dummy.doc." Then it builds another index entry that says, "the word *jack* is in Woody da Dummy.doc." And so on. When you ask for all the files that contain the word *jack,* any program looking at the index realizes immediately that Woody da Dummy.doc should be included on the list.

In practice, indexing is one whole heckuvalot more difficult than you might imagine. The biggest problem Microsoft had, for years, was the intrusiveness of the bloody indexer: You'd be typing along, pause a few seconds to think, and WHAM! All of a sudden, this crazy program had taken over your machine. Resume typing, and you had to wait an eternity to regain control of your PC.

Before Vista, if you used Windows to look for something, you really had to scan. Why? Because the indexer built into Windows XP (and all previous versions) was a bug-laden joke. The so-called "indexing service" skipped documents for reasons nobody ever figured out. It soaked up computer cycles with glee and crashed with astonishing regularity. You could get into the indexing service through the Microsoft Office applications, but nobody who ever used the Windows approach directly ever tried it more than twice.

Desktop search

With Microsoft showing no interest in search, an add-on industry grew up to help folks index and look up the contents of Windows systems — so-called "desktop search" products like Magellan became a mainstay for many Windows users.

Then came Google — Google Desktop Search, to be precise. When the Googlies brought their prodigious searching capabilities to the average Windows XP user, Microsoft finally sat up and paid attention. Suddenly, Microsoft decided that maybe people should be able to search for stuff on their computers. Imagine that. The resulting Microsoft product, named — I kid you not — *MSN Search Toolbar with Windows Desktop Search* demonstrated all the savvy its obfuscating name would imply. MSN died, or at least faded into well-deserved obscurity. The MSN toolbar died. But MSN Search Toolbar with Windows Desktop Search lives on, albeit modified, in Vista.

Magellan, Google Desktop Search, MSN Search Toolbar with Windows Desktop Search, and a dozen other products in the same genre lacked one key feature: They weren't part of the operating system. Because they all had to operate as plain-vanilla applications, running on top of Windows, you had little hope of making any of them operate unobtrusively and reliably. Indexing takes a lot of heavy lifting. Finally, with Vista, indexing gets relegated to the operating system, where it belongs.

Wither, er, whither WinFS

Fancy relational databases have been around for a decade or two: Computers can be taught to extract information from files and link the information in useful ways. Windows' various file systems, over the years, have treated files like dumb blobs: No attempt has been made to look inside the files and aggregate useful information, and precious little attempt has been made to keep track of even the simplest information about a file's contents — so-called *metadata* — like the type of file (Word document, Excel spreadsheet, Manitoba wingless flyspeck), the person who created the file, the artist who recorded the song, or the photographer who took the shot.

WinFS, or *Windows Future Storage,* was supposed to change all that. Starting in 2003, Microsoft began developing a relational database system that would hold all the files on a Windows PC and help you find what you wanted using advanced database technology. Those of us who follow such things never knew what WinFS would do, really, but the concept seemed tantalizing: bring advanced database capabilities to Windows' creaky NT File System (NTFS). Several eternal optimists (present company included) thought that WinFS would finally make it easy to store, organize, manipulate, and most of all, find the files we needed when we needed them. For years, WinFS was touted as one of the Big New Important Features in Windows Vista. And in June 2006, when Vista was far down the beta testing trail, Microsoft killed it.

Much of the disarray you see in Vista's searching capabilities can only be understood when you realize that *it was all cobbled together at the last minute.* Vista was supposed to have this fancy new relational file system, and it disappeared, vanishing into thin vapor. If you see something that doesn't make sense, well, now you know why.

**Book IV
Chapter 3**

**Searching on
Your Desktop**

Searching Basics

Maybe you need to find all the handouts you typed for your Porcine Prevaricators seminar. Maybe you remember that you have a recipe with tarragon in it, but you can't remember where in the world you put it. Maybe you accidentally moved or deleted all the pictures of your trip to Cancun, or Windows Media Player suddenly can't find your MP3s of the 1974 Grateful Dead tour.

Good. You're in the right place.

People generally go looking for files or folders on their computers for one of two reasons. Perhaps they vaguely remember that they used to have something — maybe a Christmas letter, a product description, or a great joke — and now they can't remember where they put it. Or, they have been playing around with Windows Explorer, and whatever they thought was sitting in a specific place isn't there anymore. In either case, the solution is to make Vista do the work and go searching for your lost files or folders.

Vista packs search boxes everywhere, most noticeably in the upper-right corner of every Windows Explorer window.

If you type something in a Search box, Vista immediately runs to the index, looking for matches in the current folder and all the folders underneath the current folder. It searches for all kinds of files — documents and text files, of course, but also pictures and music, e-mail messages, even the contents of Web pages.

The result frequently reminds me of listening for a specific conversation in a packed room — or a mosh pit.

Here's a simple example of a relatively tame search:

1. **Choose Start⇨Documents.**

   Windows Explorer opens your Documents folder.

2. **In the upper-right corner, where it says *Search,* type a word that might appear inside your Documents folder or one of its subfolders.**

   The word can be inside a file (providing that Vista recognizes the file type), be part of the file's name, or appear as metadata (such as the author or artist) attached to a file.

   In Figure 3-1, I type **water** and Vista finds all the files in my Documents folder (and subfolders) that contain the text *water,* or where *water* appears in the filename or in a file's metadata.

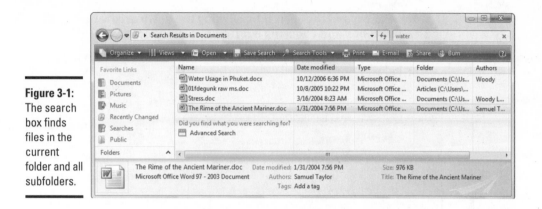

Figure 3-1:
The search
box finds
files in the
current
folder and all
subfolders.

3. **Click the Search Tools button and choose Search Pane. Then click the down arrow next to Advanced Search. (Equivalently, click the Advanced Search link at the bottom of the list of files.)**

   Vista shows you the Advanced Search pane shown in Figure 3-2.

4. **You can narrow the search to a specific kind of file by clicking one of the Show Results For buttons.**

   Clicking a Show Results For button limits the search to specific filename extensions (see Book II, Chapter 1).

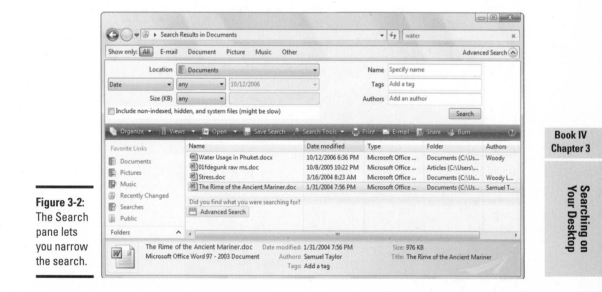

Figure 3-2:
The Search
pane lets
you narrow
the search.

**Book IV
Chapter 3**

**Searching on
Your Desktop**

5. **You can expand the search by clicking the down arrow next to the Location box and choosing a different search location.**

If you choose Indexed Files (see Figure 3-3), Vista looks at everything in its index.

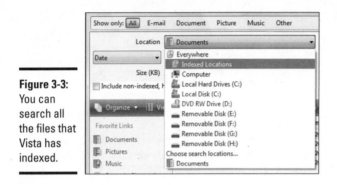

Figure 3-3: You can search all the files that Vista has indexed.

6. **For more advanced search options, follow these steps first:**

6a. **Click the Search Tools button and choose Modify Index Locations.**

The Indexing Options dialog box appears (see Figure 3-4). To make meaningful changes to Vista searches, you must first know which parts of your hard drive(s) have been indexed, and that's what this dialog box tells you. The dialog box lists every location that's used in building Vista's index.

Figure 3-4: Vista indexes all the folders included in this dialog box.

This dialog box is very confusing. In particular, the Exclude Default entry tells the Vista indexer that you want to index all the folders in the Users folder — basically all the documents, desktops, pictures, and the like for every user — but you want to exclude the hidden \Users\Default folder, which includes entries used as the "Default" when you create a new user.

If you really, really want to force Vista to index another hard drive, or another folder on your main hard drive, click the Modify button and follow the instructions to expand the indexed locations.

6b. In the Indexing Options dialog box, click Advanced.

On the Advanced Options dialog's Index Settings tab (see Figure 3-5), you have an opportunity to index encrypted files. You can change where the index is stored. You can also rebuild the index, if Vista's search just isn't finding the files it should be finding.

Watch out. Rebuilding an index can take hours. Or days.

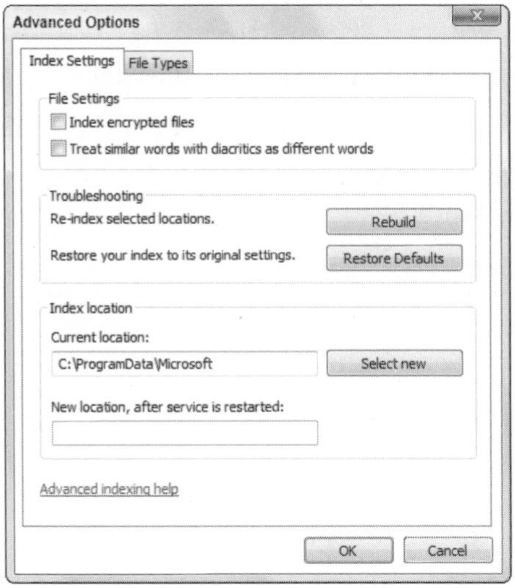

Figure 3-5:
Force Vista
to rebuild its
index here.

Advanced Options

Index Settings | File Types

File Settings
☐ Index encrypted files
☐ Treat similar words with diacritics as different words

Troubleshooting
Re-index selected locations. **Rebuild**
Restore your index to its original settings. **Restore Defaults**

Index location
Current location:
C:\ProgramData\Microsoft **Select new**

New location, after service is restarted:

Advanced indexing help

OK | Cancel

6c. In the Indexing Options dialog box, click the File Types tab.

You see the list of indexed file types shown in Figure 3-6.

6d. Vista should be set to index PDF files. Make sure the PDF box (with the description PDF IFilter) is checked, and select the Index Properties and File Contents option. Then click OK, and Close, to get back to the Advanced Search dialog in Figure 3-2.

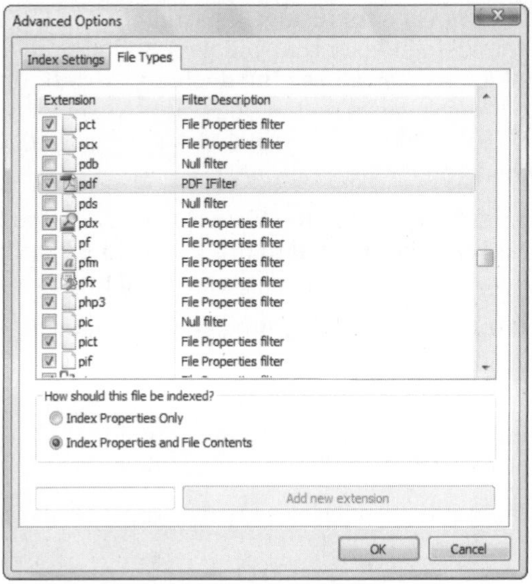

Advanced Options

Index Settings | File Types

Extension	Filter Description
☑ pct	File Properties filter
☑ pcx	File Properties filter
☐ pdb	Null filter
☑ pdf	PDF IFilter
☐ pds	Null filter
☑ pdx	File Properties filter
☐ pf	File Properties filter
☑ pfm	File Properties filter
☑ pfx	File Properties filter
☑ php3	File Properties filter
☐ pic	Null filter
☑ pict	File Properties filter
☑ pif	File Properties filter

How should this file be indexed?
○ Index Properties Only
● Index Properties and File Contents

Add new extension

OK   Cancel

Figure 3-6: Have Vista index the contents of your PDF files.

You now know which folders, and which files, feed Vista's indexer.

6e. **Click the Search Tools button and choose Search Options.**

Vista opens the Folder Options dialog box and shows you the Search tab, as shown in Figure 3-7.

This dialog box is very confusing. In spite of the title of the box, the settings here don't refer to search options for a specific folder. Rather, they're system-wide settings for *all* searches.

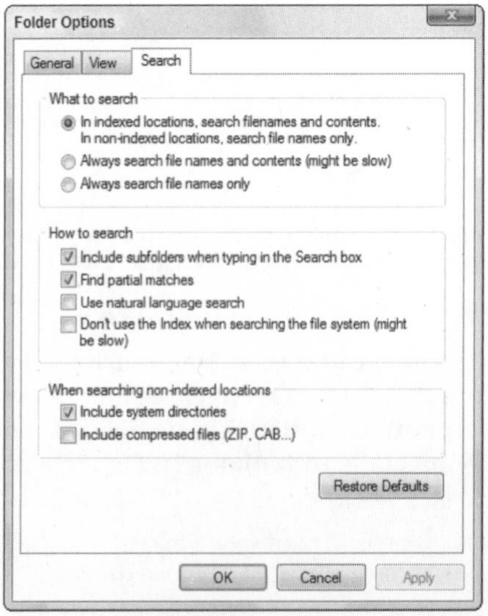

Folder Options

General | View | Search

What to search
● In indexed locations, search filenames and contents. In non-indexed locations, search file names only.
○ Always search file names and contents (might be slow)
○ Always search file names only

How to search
☑ Include subfolders when typing in the Search box
☑ Find partial matches
☐ Use natural language search
☐ Don't use the Index when searching the file system (might be slow)

When searching non-indexed locations
☑ Include system directories
☐ Include compressed files (ZIP, CAB...)

Restore Defaults

OK   Cancel   Apply

Figure 3-7: Set most search options in this dialog box.

6f. **Make changes to the search settings, following the guidelines in Table 3-1. When you're done, click the OK button.**

Personally, I tell Vista to include system directories but accept all the other defaults.

Your search settings will apply to all subsequent searches.

7. **With the advanced settings nailed down in Step 6, you are now ready to perform an advanced search. Use the boxes in the Advanced Search pane to set up the search any way you like. When you're ready to search, click the Search button.**

8. **Click the red *X* to exit Windows Explorer.**

Table 3-1	Search Options
Setting	*What It Means*
In Indexed Locations, Search File Names and Contents	Uses the index that you set up in Step 6. Vista doesn't scan or index the contents of files outside the indexed locations, but it does scan and index file names, no matter where the file may be located. You probably want this setting.
Always Search File Names and Contents	Uses the index but also scans inside files that aren't in the index (very slow).
Always Search File Names Only	Uses the Windows XP approach, where file contents and meta-data are ignored. This approach doesn't use the index but is fast.
Include Subfolders	Looks inside subfolders (and sub-subfolders) when searching from Windows Explorer.
Find Partial Matches	If you search for *water,* you also get *watering* and *watered-down.*
Use Natural Language Search	Tries to figure out what you're looking for based on the description you type. Doesn't work very well.
Don't Use the Index When	Ignores the index entirely (painfully slow).
Include System Directories	Includes system and hidden folders in the search.
Include Compressed Files	Also scans inside compressed files.

After you've run a search, you can slice and dice the results in many different ways. Click a column heading (refer to Figure 3-1) and re-sort or group the results. In particular, if you click the down-arrow to the right of the column heading, you can do the following:

✦ **Sort** in ascending or descending order (say, A to Z, Z to A, or oldest to newest).

✦ **Group** so that like items (say, all the documents written by a particular author) appear listed together.

✦ **Stack** so that like items appear in folders constructed on the fly. This is a good choice if you have a lot of results and need to sift through them by hand.

The following are a few school-of-hard-knocks tips:

✦ Your search options settings (and the list of locations included in Vista's index) have an enormous influence on what can be found and what will appear in the search results. If you can't find a file that you know must be on your PC, check your options.

✦ If you're looking for photographs, don't use Vista search. Pop into the Photo Gallery (see Book VII, Chapter 4).

✦ If you're looking for music, don't use Vista search. (See a pattern here?) Use Windows Media Player, iTunes, WinAMP, or whatever player happens to ring your chimes. The tools there are much better suited to music searches. If you're looking for video, use Media Center, not Vista search. The tools there are much better . . . aw, you get the idea.

Saving and Reusing Searches

You probably know that you can save and reuse searches: Set up a search once, and you can bring it back with the click of a mouse.

You probably didn't know that Vista doesn't actually *save* much of anything. When you bring up a saved search, Vista runs the search again. Confusingly, it uses the search options settings (see the preceding section) currently in effect. So if you saved a search with a specific bunch of search options, and then you bring the saved search up a week later, you may get an entirely different set of results.

Saved Search is one of those features that originated in the days of WinFS (see the section "Wither, er, whither WinFS," earlier in this chapter). During Vista's development, WinFS-style relational database indices morphed into "Virtual Folders," but when Microsoft found that the performance of Virtual Folders, uh, virtually brought most PCs to their knees, it abandoned that idea, too. In the end, what you see — Saved Searches — doesn't make much sense.

A saved search is actually a kind of text file, called an Extensible Markup Language (XML) file, that's stuck in the C:\Users\<*username*>\Saved Searches folder. From there you can move the entire folder to another location, drop it on the desktop, or whatever. The individual "found" items in the folder — the documents, files, e-mail messages, and so on — behave a little bit like shortcuts, but if you click and drag one of them to a new location, the file gets yanked out of its original location (wherever that may be) and gets relocated to wherever you drop it.

To save a search, follow these steps:

1. Follow the steps in the preceding section to hone your search.

2. Click the Save Search button.

Vista shows you the Save As dialog box (see Figure 3-8).

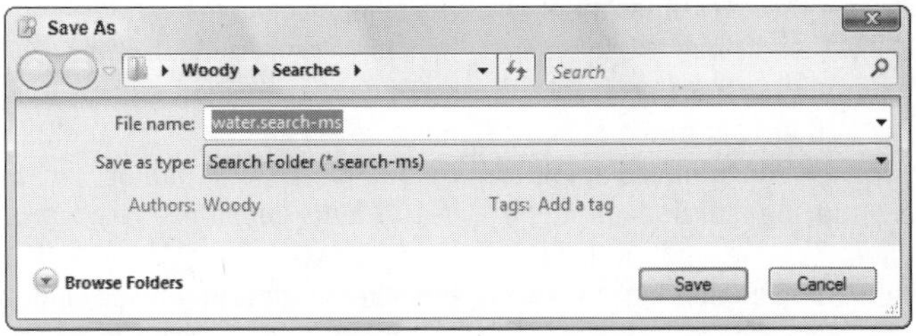

Figure 3-8:
Saving a
search is
easy (but of
dubious
value).

3. Type a descriptive name in the File Name box.

4. Click the Save button.

Vista adds your saved search to the Searches list in the Favorite Links section (see Figure 3-9) and makes it available several places in Windows Explorer.

Figure 3-9:
Saved
searches
appear in
several
places in
Windows
Explorer.

**Book IV
Chapter 3**

**Searching on
Your Desktop**

Search changes in Vista Service Pack 1

It didn't take long. Shortly after Windows Vista hit the ether, Google screamed bloody murder about Vista's locked-in desktop search. Behind the scenes, the Googlies filed a confidential formal complaint with the US Department of Justice saying that Microsoft was taking unfair advantage of its operating system monopoly to squeeze Google and others out of the desktop search market. Chief among the complaints was that Vista's indexing service can't be turned off, so anybody running a non-Microsoft product had to endure two competing indexers sucking up cycles simultaneously. Add the fact that Microsoft's Search appeared hard-wired all over the place — in the upper-right corner of most Explorer windows, just above the Start button, on the right side of the Start menu — and, clearly, Microsoft was playing dirty. Again.

In June 2007, a series of events came to light. Word of Google's confidential complaint leaked. Then we learned that the man in charge of DOJ's antitrust division circulated a memo to state attorney generals asking them to reject Google's complaint. Odd, considering he had been the vice chair of the antitrust and consumer protection group at a Washington DC law firm that represented Microsoft during the Netscape antitrust trials. Microsoft's General Counsel Brad Smith was then quoted as saying, "We've made a decision to go the extra mile to be reasonable . . . . The discussions between the company and the various government agencies have been quite fruitful." Microsoft filed a document with DOJ saying it "will create a mechanism for end users and OEMs to select a default program to handle desktop search . . . the default desktop search program will be launched whenever Windows launches a new top-level window to provide search results. This will include an existing location on the Start menu that a user can select to display additional search results in a new window." If you read that closely, it doesn't promise much, but nevermind.

Fast forward to March, 2008. Vista Service Pack 1 (see Book I, Chapter 3) rolled out. The Search entry on the right side of Vista's Start menu disappeared — if you can see Search on the right side of your Start menu, you haven't yet installed Service Pack 1. But, as best I can tell, none of the other changes promised to the DOJ surfaced. You can bet that the lawyers are burning the midnight oil on this one. We haven't heard the last.

Chapter 4: Beating and Cheating Vista's Games

In This Chapter

✔ Playing the Vista Games

✔ Beating the Vista Games

✔ Cheating the Vista Games

*Y*ou really bought this book because you heard it had all the game cheats, didn't you? C'mon, admit it.

What? Your boss doesn't like you playing games on the company PC? Remind her that Windows games are, singularly, the best way to brush up on your mousing skills, take your mind off work for a brief spell, and take a break from all the typing. How do you spell *Repetitive Motion Syndrome?*

Windows Vista ships with nine games (see Figure 4-1), many of which are quite good. If you can't see all the games, and your network admin hasn't blocked them, you may be able to retrieve some by choosing Start⇨ Control Panel⇨Programs⇨Turn On or Off Windows Features and selecting the appropriate check boxes in the Games category. If you have more than nine games, you're playing with Vista Ultimate, and I salute you.

Figure 4-1:
Vista's
games
range from
kid-friendly
to utterly
fiendish.

Solitaire

The venerable classic *Solitaire,* the oldest Windows game of all (see Figure 4-2) — dating back to the prehistory of Windows 3.0 — still captures the hearts and spare cranial cycles of millions. To get it going, choose Start➪Games and double-click the Solitaire icon. But you've probably done that a hundred times already, haven't you?

If you don't know the rules for Solitaire in general, ask the guy sitting next to you on your next flight. The Windows version of Solitaire has the following rules:

✦ Doesn't let you pull a card from inside a stack but does let you move a card from one of the suit stacks back onto the playing table

✦ Lets you undo any move or group of moves (press Ctrl+Z)

✦ Restricts you to putting Kings in open stacks

You probably know that if you double-click a card that's eligible to go into a suit stack, Windows moves the card for you. But you probably didn't know that if you press Ctrl+A, or right-click the playing table, Windows moves *all* the eligible cards from the main playing table onto the suit stacks.

Solitaire can give you a hint, if you want it: Press H. Just don't expect a *good* hint. Solitaire's advice comes free and is worth every penny.

Choose Game → Change Appearance to change the picture on the back of the card

Click here to deal

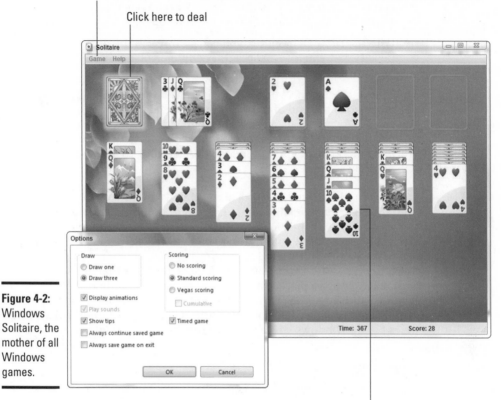

Figure 4-2:
Windows
Solitaire, the
mother of all
Windows
games.

Drag and drop cards to move them

Scoring a Solitaire game makes cricket look like child's play.

Standard scoring

Solitaire standard scoring goes like this:

✦ Add 5 points when you move a card off the deck or if you turn over a card.

✦ Add 10 points when you move a card to one of the suit stacks.

✦ Subtract 15 points when you move a card from one of the suit stacks back to the playing table. (But note that if you press Ctrl+Z to undo a move, you only lose the points from that move.)

✦ With the Draw Three option (see the option button in Figure 4-2), you can go through the deck three times with no penalty, but then you lose 20 points each additional time you go through.

✦ With the Draw One option, you can go through the deck once with no penalty, but you lose 100 points each time you go through the deck afterward.

✦ With a timed game, you lose 2 points every 10 seconds, but a bonus is awarded at the end of the game that depends on how quickly you finished. (You don't get any bonus points if the game took less than 30 seconds, but if it took more than 30 seconds, you get a bonus of 700,000 divided by the number of seconds.) According to Microsoft, the highest possible score is 24,113.

With standard scoring, you get a bonus if you can move a card from the deck onto the main playing table (5 points) and from there up to the suit stack (an additional 10 points, for a total of 15), as opposed to moving a card straight from the deck onto the suit stack (which only scores 10 points).

If you use the Draw Three option, a cheat is available that allows you to turn over one card at a time. If you press Ctrl+Alt+Shift and then click the deck, Windows turns over one card at a time. If you are running with standard scoring and use this trick, you can go through every card in the deck three times before Windows sticks you with the 20-point-per-deck penalty.

Vegas scoring

Vegas scoring is simpler to explain — but harder to master.

When you start a Vegas game, you "pay" the house $52. Each time you move a card onto a suit stack, you "make" $5. That's all there is to it.

The guy who invented Solitaire

Bet you thought that the guy who created the first version of Windows Solitaire is kicking back on a holiday island somewhere, sipping mai tais, working on that tan, and generally enjoying the good life, eh? Guess again.

Wes Cherry wrote the original Windows Solitaire in 1989. Wes was working as an intern for Microsoft during his senior year at college. He wrote it as a means to learn Windows programming and never made any money from it. You can find an intriguing interview at www.b3ta.com/interview/solitaire.

With the Draw Three option (see the radio button in Figure 4-2), you can go through the deck three times. With the Draw One option, you only go through once.

The Ctrl+Alt+Shift cheat for standard scoring also works for Vegas scoring, but in a different way. If you press Ctrl+Alt+Shift and click the deck, Windows turns over one card at a time. If you use the Ctrl+Alt+Shift trick and turn over one card at a time, you can go through the entire deck three times — a real boon for Vegas scorekeeping.

FreeCell

FreeCell, Microsoft's first Solitaire variant, mimics the card game of the same name. To get it going, choose Start⇨Games and double-click the FreeCell icon. (The result is shown Figure 4-3.)

Park your cards here   Stack cards in order here

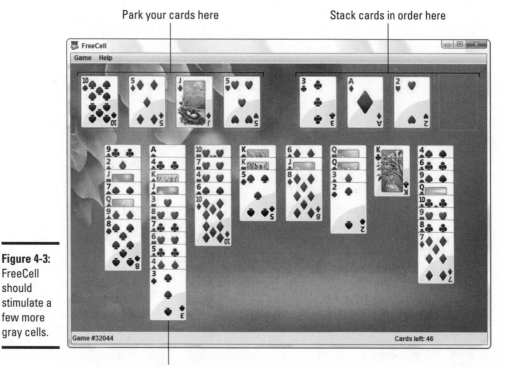

Figure 4-3: FreeCell should stimulate a few more gray cells.

Add cards to the columns, as in classic Solitaire

Book IV
Chapter 4

Windows Mail and
the Alternatives

Game play in FreeCell resembles "regular" Solitaire in the following ways:

- ✦ You try to expose aces, moving them to one of the upper-right suit stacks; after you start a stack with an ace, you build each stack sequentially, with a 2, 3, 4, and so on.

- ✦ You can move a card at the bottom of a column so that it sits on top of a card that's one higher in rank, and of the opposite color, much like playing "regular" Solitaire.

- ✦ You can move a card from the bottom of a column to an empty slot in the upper-left corner of the table.

- ✦ You can move any free card to an empty column on the table. (Some people mistakenly believe that you can only move Kings. Not so. Any card can go into an empty row.)

You can find a detailed explanation of the rules, along with a step-by-step example, at www.solitairelaboratory.com/tutorial.html.

FreeCell lets you replay the same hands, over and over, by assigning numbers to specific starting-card combinations. To play hand number 50,000, for example, choose Games⇨Select Game, type **50000**, and click the OK button. That's a nifty trick if you want to play the same hand at home and then do it again at work, or if you want to challenge a friend on a different machine to a duel.

Vista's version of FreeCell supports hands numbered from 1 to 1,000,000 — which should keep you rather well occupied. You also find four additional, fascinating, symmetrical hands, numbered –1, –2, –3, and –4. Games –1 and –2 can't be won. Games –3 and –4 win all by themselves: Just drag an ace onto one of the suit stacks, and Windows takes care of the rest.

All the hands numbered from 1 to 1,000,000 are winnable, except for eight hands: 11,982, 146,692, 186,216, 455,889, 495,505, 512,118, 517,776, and 781,948. Yes, some people study these things. No, they don't have lives.

FreeCell keeps track of how many hands you've won and lost, and how long your current winning (or losing) streak may be. To get to the scores, choose Game⇨Statistics. You see a list like the one shown in Figure 4-4.

What's the easiest way to run up your winning statistics? Play a whole bunch of games using hands numbered –3 and –4. You don't need to finish the game to have it show up as a "win." Simply drag an ace onto one of the suit stacks and wait for the cards to start crashing against the bottom of the screen. Then choose Game⇨Select Game, and you'll rack up another effortless win.

Figure 4-4:
FreeCell
keeps tabs,
but you can
stack the
deck.

> FreeCell Statistics - Woody
>
> Games played: 10
> Games won: 9
> Win percentage: 90%
>
> Longest winning streak: 7
> Longest losing streak: 1
> Current streak: 7 wins
>
> [Close] [Reset]

 Vista stores your FreeCell scores in a file called `C:\Users\<username>\AppData\Local\Microsoft Games\FreeCell\FreeCellSettings.xml`. If you're feeling very adventurous, you can try to hack your way to a breath-taking score. I haven't figured out how to alter the file and still get FreeCell to open it — I think Microsoft (more accurately, Oberon Games, which did the programming) has some sort of check sum buried in the file. If you figure out how to crack it, shoot me an e-mail, okay? `Woody@AskWoody.com`.

Spider Solitaire

When you get the hang of it, Spider Solitaire is every bit as addictive as the two older Windows Solitaire siblings. Get Spider going by choosing Start➪Games and double-clicking the Spider Solitaire icon.

The easiest way to learn Spider Solitaire is to start with a single suit — Spider gives you that option when you start. Basically, you have to move cards around in descending order (see Figure 4-5), and you can mix and match suits to your heart's content (pun intended). When you have a descending sequence (K to A) in a single suit, the entire sequence gets removed. When you get stuck, click the Spider card deck and Spider Solitaire deals another row of cards.

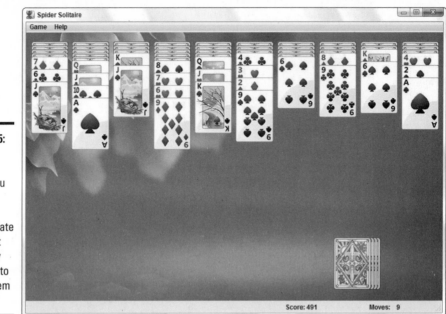

Figure 4-5:
Spider Solitaire allows you to mix suits in intermediate steps, but ultimately you have to match them to win.

Like FreeCell, Vista stores your Spider scores in `C:\Users\<username>\AppData\Local\Microsoft Games\Spider Solitaire\Spider SolitaireSettings.xml`. I had very little luck hacking that file, but you may be able to crack it.

If you don't like the way the cards were dealt, you can press F2 before moving any cards and Spider Solitaire will deal again — without adding a loss to your statistics.

Minesweeper

One of the most absorbing, simple games ever created — and a longtime personal favorite of Bill Gates — Minesweeper has been around since the days of Windows 3.1.

The concept is pretty simple: Click a square and a number appears, indicating the number of adjacent squares that contain mines (see Figure 4-6). (The Intermediate level is discussed later in this section.) Click a square that contains a mine and you lose. Play against the clock.

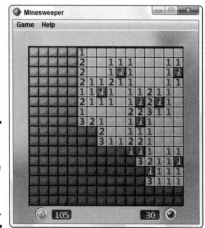

Figure 4-6:
The
Intermediate
Mine-
sweeper
playing field.

The Vista version of Minesweeper includes a kinder, gentler face — a flower garden, optionally played on a green field — that you can summon by choosing Game⇨Change Appearance.

If you've never tried Minesweeper, you're in for a treat — even inveterate computer-game-haters take a liking to this one.

Minesweeper holds oodles of options:

✦ Click Game and choose from Beginner (a 9-×-9-box playing field with 10 mines), Intermediate (a 16-×-16 field with 40 mines), and Expert (16 × 30 with 99 mines). Minesweeper automatically keeps high-score figures for each.

✦ Alternatively, you can choose Game⇨Custom and tell Minesweeper how many squares you want to see and how many mines should be scattered on the field.

✦ If you think a square contains a mine, and you want to, uh, remine yourself of that fact, right-click the square. A flag appears, warning you that once upon a time, you thought a mine might be there. Right-click the same square a second time, and you see a question mark — probably to remind you that you once thought a mine was there, but now you're not so sure, and maybe you really ought to click the sucker to see whether it blows up. Right-click the square a third time, and it goes back to normal.

Whenever you want to see the best times and who holds the records, choose Game⇨Statistics.

**Book IV
Chapter 4**

**Windows Mail and
the Alternatives**

It's easy to "stop the clock" in Minesweeper if you have the Aero version of Vista (that is, if you didn't get duped into buying Vista Home Basic). Minimize the Minesweeper window by clicking the Minimize icon in the upper-right corner or by pressing Windows Key+D. Then hover your mouse over the Minesweeper button on the Windows taskbar, or do the "3D Flip" by holding down the Windows Key and pressing Tab repeatedly, as shown in Figure 4-7. You may have to squint a bit, but you should be able to make out the details. When you figure out where you want to click next, bring the screen back up by clicking the Minesweeper button on the Windows taskbar or by releasing the Windows Key.

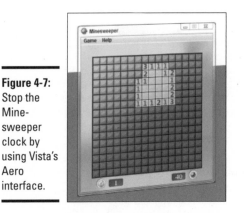

Figure 4-7:
Stop the Mine-sweeper clock by using Vista's Aero interface.

A well-known cheat used to work for Minesweeper in older versions of Windows but doesn't appear to work in Vista. (At least, we here at Dummies Central can't get it to work.) Maybe you'll be luckier. In older versions, anytime Minesweeper is running, you can type **xyzzy** and press Shift+Enter. From that moment on, every time you hover the mouse over a "good" square — one that doesn't contain a mine — Minesweeper flashes a tiny single white dot in the far upper-left corner of the Windows desktop. And every time you hover the mouse over a "bad" square, Minesweeper puts a single black dot in the far upper-left corner. You may have to change your background or wallpaper to see it, but it was there — in earlier versions of Windows. Click when you see the white dot, and you'll win every time.

Minesweeper cheats in your favor. Your first click is free: Minesweeper always arranges things so that you never hit a mine on your first click (unless you choose to restart a game, in which case the mines appear in the same location as in the previous game).

Think you have a good score? Ha! Take a look at `http://planet-minesweeper.com/bestever.php?p=ranking` for the "best ever" Minesweeper scores. And make sure that your jaw is firmly attached before you hit the page.

Yep, Minesweeper's top scores are stored in `C:\Users\`*<username>*`\AppData\Local\Microsoft Games\Minesweeper\Minesweeper Settings.xml`. Nope, I never did figure out a way to crack it.

The Other Games

Vista Home Premium, Business, Enterprise, and Ultimate come with several additional games that are worthy of your perusal — or hours of introspection, as the case may be. The stellar cast includes:

- ✦ **Chess Titans** combines a very strong chess playing engine with admirable 3D graphics. You can play against a human opponent or against the computer, and the computer can be set at ten different levels of difficulty. Yes, you can castle on both the king and queen sides, and pawns can capture *en passant*.

- ✦ **Mahjong Titans** is based on the traditional Mahjong tile game (and not the game you hear clacking at all hours of the day and night on the side-streets of Hong Kong). Your goal is to remove all the tiles by matching pairs of exposed tiles, which is to say, tiles that have empty spaces to the left or right.

- ✦ **InkBall** originated on the TabletPC and, well, it acts like a game for a TabletPC. If you don't have a Tablet, don't bother.

- ✦ **Purble Place** consists of three different games for the preschool and elementary crowd. Pattern recognition, memory stretches and elimination exercises will keep kids going for hours.

Book V

Vista on the Internet

The 5th Wave   By Rich Tennant

"Ms. Gretsky, tell the employees they can have internet games on their computers again."

Contents at a Glance

Chapter 1: Getting the Most from the Internet 347

Chapter 2: Finding Your Way around Internet Explorer (And Firefox) 363

Chapter 3: Making Internet Explorer Your Own...387

Chapter 4: Windows Mail and the Alternatives 399

Chapter 5: Working Together — IM OK, You're OK 413

Chapter 6: Searching on the Internet..425

Chapter 1: Getting the Most from the Internet

In This Chapter

✔ Getting a quick overview of the Internet

✔ Dialing with dollars

✔ Finding important Internet resources

*I*nternet this. Web that. E-mail today. Hair (or at least spam about hair products) tomorrow.

Vista makes it easy to get online. That means you can dash off a quick message to your daughter, send a birthday card to your mom, pick up the latest baseball scores and news headlines, glance at the stock market, look up show times and locations at a dozen local theaters, compare features and prices on the latest mobile phones, and check out the weather in Phuket (pronounced *Poo-KET,* by the way), Thailand, all in a matter of minutes — if your Internet connection is fast enough.

Five years from now (although it may take ten), the operating system that you use will be largely irrelevant, as will be the speed of your computer, how much memory you have, and how many terabytes of storage hum in the background. Microsoft will keep milking its cash cow, but the industry will move on. Individuals and businesses will stop shelling out big bucks for Windows and the iron to run it.

Instead, the major push will be online. Rather than spending money on PCs that become obsolete the week after you purchase them, folks will be spending money on big data pipes: It'll be less about "me" and more about "us." Why? Because so much more is "out there" than "in here." Count on it.

But what is the Internet? This chapter answers this burning question (if you've asked it). For those of you who don't necessarily wonder about the Internet's place in space and time, know that this chapter also explains how to get connected to the Internet. Of course, the easiest way to do that is with Internet Explorer (IE), the Web browser that comes (surprise, surprise) packaged with your version of Vista — at least until a federal judge says otherwise — or with Firefox, the scrappy, free upstart that took on Goliath and showed the lumbering giant a thing or three.

I explain how to download and install Firefox — my browser of choice, and free to boot — in Book V, Chapter 2.

Connecting with IE or Firefox is, thankfully, a pretty straightforward process. You aren't likely to encounter many superhuman challenges along the way — perhaps an unrecognized modem or a misplaced password, or you might need to kick your cable guy, but nothing insurmountable. This chapter walks you through the basics of making that initial IE connection and helps you anticipate and hopefully avoid any potential trouble spots along your path.

You may already be an old hand at making Internet connections. If that's the case, go to the head of the class and move along to the next chapter.

What Is the Internet?

You know those stories about computer jocks who come up with great ideas, develop the ideas in their basements (or garages or dorm rooms), release their product to the public, change the world, and make a gazillion bucks? This isn't one of them.

The Internet started in the mid-1960s as an academic exercise — primarily with the RAND Corporation, MIT, and the National Physical Laboratory in England — and rapidly evolved into a military project, under the U.S. Department of Defense's Advanced Research Project Agency (ARPA), designed to connect research groups working on ARPA projects.

By the end of the 1960s, ARPA had four computers hooked together — at UCLA, SRI (Stanford), UC Santa Barbara, and the University of Utah — using systems developed by Bolt Beranek and Newman, Inc. By comparison, right now more than a billion people can get on the Internet from home — mind-boggling.

Today, so many computers are connected directly to the Internet (including all of you who run digital subscriber line [DSL] or cable modems) that the Internet's addressing system is running out of numbers, just like your local phone company is running out of telephone numbers. The current numbering system — called IPv4 — can handle about 4 billion addresses. The next version, called IPv6 — and bundled in Vista — can handle 340,000,000,000,000,000,000,000,000,000,000,000,000 addresses, which should last us for a while, doncha think?

Ever wonder why you rarely see hard statistics about the Internet? I've found two big reasons: Defining terms related to the Internet is devilishly difficult these days. (What do you mean when you say "*X* number of computers are connected to the Internet"? Is that the number of computers up and running at any given moment? The number of different addresses that are active? The number that *could be* connected if everybody dialed up at the same time? The number of different computers that get connected in a typical day or week or month?) The other reason is that the Internet is growing so fast that any number you publish today will be meaningless tomorrow.

Getting Inside the Internet

Some observers claim that the Internet works so well because it was designed to survive a nuclear attack. Not so. The people who built the Internet insist that they weren't nearly as concerned about nukes as they were about making communication among researchers reliable, even when a backhoe severed an underground phone line or one of the key computers ground to a halt.

As far as I'm concerned, the Internet works so well because the engineers who laid the groundwork were utter geniuses. Their original ideas from 40 years ago have been through the wringer a few times, but they're still pretty much intact. Here's what the engineers decided:

✦ **No single computer should be in charge.** All the big computers connected directly to the Internet are equal (although, admittedly, some are more equal than others). By and large, computers on the Internet move data around like kids playing hot potato — catch it, figure out where you're going to throw it, and let it fly quickly. They don't need to check with some uber-computer before doing their work; they just catch, look, and throw.

✦ **Break the data into fixed-size packets.** No matter how much data you're moving — an e-mail message that just says "Hi" or a full-color, life-size photograph of the Andromeda galaxy — the data is broken up into packets. Each packet is routed to the appropriate computer. The receiving computer assembles all the packets and notifies the sending computer that everything came through okay.

✦ **Deliver each packet quickly.** If you want to send data from Computer A to Computer B, break the data into packets and route each packet to Computer B using the fastest connection possible — even if that means some packets go through Bangor and others go through Bangkok.

Taken together, those three rules ensure that the Internet can take a lickin' and keep on tickin'. If a chipmunk eats through a telephone line, any big computer that's using the gnawed line can start rerouting packets over a different telephone line. If the Cumbersome Computer Company in Cupertino, California, loses power, computers that were sending packets through Cumbersome can switch to other connected computers. It all works quickly and reliably, although the techniques used internally by the Internet computers get a bit hairy at times.

Big computers are hooked together with high-speed communication lines: the Internet *backbone*. If you want to use the Internet from your business or your house, you have to connect to one of the big computers first. Companies that own the big computers (Internet Service Providers [ISPs]) get to charge you for the privilege of getting onto the Internet through their big computers.

What Is the World Wide Web?

People tend to confuse the World Wide Web with the Internet, which is a lot like confusing the dessert table with the buffet line. I'd be the first to admit that desserts are mighty darn important — life-critical, in fact, if the truth be told. But they aren't the same as the buffet line.

To get to the dessert table, you have to stand in the buffet line. To get to the Web, you have to be running on the Internet. Make sense?

The World Wide Web owes its existence to Tim Berners-Lee and a few co-conspirators at a research institute called CERN in Geneva, Switzerland. In 1990, Berners-Lee demonstrated a way to store and link information on the Internet so that all it took was a click to jump from one place — one Web page — to another. Nowadays, nobody in his right mind can give a definitive count of the number of pages available, but it almost certainly exceeds 20 billion.

Like the Internet itself, the World Wide Web owes much of its success to the brilliance of the people who brought it to life. The following are the ground rules:

✦ Web pages, stored on the Internet, are identified by an address, such as `http://www.dummies.com`. Although you're probably accustomed to seeing addresses that start with `http://` or `www` and end with `.com`, `.org`, or `.edu`, plenty of addresses don't.

✦ Web pages are written in a funny kind of language called *HyperText Markup Language* (HTML). HTML is sort of a programming language, sort of a formatting language, and sort of a floor wax, all rolled into one. Many products claim to make it easy for novices to create powerful, efficient HTML. Some of them are getting close.

✦ To read a Web page, you have to use something called a Web browser. A *Web browser* is a program that runs on your computer and is responsible for converting HTML into something you can read and use. The majority of people who view Web pages use Internet Explorer as their Web browser, but more and more people (including me!) prefer Firefox (see `www.mozilla.org`). Unless you live under a rock in the Gobi

Desert, you know that Internet Explorer is part of Vista. Today, anyway. Heaven only knows what the courts will do. You may not know that Firefox can run right along side Internet Explorer, with absolutely no confusion between the two. In fact, they don't even interact — Firefox was designed to operate completely independently, and it does very well playing all by itself.

One unwritten rule for the World Wide Web: All Web acronyms have to be completely, utterly inscrutable. For example, a Web address is called a URL, or Uniform Resource Locator. (The techies I know pronounce URL "earl." Those who don't wear white lab coats tend to say "you are ell.") I describe the HTML acronym in the previous list. On the Web, a gorgeous, sunny, palm-lined beach with the scent of frangipani wafting through the air would no doubt be called SHS — Smelly Hot Sand. Sheeesh.

The best part of the Web is how easily you can jump from one place to another — and how easily you can create Web pages with *hot links* (also called *hyperlinks* or just *links*) that transport the viewer wherever the author intends. That's the *H* in *HTML* and the original reason for creating the Web so many years ago.

Who Pays for All This Stuff?

That's the $64 billion question, isn't it? The Internet is one of the true bargains of the 21st century. When you're online — for which you probably have to pay EarthLink, Comcast, Verizon, NetZero, Juno, Netscape, AOL, MSN, Qwest, your cable company, or some other Internet Service Provider a monthly fee — the Internet itself is free.

Internet Explorer is free, sorta, because it comes with Vista, no matter which version you buy. Firefox is free as a breeze — in fact it's the poster boy for "open source" programs, because everything about the program, even the program code itself, is free.

Most Web sites don't charge a cent. They pay for themselves in any of the following ways:

✦ **By reducing a company's operating costs:** Banks and brokerage firms, for example, have Web sites that routinely handle customer inquiries at a fraction of the cost of H2H (er, human-to-human) interactions.

✦ **By increasing a company's visibility:** This means that the Web site gives you a good excuse to buy more of the company's products. That's why architectural firms show you pictures of their buildings and food companies post recipes.

✦ **By drawing in new business:** Ask any real estate agent.

✦ **By contracting advertising:** Google's made a fortune.

✦ **By using bounty advertising:** Smaller sites run ads, usually selected from a pool of advertisers. The advertiser pays a bounty for each person who clicks on the ad and views its Web site — a so-called *click-through*.

✦ **By affiliate programs:** Smaller sites may also participate in a retailer's affiliate program. If a customer clicks through and orders something, the Web site that originated the transaction gets a percentage of the amount ordered. Amazon.com is well known for its affiliate program, but many others exist.

Some Web sites have an entrance fee. For example, if you want to use the Oxford English Dictionary on the Web (see Figure 1-1), you have to part with some substantial coin — $295 per year for individuals, the last time I looked. Guess that beats schlepping around 20 volumes.

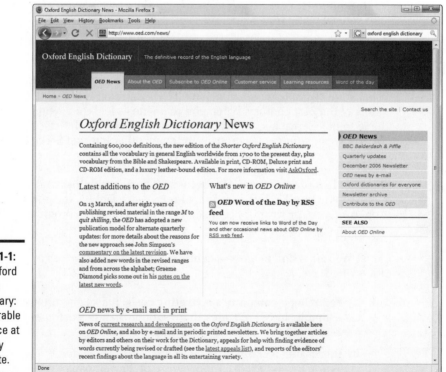

Figure 1-1: The Oxford English Dictionary: a venerable resource at a pricey Web site.

Connecting through Dialup or Broadband Services

DSL, asymmetric digital subscriber line (ADSL), integrated services digital network (ISDN), cable, and so on are called *broadband connections* because they're faster than a dialup modem. At least, theoretically. *(Definition: A broadband connection is any Internet connection that's faster than the one you have. Heh heh heh.)*

Here's the most important speed-up tip in this book: If you don't have a broadband line, get one. If you need an excuse, take a look at Google Earth or any of a hundred other data-sucking, marvelous, phenomenal free services that only make sense if you have data pipes big enough to handle them (see the section "Uses and excuses for broadband," later in this chapter). Believe me, if you're reading this book, you'll get broadband sooner or later. It might as well be sooner.

The computer business is full of inscrutable terms, but the online world is even worse. If you need an accurate definition for a technical term, or you want to compare acronyms like ADSL and SDSL and xDSL and DSL (see Figure 1-2), your best bet is to hit Wikipedia, www.wikipedia.com. If you figure out the difference between ISDN/BRI and ISDN/PRI, let me know, okay?

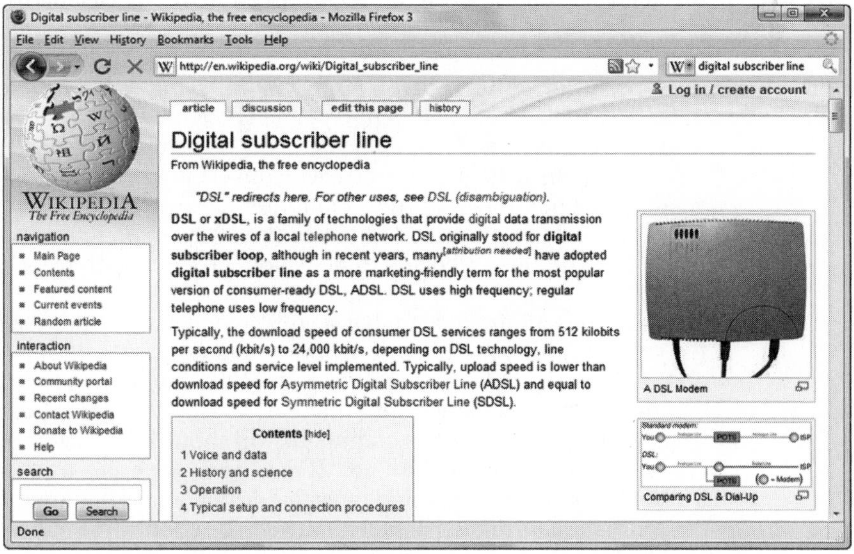

Figure 1-2: Wikipedia, the fount of all techie knowledge.

The last mile

The only real difference between DSL and a regular old dialup modem connection lies in the "last mile" between your house or office and the telephone switch. The phone and cable companies already use digital technology everywhere. If you use a dialup modem, your computer has to step back in history about a hundred years and contend with antiquated telephone technology. The following paragraphs describe what's really happening.

Your computer really, really wants to talk to other computers. If you hook up your computer to another computer with a fairly short cable, they can talk digitally, sending 1s and 0s over the cable to each other. Cool. But if your computer has to talk over the telephone line, that's another story entirely.

Back in the early days of telephones, all connections were analog: You talked into a mouthpiece, that caused a varying amount of electricity to travel through the telephone line, and the earpiece on the other end of the telephone line picked up the electrical changes and converted the impulses back into sound. Those phones acted a bit like tying a piece of string to two paper cups — the sound pulses in the cup on one end made the string vibrate, and the cup on the other end converted the vibrations back to sound.

Nowadays, telephone systems are entirely digital. (Well, almost entirely digital. I come back to that in a second.)

Computers are digital beasts — they talk in 1s and 0s. If you use your computer with a plain, old dialup phone line and a modem, the computer has to work like a telephone. Telephones are analog beasts — they want varying pulses. Modems bridge the gap. They convert digits into pulses and vice versa. Think of it this way: Your computer has a string of 1s and 0s that it wants to send to your friend Moe's computer — say, 11001. You and Moe, being game Dummies, decide to play modem. (Bear with me, okay?)

You call Moe and exchange pleasantries. When you're both ready, you both tell your computers to have at it. Your computer starts flashing the 1s and 0s on the screen that it wants to send to Moe's computer. You see a 1 on your computer's screen and yell into the telephone, "ONE!" Moe hears you say "one" and types a 1 into his computer. You shout "ONE" again, and Moe types another 1. Then you shout "ZERO," and Moe types a 0. "ZERO" again, 0 again. Then "ONE," and Moe types a 1. When your computer finishes, it flashes a message on the screen. You yell, "I'm done Moe; did you get it?" Moe yells back, "Yep, I got it!"

That's what a modem does. When it's sending data, it takes the 1s and 0s that the computer wants to send and shouts into the phone line "ONE" or "ZERO." When it's receiving data, it listens for "ONE" and "ZERO" and relays the appropriate number to the computer. Some extra work is involved — exchanging pleasantries and making sure that all the data came through — but at its heart, a modem alternately yells and listens.

Here's the ironic part: Although the telephone system used to be entirely analog, these days it's almost entirely digital. The only analog part is the short distance — called the *local loop* — from your house to the closest telephone switch. Nowadays, when you talk into the telephone, a varying amount of electricity (an analog signal) is sent on the phone line that only goes as far as the switch — typically a few hundred yards. When your voice hits the switch, it's digitized and sent to the receiving switch, where it's converted back to analog so that it can travel the final few hundred yards to Moe's house. In essence, your slow-as-a-snail modem exists only to make the trip from your house to your local telephone switch. Everything else travels at blazing speeds.

DSL technology simply leapfrogs that final few hundred yards. Instead of converting your PC's digital 1s and 0s to analog ONEs and ZEROs, the DSL box makes sure that the digital data that your PC generates gets patched directly into the already-digital network. Cable modems hook into the already-digital cable TV line that probably goes to your house. Easy, eh?

Uses and excuses for broadband

Need an excuse to get broadband? No doubt you already know that you can use a broadband connection to make free — or at least very cheap — high-quality long-distance telephone calls (see, for example, www.skype.com). You've probably struggled with some Web sites with stunning content (say, www.nasa.gov or www.louvre.fr) that make slow connections positively painful. Maybe you've heard about sites (say, www.youtube.com or http://adcritic.com) with funny videos that beg for fast Internet access. Need a bigger excuse? Have you seen Google Earth?

Google Earth (http://earth.google.com) takes mapping into the third dimension, with incredibly detailed satellite photos all stitched together in a way that makes it easy to zoom in or out, pinpoint a location, or even — you have to see this to believe it — angling the view from the tops of buildings, down to look at the side, or even take in long vistas with mountains and rivers and trees and superhighways (see Figure 1-3). You'll be absolutely floored by the ability to, oh, type **Phuket, Thailand** in the Search bar, and watch as the earth rotates, and gets closer and closer, until finally you can see . . . Phuket. Then you can "grab" the map and move down roads, identifying the landmarks as you fly, and "tilt" the camera so that you see the tops or different angles of the fronts of buildings. Google Earth satellite photos cover most of the inhabited parts of the world. Most of Europe and North America boast incredibly high-resolution photos. If you like, metropolitan areas can have the outlines of roads superimposed on the photos, with road names clearly marked.

For many people, Google Earth, all by itself, justifies the added expense of a broadband line. I bet you can find many more excuses.

Figure 1-3:
For many people, Google Earth alone justifies the cost of a broadband connection.

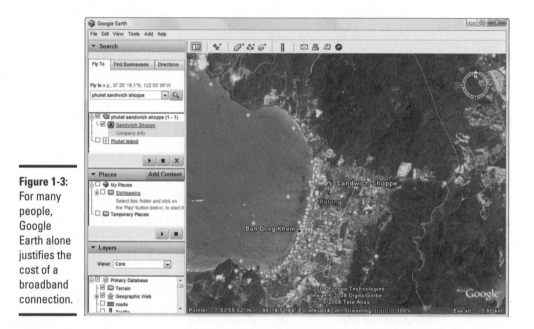

Setting Up an Internet Connection

For most people, setting up an Internet connection is as simple as contacting an Internet Service Provider (commonly a phone company or cable TV company), arranging to have the Cable Guy come by at a time that you're home (good luck), sacrificing your credit card for a moment, and turning on your computer. If the installer did a good job, you don't have to sweat any of the details — Internet Explorer and, if you so choose, Firefox jump up and greet you when you double-click them.

It may go without saying, but don't let the Cable Guy (or whomever) leave your house until you turn on your PC, crank up IE, and make sure that your Internet connection is working.

Dialup connections are a little trickier. You need a modem (your computer probably has a built-in one already), and a telephone cable that plugs into your computer and the phone jack on the wall. You also need to set up a subscription with a dialup service, which you can do at any store that sells computers.

The dialup service company (your Internet Service Provider, or ISP) has an instruction booklet that tells you precisely how to get connected to its service. They need to give you a telephone number to dial, a logon ID, and a password.

You may also receive the names of the computers that accept and send out your mail (so-called POP3 and SMTP servers), which you need to set up e-mail accounts that go through the ISP.

The booklet should step you through the rest of the process, but a few little details may be missing:

✦ Vista's **Connect to the Internet Wizard** can help you establish a dialup connection. To bring up the Connect to the Internet Wizard, choose Start➪Control Panel, click the Network and Internet icon, and then click the Network and Sharing Center icon. In the Network and Sharing Center, click Set Up a Connection or Network link. Then double-click Set Up a Dial-Up Connection link.

✦ If you need to change details about the connection after you've gone through the Connect to the Internet Wizard, choose Start➪Connect To. Your dialup connection appears in the network list. Right-click it and choose Properties. After you click through a User Account Control security box, you see a Dial-up Connection Properties dialog box. In that dialog box, you can change the phone number, pick a second modem (if you have one), control how often Vista re-dials, or (as shown in Figure 1-4) make the dialup connection available to anybody logged on to your computer.

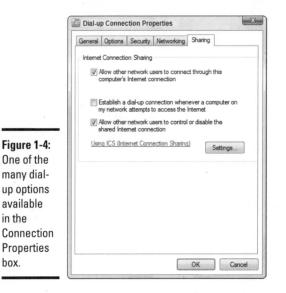

Figure 1-4:
One of the many dial-up options available in the Connection Properties box.

✦ If you need to change general dial-up options after you've gone through the Connect to the Internet Wizard — say, you suddenly realize that you need to dial 9 to get an outside line — choose Start⇨Control Panel⇨ Hardware and Sound, then Phone and Modem Options icon. Yeah, that's where it's hidden.

✦ If you aren't getting a dial tone (you should be able to hear it), the problem's usually something simple, such as a not-quite-connected phone line. First, check your hardware connections. Is the phone line plugged into the wall and all the way into the computer? Next, make sure you're using a functioning phone cord. Phone cords sometimes get a small stress break somewhere near the middle. You can also try plugging a phone into the connector to make sure the phone line is working the way it should.

✦ If the phone rings and the ISP doesn't answer (again, you can hear it), check the clock. If you're dialing into your ISP at a time of high traffic — usually between 8:00 a.m. and 11:00 a.m. and between 1:00 p.m. and 5:00 p.m. — your ISP may simply be swamped with incoming calls. Get yourself a cup of coffee and try again in a few minutes. If you try continually and are unable to get a rise out of your ISP, give its tech support line a call. The server may be down or — worst-case scenario — your modem could be failing and not giving the ISP's server the "handshake" it's looking for.

✦ When all else fails, call your ISP and ask tech support to walk you through the connection process. That's what tech support is for.

If you decide that you want to connect several computers together with either a wired or wireless network, I have detailed instructions in Book IX.

Finding Internet Reference Tools

I get questions all the time from people who want to know about specific tools for the Internet. Here are my choices for the tools that everyone needs.

DSLReports

Everybody, but everybody, needs (or wants) to measure his or her Internet speed from time to time. The site I always use for testing: `www.dslreports.com/stest`.

A million different speed tests are available on the Internet, and two million different opinions about various tools' accuracy, reliability, replicability, and so on. All I know for sure is that DSLReports produces results that match what I see and feel, and does so day after day, year after year.

DNSStuff

Ever wonder whether the Web site `BillyJoeBobsPhishery.com` belongs to BillyJoeBob? Head over to `DNSStuff.com` (see Figure 1-5) and find out. You give DNSStuff a domain name and DNSStuff divulges all the public records about the site, commonly known as a *whois:* who owns the site (or at least who registered it), where the rascals are located, and whom to contact.

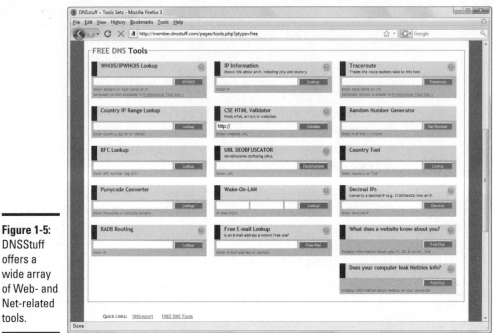

Figure 1-5:
DNSStuff
offers a
wide array
of Web- and
Net-related
tools.

DNSStuff also tells you the official "abuse" contact for a particular site (useful if you want to lodge a complaint about junk mail), whether a specific site is listed on one of the major spam databases, and much more.

DNSStuff can also run a *ping,* to show you how long it takes to get from point A to point B, or a *traceroute,* to see what tortured path your packets plod. Good stuff, all in one place.

The Wayback Machine

He said, she said. We said, they said. Web pages come and go, but sometimes you just have to see what a page looked like last week, or last year. No problem, Sherman; just set the Wayback Machine for November 29, 1975. (That's the day Gates first used the name "Micro Soft.")

If you're a Mr. Peabody look-alike and you want to know what a specific Web page really said in the foggy past, head to www.archive.org, where the Wayback Machine has more than 55 billion Web pages, archived and indexed for your entertainment (see Figure 1-6).

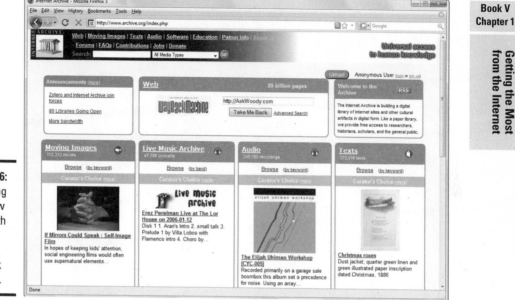

Figure 1-6:
Everything
old is new
again with
Archive.
org's
Wayback
Machine.

Chapter 2: Finding Your Way around Internet Explorer (And Firefox)

In This Chapter

✔ Internet Explorer ain't the only game in town

✔ Tabbing through the IE window

✔ Protecting yourself from phishers

✔ Playing hide-and-seek with IE

*F*or hundreds of millions of people, "The Web" and "Internet Explorer" (IE) are synonyms. It's fair to say that IE has done more to extend the reach of PC users than any other product — enabling people from all walks of life, in all corners of the globe, to see what a fascinating world we live in.

At the same time, IE has become an object of attack by spammers, scammers, thieves, and other lowlifes. As the Internet's lowest (or is it greatest?) common denominator, IE draws a lot of unwanted attention.

This chapter concentrates on showing you how to use Internet Explorer to do what you want to do. (At the same time, it also gives you hints about using Firefox, Internet Explorer's No. 1 competitor.) The next chapter delves deeper into the inner workings of IE, showing you how to customize and cajole the beast into behaving more in tune with your desires.

Exploring Internet Explorer Alternatives

Before I get started with Internet Explorer, let me say this loud and clear: You can find good, free alternatives to IE, and you should consider using them. Why? *They ain't from Microsoft.* They don't draw the lion's share of attention from malware writers. Using a product other than Internet Explorer prods Microsoft out of its developmental lethargy. The IE alternatives keep competition alive and thriving, bringing fresh ideas and approaches into the mainstream. I use Firefox (see Figure 2-1) almost all the time, and I recommend that you do, too.

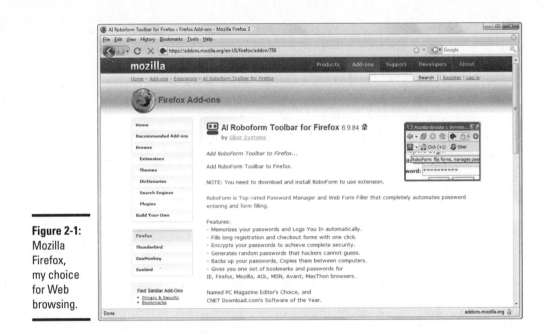

Figure 2-1:
Mozilla
Firefox,
my choice
for Web
browsing.

A bit of history, if you will.

More than any other product, Internet Explorer reflects Microsoft's odd and tortured approach to the Web. After largely ignoring the Internet for many years, Microsoft released the first version of Internet Explorer in 1995, as an add-on to Windows. In 1996, Microsoft built Internet Explorer version 3 into Windows itself, violating antitrust laws and using monopolistic tactics to overwhelm Netscape Navigator.

Having illegally pummeled its competitor in the marketplace, Microsoft made almost no improvements to Internet Explorer between August 2001 and August 2006 — an eternity in Internet time. IE became the single largest conduit for malware in the history of computing, with major security patches (sometimes several) appearing almost every month.

And then there was Firefox. Dave Hyatt, Blake Ross (who was a sophomore at Stanford at the time), and hundreds of volunteers took on the IE behemoth, producing a fast, small, free alternative that quickly grabbed a significant share of the browser market. Microsoft responded by incorporating many Firefox features into Internet Explorer, ultimately releasing the version that you see in Vista today.

You can install Firefox without disturbing Internet Explorer — they coexist peacefully, and you can run either, or both, at any time. Here's how to get Firefox:

1. **Start Internet Explorer and go to** www.mozilla.com/firefox.

2. **Click the Download Firefox link.**

3. **Follow the instructions on the page to download and install the latest version of Firefox.**

4. **When you first start Firefox, it asks whether you want to make it your default browser (see Figure 2-2). I suggest you select the Always Perform This Check When Starting Firefox check box, and click the Yes button.**

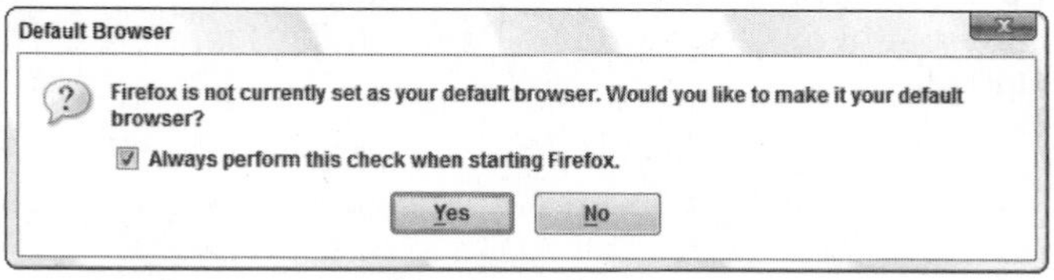

Figure 2-2:
Making
Firefox your
default
browser.

That makes Firefox your browser of choice in almost all situations, except when Microsoft insists that you use Internet Explorer (for example, when checking for Windows or Office updates).

All the concepts, and many of the tips, that apply to Internet Explorer also apply to Firefox. Even if you use Firefox, you should follow along in this chapter. Where differences between Firefox and IE exist, I note them in parenthesis.

Ready, Set, Browse!

As soon as you're connected to the Internet, you can begin browsing. To launch IE, click the Internet Explorer icon on the taskbar or choose Start⇨Internet. (Firefox has icons on the taskbar and on the desktop.)

Internet Explorer launches, and after a relatively brief moment (how brief depends primarily on the speed of your Internet connection), a Web page appears. What that page contains depends on whether your computer is set up to begin with a specific page, called a *home page*. Microsoft sets up www.msn.com as IE's home page by default, if you installed Windows from the original CD. Most PC manufacturers set the home page to display something related to their systems. Firefox takes you straight to Google.

If you end up on Microsoft's phishing settings page, make sure that you sign up for protection from phishing. I talk about Microsoft's anti-phishing support in the section "Thwarting Phishers," later in this chapter.

Changing the default home page

If MSN's ditzy, ad-laden home page (see Figure 2-3) leaves you cold, or if your PC manufacturer's idea of a good home page doesn't quite jibe with your tastes, or if Google doesn't ring your chimes, it's easy to change the home page. Follow these steps:

1. **Navigate to the Web page that you want to use as your home page.**

If you're adept at tabs (see the section "Pick a Tab, Any Tab," later in this chapter), open all the pages you wish to use as a home "page."

2. **Click the down arrow next to the Home icon on the IE taskbar and choose Add or Change Home Page. (In Firefox, choose Tools⇨ Options.)**

Figure 2-3:
The MSN home page can be long on advertising and short on useful information.

3. **Select the Use This Webpage as Your Only Home Page or the Use the Current Tab Set as Your Home Page option, and then click the Yes button. (Firefox: Choose Use Current Page, and then click the OK button.)**

   From that point on, whenever you start IE, it loads the page or pages you've designated as "home."

If you don't want any home page — thus allowing your browser to appear on the screen faster — click the down arrow next to the Home icon, choose Remove, and click the home page. (Firefox: Choose Tools⇨Options, and then select the Show a Blank Page option in the When Firefox Starts list.)

Switching the default search service

When you type something into the Search box in the upper-right corner of your browser, IE or Firefox runs out to your default Web search service, looks up what you typed, and presents you with the results, ready for you to click. Although Firefox uses Google as its default Web search service, unless the people who sold you your computer changed it, Internet Explorer uses Microsoft's own Windows Live (you were expecting something else?). Fortunately, that, too is easy to change by following these steps:

1. **Click the down arrow on the Search bar — the one that probably says "Live Search" — and choose Find More Providers.**

   IE opens a page on www.microsoft.com that lists available Web-search providers (see Figure 2-4).

2. **Click the Google link.**

   Internet Explorer asks "Do You Want to Add the Following Search Provider to Internet Explorer? / Google."

3. **Select the Make This My Default Search Provider check box, and then click the Add Provider button.**

   Google becomes your default search provider. You can verify that by looking at the text on the Search bar. It better say "Google."

Taking a Walk around the IE Window

One of the great things about Internet Explorer (and Firefox) is that you can be an absolute no-clue beginner, and with just a few hints about tools and so on, you can find your way around the Web like a pro. Figure 2-5 gives you a diagram of the basic layout of the Internet Explorer window.

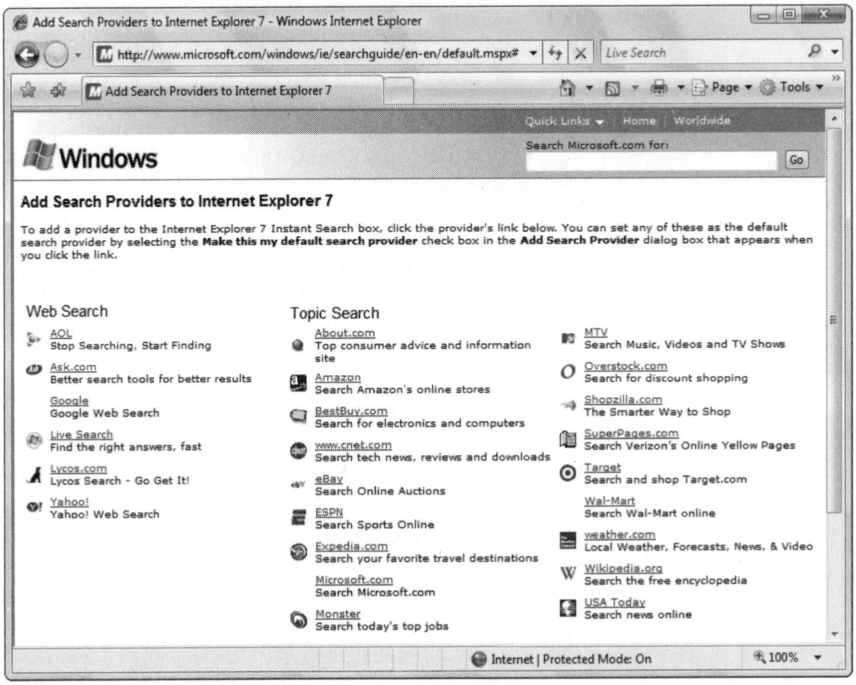

Figure 2-4: Making Google your default search engine takes a few clicks.

As you can see, IE packs lots of possibilities in that small space. The items you'll use most often are these:

✦ **Address bar:** Enables you to type the Web address of a page that you want to move to directly.

✦ **Command bar:** This bar contains seven commands: Home, RSS Feed, Print, Page, Tools, Help and, if you have Microsoft Office installed, Research. Each menu includes a different set of commands related to working with Web sites. (See Table 2-1 for a description of the various commands.)

✦ **Search box:** Includes tools you use to find your way around the Web and work with the Web pages that you find. (See the preceding section for instructions on changing your default Web search engine.)

✦ **Status bar:** Displays information about Web pages, links, security, or actions that you can take while visiting a site.

Table 2-1	The Fare on Internet Explorer's Command Bar
Icon	*Description*
Home	Opens the home page (or pages). Click the down arrow to set a new home page.
RSS Feed	Opens the *RSS (Really Simple Syndication)* feed for the current site. I talk about RSS in Book V, Chapter 3.

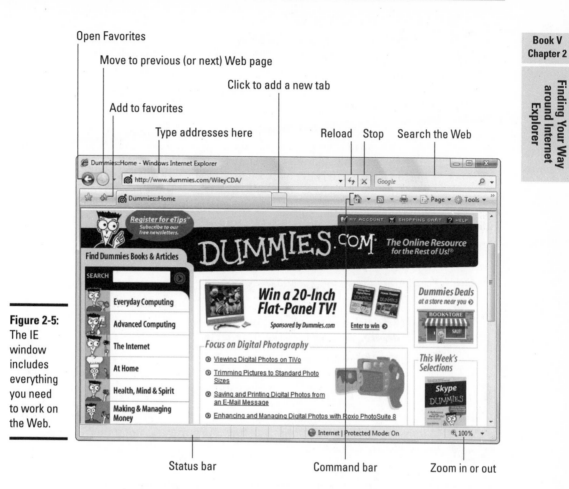

Open Favorites

Move to previous (or next) Web page

Click to add a new tab

Add to favorites

Type addresses here   Reload   Stop   Search the Web

Figure 2-5:
The IE
window
includes
everything
you need
to work on
the Web.

Status bar   Command bar   Zoom in or out

Icon	Description
Print	Gives you some flexibility in printing Web pages. See the section "Printing Web pages," later in this chapter, for ideas.
Page	A catchall icon that includes the ability to send a Web page by e-mail, to edit the page, or to view its HyperText Markup Language (HTML) source in all its glory. See the section "Doing Stuff with Web Pages," later in this chapter, for details.
Tools	Adjusts the built-in pop-up blocker and phishing filter, manages Internet Explorer add-ons, and more.
Help	Links to the Internet Explorer Help file.
Research	Opens the Office Research pane, where you can look up words or phrases in dictionaries, thesauri, encyclopedias, and so on. Only available if you have Microsoft Office installed.

If you want to see the old-fashioned File/Edit/View/ . . . /Help menus in Internet Explorer, press Alt. Yep, that's how you get to IE's inner workings.

Surfing with Style

No doubt you're familiar with basic browser functions: type an address in the Address field to go to a Web page, click the Reload button to make sure that a page's information is the most up to date it offers, click the Stop button if the page is taking too long to load and you want to move on, and click the Back (or Next) button to move back (or forward) to a page you've already visited. But you might not know about some of these finer points:

✦ Click a link and the Web page decides whether you move to the new page in the current browser window or whether a new browser window appears with the clicked page loaded.

✦ Shift+click and you always get a new browser window with the clicked page loaded.

✦ Ctrl+click and the clicked page appears on a new tab in the current browser window (see the next section in this chapter).

✦ Even if the Web page "hijacks" your Backward and Forward arrows, you can always move backward (or forward) by clicking the down arrow next to the directional arrows and choosing the page you want.

Rarely, a Web page manages to hide your Address bar and navigation buttons. If that happens, right-click the appropriate icon on the Windows taskbar and choose Close.

History in the making

Some parents (okay, and maybe spouses) use the History files to make sure that other family members are surfing on the straight and narrow. Your employer is probably doing the same thing (but probably with a piece of software designed to spot policy infractions).

Whether your weakness is *Dilbert,* sports stats, or Ru Paul's fashion advice (oy!), remember that sneaking always shows up in the wash. The moral? Big Brother is watching. You're safest to stick with the sites that you would visit even if your mother were looking over your shoulder. And for those times when the temptation is just too great (everybody needs a good David Letterman fix once in a while), at least shred the evidence in your History folder by holding down the Alt key, and then choosing Tools⇨Delete Browsing History (in Firefox, choose Tools⇨Clear Private Data). That won't necessarily keep your boss from finding where you've been surfing, but it'll probably stall your teenage son.

Saving space — losing time

Increasing or decreasing the number of days of History that IE stores doesn't have much effect on the amount of data stored on the hard drive — even a hyperactive surfer will have a hard time cranking up a History folder that's much larger than 1MB. By contrast, Temporary Internet Files on your computer can take up 10, 50, or even a 100 times that much space.

Those Temporary Internet Files only exist to speed your Internet access: When IE hits a Web page that it's seen before, if a copy of the page's contents appears in the Temporary Internet Files folder, IE grabs the stuff on the hard drive

instead of waiting for a download. That can make a huge difference in IE's responsiveness (particularly if you use a dialup modem), but the speed comes at a price: the 10, 50, or 100MB of space you have to give to IE's brain.

To clear out IE's Temporary Internet Files, hold down the Alt key, and then choose Tools⇨ Delete Browsing History and click the Delete Files button. (In Firefox, choose Tools⇨Clear Private Data, select the Cache check box, and click the Clear Private Data Now button.) You won't hurt anything, but revisited Web pages will take longer to appear.

You can bring up a history of all the pages you've visited in the past few weeks by pressing Ctrl+H. You can also refer to all the Web addresses you've entered by clicking the down arrow to the right of the address box — the latter being particularly helpful if you want to make a small change in an address.

To search for a particular word or phrase on a page, press Ctrl+F. Force your browser to *refresh* a Web page (retrieve the latest version, even if a version is stored locally) by pressing F5. If you need to make sure that you have the latest version, even if the time stamps could be screwed up, press Ctrl+F5.

Pick a Tab, Any Tab

If you've never used browser tabs before, you might wonder what all the fuss is about. It doesn't seem like there's much difference between opening another window and adding a tab (see Figure 2-6). But after you get the hang of it, tabs can help you organize pages and jump to the one you want.

Add a tab in any of the following ways:

✦ Ctrl+click a link to open the linked page in a new tab.

✦ Press Ctrl+T to start a new tab. When the tab is open, you get to navigate manually, just as you would in any other browser window.

✦ Right-click a link and choose Open in New Tab.

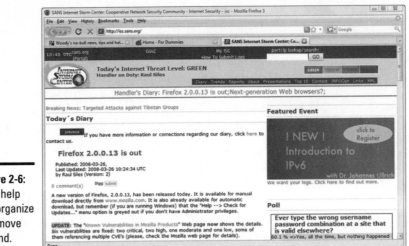

Figure 2-6: Tabs help you organize and move around.

In addition, Internet Explorer lets you click a blank tab and navigate from there.

Why do I like tabs? I can set up a single window with a bunch of related tabs, and then bookmark the whole shebang. That makes it one-click easy to open all my favorite news sites, research sites, or financial sites. While my browser's out loading pages, I can go do something else and return to the tabbed window when everything's loaded and ready to go.

If I'm trying to research two different topics at the same time, I frequently start Firefox and create tabs to hunt down the first topic, then start Firefox again — start it in a different window — and traipse through the second topic.

You can reorganize the order of tabs by simply clicking a tab and dragging it to a different location.

Thwarting Phishers

Internet Explorer and Firefox both attack phishing with a vengeance. *Phishing* is an attempt to acquire information — passwords, account numbers, and so on — fraudulently, usually via an e-mail message that appears to come from a reliable source, but points you to a bogus Web site. I talk about phishing threats in Book III, Chapter 1.

Some phishing messages, like this one, make me roll my eyes:

This E-mail was sent by the Wells Fargo server to verify your account information. You must complete this process by clicking the link below and entering your account information. This is done for your protection, because some of our members no longer have access to their online access and we must verify it. To verify your identity and access your bank account, click on the link below.

But other phishing messages these days are so well crafted that many a grizzled computer veteran — present company most certainly included — has been known to click through, only stopping at the last moment, when asked to type an account number and password. How good are the phishing attempts? Take a look at Figure 2-7, which is a genuine PayPal logon page, and compare it to Figure 2-8, which no doubt originated with a pimply faced underachieving apparatchik in Kazbukistan. . . who's soon to become a *wealthy* pimply faced underachieving apparatchik on the Kazbukistan Riviera.

Figure 2-7:
This is a genuine PayPal logon page.

As you can see in Figure 2-8, the latest version of IE second-guesses this site and displays a warning message. Firefox offers similar tools to combat phishing, as well. Basically, these anti-phishing tools enable you to provide immediate feedback about dubious destinations online; your feedback is aggregated with data from every other user who decides to use these tools.

The most sophisticated phishing sites go up and come down in 24 hours or less — the perpetrators vanish that quickly. By automating the enormous task of identifying potentially dangerous sites, and employing the votes of thousands of would-be victims, both Internet Explorer and Firefox have, uh, raised the phishing bar. These are important, albeit imperfect, tools. Your considered opinion may help save a naive person's tail. I strongly urge you to opt in and turn on the automatic Phishing Filter.

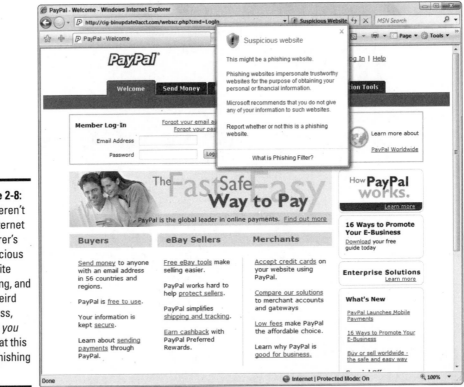

Figure 2-8: If it weren't for Internet Explorer's Suspicious Website warning, and the weird address, could *you* tell that this is a phishing site?

The consequences of anti-phishing

Here's the rub. An anti-phishing filter can only give you up-to-the-nanosecond information about potentially bad sites if your Web browser checks *each and every site* that you visit. If you use Internet Explorer's anti-phishing filter (which I recommend), you must resign yourself to the fact that Microsoft can (and probably does) track every single Web page that you visit — the anti-phishing filter simply has to send both your computer's address (your IP address) and the site you're visiting to Microsoft's giant servers. Your visit is logged, unless you go to great lengths to hide your IP address. (I talk about hiding IP addresses using a technology called anonymizing in *Windows Vista Timesaving Techniques For Dummies*.)

By default, Firefox doesn't send your address to the Firefox database in the sky — but then again, you don't get the most accurate, most up-to-date anti-phishing information. By default, Firefox 3 warns you about "attack" sites and phishing "forgery" sites (see the section "Fighting phishing with Firefox"), but Firefox 3 doesn't gather a list of the sites you visit, or send them to that great Big Brother database in the cloud. Instead, Firefox 3 updates its blacklist of suspected attack and forgery sites every thirty minutes, as long as you're online, and stores that list in abbreviated form on your computer.

In the end, you can't have your cake and eat it, too. Specifically:

✦ If you trust Microsoft, and don't mind leaving a full history of your browsing activities in Microsoft's database, use Internet Explorer with its Phishing Filter turned on. (See the next section.)

✦ If you can live with the idea that your antiphishing (er, forgery) and attack site protection can be 30 minutes out of date, use Firefox 3. (Note that Firefox 2, the older version, works in a completely different way.)

✦ If you aren't overly worried about phishing sites (or attack sites), use either IE with the Phishing Filter turned off, or Firefox 3 with forgery and/or attack site identification turned off. Details in the next two sections.

Personally, I use Firefox 3 with both forgery and attack site identification turned on.

Using the Internet Explorer filter

Here's how Internet Explorer's Phishing Filter is supposed to work (Firefox's filter works a bit differently; see the next section):

1. **You receive a clever e-mail message that looks like it comes from, oh, Wells Fargo. You, being a trusting kind of person, and more than a little distracted and overworked, click the link provided and end up on a Web site that looks a whole lot like the Wells Fargo logon page. But it isn't.**

2. **The Phishing Filter examines the page (as it does every page) and checks for these three things:**

   - **Is the Web site on the IE "white list"?** If so, you're allowed through with no impediments. The white list is stored on your computer.

   - **Does the Web site look flaky?** Microsoft doesn't divulge the method it uses for determining flakiness — *flaky* being one of those high-falutin' technical terms I made up, okay? — but if the Web address doesn't look right or the Web page asks for information that seems out of place, you get a warning (refer to Figure 2-8).

   - **Is the Web site on the IE "black list"?** With your permission, IE phones home and checks to see whether the particular site you've just contacted has been reported as a phishing site. If you've hit a reported phishing site, IE gives you the notice shown in Figure 2-9.

3. **If you land on a questionable site, click the Report Whether or Not This Is a Phishing Website link shown in Figure 2-8.**

   IE responds with the survey form shown in Figure 2-10.

4. **If you think you hit a phishing site, click the I Think This Is a Phishing Website button and then click the Submit button.**

   Microsoft aggregates your response with other users and may decide to move the site onto its "black list."

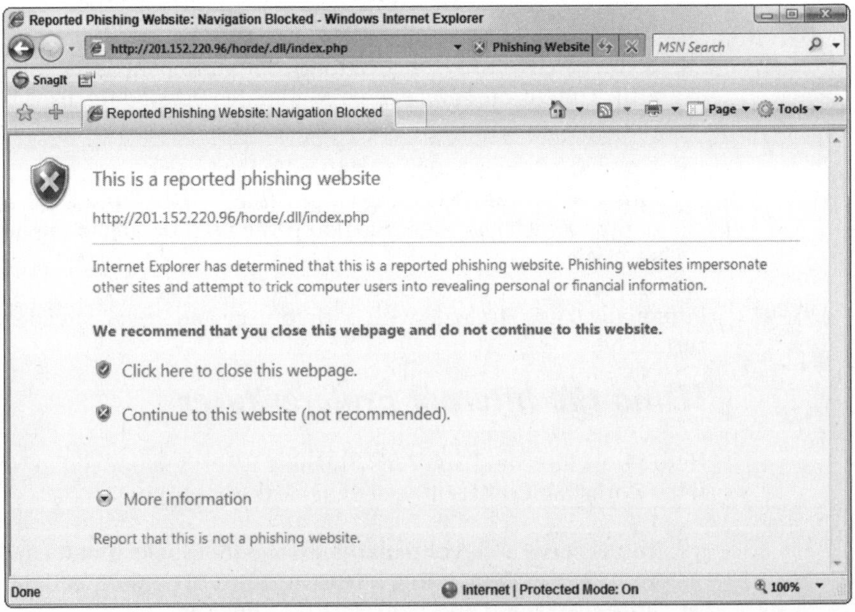

Figure 2-9:
This message tells you that other people have lodged complaints about this site, identifying it as being a phishing site. The warning isn't definitive, but it certainly should give you pause.

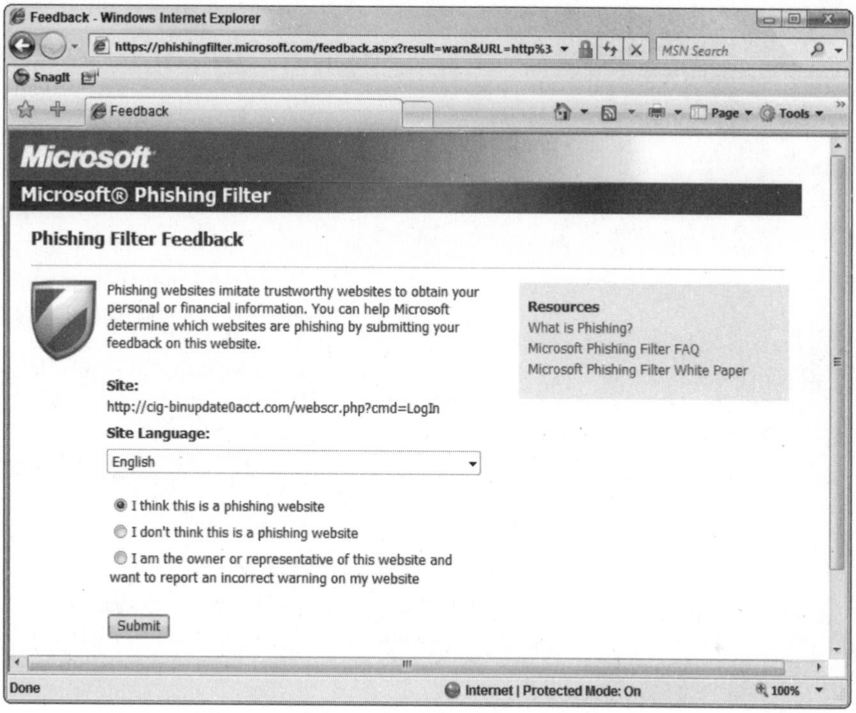

Figure 2-10:
Report
phishing
sites to
Microsoft.

To change your Internet Explorer Phishing Filter settings, follow these steps:

1. **Start Internet Explorer.**

2. **To manually check a Web site, navigate to the site.**

3. **Hold down the Alt key, then choose Tools⇨Phishing Filter.**

4. **To check the current Web site — see whether it's on the "black list" — click the Check This Website entry.**

IE warns you that it's sending information to Microsoft and then reports on the status of the site.

5. **To report a potential phishing site, or to report a misdiagnosed phishing site, click the Report This Website entry.**

IE shows you a form that lets you vent your spleen.

6. **If you have Automatic Website Checking turned off, turn it on by selecting the Turn On Automatic Website Checking entry, then selecting the Turn On Automatic Phishing Filter option, and then clicking OK.**

This is one of the few places where I recommend that you allow Microsoft to proceed automatically.

What happened to pop-ups?

Both Internet Explorer and Firefox include sophisticated blockers that prevent most obnoxious Web sites from plastering pop-ups all over your screen. A *pop-up* is a browser window — typically containing advertising — that's spawned when you simply go to a Web site.

The pop-up filters in IE and Firefox work so well that it's getting harder to find a site with the temerity to put an advertising pop-up on the screen. Far more frequently, Web sites use pop-ups in ways that may actually be beneficial: The pop-up on www.cnn.com, for example, allows you to choose between U.S. and International editions; many download sites use pop-ups to start downloads.

If IE or Firefox detects a pop-up, it blocks the pop-up and displays a bar across the top of the page, inviting you to manually allow the pop-up. If you're looking at a reputable site, you might want to unleash the pop-up, just to see whether it does something that you want it to!

Fighting phishing with Firefox

Microsoft's Phishing Filter in Internet Explorer gathers detailed information about every site that you visit. If you turn on the IE Phishing Filter, you leave a list of all the sites you've visited in Microsoft's giant database.

Firefox 3 works in a completely different way. By default, Firefox maintains two blacklists on your computer @@md a list of sites thought to harbor malicious software (so-called attack sites) and a list of sites that have been reported as phishing sites (forgery sites). Google maintains the master lists on its servers. Firefox automagically updates the lists on your computer, using the data from Google, every 30 minutes.

Each time you try to venture out to a new Web site, Firefox 3 looks for the address of the site in its blacklists. If the address appears on one of the blacklists, Firefox 3 double-checks the Google database to make sure the site is still in a state of ill repute and, if so, puts a Reported Attack Site! or Reported Web Forgery! notice on the screen. (See Figure 2-11.) If the address isn't in the blacklist on your computer or the master Google list gives the all-clear, Firefox goes straight to the indicated Web site. It all happens behind the scenes. You don't have to do anything. And your personal web surfing history never gets leaked anywhere.

Here's how to adjust Firefox's anti-phishing settings:

1. **Start Firefox 3. Choose Tools⇨Options⇨Security.**

   You see the security options in Figure 2-11.

Figure 2-11:
Firefox 3 works with two blacklists, helping to protect you from phishing and "attack" sites.

2. **If you want Firefox to use the blacklists, check the boxes marked Tell Me if the Site I'm Visiting is a Suspected Attack Site, and Tell Me if the Site I'm Visiting is a Suspected Forgery.**

   Checking the boxes sets up the blacklists, and tells Firefox to update them every 30 minutes.

3. **Click OK to get out of the Security Options box.**

   Your changes take effect immediately.

Doing Stuff with Web Pages

Viewing Web pages is easy. Working with them is hard. Nawwww. Not really. Not if you know the tricks.

Saving Web pages

If you find one of those invaluable articles that backs up every argument you've ever made about buying quality running shoes (ammunition guaranteed to convince your mate), by all means, save it! Or — if you finally find that sparkling New! icon you've seen on other people's sites, you can capture it to use on your own pages by saving the image to a file. This section explains how to save pages — and graphics items — for your own use later.

Saving to a file

There's no mystery to saving a Web page. It's not a whole lot different than saving any document in any program anywhere. Ready for the process? Don't blink — you may miss it:

1. **Navigate to the Web page you want to save.**

2. **Hold down the Alt key, then choose File⇨Save As (in Firefox, choose File⇨Save As).**

   The Save Webpage dialog box appears, as shown in Figure 2-12.

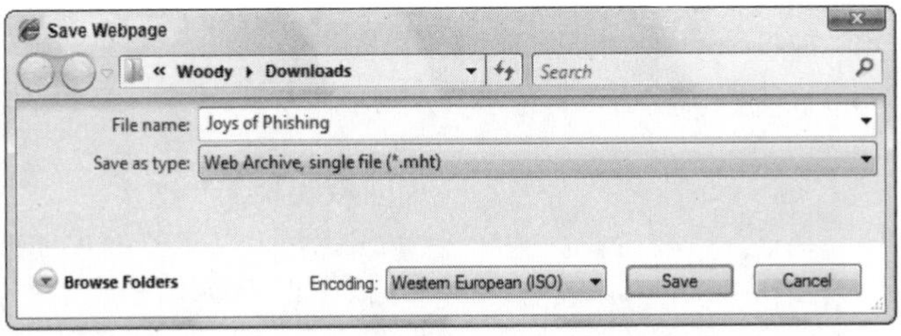

Figure 2-12: With IE, save pieces of a Web page in a single MHT file.

Save Webpage	
« Woody ▸ Downloads	Search
File name:	Joys of Phishing
Save as type:	Web Archive, single file (*.mht)
▼ Browse Folders	Encoding: Western European (ISO) ▾ [Save] [Cancel]

3. **Navigate to the folder in which you want to save the page.**

4. **In the Save as Type drop-down list box, choose Web Archive, Single File (*.mht).**

   That forces Internet Explorer to save all the pieces of the Web page — including the graphics — in a single file. If you stick the whole page in one file, it's easy to move the file around without losing the pieces. (Firefox doesn't have this option because MHT is a Microsoft-proprietary file format.)

5. **Enter a name for the file if you want to change it from its default.**

6. **Click the Save button.**

   Internet Explorer saves the file in the folder you specified.

Saving an image

Suppose that you run across a picture that you really love, an icon that you must have, or a banner that you want to remember. You can save the image to your hard drive by following these steps:

1. **Right-click the image that you want to save and choose Save Picture As.**

Windows opens the Save Picture dialog box.

You are allowed to save the file in its original format (typically JPG or GIF) or as a bitmap (BMP) file. Avoid saving pictures as bitmaps — the quality won't be any better than the original, and the file size can expand greatly.

2. **Navigate to the folder in which you want to save the file.**

3. **Enter a name for the file, if needed.**

4. **Click the Save button to save the file.**

A word about copyright laws: If you didn't create the picture, it doesn't belong to you. Taking images from the Web may be fine for your personal use (sending a picture in a recipe to Aunt Edna is probably okay as well), but if you use images, text, ideas, pages, diagrams, music, or more as part of your business or as part of something you intend to make money on, you may be in danger of copyright violation. When in doubt, check it out: `www.benedict.com/info/info.aspx` is a great place to find more information on copyrights.

Printing Web pages

When you display a page that you want to print, *don't* click the Print icon. You probably won't like the junk that comes out your printer.

Instead, click the down arrow next to the Print icon and choose Print Preview. (In Firefox, choose File➪Print Preview.) From the Print Preview window (see Figure 2-13) you stand a fighting chance of figuring out how to manipulate IE into printing only the information that you want. Given the price of color printer cartridges, this tip alone could pay for this book in a week!

Can't get Internet Explorer (or Firefox) to print exactly what you want? Select the stuff you want, press Ctrl+C, and copy the good stuff to Word or WordPad. It's much easier to, say, delete an unwanted advertisement or squish a graphic down to size inside Word — especially if you're used to working in these programs.

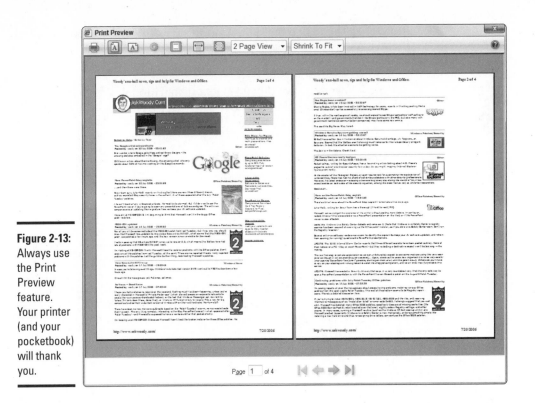

Figure 2-13:
Always use the Print Preview feature. Your printer (and your pocketbook) will thank you.

Playing Favorites

As your surfing savvy increases, you'll begin to find pages that are keepers — Web sites with information that you know you'll want to be able to find later. Internet Explorer gives you an easy way to collect and organize those sites in a feature called Favorites. (In Firefox, the feature is called Bookmarks.)

When you start Internet Explorer for the first time and click the Favorites "star" just below the Address bar, you may notice that Microsoft (or the company that sold you the computer) splays a whole slew of folders covering a variety of topics, from home and health to banking and sports. You may also see a number of strategic alliances represented there: Many third-party vendors involved in "partnering" with Microsoft and hardware manufacturers get their links built right into the default Favorites folders. And they pay dearly for the privilege.

But the steps for displaying, selecting, adding, and organizing Favorites all work the same way, no matter how many preset Favorites you find in your folders.

To explore the Favorites that Microsoft or your hardware manufacturer has, uh, thoughtfully arranged for you, follow these steps:

1. **Start Internet Explorer.**

2. **Click the Favorites "star" just below the Address bar, and then click the Favorites button.**

A list of Microsoft-and-your-hardware-manufacturer's Favorites folders appears.

3. **Right-click any of *their* Favorites that aren't *your* Favorites, and choose Delete.**

It's your Favorites menu. Give all the slimy advertisers the boot.

4. **Click any folder that interests you.**

A submenu of sites appears. Right-click any of them that deserve to go into the bit bucket, and choose Delete for them, too.

5. **If you see a site that you think might be useful, click its name in the Favorites list.**

Internet Explorer goes to the site. If you click the right-facing arrow to the right of the site's name, it'll open in a new tab.

Adding Favorites of your own

When you find yourself viewing a site that you want to go back to later, you can add the site to your Favorites folder. Internet Explorer enables you to add sites to the preset folders, or you can create a new folder that is specific to your needs. Follow these steps to add a Favorite of your own:

1. **Go to the Web site that you want to stick in your Favorites list.**

2. **Click the Add to Favorites "plus" sign below the Address bar and click the Add to Favorites line.**

IE shows you the Add a Favorite dialog box, as shown in Figure 2-14.

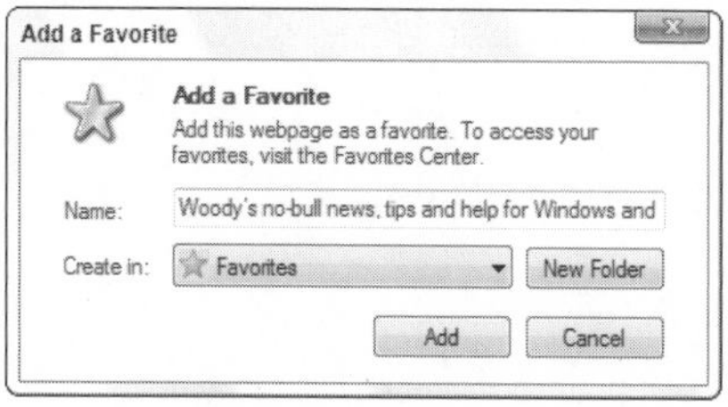

Figure 2-14:
Add a Web
site to your
Favorites
folder.

> **Add a Favorite**
>
> ☆ **Add a Favorite**
> Add this webpage as a favorite. To access your
> favorites, visit the Favorites Center.
>
> Name: Woody's no-bull news, tips and help for Windows and
>
> Create in: ☆ Favorites ▾   [New Folder]
>
> [Add]   [Cancel]

3. **Navigate to the folder in which you want to store the site, or create a new folder by clicking the New Folder button.**

To create a new folder to store the Web page you're adding, click the New Folder button in the Add a Favorite dialog box. The Create New Folder dialog box opens. Type a name for the folder (spaces and punctuation characters are okay) and click OK. IE adds the folder to the Create In list in the Add a Favorite dialog box, and you can select it as you would any of the existing folders.

4. **Click OK to save the link and close the dialog box.**

Organizing your favorites

Sometimes surfing presents you with so many exciting things to look at that you may simply save pages right and left without taking the time to put them in folders. Over time, this creates a mess of pages on your Favorites menu and means that you have to go scrolling through many pages to find the page you want.

To straighten out your folders and your life, follow these steps:

1. **On the IE toolbar, click the Add to Favorites "plus" button and then choose the line marked Organize Favorites.**

The Organize Favorites dialog box appears, as shown in Figure 2-15.

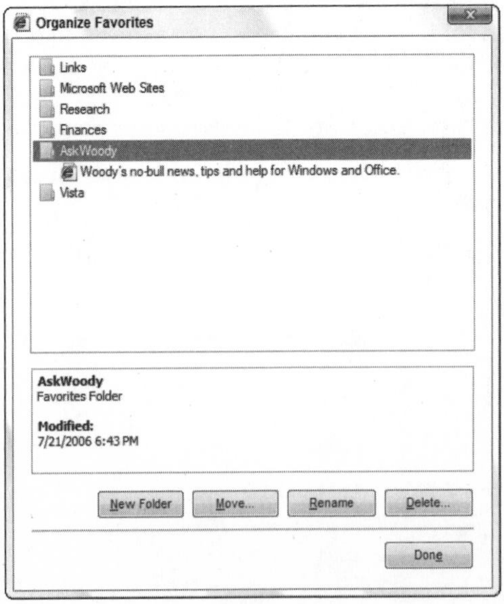

Figure 2-15:
You can add your own folder and reorganize entries in the Organize Favorites dialog box.

> Organize Favorites
>
> Links
> Microsoft Web Sites
> Research
> Finances
> AskWoody
>   Woody's no-bull news, tips and help for Windows and Office.
> Vista
>
> AskWoody
> Favorites Folder
>
> Modified:
> 7/21/2006 6:43 PM
>
> [New Folder] [Move...] [Rename] [Delete...]
>
> [Done]

2. **In the folder list, select the folder containing the link(s) that you want to change.**

3. **Click and drag entries to move them into and among folders. Alternatively, click one of the following command buttons:**

   - **New Folder:** Creates a new folder to store the page. A new folder appears in the list; type the name for the folder and press Enter.

   - **Move:** Allows you to choose a new location for the link. The Browse for Folder dialog box opens so that you can select the folder to which you want to move the link.

   - **Rename:** Allows you to enter a new name for the link (or folder). The link that you selected appears with the name highlighted; simply type the new name and press Enter.

   - **Delete:** Removes the link (or folder). The Confirm Folder Delete message box appears so that you can confirm that you want to delete the selected link. Click the Yes button to continue.

4. **Click the Done button.**

Chapter 3: Making Internet Explorer Your Own

In This Chapter

✔ **Making IE work your way**

✔ **Understanding RSS feeds**

✔ **Turbocharging your surfing**

✔ **Blogging and IE**

✔ **Digging up the truth about cookies**

I hear the same questions over and over again about making Internet Explorer (IE) run faster (you can't do much); bypassing some of IE's more, uh, idiosyncratic behavior (a few solutions exist); and knowing whether RSS is worth the effort (if you regularly read a "newsy" site, the answer's a resounding "yes").

In this chapter, I take you through the tricks that can help you get the most out of IE, even if you have to drag it kicking and screaming into the 21st century. I fill you in on RSS. I tell you the truth about cookies. I show you how to customize IE. And — if all else fails and you've made a mess of things — you can return your IE settings to the way they were before you made all the modifications. At the end of this chapter, I tell you how.

Getting the Most from Internet Explorer (And Firefox)

A handful of Internet Explorer (and Firefox) tricks can make all the difference in your productivity and sanity. Every IE/Firefox user should know the following shortcuts:

✦ You rarely need to type www in the Address bar at the beginning of an address, and you never need to type http://.

Almost every site these days just lets you type the name of the site, as long as you include the part at the end. So you can type http://www.dummies.com if you really want to, but dummies.com works just as well.

If you hit a site that forces you to type www at the beginning of an address — say, if you type someplace.com and you get a "Page not found" error — write to the Webmaster (in this case, send an e-mail to webmaster@someplace.com) and tell him that he needs to get into the 21st century. It's a sign of really sloppy Web site design.

✦ IE (and Firefox) automatically stick http://www. on the front of an address that you type and .com on the end if you press Ctrl+Enter. So, if you want to go to the site http://www.dummies.com, you really only need to type **dummies** in the Address bar and press Ctrl+Enter. (No, you don't need the http:// and most post-Neolithic sites don't require the www either. But the com is necessary.)

✦ With extremely rare exceptions, an address's capitalization doesn't matter. AskWoody.com and askwoody.com both get you to my Web site — as does asKwoodY.cOm. On the other hand, - hyphens and _ underscores aren't interchangeable: some-site.com and some_site.com are two completely different sites. Similarly, the number 0 isn't the same as the letter o, the number 1 isn't a letter l, and radishes aren't the same as turnips. Or so my niece tells me.

✦ Sometimes you really want IE to open a new window and leave your current window where it is so that you can easily refer to it. Usually, the Web page you're on has control over whether clicking a link opens a new window, but you can override the page's setting. To make IE (or Firefox) open the linked page in a new tab, hold down Ctrl when you click a link. To make IE (or . . . well, you get the idea) open a new window, hold down Shift when you click a link. Alternatively, you can right-click a link and choose Open in New Tab or Open in New Window.

✦ Depending on the size of your monitor and the quality of the display, the Web content that you see may be a bit of a strain to read. Some site designers try to cram as much information as possible on a page, crushing ten pounds of text into a five-pound space. You can control this to some degree by making the size of the text larger and easier to read. Click the Page button, and under Text Size, choose Largest or Larger.

One trade-off when you enlarge the text size is that less information fits on the screen, which means that you have to do more scrolling to read through articles that capture (and hold) your interest.

✦ If you find yourself working on pages with lots of content, you might want to flip your browser into Full Screen view, thus minimizing the amount of overhead impinging on the good stuff. To do so, press F11 or choose Tools➪Full Screen (View➪Full Screen in Firefox). When you want the navigation buttons back in IE, slide your mouse up to the top of the screen.

✦ Keeping track of passwords rates as the single biggest pain in the neck in any browser. You have passwords for, what, a hundred different sites? If you haven't discovered Roboform yet (www.roboform.com), you need to. Roboform memorizes the passwords of all your sites, stores them securely, automatically recognizes password-requesting pages when you get to them, and fills in the user ID and password with just a click. Where you had to memorize (or write down) a hundred different user IDs and passwords before Roboform, after you install the (free!) package, you only need to provide the single Roboform password, and everything else gets filled in automatically.

Making IE Run Faster

In general, if you want IE to run faster, you need to get a faster Internet connection. Beefing up your computer, adding more memory, getting a larger hard drive — none of that stuff really does much to make Web surfing faster. The bottleneck is your Internet connection.

If you're stuck with a slow connection, and you're a bit desperate, one trick can speed up IE — but at a price. You can turn off graphics. When you tell IE to load a page without the graphics, the browser displays an empty box where the image would be. That's a bit like going to the Louvre and seeing only empty picture frames, but if you want to get through quickly, it may help.

Here's how to turn off graphics in IE:

1. **Click the Tools button and then choose Internet Options.**

   The Internet Options dialog box opens.

2. **Click the Advanced tab.**

3. **Scroll down to the Multimedia section (shown in Figure 3-1), and deselect the Show Pictures check box.**

4. **Click OK to close the dialog box.**

   When you restart Internet Explorer, it no longer shows pictures.

In Firefox, you can block images, too: Choose Tools⇨Options⇨Content and deselect the Load Images Automatically check box.

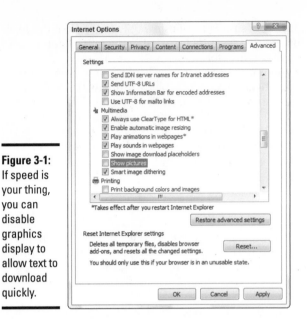

Figure 3-1:
If speed is
your thing,
you can
disable
graphics
display to
allow text to
download
quickly.

Just the facts, ma'am! If you're interested only in information, you can further reduce download times by deselecting the Play Animations in Webpages and Play Sounds in Webpages check boxes. This reduces your Web pages to straight text information, which may not be much fun but makes surfing much faster.

Even after you turn off the display of pictures, you can still view a picture if you choose. When the Web page appears, simply right-click the image placeholder (which is usually a small box surrounding a red *X*). When the shortcut menu appears, choose Show Picture, and the image appears on the page.

You turned the display of graphics back on, but they still aren't appearing. What gives? Press F5 to refresh the display, and IE reloads the page, which includes downloading the graphics as expected.

One other way to boost IE performance is to increase the amount of storage space allowed for those Temporary Internet Files. I have never been able to *feel* a difference when I jack up the space — that's my criterion for a good performance boost — but your results may vary. Here's how to increase your storage space:

1. **In Internet Explorer, click the Tools button, choose Internet Options, and in the middle of the General tab, in the Browsing History area, click the Settings button.**

You see the Temporary Internet Files and History Settings dialog box shown in Figure 3-2.

Figure 3-2:
More
room for
Temporary
Internet Files
means that
IE doesn't
have to
download
Web pages
as fre-
quently,
thus saving
you a (small)
amount of
time.

2. **Crank up the MB allotted in the Disk Space to Use box.**

If you have a lot of room on your hard drive, you can afford to let IE get a little sloppy. But remember that the gains you'll experience, day to day, aren't really that great.

3. **When you're happy with your choice, click OK twice.**

Using Links

Both IE and Firefox can display a Links toolbar (in Firefox 3, it's called a Bookmarks toolbar), which you can load with your favorite shortcuts (er, bookmarks). It's a great timesaving trick that everyone can use.

In Firefox 3, the Bookmarks toolbar appears by default, with three prede-fined links: Home, Smart Bookmarks (which are automatically generated to make your surfing faster), and Latest Headlines. Click the Latest Headlines icon, and you see a drop-down list of RSS-based news entries, tied to the BBC news feed. (See "Working with RSS Feeds," later in this chapter.)

In IE, you may have to bring up the Links toolbar. Follow these steps to do so:

1. **Right-click any empty spot on a toolbar.**

For example, you can right-click to the right of the last tab.

2. **Select the Links option so that a check mark appears next to it on the menu.**

3. **You may need to deselect the Menu Bar option to give the Links bar enough room so that you can see it.**

To put a shortcut on the Links bar, follow these steps:

1. **Navigate to the page you want to immortalize.**

2. **Click the icon to the left of the address (see Figure 3-3) and drag it to the Links toolbar.**

3. **After the icon is on the Links toolbar, you can click it to be propelled immediately (more or less) to the indicated Web page.**

To change or delete a link, right-click it and choose the appropriate command.

Figure 3-3:
Click and drag the icon to the left of the Web address, placing it on the Links toolbar.

Dealing with Cookies

Cookies are small text files that Web pages store on your computer to keep information about your choices and preferences. Cookies are small files but, depending on the number of sites you visit (and the way in which you've set your preferences to allow cookies), they can quickly accumulate in the space reserved for your Temporary Internet Files.

Do you need cookies? Mostly, no. If you subscribed to a site (such as *The New York Times*) and provided a username and password, that information may be stored in a cookie on your computer. When you go to the site, the site reads the cookie, and you can log on without entering your username and password each time. But the majority of cookies are simply files that Web pages put on your computer that have nothing to do with making things more convenient for you — and everything to do with marketing, marketing, and more marketing. Those are the ones you can delete without a second thought.

Cookies don't have anything to do with spam — you'll get the same junk e-mail even if you tell your computer to reject every cookie that darkens your door. Cookies don't spy on your PC, go sniffing for bank accounts, or keep a log of those, ahem, artistic Web sites you visit. They do serve a useful purpose, but like so many other concepts in the computer industry, cookies are exploited by a few companies in questionable ways. I talk about cookies extensively in Book III, Chapter 1. If you're worried about cookies and want to know what's really happening, that's a great place to start.

In Internet Explorer, to delete all cookies, press Alt, choose Tools➪Delete Browsing History. Click the Delete Cookies button. A message box appears, asking whether you want to proceed. Click OK to clear all cookies.

In Firefox, choose Tools➪Clear Private Data. Make sure that the Cookies check box is selected, and click the Clear Private Data Now button.

Blogging with Internet Explorer

For many people, Internet Explorer and Firefox reach their epitome in the blog space. A *blog,* short for *Web log,* is a specific kind of Web site, characterized by numerous articles listed with the newest entry first. Blogs are quick and easy to update, and resemble an ever-evolving diary more than a fixed reference.

Blogs span the entire range of human endeavor:

✦ Political blogs have been credited with helping politicians and their causes — as well as bringing down journalists.

✦ Tech blogs hold a special place in my heart because of my long involvement with AskWoody.com, a kinda-sorta blog.

✦ Literature blogs slice and dice every literary topic, sometimes with (unwittingly) humorous effect.

✦ Travel blogs deliver the lowdown on every place you could imagine, kind of like sitting in the garden and eavesdropping on conversations at the Kathmandu Guest House.

✦ You can also find sports blogs, Grumpy Old Men blogs, angst-filled teen blogs, How to Raise Goldfish blogs, I Hate (fill in the blank) blogs, I Love (fill in the blank) blogs, and Blogs about Blogs blogs.

If you're just starting out with blogs — looking for a specific type of blog, or thinking about writing one — you should take a look at Blogger, `www.blogger.com` (see Figure 3-4).

Figure 3-4: Blogger makes creating a blog — and searching for one — significantly less difficult.

Blogger can take you through the steps to create and maintain a blog. It can help with utilities like the "Blogger for Word," which lets you create your blog articles in Word (specifically with its spell checker and easy-link generator) and then post the article in your blog.

Working with RSS Feeds

At the risk of repeating myself repetitively, *RSS* — Really Simple Syndication — is, uh, really simple. There. Did that clear up any confusion you might have? Actually, RSS is a whole lot easier to see than it is to explain.

If you've ever used Firefox, you've seen RSS in action. The "Latest Headlines" Live Bookmarks button on the Bookmark toolbar uses an RSS feed from the BBC. In Figure 3-5, I clicked the Latest Headlines Live Bookmarks button, and I can read the headlines of the most recent news items posted on the BBC Web site.

If I click a headline from the Latest Headlines drop-down list, Firefox heads over to the BBC Web site and brings up the corresponding BBC news articles.

It's really just that simple.

(Internet Explorer uses a slightly less flexible method, which I discuss later in this section.)

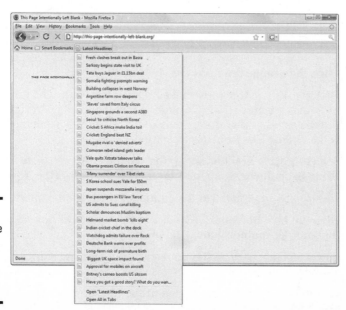

Figure 3-5:
Firefox's Live Bookmarks feature works with RSS feeds.

Here's how RSS works in Firefox:

1. **A Web site (usually with "newsy" topics, but sometimes just a site that wants to get noticed) creates a specific kind of file called an *RSS feed.***

   The RSS feed file has to be constructed in a precise way and needs to be shuffled to the correct place, but you don't have to worry about those details.

2. **When the Web site has, uh, new news, it adds the new item to the beginning of the RSS feed file and drops the last item off the end.**

   That keeps the RSS feed short and simple and reasonably up to date.

3. **If you go to a Web site that maintains an RSS feed, Firefox can tell that it has an RSS feed, and a little orange box with "radio waves" appears to the right of the Web page's address.**

   In Figure 3-6, I navigated to `http://slashdot.org`, which was one of the first tech news sites to sport an RSS feed. The orange RSS feed button appears to the right of its address.

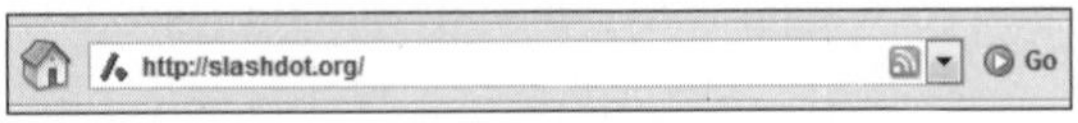

Figure 3-6:
A "radio wave" button shows that Slashdot has an RSS feed.

4. **Click the orange "radio wave" button.**

   Firefox asks you to choose a feed reader, per Figure 3-7. A *feed reader* is a program or feature that can understand and display RSS feeds. By far the easiest (and therefore, in my opinion, the best) RSS feed reader is the Firefox Live Bookmarks feature.

5. **Select the Live Bookmarks option from the Subscribe to This Feed Using drop-down menu, and then click the Subscribe Now button.**

   Firefox asks for a name and location for the Live Bookmark.

6. **Give the Live Bookmark a name. In the Create In box, choose to Bookmarks Toolbar, and click OK.**

   A new icon appears on the Bookmarks toolbar. In Figure 3-8, I put Slashdot on the toolbar.

7. **Anytime you want a quick look at the latest entries from the chosen site, click its Live Bookmark.**

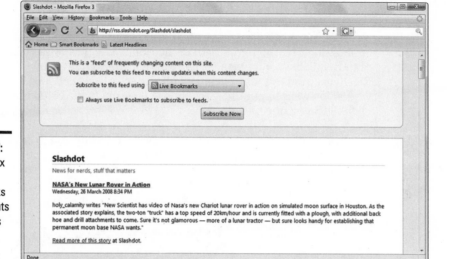

Figure 3-7:
The Firefox
Live
Bookmarks
feature puts
RSS feeds
at your
fingertips.

Note that you don't have to be looking at the site to take advantage of the
Live Bookmark. RSS feeds work no matter where your browser is pointed.

The contents of the site's RSS feed — which probably match the latest
entries on the site — appear in a drop-down list. You can click any item
in the list and the corresponding article should appear.

Figure 3-8:
Slashdot's
RSS feed —
the latest
headlines
from
Slashdot.
org —
appears
when you
click its Live
Bookmark,
even if you're
looking at a
different site.

RSS feeds in Internet Explorer are a bit more, er, clunky.

To view a site's RSS feed, navigate to a site with a feed and then click the "radio wave" button to the right of the Home icon. IE shows you a summary of the available contents (see Figure 3-9). If you want to keep updated with RSS items from this site, click the Subscribe to This Feed link. When IE asks where you want to put the feed, choose Feeds in the Create In box and then click the Subscribe button.

RSS feeds can save you gobs of time, first by allowing you to peek at headlines without opening a Web page and second by showing you all the new stuff so that you don't have to scroll through the flotsam (never mind the jetsam). Use RSS feeds whenever you can.

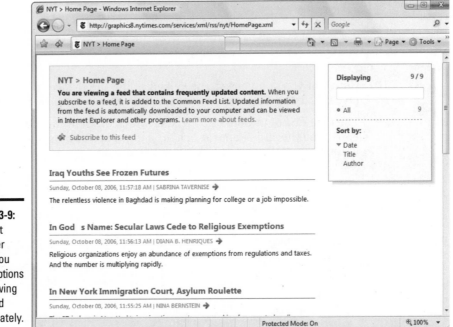

Figure 3-9:
Internet Explorer gives you more options for viewing the feed immediately.

Want a very fast and easy way to keep on top of the RSS feeds that concern you most? Take a look at `igoogle.com`. The Googlies have created a very powerful program that lets you put together your favorite RSS feeds and dish them all up on one page. Turn your personalized iGoogle page into your Web browser's Home page, and you get all of your RSS feeds in yer face, every time you crank up your browser.

Chapter 4: Windows Mail and the Alternatives

In This Chapter

✔ Choosing the right e-mail program

✔ Using Vista's free e-mail program — Windows Mail

✔ Putting together decent e-mail messages with a minimum of hassle

✔ Keeping on top of your contacts

What happened to Outlook Express?

If you used Windows B.V. (Before Vista), you might be surprised to discover that Outlook Express no longer exists. It's been tarted up a bit and renamed. Welcome to Windows Mail.

Microsoft now has four — count 'em, four — different e-mail programs. Windows Mail rates as the dinosaur of the bunch. Outlook Express, er, Windows Mail hasn't really been updated in a decade or more. Why? Because it doesn't make Microsoft any money. (Of course, you can't really say it's *free* if you consider it to be part of the price you paid for Vista.) Microsoft kept Mail in Vista because many people still use it — call it the inertia factor.

This chapter gives you a no-bull rundown of the four Microsoft e-mail programs and several good alternatives. In the end, if you decide to stick with the devil ye ken, this chapter also takes you through the high points of the latest incarnation of Outlook Expr . . . er, Windows Mail.

Just don't expect anything spectacular, okay? Microsoft saves all the good stuff for the products that make money.

Choosing an E-Mail Program

You have three good reasons to use Windows Mail: inertia, inertia, and inertia. All the other reasons aren't very convincing. If you're stuck with Windows Mail because you have a big collection of old Outlook Express (OE) messages (which Vista obligingly automatically converts to Windows Mail messages), or because you know OE and don't want to learn anything new, you have my sympathies.

Microsoft currently offers the following four very different e-mail programs (and countless variants):

✦ New in Windows Vista, **Windows Mail** is just the old Outlook Express with a thin coat of fresh paint. Two of the new features — junk-mail filtering and a phishing philter (see Figure 4-1) — are worth the effort, and another — mail search indexing — kinda comes along with the rest of the Vista ride.

Figure 4-1:
Windows
Mail
includes a
reasonably
capable
phishing
filter.

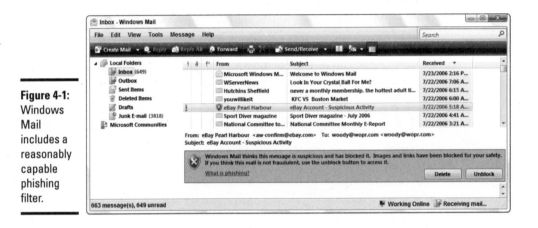

Windows Mail stores incoming messages on your computer, like a traditional e-mail program. Windows Mail can be jury-rigged to pick up messages from a Hotmail (er, Windows Live Mail), Gmail, AOL, Yahoo! Mail, and any regular "POP3" (see the nearby sidebar) e-mail account. When you retrieve messages from any of those services, they're moved onto your PC, so your mail doesn't hang around on the Internet indefinitely.

✦ **Microsoft Office Outlook,** in a dozen different flavors (Outlook 2000 SP3, Outlook 2003 SP1 and SP2, Outlook 2007, you get the idea), rates as the biggest, most bloated, most capable e-mail program available.

Outlook has absolutely nothing in common with Windows Mail — or Outlook Express before it — except that both programs (usually) download mail and store it on your computer, as opposed to leaving your mail sitting around on the Internet. Most people get Outlook as part of Microsoft Office.

To further add to the confusion: Outlook *was* part of Office 2003 Student & Teacher Edition, the low-cost version of Office that sold like hotcakes. But the new, improved Office 2007 Home & Student Edition doesn't have Outlook. The price of progress, I guess.

✦ **Windows Live Hotmail,** formerly known as **Hotmail** (and once known, very confusingly, as **Windows Live Mail**; see nearby sidebar) has hundreds of millions of users worldwide. The big advantage to Hotm . . . er, Windows Live Hotmail: You can get at your mail using any convenient Web browser. Your messages stay on the Internet, so you can play with your mail while you're logged on at LAX and pick up right where you left when you log on in the air, or in Timbuktu.

Every few months, Microsoft releases a new version of Hotmail (uh, Windows Live Hotmail), invariably emphasizing how it's "just like Outlook" — a damning indictment if ever there were. In fact, Windows Live Hotmail isn't anything at all like Outlook.

✦ **Windows Live Mail** (formerly called **Windows Live Mail Desktop**) which — tell me if you've heard this one before — isn't anything like Windows Live Hotmail or Outlook. Instead, it resembles the original Windows Mail, the program that ships with Vista, which in turn is almost indistinguishable from the old Outlook Express, which shipped with Windows XP.

Are you confused yet? Let me throw another one at you. For many months, Microsoft used the name "Windows Live Mail" for what we now know as "Windows Live Hotmail" (or, more frequently, just plain "Hotmail"). So if you see references to Windows Live Mail in books or on the Internet, you need to check and make sure that they're talking about this Windows Live Mail, and not the older Windows Live Mail, the one you know as Hotmail.

No, I don't make this stuff up.

Microsoft really, really wants Vista customers to dump Windows Mail and use Windows Live Mail. Why? Several reasons. Windows Mail and Outlook Express teem with bugs that will never be fixed. They're hooked into Windows and Internet Explorer at the wrists and ankles. They're part of the Windows development cycle, so it's very hard to update them. And . . . perhaps most importantly . . . Microsoft doesn't have any advertising or tie-in opportunities with Windows Mail or Outlook Express: Windows Live Mail connects directly to Windows Live Messenger (see Book V, Chapter 5), Windows Live Spaces blogging, the Microsoft RSS Feeds, and so much more. Ah, the marketing opportunities!

You can take Microsoft's advice and download Windows Live Mail, if you like. Go to `get.live.com/wlmail/overview` and follow the instructions. If you already use Windows Mail, or you know Outlook Express and don't see any particularly good reason to switch, this chapter should help.

Better the devil ye ken, eh?

E-mail client, POP3, and bafflegab

It's hard to keep up with all the e-mail buzzwords. Here's a quick little list that should get you through the major twists and turns of installing and using an e-mail *client* (that is, an e-mail program that runs on your computer) and getting it to retrieve your mail.

In a traditional e-mail client, you type a message, list which addresses you want to receive the message, and then *send* it. When your computer sends the message, it connects to a specific kind of computer attached to the Internet called a *Simple Mail Transfer Protocol (SMTP) server.* The SMTP server is responsible for getting the message out onto the internet, destined for the intended recipient.

The Internet *routes* messages based on the e-mail address of the recipient(s). The last part of your e-mail address — the part after the @ sign — is your *domain name.* In `Woody@`

`AskWoody.com` (yes, that's my e-mail address; no, capitalization doesn't matter), `AskWoody.com` is my domain name. A message sent to me actually ends up on a particular kind of computer called a *Post Office Protocol 3 (POP3) server* that's tasked with handling messages sent to AskWoody.com.

When you tell your computer that you want to *receive* messages, it goes out to your POP3 server and *downloads* all the messages waiting for you in its *queue.* In most cases, after the messages are downloaded to your computer, they're deleted from the POP3 server.

Attachments to messages (pictures, files, and so on) actually travel as text, and your e-mail client (or the Web program that you use to send and receive mail) takes care of the details using a specific set of rules called *Multipurpose Internet Mail Extensions (MIME).*

More and more people are finding that the two big online e-mail services, Gmail (`http://mail.google.com`) and Yahoo! Mail (`http://mail.yahoo.com`) offer all the services they need at a very good price — free. I've been using Gmail for ages. My Dad uses it, too. Simple. Powerful. And it's always there.

Getting Started with Windows Mail

All you need to start Windows Mail is a connection to the Internet. When you're online, just click the little Windows Mail icon on the Windows taskbar at the bottom of your screen or choose Start➪All Programs➪Windows Mail.

The first time you start Windows Mail, you need to enter your name, your e-mail address, and the details of your sending and receiving mail servers (see the nearby sidebar, "E-mail client, POP3, and bafflegab"). Your Internet Service Provider (ISP) should've given you all that information.

When you finally get through, the Windows Mail window appears, as shown in Figure 4-2, filled with (what else?) spam.

An identified likely phishing message

Folders that store your mail   Individual messages received

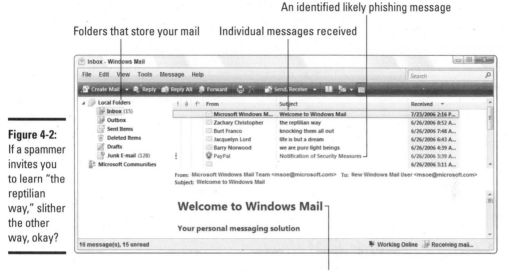

Figure 4-2:
If a spammer
invites you
to learn "the
reptilian
way," slither
the other
way, okay?

Text of the selected incoming message

The Windows Mail window is pretty easy to figure out. At the top of the
window, you find the familiar title bar and menus; beneath that, you find the
Windows Mail toolbar. Table 4-1 provides an overview of the Windows Mail
tools, from left to right on the toolbar. The screen is divided into these three
different panels:

✦ The Folders panel displays all the folders you've created in Windows
  Mail and some you have not created. The Inbox, Outbox, Sent Items,
  Deleted Items, Drafts, and Junk E-mail folders have been created auto-
  matically for you.

✦ The messages list in the upper-right panel shows all the messages in the
  currently selected folder.

✦ The individual message panel shows the contents of the message that is
  highlighted in the messages list.

Table 4-1	Windows Mail Tools
Name	*Description*
Create Mail	Displays the Create Mail window so that you can compose a new message
Reply	Enables you to respond to the current message
Reply All	Lets you respond to all the recipients of the current message

(continued)

Table 4-1 *(continued)*

Name	Description
Forward	Forwards the current message to the new recipient(s) that you choose
Print	Displays the Print dialog box so that you can print the current message
Delete	Deletes the current e-mail message
Send/Receive	Sends any mail you've created and checks your mail server to see whether you have any new mail
Contacts	Displays the Address Book so that you can add, edit, or delete contacts
Find	Enables you to search for a message that you've sent or received, people on the Web, or specific text phrases
Folder List	Toggles (turns on and off) the list of folders on the left

Conversing with E-Mail

When you start Windows Mail for the first time, you are asked for the ISP information and e-mail account information.

The process of setting up mail accounts — and you can set up dozens, if you choose — is a simple one. Get your accounts in order, and you're free to create, send, and receive e-mail messages at will.

Setting up mail accounts

How many e-mail accounts do you need? Many people have several e-mail addresses — perhaps one for work, one for school, and one for personal use. And let's not forget the kids' e-mail addresses.

To add other e-mail accounts or modify your existing one, follow these steps:

1. **Start Windows Mail.**

2. **Choose Tools↪Accounts.**

The Internet Accounts dialog box appears, as shown in Figure 4-3.

3. **Click the Add button, select the E-mail Account option, and click Next.**

The wizard then steps you through all the information that you need for a new account — your e-mail address, mail server addresses, passwords, and so on. All this information should come from your Internet Service Provider.

Figure 4-3:
Add a new
e-mail
account
here.

Although Windows Mail offers to subscribe you to newsgroups — the original
Internet-based bulletin boards that cover millions of different topics — very
few people use Windows Mail to get into the newsgroups. Far more common —
and far more usable — is the Google newsgroup engine, which you can find
at http://groups.google.com.

Retrieving messages and attachments

When you want to check your e-mail, click the Send/Receive button on
the Windows Mail toolbar. A notice appears in the lower-right corner
of the Windows Mail window, advising that you are receiving mail. Click the
Receiving Mail line, and you can watch the details as Windows Mail downloads your massive missives.

If you want to only receive (or send) messages, you can click the down
arrow to the right of the Send/Receive button and choose Receive All
(or Send All) from the menu that appears. That's the easy part.

The hard part lies in retrieving files that are attached to your e-mail messages.

In the normal course of events, you click an incoming message with an
attached file, and a paper-clip icon appears to the right of the message body,
indicating that a file is attached. Click the paper clip, and Windows Mail tells
you the name(s) of the file(s) attached (see Figure 4-4). And whoa — the

`.zip` extension tells you `woody@wopr.com` is *not* an e-mail address. This extension actually represents a compressed file, which may contain unsavory programs that, if opened, could spill all over your carefully guarded machine (because you are taking the security precautions I discuss in Book III, Chapter 1, right?).

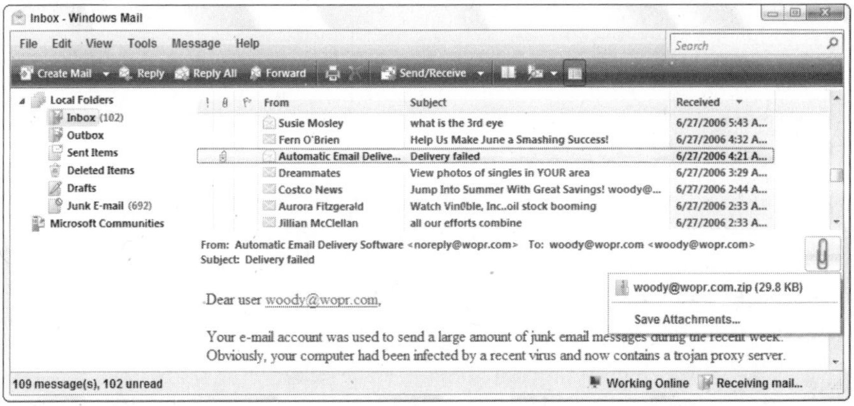

Figure 4-4:
Danger, Will Robinson! If you unzip this attachment, you may accidentally run a program.

The latest version of Windows Mail blocks certain kinds of files, based on the filename extension of the attached file. (See Book II, Chapter 1 for a discussion of filename extensions — and why you need to make Vista show them to you.)

If Windows Mail receives a message with a file attached to it, and the filename extension of the attachment is in Table 4-2, Windows Mail grays out the name(s) of the attached file(s) and you can't click them.

Table 4-2   Blocked "Unsafe" Attachments in Windows Mail

Attachments with These Filename Extensions May Contain Viruses or Malware

.ad	.adp	.asp	.bas	.bat	.chm	.cmd	.com	.cpl
.crt	.exe	.hlp	.hta	.inf	.ins	.isp	.js	.jse
.lnk	.mdb	.mde	.msc	.msi	.msp	.mst	.pcd	.pif
.reg	.scr	.sct	.shb	.shs	.url	.vb	.vbe	.vbs
.vsd	.vss	.vst	.vsw	.ws	.wsc	.wsf	.wsh	

Why does Windows Mail block pictures?

Unless you specifically tell Windows Mail that you want it to download and show you pictures inside e-mail messages, it won't. There's a reason why — and it has nothing to do with all the, uh, shall we say, er, creative pictures floating around on the Internet these days.

Pictures can be put inside e-mail messages in one of two ways. Either the whole picture goes in the message, or a *link* to the picture goes inside the message. The link points to a place on the Internet where Windows Mail can retrieve the picture, if you ask it to. If the whole picture is inside the message, Windows Mail shows it. But if a link exists, Windows Mail won't retrieve the picture unless you tell it to.

Why? Something called a "Web beacon." Spammers learned long ago that they could put

unique pointers inside e-mail messages, referring to pictures on their Web sites. When Windows Mail reaches out and grabs the picture, it leaves behind a trace of where it came from — and that trace can be linked to the e-mail address of the person who received the message. Spammers send out millions of messages with Web beacons, and they're rewarded with a list of all the e-mail addresses of the people who opened the messages.

Windows Mail doesn't follow the picture links — and thus it doesn't confirm the validity of your e-mail address to spammers — unless you choose Tools⇨Options, click the Security tab, and deselect the Block Images and Other External Content in HTML E-mail check box.

If you receive an e-mail message and you need to get at a blocked file attached to the message, here's how to do it:

1. **By far the safest, fastest, easiest way to get the attachment is to e-mail the person who sent you the message and ask him or her to zip the file and send it to you again.**

   If your friend is using Vista or Windows XP, have him or her choose Start⇨My Computer and navigate to the file, right-click the file, and choose Send To⇨Compressed (Zipped) Folder. Windows creates a compressed file with a .zip filename extension, which you can open immediately when you get it.

2. **If you can't get the file resent to you, or you're in a big hurry, use Steps 3 through 7, but be careful to *finish all the steps*.**

   In particular, make sure that you turn security on again when you're done, as I describe in Step 7.

3. **In the main Windows Mail window (refer to Figure 4-1), choose Tools⇨Options and then click the Security tab.**

Windows Mail shows you the Options dialog box shown in Figure 4-5.

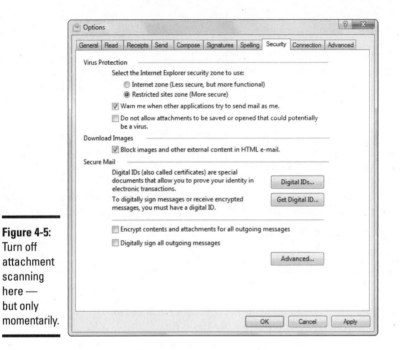

Figure 4-5:
Turn off
attachment
scanning
here —
but only
momentarily.

4. **Deselect the Do Not Allow Attachments to Be Saved or Opened That Could Potentially Be a Virus check box, and then click OK.**

Windows Mail returns to the main window.

5. **Double-click the message that has the attachment that Windows Mail blocked.**

The Windows Mail paper clip should make the file available to you, without graying it out.

6. **At this point, you can click the file to run it, right-click the file and save it, or choose Save Attachments from the paper-clip menu and save the file.**

Be very, very cautious if you run the file by double-clicking it, okay? That's how machines get infected with viruses. It's far better to save the file and use your (recently updated!) antivirus program to scan the file, individually, before you open or run it. *I warned you. . . .*

7. **Turn attachment security back on. Back in the Windows Mail main window, choose Tools➪Options➪Security, select the Do Not Allow Attachments to Be Saved or Opened That Could Potentially Be a Virus check box, and then click OK.**

Don't forget the last step. It's important.

Creating a message

When you're ready to create a message, follow these steps:

1. **Click the Create Mail button on the Windows Mail toolbar.**

The New Message window appears so that you can create the message you want to send (see Figure 4-6).

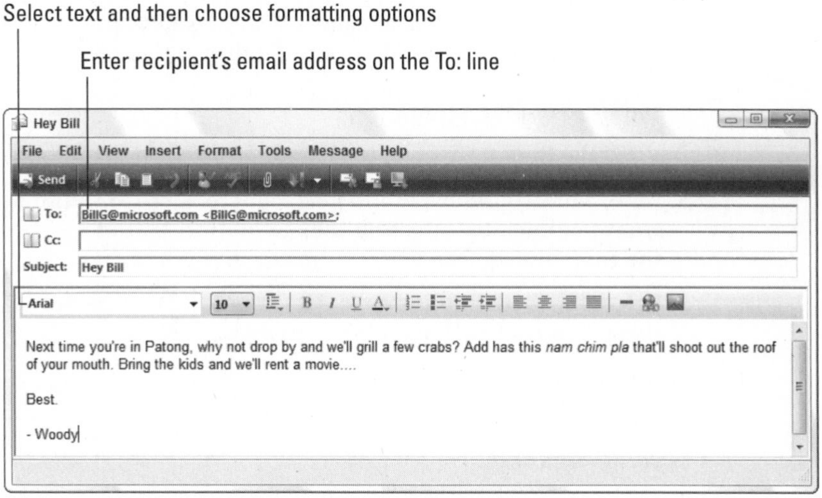

Select text and then choose formatting options

Enter recipient's email address on the To: line

Figure 4-6:
Writing
a new
message.

2. **Choose who you want to send the message to.**

You can enter the person's e-mail address in two different ways:

- You can type the e-mail address in the To: line.

- You can click the Address Book icon to the left of the To: line and select the recipient you want from the Address Book. (To select a recipient, click the contact from the list on the left, click the To button, and then click OK.)

Windows Mail then adds the contact name or e-mail address in the To line.

3. **Enter a subject for your message. For best results, keep it fairly short and make it descriptive.**

4. **Type the body of your message.**

You have a wide-open space to do just that. You can enter the words the way you want them without any fancy formatting, or you can change the look of the text by choosing a different font and size, changing colors, indenting information, and more.

See the following sections if you want to add a signature, check spelling, or attach files before you send.

Adding a signature automatically

Many people have little catch phrases, business mottos, *bon mots,* snips of *bathos,* kinky double entendres, explicit . . . well, you get the idea . . . and more that they like to stick on the end of their e-mail messages. If you're into these kinds of signatures, you can let Windows Mail add a signature for you automatically. Here are the steps for adding a signature:

1. **Choose Tools⇨Options.**

2. **Click the Signatures tab, and then click the New button.**

3. **Enter your signature in the Edit Signature box or add the file that you want to attach by selecting the File option button and browsing to the file that you want to use.**

4. **Select the Add Signatures to All Outgoing Messages check box to add the signature to all outgoing messages.**

5. **Click OK.**

Checking spelling

Have you ever dashed off a quick e-mail message, only to discover later that you misspelled a critical word? You can avoid embarrassing moments like that by running Windows Mail's spelling checker before you send your messages. To check spelling, simply complete your message and then choose Tools⇨Spelling. If the program suspects a misspelling, the Spelling dialog box appears, and you can choose the spelling that you want or enter a new spelling. Click the Cancel button to close the dialog box.

Windows Mail doesn't have its own built-in dictionary. Instead, it hijacks the dictionary used by Microsoft Office. You can run a spell check only if you have Word, Excel, or PowerPoint installed.

If youre spulling is as louzy as mine, you probbly want Windows Male to chek it every time you put togethr a mesage. To do so, back on the main Windows Mail toolbar, choose Tools⇨Options, click the Spelling tab, and select the Alwayz Chck Spullng Befour Snding check box. Or something like that.

Attaching files

Want to piggy-back a file onto your message? No sweat. Just keep in mind that the person receiving your message may be under the same filename restrictions that you must endure — as shown in Table 4-2 — or maybe even worse.

When you want to attach files, the process is simple. Follow these steps:

1. **Follow the steps earlier in this section to create your message.**

2. **Click the Attach File to Message button on the Windows Mail toolbar —
   the one that looks like a paper clip.**

   The Open dialog box appears, as shown in Figure 4-7, from which you can select your files.

3. **Navigate to the folder where the file is stored.**

4. **Click the file that you want to attach.**

5. **Click the Open button to add the file.**

Figure 4-7:
Attach a file to your message.

Note that Windows Mail allows you to attach any file you like to an outbound message. Problems may arise on the receiving end, though, if the person you're sending the message to has an e-mail program (like Windows Mail or Outlook or any of the online mail programs) that blocks certain kinds of files.

You can easily add more than one file to your e-mail message. To select multiple files in the same folder, press and hold Ctrl while you click.

Sending a message

Okay. Ready, set, send! Just click the Send button in the Windows Mail window. If you want to save the message that you created and send it later, choose File⇨Send Later. Windows Mail tells you that it is saving the message in your Outbox folder and you can send it when ready by clicking the Send/Receive button.

If you want to save a message and work on it again before you send it, choose File⇨Save. This places the message in your Drafts folder. When you want to continue working on it, simply open the Drafts folder and double-click the message.

Chapter 5: Working Together — IM OK, You're OK

In This Chapter

⊯ **Introducing Windows Live Messenger**

⊯ **Using Messenger effectively**

⊯ **Working with voice, pictures, and more**

⊯ **Windows collaboration — sharing folders**

*I*n the preceding chapter, I talk about the sorry state of Windows Mail: Microsoft now has four distinct mail programs, each with its own wrinkles and each with a basketful of pluses and minuses. And double minuses.

Instant messaging (IM) in the Microsoft milieu used to have the same problem. When Windows XP ruled the roost, we had Windows Messenger, MSN Messenger, and .NET Messenger, all from Microsoft, each with its own foibles and bumbles. Some versions of some Microsoft IM programs wouldn't even talk to others.

With Vista, some sanity has returned to Microsoft's instant messaging mess: Now exactly one (recent) offering exists, although it has a funny name — Windows Live Messenger — and you have to keep downloading and installing new versions. Never mind.

Like every "Windows Live" application, Windows Live Messenger isn't part of Windows. It's an add-on program that marches to the tune of its own drummer.

This chapter touches on the high points of Windows Live Messenger, particularly where the Messenger hooks into Windows itself.

Exploring the Alternatives

What can I say? I don't use an instant messenger unless I have to. I find instant messaging intrusive, distracting, and disruptive — even more than the phone, and very few people have my direct phone number. E-mail is much better for a lot of reasons.

The historic Messenger mess

Because so many Microsoft Messengers are floating around, it's hard to keep track without a scorecard. Unfortunately, if you're trying to communicate with different versions of Messenger, you might run into problems: They don't all talk to each other.

Over the past seven years, we've seen the names Windows Messenger (now known as Windows Dead Messenger?), MSN Messenger, .NET Messenger, and most recently, Windows Live Messenger all applied to essentially the same product, its derivatives, and its plumbing. I'll forgive you if you don't get the names straight.

The original MSN Messenger first appeared in 1999. Microsoft made it fully compatible with AOL Instant Messenger (AIM), which was the only messenger on the block. The folks at AOL didn't like Microsoft crashing its party, changed a few things, and rendered MSN Messenger incapable of talking to AIM customers. Lawsuits ensued. When the dust settled, AOL had its network, Microsoft had a different one, and Yahoo! had another. Google Talk came out with Jabber, an (arguably) open network. Trillian talked to all of them, to a greater or lesser extent. Microsoft apparently forgot its original court claims that IMing should be open to all and knocked Trillian off the MSN network repeatedly.

In 2001, Microsoft "forked" Windows Messenger, diverting that version from the MSN Messenger mainstream, to handle NetMeeting and videoconferencing in Windows XP. Windows Messenger was dependable, if boring. New versions appeared every year or two, whether we needed them or not.

MSN Messenger, the progeny of Microsoft's rapid-development, rapid-deployment crew, barreled ahead. We saw steady improvement in the product, delivered in a much more timely fashion. Too timely, in fact. New minor MSN Messenger versions seemed to roll out every week. Some versions of MSN Messenger didn't even communicate with Windows Messenger itself. Office 2003 hooked into Windows Messenger, not MSN Messenger.

Now, we're seeing history repeat itself. Some versions of Windows Live Messenger don't communicate with older versions of MSN Messenger — and heaven only knows whether Windows Messenger can talk with either of them.

But, truth be told, sometimes I do use IM — but only if I've made an appointment with the other party in advance. Maybe I'm an old fuddy-duddy, but there are, oh, about a hundred thousand things I'd rather do than deal with IM interruptions all day. Oy!

If you must use an instant messaging program, you and the person you're talking to have a fairly limited number of options:

✦ You can both use **AOL Instant Messenger (AIM)** or **ICQ** (which is owned by AOL). AIM was the original instant messenger (see the nearby sidebar). Depending on whom you believe, as of this writing, AIM users account for about half of all IM users.

✦ If one of you uses **Windows Live Messenger,** the other one can use Windows Live Messenger, MSN Messenger (some versions; see the nearby sidebar), Windows Messenger, or the latest version of Yahoo! Messenger with Voice.

✦ If one of you uses the latest **Yahoo! Messenger with Voice,** the other can use Windows Live Messenger or any of the recent Yahoo! Messenger versions.

✦ If one of you uses **Trillian,** the other can most likely use just about any instant messaging program. Trillian is the "universal donor," if you will, of the IM polyglot mess.

✦ If one of you uses **Google Talk,** the other can use any program that understands Jabber, the only more-or-less open, standards-based network. Unfortunately, at this moment, only Google Talk and a handful of less-well-known programs speak Jabber.

Things are changing quickly. As of this writing, Google owns 5% of AOL. I think it's a sure bet that Google and AIM will find a way to talk to each other. Keep an eye on AskWoody.com for all the latest news.

Given the current deplorable polyglot state of affairs, I have several recommendations:

✦ **If you need to IM with someone who's already hooked up with a specific IM service, join that service.**

That way, you get all the bells and whistles and smileys.

You don't need to use or pay for (yech!) AOL to run AIM. Drop by www.aim.com and download your free copy.

✦ **If you feel a general need to IM, go for Trillian (**www.cerulean studios.com**).**

That gives you the maximum flexibility, although occasionally some IM services knock out Trillian. Trillian isn't the most exciting IM program, but it gets the job done.

✦ **If you want to get into IM for the long term — that is, start using an ID that'll still be usable a few years from now — go for Google Talk** (http://talk.google.com**).**

Google and AOL together should prove formidable, and the fact that they're both based on a more-or-less open network makes the situation even more inviting.

Maybe Microsoft and Yahoo! can come up with compelling reasons for people to sign up for their advertising-laden proprietary services. I certainly haven't seen anything that would convince me.

Making Windows Live Messenger Work

So you want to use Windows Live Messenger. Fair enough. Here's the easy way to do it:

1. **Sign up for a Windows Live ID, preferably using a bogus name and dubious personal information.**

   Point your favorite Web browser to `http://get.live.com/getlive/overview` and click the Sign Up button. Follow the instructions. Bonus points are awarded if you give your name as William Gates III, residing in Washington State, zip code 98572, born in 1955.

   Although I have no problem giving *you* my e-mail address — it's `woody@AskWoody.com` — I'll be hanged if I'm going to put my real e-mail address in Microsoft's giant Live database. Microsoft has enough information about me already. Far better, in my opinion, is to sign up for a new Hotmail account, er Windows Live ID, with a completely bogus name and use that account for Windows Messenger, er, Windows Live Messenger.

   If you already have a bogus Windows Live Mail, MSN Hotmail, MSN Messenger, or Microsoft Passport account, you already have a Windows Live ID. Go on to Step 2.

2. **Download Windows Live Messenger.**

   Head over to `http://get.live.com/messenger/overviewhttp://get.live.com/windowsvista/messenger`. Click the Get It Free button. When asked whether you want to run or save the file, choose Save (you might want to run it again).

3. **When the file has downloaded, click the Run button to run the Windows Live Messenger installer.**

   You see the splash screen shown in Figure 5-1.

4. **Click Next.**

   The installer goes on for a bit, and then you see the screen shown in Figure 5-2.

5. **Deselect all the check boxes except the first one (Windows Live Messenger Shortcuts), and then click Next.**

   You can change your home page to MSN manually, if you really want to. See Book V, Chapter 3 for details.

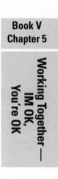

Figure 5-1:
Windows Live Messenger isn't a part of Windows; it must be downloaded and installed separately.

Figure 5-2:
Windows Live Messenger politely asks you to let it intrude.

Do you wonder why Rhapsody — the online music service from RealNetworks — is offered here, while URGE — the online music service from MTV — rates as the music service of choice in Windows Media Player (see Book VII, Chapter 2)?

Maybe it's because of the antitrust action brought by RealNetworks. In October 2005, Microsoft agreed to pay RealNetworks $460 million in cash and promised another $301 million "to support Real's music and game efforts." Microsoft gets credit toward that $301 million debt for every chump, er, customer that it signs up for Rhapsody. Now you know the rest of the story.

Figure 5-3:
Use your
bogus
Windows
Live ID to
sign in to
Messenger.

6. **When Windows Live Messenger says it's been installed, click Finish.**

Windows Live Messenger springs to life, and you see the sign-in screen shown in Figure 5-3.

7. **Type the Windows Live ID you received in Step 1 and your password. Select the Remember Me check box and deselect the other two (Remember My Password and Sign Me in Automatically). Then click the Sign In button.**

Windows Live Messenger (WLM) logs you in, and you see both the WLM main page and the gratuitous MSN Today screen (see Figure 5-4).

8. **Click the Add a Contact button, which is to the right of the Find a Contact or Number box.**

Messenger invites you to fill out the information for your messenger-enabled contact (see Figure 5-5).

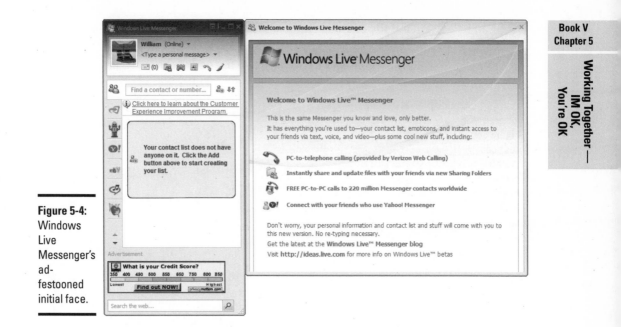

Figure 5-4:
Windows
Live
Messenger's
ad-
festooned
initial face.

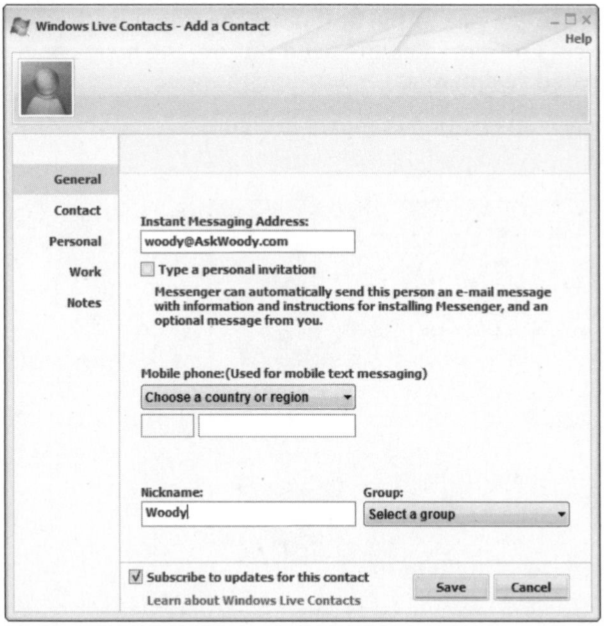

Figure 5-5:
Enter
contact
information
here.

9. **Fill out the contact's information, and then click the Save button.**

When you add a contact, and that contact doesn't yet have you on her buddy list, *she* gets a message, like the one shown in Figure 5-6. The contact gets to choose whether she want you to "see" her.

Figure 5-6:
Your contacts must give permission before you can see them.

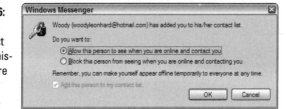

That means you can add someone to your Contact list, do everything properly, and have her show up on your Contact list — but you may never be able to connect to her because she told Messenger that she didn't want to be visible to you. Tough luck, eh?

10. **To start a conversation, double-click the contact's name. Type your message in the box at the bottom of the Conversation window. When you press Enter or click the Send button, the message gets sent to the designated recipient(s).**

A typical conversation is shown in Figure 5-7.

Figure 5-7:
Bill and Duangkhae have a little chat.

Although you're limited on the amount of text you can type in the message box, if you press Enter, you can keep on typing. You can copy text from just about anywhere and paste it into the message box: Windows Live Messenger treats it as if you typed it all out.

11. **When you're done chatting with this contact, click the *X* (Close) button to exit the conversation.**

    Alternatively, you can click the down arrow next to the Minimize button and choose File⇨Close, as shown in Figure 5-8.

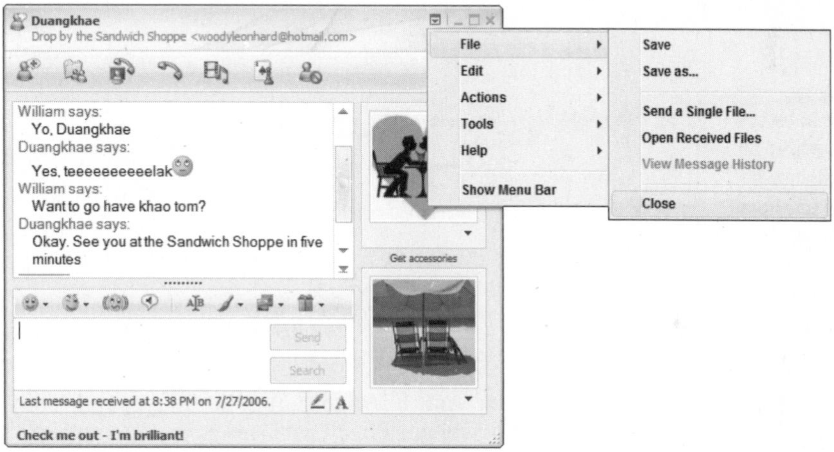

Figure 5-8: You can get at the menu by clicking the down arrow or by pressing Alt.

12. **When all your conversations are over and you're done with Windows Live Messenger, click the *X* (Close) button or click the down arrow, and then choose File⇨Close.**

    Even if you've closed Windows Messenger, it's still active — still lurking in the background listening for incoming messages, still waiting to interrupt what you're doing with a ripply *garururump* sound. If you want to *really* turn the bloody thing off, right-click the Messenger icon in the system tray (next to the clock) and choose Exit.

Tweaking Settings in Windows Live Messenger

Windows Live Messenger has lots of settings, some of which actually make sense. To get to the mother lode, click the down arrow next to the Minimize button and then choose Tools⇨Options. From that vantage point (see Figure 5-9), you can change your display name and choose from myriad additional settings.

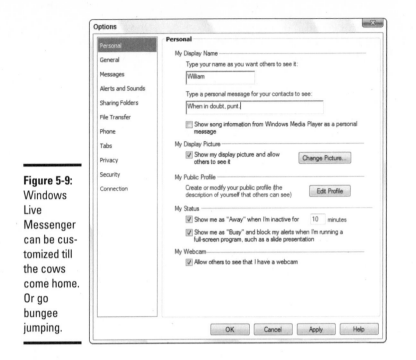

Figure 5-9:
Windows
Live
Messenger
can be cus-
tomized till
the cows
come home.
Or go
bungee
jumping.

If you don't yet! have your fill! of exclamation points! and really! cool! stuff!
head over to the Messenger Plus! Live site (`http://msgpluslive.net`)
and download a potful of Windows Live Messenger extensions. The extensions let you use tabbed chats (much like Internet Explorer's tabbed Web
pages), auto-replace text, and change your sounds, colors, and formatting.
You even find an auto-responder that kicks in while you're away. Just
make sure that you "opt out" of the adware when given a chance during
installation.

Sharing Folders

One advanced feature in Windows Live Messenger might prove useful. No,
I'm not talking about the shaking "wink" command or the really neat extra-
cost, extra-hassle cute icons. I'm not even talking about the ability to spend
money with Verizon for Internet-based telephone service (you can probably
get it cheaper with Skype) or the Webcam capabilities that deliver grainy pictures at grass-growing speeds.

Windows Live Messenger includes a feature called Shared Folders, and if you need to pass a file around to a small group of people, it beats the living daylights out of many alternatives (including, in many cases, Sharepoint Server, which costs about a gazillion times as much).

To get Shared Folders working, follow these steps:

1. Right-click a contact and choose Create a Sharing Folder.

Windows Live Messenger shows you the Sharing Folders dialog box shown in Figure 5-10.

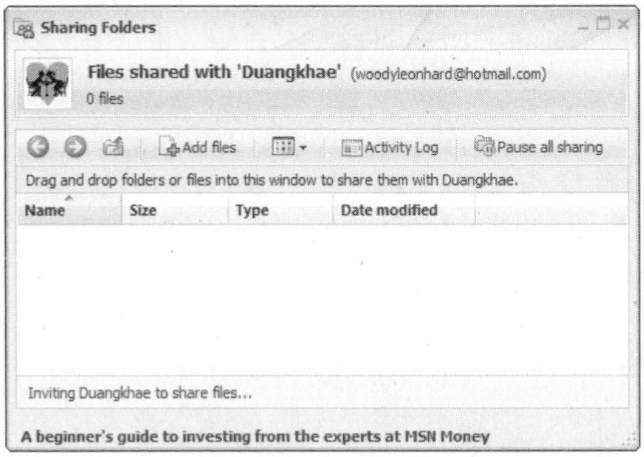

Figure 5-10:
Share files carefully, keeping in mind that destructive programs can be passed this way.

> **Sharing Folders**
>
> **Files shared with 'Duangkhae'** (woodyleonhard@hotmail.com)
> 0 files
>
> | | | Add files | | Activity Log | Pause all sharing |
>
> Drag and drop folders or files into this window to share them with Duangkhae.
>
> | Name | Size | Type | Date modified |
> | --- | --- | --- | --- |
>
> Inviting Duangkhae to share files...
>
> A beginner's guide to investing from the experts at MSN Money

2. The person you're sharing files with receives a message that says you are trying to share files, asking whether you want to set up a shared folder. If she wants to share files, she should click the Yes button.

If she agrees, she, too, sees a Sharing Folders dialog box like the one shown in Figure 5-10.

3. Click and drag any files you wish to share into the Sharing Folders dialog box.

Windows Live Messenger makes a copy of the file(s) — the originals aren't touched — and makes the copy available to the person you're sharing with.

Each of you can make modifications to the files. When you close the file, Windows Live Messenger synchronizes the files on both machines by copying the newer version to the PC with the older version.

It isn't fast. It isn't fancy. But it does work.

Note that this isn't "whiteboard" sharing — you can't make changes to the file while others watch the changes being made in real time. It's just simple synchronization using the Windows Live Messenger connection.

Windows Live Messenger (in)security

If you use Windows Live Messenger and you haven't updated it since September, 2007, you better do so now. WLM version 8.1 and earlier are susceptible to a security problem that crops up when you accept a webcam or video chat invitation from a miscreant. There's a detailed discussion in Microsoft Security Bulletin MS07-054 (www.microsoft.com/technet/security/Bulletin/MS07-054.mspx).

All the usual admonitions about not opening a file or clicking a link in an e-mail message apply to instant messages, too. In spades. "Get surprise at http://www.messengerxxx.info/ Unbelievable!" "U have deleted me! Look here http://www.messengerxxx.info" and "Hey, http://www.messengerxxx.info/ helps u find out who is your friend!" are all come-ons designed to get you to look at an ad-filled site. More and more viruses and worms are reaching out over IM networks. Play it safe. Use the same precautions with Windows Live Messenger as you would with any e-mail program. The computer you save may be your own.

Chapter 6: Searching on the Internet

In This Chapter

✔ Google ain't the only game in town — but neither is Microsoft Live Search

✔ Setting browser defaults in IE and Firefox

✔ Using Google pet tricks

✔ Searching quickly and effectively

Internet searching can be a lonely business. You're out there, on the Internet range, with nothing but gleaming banner ads and text links to guide you. What happens when you want to find information on a specific subject but you're not sure where to start? What if Google leads you on a wild goose chase?

Microsoft's been gunning for Google for years as though it's the only big search engine in town, but the fact remains that alternatives to Google abound. You don't need to develop a religious attachment to a single search engine. Look around, and go with what works best for you.

We cover search engines with, uh, religious fervor at AskWoody.com.

This chapter helps you get the most from Google, yes, but it also shows you many alternatives that can really come in handy, whether you use Google or not.

Choosing a Search Engine

It ain't easy being the biggest, baddest search engine around. A decade or so ago, Google (then called BackRub) amounted to little more than a simple idea: If a lot of Web sites point to a particular Web page, the page being pointed to probably contains information that many people would find interesting.

Stanford grad students Larry Page and Sergey Brinn, BackRub's founders, scrimped together enough money to build a working prototype in a Stanford dorm room. By 1998, the (ahem!) PageRank system was generating a lot of interest on campus: Students could actually find the stuff they wanted without slogging through endless lists of categories. In September 1998, Page and Brinn adopted the name Google and opened a real office with a cool $1 million in initial capital. Truth be told, the "office" was in a garage, which came with a washing machine, dryer, and hot tub. They blew all the money on computers. My kind of people.

Google has gone from one of the most admired companies on the Web to one of the most vilified, and the PageRank system, which tries to assign a number that predicts the relevance of a page to a specific query, has been demonized in terms rarely heard since the Spanish Inquisition. Few people now believe that PageRank objectively rates the "importance" of a Web page — millions of dollars and thousands of months have been spent trying to jigger the results. But, like it or not, Google just works. Google's *spiders,* which crawl all over the Web night and day looking for pages, have indexed billions of pages, feeding hundreds of millions of searches a day. For example, in Figure 6-1, check out the results of Google's search for the longest river in Asia. The No. 1 result says the longest is the Yangtze (known locally as the "Chang Jiang"), at 3,964 miles long.

As this book went to press, Google was worth about $120 billion, the verb "to google" had been embraced by prestigious dictionaries, Google was taking on Microsoft *mano a mano* in many different areas, and many other search engines offered decent alternatives to the once-almighty Google.

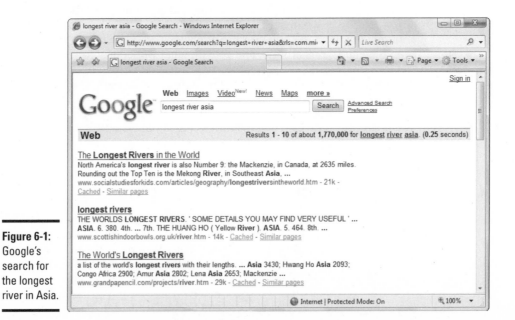

Figure 6-1: Google's search for the longest river in Asia.

I don't use Google as my primary search engine. Or perhaps I should say that I use Google in addition to others, either via Firefox's multiple search-engine capabilities (see the section "Changing the Search Engines — the Advanced Course," later in this chapter) or with a composite search site called Dogpile.

If you're stuck in a searching rut, try one of these alternatives:

✦ **Dogpile** (www.dogpile.com) automatically combines the search results of Google, Yahoo! Search, Windows Live Search (formerly MSN Search), and Ask.com (formerly Ask Jeeves), with a proprietary ranking formula that frequently gives excellent results. As shown in Figure 6-2, Dogpile's top result is more detailed than Google's, giving the length as 3,720 miles. The No. 2 result is an ad. Dogpile doesn't show Google ads. Bonus points, eh?

✦ **Windows Live Search** (http://search.live.com) from Microsoft covers much of the same ground as Google, although I find its results spotty. As shown in Figure 6-3, Live Search pulls the correct answer (with no details) from the Encarta Encyclopedia, but the next two results don't apply at all. You don't get much detail until the fourth entry.

Windows Live Search's image search presents results in a unique, and very usable, way.

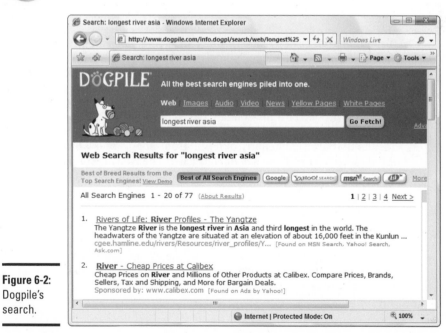

Figure 6-2:
Dogpile's
search.

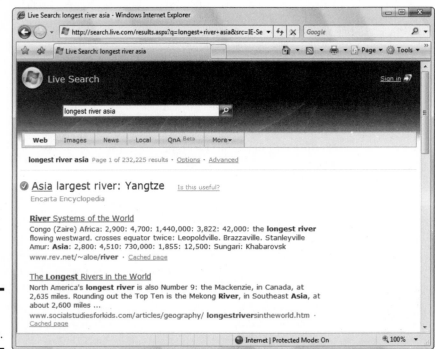

Figure 6-3:
Windows
Live Search.

+ **Yahoo! Search** (`http://search.yahoo.com`) has an interesting and different history. Years ago, Yahoo! drew much acclaim for its directory — kind of an Internet Yellow Pages. In 2002, Yahoo! bought Inktomi, which had one of the best search engines at the time, and in 2003, it acquired AltaVista. Yahoo!'s search site used the Google search engine until 2004, when it switched to a new engine based on the offerings from the acquired companies. As a result, Yahoo! frequently comes up with results that are significantly different from Google's — which may be good or bad, as you can see in Figure 6-4. The No. 1 result is an ad with no useful information. The No. 2 result is the same as Windows Live Search's No. 1 result.

+ **Ask.com** (`www.ask.com`), formerly Ask Jeeves, developed a small following because of its ability to work with natural-language questions. My search for the longest river in Asia (see Figure 6-5) yielded a #1 answer that doesn't answer the question, but the #2 and #3 answers were both spot-on. When I clicked through, I discovered that both of the sites had precisely the same text.

Figure 6-4:
Yahoo!
Search
results for
the longest
river in Asia.

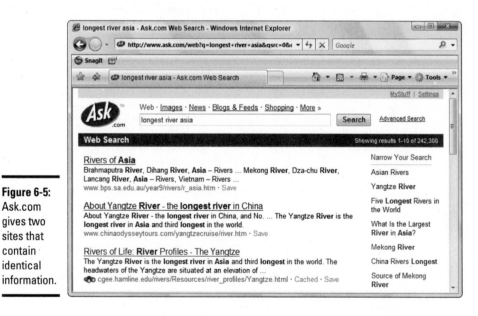

Figure 6-5:
Ask.com
gives two
sites that
contain
identical
information.

Surprisingly, none of the search engines brought up the Wikipedia entry for the Yangtze River (`www.wikipedia.org/wiki/Yangtze_River`), a very thorough and detailed reference.

Other search engines, which rely more on audience participation than on automated scanning and gathering, are worth mentioning. Check out these examples:

✦ **Technorati** (`http://technorati.com`) specializes in scanning and indexing blog entries. It includes a kind of audience-participation engine that makes it easy to find the most popular blog entries: You're invited to vote for blog postings that ring your chimes. The emphasis is on technical topics.

✦ **Digg** (`http://digg.com`), like Technorati, relies on user votes to bring news stories and specific postings to your attention. Unlike Technorati, Digg doesn't scan or index entries, relying on submissions from the world at large. Digg's emphasis is on news, broadly defined, in technology, science, world/business, videos, entertainment, and games.

✦ **del.icio.us** (`http://del.icio.us`) makes it easy for you to bookmark sites, and then leaf through other folks' bookmarks, with popularity rankings and affinity scores.

Which search engine is best? That's easy. None of them. If you don't find what you want in a few minutes, switch search engines. At the very least, you'll get a different perspective — and you might just find the answer you need.

Changing Search Engines — the Advanced Course

Internet Explorer, right out of the box, uses Windows Live Search as its search engine: When you start IE, it goes straight to the Windows Live Search page; when you type something in the IE search box in the upper-right corner, IE uses Windows Live Search to perform the search. Microsoft came under a lot of legal fire for that decision, but (at least as of this writing) when you first start IE, you're hooked up with Windows Live Search and the wrists and ankles.

Your PC manufacturer might have already changed search engines for you — you might even find an engine you like. Stranger things have happened.

You can change your IE search engine quickly and easily, and with absolutely no ill side effects and no bad feelings. If you're using Internet Explorer (as opposed to Firefox), I recommend that you switch to Google. I explain how to do that in Book V, Chapter 2.

Changing Firefox's search engine is just as easy, but there's a very cool twist: Firefox lets you use just about any search engine.

If you hook Firefox into Dogpile, you can use the combined force of multiple search engines, simultaneously. Even though Dogpile isn't one of the pre-configured Firefox choices, you can coerce them into working together. Here's how:

1. **Start Firefox. Click the down arrow to the left of the search box, in the upper-right corner.**

2. **Choose Manage Search Entries.**

   Firefox shows you the Search Engine Web page.

3. **Select the Get More Search Engines option.**

   Firefox takes you to the Search Engine Firefox Add-Ons page, as shown in Figure 6-6.

Figure 6-6:
New search engines are treated much the same as any other add-on in Firefox.

4. **Scroll down to the Additional Resources section and click the Browse through More Search Engines at Mycroft.Mozdev.org link.**

The Mycroft open-source site (named after Sherlock Holmes's brother, my dear Watson) has a large collection of search-engine plug-ins that work with Firefox and (reportedly) Internet Explorer 7.

5. **In the Site Name search box, type** Dogpile **and press Enter.**

Mycroft returns a handful of results, as shown in Figure 6-7.

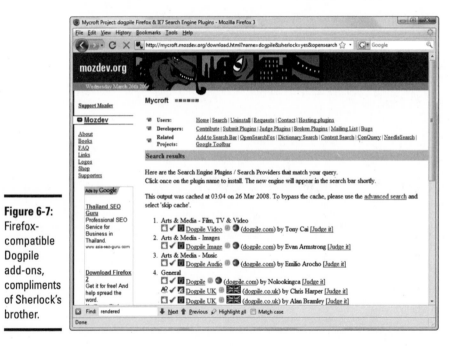

Figure 6-7:
Firefox-
compatible
Dogpile
add-ons,
compliments
of Sherlock's
brother.

6. **Click one of the Dogpile choices in the General category.**

Firefox asks whether you want to add Dogpile to the list of engines available in the Search bar.

7. **Select the Start Using It Right Away check box, and then click the Add button.**

Dogpile replaces Google as the default search engine in the Firefox search box, as shown in Figure 6-8.

**Book V
Chapter 6**

Figure 6-8:
It's easy to
have Firefox
use Dogpile
as its default
search
engine.

TIP

Another Firefox option called Rollyo allows you to add just about any search engine, or groups of search engines to the Firefox repertoire. For example, Rollyo has predefined searches that hit all the major news organizations, political blogs, major travel sites, or health-related sites. If you choose the predefined travel search, you get results from dozens of major travel sites, such as `Frommers.com` and `Travel.Discovery.com`. Follow the preceding steps, and in Step 4, choose Rollyo.

Googling Tricks

Google searches for much more than text. If you run a standard Google search using the search box, with the results shown in Figure 6-1, you are presented with a number of options above the Google search box:

✦ **Google maintains an enormous database of pictures, called** *Google Images.* Click the Images link above the search box, and you see pictures on the Web that appear near the given text. In Figure 6-9, Google shows you pictures that are, to a greater or lesser extent, associated with the phrase "longest river asia."

Figure 6-9:
Search for
pictures,
more or less
related to
the topic
at hand.

Similarly, you can click the Images link in Dogpile and see pictures associated with the search text. In Figure 6-10, Dogpile returns images that Google Images missed. In this case, Dogpile is also better at sticking to the requested topic — the Google Images result included many pictures that had nothing to do with the longest river in asia.

✦ **Google owns newsgroups.** If you're looking for Internet newsgroups — the largely unmonitored postings of millions of Internet users, on every topic under the sun — use the search box and then click the Groups link. Google literally owns the newsgroup archives, to a first approximation, anyway. Google's newsgroup tools and interface run rings around anything Outlook Express can deliver.

✦ **You may also like Google News.** Google News competes with CNN.com and other newsy sites — click the News link above the search box. Click the More link for a bunch of additional Googlethingies. Froogle tries to sell you things. Blog Search blogs the blogs. You can also find finance topics, mail-order catalog listings, and so on.

Google has many tricks up its sleeve. For example:

✦ If you want to find the status of your UPS, FedEx, or USPS delivery, just type the package number (digits only) in the Google search box and press Enter.

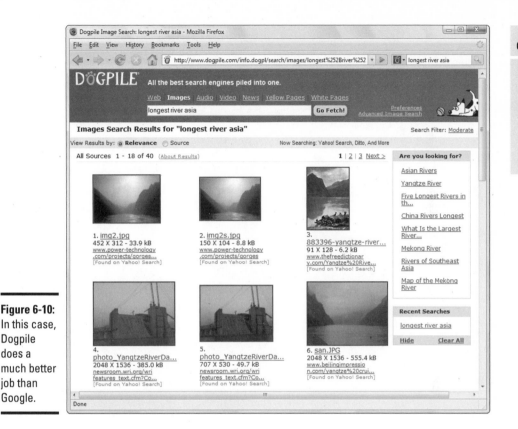

Figure 6-10:
In this case,
Dogpile
does a
much better
job than
Google.

✦ **The search box is a stock ticker:** Type a symbol such as **MSFT** or **SCBSET**.

✦ **It's a calculator:** Type **123*456** in the Google search box and your answer appears.

✦ **It converts:** Try entering **26 inches in centimeters**, **5 liters in gallons**, **3 oz in kg**, or **27 USD in Euro**.

To get a feel for some of the esoteric services Google provides, click the More link on the main page and then click the Web Search Features link on the page that appears.

I cover Google tricks extensively in *Windows Vista Timesaving Techniques For Dummies* (published by Wiley).

Book VI

Adding Cool Hardware

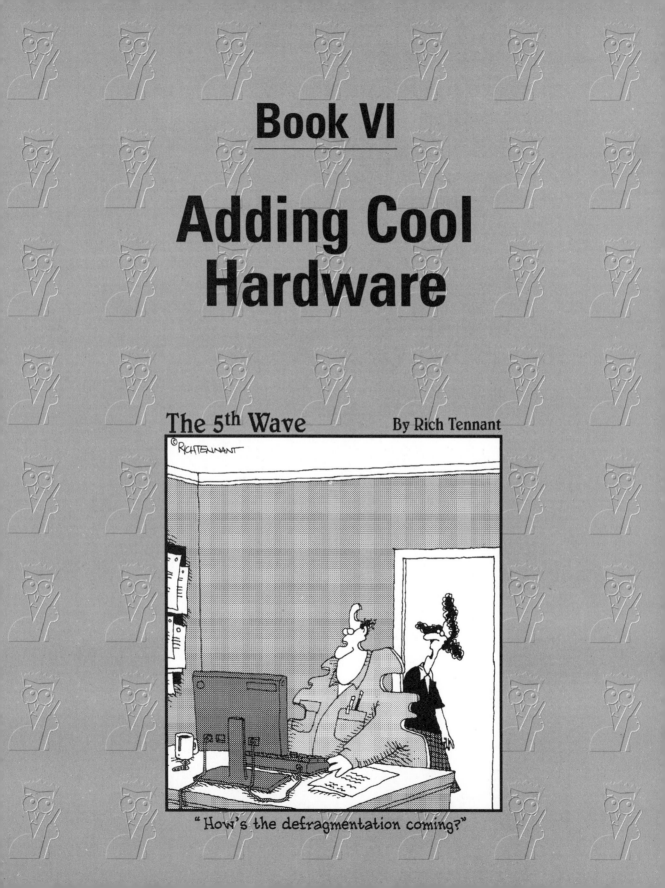

The 5th Wave   By Rich Tennant

"How's the defragmentation coming?"

Contents at a Glance

Chapter 1: Finding and Installing the Hardware You Want..439

Chapter 2: iPimping iPods and iTunes...465

Chapter 3: Adding a Second (Or Third) Hard Drive...485

Chapter 4: Picking Printers and Printer/Scanner/Faxers...493

Chapter 1: Finding and Installing the Hardware You Want

In This Chapter

- Finding out what hardware is available
- Figuring out how it works
- Choosing a new monitor
- Is ReadyBoost worth the effort?

*L*et's face facts: You don't need all the fastest, most expensive gadgets to get value out of your computer. On the other hand, equipment that fits your needs can help you do more and better work in less time.

You can spend a whole lot of money on toys and gewgaws that, ultimately, end up collecting dust. You can spend a pittance on items that you'll use every day. Unfortunately, it's hard to tell in advance whether a specific, fancy new WhipperSnapper II belongs to the former group or the latter.

This chapter reviews the common computer thingies currently available to help you decide whether any of them would be valuable to you. I take a special look at the hardware that's supposed to make Vista work faster. The results? Uninspiring.

In subsequent chapters, I take a specific look at iPods, hard drives, and printers and multifunction devices (you know, copier/scanner/faxer/coffee-warmer/foot-massager appliances).

Understanding Hardware Types

Before you can make an informed decision about adding a new piece of hardware to your computer or network, you have to understand how hardware connects to your PC and what you need to make that sparkly new toy work.

Juggling internal and external devices

An *internal device* is one that goes inside your computer's case. An *external device* has its own case and is connected to your computer by a cable.

An internal device is more convenient to use. If you have to move your computer, the internal device goes right with it. There's no cable or separate power cord to get tangled and catch dust. But you have a physical limit on the number of internal devices you can cram into a box, and the heat generated by many devices can shorten the life of everything in the box.

On the other hand, an external device is often more flexible — and it's almost always more expensive. If you have more than one computer, you can move an external device from one to another as the need arises.

An internal device may be an *adapter card* that plugs into one of the *slots* on your computer's motherboard, or it may be connected to a *controller* by an internal cable. All external devices are connected to a controller.

The type of *interface* that a device has determines the type of controller it needs. (The next section explains interfaces.) A single controller can operate several devices with the same type of interface. Most types of controllers are built into the motherboard; some — especially the more esoteric ones — can be added as adapter cards.

Choosing an interface

Any device connected to your computer uses some type of *interface* to move data back and forth. The interface is just a physical connection — a plug, if you will. Many types of devices are sold with a choice of interfaces, and you need to know enough about the different interfaces to choose the right one for your needs.

Traditionally, interfaces are generally broken into two categories: *internal interfaces* (ones that are designed to support stuff inside your computer) and *external interfaces* (ones that let you hook stuff to the outside). More and more, though, the distinctions are blurring.

In Book VI, Chapter 3, I talk about hard drives — they have their own interface peculiarities.

Internal interfaces

Adapter cards (computer cards that plug straight into the PC's motherboard) use one of four types of interfaces, corresponding to the four types of slots on the motherboard. The names of the slots are pretty weird, but don't let the terminology put you off. There were reasons for the names, once upon a time, but they don't really mean much nowadays. Like, oh, "New York." Know what I mean? Here are the four types you'll find:

✦ The *Peripheral Component Interconnect (PCI) interface* gets the nod for most adapter cards other than video cards. It's physically strong (so you'll have a hard time breaking the sucker when you stick a card in the slot), and lots of electrical contacts are inside. PCI supports *Plug and Play* operation, which means that Vista can detect the properties of an adapter card and do much or all of the software installation automatically. Most Windows computers have three, four, or five PCI slots.

✦ The *Accelerated Graphics Port (AGP) interface* is for video adapter cards only — that is, cards that slap stuff up on your screen. An AGP slot is shorter than a PCI slot. Some AGP slots have a little lever that flips up on the back to hold the card in tighter. Video adapters with the AGP interface can offer better performance than those with the PCI interface. AGP is also a Plug and Play interface.

✦ The newer *PCI Express* or *PCIe* (sometimes called *PCI-2*) *interface* runs 10 to 20 times faster than PCI, and (at least theoretically) twice as fast as AGP. Although the name sure sounds a lot like "PCI" and the technology is similar, PCI Express and PCI are two entirely different interfaces: Cards built for one don't work with the other.

✦ You might stumble onto an interface called *PCI-X*. It's old technology, primarily used for servers. Avoid it. You can't use a PCI-X card in a PCI Express slot.

Confusingly, PCI Express slots and cards come in four different sizes, called x1, x4, x8, and x16. Video cards always use x16 — the size with the biggest data pipe — and you should look for x16 slots when you buy a new computer.

Graphics card manufacturer nVidia developed a technique it calls *SLI*, or *Scalable Link Interface*, that lets you use two (or in some cases three) identical video cards in two (or three) PCI Express slots in a single computer to boost video-system performance. SLI isn't a new kind of hardware interface; rather, it's an adaptation of the PCI Express interface: As long as your computer has two PCI Express x16 slots, you can use two SLI cards. Similarly, AMD/ATI's Crossfire relies on two PCI Express slots. New Quad SLI products and other multi-graphics-processing-unit devices are just reaching the market. Check www.tomshardware.com before you shell out exorbitant amounts of money.

Before you buy a new graphics card for your computer, make sure you know what kind of interface your computer can handle. An AGP card without an AGP slot is about as useless as a kite without a string, and an SLI card needs two PCIe x16 slots.

The *ISA interface* is a much older interface, and it's not a Plug and Play interface. Most modern Windows computers have just one ISA slot or none at all.

Do not buy an adapter card with an ISA interface unless you need something unusual that is only available in ISA. If you buy an ISA card, expect to spend lots of hours wrestling with arcane topics, such as IRQs, DMA channels, and base I/O addresses — all three of which were government plots designed to keep computers out of the hands of "normal" people. You'll have a hard time finding ISA cards nowadays for a reason. Let them die a well-deserved death.

External interfaces

The *USB interface* ranks as the closest you can get to a universal controller. The original USB 1.0/1.1 standard was slow as a slug, but "hi-speed" USB 2.0 connections run at 480 megabits per second — not as fast as Serial Advanced Technology Attachment (SATA) but as fast as many other connections *inside* your computer. All modern Windows computers have a built-in USB 2.0 controller, many with four or six available USB slots.

You'll have no problem plugging USB 1.1 devices (such as a printer, scanner, or camera) into USB 2.0 ports: The devices just go at the slow USB 1.1 rate.

The USB interface is used only for external devices. It is the most flexible interface for such devices, and the easiest to use. You can plug in or remove a USB device without restarting your computer: Just click the Safely Remove Hardware icon in the system tray (near the clock), choose the USB device you want to remove, and click the Stop button (see Figure 1-1).

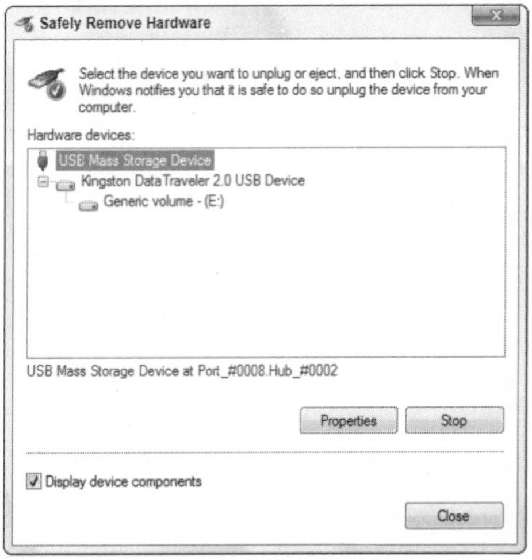

Figure 1-1:
Make sure
that you tell
Vista before
you unplug a
USB device.

Safely Remove Hardware
Select the device you want to unplug or eject, and then click Stop. When Windows notifies you that it is safe to do so unplug the device from your computer.
Hardware devices:
USB Mass Storage Device
Kingston DataTraveler 2.0 USB Device
Generic volume - (E:)
USB Mass Storage Device at Port_#0008.Hub_#0002
Properties   Stop
☑ Display device components
Close

FireWire slots — sometimes called *1394 slots* because they're based on the standard IEEE 1394 — used to look like the wave of the future. With the emergence of USB 2.0, though, few manufacturers do much with FireWire: It runs about the same speed as USB 2.0 and it's Plug and Play compatible like USB, but it doesn't appear that FireWire holds many advantages over USB 2.0.

FireWire grew up around the camera/video industry, and that appears to be the extent of its support, although you'll find it in widespread use on Macs. Someday you may find yourself with a digital video camera or digital camcorder that demands FireWire. If so, you can buy a FireWire–to–USB 2.0 converter plug that should solve the problem.

Old-fashioned *serial* and *parallel* external interfaces are used mainly for vintage printers (ah, my LaserJet II, I remember it fondly), scanners, and external dialup modems. Parallel interfaces contain 25-pin plugs, typically used to attach a printer to a PC. Serial interfaces employ 9-pin plugs; you frequently see them used with external dialup modems. Both parallel and serial interfaces are much older than the other types of external interfaces described previously, and they're becoming much less common — USB is simpler, faster, cheaper, and better.

Almost all Windows computers have a parallel interface (good for one device), and most have one or two serial interfaces (good for one device each). Avoid them if you can.

Upgrading the Basic Stuff

You probably have a printer, but it may not suit your needs — heck, photo-quality printers are so good and cheap nowadays that I'm frequently tempted to throw my old printer out the window. Your monitor may have died — or you might've noticed that gorgeous 21-inch flat-panel monitor winking at you across the aisle at your local Comput-O-Rama. Perhaps that giant 60GB hard drive that you bought two years ago doesn't look so gigantic anymore — particularly because the kids discovered how easy it is to transfer pictures taken on the digital camera.

Be of good cheer. For the most part, basic upgrades under Vista go slick as can be.

I talk about choosing and installing new hard drives in Book VI, Chapter 3, and about new printers/copies/scanners/faxers in Book VI, Chapter 4.

Dealing with drivers

Most types of devices raise the question of compatibility: Will this gadget work with Vista? You can dissect that question a thousand different ways, but the real acid test is a simple one: Is a good driver available for the hardware? (A *driver* is a program that allows Vista to interact with the hardware.)

In most cases, the answer is yes, simply because Microsoft now hounds hardware manufacturers who have the temerity to distribute bad drivers. (Video board manufacturers seem to be immune to this rule, however — I *still* have no end of trouble with video drivers.)

A high-level 'Softie I know once told me that 50 percent of all the tech support calls Microsoft had to answer dealt with bad drivers. That's powerful incentive — and the main reason why Vista wants to "phone home" when it crashes.

Most Vista crashes, and a big part of Microsoft Product Support's workload, stems from bad device drivers — which Microsoft didn't write!

Hard as it may be to believe, that new piece of hardware you just bought may require no driver because its interface to the computer is completely standardized so that Vista can operate any device of the same type. Most (but not all!) keyboards, monitors, and mice work like that. Any such device may have unique features that are available only with an appropriate driver, though.

Choosing a new monitor

Once upon a time, cathode ray tube (CRT) screens ruled the roost: They were hot enough to fry an egg and were prone to flicker and have wavy lines; the big ones weighed as much as an elephant. A big elephant. Nowadays, CRTs have one big advantage over flat-panel liquid crystal display (LCD) screens: They're cheap.

Before you buy a new monitor, make sure that you read an unbiased review (or ten) written by people who sit down in front of a bunch of monitors and compare them all side by side. The best reviews I've found, year after year, appear on the Tom's Hardware Web site, www.tomshardware.com. You might also want to use Google.

LCD monitor considerations

If you opt for an LCD monitor — and most people do — consider the following items:

✦ If you play games or work with fast-moving images, make sure that you can put up with a specific LCD's refresh rate before you buy it. LCDs are notorious for not keeping pace with some games, turning crisp images of, oh, smashing taxi cabs into mushy blobs of smashing taxi cabs. Come to think of it, maybe there isn't all that much difference.

✦ The manufacturing process occasionally produces screens with dead pixels. A *dead pixel* shows up as a black spot (or some other nonmatching color) in the image. Most manufacturers consider an LCD display functional if it has no more than three dead pixels, but a single dead pixel may drive you crazy, especially if it sits near the middle of the screen. If you look at a screen and immediately notice its dead pixel(s), pass it by.

✦ An LCD can be difficult to read from certain angles, particularly far from the screen's centerline. This can be a problem if several people have to watch the computer screen at once.

Aspect ratio

If you've ever wondered why movies appear on-screen with a black band at the top and bottom, or why your photos get cut off a little differently on 8-by-10 prints as opposed to 6-by-9s, you've bumped into the effects of the *aspect ratio*.

Digital Visual Interface

CRT monitors live in an analog world: They're controlled by signals that vary in strength, much as a television attached to a Nintendo gets driven by three cables controlling the red, green, and blue colors.

LCD monitors, on the other hand, are all digital, all the time. Internally, they control each dot on the screen with 1s and 0s, on and off, just like your computer.

The video card was invented specifically because the bits inside your computer needed to drive an analog monitor. The video card translated 1s and 0s inside the computer into varying-intensity red, green, and blue dots on the screen. In short, video cards served as digital-to-analog converters, feeding signals to CRT monitors.

Times have changed. It doesn't make any sense for the video card to translate bits into an analog signal, only to have an LCD monitor translate the analog signal back into bits. That's the crux of the Digital Visual Interface (DVI) plugs: Eliminate the video-card middleman.

More and more LCD monitors come equipped with DVI plugs. More and more video cards come equipped with DVI ports. Unlike the old D-shaped VGA plugs, which have 15 round pins arranged in 3 rows of 5 each, the much larger and more rectangular DVI plugs have a single flat pin and (usually) 24 round ones, in an asymmetrical pattern.

If you have a choice, go with DVI. It's faster and more reliable — and the pins are less likely to get crunched when your ham-fisted cousin starts switching around monitors.

The aspect ratio of a picture is the ratio of the picture's width to its height. For many years, televisions and (almost) all computer screens used the 4:3 aspect ratio, where the ratio of a screen's width to height is 4 to 3. In Figure 1-2, you see a photo taken with a typical electronic camera. It produces pictures in a 4:3 aspect ratio.

The earliest movies were shot at 4:3, but Hollywood quickly found that wider screens led to more spectacular films. Over time, the aspect ratio for movies changed, but TV stayed the same — and computer screens aped TV.

Nowadays Hollywood movies use several different aspect ratios, but home theaters all over the world have pretty much settled on the 16:9 aspect ratio, which has become the standard for High-Definition TV (HDTV) (see Figure 1-3).

Figure 1-2:
A typical shot from an electronic camera at a 4:3 aspect ratio.

Figure 1-3:
The High-
Definition
TV's
standard
16:9 ratio
lends itself
to more
dramatic
images.

Choosing a screen resolution

A flat-screen monitor's native *resolution* is the number of image-forming dots, or *pixels,* that the monitor can display horizontally and vertically. Although you can adjust the resolution on CRT displays to infinitesimal sizes and squint with the consequences, for the most part, adjusting an LCD screen to any resolution other than its native resolution leaves your eyes begging for mercy.

The grid of dots in a flat-panel display is fixed — the modified screen resolution is a sleight of hand, performed by interpolating among dots on the grid. So it's important to choose a monitor with a native resolution that you can live with.

Smaller and older screens conform to the 4:3 aspect ratio: 800-×-600 and 1024-×-768 resolutions are both 4:3 aspect ratios. Typical 15-inch screens run at 1024×768, while some truly tiny screens scrimp along at 800×600. Most 17-inch and 19-inch screens run at a native 1280×1024, which isn't exactly 4:3 (it's actually 5:4), but you don't notice much distortion when viewing material meant to be seen at 4:3.

I think the easiest way to understand the effect of changing screen resolution is to consider the effect of screen resolution on a plain-vanilla Excel 2007 spreadsheet:

✦ At 800-x-600 resolution, you can see cells A1 through L19 — or 228 cells — on a virgin spreadsheet.

✦ At 1024 × 768, you can see cells A1 through O27, or a total of 405 cells. That's 78 percent more usable cells than the 800-x-600 resolution offers.

✦ At 1280 × 1024, Excel 2007 shows cells A1 through S40, for a grand total of 760 cells. That's 88 percent more cells than at 1024 × 768 and more than three times as many as 800 × 600 offers.

Although you probably won't spend most of your time sweating over thousand-cell spreadsheets, this little comparison combined with a lot of experience leads me to a few simple generalizations:

✦ Any modern monitor you buy can handle 1024-x-768 resolution just fine. At 1024 × 768, you can see two-thirds of a page in Word or Excel. For most Windows users, that's good enough.

✦ If you move up to 1280 × 1024, you can see almost an entire page in Word. In Excel, you almost double the number of cells that you can see in a spreadsheet, compared to the 1024-x-768 resolution. Because of that, 1280 × 1024 makes sense for most people who use a monitor all day long.

✦ Resolutions above 1280 × 1024 come in handy if you commonly need to work on more than one Word document at a time or if you're struggling with really hairy spreadsheets.

Wide-screen monitors

NEC, the monitor manufacturer, funded a study at the University of Utah that discovered (perhaps to no-one's surprise) that bigger screens increase productivity. Folks who move from a 17-inch or 18-inch monitor to dual 20-inch widescren monitors increase their performance by 44 percent in text editing and by 29 percent in spreadsheet editing. Folks who move from a 17-inch or 18-inch monitor to a single 24-inch widescreen LCD, on average, see their performance increase by 52 percent in text editing and 26 percent with spreadsheets.

The University of Utah study didn't find any increase in productivity with a 26-inch monitor. My guess is that they were using a test regimen that didn't lend itself to huge screen real estate.

Ben Worthen at the Wall Street Journal has a thorough recap of the study and its findings at `blogs.wsj.com/biztech/2008/03/10/` `bigger-computer-monitors-more-productivity`.

When you move into the realm of wide-screens, standards get thrown to the wind. Most movies come in 16:9 HDTV wide-screen format, but true theatrical-release movies frequently need a 12:5 aspect ratio.

It's not unusual to find wide-screen computer monitors running at 1440-x-900, 1680-x-1050, or 1920-x-1200 resolution. All those screen resolutions look more like 16:10 than 16:9. No harm done, but you'll notice a small band at the top and bottom of the screens when you play HDTV movies.

You can also look into the possibility of running two monitors side by side — doubling the amount of screen you can see at the expense of exercising some neck muscles. Windows Vista makes setting up two monitors easy, but your video card(s) have to support two monitors.

Changing resolutions

To change your screen resolution (and set up a second monitor), follow these steps:

1. **Right-click in any blank place on the Windows desktop and choose Personalize.**

Vista opens the Personalize Appearance and Sounds dialog box.

2. **At the bottom, click the Display Settings link.**

Vista opens the Display Settings dialog box, as shown in Figure 1-4. The Resolution slider shows the display's current resolution.

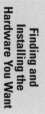

**Book VI
Chapter 1**

Finding and
Installing the
Hardware You Want

Figure 1-4:
The Display
Settings
dialog box
lets you
change
resolution.

> **Display Settings**
>
> Monitor
>
> Drag the icons to match your monitors.   [Identify Monitors]
>
> **1**   **2**
>
> 1. Generic Non-PnP Monitor on NVIDIA GeForce 7600 GS (Microsoft Corpo ▼
>
> ☑ This is my main monitor
> ☑ Extend the desktop onto this monitor
>
> Resolution: Colors:
> Low ———————▯——— High   Highest (32 bit) ▼
>   1280 by 1024 pixels
>
> How do I get the best display?   [Advanced Settings...]
>
> [OK]   [Cancel]   [Apply]

3. **To change the resolution, move the slider to the setting you want. If you don't want to change the resolution, you may skip to Step 7.**

   This is where you can set up multiple monitors. Click the "1" box to set up your first monitor and "2" to set up the second. If you can't figure out which monitor is which, click the Identify Monitors button and Vista will put a big **1** on monitor 1.

4. **Take a look at the Colors drop-down list.**

   If Vista set it to a lower value than you want when you moved the slider, you may have to upgrade or replace your display adapter. (See the next section in this chapter.)

5. **Click the Apply button.**

   Vista changes the display's resolution.

6. **If Vista opens a dialog box that asks whether you want to keep the new settings, click the Yes button to keep the new settings or No to return to the old ones.**

   If the display disappears or becomes unreadable, press Esc to return to the old settings. (Or, if you wait 15 seconds, Vista returns to the old settings automatically.) This means you chose a resolution your monitor can't display: You're trying to pump ten pounds of video out of a five-pound card. You have to choose a lower resolution.

7. **When you're done, click the OK button to close the Display Settings dialog box.**

Picking a video adapter

Windows Vista places high demands on your video card. Many people find that upgrading their video card delivers more noticeable punch than almost any other hardware improvement.

You may want to replace your video adapter card to get higher resolution and a higher refresh rate, better performance, or additional features. Some graphics cards promise faster rendering of three-dimensional objects in several popular games. Many graphics cards fail to live up to their promises.

Once again, I trust the reviews at Tom's Hardware, www.tomshardware.com.

When you choose a new video adapter, consider the following points:

✦ If your computer's motherboard has an AGP adapter slot, get an adapter with an AGP interface. If it has PCIe, get PCIe. (See the section "Internal interfaces," earlier in this chapter.)

✦ If your monitor has a Digital Visual Interface, get a video card with a DVI port. It's worth paying extra. Trust me.

✦ If you want to watch TV on your computer, or use the computer to cap-ture video from a TV signal or VCR, choose a card that supports TV input and output. See Book VIII, Chapter 2 for details.

In my experience, the single greatest source of frustration with Windows since its inception has been lousy video drivers. I've seen it happen year in and year out, in every version of Windows, with every video-card manufac-turer. Vista is no exception. Video-card manufacturers take a long time to come out with decent drivers for their wares — and when they have a stable driver, the pressure to incorporate new features frequently leads to unstable newer versions. If you buy a new video card, make sure that you check the manufacturer's Web site for the latest Vista driver prior to installing the card. And always keep your old video card, just in case the new one simply doesn't work.

Heat has become a major problem with video cards. Some cards produce as much heat as the main computer chip on your motherboard. Most Vista-class video cards come with a built-in fan and heat sink, which draws heat away from the processing unit and video memory, dumping it into your computer's main case. If you're having heat problems, consider buying a dual-slot video card, with an oversize fan that forces air out of the case, via openings in the second slot's mounting bracket.

If you're feeling handy, you can also buy and install a video-card cooler, com-plete with its own heat sink, fan, and exhaust mounting bracket. For an example, see www.driverheaven.net/guides/videocooling.

Upgrading keyboards

Face it. The keyboard that came with your computer wouldn't even make a decent boat anchor. Don't get me wrong. Those mushy, squishy, Tinkertoy keyboards would make fine Cracker Jack prizes, and casual computer users can get by with them for years. I wouldn't look down *my* nose at your flimsy, somnambulant, ludicrous excuse for a keyboard. Sniff.

Seriously, if you spend more than a few hours a day at the computer, you're probably wondering why your fingers hurt and why you make so many mis-takes typing. There's a good reason why. That keyboard you're using probably cost a dollar. Maybe less. Getting a new one can make a big difference in how well you type and can speed your computing enormously. You know — so you can get a life. . . .

Several companies now make *ergonomic* keyboards, which are contoured to let you type with your hands in a position that (supposedly) reduces the stress on them. These keyboards take some getting used to, but some users swear by them. Personally, I swear *at* them. You can get a wireless keyboard. You can also get a keyboard with a built-in pointing device to replace the mouse. Heck, you can probably get one that *looks* like Mickey Mouse.

If you're serious about replacing your tin-can keyboard, keep these points in mind:

✦ Look for a keyboard that feels right. Some folks like quiet keys. I like 'em loud. Some people prefer keys with short throws — ones you don't have to push very far. I like long throws. Some prefer minimal tactile feedback — when you push the key, it doesn't push back. I like lots of tactile feedback. Most current keyboards have a row of function keys across the top. I like mine on the left. Everybody's different, and the only way you're going to find a keyboard that you like is to try dozens of them.

✦ If you've been using a "straight" keyboard, make sure that you can get used to a split ergonomic keyboard before you buy one. I know a lot of people who have given up in disgust when their fingers couldn't adapt to the ergonomic split.

✦ Wireless keyboards have batteries that wear out. With regular wired keyboards, you don't have to worry about interference or blocked sensors. Sure, cables are ugly, but they're very reliable.

✦ Expensive keyboards aren't necessarily better than cheap ones. Big-name keyboards aren't necessarily better than generics.

✦ Heavy keyboards are better than light ones, unless you're going to schlep your keyboard with you on your travels through Asia. Heavy keyboards with rubber feet stay put.

What keyboard do I use? An old Northgate OmniKey Ultra, which is surely the Sherman Tank of the keyboard biz. The beast weighs almost as much as a portable computer, and it costs just under two hundred bucks. You can't find new ones anymore — have to buy them refurbished. It's ugly, it's retro, and it's decidedly un-hip. But it keeps goin' and goin'.

Choosing a mouse — or alternatives

Mice are probably available in more varieties than any other computer accessory. You can get mice with special ergonomic profiles, colored mice, transparent mice, special mice designed for kids, and on and on.

Optical mice now rule the roost. An *optical mouse* uses a light source and sensor to detect movement over a flat surface. It has no rolling ball to slip or stick, and it rarely needs to be cleaned. You may find this particularly helpful if you have furry pets and your mouse tends to get clogged by their hair.

Some folks prefer a *trackball* to a mouse. A trackball is a stationary device with a large ball resting in a cup on the top. You operate it by turning the ball with your palm or thumb. I hate 'em.

Some folks like to use a *graphics tablet* instead of or in addition to a mouse. You control software with a graphics tablet by touching its surface with a special stylus. Unlike a mouse, the graphics tablet detects position, not motion, so you can literally point at the item you want. You can even write or draw with the stylus. Graphics tablets are popular with serious users of photo editors and other graphics software, and they're becoming more popular since Microsoft started producing "digital ink" programs like OneNote, which can read what you write, to a first approximation anyway. Many of these applications have special graphics tablet support and can detect the amount of pressure you're applying to the stylus. Thus you can press hard to draw a wide line, for example, or lightly to draw a thin line.

Tablet PCs — the kind that are designed to be used with a stylus and (almost invariably) OneNote — aren't for everyone. Some people love them. Most people don't get used to them. I count myself among the latter. If you ever think about buying a Tablet PC specifically for its note-taking capabilities, try to borrow one for a day or two before you plunk down the cash. You may find that the reality doesn't live up to the glitz. Or you may find that you love it!

A *touchpad* is similar to a graphics tablet, but you control it with your fingertip instead of a stylus. You "click" by tapping the pad. A touchpad is very convenient for moving the pointer around the screen, but because most people's fingers are less pointy than a stylus, it's not very good for drawing or writing. Touchpads usually are just a few inches long and wide, and cost $20 to $50, whereas graphics tablets are larger and cost $100 or more.

Touchpads are available with a serial interface, a USB interface, or the funny round plug used by most keyboards and mice (called a *PS/2 connector*). You can also buy a keyboard that has a touchpad built in, and which needs only the keyboard's usual connector. And, of course, touchpads and belly buttons (er, pointer sticks) are common on notebook computers.

All mice designed for Windows computers are compatible with Vista. Specialized devices such as graphics tablets may require special drivers; make sure that the device you buy is Vista compatible.

Key Drives, SuperFetch, and ReadyBoost

Although Windows has been *prefetching* data — going out to the hard drive and loading certain files that the system feels are likely to be needed — since the days of Windows XP, Vista brings a new capability to the table. *SuperFetch,* as the new technique is called, keeps track of the data and programs that you commonly use on your machine and tries to load that data before it's used.

Prefetching doesn't help much if you don't have a lot of system memory: The stuff that's prefetched has a nasty habit of turning stale and getting shuffled off to Buffalo, er, sent back to the hard drive, thus negating any benefit of prefetching it. Vista lets you use a USB key drive as kind of a scratch pad for prefetching: Instead of prefetching files from the hard drive and sticking them in main memory before they're needed, Vista can retrieve the files and store them on a dedicated chunk of real estate on a key drive. Because grabbing data from a key drive is about 10 or 20 times faster than pulling it in off a rotating platter, this *ReadyBoost,* as it's called, can make fetching work better. ReadyBoost also works independently of SuperFetch, as kind of a super-fast cache.

After playing with it a bit, I've come up with a simple rule of thumb: If your computer has less than 512MB of memory, and it would cost a fortune to add more memory, use a 512MB or 1GB key drive for ReadyBoost. Otherwise, fuhgeddaboutit.

Understanding flash memory and key drives

Regular computer memory — RAM — needs a constant supply of power to keep going. *Flash memory* is a special kind of computer memory that doesn't self-destruct when the power goes out. Technically a type of EEPROM (Electronically Erasable Programmable Read-Only Memory), flash memory comes in many different kinds of packages.

If you've spent any time with electronic cameras, you probably know about all about memory cards — SD (Secure Digital), CF (Compact Flash), and SM (Smart Media) cards — and if you've been around Sony equipment, you also know about Memory Sticks. All of them rely on flash memory.

For us computer types, flash memory also comes in a little package — frequently the size and shape of half a pack of gum — with a USB connector on the end. You can call it a USB flash memory stick, a key drive, a key-chain drive (people really use them as key chains? I dunno — my favorite key chain looks like Watto from *Star Wars*), a pocket drive, a pen drive, a USB key, or a USB stick (that's what my cables do when they get old).

If you have your USB drivers up to date, here's how hard it is to use a USB flash memory stick:

1. **Plug the USB flash memory key drive into a USB slot.**

2. **You're done.**

   The data on the drive looks like data on any other drive. Choose Start⇨ Computer and you can look at it. Or, you can open a file on the stick with any program.

The salespeople would have you believe that it's cool to have color-coded sticks (I just put a sticker on mine), fancy encrypted memory (so that if somebody steals the stick, it takes him ten minutes to look at the data instead of ten seconds), designer outsides, and on and on. Here's what I say:

✦ Buy twice the amount of memory you think you need — you'll use it some day.

✦ Go for the lowest price.

If you need to read the other kinds of flash memory — memory cards, the kind normally used in cameras or MP3 players — buy a cheap generic USB multiformat memory card reader. It shouldn't set you back more than ten bucks, and it can come in very handy.

Beware of U3 autoplay

Many companies now make USB key drives that can pose a security risk. So-called U3 drives are formatted into two parts: a read-only part holds applications that can run without being installed, and a regular read-write part that holds data. The read-only part is set up to look like a CD drive. When you stick a U3 key drive into a USB slot, Vista thinks you've inserted a CD and may "autoplay" the read-only part, thereby running a program that you may not want to run.

Although it's generally true that anybody who has physical control over your computer can get almost anything he wants, U3 presents a

particularly vexing problem because it works silently. One group of white hat hackers left a bunch of U3 key drives scattered around a certain company's parking lot. Within a matter of minutes, the hackers' Web site lit up with data being transmitted from computers all over the company. Employees figured they'd picked up a free USB key drive. The hackers had a field day.

You can always disable autoplay by holding down the Shift key as you insert a USB key drive into a USB slot. You can permanently disable autoplay by clicking the Set AutoPlay Defaults in Control Panel link shown at the bottom of Figure 1-5. Might not be a bad idea, eh?

Setting up ReadyBoost

Using a key drive as additional "scratch" memory for Vista's prefetch, and as a super-fast system cache, couldn't be simpler. But before you go to the bother, make sure that your system can actually benefit from the boost:

✦ If you already have 1GB or more of memory inside the computer, you don't need ReadyBoost. Even at 512MB, you probably won't see much benefit from ReadyBoost.

✦ If you can upgrade your computer's memory without spending a fortune, do it. Forget about ReadyBoost. Additional main memory can help with every part of Windows. ReadyBoost only tackles a piece of the problem.

That said, if you have a computer with limited main memory and you want a quick and easy performance boost, here's how to get ReadyBoost going:

1. **Plug a USB flash memory key drive into a USB port.**

Vista responds with the AutoPlay dialog shown in Figure 1-5.

Figure 1-5: Setting up ReadyBoost as an AutoPlay option.

2. **Click the Speed Up My System Using Windows ReadyBoost icon.**

Vista brings up the Properties dialog box for the key drive, open to the ReadyBoost tab (see Figure 1-6).

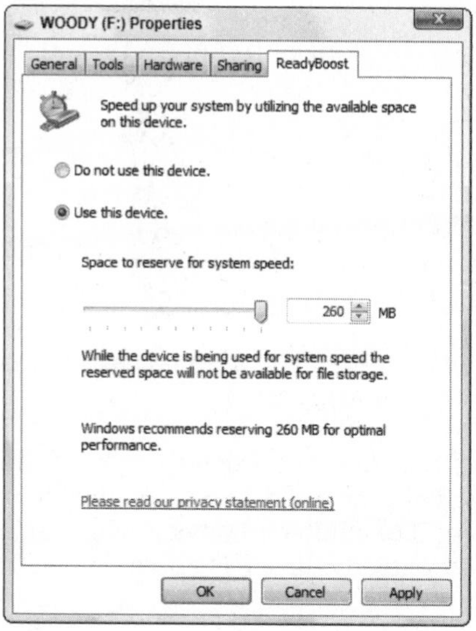

WOODY (F:) Properties

General | Tools | Hardware | Sharing | ReadyBoost

Speed up your system by utilizing the available space on this device.

◯ Do not use this device.

◉ Use this device.

Space to reserve for system speed:

260 ⇕ MB

While the device is being used for system speed the reserved space will not be available for file storage.

Windows recommends reserving 260 MB for optimal performance.

Please read our privacy statement (online)

OK | Cancel | Apply

Figure 1-6:
ReadyBoost
is part of the
properties of
a USB drive.

3. **Select the Use This Device option. Adjust the slider if you like, to reserve more or less space.**

4. **Click the OK button.**

   ReadyBoost lops off the indicated amount of space on the key drive (so that you can't use that space for data), and ReadyBoost kicks in.

ReadyBoost stores data on the key drive in a 128-bit encrypted form — anyone who gets the key drive can't decrypt it.

You can remove the key drive at any time. ReadyBoost turns itself off, with no untoward effect on the system.

USB Hubs

Your Windows computer probably has two, four, or six USB ports, but you can attach many more USB devices to it than that. In theory, you can attach 127 USB devices to one computer. If you keep that many devices, you probably have no space left to sit down!

To attach additional devices, you need the USB equivalent of a power strip to turn one connector into several. That device is called a *USB hub*.

A USB hub has one USB connector to attach it to a computer and several connectors to attach it to devices. Hubs most often have either four or seven device connectors.

If you run out of USB ports, get a powered USB hub — one that draws electricity from a wall plug. That way, you protect against power drains on your computer's motherboard. If possible, plug your USB hub into an uninterruptible power supply (UPS) so that a sudden loss of power doesn't cause a surge down the USB hub's power supply.

You can plug one USB hub into another — daisy-chain them — to attach more devices than a single hub can support.

The maximum length of a USB cable is not precisely defined, but the figure of 5 meters (about 16 feet) is widely accepted. This is the maximum length of a cable from a computer or a hub to a hub or a device. The maximum total length between the computer and any device is about 25 meters, or 80 feet.

Installing New Hardware

If you have a USB device — a printer, hard drive, scanner, camera, flash memory card, foot massager, water desalination plant, or demolition machine for a new intergalactic highway — just plug the device into a USB port, and you're ready to go.

Okay. I exaggerated a little bit.

Two fundamentally different approaches to installing new hardware exist. It amazes me that some people never even consider the possibility of doing it themselves, whereas other people wouldn't have the store install new hardware for them on a bet!

Have the store do it

When you buy a new hard drive or video card, or anything else that goes inside your computer, why sweat the installation? For a few extra bucks, most stores can install what they sell. This is the easy, safe way! Instead of messing around with unfamiliar gadgets, which may be complicated and delicate, let somebody experienced do the work for you.

Different types of hardware present different levels of difficulty. It may make plenty of sense for you to install one type of device but not another.

At one end of the scale, installing a new video card or hard drive can be rather difficult and is best done by an expert. At the other end, speakers don't need any installation; you just plug them in and they work. The store can show you where the connectors go, but you have to plug them in yourself when you get home.

Here are some guidelines to help you judge how difficult an installation is likely to be:

✦ Any device that goes inside your computer is best left to the store unless you have experience with that specific kind of computer hardware.

✦ A device with a USB interface is usually easy; nine times out of ten, you just plug it in and it works.

✦ Most modern wireless networking systems go in with nary a hiccup.

A cable modem should be installed by the communication carrier's technician if at all possible. Digital subscriber line (DSL) modems are easier to install, but you have to know whether your phone line is ready. The modem just plugs in, but the telephone line or cable may require configuration or rewiring to deliver the signal properly.

If you're unsure whether to install something yourself, ask the store what's involved. If you decide to try it, but the instructions confuse you or scare you when you read them, don't be embarrassed to go back and ask for help. I do.

Do it yourself

If you decide to install a device yourself, the job is more likely to go smoothly if you observe these guidelines:

✦ **Don't just dive in — read the instructions first!** Pay attention to any warnings they give. Look for steps where you may have trouble. Are any of the instructions unclear? Does the procedure require any software or parts that appear to be missing? Try to resolve these potential problems ahead of time.

✦ **Back up your system before you start.** It's unlikely that your attempt to install a new device will disturb your system if it fails, but a backup is a good insurance policy in case something bad happens. You need to back up your data files. Vista can create a system checkpoint and back up all the internal stuff.

✦ **Write down everything you do in case you need to undo it or ask for help.** This is particularly important if you're opening your computer to install an internal device!

✦ **If the device comes with a Vista driver, check the manufacturer's Web site to see whether you have the latest version.** A company usually keeps drivers on one or more Web pages that you can find by clicking a link for Drivers, Downloads, or Support. If you discover a version that is newer than the one packaged with the device, download it and install it instead.

If you can't tell whether the version on the Web site is newer because you can't tell what version came with the device, you have two choices:

- Download and install the Web site's version just in case. It's unlikely to be older than the one that came with the device!

- Install the one that came with the device. Then check its date and version number. (See the next section.) If the one on the Web site proves to be newer, download the newer one and install it. Read the instructions; you may need to uninstall the original driver first.

Checking a driver's version

To check the version number of a driver, follow these steps:

1. **Click the Start button. Right-click Computer and choose Properties.**

2. **On the left, click the Device Manager link.**

You have to jump through a security warning, but then Vista opens the Device Manager window, as shown in Figure 1-7.

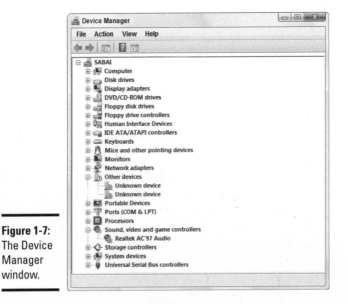

Figure 1-7: The Device Manager window.

3. **Click the plus sign next to the heading that contains the device you want to check.**

   Vista expands that heading to show its devices, as shown in Figure 1-8.

Figure 1-8:
Click the
plus sign to
expand a
heading.

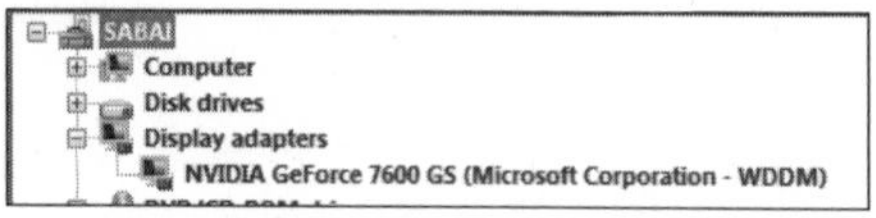

   You may have to try several headings to find the right one. If you guess wrong, just click again to collapse the heading you expanded.

4. **Double-click the device to open the Device Properties dialog box.**

5. **Click the Driver tab to display details about the driver, as shown in Figure 1-9.**

   You should be able to identify the latest driver by its date, its version number, or both.

Figure 1-9:
The driver
date and
version are
easy to see.

If anything goes wrong

If your installation is unsuccessful, try these things in any order that makes sense to you:

✦ Review the instructions. Look for a section with a title such as "Troubleshooting" for suggestions on how to proceed.

✦ Call or e-mail the manufacturer's technical support service for help. The manual or the Web site can tell you how.

✦ Call the store, or pack everything up and take it in. If you happen to have a seven-foot-tall friend named Guido who drags his hairy knuckles on the ground, take him along with you. Moral support, eh?

If your computer no longer works correctly, restart Vista with the last known good configuration. (See the instructions in the next section.)

Restarting with the last known good configuration

When you install a new device driver, you change Vista's *configuration*. The next time you restart your computer, Vista tries to use the new configuration. If it succeeds, it discards the old configuration and makes the new one current.

Sometimes you install a new device driver, and everything goes to heck in a handbasket. If that happens to you, restart Vista and tell it to use the "last known good configuration" — which is to say, Windows should ignore the changes you made that screwed everything up and return to the state it was in the last time it started. That effectively removes the new driver from Vista.

To start Windows with the last known good configuration, follow these steps:

1. **If your computer is operating, click the Start button, click the right-facing arrow to the right of the little lock, and choose Restart.**

   Vista restarts. Skip to Step 3.

2. **If your computer isn't operating, press the power button to turn it off.**

   If that doesn't work, try pressing the button again and holding it in for several seconds. If that doesn't work either, pull the power cord out of the back of the computer; wait a few seconds, and then plug it in again. If you're working with a portable, you may have to remove the battery. Yes, it happens.

3. **Press the power button again to turn the computer back on.**

4. **As soon as the computer starts to come back to life, press and hold down F8.**

   Vista displays a menu of special start-up options that you can choose.

5. **Use the up-arrow and down-arrow keys to move the menu's highlight to Last Known Good Configuration (Advanced), and then press Enter.**

6. **Finish the startup procedure as usual.**

If this procedure restarts your computer successfully, Vista discards the "new" screwed-up configuration and returns permanently to the last known good configuration.

Installing USB hardware

Nine times out of ten, when you install a new USB device in a Vista computer that has all the latest fixes, everything works easily. The general procedure works as follows:

1. **Read the manual.**

   Some hardware installs automatically: Plug it in, and it works. Most hardware needs a little help: You have to put a CD in the CD drive shortly after you plug it in and let Windows pull the driver off the CD. Some hardware, though, takes a little extra help, and you have to run an installation program from the product's CD before you plug it in.

   The only way to know for sure which approach works for the specific piece of hardware that you bought is to read the furshlinger manual! Look for the section with instructions on installing the hardware on a Vista computer. Follow the instructions.

2. **After you've read the manual and done what it says, plug the USB device into any handy USB slot.**

   Windows realizes that you've just installed a new USB device and cranks up the Found New Hardware Wizard.

3. **Select the Yes, This Time Only radio button to let Microsoft see whether it has a new driver for the hardware, and then click the Next button.**

4. **Follow the rest of the steps in the wizard, and at most times, you'll end up with a functioning device.**

5. **If you can't get the device working, check Microsoft's Knowledge Base article for troubleshooting USB devices.**

   You can find it at `http://support.microsoft.com/?kbid=310575`.

Chapter 2: iPimping iPods and iTunes

In This Chapter

- ✔ **Getting your iPod to work**
- ✔ **Getting your iPod to work right**
- ✔ **Copying songs from your iPod to your computer**
- ✔ **Solving the problems everyone has with iPods and Windows**

So you went out and splurged on a brand new iPod, eh? Yeah. Me, too. Four times.

No doubt you've discovered that the iPod works fine with Windows — as long as you use Apple's software and buy from Apple's music store, and you don't want to do anything Apple doesn't want you to do. B-o-r-i-n-g.

Look. You bought your iPod. You paid for your music (or you got it free, legitimately). You bought your PC. You paid for Vista. So why in the heck are you treated like a criminal every time you want to do something reasonable?

In Book VII, Chapter 1, I talk about the ways Microsoft and Apple use their proprietary music formats to try to squeeze every last cent, ruble, and zloty out of your pocket, and ways that you can fight back. It's all about CRAP music; see that chapter for details. In the same chapter, I also talk about using other players, like Zunes, with Windows Media Player. In Book VII, Chapter 2, I talk about podcasting, which, in spite of the name, really doesn't have anything to do with iPods.

In this chapter, I concentrate on what you can do to liberate your iPod from the clutches of both Apple and Microsoft, the Evil eMP3ires.

What You Can't Do

I bet you've shed more than a few tears (and sworn more than a few syllables) trying to figure out why these things happen:

+ **You can't use Windows Media Player to put music on your iPod.**

    Why? No way will Microsoft do anything to support iPod. Well, okay, maybe if UFOs invaded Lake Washington and a hundred little green aliens marched into Bill G's living room chanting "I Pod, U Pod, We all Pod for I Pod". . .

+ **You can't upload music from your iPod to your PC, using either iTunes or Windows Media Player.**

    Why? Apple wants you to buy more music from the iTunes Music Store. Microsoft wants you to buy more from URGE. Neither Microsoft nor Apple nor the music companies want you to use your iPod to move music from one PC to another, even if you've bought and paid for the music. Ka-ching. But a solution exists. See the section "Copying Songs to Your PC," later in this chapter.

+ **You can't play music that you bought on other services, even though it "Plays for Sure."**

    Why? Because Microsoft's "Plays for Sure" advertising campaign overlooked one tiny fact: The music that Microsoft says "Plays for Sure" doesn't play on an iPod. For sure. You have to convert music recorded in Microsoft's proprietary Windows Media Audio (WMA) format with iTunes first.

+ **You can't add music from two computers to the same iPod.**

    Why? When you connect an iPod to a computer it becomes "tethered" to that computer. As long as you only plug it into the same computer, everything (usually) works as advertised. But when you move the iPod to a second computer, iTunes wants to erase all the old music and sync with the music on the second computer. Of course, Apple stands to make more money that way.

+ **You plug your iPod into your computer, and all of a sudden, some songs that you had on your iPod disappear.**

    Why? Apple built it that way, to enforce its digital rights management scheme. It's called auto-sync. I talk about how to disable it — or at least make it work for you, instead of against you — in the section "Synching," later in this chapter

✦ **You can't play music that you bought from the iTunes Music Store on another computer.**

Why? Apple built it that way, to enforce its digital rights management scheme. (Do you hear an echo in here?) Actually, you can copy and play the music that you bought on up to five different computers (if you know the trick), but you can't mix 'n' match — the five computers all have to be "locked in" to the same iTunes Music Store account. See the sidebar "The five-PC limit for iTunes songs," later in this chapter.

But you can play regular, old MP3 music files on your iPod, even if you borrowed those files from your maiden aunt's long-suffering hairdresser's underworked and overpaid boyfriend or bought your MP3s from Amazon.com, emusic.com, or MP3.com.

Why? Because Apple would lose most of its market share overnight if it blocked the most popular open music file format.

It's surprisingly difficult to get surprisingly simple things done, eh?

Fortunately, decent workarounds exist for all those problems, and many more.

The rest of this chapter not only explains the "official" way to work with your iPod, but it also takes you behind the scenes to see how the pros make iPods dance the hurdy-gurdy, whether the folks in Redmond or Cupertino like it or not.

iPod the Apple Way

So you pulled your iPod out of its cavernous box and you're ready to boogie. Fine. Just don't bother slipping the iPod driver CD into your computer. The stuff on the CD is obsolete by now, and you're going to want the latest.

Even if you've already installed anything and everything Apple has to offer, your very first stop should be the Apple Web site.

In the following sections, you find out the best way to break in your new iPod by getting the software you need, setting up iTunes, and filling the iPod with songs.

Bringing everything up to date

You need to make sure that you have the latest version of the iPod's internal software (called *firmware*) and the latest version of iTunes. You don't need to do this every week, but you probably should check things out every few months. Here's how to do that:

1. **Crank up your favorite browser and head to** `http://docs.info.apple.com/article.html?artnum=61688`. **Find your iPod, and make sure that you know its model number.**

   Although having the model number isn't an absolute requirement for updating the software, you will need it in many other situations.

   In Figure 2-1, you see the list of iPods. Click the name of a particular model to see a full-size picture and details about the model.

2. **Click the Current iPod Software Version column heading.**

   You're sent to the iPod download site. If you don't yet have an Apple ID, fill in the sign-up sheet at the bottom of the page. *Remember to deselect the nag check boxes.* If you do have an Apple ID (and can remember it), type your ID and password and click the Sign In button.

3. **Click the Download iPod Software Update button.**

   Follow the instructions to download the file `iPodSetup.exe`.

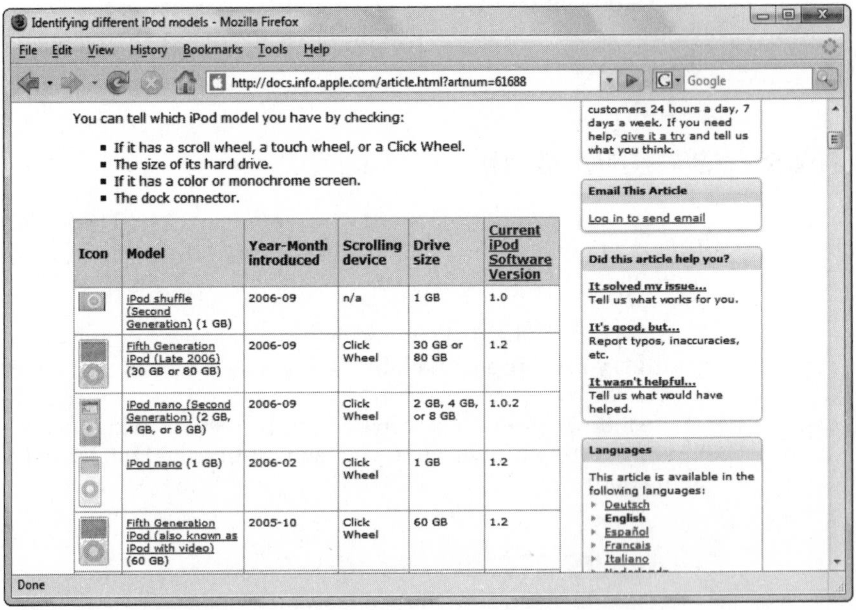

Figure 2-1: Start by identifying your iPod.

4. **Run** `iPodSetup.exe` **and follow the installation instructions.**

   You have to click through a couple of security warnings. In the end, iPodSetup has you reboot your computer.

5. **When the computer comes back up, log on as usual. If the Updater doesn't start automatically, choose Start⇨All Programs⇨iPod⇨ iPod Updater and run the version of iPodUpdater that you just downloaded.**

   The Updater appears and tells you to plug in your iPod. Do so. (If you get an AutoPlay notification offering to Open Folder to View Files, click the red *X* to exit the notification.) You see an iPod Updater dialog box, like the one shown in Figure 2-2.

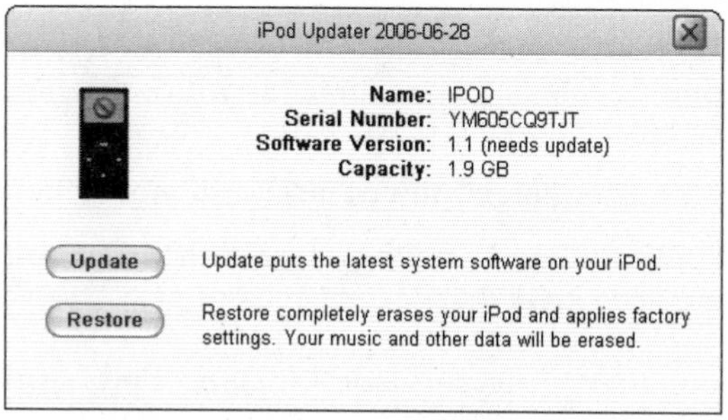

Figure 2-2:
The Updater
tells you
whether you
need to
update
your iPod.

iPod Updater 2006-06-28	✕

	Name: IPOD
	Serial Number: YM605CQ9TJT
	Software Version: 1.1 (needs update)
	Capacity: 1.9 GB

Update — Update puts the latest system software on your iPod.

Restore — Restore completely erases your iPod and applies factory settings. Your music and other data will be erased.

6. **If the Update button is available (which is to say, if it isn't grayed out), click it.**

   The process may take a few minutes or more, but sooner or later your iPod gets updated, and you are told to leave it plugged in until the update finishes. Follow the instructions and remain patient. The whole process can take ten minutes or more.

   Resist the urge to click the Updater's Reset button unless you're prepared to lose all the music on the iPod. (If you have copies of all the songs on your PC, you have no cause for concern.) Reset wipes out everything on your iPod; it's only there for emergencies. If you really want to reset and you don't have good copies of all your music, cancel out of the Updater — click the "X" in the upper right corner — then follow the instructions in the section "Copying Songs to Your PC," later in this chapter, to pull the music off the iPod; and go back to Step 5.

7. **Click the red *X* to exit the Updater.**

   Your iPod is now up to date.

8. **Point your favorite browser to** `http://apple.com/itunes/` `download`. **Fill out the form (deselect the nag boxes), and then click the Download iTunes - Free option.**

   Download the file `iTunesSetup.exe`.

9. **Run** `iTunesSetup.exe`.

   You have to click through one or more security messages, and then the iTunes + QuickTime installer does its thing.

   QuickTime, a large Apple program best known for playing video (and its quirky, buggy behavior in almost every version of Windows), comes along for the ride: iTunes requires QuickTime.

10. **Follow the installation wizard, but when the time comes, deselect the Use iTunes as the Default Player for Audio Files check box and deselect the Use QuickTime as the Default Player for Media Files check box.**

    That leaves Windows Media Player intact as your default music and video player.

11. **Click the Finish button to exit the wizard, and you're done.**

    Your iPod has been updated, and the latest versions of both iTunes and QuickTime have been installed.

Now would be a good time to run through the Apple iPod tutorial. Even if you've been using an iPod for years, you might pick up on some nuances that could prove to be fun — or even useful. Start at `www.apple.com/` `support/ipod/tutorial` and click the Start Tutorial link.

With the latest versions ready, and a bit of Apple Party Line orientation under your belt, it's time to fill your iPod.

Getting iTunes ready to feed your iPod

The first time you use iTunes, you have to make a few choices. Here's how to minimize your ongoing headaches:

1. **Double-click the iTunes icon to run iTunes for the first time.**

   You have to agree to a bunch of dense gobbledygook that's only slightly shorter than the U.S. Tax Code.

2. **Click the Next button when you are prompted by the iTunes Setup Assistant.**

   Yeah. Rocket science. The Assistant presents you with the dialog box shown in Figure 2-3.

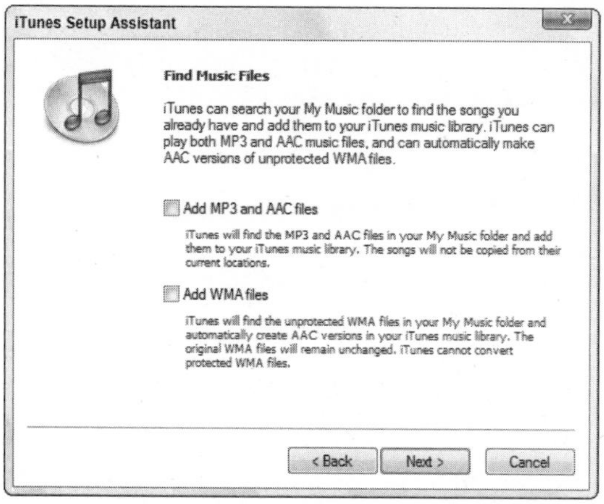

iTunes Setup Assistant

Find Music Files

iTunes can search your My Music folder to find the songs you already have and add them to your iTunes music library. iTunes can play both MP3 and AAC music files, and can automatically make AAC versions of unprotected WMA files.

☐ Add MP3 and AAC files

iTunes will find the MP3 and AAC files in your My Music folder and add them to your iTunes music library. The songs will not be copied from their current locations.

☐ Add WMA files

iTunes will find the unprotected WMA files in your My Music folder and automatically create AAC versions in your iTunes music library. The original WMA files will remain unchanged. iTunes cannot convert protected WMA files.

< Back   Next >   Cancel

Figure 2-3:
Don't let
iTunes scan
for existing
music yet.

3. Deselect both check boxes — don't let iTunes scan for existing music just yet. Then click the Next button.

Later, in Steps 6 and 7, you can change the automatic scanner so that it generates MP3 files (which can be used anywhere) instead of Advanced Audio Coding (AAC) files (which are only good, really, in the Apple world) when it automatically converts Microsoft-formatted (WMA) music files. You don't need to run the scan now and create a bunch of files you'll never use.

The Assistant asks whether you want iTunes to maintain its own music folder.

4. Select the Yes, Keep My iTunes Music Folder Organized check box and click the Next button.

Allowing iTunes to maintain its own music folder (which is kept in your \Music\iTunes folder) can help keep things straight on your iPod. iTunes is actually quite good about not creating extraneous copies of music files — the folder only gets used when you convert music file formats or change the names of songs.

The Assistant asks <cough, cough> whether you <ahem> want to go to the <wink, wink> iTunes Music Store right now <nod, nod>.

5. Resist the temptation; be still my heart. Click the No, Take Me to My iTunes Library button, and then click the Finish button.

iTunes appears in all its naked glory — without a song to be seen — as shown in Figure 2-4.

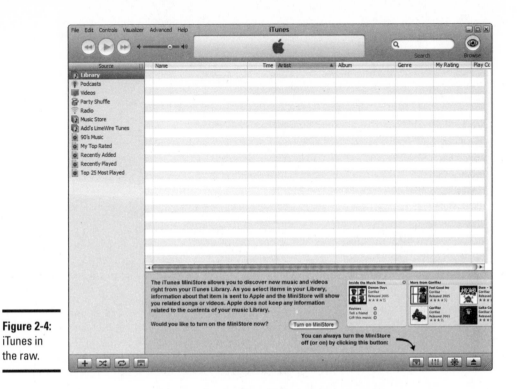

Figure 2-4:
iTunes in
the raw.

6. **Immediately choose Edit➪Preferences. In the dialog box that appears, click the Advanced tab and then click the Importing tab.**

7. **In the Import Using drop-down list, choose MP3 Encoder. For a setting, use High Quality (160 kbps). And select the final two check boxes at the bottom, as shown in Figure 2-5. Then click the OK button.**

By doing so, you ensure that iTunes always rips songs into the MP3 format (see Book VII, Chapter 1 for a description of why that's beneficial). You also ensure that when iTunes encounters a nonprotected WMA file, it converts the WMA file into an MP3 file. (WMA is the Microsoft-proprietary music format.)

You may want to have iTunes play songs while it's ripping them. I like to have filenames include the track number, but it's a personal preference. And I strongly recommend that you use error correction when ripping audio CDs, even if it takes more time, because that minimizes your chances of coming up with ripped tracks that are screechy and skippy. Ya know, like peanut butter.

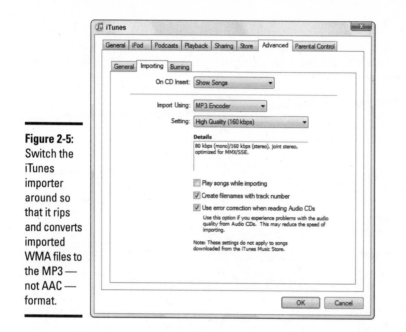

Figure 2-5:
Switch the
iTunes
importer
around so
that it rips
and converts
imported
WMA files to
the MP3 —
not AAC —
format.

8. **You can click the Turn on MiniStore button, down at the bottom, if
you like. It'll soak up some bandwidth on your Internet line, but it's
moderately amusing at times.**

Now it's time to import your music into iTunes. (Note that your music
won't be moved — iTunes just collects pointers to the song files.)

9. **Choose Start➪Music, click any albums or songs that you want to add
(or press Ctrl+A to select everything in your Music folder), and drag
the albums into iTunes.**

If iTunes bumps into songs in the WMA format, it warns you (see
Figure 2-6). Click the Convert button, and iTunes creates an MP3
version of the song, placing it in the iTunes folder, `<your username>\
Music\iTunes\iTunes Music`.

Figure 2-6:
iTunes
converts
WMA songs
to MP3
format auto-
matically.

Your WMA file remains intact — iTunes doesn't touch it.

10. **Gather all the music you like — and avoid the music that you don't particularly want on your iPod (you can use Windows Media Player to mess around with that stuff).**

In the end, you should have a sizable collection of music. If you gather more than can fit on your iPod (as you can confirm by the status bar at the bottom of the iTunes window; see Figure 2-7), not to worry. iTunes can help.

If you ever discover that iTunes failed to pick up a new song — one that you've ripped off a CD, downloaded from the Internet, or bought from an online service — simply locate the song file or album folder and drag it into iTunes, precisely as you did in Step 9.

The five-PC limit for iTunes songs

When the iTunes Music Store says you can play the songs you buy on five machines, the details get a bit hairy. Each computer (PC or Mac) gets branded with an Apple ID (which does double duty as an iTunes Music Store account number). Up to five computers can be branded with the same Apple ID. Songs can only be played on computers that are branded with the original, downloading computer's Apple ID. Confused? Here's how it works.

Say you buy a song at the iTunes Music Store with an Apple ID of myaccount@someplace. com and password 123456789. You give a copy of the song to your son. When he tries to play it, iTunes asks for *authorization*. Your son has to type in **myaccount@someplace.com** and the password **123456789**, and his computer is then "branded" with that account number. (Not so coincidentally, he now has your iTunes Music Store ID and password.) You and your son can share songs bought with that iTunes Music Store account number till the cows come home.

You can copy the file without restriction. But the song won't play on any PC unless the person who tries to play the file can provide the correct authorization — myaccount@someplace. com and password 123456789. And at most five PCs, at any one time, can be branded with that Apple ID.

Because a computer can only be branded with one Apple ID, you can't mix and match songs — if your computer is branded with myaccount@ someplace.com, you can't play songs that were bought with, oh, anotheraccount@ someplaceelse.com. It's an either-or situation.

To *deauthorize* a computer, go into iTunes, choose Advanced➪Deauthorize Computer, choose the Deauthorize Computer for Apple Account option, type in your Apple ID and password, and click the OK button. That frees one of the five available copies.

Figure 2-7:
iTunes now
has 2.19GB
of songs,
according
to the
status bar.

If you feel so inclined, you can always buy music at the iTunes Music Store.
Just remember that the music you buy (the filenames end with .m4p) is subject to the following restrictions:

✦ The songs are in a protected Apple-controlled format. Unless you use
   nefarious (illegal?) means to crack the songs and convert them to MP3
   format, you have no control over them.

✦ Song files can be copied to any number of computers, but only five computers can play the songs at the same time (see the nearby sidebar).

✦ You can only play the songs you bought with iTunes or with an iPod.
   Encrypted AAC files don't work anywhere else.

✦ You can burn a given playlist (in other words, you can create a CD with a
   specific set of songs) no more than seven times, if you have just one purchased song in the bunch.

✦ Here's the kicker: Apple reserves the right to change its restrictions at
   any time. Yes, it can do that. Apple did it in April 2004, when it reduced
   the number of times you could burn a specific playlist.

Automatically update your songs?

I have iTunes update my iPod automatically. Why? Because I use Windows Media Player to work with most of my music; I only put the songs that I want on my iPod in iTunes. I add or remove songs in iTunes as the mood strikes. That way, when I plug my iPod into my computer, I know exactly what songs will get synched.

There's a downside to automatically updating your songs: If you remove a song from iTunes (even accidentally), or if something catastrophic happens to your iTunes database, the next time you plug your iPod into you computer, it's synchronized quite precisely: Any songs that are in your iPod, but aren't in iTunes, disappear.

You can update your iPod manually, or you can specify that only certain playlists should be synchronized when you plug in your iPod. See the nearby section "Synching" for details.

You can always burn your purchased music onto a CD and rip it back into MP3 format — but invariably you suffer a loss of quality in the round trip.

For the straight story, see the Electronic Freedom Foundation's discussion of online music digital rights management at www.eff.org/IP/DRM/guide.

Moving music to your iPod

Have all the songs you want in your iTunes library? Good. It's time to transfer them to your iPod. Here's how:

1. **Get iTunes going and plug your iPod into your USB port.**

   If you get an AutoPlay notice, click the red *X* to get rid of it.

   The iPod Setup Assistant makes an encore appearance, as shown in Figure 2-8.

2. **Give your 'Pod a good name. Consider whether you want your iPod to be updated automatically (see the nearby sidebar). Click the Next button.**

   Apple asks you to register your iPod.

3. **Register your iPod if you like (there doesn't seem to be any compelling reason to do so).**

   If you decide to register, you'll need your serial number (engraved on the back of the iPod), and you'll be given an opportunity to create an Apple ID — which doubles as your iTunes Music Store account. How thoughtful. When you're done, click the Finish button.

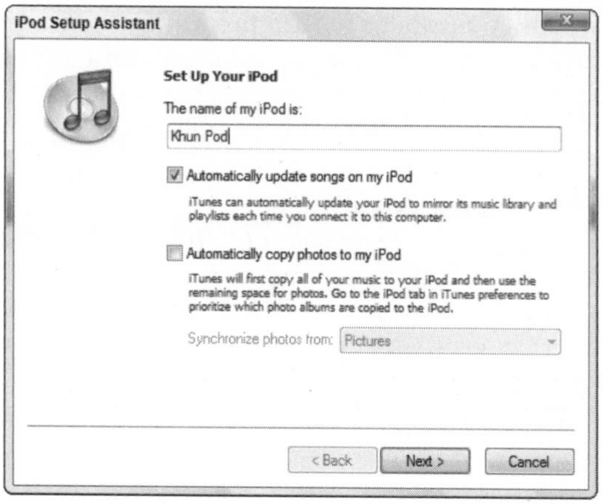

Figure 2-8:
Set up your
iPod for the
first time.

iTunes lists the name of your iPod on the left, in the Source area. It also
tells you that it's updating the iPod and that you shouldn't disconnect it
(see Figure 2-9).

The name of your iPod

Update is in progress

Figure 2-9:
Update in
progress —
don't dis-
connect.
No, really.

iTunes helpfully tosses you into the music store

4. If you have too much music to fit into the iPod, iTunes detects a blivet condition (that's a technical term, never mind) and asks whether it can choose a selection of songs to copy to the iPod. If you see that dialog box, click the Yes button.

If you tried to put more music on your iPod than the iPod can handle, iTunes automatically creates a new playlist called *<your iPod's name>* Selection (in my case, Khun Pod Selection). It trims down the list of songs that you tried to put on the 'Pod, removing songs from the bottom of the list, and that truncated list of songs becomes the new playlist, *<your iPod's name>* Selection. iTunes then automatically sets itself up so it synchronizes the *<your iPod's name>* Selection playlist with your iPod. If iTunes successfully accomplishes all of that, you see the message in Figure 2-10.

Figure 2-10:
Too many
songs
prompts
this dialog.

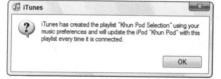

The process sounds complicated, but it's about the only thing iTunes can do. If you've ever wondered why your iPod synchronizes with a weird playlist that you didn't personally create, now you know why.

5. If you tried to put too much music on your iPod, and you get the message in Figure 2-10, click OK.

iTunes starts downloading songs to your iPod.

6. If you want to watch the progress as iTunes downloads songs to your iPod, click the iPod (or the name of the automatically generated Selection under the iPod).

Ten or 15 minutes (or an hour or two) later, iTunes finishes the sync. Your iPod is ready to rock 'n' roll, as shown in Figure 2-11.

If you've set up your iPod for automatic updating (also known as *auto-sync*), the next time you plug it into your computer, the songs on the iPod get synched with the songs in iTunes. (If you didn't have enough room on your iPod for all the songs, your iPod gets synched with the *<iPod's Name>* Selection playlist; see the next section.) If you remove all the songs from iTunes (or if you had too many songs and you delete the *<iPod's Name>* Selection playlist), all the songs in your iPod go bye-bye.

File	Edit	Controls	Visualizer	Advanced	Help	iTunes

iPod update is complete.

Search   Browse

		Source		▲	Name		Time	Artist		Album		Genre		My Ra
		Library		1.	☑ Broken Home	◎	3:39	Papa Roach	◎	DreamWorks Dem...	◎	Rock	◎	
		Podcasts		2	☑ Juanita	◎	3:50	Shania Twain	◎	Up! Disc 2	◎	Country		
		Videos		3	☑ Forever and for Always	◎	4:43	Shania Twain	◎	Up! Disc 2	◎	Country		
		Party Shuffle		4	☑ Ain't No Particular Way		4:25	Shania Twain	◎	Up! Disc 2	◎	Country		
		Radio		5	☑ It Only Hurts When I'm Breathing	◎	3:20	Shania Twain	◎	Up! Disc 2	◎	Country		
		Music Store		6	☑ Nah!		4:14	Shania Twain	◎	Up! Disc 2	◎	Country		
▼		Khun Pod	⬆	7	☑ (Wanna Get to Know You) Tha...	◎	4:31	Shania Twain	◎	Up! Disc 2	◎	Country		
	🎵	Khun Pod Selection		8	☑ C'est la Vie	◎	3:39	Shania Twain	◎	Up! Disc 2	◎	Country		
		Woody's Music		9	☑ I'm Jealous	◎	3:59	Shania Twain	◎	Up! Disc 2	◎	Country		
		90's Music		10	☑ Ka-Ching!	◎	3:20	Shania Twain	◎	Up! Disc 2	◎	Country		
		My Top Rated		11	☑ Thank You Baby (For Making S...	◎	4:01	Shania Twain	◎	Up! Disc 2	◎	Country		
		Recently Added		12	☑ Waiter! Bring Me Water!		3:20	Shania Twain	◎	Up! Disc 2	◎	Country		
		Recently Played		13	☑ What a Way to Wanna Be!	◎	3:33	Shania Twain	◎	Up! Disc 2	◎	Country		
		Top 25 Most Played		14	☑ I Ain't Going Down	◎	3:45	Shania Twain	◎	Up! Disc 2	◎	Country		
	🎵	Khun Pod Selection												

Used: 1.77 GB   Free: 52.3 MB 🔒   0 photos

318 songs, 23.1 hours, 1.77 GB

Figure 2-11: iTunes finishes its sync, and you can grab your 'Pod and go.

Synching

When you plug your 'Pod into your PC, iTunes "synchronizes" the iPod with iTunes. Unless you change the way iTunes syncs, here's what happens:

✦ All the songs (videos, pictures) that iTunes knows about — which is to say, all the songs (videos, pictures) you can see inside iTunes — get copied to your iPod.

✦ If you have any songs on the iPod that aren't known to iTunes, they're deleted from the iPod. That can be disastrous.

As I describe in the preceding section, if you have too much music to fit in your iPod, iTunes takes it upon itself to create a new playlist that holds as much music as possible. It then sets things up so you sync with that playlist every time you plug in your iPod. This artificially generated playlist is called *<your iPod's name>* Selection. On my "Khun Pod" iPod, it's Khun Pod Selection.

The term "sync" is something of a misnomer. That's why Apple generally avoids using the word. In fact, music (videos, etc.) gets copied to your iPod, and some music may be deleted from the iPod. It isn't a two-way street.

Many people are surprised to discover that iTunes allows you to control the iPod synching process to a fairly refined degree. Here's how:

1. **Get iTunes running and connect your iPod by plugging in the USB cable.**

If you get an AutoPlay notice, click the red *X* to get rid of it.

You see your iPod on the left, in the Source list (refer to Figure 2-9).

2. **Choose Edit⇨Preferences. Click the iPod tab.**

Your iPod is identified by name, as shown in Figure 2-12.

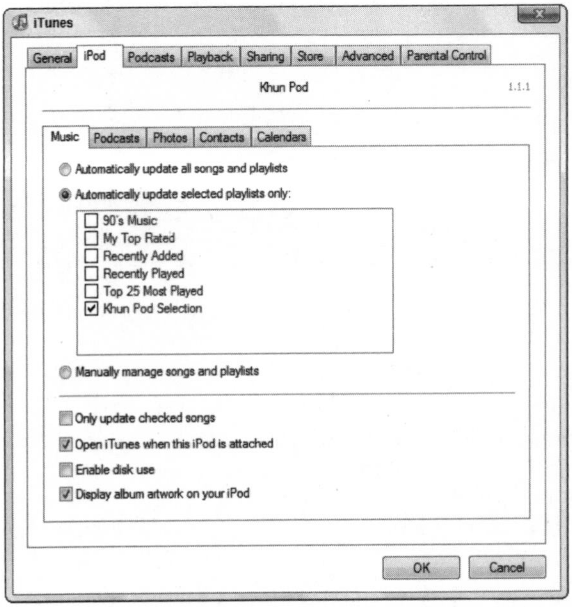

Figure 2-12:
You have a
fair amount
of control
over
automatic
updating if
you know
where
to look.

Because I occasionally store more music in iTunes than I could ever fit on my iPod (hope springs eternal, eh?), Figure 2-12 shows that I've been set to synchronize with the *<your iPod's name>* Selection playlist — the Khun Pod Selection playlist.

3. **Select the playlist(s) that you want to sync with your iPod.**

You can stay with the playlist that was created for you, or you can choose any playlist (or combination of playlists) that you like.

4. **Alternatively, if you want to manage the contents of your iPod manually (a real pain in the neck), select the Manually Manage Songs and Playlists option.**

To manually manage songs and playlists, back in the main iTunes window (Figure 2-9), you have to click and drag songs and playlists from the song list on the right to the iPod on the left. Manually managing songs can be quite, uh, tedious.

5. **Click the OK button.**

Your iPod is updated according to the settings you chose.

Sometimes your iPod will flash "Do Not Disconnect" while iTunes says "iPod Update is Complete / OK to Disconnect." (A bit of iPodding cognitive dissonance, eh?) If that ever happens to you, click the Eject iPod icon in the lower-right corner of the iTunes window. Give it a few seconds, and as long as the battery's charged, the iPod should say "OK to Disconnect."

Copying Songs to Your PC

Here's one question I hear, over and over: How do I take songs off the iPod and copy them back to my PC?

It's really very easy. In fact, if you followed my instructions in Book II, Chapter 1 and told Vista that you wanted to see hidden files, you're basically done. Here's how to copy songs back to your PC:

Book VI Chapter 2

iPimping iPods and iTunes

1. **Plug your iPod into your computer's USB port.**

2. **If you receive an AutoPlay notification, click the Open Folder to View Files Using Windows Explorer link.**

If you don't receive an AutoPlay notification, choose Start⇨Computer and double-click your iPod "drive."

You may have to guess a little bit to see which drive is actually your iPod. Go ahead and click around. Windows Explorer should look like Figure 2-13.

3. **If you can't see the iPod_Control folder, press Alt and then choose Tools⇨Folder Options⇨View. Select the Show Hidden Files and Folders check box, then click OK.**

And while you're here anyway, deselect the Hide Extensions for Known File Types check box. Click the OK button.

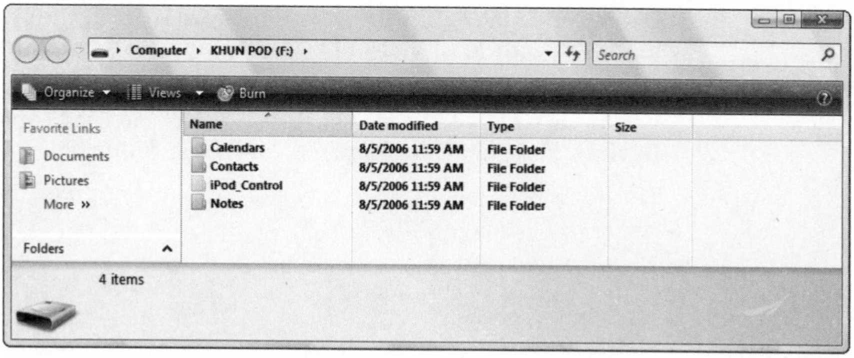

Figure 2-13:
Your music
is in a
hidden
folder called
iPod_
Control.

Name	Date modified	Type	Size
Calendars	8/5/2006 11:59 AM	File Folder	
Contacts	8/5/2006 11:59 AM	File Folder	
iPod_Control	8/5/2006 11:59 AM	File Folder	
Notes	8/5/2006 11:59 AM	File Folder	

Computer ▸ KHUN POD (F:) ▸   Search

Organize ▾   Views ▾   Burn

Favorite Links
Documents
Pictures
More »

Folders

4 items

The details are in Book II, Chapter 1, but every Vista user really needs to be able to see her hidden files and folders, and full filename extensions.

4. **Double-click to navigate to the `iPod_Control\Music` folder and then double-click one of the subfolders — on an iPod nano, they're marked F00, F01, and so on.**

5. **Right-click one of the columns and choose More. Select the Album Title and Title check boxes. Click the OK button.**

   Windows Explorer shows you the (inscrutable) iPod filename, plus the album title and the song's title, as shown in Figure 2-14.

Computer ▸ KHUN POD (F:) ▸ iPod_Control ▸ Music ▸ F00
Search
Organize
Views
Play
Burn
Favorite Links
Documents
Pictures
Music
More »
Folders
Name
Date modified
Type
Size
Album title
Title
EMOM.mp3 3/8/2006 7:40 AM MP3 Form... 2,743 KB Meteora From the Inside
EXJR.mp3 8/4/2006 3:51 PM MP3 Form... 3,421 KB Elephunk The APL Song
EYDB.mp3 6/2/2005 1:37 PM MP3 Form... 3,366 KB Meteora Somewhere I Belong
EZYG.mp3 8/3/2006 3:47 PM MP3 Form... 8,917 KB DIDO Greatest hits 2004 This land is mine
FJZB.mp3 6/4/2005 6:48 PM MP3 Form... 3,387 KB All Wound Up Bad Religion
FKTA.mp3 6/20/2006 10:28 AM MP3 Form... 4,117 KB PCD (Special Edition) Flirt
FYHO.mp3 6/9/2006 9:00 PM MP3 Form... 10,304 KB Crow Left of the Mur... Pistola
EMOM.mp3
MP3 Format Sound
Artists: Linkin Park
Album title: Meteora
Genre: Rock
Length: 00:02:55
Rating:
Year: 2003
Size: 2.67 MB
#: 10
MP3

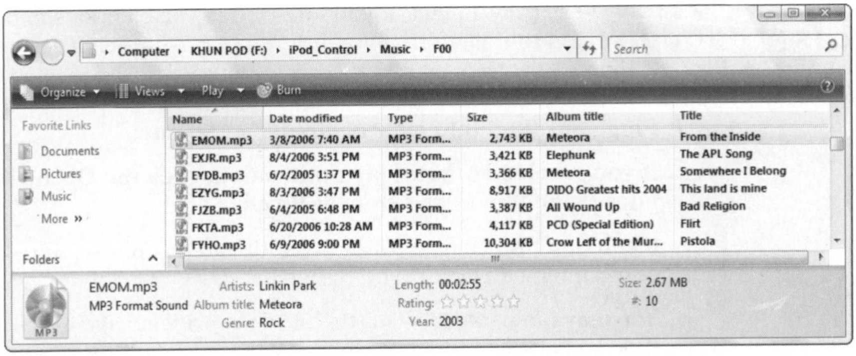

Figure 2-14: You can see the track name and the album title for every song.

You can treat the files on your iPod like any other files — select, click, drag, copy, and so on — to copy them back to your PC.

WARNING!

But don't move or delete them! The iPod keeps its own database. It ain't nice to fool with mother nature. If you want to remove a song, use iTunes.

6. **When you're done, click the red *X* to exit Windows Explorer.**

7. **Double-click the Safely Remove Hardware icon, in the system tray next to the clock. (It looks like a USB plug with a green check mark.)**

8. **Select the Display Device Components check box to make sure that you know which device is your iPod. Select the iPod (Apple iPod USB Device). Then click the Stop, OK, and Close buttons.**

   The Do Not Disconnect icon may still show on your iPod, but you can go ahead and disconnect it anyway.

The iPod Ecosystem

An entire industry has grown up around the iPod: cute little fuzzy things that warble and squeak; cases that can withstand a point-blank blast from an Abrams M1A2 tank; and lots of software that can turn your iPod into an air-traffic control system — or a puddle of useless iron. A cool puddle, yes, but a puddle nonetheless.

If you're interested in keeping up on the latest, permit me to recommend a few Web sites:

✦ www.ipodhacks.com does a good job of dishing out iPod news. It's a bit Mac-centric for my tastes, but that's just me. Its forums cover just about every nook and cranny of iPod-dom.

✦ www.ilounge.com covers the news, but more from an industry perspective. Its free iPod Book is well worth the download. You'll find lots of information.

✦ www.ipoding.com concentrates on news about iPod accessories. Some of the material is dated, but it's worth a look.

If you have an iPod, you should also read *iPod & iTunes For Dummies, 4th Edition,* by Tony Bove and Cheryl Rhodes (published by Wiley).

Will Digital Rights Management go the Way of the Dodo?

It warms my heart to see cut-throat competition in action, especially when we consumers are the ones who win.

In January, 2008, Amazon announced that it was about to start selling real, legitimate music from four of the major music labels without the copy restrictions foisted on customers by Microsoft and Apple. Although several other companies — notably emusic.com — had been selling restriction-free MP3s for years, Amazon was the first distributor with enough clout to get the major labels to agree that people who buy digital music should have the same capabilities as people who buy music on CD.

Within weeks, several other companies (notably Google) were rumored to be considering the same approach. Then, amazingly, Apple announced it, too, would start selling some music (a very limited subset) in un-protectable MP3 format.

Do yourself and the industry a favor. If you're going to buy music, either buy MP3 files, or buy a CD and rip it into MP3 format. That way you can be sure that you can play the music you pay for. And you can help fight Apple's and Microsoft's grand designs to take control of the future of music distribution.

Chapter 3: Adding a Second (Or Third) Hard Drive

In This Chapter

✔ **Cutting through the IDE/EIDE/SCSI/SATA/SATA2 BS**

✔ **Installing a SATA2 drive**

✔ **Getting Vista to recognize a new drive**

*D*o you find yourself collecting bits? They're like dust bunnies or clothes hangers — every week it seems you have twice as many as you did the week before. My bit bucket runneth over.

Everybody needs a new hard drive from time to time. Can't do much about it. If your bit collection is busting at the seams, follow the nostrums in this chapter to pick a decent drive, and find out how to get Vista to recognize it.

Choosing a Second Hard Drive

All Vista computers have a hard drive, but you can add a second one if you need more storage space.

Hard drive capacity is measured in *gigabytes,* abbreviated *GB.* One gigabyte is 1,000 megabytes, or 1,000,000,000 bytes, give or take a power-of-two roundoff error. (Yes, lawsuits have been fought and won on the roundoff.)

Once upon a time, removable storage was dominated by Zip disks and other contraptions with adapter kits that let you "plug in" a hard drive by sliding it into a slot in your computer's front panel. Fast USB has nearly made those beasts obsolete, although in a few cases *hot-swappable* hard drives have their place.

Your second hard drive can go inside or outside your computer. Here's a quick guide to the configurations:

✦ If you only need a gigabyte or so, don't get a hard drive. Look at USB flash drives or Memory Sticks (see "Key Drives, SuperFetch, and ReadyBoost" in Book VI, Chapter 1). Also consider archiving your little-used data to CD or DVD, or setting up a network and just transferring data you don't need very often to a different computer.

✦ If you decide to go with a second hard drive, get at least twice as much hard-drive space as you think you'll need. If you're shooting and storing a lot of pictures and videos, get four times as much as you think you'll need.

✦ Don't overlook external hard drives. For a few dollars more, you can frequently get a drive that plugs into your USB port, runs almost as fast as a "normal" hard drive, requires basically zero effort to install — and is completely portable. External hard drives have saved my tail more than once when my computer went belly-up and I needed to get at its data.

✦ You'll always find a "sweet spot" for hard drives, a point at which the cost per gigabyte is lowest. (The very largest hard drives always command a premium, and small hard drives don't give the best byte-fer-the-buck.) When comparing hard drives, always compare the cost per gigabyte, and go for the cheapest. Yes, I know the experts will tell you that the rotational speed is important, that the Mean Time Between Failure rating rules, or that brand X is more reliable than brand Y. In my experience, none of that really matters. Go for cheap.

You can also replace your first hard drive with a larger one, but then you have to reinstall Vista, reinstall all your applications, and transfer your data. (There are ways to transfer the operating system and applications intact, but they require special hardware or software.) You don't need the bother. Ain't broke, don't fix.

If you go with an internal hard drive, be sure to buy a hard drive with the same type of interface as the disk controller in your computer. See the next section for details.

Interfaces for Disk Drives

Disk drives have to plug into and talk to your computer's motherboard. They do so through an *interface*. You need to find out what type of interface your motherboard has so that the new drive you buy can speak your motherboard's language.

The only reliable way to find out what kinds of interfaces exist inside the belly of your beast is to consult the documentation that came with the PC — or have a knowledgeable friend open it up and look at the slots. Sounds drastic, but that's the most direct, most accurate way.

Whether you learn about it by divine inspiration, mental telepathy, or buying your niece's smelly boyfriend a pizza, you'll find that your motherboard has one or more of the following types of disk-friendly interfaces:

✦ EIDE or its predecessor, IDE

✦ Serial ATA

✦ SCSI

The *Enhanced Integrated Drive Electronics (EIDE) interface* controls the hard drive on most older Windows computers. Often it controls the CD-ROM drive or DVD drive as well. All modern Windows computers have a built-in EIDE controller or two, sitting on the motherboard. Older computers frequently sport big, ugly 40- or 80-wire ribbon cables that connect the motherboard to all the hard drives and CD drives in the PC.

The *Integrated Drive Electronics (IDE) interface* is an ancestor of EIDE, and you still find hard drives that are designed to run with IDE. If your computer has an EIDE interface, you can probably plug an IDE hard drive into it, but you're talking slug city.

The *Serial Advanced Technology Attachment (SATA)* approach replaces those 40- or 80-wire dinosaur ribbons with a single cable that looks like a stereo patch cord. Of course, SATA is faster, smarter, and better than its predecessors. Of course, it's completely incompatible — you need SATA hard drives, CD drives, and so on to go on one end of the cable, and your PC has to have SATA sockets on its motherboard. But SATA runs rings around the competition.

The first version of SATA — called, variously, SATA I, SATA/150, and just plain SATA — runs at 1.5 gigabytes per second (1.5 billion bits per second, give or take a couple of roundoff errors). Most of the SATA devices you see advertised nowadays call themselves *SATA II.* That designation generally refers to devices that run the SATA specification at 3 gigabytes per second. You should be able to use SATA II drives in PCs with SATA I controllers, because SATA II devices are required to "fall back" to the slower SATA I speed automatically.

The standards organization responsible for such things takes umbrage at the name "SATA II" because (a) that was the name *of the organization,* not the name of the interface and (b) the SATA II organization promulgated several standards, of which the SATA 3-gigabytes-per-second spec was just one. It's all rather academic at this point, but with a new SATA 6-gigabytes-per-second standard coming soon, the naming could get a little hairy.

The *Small Computer System Interface (SCSI)* (pronounced *scuzzy*) is for fast devices such as high-performance disk drives and tape drives. Very few Windows computers have a SCSI controller built in. Here's the reason why: Although SCSI is theoretically faster than EIDE, and possibly faster than SATA, in practice, very few people recognize much of a speed improvement when moving "up" to SCSI. But SCSI is almost always (and sometimes quite considerably) more expensive.

IDE and EIDE interfaces are rarely used for external devices because the length of the cable connecting the controller to the device is quite limited. SATA and SCSI work with both internal and external devices, although USB and FireWire (see the discussion in Book VI, Chapter 1) have largely taken over external connections.

Here's the bottom line: If you need a new hard drive and you don't want an external hard drive (either because they're too expensive or too cumbersome), and your computer's motherboard supports SATA drives, you should definitely buy a SATA II drive. Try to buy twice (or four times) as much storage space as you think you need, and choose among the major brands based on cost per gigabyte.

Installing a New SATA Drive

Installing a new SATA hard drive is a piece of cake — if you know the tricks:

1. **Make sure that you have a spare hour or two to let Vista format the hard drive. When you're ready, turn off your computer and crack open the case.**

   You may have to refer to the instructions that came with the computer.

2. **Find an empty 3.5-inch spot for your new hard drive.**

   If possible, look for a location that isn't right next to some other piece of hardware.

3. **Slide the drive into the bay. Make sure that the electrical connections are pointed outward so that you can get to them. Gently screw the drive into place using four screws (some computer cases just use a slider tab to secure the drive).**

4. **Connect a power cable to an available power connector inside your computer, and then slide the SATA side of the power cable onto the hard drive.**

   A SATA drive needs two cables. The wider one is for power, and the narrower one is for data. It only fits one way.

5. **Connect one end of a SATA data cable onto your hard drive and the other end into a SATA slot on your motherboard.**

Again, they only fit one way. You can use any available SATA slot.

If you're accustomed to installing IDE hard drives, you might be wondering at this point about master and slave jumper settings, attaching the correct end of the cable to the drive, and so on. Not to worry. With SATA, each drive gets its own data cable, and the wires only fit one way. Brilliantly simple.

6. **Close your computer case and turn on the power.**

When Vista comes back up, it identifies the SATA drive and automatically installs the drivers. You see a notification like the one shown in Figure 3-1.

You might think that you're done, but you aren't. Here's the part where you need to know the trick.

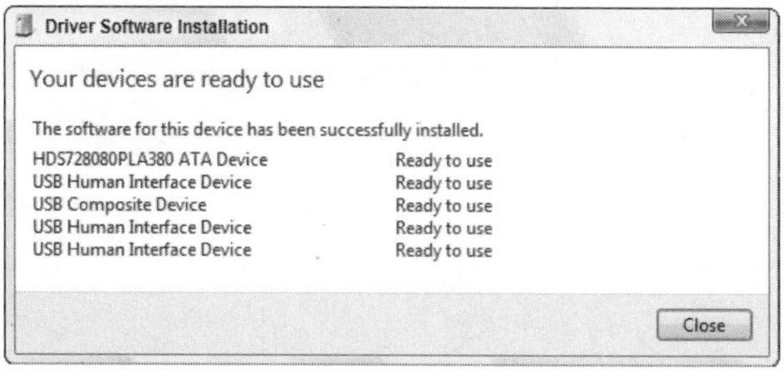

Figure 3-1:
Vista automatically installs drivers for SATA drives.

7. **Click the Start button, right-click Computer, and choose Manage. On the left, under Storage, double-click the line marked Disk Management.**

Vista presents you with the Initialize Disk dialog box shown in Figure 3-2. Your new disk may be identified as "Disk 0" (if you're adding a SATA drive to a computer that already has an IDE drive) or "Disk 1" (if you're adding a SATA drive to a computer that already has a SATA drive). Don't let the numbers spook ya.

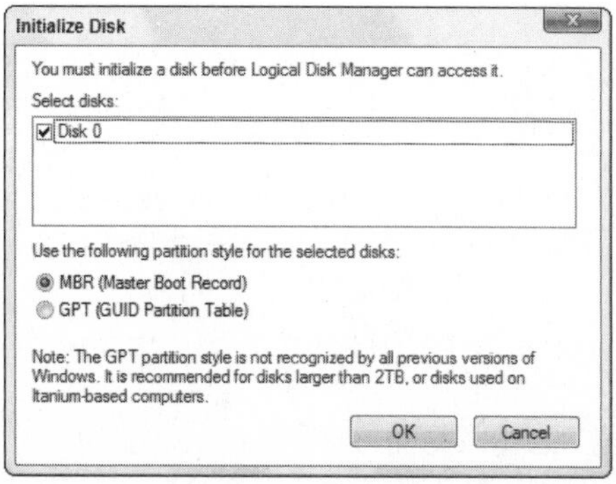

Figure 3-2:
Vista offers to initialize the hard drive, which it may or may not actually do.

8. **Select the MBR (Master Boot Record) partition style option and then click the OK button.**

Vista may start the New Simple Volume Wizard. If it doesn't, you see the Computer Management screen shown in Figure 3-3.

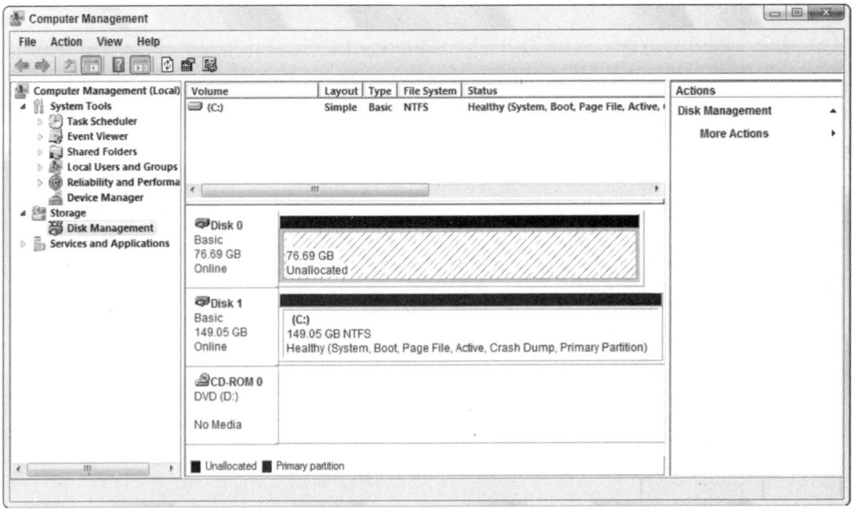

Figure 3-3: If the New Volume Wizard doesn't start auto-matically, you see an "Unallo-cated" drive.

9. **To start the New Simple Volume Wizard, if it doesn't kick in automatically, right-click the Unallocated partition and choose New Simple Volume.**

That gets the New Simple Volume Wizard going, as shown in Figure 3-4.

Figure 3-4: The New Simple Volume Wizard gets going sooner or later.

10. **Follow the steps in the wizard, give the new drive a letter, choose to format the volume as NT File System (NTFS), choose a default allocation unit size, and type in a volume label. At the end of the wizard, click the Finish button.**

And wait. Formatting a new hard drive can take a long, long time — and the bigger the drive, the longer it takes.

11. **When Vista finishes, click the red *X* to exit the Computer Management console.**

Your new SATA hard drive is ready to use (see Figure 3-5).

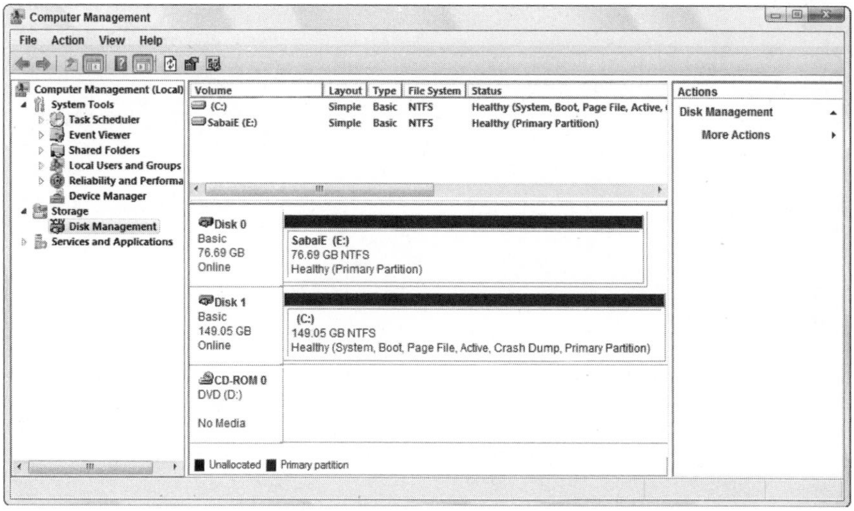

Figure 3-5:
Vista
formats the
hard drive
and marks it
as Healthy.

It takes a while, and you have to know where the Initialize Disk dialog box is hidden. But by and large, installing a new SATA drive in your Vista PC is like falling off a log.

Chapter 4: Picking Printers and Printer/Scanner/Faxers

In This Chapter

✔ **Choosing a printer**

✔ **Attaching a new printer to your PC or network**

✔ **Solving print queue problems**

✔ **Troubleshooting other problems with printers**

Ah, the paperless office. What a wonderful concept! No more file cabinets bulging with misfiled flotsam. No more hernias hauling cartons of copy paper, dumping the sheets 500 at a time into a thankless plastic maw. No more trees dying in agony, relinquishing their last gasps to provide pulp as a substrate for heat-fused carbon toner. No more coffee-stained reports. No more paper cuts.

No more . . . oh, who the heck am I trying to kid? No way.

Industry prognosticators have been telling us for more than a decade that the paperless office is right around the corner. Yeah, sure. Maybe around your corner. Around my corner, I predict that PC printers will disappear about the same time that *Star Trek* reruns go off the air. We're talking geologic time here, folks.

Vista has great printer support. It's easy after you grasp a few basic skills.

Evaluating Printers

Most popular modern printers come in one of two types:

✦ **Inkjet printers:** These work by spraying tiny droplets of ink on paper. Inkjet printers tend to be small, light, and inexpensive. They make less noise than laser printers and consume far less power. Photo-quality printers need expensive paper, but they produce pictures that rival quickie photo labs.

✦ **Laser printers:** These work by fusing powdered toner onto the paper, essentially the same way a photocopier works. Laser printers tend to be larger and heavier than their inkjet cousins, and they cost more too. On the other hand, laser printers tend to be faster than inkjet printers, and any monocolor laser printer worth its salt produces much sharper results than an inkjet on normal (read: cheap) paper.

Once upon a time, choosing between inkjet and laser boiled down to a question of the cost of consumables: Inkjet cartridges were (and are) considerably more expensive, per printed page, than laser toner cartridges. Now that many of the major inkjet printer manufacturers make printers with ink tanks, the cost per page for inkjets and lasers has narrowed considerably.

Printing photos

Most modern inkjet printers produce prints that rival quickie photo shops. They're cheap to buy and easy to use.

Color laser printers, on the other hand, are more expensive. Like other laser printers, color laser printers are faster than color inkjet printers and are cheaper to operate. The quality of the best color laser printers rivals inkjets — but only on plain paper.

Dye sublimation printers produce the highest-quality photographic output, yielding results as good as a conventional photographic print or better. They are expensive, though, and they require special paper and dye/ink, both of which are also expensive. The materials for a single print can cost several dollars. For this reason, dye sublimation printers are generally suitable only for photo printing, or for low-production, high-quality brochures and so on, not for general printing.

Considering multifunction devices

Several companies sell *multifunction devices* that can do two or more functions, such as printing, photocopying, faxing, and scanning.

A multifunction device saves space and usually costs less than several separate devices. On the other hand, it is a compromise; it can't be designed to perform any of its functions as well as a single-purpose device would. Also, you must deal with the inconvenience of not being able to use more than one of the device's functions at a time, and you run the risk that a breakdown will take away your ability to do several things.

A multifunction device can be a real convenience if you use each of its functions lightly. If you use one function frequently, you're better off buying a dedicated device to perform that function. On the other hand, if you need to print, copy, scan, and fax, getting one machine to cover all the bases makes a great deal of sense.

Exploring exotic features

You can easily find printers that accept paper up to 11 inches wide. Wide-carriage inkjet printers cost a few hundred dollars extra; wide-format laser printers cost a thousand dollars or more extra. Even larger-format printers are available from specialized suppliers (at specialized prices).

Many laser printers and some inkjet printers can print a page and then turn it over and print the other side. This is called *duplex printing*. It's a valuable feature if you print proposals or reports whose appearance is important, or if you mail a lot of documents and would like to save postage by reducing weight.

Some applications, notably Microsoft Word, include rudimentary support for duplex printing on a standard printer — if you don't mind taking a stack of printed pages out of the printer, flipping it over, and feeding it back in. The trick lies in figuring out which pages to print first (odd or even), whether they should be printed in normal order (pages 1, 3, 5, and so on) or reverse order (pages 5, 3, 1), and exactly how the stack needs to be flipped (face up, face down, rotated, or not). With a bit of experimenting and a bit of time spent on the File➪Print dialog box (see Figure 4-1), you can undoubtedly coax your standard printer into doing duplex, particularly if you select the Manual Duplex check box.

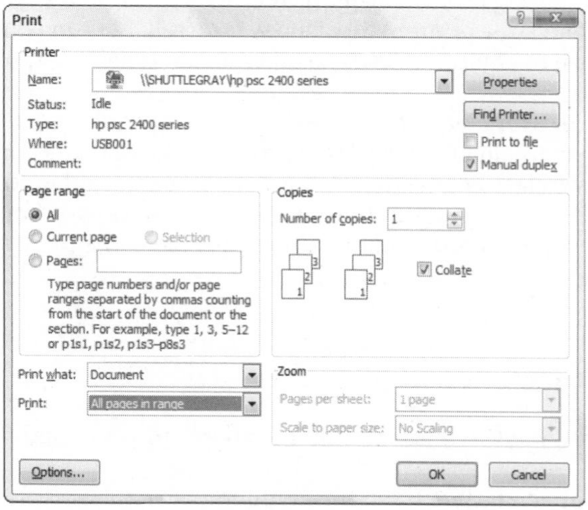

Figure 4-1:
Word 2002, 2003, and 2007 all include a Manual Duplex check box.

An almost endless list of printers exists to meet specialized needs. For example, banner printers print on wide rolls of paper; drafting printers can print architectural drawings and similar documents on paper up to several feet wide; label printers can produce mailing labels one at a time; and more. If you need something unusual, look for it on the Web or ask people who deal with equipment for your business or hobby. If you can imagine a printer with some specialized feature, somebody probably sells one.

Making a final decision

After a lot of years advising people and companies about printers, I've come to a handful of very simple conclusions:

✦ If you don't print a lot, get a good color inkjet printer from one of the major manufacturers. You can't go wrong with any of them.

✦ If you do print a lot — say, more than a dozen pages a day — and you only need one color, get a laser. It costs less in the long run, although the initial expense is higher. For the occasional color print, find a company nearby that lets you run your pictures through its color inkjet.

✦ If you expect to print a lot of color photos, get an inkjet printer with an individual tank for each color of ink. You can't beat the quality, and the price probably isn't as steep as you fear.

✦ If you want to print in color, but photographic quality isn't a priority, get a color laser printer. Color lasers are a great choice for small offices that want to print color flyers, but rarely need to print photos.

✦ If you need to print color photos *and* a lot of black-and-white documents, consider getting both an inkjet printer with individual tanks and a laser printer. The laser printer still can pay for itself, it'll run faster, and you won't have to compromise the quality of one type of output to get both.

If you have a network, you could consider getting a printer (or an adapter) that allows you to plug the printer directly into the network, either through a hub or via a wireless connection. A normal USB cable–tethered printer has to be plugged into a computer that's running whenever you want to print. Although most people won't find that a big problem, the price of network-ready printers has fallen dramatically.

Installing a Printer

You have three ways to make a printer available to your computer:

✦ You can attach it directly to the computer.

✦ You can connect your computer to a network and attach the printer to another computer on the same network.

✦ You can connect your computer to a network and attach the printer directly to the network's hub, either with a network cable or via a wireless connection.

Connecting a computer directly to a network hub isn't difficult, if you have the right hardware. Each printer controller is different, though, so you have to follow the manufacturer's instructions.

Attaching a local printer

So you have a new printer, and you want to use it. Attaching it locally — which is to say, plugging it directly into your PC — is the simplest way to install a printer, and the only option if you don't have a network.

Printers usually have either a USB connector or a parallel connector that plugs into your computer:

✦ **If the printer uses a USB connector,** simply plug the connector into your PC's USB port. (I walk you through the details of installing a USB printer a little later in this section.)

✦ **If the printer uses a serial or parallel connector,** turn your computer off, plug in the connector, and turn the computer back on.

If you have a parallel or serial printer — one that connects with a large D-shaped plug to your computer — Vista may detect and install it automatically when you restart the computer. If that doesn't happen, you have to haul out the big guns and manually install the printer driver, following the manufacturer's directions.

✦ **If you have a printer that lets you choose between USB and parallel connections,** always use the USB connection, even if you have to buy a USB hub to get another USB port (see Book VI, Chapter 1). USB is faster, easier to set up, and easier to maintain than a parallel-port connection.

After you connect your printer to the computer, you must make Vista recognize it. That's what "installing the printer" means, eh?

If you have a USB printer, Vista will almost always detect it and install it automatically when you turn the printer on. But then again, you may need a driver, and you should probably check whether a newer driver is available for the printer before you fire up the printer installation wizard. Table 4-1 has the Web addresses you should visit to search for new printer drivers. You're welcome.

**Book VI
Chapter 4**

Picking Printers and Printer/Scanner/ Faxers

Table 4-1	Driver Sites for the Major Printer Manufacturers
Printer Manufacturer	*Find Drivers at This URL*
Brother	www.brother.com/E-ftp/info/index.html
Canon	www.usa.canon.com/html/conCprSupport.jsp?type=xp

(continued)

Table 4-1 *(continued)*

Printer Manufacturer	Find Drivers at This URL
Dell	`http://support.dell.com/filelib/criteria.aspx?c=us`
Epson	`www.epson.com/cgi-bin/Store/support/SupportIndex.jsp`
HP	`http://welcome.hp.com/country/us/en/support.html`
Lexmark	`http://support.lexmark.com/cgi-perl/selections.cgi`

If you have to use an old-fashioned parallel or serial cable to connect your printer, make sure you have the manufacturer's installation instructions handy, and follow their advice religiously.

If you have a USB printer, you may be able to let Vista do all the heavy lifting. Try this:

1. **Choose Start⇨Control Panel, and under the Hardware and Sound heading, click the Printer link.**

   Vista shows you the current Printers list, as shown in Figure 4-2. It's a good idea to check and see whether the printer you're about to install is already installed!

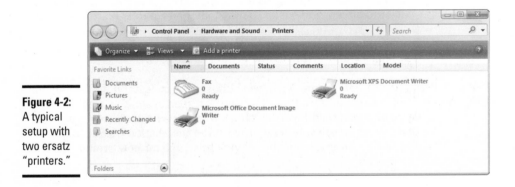

Figure 4-2: A typical setup with two ersatz "printers."

2. **Turn on your printer, and plug in the USB cable.**

   Vista identifies the printer and starts the Found New Hardware Wizard, as shown in Figure 4-3.

Figure 4-3:
Vista senses
your printer
as soon as
you plug it in.

3. **Click the Locate and Install Driver Software (Recommended) icon.**

   You may have to click through a security nag screen or three, but the wizard asks you to insert the disc that came with your printer. Alternatively, you can tell Vista that you don't have the disc.

4. **If you have the disc that came with the printer, insert it into the CD drive. Otherwise, click the I Don't Have the Disc / Show Me Other Options line.**

   If you don't have the disc, Vista asks you whether it can check for a solution (which, in my experience, doesn't succeed very often) or whether you want to browse your computer for the driver software.

   At this point, if you don't already have the driver sitting somewhere on your computer (or on your network), it's a good idea to run to the manufacturer's Web site (see Table 4-1), download the software, and resume the wizard at this point. You don't need to shut down the wizard while you're off snagging the driver.

5. **If Vista asks you to pick the best match for your hardware (see Figure 4-4), do so. Click the Next button.**

   At some point, Vista gets the hint and installs the printer. You can tell that the printer's ready by looking in the Printers list (see Figure 4-5). The green check mark signifies that this is the default printer.

6. **To share this printer on your network, right-click the printer, choose Rename, and give it a short name.**

   Short printer names (such as PSC2400, LJ4, or DJ930C) are easier to remember and harder to mistype.

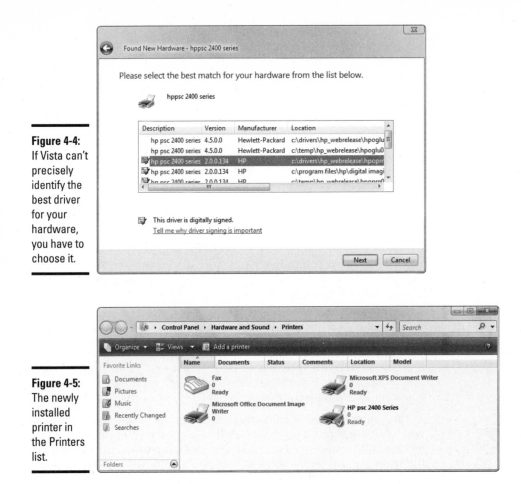

Figure 4-4:
If Vista can't precisely identify the best driver for your hardware, you have to choose it.

Figure 4-5:
The newly installed printer in the Printers list.

7. **To share the printer, right-click it and choose Sharing. Then click the Change Sharing Options button.**

   You have to click through yet another security dialog box, and then Vista opens the Properties dialog box for the printer, set to the Sharing tab (see Figure 4-6).

8. **To set up the printer for sharing, give the printer a Share Name and click the OK button.**

   You know that the printer is shared when a small picture that looks vaguely like two people appears to the lower left of the printer name.

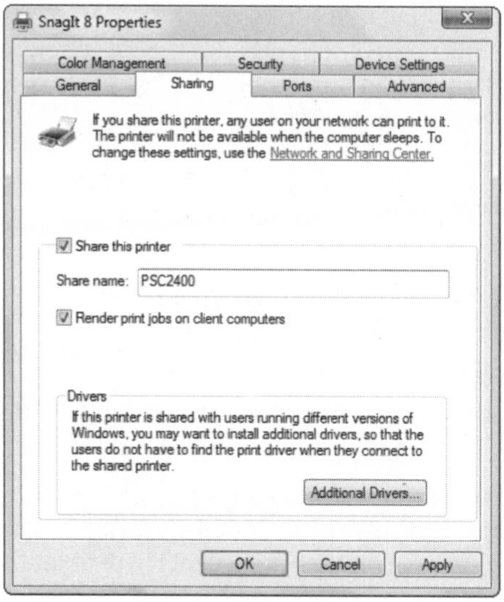

SnagIt 8 Properties

| Color Management | Security | Device Settings |
| General | Sharing | Ports | Advanced |

If you share this printer, any user on your network can print to it. The printer will not be available when the computer sleeps. To change these settings, use the Network and Sharing Center.

☑ Share this printer

Share name: PSC2400

☑ Render print jobs on client computers

Drivers
If this printer is shared with users running different versions of Windows, you may want to install additional drivers, so that the users do not have to find the print driver when they connect to the shared printer.

Additional Drivers...

OK   Cancel   Apply

Figure 4-6: To share the printer on your network, give it a Share Name.

9. **To make sure that the printer is working correctly, right-click the printer, choose Properties, and then click the Print Test Page button.**

If the printer prints, it, uh, works.

Connecting a network printer

Vista networks work wonders. I talk (and talk and talk) about them in Book IX. If you have a network, you can attach a printer to any computer on the network and have it accessible to all the users on all the computers in the network. You can also attach different printers to different computers, and let the network users pick and choose the printer that they want to use as the need arises.

Before other computers on a network can use a printer, the printer must be officially shared. To share a printer, an administrator has to go to the *host PC* — that is, the PC to which the printer is physically attached — and tell Windows that the printer should be shared. I explain how to do that in Steps 7 and 8 in the preceding section.

Sometimes Vista is smart enough to identify printers attached to your network and install them right on the spot, and you don't have to lift a finger. When you look at a list of printers in Vista, it identifies these automatically recognized printers as "Auto" printers — Auto HP DeskJet on Shuttlegray, for example. Slick.

Sometimes (and for the life of me, I don't know why), Vista doesn't automatically recognize all the printers on a network. For those special occasions, you need to install the printer manually on any PC that wants to use it. To do so, follow these steps:

1. **Make sure that the printer is installed on the host PC — that is, go over to the PC that the printer is attached to and make sure that you can use it.**

   Try firing up a word processor and print a page, or something along those lines. If the printer doesn't work on the host PC, start at the beginning of this chapter and get the printer going.

2. **Follow the steps in the preceding section to make sure that the printer is officially designated as a shared printer.**

   At least 90 percent of the time, if you can't get a PC to recognize a printer attached to the network, either the printer itself isn't working on the host (see Step 1) or the printer isn't properly designated as a shared printer (see Step 2).

3. **On the computer that doesn't automatically recognize the printer, choose Start➪Control Panel, and under the Hardware and Sound heading, click the Printer link.**

   This opens the Printers list (refer to Figure 4-2).

4. **Click the Add a Printer icon.**

   Vista asks whether you want to add a local printer or a network/wireless/ Bluetooth printer.

5. **Click the Add a Network, Wireless or Bluetooth Printer button.**

   The wizard starts searching for printers. Sometimes it finds the printer you want. Sometimes it doesn't.

6. **If the wizard doesn't identify the printer you want within a minute or two, click the Stop button and then click the link The Printer That I Want Isn't Listed.**

   The wizard displays the dialog box shown in Figure 4-7.

7. **If you need to find the printer, click the Browse button and then locate the printer on your network. Select the printer, click the OK button, and then (back in Figure 4-7) click the Next button.**

   If the wizard does not display the printer that you want to install, you can install it anyway, but you must type its name into the Printer text box under the Select a Shared Printer by Name option. The name has this form:

   `\\host\printer`

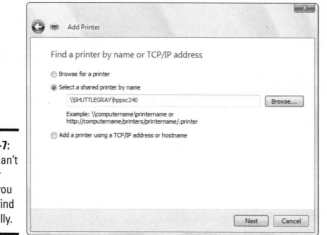

Figure 4-7:
If Vista can't find your printer, you have to find it manually.

For *host,* substitute the name of the host computer as it appears in the Shared Printers dialog box. For *printer,* substitute the share name of the shared printer (which you can find on the host computer's Printers list). You get something like \\Dimension\LJ4.

8. Vista displays a warning about the potential presence of viruses in printer drivers. Click the Yes button to continue installing the driver.

If you connect successfully, the wizard asks whether you want to make this printer your default printer (that is, the one that an application uses unless you explicitly tell it otherwise).

9. Click the Next and then the Finish buttons to finish the wizard.

File and printer sharing has to be allowed on both the *host* computer — the one with the printer physically attached to it — and on the other computer from which you want to be able to use the printer. To make sure that file and printer sharing is enabled, choose Start➪Control Panel and, under the Network and Internet icon, click the Set Up File Sharing link.

Using the Print Queue

You may have noticed that when you print a document from an application, the application reports that it is done before the printer finishes printing. If the document is long enough, you can print several more documents from one or more applications while the printer works on the first one. This is possible because Vista saves printed documents in a *print queue* until it can print them.

Changing the printer temporarily

If you want to print to a particular printer once, changing the default printer and then changing it back is inconvenient. In most applications, you can change the printer temporarily.

For example, in any Microsoft Office application, if you choose File⇨Print, the Print dialog box shows the default printer, but you can click the down arrow next to the printer name, or click the Find Printer button, to temporarily shift to a different printer. The change only takes effect for the application — not for Vista itself.

If more than one printer is installed on your computer or on your network, each one has its own print queue. The queue is maintained on the host PC — that is, the PC to which the printer is attached.

Vista uses print queues automatically, so you don't even have to know that they exist. If you know the tricks, though, you can control them in several useful ways.

Displaying a print queue

You can display information about the document that a printer is currently printing and about any other documents in a printer's print queue by following these steps:

1. **Go to the printer's host computer. Choose Start⇨Control Panel, and under the Hardware and Sound heading, click the Printer link.**

2. **Click the printer whose queue you want to display, and then click the See What's Printing button.**

   The Control Panel opens a printer queue window, as shown in Figure 4-8.

The jobs in the print queue are listed from the oldest at the top to the newest at the bottom. The Status column shows which job is printing.

You can close the Control Panel window and keep the print queue window open for later use. You can minimize the print queue window and keep it in the taskbar. That can be very handy if you're running a particularly long or complex print job — Word mail merges are particularly notorious for requiring close supervision.

If several users are printing documents to the same printer, Vista does not let them interfere with each other's work. Thus, you can control the documents that *you* placed in the queue; you cannot control other users' documents, nor can they control yours.

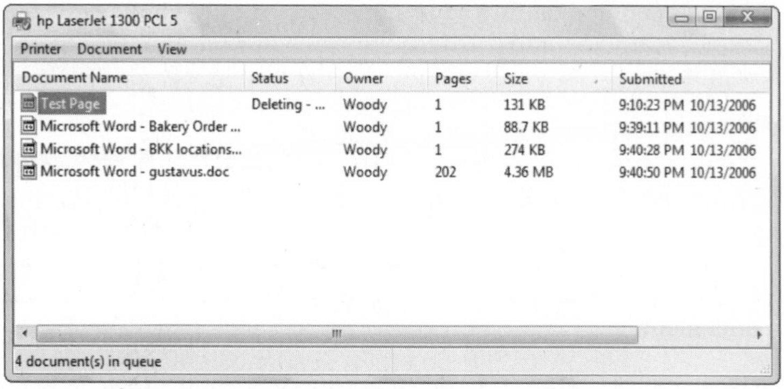

hp LaserJet 1300 PCL 5					
Printer Document View					
Document Name	Status	Owner	Pages	Size	Submitted
Test Page	Deleting - ...	Woody	1	131 KB	9:10:23 PM 10/13/2006
Microsoft Word - Bakery Order ...		Woody	1	88.7 KB	9:39:11 PM 10/13/2006
Microsoft Word - BKK locations...		Woody	1	274 KB	9:40:28 PM 10/13/2006
Microsoft Word - gustavus.doc		Woody	202	4.36 MB	9:40:50 PM 10/13/2006

4 document(s) in queue

Figure 4-8:
The printer queue lists all the documents to be printed.

Pausing and resuming a print queue

When you *pause* a print queue, Vista stops printing documents from that print queue. If a document is printing when you pause the queue, Vista tries to finish printing that document and then stops. When you *resume* a print queue, Vista starts printing documents from the queue again. Follow these guidelines to pause and resume a print queue:

✦ **To pause a print queue,** when you're looking at the print queue window, choose Printer⇨Pause Printing.

✦ **To resume the print queue,** choose the same command again. The Pause Printing command has a check mark next to it when the queue is paused.

Why would you want to pause the print queue? Say you want to print a page for later reference, but you don't want to bother turning your printer on to print just one page. Pause the printer's queue, and then print the page. The next time you turn the printer on, resume the queue, and the page prints.

Sometimes Windows has a hard time finishing the document — for example, you may be getting print buffer overruns (see the "Troubleshooting" section, later in this chapter), and every time you clear the printer, it may try to reprint the overrun pages. If that happens to you, pause the print queue and then turn off the printer. As soon as the printer comes back online, Windows is smart enough to pick up where it left off.

Also, depending on how your network is set up, you may or may not be able to pause and resume a print queue on a printer attached to another user's computer.

Pausing, restarting, and resuming a document

Why would you want to pause a document? Say you're printing a Web page that documents an online order you just placed and the printer jams. You've already finished entering the order, and you have no way to display the page again to reprint it. Pause the document, clear the printer, and restart the document.

Here's another common situation where pausing comes in handy. You're printing a long document and the phone rings. To make the printer be quiet while you talk, pause the document. When you're done talking, resume printing the document.

Here's how these three different actions work:

✦ **When you *pause a document,* Vista is prevented from printing that document.** Vista skips the document and prints later documents in the queue. If you pause a document while Vista is printing it, Vista halts in the middle of the document and prints nothing on that printer until you take further action.

✦ **When you *restart a document,* Vista is again allowed to print it.** If the document is at the top of the queue, Vista prints it as soon as it finishes the document that it is now printing. If the document was being printed when it was paused, Vista stops printing it and starts again at the beginning.

✦ **Resuming a document is meaningful only if you paused it while Vista was printing it.** When you *resume a document,* Vista resumes printing it where it paused.

To pause a document, right-click the document in the print queue and choose Pause. The window shows the document's status as Paused. To resume or restart the print document, right-click that document and choose Resume.

Canceling a document

When you *cancel a document,* Vista removes it from the print queue without printing it. You may have heard computer jocks use the term *purged* or *zapped* or something totally unprintable.

Here's a common situation when document canceling comes in handy. You start printing a long document, and as soon as the first page comes out, you realize that you forgot to set the heading. Cancel the document, change the heading, and print the document again.

To cancel a document, select that document. In the print queue window, choose Document⇨Cancel. Or, right-click the document in the print queue window and choose Cancel. You can also select the document and press Delete.

When a document is gone, it's gone. No Recycle Bin exists for the print queue.

Conversely, most printers have built-in memory that stores pages while they're being printed. You may go to the print queue looking for a document only to discover that it isn't there. (As I was walking up the stair / I met a doc that wasn't there . . .) If the document's already been shuffled off to the printer's internal memory, the only way to cancel it is to turn off the printer.

Troubleshooting

The following list gives some typical problems with printers and the solutions to those sticky spots:

✦ **I'm trying to install a printer. I connected it to my computer, and Vista doesn't detect its presence.**

Be sure that the printer is turned on and that the cable from the printer to your computer is properly connected at both ends. Check the printer's manual; you may have to follow a procedure (like push a button) to make the printer ready for use.

✦ **I'm trying to install a printer that's connected to another computer on my network, and Vista doesn't detect its presence. I know that the printer is okay; it's already installed and working as a local printer on that system!**

The printer may not be shared. See the section "Connecting a network printer," earlier in this chapter.

If the host PC reports that the printer is shared, look at the computers attached to your network by choosing Start⇨Network. If no computers show up, something is wrong with your network connection. If computers are shown but the printer's host is not among them, something is wrong with *its* network connection.

If the printer's host is visible on the network, you should be able to install the printer by typing in its name. The section "Connecting a network printer," earlier in this chapter, explains how to do this.

Finally, you may have disabled file and printer sharing on one of the PCs or both. See the tip at the end of the "Connecting a network printer" section for help.

✦ **I can't use a shared printer that I've used successfully in the past. Vista says it isn't available when I try to use it, or Vista doesn't even show it as an installed printer anymore.**

This can happen if something interferes with your connection to the network or the connection to the printer's host computer. It can also happen if something interferes with the availability of the printer — for example, if the host computer's user has turned off sharing.

If you can't find a problem, or if you find and correct a problem (such as file and printer sharing being turned off) but you still can't use the printer, try restarting Vista on your own system. If that doesn't help, remove the printer from your system and then reinstall it.

To remove the printer from your system, open the Control Panel's Printers list, right-click the printer, and choose Delete from the shortcut menu. Vista asks whether you're sure that you want to delete this printer. Click the Yes button.

To reinstall the printer on your system, use the same procedure that you used to install it originally. See the "Connecting a network printer" section, earlier in this chapter.

✦ **I printed a document, but it never came out of the printer.**

Check the printer's print queue, over on the host PC (the one directly attached to the printer). Is the document there? If not, investigate several possible reasons:

- The printer isn't turned on. In some cases, Vista can't distinguish a printer that is connected but not turned on from a printer that is ready, and it sends documents to a printer that isn't operating.

- You accidentally sent the document to some other printer.

- Some other user unintentionally picked up your document and walked off with it.

- The printer is turned on but not ready to print, and the printer (as opposed to the host PC) is holding your whole document in its internal memory until it can start printing. A printer can hold as much as several dozen pages of output internally, depending on the size of its internal memory and the complexity of the pages.

If your document is in the print queue but isn't printing, check the following:

- The printer may not be ready to print. See whether it is plugged in, turned on, and properly connected to your computer or its host computer.

- Your document may be paused.

- The print queue itself may be paused.

- The printer may be printing another document that is paused.

- The printer may be "thinking." If it is a laser printer or some other type of printer that composes an entire page in internal memory before it starts to print, it will appear to be doing nothing while it processes photographs or other complex graphics. Processing may take as long as several minutes.

  Look at the printer and study its manual. The printer may have a blinking light or a status display that tells you it is really doing something. As you become familiar with the printer, you get a feel for how long various types of jobs should take.

- On the other hand, the printer's status display may tell you that the printer is offline, out of paper, jammed, or unready to print for some other reason.

✦ **I tried to print a complex document, and only part of it came out. I got an error message that said something like "Printer Overrun," either on the last printed page or on the printer's status display.**

This can happen with laser printers and other printers that compose a whole page at a time in internal memory. The error occurs if a page is too complex for the amount of memory in the printer.

The following procedure corrects the problem in most cases, although details may vary with the type of printer you use:

1. **Press the printer's Reset control, or turn the printer off and then back on.**

2. **In Vista, open the printer's Properties dialog box and click the Device Settings tab.**

3. **Look for a property named Page Protection. Its setting should be Off for this problem to have occurred.**

4. **Click the Page Protection property to turn it on.**

With page protection turned on, the printer assembles each page in the printer's memory before printing it. With page protection turned off, the printer can start printing a page and get halfway through before discovering that it doesn't have enough memory to print the whole page. It happens, from time to time, with complex graphics, especially on older printers.

Book VII

Joining the Multimedia Mix

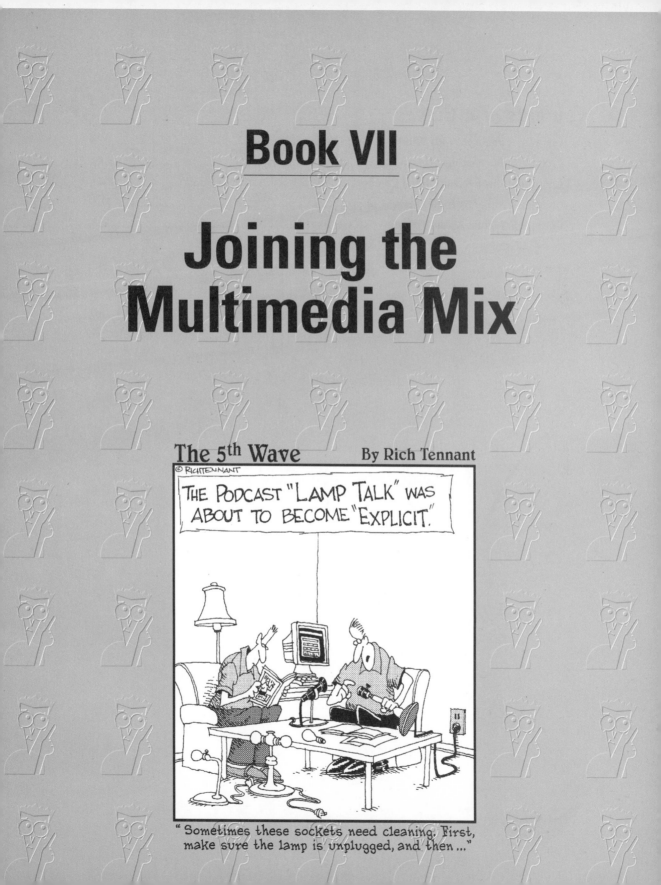

The 5th Wave   By Rich Tennant

THE PODCAST "LAMP TALK" WAS ABOUT TO BECOME "EXPLICIT."

"Sometimes these sockets need cleaning. First, make sure the lamp is unplugged, and then ..."

Contents at a Glance

Chapter 1: Jammin' with Windows Media Player...513

Chapter 2: Podcasting 553

Chapter 3: Discovering Digital Cameras 563

Chapter 4: Mugging in the Photo Gallery 581

Chapter 5: Lights! Action! Windows Movie Maker 595

Chapter 1: Jammin' with Windows Media Player

In This Chapter

✔ Understanding C.R.A.P. music and video formats

✔ Getting the latest version of Windows Media Player

✔ Copying music from a CD

✔ Finding the Media Library: Where your music is kept

✔ Copying music to a CD or digital player

✔ Customizing Media Player

*W*indows Media Player (WMP) is da *MAN*. Er, uh. Wait a sec. Let me start over. WMP *sucks*. No, that's not what I meant. Hold on. I have this loud thud coming from my speakers, the Water Ambience visualization looks like smoke in Godzilla's eye, and Trent Reznor is screaming "You can't take it away from me." Lemme turn the volume down. There. Yeah. That's better.

What I meant to say is that Windows Media Player *sucks you in* from the moment you start it. As Vista's built-in boom box, it plays CDs, of course, but it also lets you play, organize, and generally enjoy almost any kind of music and most videos stored on your computer, whether the tunes or vids came from CDs, an online store, the Internet, or that smelly guy with a big baseball cap at the flea market.

But wait! Before you buy more music or videos online, there's something you need to know: the industry's dirty little secret. Much of the music and videos you can buy online today are protected by Digital Rights Managerment (DRM), although some more-enlightened companies have started selling music and videos without onerous restrictions. If you buy DRM-hobbled media, the companies that pull the strings can dictate not only how and when you listen to the music (or view the videos), but they can also change the rules, retroactively, after you've paid for the music, and you can't do a thing about it. The solution? Demand unprotected movies and videos (MP3s and MPVs, for example), or rip them yourself. The next section of this chapter goes into more details.

What You Need to Know about C.R.A.P.

Digital Rights Management doesn't add any value for the artist, label (who are selling DRM-free music every day — the Compact Disc), or consumer; the only people it adds value to are the technology companies who are interested in locking consumers to a particular technology platform.

— Ian Rogers, Yahoo! Music Blog

ZDNet Executive Editor David Berlind calls it C.R.A.P. — Content Restriction, Annulment, and Protection (`http://blogs.zdnet.com/BTL/?p=2428`). You may know it by the politically correct *Digital Rights Management.* By whatever name, you're the one getting nailed. Don't buy C.R.A.P.

In the big-time audio arena, C.R.A.P. music comes in two versions: Apple's Advanced Audio Coding (AAC) with FairPlay encryption (`.m4a` file extensions) and Microsoft's Windows Media Audio (WMA) format (`.wma` files). On the video side of the fence, Apple's FairPlay (`.m4v`) and Microsoft's Windows Media Video (WMV) (`.wmv`) files frequently contain digital rights restrictions. In other words, if you paid for an `.m4a`, `.wma`, `.m4v`, or `.wmv` file, you may not have control over how the file is used. CRAPpy, eh?

Music comes in many different *formats* — think of them as different methods for converting sound into bits. The formats are all different, and translating a song from one format to another can really put a crimp on the quality of the recording.

Back in the dark ages, if you wanted to record music on a computer, you used the MP3 format. It wasn't (and isn't) the fanciest format on the street; it makes files that are bigger than they need to be, and it doesn't support some really cool capabilities found with newer formats (such as Dolby-style 5.1 or 7.1 channel recording). With all its shortcomings, MP3 took off and became the universal language of digital music. If you have something that plays digital music — whether it's an old PC, an ancient portable audio player (there's a reason why they're called "MP3 players"), a 200GB iPod, or a Galactic Zune — it'll understand MP3.

WMA (for audio files) and WMV (for video files) are proprietary formats: Microsoft owns them, lock, stock, and digital barrel. Microsoft wants you to use the WMA format. It wants to see WMA supplant MP3 as the audio file format of choice for all computer users, everywhere. Microsoft has plenty of reasons why it wants to control the format of digital media — and almost all of them are spelled with dollar ign.

Similarly, Apple wants you to buy music that can play only on an iPod. As of this writing, most of the items for sale at the iTunes Music Store can only play on a computer running Apple's QuickTime, or on an iPod. That's it. If you buy Apple's C.R.A.P. music or videos, you're locked in to Apple's hardware and software.

Worse yet, the restrictions on using C.R.A.P. music or video can change — *unilaterally.* With no notification to you or anybody else. No consent required. No consent requested. If Apple suddenly decides tomorrow that you should only be able to "burn" a list of songs onto a CD three times, the magic of C.R.A.P., er, DRM, allows Apple to reach into your computer and make that restriction come true. It's scary.

Everybody and his brother have tried to introduce a format that's better than MP3, and almost all of them have succeeded, technically. But none of them have even approached MP3's colossal share of the market and minds of the world's music consumers — until Microsoft and Apple launched their C.R.A.P. formats.

Long the stalwart of MP3 truth and C.R.A.P.-free light, eMusic (www.emusic.com) still offers unencumbered, unencumberable MP3s. In late 2007, Amazon jumped on the, uh, bandwagon and started peddling MP3s from most of the major music labels. Apple then dipped its toe in the water, offering some songs without DRM restrictions. (Steve Jobs published a fascinating analysis of the situation in February, 2007; see it at www.apple.com/hotnews/thoughtsonmusic.) Clearly, C.R.A.P. music is on the decline. Don't get sucked into supporting a dinosaur.

Adjusting WMP Privacy Settings

If you haven't specifically gone fishing for the latest version of Windows Media Player (affectionately known as *WiMP* to its fans), you should take a

---

Got the URGE?

Microsoft and MTV teamed up to create URGE, the online music store that's supposed to compete with Apple's iTunes. It's easy to buy music from URGE — you don't even need to leave Windows Media Player. But before you buy any music from URGE, make sure that you understand the C.R.A.P., er, the Digital Rights Management restrictions that apply:

"We . . . are permitted to transmit and arrange for automatic installation of any and all updates, modifications, and/or even full re-installations of the Software to address security, digital

rights management, interoperability, and/or performance issues . . . The Software . . . [can] automatically identify your computer . . . and manage some or all of the digital rights associated with Content . . . Re-installations and other modifications to the Software can occur periodically or when necessary and without any notice to you."

That's what the URGE license agreement says. (Or, at least, said. Heaven knows how it's been changed by now.) Are you sure you want to buy anything from URGE?

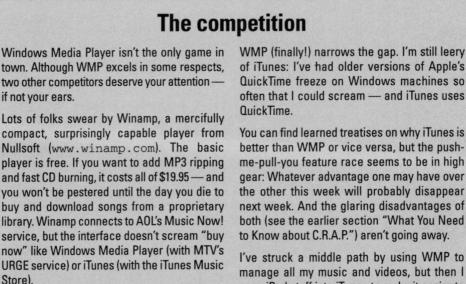

The competition

Windows Media Player isn't the only game in town. Although WMP excels in some respects, two other competitors deserve your attention — if not your ears.

Lots of folks swear by Winamp, a mercifully compact, surprisingly capable player from Nullsoft (www.winamp.com). The basic player is free. If you want to add MP3 ripping and fast CD burning, it costs all of $19.95 — and you won't be pestered until the day you die to buy and download songs from a proprietary library. Winamp connects to AOL's Music Now! service, but the interface doesn't scream "buy now" like Windows Media Player (with MTV's URGE service) or iTunes (with the iTunes Music Store).

Apple's iTunes once ruled the roost in the music-playing biz, but the latest version of WMP (finally!) narrows the gap. I'm still leery of iTunes: I've had older versions of Apple's QuickTime freeze on Windows machines so often that I could scream — and iTunes uses QuickTime.

You can find learned treatises on why iTunes is better than WMP or vice versa, but the push-me-pull-you feature race seems to be in high gear: Whatever advantage one may have over the other this week will probably disappear next week. And the glaring disadvantages of both (see the earlier section "What You Need to Know about C.R.A.P.") aren't going away.

I've struck a middle path by using WMP to manage all my music and videos, but then I copy iPod stuff into iTunes to make it easier to manage the 'Pod. I tell you all about it in Book VI, Chapter 2.

look and see what Microsoft has available. Drop by www.microsoft.com/windows/windowsmedia and make sure that you have the latest and greatest.

The download is free — you already paid for Windows Media Player when you bought Vista. More to the point, Microsoft keeps adding new "features" to WiMP that try to sell you something, so the upgrades come frequently and invariably at no charge. If you find a newer version of WMP, download the file and run it.

Setting options when you install WMP

If you haven't run WMP yet, here's how to get off on the right foot:

1. **Choose Start⇨Windows Media Player or Start⇨All Programs⇨Windows Media Player.**

   The installer appears.

2. **Click the Custom Settings button, and then click the Next button.**

   WMP shows you the Select Privacy Options dialog box shown in Figure 1-1.

3. **Select or deselect the various check boxes, depending on your preferences.**

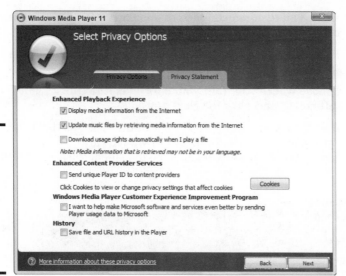

Figure 1-1:
Given
WMP's
checkered
past, it's a
good idea
to limit its
snooping
abilities.

Microsoft has a long, tumultuous history of using Windows Media Player to gather all sorts of personal information about you and your media-playing habits. Approach this dialog box with skepticism. I only select the Display Media Information from the Internet and the Update Music Files by Retrieving Media Information from the Internet check boxes. You may want to send Microsoft more, but unless you have an over-whelming reason to do so, I suggest you limit your exposure. Of course, if you opt to Display Media Information from the Internet, Microsoft keeps tabs on you, too. Guess it all boils down to a question of how much privacy you're willing to give up to get the cool features like auto-matically downloaded album covers and correct song titles.

If you select the Download Usage Rights Automatically When I Play a File check box, each time that you try to play or sync a protected file (typi-cally a song in Microsoft's proprietary WMA format or a video in WMV format) on your computer, if the rights have expired, Windows Media Player will go out to the company that owns the copyright on the file and ask for a license. (See the section "What You Need to Know about C.R.A.P.," earlier in this chapter, for details.) In other words, if you try to play a protected WMA file that you don't have rights to play, Microsoft and the copyright holder are notified. Part of the notification includes a number that identifies your computer uniquely and your IP address, which may or may not identify your location uniquely. You usually end up on a Web page that asks you to buy something. Bah. Humbug. Turn this option off so that WMP asks for your permission before it goes out to retrieve rights information. That way you'll know in advance that you're trying to play C.R.A.P. music, before Windows Media Player phones home.

4. **When you're comfortable with your privacy choices, click the Next button.**

   The WMP installer asks whether you want shortcuts on the desktop and/or Quick Launch toolbar.

5. **Choose where you want your shortcuts (the Quick Launch toolbar is sufficient), and click the Next button.**

   WMP then asks whether you want it to be used as the default music and video player (see Figure 1-2). I use WMP as my default player, but you may prefer iTunes or Winamp (see the sidebar "The competition").

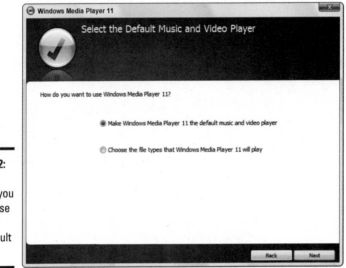

Figure 1-2: Consider whether you want to use WMP as your default player.

6. **Choose whether you want WMP to be your default player, and click the Next button.**

   WMP asks whether you want to set up MTV's URGE music shop so that you can buy C.R.A.P. music easily from Microsoft's preferred partner.

7. **Select the Whasammatayounuts? er, Don't Set Up a Store Now option, and click the Finish button.**

   WMP springs to life with some free sample music (in protected WMA format, of course) in the Library, as shown in Figure 1-3. WMP immediately begins scanning your Music folder, adding songs as it bumps into them. Note that URGE is listed on the main toolbar, but as long as you don't do anything to bring the beast to life, it's effectively disabled.

Figure 1-3:
WMP immediately begins scanning your Music folder for songs.

No doubt you're wondering why WMP needs to scan your computer to set up the Media Library — after all, Windows Media Player is part of Windows, and Windows should know which songs and videos are already on your hard drive, right? Well, no. Although WMP tries to convince you otherwise, the Media Library isn't a separate place on your hard drive where the media files are stored. In fact, the Library is an ad hoc catalog of media files that may reside anywhere on any hard drive. The Media Library may or may not accurately reflect which files are actually on the hard drive at any given moment. See the section "Organizing Your Library," later in this chapter, for details.

The sample music provided by WMP sits in your `\Public\Public Music\ Sample Music` folder.

Tweaking options after installation

If you've already installed WMP, or the latest version came preinstalled on your PC, take a moment now to turn the $#@! Acquire Licenses setting off. Follow these steps to do so:

1. **Start Windows Media Player.**

2. **Press Alt to bring up the main menu (bet you wondered where it was hidden), and then choose Tools⇨Options and click the Privacy tab (see Figure 1-4).**

3. **Deselect the Download Usage Rights Automatically When I Play or Sync a File check box.**

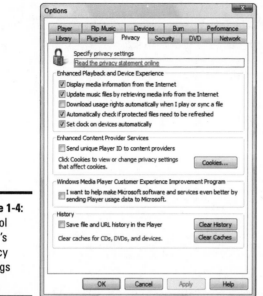

Figure 1-4:
Control
WMP's
privacy
settings
here.

You might be wondering about the Automatically Check if Protected Files Need to Be Refreshed and the Set Clock on Devices Automatically check boxes. Both of those are related to subscription services — where you pay by the month for the ability to play music (or video) files. The first check box tells WMP that it should check to see whether you've paid for your subscription before the right to play the music expires. The second check box tells WMP that it should set the secure clock on MP3 players as soon as they're attached to your PC — an important step in verifying that you've paid your subscription fee and can continue to play the music you're renting, you scofflaw.

If you rent your music, you probably want to select both of those check boxes. If you don't, the boxes don't mean anything.

4. **Click the OK button.**

   Your changes take effect immediately — although, if you didn't make the changes soon enough, Microsoft may already have your unique player ID on file.

If you have questions about the other tabs in the Options dialog box, see the section "Customizing WMP," later in this chapter.

Playing with Now Playing

To start Windows Media Player, choose Start⇨All Programs⇨Windows Media Player. If you told the WMP installer to put an icon on the Quick Launch toolbar, it's much easier to start WMP from there.

You control Windows Media Player with the row of buttons that runs across the top of the window. Although you can't see them until you hover your mouse in the right place, each button has a down arrow that displays multiple options.

Click the Now Playing button, and you see something like Figure 1-5.

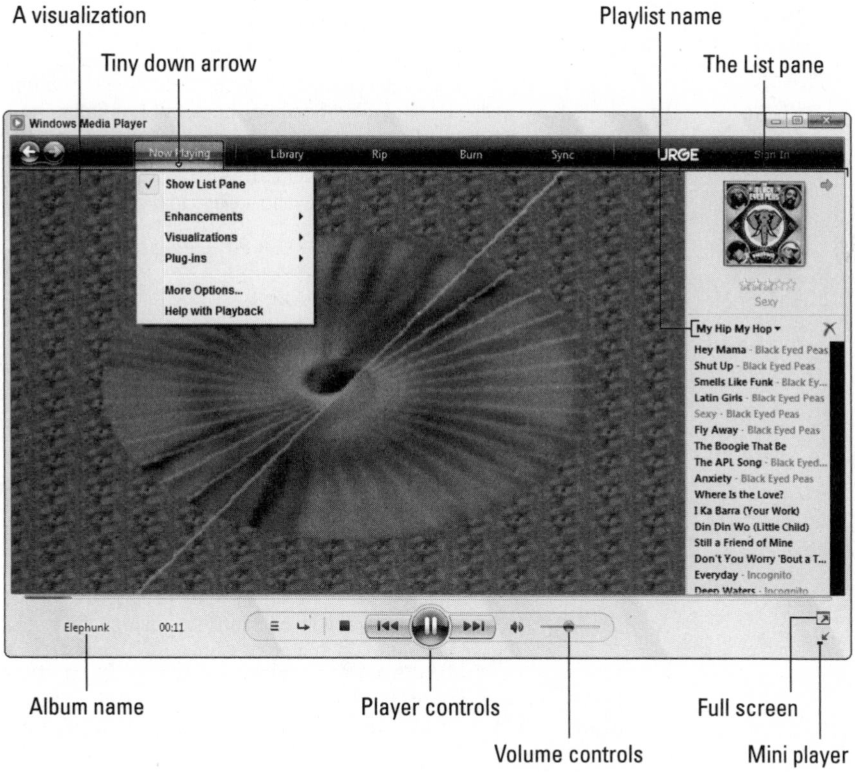

A visualization

Tiny down arrow

Playlist name

The List pane

Figure 1-5:
The Now
Playing
view, with
options
connected
to that tiny
down arrow.

Book VII
Chapter 1

Jammin' with
Windows
Media Player

Album name

Player controls

Volume controls

Full screen

Mini player

The right side of the Now Playing window displays a *playlist,* which is just a sequence of tracks. You can create your own playlists or rely on the ones built into WMP. The Now Playing playlist, for example, is the list of tracks that are currently queued up to play, one after the other. To play a different track from the current playlist, double-click the track down in the list of playlist contents.

Playback buttons

The buttons along the bottom of the window control the Now Playing screen. As shown in Table 1-1, they are very similar to the buttons on a conventional CD player.

Table 1-1	Playback Buttons for Windows Media Player
Button	*What It Does*
	The Pause button pauses the playing. When playing is paused, the Pause button toggles to a Play button. Click it again to make playing resume.
	The Stop button stops the playing. Click the Play button to start playing again. Unlike Pause/Resume, the Stop/Start button returns to the start of the track. To start a different track, double-click that track in the playlist.
	The Previous Track button skips to the start of the previous track. From the first track in the playlist, it skips to the beginning of the last track on the playlist.
	The Next Track button skips to the start of the next track. From the last track in the playlist, it skips to the first.
	The Mute button silences the sound. Click the button again to restore the sound. Unlike the Pause button, the Mute button does not halt playing. If you mute the sound for ten seconds, you miss hearing ten seconds of the track. If you mute Eminem for ten seconds, you get unwrapped (hardy har har).
	The little slider to the right of the buttons controls the volume.
	The skinny slider above the buttons shows WMP's position in the current track. As the track progresses from beginning to end, the slider moves from the left to the right. While WMP is playing a track, you can shift it to any point in the track by clicking that point on the track or by dragging the slider control to that point.

That's about all you need to know to play music from a playlist. Rocket science.

Playing a CD

Want to play a CD? That's hard, too. Here's how:

1. Take the CD out of its plastic case, if it's in one.

2. **Wipe the pizza stains off the shiny side (don't worry about the other side).**

3. **Stick the CD in the PC's drive and close it.**

4. **If Windows asks whether you want to Play Audio CD Using Windows Media Player (see Figure 1-6), click the No, I'd Rather Clip My Toenails What Did You Think I Wanted to Do? button and then click the OK button.**

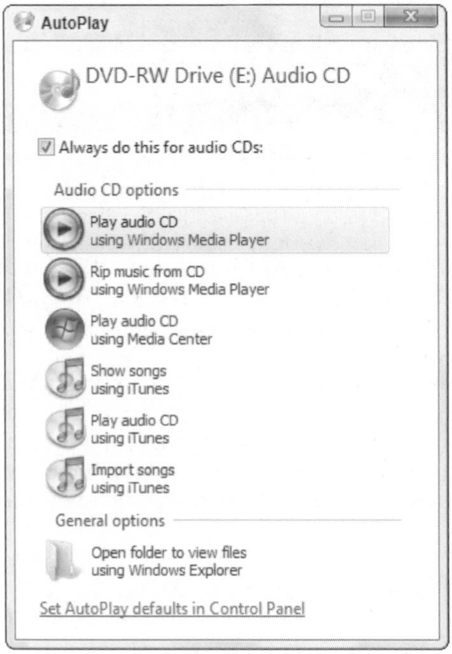

Figure 1-6:
Vista asks whether you want to play the CD you just inserted into your CD drive. Yes, you probably do.

If WMP isn't running already, it starts all by itself. Then you wait a few seconds, and WMP starts playing the first track, using the Now Playing window, showing you the last visualization you chose. If the album is in Microsoft's big database in the sky, album info appears magically in the Now Playing screen, as shown in Figure 1-7.

You can use the control buttons the same way for a CD as you do for a playlist — to pause and resume playing, select different tracks, and so on.

To WMP, the CD *is* a playlist. The tracks on the CD appear in the playlist area on the right side of the window. Look at the drop-down list of playlists in the upper-right corner of the window; the name of the CD appears as the selected item.

Figure 1-7:
WMP
correctly
identifies
the album.
Man, I'm
impressed.

How does WMP know what's on the CD? After it identifies the CD from infor-mation encoded along with the recorded tracks, it gets the CD's description and track titles through the Web, from a database maintained for that purpose.

If a CD is quite obscure — or really good — it may not be in Microsoft's data-base. Then WMP can display only the information it finds on the CD itself: the number of tracks and the playtime of each track. If a CD isn't in Micro-soft's database, you can enter the names of the songs manually. (To do so, right-click any song and choose Edit, and then type in a new name.)

Copying from a CD (Also Known as Ripping)

Before you copy music from a CD onto your computer, take a few minutes to find out more about MP3 and the reason why you don't want to add to the world's accumulation of C.R.A.P. music. See the section "What You Need to Know about C.R.A.P.," earlier in this chapter.

Here's how to *rip* a CD — that is, convert the audio tracks on the CD into files that your computer can work with:

1. **Put the audio CD that you want to copy into the CD drive.**

Vista may ask whether you want to play the CD or whether you want to rip it (see Figure 1-6). *Don't click the Rip Music from CD Using Windows Media Player icon.* That starts the ripper without giving you a chance to choose your settings. Instead, choose to play the CD using Windows Media Player.

2. **Click the tiny down arrow below the Rip button at the top of the WMP screen.**

   WMP brings up a list of options, as shown in Figure 1-8.

Figure 1-8:
Make sure
that you tell
WMP to rip
in MP3
format.

3. **Choose Format and select MP3 from the submenu that appears.**

   That ensures that WMP will rip into the unprotected MP3 format. This is a "sticky" setting, so you should only have to choose it once.

4. **Click the Rip button.**

   WMP lists all the tracks on the CD, as shown in Figure 1-9.

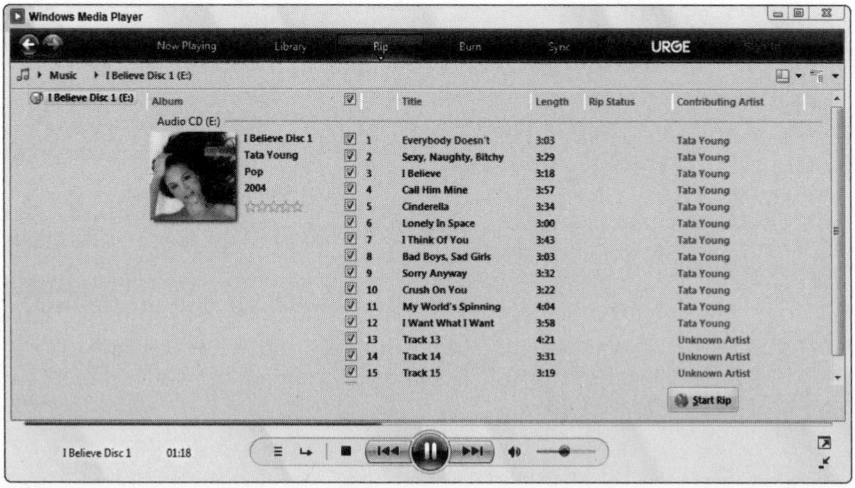

Figure 1-9:
The Rip list.

5. **If some of the information is missing (see, for example, Track 13 in Figure 1-9), right-click the missing piece and choose Find Album Info.**

   WMP goes out to www.windowsmedia.com (or your music vendor of choice) and tries to retrieve the missing information. Unfortunately, www.windowsmedia.com doesn't always have the missing information — as is the case with the missing tracks in Tata Young's album, shown in Figure 1-9.

   If you know the names of missing tracks, you can help fill in the gaps in Microsoft's database by following the indicated steps to add new data to the database. That way, you'll not only help other people who may be looking for the song info, but you'll also automatically have your Windows Media Player entries updated.

6. **To rip all the tracks (er, copy all the songs) on the CD, you don't need to do anything. But if you want to choose specific songs to copy, select the check boxes to the left of each track that you want to copy and deselect the check boxes next to the ones you want to leave behind.**

   In Figure 1-10, I decide to copy all of Tata Young's *I Believe* album. Great stuff.

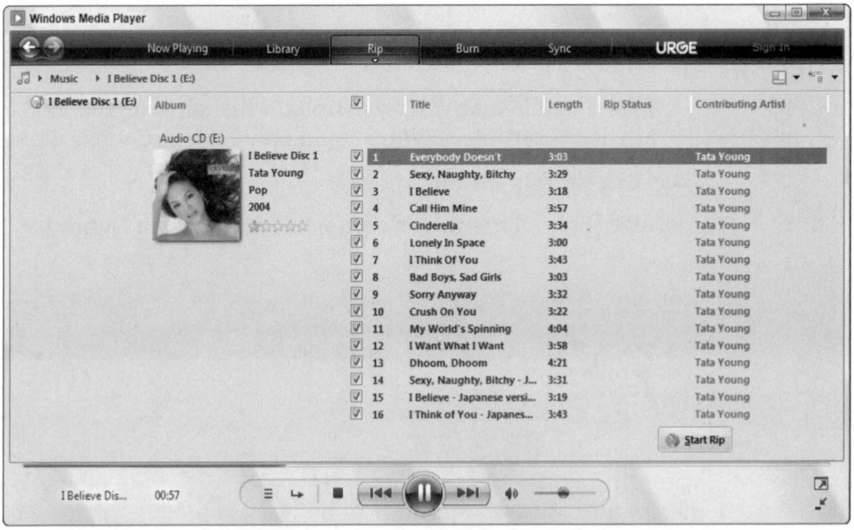

Figure 1-10: All the information is filled in, ready to rip.

7. **Click the Start Rip button, at the bottom of the rip list.**

   Windows Media Player dutifully copies the tracks you've selected, placing the "ripped" files in the default folder, which is most likely your Music folder.

WMP makes a folder for each artist, and inside the artist's folder, it makes a subfolder for each album. The music tracks go into the album's folder. If you're connected to the Internet, WMP grabs all the associated album information — track titles, album cover art, and artist — and sticks it in the folder along with the music. Very sweet.

8. **Copying can take a while, so sit back and listen to the music or go grab a latte or two.**

   When WMP is done, all the tracks will be marked Ripped to Library, as shown in Figure 1-11.

Figure 1-11:
All the tracks have been converted to MP3 files and placed in the Music folder.

Your newly ripped album appears in Windows Media Player's Library list.

Organizing Your Library

WMP uses its Library to organize soundtracks, videos, TV shows, and so on. When you understand how the WMP Library works, you can organize your music just the way you want.

Where the Library comes from

It's easy to get confused about the relationship among tracks — files on your computer — the Windows Media Player Library, and playlists. Here's my favorite analogy, with books and brick-and-mortar (or concrete and steel) libraries. I'm kinda partial to books, ya know.

Book VII
Chapter 1

Jammin' with
Windows
Media Player

Say that a track or video is roughly analogous to a book. Your computer is like a brick-and-mortar library. A big library. Windows Media Player's Library corresponds to the library's card catalog — although now it's likely stored in a database instead of on cards. Each playlist is like a special-purpose card catalog.

If you keep that analogy in mind, it's easy to understand the following points:

✦ When the world's perfect, every track (audio, video, or TV recording) on your computer (or network) is in Windows Media Player's Library, and every track in the WMP Library and every track in every playlist is on your computer (or network). But the best laid plans o' mice 'n' men gang aft agley . . . .

✦ You might have a track on your computer that isn't in Windows Media Player's Library. (That's analogous to the situation where you have a book in the library that isn't in the card catalog.)

✦ You can remove a track from the WMP Library without taking it off your computer. (In the analogy, you can yank a card out of the catalog without pulling the book out of the library.)

✦ You can have entries in the WMP Library that refer to tracks that have been deleted or aren't available because, for example, they may refer to a folder that's offline. (Analogously, you can have a card in the card catalog that refers to a book that's been checked out — or chucked out.)

✦ Surprisingly, you can also have tracks in a playlist that aren't in WMP's Library. (Analogously, you can have a card in a special-purpose card catalog that refers to a book in the library — but the book doesn't have a card in the main catalog.)

Windows Media Player does a credibly good job of keeping everything in sync by continuously scanning specific folders on your computer (and possibly on your network) to see what's been added or deleted. You have control over which folders feed the WMP Library. To see what's being tracked, follow these steps:

1. **In Windows Media Player, click the tiny down arrow under Library.**

2. **Choose Add to Library, and then click the Advanced Options button.**

WMP opens the Add to Library dialog box and shows you the advanced options at the bottom, as shown in Figure 1-12.

Don't trust the radio buttons at the top: They're very simplistic and not very accurate. Instead, look at the list of Monitored Folders. If you know of a folder that you would like to monitor, click the Add button and add it to the list.

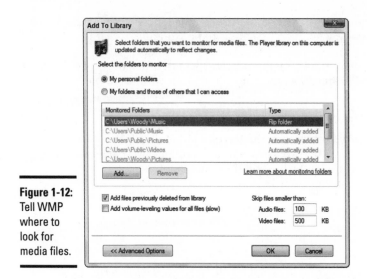

Figure 1-12:
Tell WMP
where to
look for
media files.

Be aware of the fact that it can take a long, long time to scan a folder that contains a lot of media.

3. **Make sure that the Add Files Previously Deleted from Library check box is selected.**

4. **Click the OK button and, if you added a folder with a lot of music or videos, go out for lunch.**

When you come back, Windows Media Player's Library should be rebuilt, leaving the dialog box shown in Figure 1-13.

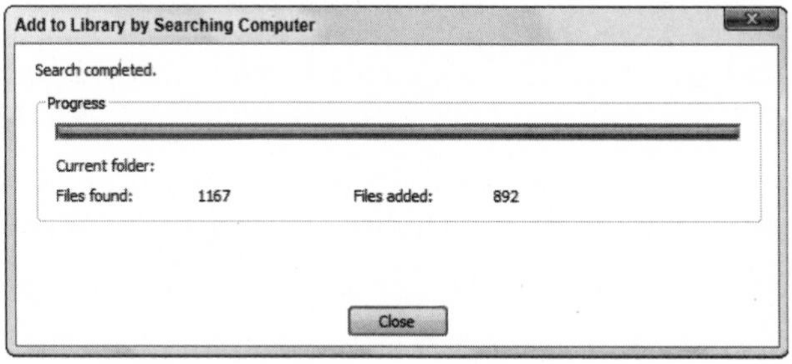

Figure 1-13:
Scanning a
lot of media
files can
take quite
a while.

5. **Click the Close button, and Windows Media Player comes back, good as new.**

Note that when you add a file or a Web site to the Library, you're not storing a copy of the sound recording in the Library; you're just storing a *reference* to it. When you play the recording through the Library, WMP actually plays the original copy, wherever it happens to be stored.

If you add a file to the Library and later delete or move the original file, the entry for the file still appears in the Library, but WMP can't play the file.

Leafing through the WMP Library

Click the Library button up at the top of WMP to display Windows Media Player's Library. WMP displays a window split into two panes, with the Library's structure on the left and the contents of the selected item on the right, as shown in Figure 1-14.

Choose a new category by clicking here

Figure 1-14: My WMP Library (or at least a small part of it).

The Library is organized into folders, just like the Vista file system. Unlike the file system, the Library has a fixed set of categories. You can choose from among the categories by clicking the right-facing arrow next to the musical note. Here's the rundown of categories you'll find:

✦ **Music:** Contains all the audio tracks that are in the WMP Library, such as those you have ripped from CDs. You can get at audio tracks by artist, composer, album, genre (rock, classical, comedy, folk, jazz, dance, Cajun, and so on), year released, the star rating that you've assigned to individual tracks, or the parental rating. A, uh, special place is also available for music that you've bought using WMP's connection to URGE or other online stores.

An album is "in" the Media Library if you have copied at least one track from that album with the Copy from CD operation, or if you have dragged a folder containing music into the Music folder.

+ **Pictures:** Contains various kinds of image files that happen to be located in folders scanned by WMP. You will undoubtedly find it much easier to manage pictures using Windows Photo Gallery, which I discuss in Book VII, Chapter 4.

+ **Video:** Contains video recordings, discussed in Book VII, Chapter 5. WMP can play video files in almost any format, including MPG, AVI, ASF, WMV, and many others — but not the Apple protected M4V format.

+ **Recorded TV:** Includes all TV shows that you've recorded using Windows Media Center Edition, as Book VIII, Chapter 3 explains. Shows are listed by title, series, genre, date recorded, actors, or your star ratings.

Windows Media Center Edition uses a weird file format called DVR-MS for recorded television programs (so-called `.dvr-ms` files). As of this writing, several companies are trying to crack the format and/or make "official" translators that change DVR-MS files into other kinds of files that the rest of the computer industry can work with. Until that happens, the only programs that can play your DVR-MS files are Windows Media Player and Windows Media Center (which actually uses WMP to do the playing), and the Windows Movie Maker — which can actually translate DVR-MS files into WMVs, which are a fraction of the size. See Book VII, Chapter 5 for details.

+ **Other Media:** This is a catch-all for future media types.

Finding the tracks you want

Windows Media Player's Library folders are powerful tools for keeping your recordings organized because they offer so many different ways of looking at the same information.

It behooves you to keep your data clean. Misfiled and misidentified songs lead to endless frustration when you can't find a song that you know should be in the Library. If you want to change the data associated with a bunch of songs (say, for example, the songs are all by the same artist or on the same album), follow these steps:

1. **Find them in the Library, and get the Library to list the individual songs. (Typically you can do that by double-clicking an album or by choosing Recently Added, Songs, or Genre from the Library list on left; refer to Figure 1-14.)**

2. **Select the songs (Ctrl+click to select individual songs or Shift+click to select a group of songs).**

3. **Right-click one of fields (for example, the Album or the Artist) and choose Edit.**

4. **Type in the new value and press Enter, and all the selected songs are changed at the same time.**

WMP also provides a tool to edit data that works on one song at a time (see Figure 1-15). It's slow, but it works. To use it, right-click a misidentified track and choose Advanced Tag Editor.

Figure 1-15:
Windows
Media
Player's tool
for editing
"Tag"
information
is rudimen-
tary but it
works.

Rating songs

One of WMP's most powerful capabilities, the ability to create and manipulate playlists based on your own ratings of individual songs (or movies or TV shows), only works if you take the time to rate your songs! To rate any track or album at any time, right-click it, choose Rate, and give it a rating from 1 to 5 stars. You can even select multiple tracks or albums and rate them all in one fell swoop.

Sorting

You can sort all the albums or tracks on the right of the WMP screen. For example, bring up the Music category (at the upper left) and double-click Artist (under Library on the left) to display an alphabetized list all of the albums in your Library, sorted by artist name. Now click the Rating column and the list gets shuffled, displaying your highest-rated albums first.

If you have WMP show you albums, instead of individual songs, the really cool rating system doesn't work as well. When WMP rates an album, it uses the average rating of all the songs in the album. So if you have an absolutely great song inside a rather dull album, if you sort the albums by rating, you might not even get around to that really great song. The only solution? Lie. Rate all of the songs in the album as five-star. That way the album floats to the top of the charts.

You have a great deal of flexibility in the ways you can sort. If you want to look at all your Rap & Hip Hop albums, for example, make sure that you're looking at the Music category (at the upper left) and then double-click Album to list all your albums by album name. Now click the top of the Genre column to sort the list of tracks by genre (see Figure 1-16), going from A to Z. Click Genre again to sort the list backward.

Figure 1-16: Sorting by genre can help you see your collection differently.

Book VII
Chapter 1

Jammin' with
Windows
Media Player

If your collection of recordings is large, sorting the list in different ways can help you find items you want. Microsoft claims that Windows Media Player can handle tens of thousands — even hundreds of thousands — of tracks. Go ahead. Put it to the test.

Searching

You can search the Windows Media Player Library for items that have certain words in their titles or for artist names, album names, composer names, conductor, date, or genres. When your collection of recordings becomes too large to inspect easily, this is a convenient way to find things in it.

Searching the WMP Library is much like searching in Windows Explorer — no doubt because they use the same search engine. To find what you want, simply start typing in the Search box, in the upper-right part of the screen. WMP responds immediately, narrowing its list of found items as you type. In Figure 1-17, my search for **guil** brought up Billie Holiday's song *Guilty,* as I would expect, but also Avril Lavigne's *Tomorrow.* Why? Because one of the composers of *Tomorrow* is Guillermo Breer.

Figure 1-17: Searches look for titles, artist names, album names, genres, composers, and other ancillary "meta" information.

Depending on where you perform the search, WMP may display a list of how many artists, albums, or songs match the search criteria. In that case, simply click the underlined link to view the results.

If you're looking for the same kind of advanced searching — saved searches and the like — that exist in Vista's Windows Explorer, forget about it. WMP isn't that smart. You can use AND, OR, and NOT in the Search box, though: a search on `"Willie Nelson"` AND `Minuet` brings up Willie's *Bach Minuet in G* from his album *The Promiseland.* No, I'm not kidding.

Playing tracks in the Library

You can play a track directly from the Library. Just select the track and click the Play button at the bottom of the WMP window — or double-click the track and WMP cuts straight to it.

You can even play a group of tracks by selecting the group. To play all the songs by a given artist, for example, double-click Artist on the left, click to select the stack of albums performed by your chosen artist, and click the Play button.

Nailing Track 6, Unknown Artist, Unknown Album

You probably already know that if you rip a CD while your PC isn't connected to the Internet, the Windows Media Web site may not be able to provide the track name, artist, and so on. In that case, the Media Library lists the track number as the track name and shows the artist, album, and genre as "Unknown" (see Figure 1-18). Blech.

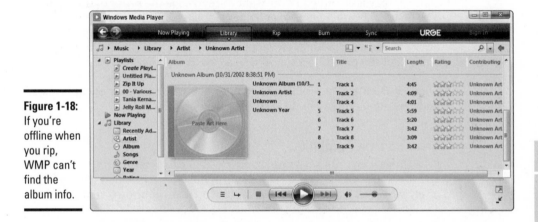

Figure 1-18: If you're offline when you rip, WMP can't find the album info.

Book VII Chapter 1

Jammin' with Windows Media Player

Although many CDs these days include album cover art and other identifying information, Windows Media Player may or may not be able to pick up that information when it's ripping — and if you have an Internet connection that's, uh, less than 100 percent reliable, you may soon find yourself with a bunch of songs that claim to be "Track 6, Unknown Artist, Unknown Album." Fortunately, with WMP, if you can connect to the Internet, you can probably retrieve the information — unless you have a very obscure CD that isn't in the WMP database.

Follow these steps to retrieve data for an "Unknown" album:

1. **Make sure that you're connected to the Internet, and then start Windows Media Player.**

2. **Find the album in the Library.**

   Hint: It's listed among the albums under "U" for "Unknown."

3. **Right-click the album, and choose Update Album Info.**

WMP runs out to Microsoft's Web site (or your chosen music vendor's Web site) and retrieves the album information, if it can find the info.

4. **If WMP found the correct album, click the Finish button.**

WMP automatically updates the file information, replaces any information stored in the Media Library, and generally repairs all the broken pieces, without any further instruction.

Managing playlists

Er, maybe that should be *mangling* playlists.

WMP gives you all sorts of control over which songs you hear, and it does so through playlists. Did you ever want to rearrange the order of the songs on The Beatles' *White Album?* My son just about croaked when he found out he could burn a CD that plays Britney Spears' "Oops! . . . I Did It Again" immediately after Eminem's homage "Oops! . . . The Real Slim Shady Did It Again." You've got the power. Hmmm. That's a catchy tag line, isn't it?

Windows Media Player's Library enables you to create your own playlists, and you can modify them to your heart's content.

Creating a new playlist

If you have a favorite set of tracks that you like to hear in a particular order, and the tracks are in the Library, you can build a playlist that gives you precisely what you want. It's like being able to create your own custom CD.

In fact, you can use a playlist to *make* your own custom CD, if you have a CD burner (er, recorder). Nothing to it. The section "Burning CDs," later in this chapter, explains how.

To make your own playlist, follow these steps:

1. **Make sure that the Music category is showing (in the upper-left corner). Click the left-facing arrow immediately to the right of the search box.**

Windows Media Player invites you to drag items to create a new playlist, as shown in Figure 1-19.

2. **On the left, navigate to each song that you want to have on the playlist and then drag it to your preferred location on the right.**

You can use any of the navigation tools — choose an artist, album, or genre, or use the search box — everything's fair game.

Figure 1-19:
Build a new playlist by dragging tracks to the area on the right.

WMP adds the track to the playlist. In Figure 1-20, I build a playlist of rock songs by Thai artists.

Figure 1-20:
My favorite Thai rock songs.

3. **If you decide that you don't want a specific song on the playlist, right-click it and choose Remove from List. You can move the songs up and down on the playlist by clicking the up and down arrows.**

4. **When you're happy with your playlist, click the Save Playlist button.**

WMP highlights "Untitled Playlist," inviting you to type in a name for the new playlist.

5. **Type a name for your new playlist in the File Name text box and press Enter.**

WMP saves your new playlist. It appears anywhere playlists appear, anywhere in Windows Media Player.

That's how easy it is to create a new playlist.

Adding a track to a playlist

In the Library, you can add a track to any playlist, at any time. Just follow these steps:

1. Find the track.

You can use any of the navigation tricks.

2. Right-click the track and choose Add To, and then choose the playlist.

It's that easy.

Alternatively, you can bring up a playlist so that it appears on the right (say, by double-clicking a playlist on the left and then clicking the Edit in List Pane button) and then drag new tracks into the playlist. Just remember to click the Save Playlist button when you're done.

You can add the same track to any number of playlists. Just right-click it again, choose Add To, and pick a different playlist.

Don't worry about using up storage space. Playlists take almost no room. No matter how many playlists you add a track to, WMP's Library maintains just one copy of the track. Playlists are like headings in a library catalog: No matter how many headings a particular book is indexed under, just one copy of the book exists.

Renaming and deleting playlists

To change a playlist's name, simply right-click the playlist and choose Rename.

To delete a playlist, follow these steps:

1. Right-click the playlist in the Playlists list (say that ten times really fast) and choose Delete. Or just click the playlist and press Delete.

WMP responds with a confusing dialog box, as shown in Figure 1-21.

Don't worry. Removing a playlist does *not* remove the songs from your computer. Where the dialog box says Delete from Library and My Computer, it isn't referring to the songs. The songs stay on your computer no matter which choice you make. The dialog box is referring to the *playlist* — and you can delete a playlist from your computer with no ill effect.

Figure 1-21: Select an option to delete a playlist.

Windows Media Player

Are you sure you want to delete these items from the library?

◉ Delete from library only
○ Delete from library and my computer

☐ Don't show this message again

OK   Cancel

2. **When working with playlists, you can safely select either the Delete from Library Only or the Delete from Library and My Computer check box.**

   There's essentially no difference between the two choices, unless you want to copy playlists from computer to computer.

Managing the contents of playlists

Just as you can manage playlists, you can manage the contents of a playlist. You have the following options:

✦ **To make any type of change to a playlist,** double-click the playlist in the left pane of the Library and then click the Edit in List Pane button to display its contents in the right pane.

✦ **To delete a track from the playlist,** right-click the track and choose Delete from Playlist, or select the track and press Delete.

✦ **To change a track's position in the playlist,** just drag the track to the position you want or use the up and down arrows above the list.

Book VII Chapter 1

Jammin' with Windows Media Player

Deleting tracks from the Library

No matter how many playlists a track is added to, your hard drive still contains just one copy of the track. The reverse is just as true: Even if you delete a track from every playlist that contains it, the track is still on your hard drive, and the Library still has a record of the track.

However, you can remove a track from the Media Library.

If you right-click a track, an album, or even an artist or genre, and choose Delete, WMP asks whether you want to delete the track (album, whatever) from the Library only or whether you want to delete it from both the Library and your computer, as shown in Figure 1-22. This dialog box looks almost exactly like the one you see when deleting a playlist (refer to Figure 1-21), but it's not nearly as innocent. When you click a track (as opposed to a playlist), selecting the Delete from Library and My Computer check box deletes the song itself from your computer.

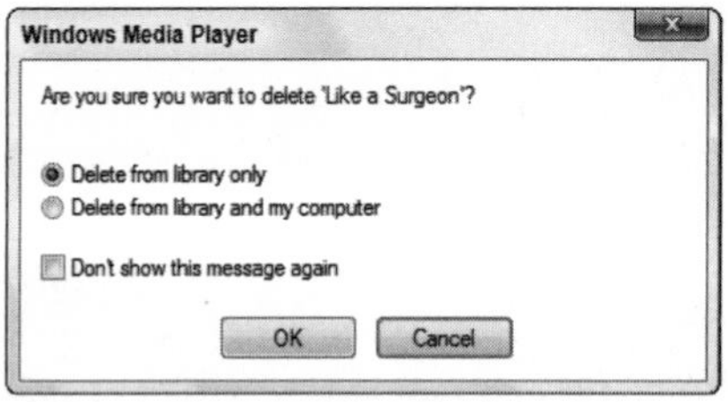

Figure 1-22: This dialog box asks if you want to delete the song itself.

> **Windows Media Player**
>
> Are you sure you want to delete 'Like a Surgeon'?
>
> ⦿ Delete from library only
> ○ Delete from library and my computer
>
> ☐ Don't show this message again
>
> [OK] [Cancel]

It's rare that you want to delete a track from your computer — although if you have 200GB of tracks (and I won't mention a certain author by name), you might want to free hard drive space by working from inside Windows Media Player. In general, choose to delete the track from the Player (so that it doesn't clutter things when you're looking for stuff you really want to play), but don't delete the track from your computer. That way, if you change your mind and want to get the track back, you can just click the tiny down arrow below the Library button, choose Add to Library, and have WMP rescan all your computer's hard drives.

Burning CDs

If your computer has a CD writer, you can create an audio CD by using tracks in the Library. Windows Media Player makes it easy.

Of course, you can also burn CDs and DVDs by using Vista itself — I talk about that in Book II, Chapter 1. The procedure is quite simple: In Windows Explorer, drag the files you want to put on the CD into the CD's folder, and then work with a wizard to transfer the files to CD. That method works great for copying, say, MP3 files onto a CD. As long as you have another computer, or a player that works with MP3, using Windows itself and copying plain old computer files makes a lot of sense.

But if you want to make an audio CD — that is, a CD that you can stick into any old CD player — you need to use Windows Media Player. Just as ripping [see the section "Copying from a CD (Also Known as Ripping)," earlier in this chapter] changes audio sound tracks into files that the computer can understand, burning with Windows Media Player transforms those files back into audio sound tracks that any CD player can play.

You may also want to use Windows Media Player to burn a *Data CD or DVD* — which is to say, a CD or DVD that contains MP3 (or WMA) files. If you have your music organized into playlists, or if you want to burn more than one CD- or DVD-full of music files, using WMP runs rings around the Windows-based click-and-drag.

Burning video DVDs — that is, transferring movies to a DVD writer — is an entirely different can of worms. I talk about burning DVDs in Book VIII, Chapter 4.

In any case, you can't use Vista to copy live feeds such as programs from radio stations. Such *streaming* programs are broadcast for listening only, so recording them would often violate the intellectual property rights of the radio station or of others.

Burning an audio CD

To a first approximation, if you're going to create an audio CD, you should use a blank CD-R disc. That maximizes the chances that your burned CD can work in almost any sentient CD player. I go into very gory detail about various ways to make your burning life more complicated in Book II, Chapter 3. If you just want to burn an audio CD, *don't* read that chapter. Grab a plain old CD-R disc, follow the instructions here, and forget about the complicated stuff.

The process of writing data to a CD is called *burning*. WMP enables you to burn a plain, old-fashioned, everyday audio CD very, very easily. Here's the quickest way I know to put together a dynamite audio CD:

1. Stick a blank CD-R disc in your CD drive.

Assuming that you have a CD drive that's capable of burning CDs, Vista responds with the AutoPlay dialog box shown in Figure 1-23.

AutoPlay

DVD-RW Drive (E:)

☐ Always do this for blank CDs:

Blank CD options

▶ Burn an audio CD
using Windows Media Player

Burn files to disc
using Windows

Create a CD
using iTunes

Set AutoPlay defaults in Control Panel

Figure 1-23:
The fastest
way to burn
a plain, old-
fashioned
audio CD.

2. Click the Burn an Audio CD Using Windows Media Player icon.

Vista opens WMP and starts a Burn List for you (see Figure 1-24).

Figure 1-24:
Ready to
burn Jimmy
Buffett.

3. Using any tricks you can muster (listing by artist or album, sorting, searching, pulling up an existing playlist, whatever), click and drag the tracks you want to burn, and arrange them on the right, in the *Burn List*.

Keep an eye on the "Remaining" number at the top of the list. WMP has been known to overestimate the available room on a CD, so it's a good idea to leave a minute or two or three left, unused, on the CD.

If you try to put too much music on a CD, WMP breaks out the Burn List, with horizontal lines marking the current disc, the next disc, next disc, and so on. When you burn a multidisc list, you just have to keep feeding CDs into the drive. Easy.

4. When you've chosen and arranged the tracks just the way you want them, click the Burn List down arrow and choose Save Playlist As.

WMP shows you the playlist Save As dialog box, shown in Figure 1-25.

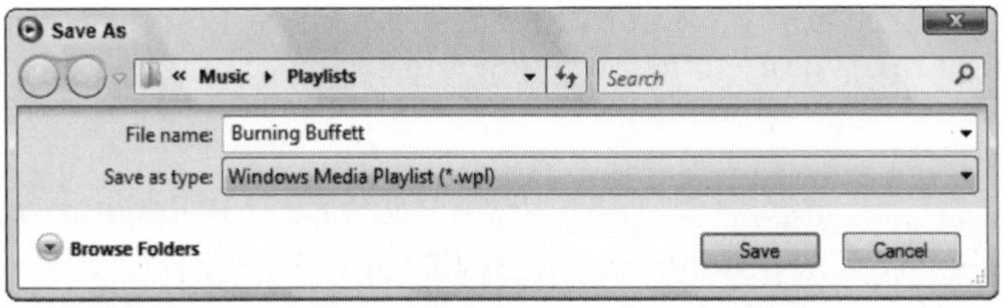

Figure 1-25:
Save your
Burn List
in case you
need it later.

5. **Type in a name for the playlist, and click the Save button.**

   WMP saves the playlist. That can come in handy if a problem exists with
   the burn that you don't find out about for a day or two or three.

6. **Click the Burn button's down arrow (see Figure 1-24). Make sure that
   Audio CD is selected (you're burning an audio CD, right?), and then
   click the line marked More Options.**

   WMP shows you the Options dialog box with the Burn tab selected, as
   shown in Figure 1-26.

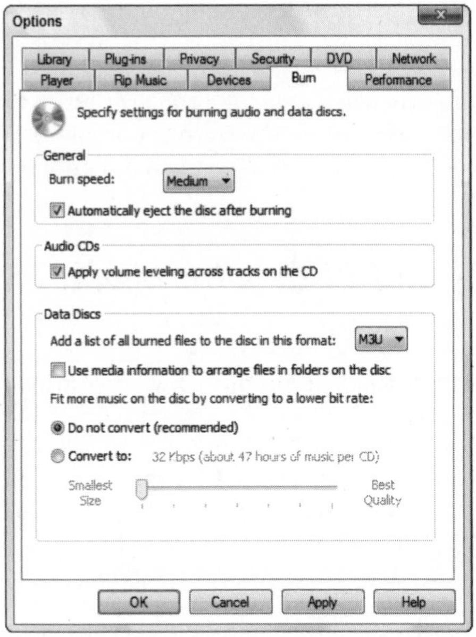

Figure 1-26:
Set the
basic burn
charac-
teristics.

**Book VII
Chapter 1**

**Jammin' with
Windows
Media Player**

7. **In the Burn Speed box, choose Medium. You can try to run Fast or
   Fastest if it looks like your CD drive is turning out good CDs, but it's
   best to start at a slower speed.**

Select the Apply Volume Leveling across Tracks on the CD check box. That takes more time, but it ensures that you don't get blasted with a rogue song.

You might want to set the Data Discs defaults now, too. I always select the Use Media Information to Arrange Files in Folders on the Disc check box. I've bumped into too many CD and DVD players that mess up when confronted with nested folders. I also like to put an M3U list on my CDs and DVDs, as sort of a roving Table of Contents.

8. When you're happy with your choices, click the OK button.

WMP goes back to the main Burn window, as shown in Figure 1-24.

9. Click the Start Burn button, at the bottom of the Burn List.

WMP processes each track in turn, converting it from a music file into data that's required on an audio CD and then burning each one.

It's really that simple. When WMP's done, pull the CD out of the CD burner and plop the CD into any CD player. The magic's the music.

The copying process takes, oh, a third to a fifth of the time it would take to play the copied tracks, the exact time depending on the speed of your CD writer.

If you interrupt the writing process by clicking the Stop Burn button or by removing the CD from the writer before the burn is complete, WMP goes bananas, and the whole process stops. A fried CD-R ain't good for anything but a coaster.

Burning data CDs and DVDs with Media Player

The procedure for burning data CD-Rs, CD-RWs, DVD-Rs, and DVD-RWs with Windows Media Player is essentially the same as that described in the preceding section, except when you click the tiny down arrow in Step 6, you need to select Data CD or DVD.

You can fit a whole lot more music on a Data CD than on an audio CD. In spite of that fact, the burning process for a Data CD can go faster than that for an audio CD. Why? WMP doesn't have to pre-process data files — doesn't need to convert them into a form that works with audio CD players.

If you already set the Data Discs options in Step 7, you've done everything you need to do to produce top-notch MP3 (er, data) CDs and DVDs.

Syncing with a Portable Player

Call it an MP3 player, if you will. Call it a Zune. (The folks at Microsoft do, but they kinda have a vested interest.) Or call it a portable digital audio player. Or a personal digital device. Moving your songs from your computer to an MP3 player has never been simpler.

Audio is only part of the story, though. The new generation of portable video machines — whether you call the device a Portable Media Center (a term trademarked by Microsoft, of course), video jukebox, digital video player, or that dern MTV thingy — seems poised to take over the toy market.

Windows Media Player handles both audio and video (including recorded TV) with aplomb. In fact, when WMP works right, transferring files to your portable player is every bit as easy as burning a CD. It's easier, actually, because you don't have to put a blank CD in the drive.

If you have an iPod, you can't use Windows Media Player. The iPod has a weird internal format, and syncing with WMP doesn't add songs to the iPod's playlists. You have to use iTunes (see Book VI, Chapter 2) or Winamp. (See *Windows Vista Timesaving Techniques For Dummies*, by yours truly.)

Moving tracks to the player

Here's how to get your tunes and flicks onto your MP3 or video player:

1. **Attach your player to one of your computer's USB ports and turn it on.**

   Vista should identify the player with the Found New Hardware Wizard. If all else fails, read the player's instruction manual and run the program on the CD that came with the player to get the drivers working. You may need to visit the manufacturer's Web site to download the latest drivers. This technology is changing fast, and drivers become obsolete overnight.

   If your MP3 player holds more than 4GB of data and your music collection is less than 4GB, Windows Media Player automatically syncs your player as soon as you plug it in. To keep WMP from auto-syncing, hold down Shift when you plug in the player.

2. **Start Windows Media Player if Vista doesn't start it for you. Click the Sync button if it isn't already clicked.**

   Vista shows you the MP3 device in the upper-right corner (see Figure 1-27) and offers to create a sync list for you.

3. **Use whatever tricks are at your disposal (clicking entries on the left, sorting, searching) to find tracks that you want to transfer to the MP3 player. Click each track and drag it to the Sync List on the right.**

Figure 1-27:
Syncing
with an
MP3 player
is easy.

See the section "Finding the tracks you want," earlier in this chapter, for details.

Watch the "remaining" counter to fill your MP3 player as far as it'll go. If you drag too many songs to the Sync List, right-click any you want to remove and choose Remove from List.

4. **To save your new playlist (and you should), click the Sync List down arrow and choose Save Playlist As. Give your playlist a name and click the Save button.**

5. **Click the Start Sync button.**

WMP copies the files in your playlist to your portable player.

If your MP3 player didn't have enough room, Windows Media Player simply states that the track(s) wasn't copied.

Note that nothing on your MP3 player gets deleted. Synching with WMP is very different from syncing with iTunes (see Book VI, Chapter 2).

6. **When the copying is done, unplug your portable player and have at it.**

Transferring songs, video, and TV shows is really that simple.

Moving tracks from the player to your PC

If you have an iPod, copying music from your iPod to your computer involves a trip through Windows Explorer, with hidden files displayed. It isn't difficult, but it's a pain in the neck. See Book VI, Chapter 2 for details.

You can use the same method to copy files from any other kind of MP3 player to your computer, but why bother? Windows Media Player makes it easy to "reverse sync" your music. Here's how:

1. **Plug your MP3 player into your computer. Windows Media Player should appear, with the Sync button clicked.**

If this doesn't happen, start Windows Media Player and click the Sync button.

2. **On the left, click the name of your MP3 player. Then navigate to the song you want to copy to your PC.**

You can use any of the typical tricks, including a search.

3. **Click the song(s) you want to retrieve, and drag them to the Sync List on the right.**

In Figure 1-28, I try to bring back Norah Jones's "Don't Know Why" by dragging it into the Sync List.

The Sync button magically turns into a Copy from Device button.

Book VII
Chapter 1

Figure 1-28:
Copying
music from
your MP3
player back
to your
computer is
amazingly
easy.

Jammin' with
Windows
Media Player

4. **After you've gathered all the songs that you want to copy to your PC, click the Copy from Device button.**

    WMP lists each song and lets you know when they've been copied.

The songs end up in your Music folder or whichever folder you've designated as your default folder for ripped music.

Deleting tracks from your player

What? You're tired of listening to the same Weird Al Yankovic song a hundred million times? Does it make you break out in hives? Zap it!

WMP makes it surprisingly easy to manually delete any song you like. But before you make any rash decisions — sorry, Al — why not create a backup copy of the song, before you send it to that big bit bucket in the sky? Here's how:

1. **Follow the steps in the preceding section to copy the songs you want to delete from your player to your PC.**

    If a particular song is already on your PC and you try to "reverse sync" it, WMP simply tells you that the song is already in the library. No biggie.

2. **When WMP finishes copying all the songs to your PC, right-click the song in the Copy from Device list on the left (see Figure 1-29) and choose Delete.**

Figure 1-29: Deleting songs from your MP3 player is easy, too — if you know the trick.

3. **When WMP asks for confirmation that you want to delete the song from the MP3 player, click the Yes button, and it's gone.**

Choosing a Skin

A *skin* is a little file that changes WMP's appearance. I'm not talking subtle changes here; I'm talking complete transformation. A skin can make WMP look like a 1950s jukebox, a *Star Trek* phaser, a funny face, or Bill G's trampoline room. If you like intriguing visual effects, skins are for you.

Skins have a practical advantage, too: Most of them make WMP occupy less screen space in *skin mode* than it does in its normal *full mode*. Skins do this by presenting only WMP's most frequently used functions, but if those are the only functions you need, why should you mind? You can always switch back to full mode when you need a function that your preferred skin doesn't provide.

Switching skin modes

Getting WMP into skin mode is easy. Just press Ctrl+2. If you want to go the long way around, press Alt, then choose View➪Skin Mode.

What does skin mode look like? Well, that depends on the skin. One that Marcus Johnson and Jennifer Young developed at Howard University looks like that shown in Figure 1-30.

To get out of skin mode, each of the skins has a Return to Full Mode button. Or, you can press Ctrl+1. The buttons move all around; no two skins seem to have the same button in the same place, but that's part of the fun, eh?

Controlling WMP's functions in skin mode can be a, uh, challenge. Who woulda thought that clicking above the right eye (see Figure 1-30) would pop the gnome's top, revealing the current playlist?

When in doubt (or if you don't find these games amusing anymore — where have I heard that phrase?), right-click the skin and you see a more-or-less normal selection of functions, including the Switch to Full Mode option.

You can also switch WMP back to full mode by pressing Ctrl+1. That should be easy to remember: Press Ctrl+2 for skin mode, Ctrl+1 for full mode.

The volume control is usually on the graphic equalizer or in the audio controls.

Figure 1-30:
A Windows
Media
Player
"Authentic
West
African
Gnome."

More skins!

Choosing a new skin while you're in "normal" full mode requires some gymnastics. Here's how:

1. **In Windows Media Player, press Alt and then choose View⇨Skin Chooser.**

   WMP shows you a handful of built-in skins.

2. **To find more Microsoft-approved skins, click the More Skins button. You'll be transported to Microsoft's skin collection, which has some truly remarkable skins, ready to download for free.**

   Or you can hit one of the thousands of sites on the Web that have skins, almost all of which are free. Try http://skinz.org or http://customize.org.

If you go surfing for skins on the Web, be careful. Many skins come bundled with scumware. Scan any downloaded skins with your anti-virus program before installing them. And if you want the low-down on a Web site before you download, run the name of the site through www.siteadvisor.com.

3. **Pick a skin you want to try and click the Download button. When the download completes, click the View Now button.**

WMP flips into skin mode, with your chosen skin.

Customizing WMP

You can customize WMP in a large number of ways. You get to most of the settings by pressing Alt and then choosing Tools⇨Options. This command displays a dialog box with a bunch of tabs for customizing many aspects of WMP's behavior:

✦ **The Player tab:** Controls general aspects of WMP's behavior, such as checking for automatic updates.

✦ **The Rip Music tab:** Controls aspects of the copying process, including most importantly the format of ripped CDs (which you set to MP3 already, right?). You can also control the amount of data compression to apply when copying a CD. (More compression makes the copied tracks occupy less space, but reduces sound quality.) It also controls the folder to which music is copied (by default, your Music folder).

✦ **The Devices tab:** Lists available devices that WMP can use (such as CD drives and portable players) and enables you to control certain aspects of their behavior.

✦ **The Burn tab:** I talk about that one extensively in the section "Burning CDs," earlier in this chapter.

✦ **The Performance tab:** Lets you control how WMP handles streaming media.

✦ **The Library tab:** Controls access to the Library by other applications. It also tells WMP which folders to monitor for additions to, and deletions from, the Library.

✦ **The Privacy and Security tabs:** Primarily control how much information you send to Microsoft every time you use WMP. See the section "Adjusting WMP Privacy Settings," earlier in this chapter.

✦ **The DVD tab:** Sets the default language used when playing DVDs.

✦ **The Network tab:** Lets you select the network protocols that WMP may use to receive streaming media. It also lets you control *proxy settings,* work protected by a firewall.

My privacy settings are shown at the beginning of this chapter, in Figure 1-4. If you decide to give Microsoft more information than the amount shown in that figure, I strongly recommend that you click the Read the Privacy Statement Online link and read the information with a thoroughly jaundiced eye.

It'll take an advanced degree in computer science to even begin to understand many of these settings. Come to think of it, I have an advanced degree in computer science, and *I* don't understand some of those settings. It's a good policy to change one of the options only if you understand it well and keep careful notes so that you can restore the original setting if anything goes wrong.

There's no harm in *looking* at the options, though. You can discover a lot by clicking the Help button on each tab of the Options dialog box.

Chapter 2: Podcasting

In This Chapter

✔ **Understanding podcasting**

✔ **Getting hooked into podcasts that you might actually want**

✔ **Playing podcasts**

✔ **Rolling your own podcasts**

*R*arely has a new technology taken hold so quickly.

In a literal sense, *podcasting* combines the words *iPod* and *broadcasting* in historic reference to the technology's roots.

In a broader sense, podcasting has absolutely nothing to do with iPods, and it bears only a tenuous relation to traditional methods of broadcasting. You can play a podcast without an iPod (in fact, more than half of all podcasts are played on a PC, not on an audio player like an iPod). Nothing goes out over the airwaves. But podcasts have rapidly become a medium of choice for people and organizations with stories to tell or songs to sing or videos to vid — and for folks like you and me who are interested in listening or watching.

If you've never heard a podcast, this chapter shows you how to get started. If you've ever thought of distributing your own podcasts, this chapter fills you in on some of the gory details.

Understanding Podcasting

Ten years ago, if you had a grunge band that wanted to get airplay, it would've taken a lot of time, friends in the business, and probably a grubby jeans pocket stuffed with hundred-dollar bills to even have your songs heard.

Twenty years ago if you wanted to create your own particular style of radio talk show, it would've taken a lot of time, friends in an even shadier business, *two* grubby jeans pockets stuffed with hundred-dollar bills, and a name like Howard Stern.

Nowadays, if you're Howard Stern, you don't want to podcast your shows because it's hard to make a buck off pirate copies, much less half a billion of them. Times change, eh?

At its heart, podcasting consists of a simple four-step process — and you don't really need two of the steps. Here's what it boils down to:

1. **You record something.**

In most cases, the "something" is a radio-talk-show–style program, music (without breaking any copyrights, of course), or the intimate sounds of frolicking dolphins (all over the age of consent, of course). Almost always, the recording is in the form of an MP3 file for audio, or an AVI or MPG file for video.

2. **You make your recording available.**

In most cases, you post the recording on the Internet, but you can also release it as a Torrent (downloadable with BitTorrent, `www.bittorrent.com`, or similar Torrent person-to-person software). Many sites let you post podcasts, both for free and for a fee.

3. **You let people know that you have a podcast available.**

You don't really need to do this, but it helps to publicize the fact that you have a podcast available. (In fact, this is the *cast* part of *podcast.*) Publicizing normally takes place via a Really Simple Syndication (RSS) feed — the same kind of feed that I talk about in Book V, Chapter 2.

A person looking for podcasts finds out about your MP3 file, either via one of the podcasting search engines or through a commercial service, such as iTunes. The search engines crawl the Web looking for podcasting files. The commercial services rely on RSS feeds, searches, and divine perspiration. You can also tell the commercial sites about your podcast. iTunes gets thousands of submissions a day.

4. **Your listener downloads the podcast and listens to it.**

If you're lucky (this is also an optional step), somebody will actually listen to or watch your podcast. iTunes (see Book VI, Chapter 2) makes it easy to discover, download, and listen to podcasts, but so do Winamp (free from `www.winamp.com`) and Nimiq (which also does BitTorrents; free from `http://nimiq.nl`).

That's the beauty of podcasting. You don't need a recording studio. Don't need an FM antenna. Don't need a public-access TV station. All you need is a computer, a five-dollar mic, and a little bit of time. Just four steps — two of them optional — and you're on the air. And you have no FCC to contend with, no thought police, no station managers, no hassle. No wonder so much poddreck is floating around. . . .

Finding and Playing Podcasts

You can find lots of podcasts using Google. Simply type **inurl:podcast** followed by whatever cast you seek in the search box. For example, to find podcasts related to coffee, try Googling **inurl:podcast coffee**.

By far the easiest and fastest way to sort through millions of podcasts, though, is with iTunes. Rumor has it that Apple built podcast support into iTunes because of the iPod name connection. (What, you never heard of WiMPcasts?) Whatever the reason, you'll soon find that iTunes has enough good podcasts to fill a thousand giant iPods.

Here's how to get into the iTunes podcast collection:

1. **Start iTunes (see Book VI, Chapter 2). On the left, under Source, select the line that says Podcasts.**

iTunes flips over to the Music Store "source" and presents you with the podcast main page, as shown in Figure 2-1.

2. **Use one of the myriad tools on offer to find a podcast that interests you.**

Figure 2-1:
The easiest way to find zillions of podcasts: iTunes.

**Book VII
Chapter 2**

Podcasting

You'll find a Top Podcasts list, a search box, featured podcasts (all of which are free), category lists, and more. I clicked the big Public Broadcasting box and arrived at the choices shown in Figure 2-2.

Figure 2-2:
A small subset of the public broad-casting podcasts.

3. **Click the name of a podcast that appears worthwhile.**

   In Figure 2-3, you see the window that appears after I selected NewsHour with Jim Lehrer. In the Podcast Description area is a brief blurb from the person or organization that originates the podcast.

Subscribe here

Figure 2-3:
The NewsHour with Jim Lehrer offers free podcasts that go in-depth on specific topics.

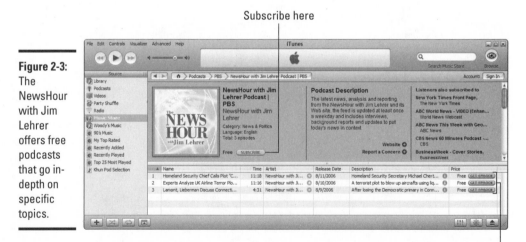

Choose a specific podcast here

4. **To listen to one specific episode, on the right, click the Get Episode button. To have iTunes download the most recent episode, and then watch and download each new episode as it becomes available, click the Subscribe button.**

iTunes downloads the podcasts you have selected, as shown in Figure 2-4.

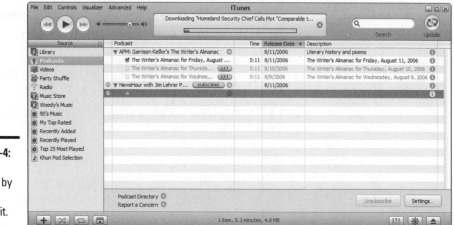

Figure 2-4:
Play a
podcast by
double-
clicking it.

The downloaded file, typically an MP3, goes into your `Music\iTunes\ iTunes Music\Podcasts` folder. It's an MP3 file just like any other MP3 file. No restrictions. No problem.

5. **To play a podcast after it's been downloaded, double-click it.**

The podcast plays just like any other audio (or video) file.

Because a podcast is just another MP3 file, you can play one simply by double-clicking it, whether you use iTunes, Windows Media Player, Winamp, or Jungle Julie's Jukeybox. The trick, of course, is that you have to find files filled with fun stuff you want to hear.

In addition to Google (which snags many podcasts along with its usual Web-crawling activities) and iTunes (which actively requests submissions from the general public), I've found four very different, very good podcast index-ers that I swear by:

✦ **Singing Fish** (`http://singingfish.com`) indexes podcasts, videos from many famous — and not so famous — artists, music, and much more. It sports a very clean and easy-to-use interface (see Figure 2-5).

Figure 2-5:
Singing
Fish is a joy
to use.

✦ **Podzinger** (`http://podzinger.com`) claims almost 300,000 podcasts available for a quick scan, including an interesting popularity rating system.

✦ **Yahoo! Podcasts** (`http://podcasts.yahoo.com`) covers podcasting from soup to nuts to podcast creation to publication, and its easy-to-navigate main page will keep you coming back. I find it even easier to discover new podcasts on Yahoo! than on iTunes.

✦ **Podscope** (`http://podscope.com`) is unique in its ability to scan the contents of podcasts and index them based on the words that are spoken. Cool. Capable. Eerie.

I also like the voting mechanism and forum built into Podcast Alley (`http://podcastalley.com`), which frequently produces fascinating podcasts that I never would've seen — er, heard — otherwise.

Publishing Your Own Podcasts

Er, maybe I should say casting your own pod. . . .

Thinking of making your own podcast? Got a good story to tell? Want to vent a little steeeeeeeam? Hey, you may only play a one-night stand (or is that a one-MP3 stand?), but it's worth a shot.

To make your own podcast, start by recording a WMA file using Vista's Sound Recorder (choose Start⇨All Programs⇨Accessories⇨Sound Recorder). But that's a little bit like writing a novel with a clay tablet and mallet. And the result will be a file that's hemmed in by Digital Rights Management restrictions and the limitations that come with proprietary formats — in Book VII, Chapter 1, I call this C.R.A.P.

Instead, you should try a free podcast-creation package, called Audacity, and the free Lame MP3 encoder, which allows Audacity to output an MP3 file, ready to be posted.

Here's how to make them work:

1. **Head over to** `http://audacity.sourceforge.net`, **and download and install the latest version of Audacity.**

Audacity is yet another example of excellent *open source* software. (To a first approximation, open source software is free to use and free to distribute, and very few restrictions are placed on the program's source code.)

2. **Go to** `www.free-codecs.com/Lame_Encoder_download.htm` **and download the Lame MP3 encoder.**

The encoder comes in a Zip file. Unzip the file and put the results in a convenient location. (You'll need to locate the file `lame_enc.dll` in Step 8.)

Audacity doesn't include an MP3 encoder because MP3 encoders have to be licensed.

3. **Start Audacity.**

4. **When you have your microphone connected and you're ready for Take 1, click the Record button.**

Audacity starts recording, and you see something like what is shown in Figure 2-6.

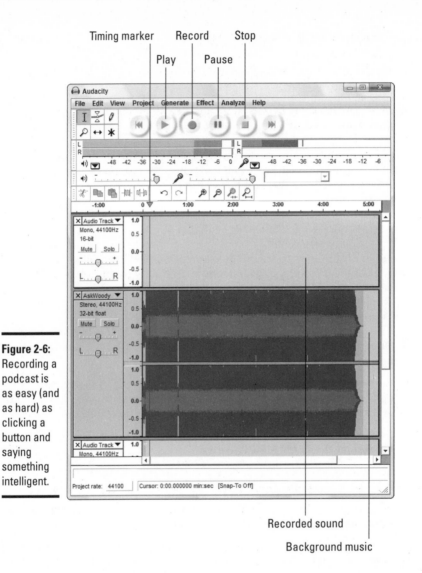

Figure 2-6:
Recording a
podcast is
as easy (and
as hard) as
clicking a
button and
saying
something
intelligent.

5. **Add background music by choosing Project⇨Import Audio and picking a music file.**

   If you intend to post the podcast, be careful about copyright restrictions and infringement, particularly for background music.

6. **Use the buttons to pause or stop. To go back and edit what you've said, click the Stop button, click in the location where you want the recorder to start again, and then click the Record button.**

TIP

You can find a detailed tutorial and reference at `http://audacity.sourceforge.net/help/documentation`.

7. **When you're done recording, click the Stop button and then choose File⇨Export as MP3.**

8. **When Audacity asks you to locate the MP3 encoder, point it to the place you used in Step 2 to store the unzipped Lame MP3 encoder.**

   Audacity asks you to type in the information for the MP3 file's ID3 tags, per Figure 2-7.

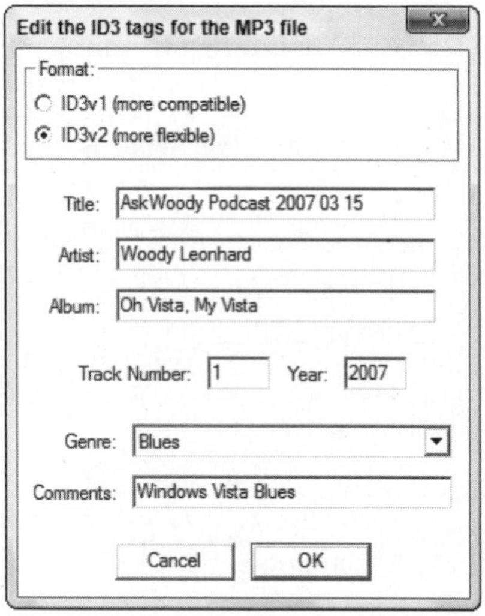

Figure 2-7:
Be sure to give your podcast proper identification. You never know who will be looking.

> **Edit the ID3 tags for the MP3 file**   ✕
>
> **Format:**
> ○ ID3v1 (more compatible)
> ● ID3v2 (more flexible)
>
> Title: `AskWoody Podcast 2007 03 15`
> Artist: `Woody Leonhard`
> Album: `Oh Vista, My Vista`
>
> Track Number: `1`   Year: `2007`
>
> Genre: `Blues` ▼
> Comments: `Windows Vista Blues`
>
> [Cancel]   [OK]

Book VII
Chapter 2

Podcasting

9. **Type in something funny or outrageous and click the OK button.**

   Audacity exports the file. Now you need to put your new MP3 file someplace where people can find it.

10. **If you already have a Web site or a blog that can easily accommodate a podcast, upload the file using the site's instructions.**

    If you don't have a site or blog with podcast-posting capabilities, check out Liberated Syndication (`www.libsyn.com`, $5 per month) or the granddaddy of Web hosting services, GoDaddy (`http://godaddy.com/gdshop/pod/landing.asp`, also $5 per month). Or, you can do a Google search for "podcast hosting" to find about a million other alternatives.

11. **Use your podcast host or blogging site's forms to come up with an RSS feed file. It's a pain in the neck, and error-prone, to try to do it manually.**

The RSS feed sounds mysterious, but it isn't. It's a specific kind of text file that has to be completed in a very exacting manner. After you've created the RSS feed file, you (or your podcast-hosting site) stick the text file on the Internet. Most podcast-hosting sites also notify the big podcast-listing services, automatically, at no additional charge.

Okay, you twisted my arm. Sheesh. If you really feel like building an RSS feed file for your podcast by hand, go to `http://podcasts.yahoo.com/publish/3` and follow the instructions very carefully.

12. **After you've completed your RSS feed file, you need to tell the major podcast-listing services (unless your podcast host does it for you). See Table 2-1 for a list of the major podcast-listing services.**

Wait a day or two, and tell all your friends to give your podcast five stars!

Table 2-1	Major Podcast Listing Services
Lister	*How to Submit*
iTunes	Start iTunes. Go to the Music Store. On the left, click the Podcasts arrow. Then click the Submit a Podcast box, near the middle of the screen.
FeedBurner	Visit `www.feedburner.com`.
iPodder	Start at `www.ipodder.org` and navigate to the topic that best describes your podcast — say Computers/Operating Systems/Microsoft. Then click the Suggest a Link link at the bottom.
Yahoo!	Visit `http://podcasts.yahoo.com/publish`.
Podcast Alley	Visit `http://podcastalley.com/add_a_podcast.php`.
Odeo	You must join Odeo and then go to `http://odeo.com/create/import-feed`.

If you're willing to shell out about $90 for podcasting software, take a look at the ePodcast Producer from Industrial Audio Software (`http://industrialaudiosoftware.com`). It covers everything from podcast creation to uploading and RSS feed creation.

Chapter 3: Discovering Digital Cameras

In This Chapter

✔ **Choosing a camera**

✔ **Buying a camera**

✔ **Moving photos and movies to your PC**

✔ **Sharing your shots**

✔ **Troubleshooting**

Microsoft spent a lot of time and money adding rudimentary but capable photo and movie features to Windows Vista. The result won't impress anyone who's accustomed to working with, say, Photoshop. But for most of us, Vista's photo and video capabilities are good enough, and they're remarkably easy to use.

The Vista Video/Photo Shtick comprises three programs that work together, more or less:

✦ The **Windows Picture and Video Import** program takes digital photos (and/or movies) out of your camera and puts them on your computer's hard drive.

✦ The **Windows Photo Gallery** works with photos on your computer (or on your network) and allows you to adjust the photos, crop, adjust for red eye, rotate, print, or burn the photos to CD. The Photo Gallery also lets you run a bunch of photos you've chosen as a slide show.

Technically, Windows Photo Gallery supports JPG, TIF and WPD files, and can support camera RAW files if you get your camera manufacturer's translation software to work. (See the sidebar "What About RAW?" later in this chapter.) GIF and BMP files — typically, clip art — aren't handled.

Although the Photo Gallery can show you videos, you can't do much with them.

✦ **Windows Movie Maker** provides tools for creating movies, editing and stitching together clips and photos, and adding sound, titles, and so on.

In this chapter, you discover everything you need to know to choose a digital camera, hook it up to your PC, and move pictures from the camera to the PC, where you can store, edit, and print them with just a couple of clicks.

Two subsequent chapters cover Windows Photo Gallery and Windows Movie Maker.

Choosing a Camera

Before you can have fun with your images, of course, you need to get them into your computer. You have a lot of options, as this list describes:

✦ You can use a *conventional (or film) camera* to record images on film and then request the film processor to return the images to you on computer media — typically a CD. Having the photo processor burn a CD while developing the film costs only a couple of bucks — and you may get a small free application thrown in to do some rudimentary editing. Or you can scan prints, if all else fails. When I talk about conventional cameras in this book, I'm talking about the kind that produce images on regular, ol' everyday film. Silver halide.

✦ You can use a *digital camera,* like the one shown in Figure 3-1, to record images in electronic memory and then transfer them to your computer. When I talk about digital cameras in this book, I mean a camera that produces images as files, one image at a time, and stores the files inside the camera.

Figure 3-1: The 10.1-megapixel Canon EOS Digital Rebel XTi with a high-quality EF-S 18–55-mm zoom lens.

Digital cameras fall into two broad categories:

- Point-and-shoot cameras combine light weight and ease of use.

- Digital *SLR*s (single-lens reflex cameras) weigh more and generally cost more, but they come with interchangeable lenses and advanced picture-composition capabilities. SLRs generally produce better pictures, but they also require more care.

✦ You can use a *webcam* (variously called an Internet camera, QuickCam, or Network Camera) to feed live images directly into your computer and capture them as either still frames or movie clips. When I talk about webcams here, I'm talking about the ones that have to be tethered to a computer. They have no capability (or very limited capability) to store images.

✦ You can use a *camcorder* (also known as a video camera or a digital video recorder), like the one shown in Figure 3-2, to record movie clips on tape and then feed them into your computer from the camera or from a playback device. When I talk about camcorders in this book, I'm talking about the kind that internally store moving images.

Figure 3-2: Canon's small, light 1080 HDV (high-definition video— 1920 x 1080 pixels) camcorder records on HDV videotape.

Strictly speaking, webcams are digital cameras. So are many video cameras. Camcorders can take still shots, just like digital cameras, and many digital cameras can make video clips — although you may be less than impressed with the quality of the results, in both cases. Then again, strictly speaking, Dummies are smart. But I digress.

Understanding digital cameras

You use a digital camera just like a conventional one, but it records images in electronic memory, not on film. Instead of sending a roll of film to be processed and printed, you simply copy the images to your computer. Then you can erase the camera's memory and use it again, or you can buy a new memory card and save the old one.

A digital camera forms its image on a sensor that contains a square grid of tiny, light-sensing areas called *pixels. Resolution* refers to the number of pixels the sensor has, measured in millions of dots, or megapixels (abbreviated MP). The more pixels, the more detail the camera can record. The more detail, the larger a print you can make without the individual pixels becoming noticeable (see Table 3-1).

Table 3-1	Resolution and Acceptable Print Size
Camera Resolution (MP)	*Produces High-Quality Prints Up To (inches)*
1	3 x 5
2	4 x 6
3	5 x 7
4	8 x 10
5	11 x 14
8	14 x 17
24	30 x 36 (or bigger)

Megapixels constitute an important part of the shopping equation, but they aren't the only part. After you get past 5 MP or so, the quality of the lens becomes even more important than the number of pixels. And at any level of detail, usability in small cameras can make all the difference, especially for people like me who have five left thumbs and six right ones.

Having more resolution than you need gives you leeway to crop out the unimportant parts of an image and still get a good-quality print. Those extra pixels cost money, of course.

Zoom lens

A *zoom lens* lets you vary the angle of view that your camera takes in by increasing or decreasing the lens's magnification. Most advanced point-and-shoot digital cameras have this feature, as do all SLRs. The better ones cover a wider range.

What about RAW?

Traditionally, most cameras save pictures in JPG format. JPG represents a decent balance between image quality and file size, and just about every kind of software recognizes JPG. JPG is a "lossy" format — some of the detail of the picture gets zapped in the process of crunching the bits.

Not so with RAW. The RAW file format (actually, it's a loosely defined bunch of formats) captures information from every single pixel inside the camera. When it comes to quality, what RAW sees is what you get. Full stop.

Unfortunately, every camera manufacturer creates RAW files in different ways, and the files themselves can be big — say, two to ten times the size of a good-quality JPG file. But if you work in the, uh, RAW, you can edit every detail

that the camera can muster directly, without bumping into the pre-editing that's inherent in JPG.

RAW files are a pain in the neck. Not every camera can generate RAW files, and for daily use, you won't want to hassle with them. In order to get Vista Photo Gallery to work with RAW files, you need to find a WIC codec (see `en.wikipedia.org/wiki/Windows_ Imaging_Component`) from your camera manufacturer that works. If you can't make your camera's WIC codec work, try Dave Coffin's open source command-line program dcraw, `cybercom.net/~dcoffin/dcraw/ dcraw.1.html` and its (free!) Windows front-end, RAWdrop, from Frank Siegert, `www.wizards.de/rawdrop`.

Most digital cameras offer *optical zoom* (where the lens physically moves) and *digital zoom* (which simply enlarges an image by making each pixel bigger). Digital zoom isn't very useful: Think of it as a marketing gimmick, not something that you'll want to use for your pictures. You can get the same result by enlarging the final image.

Focusing and stabilizing

Most modern cameras adjust the focus automatically — they *auto-focus* — to give the sharpest result at any distance. Auto-focusing cameras can generally be held closer to the subject than fixed-focus ones — sometimes down to a few inches, which can be useful if you want to photograph small objects, like flowers or coins.

As an added feature, some advanced cameras let you deal with special photo situations — where the auto-focus just doesn't work very well — by adjusting the focus manually. Typically, auto-focus has problems when the subject of the shot isn't at the middle of the picture; when the subject is very bright, very dark, or low contrast; when you're taking the picture through glass or water; or when you want to emphasize a small part of a picture by giving it the sharpest focus — a small flower standing quite some distance in front of a face, for example.

Image stabilizers work wonders, even on digital still cameras. By electronically adjusting to compensate for camera shake, a stabilizer can keep you from capturing a blurry mess. You can shoot in low light, shoot from a bus, or shoot while jumping with a bungee cord, and your pictures turn out great. Given a choice between a higher-resolution camera — one with more megapixels — and one with image stabilization, go for the stabilizer, every time.

Exposure control and flash

All digital cameras adjust the exposure automatically to suit different light levels. The better ones have more sophisticated circuits that produce good results under a wider range of conditions. Better cameras also give you some control over exposure, either by taking a picture that's lighter or darker than what the camera thinks is ideal or by allowing you to set the exposure controls (the aperture and shutter speed, for those technically inclined) yourself.

Many cameras have a built-in electronic flash that fires automatically when needed. Better cameras have more powerful and flexible flashes, and offer you various types of control. You may be able to turn off the built-in flash and attach a separate electronic flash of your choice, for example.

Digital cameras are notorious for overly powerful or utterly wimpy flash systems — and far too frequently the same flash is too powerful under one set of lighting conditions and doesn't work worth squat under slightly different conditions. If you're willing to schlep around a stand-alone flash unit (called an *external flash*), look for a camera that has a *hot shoe* (also called a *synchro-flash terminal*) — a place to plug in and control a stand-alone flash. Using an external flash with simple techniques like *bouncing* (aiming the flash at a white ceiling or wall) can make a world of difference in the quality of your pictures, and in most cases, the camera does all the work.

Image storage and transfer

Most cameras use removable memory media, often shaped like little cards. When one memory card gets full, you just pull it out and insert a new one, or you plug your camera into your computer and download all the pictures. It's best to carry an extra memory card or two: If you're at the rim of the Grand Canyon when your card gets full, an extra $25 memory card can save you a trip back to the car. Different cameras use different types of memory cards; all of them work about equally well.

The price of removable memory cards continues to fall precipitously. If you can hold off on buying an SD card, CompactFlash, xD, or Memory Stick, by all means do so. They'll only get cheaper. And bigger.

Most recent cameras have a USB interface for transferring images to your computer. USB is easy and fast, but the whole setup can be clumsy, especially if you want to plug your camera into the wall to avoid draining the batteries during file transfers.

If you buy a camera that uses memory cards, spend an extra $20 or so for a card reader that plugs into your computer's USB port. You can then slide the camera's memory card into the reader and treat it like any other disk drive. Vista will identify it immediately. I've used the Kodak 6-in-1 card reader for years, and it works like a champ, but many cheaper generic readers work well, too. Alternatively, the next time you buy a printer or other peripheral, you can look for one that takes memory cards. That way, you won't have to worry about finding the reader when you need it most.

Plugging your camera's memory card into a USB or PCMCIA reader, or into a card slot on a printer, virtually eliminates compatibility problems (see the next section). More than that, you don't have to worry about the dog tripping over the camera's power cord or USB cable, knocking the camera off your desk. I know. My beagle broke my Nikon Coolpix that way, and it cost hundreds of dollars to get it fixed. Blech!

Compatibility

Vista provides direct support for many digital cameras, but not for all of them. If you happen to own a camera that Vista doesn't support, it's not a big deal. You may have to use the application provided with the camera to move pictures to your PC instead of using the Picture and Video Import program built in to Vista itself. If you're buying a new camera, direct support in Vista is a given.

Look and feel

Yeah, cameras have look and feel, just like computer applications do. And it's important. The best camera in the world won't do you much good if you can't use it easily. If you're always pushing controls the wrong way, or you can't quite find a comfortable way to hold the camera when you're taking a shot, that camera isn't for you.

It's always wise to try out a camera in a quiet, unpressured environment before you buy it. And in case you miss something important, buy from a dealer who will let you exchange your purchase if you change your mind. For these reasons, buying from a reputable local dealer can be a good move, even if a discounter on the Web offers you a better price.

Using conventional cameras

If you have an old-fashioned film camera and don't want to buy a digital camera (hey, the investment in lenses alone could kill ya), you can take pictures with a conventional film camera and have the photofinisher digitize them. The photofinisher may return the digitized images to you on a CD-ROM or may post them on a secure Web site from which you can download them.

If you're a casual photographer, this approach lets you get your pictures online without buying a new camera. If you're an advanced user, it may be attractive because the best film cameras still produce better results than the best digital cameras. (I know those are fighting words in some corners, but my ancient Hasselblad can beat up your wimpy digital camera any day — so *there.*) By having the photofinisher do the digitizing, you get the best of both worlds: digital images for their ease of use and negatives/positives for the highest-quality results.

On the other hand, digitizing with a photofinisher is relatively slow, because you have to wait for the film to be processed. It is expensive because you have to pay for film, processing, and digitizing. And you may have to change photofinishers to get the service.

Plugging webcams

A webcam (a.k.a. Internet camera, QuickCam, or Network Camera) is like a little video camera designed to work only while attached to a computer. All modern webcams come with USB interfaces — plug one into a USB port on your PC, and you're off to the movies — or an 802.11 connection that communicates with your wireless network.

Some people use webcams to publish a continuous, live video feed through a Web site. Popular feeds include pictures of fish in a tank, waves on a shore, burglars breaking into houses, and . . . uh, let's just leave it at that. Other popular uses are videoconferencing and recording still pictures or short movie clips to include in e-mails. Yahoo! Messenger, Google Messenger, AIM, Trillian, and Windows Live Messenger all tie into webcams with a click and a sigh.

I know lots of people who comb their hair every morning, for a change, on the off chance that they'll be instant-messaged with a webcam.

Webcams are generally less expensive than digital picture–taking cameras but are also more limited because they work only when plugged into an operating computer. Their resolution is low: typically 320×240 to 640×480 pixels (with as many as 1 million pixels for snapshots). The lens, image quality, and color accuracy are adequate for the camera's intended purpose but may be poorer than a point-and-shoot camera.

If you want to get images into your computer quickly and easily and don't need high quality, a webcam may be just the thing for you. They're pretty darn cheap, to boot.

I use my webcam as a kind of 3D scanner. Instead of trying to get decent scans of small items (such as coins and computer parts), I just set the subjects on a black background and hook up the webcam, and I have a picture in a second.

Panning camcorders

Digital video recorders have taken over the earth. Where I used to see hordes of bleary-eyed tourists staring into viewfinders, snapping rolls of 35-mm film, I now see hordes of bleary-eyed tourists staring into washed-out LCDs, taking videos of stationary objects. "Wave your hand, Aunt Martha!" That's what passes for motion these days.

The camcorder field changes so quickly it's impossible to give general guidelines regarding manufacturers, styles, or even technologies, which seem to evolve from week to week. But a few issues stand out, year after year, camera after camera.

If you are looking for a camcorder, get good answers to these questions before you buy:

✦ **Will the camcorder work in low light?** This seems to be the Achilles heel of most camcorders. Don't rely on the manufacturer's claims or specifications. Look for comments from unbiased reviewers and (even better) real people.

✦ **Can you use the buttons?** Ergonomic problems bedevil still camera designers. Camcorder engineers have all their problems, and many more. Most camcorders have so many complicated controls, placed so close together, with ambiguous or nonexistent labels, that you need to lug along the owner's manual just to shoot a pic.

✦ **How long will the battery last? Really?** Camcorder batteries are notorious for going dead at the wrong time — and low batteries can lead to all sorts of anomalous behavior. If you think your camcorder needs to be fixed, try it with a new battery. You may be pleasantly surprised.

✦ **Can you see *anything* in bright light?** Those LCD screens are a lost cause when there's the tiniest bit of glare, but many cameras also use hard-to-see lights to show various settings or step you through the more complicated procedures.

✦ **What about color?** Most camcorders have a lot of trouble matching human skin tones, in particular, when moving from shady to bright locations. Shifting from natural to artificial light can turn a person green.

Here are some tips from the School of Hard Knocks:

✦ Don't even bother buying a camcorder without a stabilizer.

✦ The still shots produced by a camcorder will never measure up to (even mediocre) stills from a real digital camera — the technology is completely different.

✦ If you want decent sound, plan on paying extra for a real microphone.

✦ And, just like with still cameras, good optical zoom means something; digital zoom doesn't.

Most camcorders use regular DVDs, HDV or Mini-DV tape, or internal hard drives, but a few alternatives exist. If you go for one of the other storage media, keep in mind that it may be hard to find a mini-DVD disc or MicroMV tape in Upper Slobovistan.

You can reuse tapes, recording over old videos, dozens of times. Because the data the camera records is digital, the picture quality doesn't deteriorate — but your camcorder may need to rewrite and re-rewrite over "bad" sections of tape, reducing the available recording time and possibly leading to *dropouts,* or missed sections of video. For that reason, it's a good idea to use a new tape for important recordings. HDV tapes are specifically manufactured to reduce the number of dropouts.

Because each manufacturer uses slightly different lubricants for its tapes, and the lubricants can gunk up each other, you would be well advised to stick to one type of tape from one manufacturer, or clean the heads (with, say, a head-cleaning tape) when switching manufacturers.

How to Buy a Camera/Camcorder

Here's my 60-second guide to buying a digital camera or camcorder:

1. **Decide whether you want a still camera or a camcorder.**

Unless you can afford both a good digital camera and a good digital camcorder, this may be the most difficult decision. Ultimately, you have to decide how you want to use the pictures. Still cameras take lousy videos. Camcorders take lousy stills. If you want a telephone or a personal digital assistant (PDA), pick the phone or PDA on its own merits; digital photos just come along for the ride.

2. **Narrow your choices to two or three models.**

I recommend that you take a look at reviews in the major magazines and on Web sites such as www.pcworld.com and www.pcmag.com. Photo magazine pieces are great, too, but unless you look at a side-by-side review that compares many cameras, you may be swayed by a tiny new feature which may or may not be all it's cracked up to be.

3. Search the Web for comments.

A few minutes spent with Google — particularly Google Groups — can save you days of headaches. Although you can't believe everything you read online, if you see ten complaints about low-level-light photos with a camera you've chosen, you should think twice about buying it.

4. Search the Web for prices and keep a list of the lowest ones.

When you have a short list of cameras you're interested in, it's easy to run a quick price comparison. Everybody has his or her favorite shopping sites, but I always check www.mysimon.com, www.shopping.com, www.pricegrabber.com, www.nextag.com, and www.bizrate.com. I also drop by www.amazon.com, both to see what customers say and to see whether Amazon's prices are competitive.

Don't overlook www.nextag.com. This site shows you historical prices for the camera so that you can see how rapidly the price is decreasing (see Figure 3-3). A recent, fast descent may mean that the camera's ready to be replaced with a newer model.

Book VII
Chapter 3

Discovering Digital Cameras

Figure 3-3:
Nextag.com includes a price history graph that speaks volumes about price trends.

NexTag®	Comparison Shopping for Products Mortgages Travel Schools More ▾		Sign In

a620   **NexTag Search**

related searches: canon a620, powershot a620, sd620, a620camera, powershota620, canon a620 camera, more...

Not what you're looking for? See additional matches in Bed & Bath, Electronics or all categories.

All Categories : Electronics : Digital Cameras : Canon   Have One to Sell?

Canon PowerShot A620 Silver Digital Camera 7.1MP Digital Camera
Compact - 7.1MP - 4x Optical Zoom - 4x Digital Zoom - SD/MMC Memory Card - 32 MB Installed Memory

You have never seen anything quite like the PowerShot A620. Loaded with features, this high-performance camera has a 7.1MP CCD to give you magnificent pictures at a price that will amaze you. The crisp detail and brilliant more...

Part #: 0321B001 / POWERSHOTA620

Sellers Found: 3
Available Since: Aug 30, 2005
Lowest Price: $318.00
Set Price Alert

★★★★☆ (52 user ratings)
Read 4 Reviews | Write a Review
Rate Product
◯1 ◯2 ◉3 ◯4 ◯5
poor   excellent

Price History Oct/06 (c) NexTag
400 350 300 250 200 150
Sep Nov Jan MarMay Jul Sep Nov

Compare Prices	Read 4 Reviews	Write Product Review	Details & Specs	Price History

Seller	Seller Ratings	Description	Price	+Tax & Shipping	True Price
TECH for LESS	⚙ Trusted Seller ★★★★☆ 69 Seller Reviews	In Stock	Best Value* $320.00 Buy at Seller	To calculate TruePrice, including exact Tax and Shipping, enter your zip code below. Enter Zip Code: [ ] Go	
Wild Digital	New Seller	In Stock	$333.00 Buy at Seller		

Don't forget the batteries

Digital cameras eat batteries for lunch. The Energizer Bunny might last only 20 minutes in a normal camera, particularly one being used at night. You need rechargeable batteries.

If you have a choice in the type of battery you buy, consider the following:

- **Lithium-Ion (Li-Ion):** These batteries recharge faster and hold their charge longer. But they cost more, and you can't recharge them as many times as other types of batteries.

- **Nickel-Metal Hydride (NiMH):** These batteries are slow on the uptake and discharge quickly, but they aren't as expensive

and can be recharged many more times than Li-Ion batteries. NiMH batteries are measured in milliamp-hours (mAh) per charge: A 1,800-mAh battery will last 12.5 percent longer than a 1,600-mAh battery on one charge.

- **Nickel-cadmium (NiCad):** These batteries are the dogs — slow to charge and quick to die; they degenerate (each progressive charge gets less effective) and die much sooner than Li-Ion or NiMH.

Also, consider spending extra for a fast recharger. If you have to wait eight hours to recharge your batteries, and each set lasts 20 minutes — well, you do the math.

---

5. **After you have a good idea of what you want and how much it costs, you can shop anywhere with confidence.**

   Local discount stores may have the camera cheaper (don't forget to factor in shipping costs). Camera shops might charge a few dollars more, but their help — and the knowledge that you're supporting a local business — could well be worth spending a few extra dollars.

Moving Images to Your Computer

How you transfer images to your computer depends on the type of camera you're using.

If your brand-spanking-new camera came with a CD and a dire warning to install the camera manufacturer's program before trying to transfer pictures to your PC, fuhgeddaboutit. In my experience, file transfer applications from camera manufacturers are buggy, slow, error-prone, and a general pain in the neck. It's far better to use the program that comes with Vista.

If you're using a conventional camera and your images were scanned by the photofinisher, transferring images is easy: Simply put the CD-ROM in a handy CD drive and copy the files, or go to the photofinisher's Web site and follow its directions. Rocket science.

If you're using a video camera, you should first try the interface in Windows Movie Maker, which I discuss in Book VII, Chapter 5. If you bump into a problem and you're looking for answers, start with the camera manufacturer's Web site. See Table 3-2.

Table 3-2	Major Camera Manufacturers' Web Sites
Manufacturer	*U.S. Web Site*
Canon	www.usa.canon.com
Casio	www.casio.com
Fuji	www.fujifilm.com
Kodak	www.kodak.com
Logitech	www.logitech.com
Nikon	www.nikonusa.com
Olympus	www.olympusamerica.com
Panasonic	www.panasonic.com/consumer_electronics
Sony	www.sony.com

You can use any one of three procedures to bring images from digital cameras and Internet cameras into your PC:

✦ With webcams and digital cameras supported by Vista, plug the camera into your PC and use the Windows Picture and Video Import program (see the steps that follow).

✦ With any digital camera, you can use the file-transfer application provided with that camera, but I don't recommend these apps.

✦ With any digital camera that uses memory cards, you can transfer images by putting the card — say, a SmartMedia or CompactFlash card — into a memory card reader. Sticking the card in a reader brings up the Picture and Video Import program, and you can proceed in the same manner as if you had plugged the camera itself into the PC.

Use the Picture and Video Import program to transfer images stored in the memory of a digital camera to your PC (or to capture still images from a webcam) as follows:

1. **Plug the camera into the appropriate port on your computer.**

If it's a digital camera, turn it on. You may have to move the camera's controls to some particular setting; consult the camera's instructions for transferring images.

Vista should stumble for a few seconds, put a bubble in the notification area (near the clock) saying that it's installing the new device, and then confirm that the device is installed.

When Vista comes back up for air, it shows you an AutoPlay dialog box like the one shown in Figure 3-4.

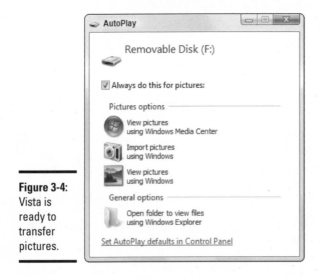

Figure 3-4:
Vista is ready to transfer pictures.

2. **Click the Import Pictures Using Windows icon.**

The Picture and Video Import program asks whether you want to tag the pictures being brought in (see Figure 3-5). If all the pictures on your camera share some theme, it's easiest and smartest to tag them now. The tag can help you find the right pictures later — and you can always add, change, or delete tags in the Photo Gallery.

Figure 3-5:
Adding a tag now is quick and easy.

3. **Type a tag that you want to associate with the pictures. If you want Windows to erase the pictures inside the camera after they've been transferred to your computer, select the Erase after Importing check box (see Figure 3-6). When you're ready, click the Import button.**

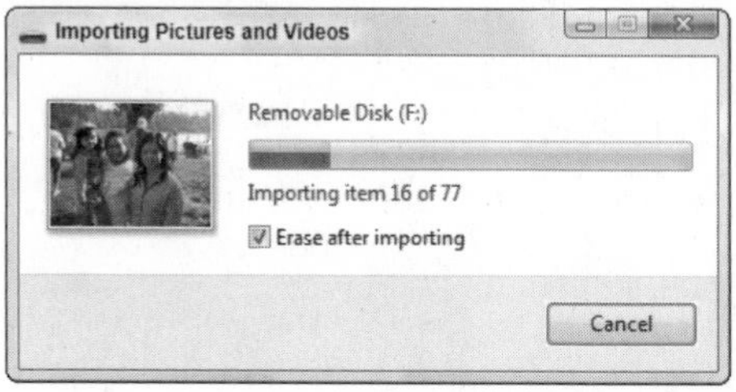

Figure 3-6: If you like, tell Windows to erase pictures after they're imported.

> **Importing Pictures and Videos**
>
> Removable Disk (F:)
>
> Importing item 16 of 77
>
> ☑ Erase after importing
>
> Cancel

Vista copies all the pictures on the camera and puts them in a folder labeled with the current date and the tag you typed in Step 3. In this case, I imported the pictures on December 31, 2006, so Vista created a new folder called \Pictures\2006-12-31 Family Reunion 2006 and put all the pictures in that folder.

If you chose to erase after importing, Vista then goes into your camera and deletes all the imported pictures.

Mission accomplished, the Picture and Video Import program opens the Windows Photo Gallery (Figure 3-7), showing you all the pictures you just imported, allowing you to work with them immediately.

I talk about Windows Photo Gallery in the next chapter, Book VII, Chapter 4.

If Vista doesn't recognize your camera, the least-hassle alternative, by far, is to use a memory card reader. These cheap little devices plug into your computer's USB port. Simply stick your camera's memory card (probably an SC card, a CompactFlash card, an xD card, or a Memory Stick) into the card reader, and Vista thinks you have a new hard drive. Files on the camera's memory card are treated just like any picture files in Windows.

If Vista still doesn't recognize your camera, you may have no choice but to try the software that shipped with the camera to transfer images from the camera to your PC. Most digital cameras come with such an application. Install the application and follow its instructions. Good luck.

If Vista *does* support your camera directly, you may still want to take a look at the camera's file-transfer application anyway. Some of these applications have useful functions that Vista does not provide, such as remotely setting some of the camera's controls.

Figure 3-7:
Vista shuffles you off to the Photo Gallery, where you can start working with your newly imported pictures.

Sharing Your Pictures on the Web

When you have some nice pictures on your computer, naturally you want to share them with other interested people. As I mention in the next chapter, it's easy to use Photo Gallery to send pictures by e-mail or to burn pictures to a CD.

Many Internet Service Providers maintain Web servers where their subscribers can post their Web sites with personal material. You can use such a Web site to "publish" your pictures. Anyone who knows where to look can see them, of course, which you may or may not consider a good thing.

Check your service provider's Web site for information about its file-hosting policies and instructions for uploading files.

More and more people are using free or very inexpensive Web sites to share pictures. It makes a lot of sense: You don't need to clog your friends' inboxes with big pics when they can browse your pics on Flickr or Smugmug, download what they like — or ignore you completely.

The following list describes the most popular picture-sharing sites:

✦ Yahoo!'s **Flickr,** www.flickr.com, the granddaddy of free photo-sharing sites, lets you upload up to 20MB of photos per month at no charge. The "Pro" package includes 2GB of monthly uploads and an unlimited amount of storage, for $24.95 per year. You can specify who can see your pics or open them to the world, and uploading photos from your camera is easy. Tags and an "interestingness" filter help you find photos from other people that might ring your chimes.

✦ **Smugmug,** www.smugmug.com, may not be as big or well known as Flickr, but it draws rave reviews for all its services, including photo printing and the ability to sell your photos online, using a full-fledged shopping cart system. Smugmug runs $29.95 per year, with a 7-day free trial — but you have to enter a credit card number to sign up for the free trial.

✦ **Fotki,** www.fotki.com, doesn't support video, but it has a very easy-to-use interface, full automated Really Simple Syndication (RSS) feeds so that you can tie your pics to your blog, and "communities" of like-minded folks.

I cover digital photography extensively (and even answer questions!) on my Web site, www.AskWoody.com. You can also pick up *Digital Photography For Dummies, 5th Edition,* by Julie Adair King (published by Wiley).

Chapter 4: Mugging in the Photo Gallery

In This Chapter

✔ **Organizing with the Photo Gallery**

✔ **Fixing Fotos**

✔ **Taking advantage of Photo Gallery quirks**

✔ **Printing at home and at the studio**

*R*emember that photo I took of Dad falling out of the fishing boat? You know, the one from 1998? Or was it 1996? Wait a sec. Gimme a minute. I have it right here. Uh . . . no, it must be over here. . . . Hmmm, maybe it's in this folder down here. . . . Is it on the network drive? Er . . . Where in the %$#@! did I put that thing?

Vista's Windows Photo Gallery brings a handful of sophisticated tools to the thorny problems of gathering, fixing, and most of all *finding* pictures on your computer.

Unfortunately, Vista can't read your mind. If you want to retrieve that shot of Dad falling out of the fishing boat, you need to mark — to *tag* — the picture with some pertinent keywords that you can later find. I don't know about you, but it'd take me a year or two to go through all my old shots and sort them out. By the time I was done, I'd have to start all over again with new shots. Like the hare and the tortoise, I'd probably never finish.

That's the fundamental problem with Photo Gallery's fancy indexing methods. Vista can't create indexes out of thin air. You have to do the work before you can reap the rewards — and it's debatable whether all the time you might invest in cataloging your pictures will ever pay off.

You have to put the garbage in before you can take it out, eh?

Leafing through the Gallery

Windows Photo Gallery appears in one of two guises:

✦ When you browse through many pictures (see Figure 4-1), you can use the navigation pane on the left to narrow the view, and (optionally) the info pane on the right to see or change information about a specific picture.

Navigation tree

Photo Gallery toolbar · · · · · · · · · · · Change view · · · Search box · · · · Information pane

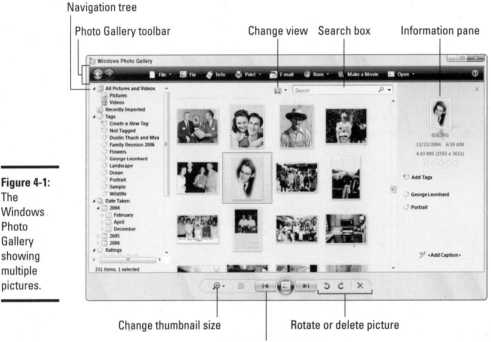

Figure 4-1:
The
Windows
Photo
Gallery
showing
multiple
pictures.

Change thumbnail size · · · · · · · · · · · · · Rotate or delete picture

Move one picture at a
time, or play slideshow

✦ When you look at just one picture (see Figure 4-2), the Photo Gallery has a small set of "Fix" tools available for you to change the color of the picture, crop it, or remove red eye.

Although the two different views of the Photo Gallery look very similar, in fact they serve two totally different masters. When you're working with multiple pictures, Photo Gallery's emphasis lies on cataloging and retrieving your pics. When you look at just one picture, Photo Gallery offers a limited set of touch-up tools.

Photo Gallery toolbar   Selected picture   "Fix" or Information pane

Figure 4-2:
The Photo
Gallery
working
with a single
picture.

Zoom   Rotate or delete picture   Undo/Redo

Navigate or
play slideshow

Microsoft's Photo Gallery development team likes to say that Photo Gallery is designed to store your "digital memories." Gag me with a RAMDAC. What they're really saying is that Photo Gallery only works with the kinds of picture files that are commonly produced by digital cameras — JPG and MPG (and to a lesser extent, TIF) files, with RAW format support promised at some point in the indefinite future — as well as BMPs. You can't use Photo Gallery to look at GIF, PCX, or WMF files. Yet another reason why it's important to have Vista show you filename extensions (see Book II, Chapter 1).

Adding Photos to the Photo Gallery

You can put photos in the Photo Gallery in the following three ways:

✦ You can use the Picture and Video Import program to pull them off a camera and add them to the Photo Gallery automatically.

✦ You can copy or move a picture (which is to say, a JPG, TIF, MPG, or MPEG file) to your Pictures folder or any folder within the Pictures folder.

✦ You can point the Photo Gallery at a folder, either on your computer or on your network (if you have one), and tell Photo Gallery to add the photos in that folder to the Gallery.

Using Vista's Picture and Video Import program

When you transfer photos from your camera to your PC, be sure to use the Windows Picture and Video Import program, as I describe in Book VII, Chapter 3. If you use Vista's importer, you're more likely to remember to tag your shots — and that can help you find them at some point in the dim, dark future.

When you use the Import program and type in a tag, Vista moves all the pictures into a folder within your Pictures folder that's stamped with the current date and the tag. For example, in Chapter 3, I import a bunch of pictures with the tag *Family Reunion 2006* and drop them in a subfolder like this:

```
\Pictures\2006-12-31 Family Reunion 2006
```

In addition, I added the tag "Family Reunion 2006" so that the filenames become `Family Reunion 2006 001.jpg`, `Family Reunion 2006 002.jpg`, and so on.

Photos that are added via the Picture and Video Import program appear in the Recently Imported category (see the navigation pane in Figure 4-1) and remain there until you import another batch of pictures.

Copying to the Pictures folder

If you already have pictures on your computer or network (and I bet you do), the mere act of copying them or moving them to your Pictures folder, or any folder within the Pictures folder, adds them to the Photo Gallery. Similarly, copying or moving videos to the Videos folder adds them to the Photo Gallery.

The Photo Gallery doesn't work with — doesn't even recognize — GIF, BMP, or WMF files. If you move a GIF file to your Pictures folder, you can't see it in the Photo Gallery.

Also, copying or moving pictures to the `\Public\Pictures` folder or the `\Public\Videos` folder — the folders that Vista sets up in your "public" shared folder — also adds them to the Photo Gallery. You don't need to lift a finger.

Perhaps surprisingly, if you click and drag a file — any file — into the Photo Gallery window, the file gets copied to your Pictures folder. That's true even if the file you drag isn't a picture file.

Adding photos from a different folder

So you have photos stored on a network drive? Yeah, me, too.

Fortunately, it's easy to tell Photo Gallery to add those photos to the gallery — without copying them to your Pictures or \Public\Pictures folder. Here's how:

1. **If Windows Photo Gallery isn't running, start it by choosing Start⇨All Programs⇨Windows Photo Gallery.**

The Photo Gallery appears, showing multiple pictures (see Figure 4-3).

Figure 4-3: The Windows Photo Gallery with multiple pictures.

Book VII Chapter 4

Mugging in the Photo Gallery

2. **Choose File⇨Add Folder to Gallery.**

Vista opens a dialog box that lets you navigate to the folder you want.

3. **Locate the folder you want to add, and click the OK button.**

Vista warns you that it's going to take a while, and the Photo Gallery might run a bit slowly, as shown in Figure 4-4. Click the OK button, and go grab a latte. By the time you come back, the Photo Gallery should show all the new pictures.

When you use this approach, the photos stay where they are — Photo Gallery doesn't copy them or touch them in any way.

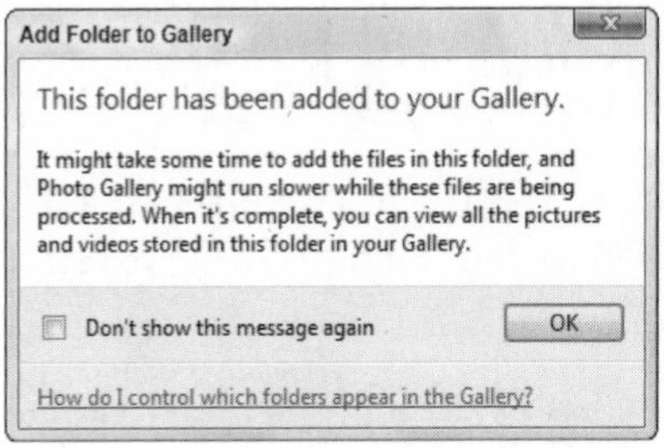

Figure 4-4:
You see this message when you add a folder to the Gallery.

Add Folder to Gallery
This folder has been added to your Gallery.
It might take some time to add the files in this folder, and Photo Gallery might run slower while these files are being processed. When it's complete, you can view all the pictures and videos stored in this folder in your Gallery.
☐ Don't show this message again   [OK]
How do I control which folders appear in the Gallery?

If you delete a photo from the Photo Gallery, Vista deletes the file — so the picture not only disappears from the Gallery, but it also disappears, period — even if the photo is located on a networked drive! If you accidentally delete a picture on your computer, you can pick it back up in the Recycle Bin. But if you delete a picture out on a network drive, it's gone. Bye-bye.

Finding Pictures

I wish I had a nickel for every new Vista user who bellyaches that the Photo Gallery doesn't show pictures "the old-fashioned way" — which is to say, arranged by folder. That simply isn't true. In fact, the Photo Gallery gives you two different ways of looking at pictures by folder, and both of them are vastly superior to anything that Windows has offered before. The following sections describe these options.

Looking by location

So you're stuck in a time warp and you really just want Photo Gallery to show you your shots based on the folder they're located in? No sweat. You have two choices:

✦ **Click the down arrow next to the Thumbnail View button, and choose Group By⇨Folder (see Figure 4-5).** The contents of every folder known to Photo Gallery appear grouped together, with the name of the folder at the top.

✦ **Alternatively, if you know which folder you want, simply click the name of the folder in the navigation pane on the left** (see Figure 4-6). That lets you "drill down" quickly.

If you've spent more than ten minutes looking for a photo, you already know that browsing for pictures based on their location on disk can drive you nuts in no time. That's why tags were invented.

Figure 4-5:
To view
photos by
folder,
use the
Thumbnail
View button.

Figure 4-6:
To drill
down to a
specific
folder,
use the
navigation
pane.

Skipping through tags

When you tag your pictures, the Photo Gallery keeps an index that makes it lightning-quick to find any pic with the specific tag. The problem, of course, is that you have to type in a tag or two or three before Photo Gallery has anything to find.

Say you took a picture of your dad falling out of a fishing boat. You might want to tag the picture with, oh, "dad," "fishing," and "boat." After you've tagged a hundred thousand pictures or so, you can tell Photo Gallery to bring up all the pics with the "dad" tag and narrow your choices considerably.

Tagging a picture

To add a tag to a picture or group of pictures, follow these steps:

1. **Open the Photo Gallery, if it isn't already open, by choosing Start⇨All Programs⇨Photo Gallery.**

2. **Click the picture that you want to tag.**

To give a bunch of pictures the same tag(s), hold down Ctrl while clicking each picture. Alternatively, if the pictures are contiguous (one right after another), you can click the first picture, hold down Shift, and click the last picture, or you can "lasso" them by clicking and dragging a box over the picture(s) you want to select.

Photo Gallery shows selected pictures with a gray border around them.

3. **Click the Add Tags icon, type in the first tag you want to apply to all the selected pictures, and press Enter.**

To add more tags to the same group of pictures, click the Add Tags icon again, type in the next tag, and press Enter. Repeat until you've given the selected pics all the tags you like.

When you click the Add Tags icon, Photo Gallery shows you a list of all the tags that you've typed. To make sure that you don't misspell a tag (with potentially disastrous results!), simply click the tag that you want to add to additional photos and press Enter (see Figure 4-7).

Tags that you assign to a picture travel with the picture. If you tag a photo as "dad," "fishing," and "boat" and you send a copy of the picture to your brother, and your brother puts the picture in his Pictures folder, he'll be able to use Vista's Photo Gallery to find the picture using any of the tags.

Finding a tagged picture

If your tags are in good shape, Photo Gallery can find the tagged pictures in a split second. You have two choices:

✦ In the search box, type the tag(s) that interest you. If you type more than one tag, Photo Gallery retrieves all pictures that match *any* of the tags — in Boolean terms, the search is an OR search (such as find "dad" OR "mountain" OR "boat").

Figure 4-7:
You can choose from tags that you've typed already by clicking the Add Tags drop-down list.

When you search using the search box, Photo Gallery looks for tags, but it also looks for filenames. So if you have a picture called `godaddy.jpg` and a tag named "dad," searching for "dad" brings up both the tagged pictures and the pic called `godaddy.jpg`.

✦ In the navigation pane, on the left, click the tag. Photo Gallery shows you all the pictures that have the specific tag.

You can combine tags with other entries in the navigation pane. For example, if you click the "dad" tag, then Ctrl+click the Date Taken entry 2005, Photo Gallery shows you all the pictures with the "dad" tag that were taken in 2005. In other words, Photo Gallery performs an AND search.

Confusingly, if you Ctrl+click to select two different tags, Photo Gallery performs an OR search. So, if you click the "dad" tag and Ctrl+click the "mom" tag, Photo Gallery shows you all the pictures with the "dad" tag, plus all the pictures with the "mom" tag — you see pictures with either "dad" OR "mom" (or both).

Rearranging the tag list

Tags are like coat hangers: Ignore them for a day or two, and all of a sudden, you have hundreds of 'em. Tags help you manage pictures. Photo Gallery helps you manage tags.

You can click and drag tags in the navigation pane, creating a hierarchy of tags. Simply click a tag and drag it to the desired location. Grouping tags in ways that make sense to you decreases the amount of hunting and clicking necessary to find the right tag.

For example, in Figure 4-8, I organized a bunch of tags that I used to keep track of pictures taken in Thailand: individual cities, places within the cities, festivals, and so on. Clicking a higher-level tag brings up all the pictures associated with the tag and all lower-level tags. So if I click "Phuket," I also get pictures of the Vegetarian Festival in Phuket. It's a powerful capability.

Figure 4-8:
Organize tags to make them easier to find.

Touching Up Pictures

Windows Photo Gallery offers a small set of the most-used photo touch-up tools, specifically designed to be easy to use and not particularly intimidating — or powerful. You may find them useful . . . or not.

The Photo Gallery "fix" tools can permanently change a picture (unless you're using Vista Business, Enterprise, or Ultimate and its ShadowCopy feature automatically saves an older version). For that reason, I strongly recommend that you make a backup copy of a picture before you apply fixes.

Here's how to safely and effectively touch up your pictures:

1. **In Photo Gallery, double-click a picture and then click the Fix icon on the toolbar.**

Vista shows you the touch-up tools on the right of the screen, as shown in Figure 4-9.

Figure 4-9: The "fix" tools appear on the right.

2. **Immediately choose File⇨Make a Copy and save a copy of the original, giving it a name that you can remember.**

3. **To let Photo Gallery try to adjust everything on its own, click the Auto Adjust icon.**

Vista analyzes the picture and automatically adjusts the brightness, contrast, and color.

If you don't like what Photo Gallery did to your picture, click the Undo button at the bottom of the Fix pane.

4. **To adjust your photo manually, click the Adjust Exposure icon to set brightness and contrast, and click the Adjust Color icon to set color temperature, tint, and saturation (see Table 4-1).**

5. **To crop the picture (cut off the edges), click the Crop Picture icon.**

You can then set the crop location manually, or you can click the Proportion drop-down list (see Figure 4-10) to crop for specific print sizes (actually, aspect ratios). When you're happy with your croppin', click the Apply button.

Figure 4-10: It's easy to crop to fit a specific print size.

6. **To fix "red eye" (see the nearby sidebar), click the Fix Red Eye icon and then drag a box around the eye that's red.**

To get the most accurate red-eye correction, you usually need to zoom in so that you can pick out the bad eye. To do so, click the Display Size icon in the lower-left corner and swing the slider up to zoom in the picture. Then hold down Alt while you click and drag the picture, moving it around so that you can get to the eye. When you have the eye in, uh, sight, release Alt and click and drag a box around the eye. Make the box as small as you can while still getting all the red. Release the mouse button, and Vista does its level best to get the red out.

When you're done, click Back to Gallery. Your changes are saved automatically. Which is why you made a copy of the original in Step 2, eh?

The touch-up tools are designed to be used in order, from top to bottom.

What is red eye?

That devilish glint of red in a photographed eye arises because your camera's flash happened so quickly that the iris of the eye didn't have a chance to close the pupil. Light from the flash gets focused by the eye's lens onto the retina, at the back of the eye. The lens then focuses the light back to the camera. All the blood in the retina results in a vivid red color.

Animals get red eye, too. Pictures of cats can have "red" eye, but it's usually green, because of a coating in the cat's eyes.

Most modern cameras have red-eye reduction modes that cause the flash to go off multiple times before the real picture gets taken. Those preliminary blasts suffice to close the pupil.

Red eye only occurs when the flash goes straight into the eye and straight back. If you have a lot of problems with red eye, try to bounce your flash — aim the flash at the ceiling or a wall — or have the person look away from the camera.

Table 4-1	A Layman's Guide to Color
Term	*What It Means*
Brightness	Makes all the pixels in the picture lighter or darker, by the same amount
Contrast	Changes the relative darkness of individual pixels
Temperature	Makes reds look more blue (sliding to the right) or blues look more red
Tint	Adjusts the green and red
Saturation	Makes the colors more or less intense

Chapter 5: Lights! Action! Windows Movie Maker

In This Chapter

- ✔ Recording and editing video
- ✔ Burning your own DVDs — within limits, anyway
- ✔ Bringing in narration and background sounds
- ✔ Creating transitions

No, you can't go down to Blockbuster, rent a DVD, take it home, and make a copy of it using Windows Movie Maker (WMM). There. That answers about 80 percent of the questions I get about WMM.

Yes, you *can* take that TV program you recorded with Windows Media Center — you know, that huuuuuuuuuuuge hour-long 4GB DVR-MS file — run it through WMM, and save the program as a 400MB WMV file. The trip through WMM will take more than an hour of computer time. But it'll reduce the size of the file by 80 to 90 percent. That answers about 80 percent of the questions I *should* get about WMM.

(No, you can't process "protected" shows you may have recorded, like the ones on the movie channels. But you can process VOB files, the files created by most camcorders.)

Windows Movie Maker brings a full-featured video-editing workshop to your PC. You can use it to create anything from a few seconds of action — say, to dress up an e-mail message — to a full-length documentary about your kid's first birthday party. Get the sound synchronization right, and you could even toss together a decent music video, sell it to iTunes, and turn into an overnight sensation.

Just remember where you got the idea, huh?

Introducing Windows Movie Maker

Windows Movie Maker doesn't look much like other Microsoft applications: It's specially built for the task at hand and doesn't make many bones about that fact. If you start Windows Movie Maker (choose Start⇨All Programs⇨ Windows Movie Maker), you see the window shown in Figure 5-1.

Follow the tasks to put a movie together

Show or hide collections

Store clips here

Preview the movie

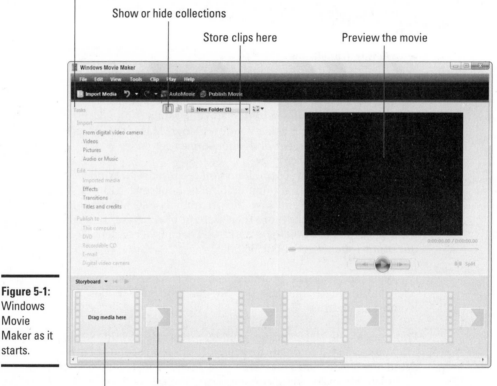

Figure 5-1:
Windows
Movie
Maker as it
starts.

Pick tranistions between clips

Drop clips in sequence

Take a moment to become familiar with the parts of the window. Up at the top, you see these three panes:

✦ The pane on the left suggests various *tasks* — steps that you can take to bring in clips, tie them together, add effects like titles, and save your movie. You won't go through every task, but this pane can help remind you of what to do next.

✦ The second pane shows *collections* of movie clips. A collection is a group of related movie clips with a name. You can use collections to organize your movie clips, much as you use folders to organize other types of files.

✦ The third pane shows you a preview of how your movie looks in its current sorry state.

If you click the Show or Hide Collections icon, the leftmost pane shows you all the collections of clips that Windows Movie Maker has at its disposal, as shown in Figure 5-2. The collections are arranged just like Windows folders — and that's the easiest way to think of them.

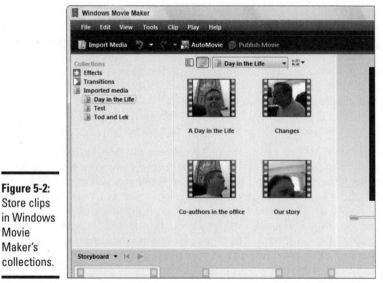

Figure 5-2:
Store clips in Windows Movie Maker's collections.

Book VII
Chapter 5

Lights! Action!
Windows
Movie Maker

Windows Movie Maker lets you put collections inside other collections, just as the Windows file system lets you put folders inside other folders. To put collection X inside collection Y, drag the icon for X on top of the icon for Y. To create a new collection inside collection Z, right-click collection Z and choose New Collection.

Below the three panes is the *workspace.* As you assemble movie clips into a whole movie, this area displays the state of your work and lets you control it. The workspace can appear as a *storyboard,* which shows the first still picture of each clip with room for transitions between the clips, or as a *timeline,* which superimposes a clock over the sequence of clips, with separate tracks for video, audio, and text titles.

Gathering Clips

Before you can edit video, you must get some clips into your computer. D'oh!

In general, you have the following four choices:

+ **Use your camcorder (or even your webcam).** WMM helps you bring in movies from any digital video camera. Whatever you can see on that tiny video screen will look great pulled into your PC — and because it's digital, the quality should be outstanding. Click the Import Media button on the toolbar and follow the instructions.

+ **Use Windows Media Center to record your favorite shows.** You can't burn "protected" material onto a DVD, but many TV shows can be used as WMM fodder. Find out all about Windows Media Center in Book VIII.

+ **Beg, borrow, or steal existing clips.** The Web's full of video clips that you can use. No doubt your friends have marvelous cute clips of Little Dufous spilling ice cream on his blue suede shoes. Any MPG, AVI, WMV, or other video file, including DVR-MS files generated when you record a TV show in Windows Media Center, and VOB files from certain kinds of camcorders; any MP3, WMA, WAV, or other audio file; any JPG, GIF, TIF, BMP, or other picture file — they're all fair game.

+ **Go analog.** Whether you're trying to retrieve old predigital camcorder clips, movies from a VCR, or even a direct feed from your television or satellite TV box, WMM can transform anything you see in the analog world into a file that can be edited and saved. But you have two major problems to deal with. First, you have to buy a gizmo that translates TV output into digital signals. (You can get cables from Pinnacle and Belkin and many other companies that plug into your camcorder's S-Video port on one end, and your USB port on the other; but you can also buy a video card or a translation box.) Second, the quality of digital video generated by analog signals tends to be, uh, less than stellar.

If the clip you want already sits on your computer (or on another computer on your network), adding it to WMM's collections is easy — just click the Import Media button.

You can mix and match clips from all those sources.

If you don't have all the gadgets you need — or don't know how to operate them — ask your dealer for assistance.

It's almost as easy as saying, "Lights! Camera! Action!" Except that you don't have to worry about blowing a $100 million budget, overrunning a 32-day shooting schedule, and/or keeping your stars out of each other's trailers.

Don't shake yer booty

Did you shoot a lot of video back before image stabilizers became all the rage — and came down in price? Yeah, me too.

If your movies shake like a Willy's in four-wheel drive (sorry, Jerry), help is at, uh, hand. A company called Goodervideo (www.goodervideo. com) offers a truly amazing program called

SteadyHand that takes the shakes out. Feed SteadyHand an AVI, MPEG, or ASF file filled with jerks and jitters, and the clip you get back looks like it was taken on a tripod bolted to the base of Cheyenne Mountain. At $66.66, Steady-Hand ain't cheap, but your old videos are worth it, aren't they?

Assembling a Movie

A *project* is a file that contains your work on a movie. In effect, a project *is* a movie, either completed or in development. A *clip* is a piece of a movie (or music or a still picture). In the preceding sections, I mention a bunch of ways to gather clips. When the clips are ready, you assemble the clips to create a project.

Creating a project

Here's how to put together a project, er, a movie:

1. **Choose Start➪All Programs➪Windows Movie Maker to start Windows Movie Maker. Immediately choose File➪Save Project, give your movie a name, and click the Save button to save the project.**

   Your project is ready to go.

2. **Choose a clip from one of your collections — or from anywhere else on your computer or network — and drag it to the storyboard at the bottom of the window.**

   To see all the collections available to you, click the Show or Hide Collections icon just below the toolbar, and WMM shows you a tiled list of collections (refer to Figure 5-2).

   An image of the clip appears in the first slot of the storyboard (see Figure 5-3).

3. **Drag one or two more clips to the unoccupied part of the storyboard.**

   An image of each one appears in the workspace.

Figure 5-3:
Drag a
movie clip
or still
picture
to the
storyboard
to start the
project.

Unless you change things, still photos dragged onto the storyboard appear in the final movie for five seconds.

It's easy to use Windows Photo Gallery to locate video clips and still photos (see Book VII, Chapter 4). If you find something you want to put in your project, click it in the Photo Gallery and drag it into Windows Movie Maker. The clip or picture gets added to the current collection. From there, it's another quick click-and-drag to move the clip to the storyboard.

You can insert a clip between two existing clips. Just drag it between the two clips.

4. **To move a clip in the workspace to a different position, click the clip, drag it to the place where you want to insert it, and release the mouse button.**

When you need to move a clip a long way, dragging can be clumsy and error-prone; the cutting and pasting technique is more convenient. To cut and paste, right-click the clip that you want to move and choose Cut. Then right-click the clip *after which* you want to place this clip and select Paste.

To delete a clip from the workspace, right-click the clip and choose Remove.

5. **To save your project, choose File⇨Save Project.**

Congratulations. You're well on your way to becoming a film legend.

Playing a clip or a movie

To play a clip, select it either in the collections pane or in the storyboard or timeline workspace. Then click the Play button under the preview area. When you've seen enough, click the Pause button to stop the playback. (See Figure 5-4.)

Pause   "Monitor" preview area

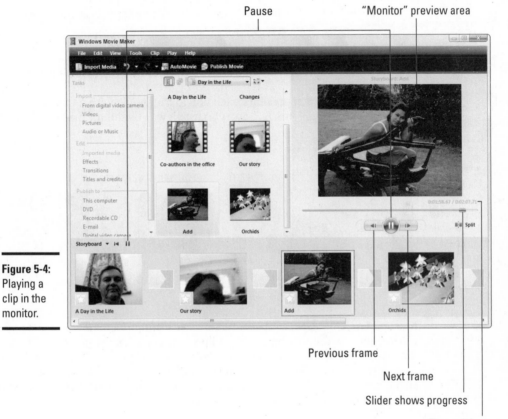

**Book VII
Chapter 5**

Lights! Action!
Windows
Movie Maker

Previous frame

Next frame

Slider shows progress

Elapsed time

Figure 5-4:
Playing a
clip in the
monitor.

As you play a clip, the slider underneath the monitor moves across the bar to show how far the monitor has progressed through the clip. The number near the monitor's lower-right corner shows the elapsed play time for the entire movie, to the nearest hundredth of a second, and the total time for the movie.

Clicking either the left or right arrow moves one frame at a time, backward or forward. You go in slow motion, until you click the Play button again.

Pressing either the left-arrow or the right-arrow key moves to the next (or previous) clip.

You can also play your entire movie in the "monitor" preview area. Choose Play⇨Play Storyboard (or Play Timeline, if the workspace shows a timeline).

Viewing the storyboard and timeline

The storyboard and the timeline are two different ways of viewing a movie.

The *storyboard* view represents each clip in the movie with a thumbnail image, as shown in Figure 5-5. Storyboard view is useful for assembling and rearranging clips.

Figure 5-5:
Storyboard view makes it click-and-drag easy to move around clips.

The *timeline* view represents each clip with a thumbnail image set in a space whose width is proportional to the clip's length, as shown in Figure 5-6. A timeline above the thumbnails helps you judge the playing time of each clip. Timeline view is useful for trimming the beginnings and ends of clips. It's also helpful for adding titles and sound. I cover how you trim clips and work with titles and sound later in this section.

Figure 5-6:
Timeline view shows three tracks: video, audio, and titles.

To switch between the storyboard and timeline view, click the Storyboard or Timeline down arrow, at the upper-left part of the pane.

Trimming a clip

Windows Movie Maker lets you *trim* individual clips — remove pieces at the beginning or end of the clip, to make it shorter. You can trim video or sound clips while in timeline view.

The hack-'n'-slash approach to trimming couldn't be simpler: While in timeline view, click the clip you want to trim and then drag either the left or the right edge of the clip inward, toward the center. WMM makes the trim quickly and easily — and it's reversible. If you ever decide to "undo" the trim, repeat the process, but drag the edge back outward, to its original position.

Making a precise trim — where you pick the exact frame that marks the beginning and the ending of the clip — doesn't take much more effort than the hack-'n'-slash approach. To trim either end of a clip with a bit of finesse, follow these steps:

1. **Make sure that Windows Movie Maker shows you the timeline at the bottom of the screen (if necessary, click the Storyboard down arrow and pick Timeline).**

2. **Click the clip in the timeline that you want to shorten.**

   The first frame of the clip appears in the "monitor" preview area.

3. **Move the slider (below the preview area) to the point where you want to trim the clip. You can choose from several ways to do this:**

   - Click the Play button and then click the Pause button when the clip reaches the right point.

   - Drag the slider's pointer to the right position. (Equivalently, you can click the appropriate time at the top of the timeline pane.) The monitor displays the frame at the spot in the clip where you release the pointer.

   - Click the Previous Frame and Next Frame buttons to move the pointer (and the monitor) backward and forward one frame at a time.

4. **When the slider's pointer is correctly positioned at the precise frame you want to use as the starting point for this clip, choose Clip➪Trim Beginning to trim the start of the clip to that point.**

5. **Move the slider to the point where you want to end the clip.**

6. **Choose Clip➪Trim End to trim the end of the clip to that point.**

When you trim a clip, the remaining part expands to fill the entire slider. If the workspace is in timeline view, the clip contracts in the timeline so that only the trimmed part is shown.

If you trim too much from a clip, choose Clip⇨Clear Trim Points to start over.

If you drag a clip from the collections pane to the workspace and trim it, and then you drag the same clip into the workspace again, the second copy is *not* trimmed. You can trim it differently if you want to.

To see more detail in the timeline view, click the + Magnifying Glass icon to zoom in. To see a larger span of time in less detail, click the – Magnifying Glass icon to zoom out.

Making transitions and adding effects

Windows Movie Maker gives you dozens of ways to manage the transition from one clip to the next. You can fade out the end of one clip while fading in the beginning of the next clip. You can wipe the screen, or shatter the last frame in a clip before moving on to the next.

Best of all, adding a transition to a movie takes only a few clicks. Here's the easiest way:

1. **Make sure that Windows Movie Maker shows you the storyboard at the bottom of the screen (if necessary, click the Timeline down arrow and choose Storyboard).**

2. **Choose Tools⇨Transitions.**

   WMM shows you the video transitions pane, in the middle, as shown in Figure 5-7.

3. **Click and drag a transition from the video transitions pane to a location between any of the clips.**

   The transition you specify is used to go from the first clip to the second.

4. **To see the effect of the transition, click the Play button on the monitor.**

   Use the Storyboard to start at any point in the presentation and check how your presentation's transitions look in the grand scheme of things. Don't like your handiwork? You can delete a transition by right-clicking it and choosing Delete.

In addition to the dozens of transitions available in Windows Movie Maker, you can also change the appearance of an individual clip: make it brighter or darker, rotate or mirror it, turn the color askew (to great effect with "old time" sepia), speed it up, or slow it down.

Figure 5-7:
Adding a
Reveal,
Right
transition.

To apply an effect to a clip, click Tools⇨ Effects and then click and drag the effect you want onto an unsuspecting clip. Click the Play button to preview the result and see what you think!

Splitting and combining clips

You can split or combine clips in two ways: In the workspace (either story-board or timeline view) and in the collections pane. When you split or combine clips in the workspace, the effect is similar to trimming a clip: Only that use of the clip is affected. When you split or combine clips in the collections pane, you actually split or combine the files that store the clips. This affects all projects that use the clips, now and in the future.

Splitting a clip in the workspace is useful if you want to insert a still picture or another clip in the middle of a clip. Combining clips in the workspace is not as common as splitting a clip, but you can do it.

Splitting/combining clips in the workspace

To split a clip in the workspace, follow these steps:

1. **Click the clip that you want to split.**

2. **Set the slider (below the "monitor" preview area) to the position where you want the split to occur.**

**Book VII
Chapter 5**

**Lights! Action!
Windows
Movie Maker**

You can click the right or left arrows to move a frame at a time, or you can bring up the timeline to set a precise time.

3. Click the monitor's Split button.

The storyboard shows two clips: one for the original clip up to the point of the split and the other for the remainder of the clip.

These clips exist only in the workspace; the clip in the collection (and on your hard drive) is not affected.

To combine two or more consecutive clips in the workspace, hold down Shift and click the first and last clip. Then choose Clip⇨Combine. Again, the clips in the collection, and on your hard drive, aren't harmed.

Splitting/combining clips in the collections pane

Splitting and combining clips in the collections pane is useful for organizing your clips. For example, you may need to split a clip because Windows Movie Maker failed to recognize a new clip between shots when recording. You may need to combine clips because Windows Movie Maker started a new clip where a new shot did not begin.

To split a clip in the collections pane, follow these steps:

1. Select the clip in that pane.

2. Move the slider to the split point that you want, and then click the Split button.

The "before the split" clip keeps its old filename. The "after the split" clip uses the same filename with a (1) afterward.

To combine clips in the collections pane, select the clips in the pane (Ctrl+click or Shift+click), right-click, and choose Combine.

You can combine clips only if they were recorded consecutively or were previously split from a single clip.

Typing titles

Superimposing text over your clips — or adding stand-alone title or credit clips — ranks as the simplest of WMM tricks, and the text formatting options boggle the imagination. Here's how to add titles:

1. Put your movie together first.

It's easiest to add titles when you nail down the location and duration of each clip in advance.

2. Choose Tools⇨Titles and Credits.

WMM asks where you want to add a title, as shown in Figure 5-8.

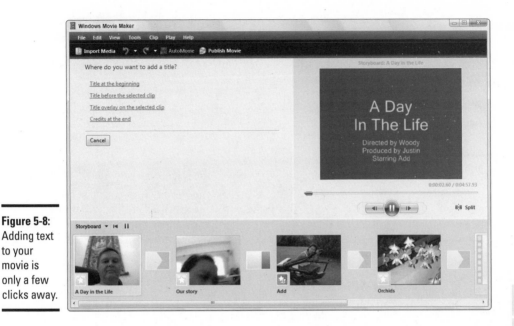

**Book VII
Chapter 5**

**Lights! Action!
Windows
Movie Maker**

Figure 5-8:
Adding text
to your
movie is
only a few
clicks away.

3. Choose the type of text you want to add.

If you want a title on a specific clip, make sure that you click the clip down in the workspace before clicking the Title Overlay on the Selected Clip link.

WMM presents you with two boxes (see Figure 5-9).

4. Type the text you want.

Text that you type in the top box appears in a larger font, near the top of the screen. Text in the lower box shows in a smaller font, underneath. Look for a preview in the monitor.

At the bottom of the Enter Text for Title pane, you'll find two options: Change the Title Animation and Change the Text Font and Color. Try both of them: Titles can fade in and out, fly, flash, or scroll, and the effect can be different if you have one or two lines. Text can appear transparent, in any color, in any font. Seriously kewl.

5. When the text looks good, click the Add Title button.

WMM places the title where you asked. To see it, use the monitor to play the movie or the clip.

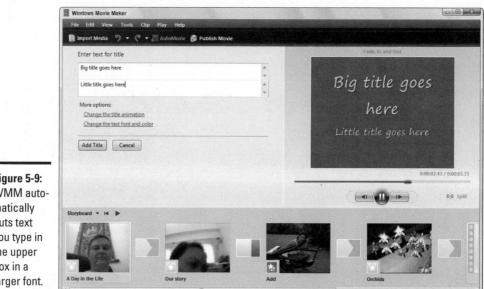

Figure 5-9:
WMM auto-matically puts text you type in the upper box in a larger font.

Using sound clips

You can narrate your movie and save the narration so that it plays whenever you view the movie. Windows Movie Maker stores the sound clip on your hard drive as a WMA audio file.

Recording a narration

To record a narration, follow these steps:

1. **Open the project you wish to narrate.**

Make sure that you're in timeline view by clicking the Storyboard down arrow and choosing Timeline if necessary.

It's easier to see what's happening if you expand the workspace at the bottom of the screen — just click the bar at the top of the workspace and drag it upward — so that you can see the Audio/Music track. That's where the narration will go.

2. **When you're ready to record, choose Tools⇨Narrate Timeline.**

Windows Movie Maker opens the Narrate Timeline dialog box, as shown in Figure 5-10.

3. **Make sure that your microphone is connected and working.**

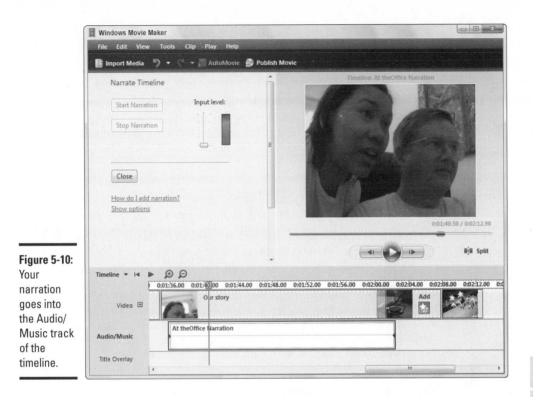

Figure 5-10:
Your narration goes into the Audio/ Music track of the timeline.

If the mic is live, you see the Input Level indicator bobbing up and down when you talk into it.

Click the Show Options link to record from a different microphone, or if you want to mute the speakers so that any sounds you currently have in the movie don't tromp over your narration.

4. **Click the Start Narration button to start recording.**

   Windows Movie Maker plays the movie as you record so that you can synchronize your narration with it.

5. **When you're done, click the Stop Narration button.**

   Windows Movie Maker opens a Save dialog box.

6. **Choose a filename and location for the recording and click the Save button.**

   After Windows Movie Maker saves the file, it returns to the main window, and your narration appears in the Audio/Music track.

   You can make another recording or click the Close button to close the dialog box.

You can't synchronize narration with a single clip selected in the workspace. To get the same effect, create a separate project that contains the clip and synchronize the narration to it.

Adding a sound clip to a movie

To add a sound clip to a movie, drag the sound clip from the current collection to the appropriate point in the workspace. This is essentially the same operation as adding a video clip, but note the following differences:

✦ Sound clips are visible only in timeline view and can be added or managed only in timeline view.

✦ Sound clips appear below video clips (refer to Figure 5-10).

✦ You can't leave spaces between video clips in the timeline, but you can leave spaces between sound clips. This enables you to set each sound clip's exact position relative to the movie's video clips.

You can play a sound clip by selecting it and clicking the monitor's Play button; the sound plays along with the video. You also can trim a sound clip the same way you would trim a video clip. Click the sound clip, and then use the monitor or the trim handles in the workspace's timeline. See the section "Trimming a clip," earlier in this chapter, for details.

Importing clips from other sources

You can use video clips, sound clips, and still pictures from other sources in your movies. For example, you can use pictures in the Photo Gallery (see Book VII, Chapter 4) or sound tracks ripped from a CD by Windows Media Player (assuming that you don't violate any copyright restrictions; see Book VII, Chapter 1). You also can download all three types of material from sources on the Web.

To import a clip or still image into Windows Movie Maker, it must reside on your computer. If the clip is on the Web, you must download it to your computer first.

The usual CYA (Cover Your, ah, Patootie) applies: If you plan to distribute your movie publicly or use it for commercial purposes, you cannot use copyrighted material without the copyright holder's permission. If in doubt, see your attorney for guidance.

When you have the file, here's how to put it in your movie, er, project:

1. **Click the Show or Hide Collections icon below the main toolbar so that you can see WMM's collections (refer to Figure 5-2).**

2. **Click the collection that you want the clip to go into.**

3. **Choose File⇨Import into Collections.**

4. **Find and select the file that you want to import, and then click the Open button.**

   Windows Movie Maker adds the file to the collection that you selected.

   Alternatively, you can simply click and drag the clip into Windows Movie Maker.

5. **When the clip or still image is in the current collection, you can click and drag away.**

The only technical restriction on importing clips is that they must be in one of the recording formats that Windows Movie Maker knows how to handle. Here is a list of the more common formats that work:

+ **Video clips:** `.avi`, `.wmv`, `.mpeg`, `.mpg`, `.mp2`, and `.wmv`

+ **Audio clips:** `.wav`, `.wma`, and `.mp3`

+ **Still pictures:** `.bmp`, `.jpeg`, `.jpg`, and `.gif`

Publishing the Movie

After you edit a movie to your satisfaction, you probably want to show it to other people. When you choose File⇨Save Project or File⇨Save Project As, Windows Movie Maker stores the movie as a project (a so-called `.mswmm` file) that can be watched only in Windows Movie Maker. Blech. If you want your friends to be able to view it, either they have to run Windows Movie Maker or you have to convert the movie into a format that other folks can use.

Vista also allows you to turn your movie into a DVD — one that can play in any DVD player — but only if you have Windows DVD Maker, and Windows DVD Maker only comes in Vista Ultimate or Vista Home Premium. Details are shown in Table 5-1.

Table 5-1	Ways to Publish a Movie
Publish Dialog Box Choice	*What It Does*
This Computer	Creates a file on your computer. You can make a DV-AVI file, which can be copied to (and used by) some camcorders. All the other options involve WMV files, ranging in quality from Windows Media Portable Device format to standard DVD quality to High-Definition TV — but they're all WMV files, which can't be played by most DVD players.
DVD	Saves and closes your project, and then opens Windows DVD Maker (see the sidebar, "Windows DVD Maker") with the movie in place so that you can burn a DVD that can be played in any DVD player. Note that Windows DVD Maker is only available in Vista Home Premium and Vista Ultimate editions.
Recordable CD	Creates a WMV file in precisely the same fashion as the This Computer option. You get to choose the quality, per Figure 5-12, and WMM then copies the newly created file to a recordable CD or DVD. Two common misconceptions exist with this option. First, you *aren't* creating a DVD (or CD) that can be played on most DVD players; all you get is a WMV file, which (in general) can only play on Windows computers. Second, you can burn the file onto either a CD or DVD, despite what the dialog box says.
E-Mail	Creates a standard WMV file, starts your e-mail program, creates a new message, and attaches the file to the message.
Digital Video Camera	Copies the movie directly to your camcorder.

Windows DVD Maker

Windows DVD Maker burns DVDs that can be played in DVD players. It ships with Windows Vista Home Premium Edition and Windows Vista Ultimate; you Home Basic, Business, and Enterprise folks need not concern yourselves.

This is probably just as well. If you've used a DVD-burning program worthy of the name, such as Nero or Xilisoft (see the sidebar, "Rip, burn, and convert movies"), Windows DVD Maker will leave you thoroughly underwhelmed. It's just about the wimpiest DVD burner you can imagine.

Windows DVD Maker lets you choose the 4:3 or 16:9 aspect ratio, NTSC or PAL format, when (or whether) you will see a DVD menu, and what the menu looks like. That's all she wrote.

You can *play* DVDs with any version of Vista. Burning — at least, burning with the built-in Windows software — is another story.

To get Windows DVD Maker going, choose Start⇨All Programs⇨Accessories⇨Windows DVD Maker.

To let others view your movie, follow these steps:

1. **In Windows Movie Maker, choose File⇨Publish Movie.**

Windows Movie Maker opens the Publish Movie dialog box, as shown in Figure 5-11.

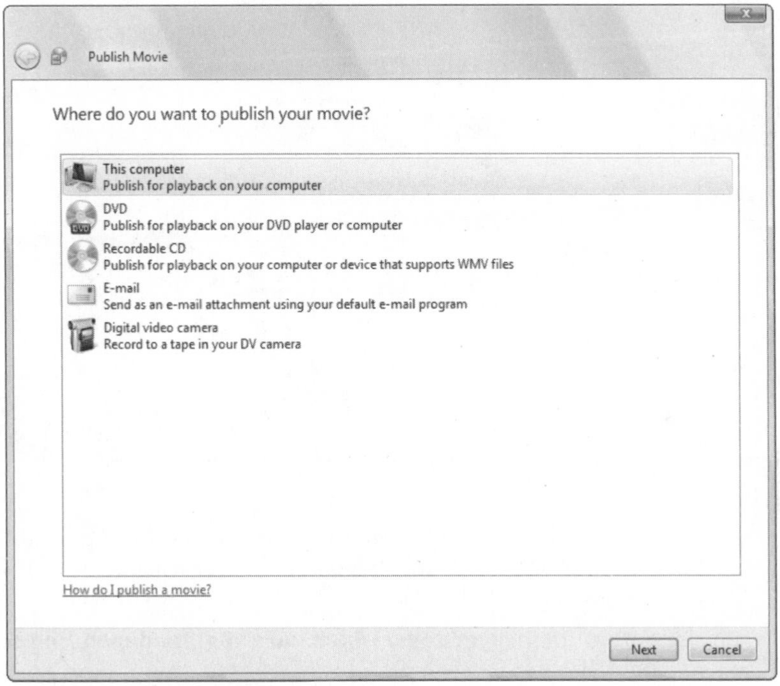

Figure 5-11:
Publishing options. For the real story, see Table 5-1.

Publish Movie

Where do you want to publish your movie?

This computer
Publish for playback on your computer

DVD
Publish for playback on your DVD player or computer

Recordable CD
Publish for playback on your computer or device that supports WMV files

E-mail
Send as an e-mail attachment using your default e-mail program

Digital video camera
Record to a tape in your DV camera

How do I publish a movie?

Next   Cancel

2. **Consult Table 5-1 to choose the best way to publish your movie, and then click the Next button.**

In Figure 5-11, I chose This Computer to publish the movie to my computer. The More Settings options in Figure 5-12 demonstrate the various WMV file qualities available.

If you choose to publish to This Computer, I recommend saving movies to some folder other than Videos. Otherwise, they are hard to distinguish from your clips, which are also stored in the Videos folder and also use the filename extension .wmv.

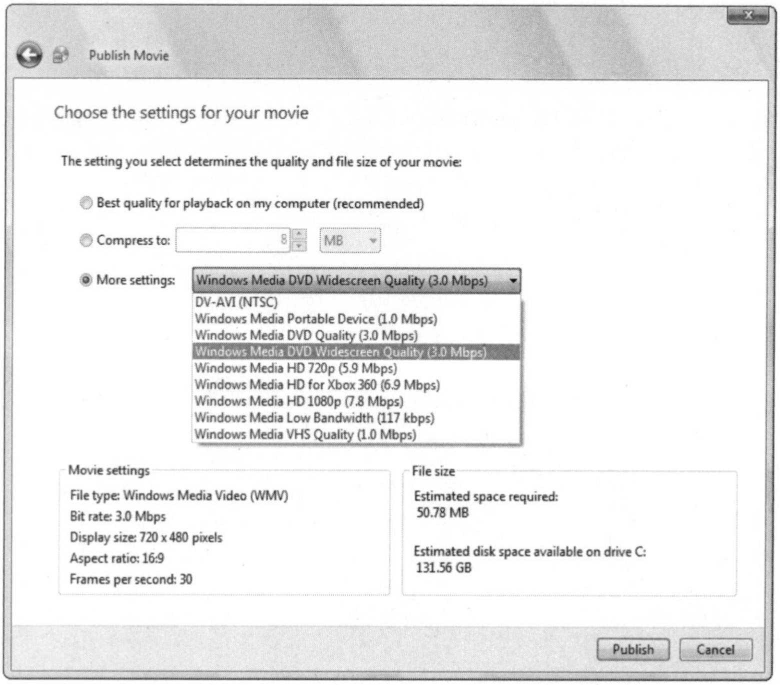

Figure 5-12:
You can set WMV file qualities when publishing to "This Computer" or "Recordable CD."

Beware of DV-AVI. A five-minute video might take up 50MB in the default WMV format. The same video could require as much as 1GB in DV-AVI format. A DV-AVI file can run *20 times* larger than WMV.

3. **Follow the instructions, which vary slightly depending on where you publish.**

   Converting the project to a movie file can take a long, long time. Several Ice Ages may pass. Ultimately, you see a dialog box that invites you to play the movie when you click the Finish button. (As if you haven't seen it enough times already.)

4. **Click the Finish button.**

If you publish the movie as a WMV file, anyone running Windows can view the movie later by double-clicking the file. This starts Windows Media Player, which plays the movie.

Rip, burn, and convert movies

The legal status of DVD ripping and burning seems pretty clear: You can't make copies of commercial movies and hand them out to your friends; you can't rent a DVD and rip a copy for your later enjoyment.

On the other hand, the legal status of making backups of DVD movies that you've bought also seems quite clear: You can probably make a backup copy for your personal use. Maybe. At least, that's the theory. In practice, it may be illegal to sell software that makes it possible to rip movie DVDs. Or maybe not. Have your lawyer call my lawyer and let them bill each other for lunch.

Windows Vista won't rip any commercial DVDs. Period. End of story. It's against the Microsoft religion. You can play a DVD on any Windows

PC. But Vista won't pull a movie off a commercial DVD and stick it in your computer. If you want to rip a DVD, you have to look beyond Vista. (There's something poetic in that statement.)

One company has been making ripping, burning, and file-format-conversion software for many years. Xilisoft Corporation, www.xilisoft.com, may have just the converter you need. If they're still in business.

By all means, try Windows Movie Maker and/or Windows DVD Maker to see whether you can convert and play video the way you want. But if you get frustrated, check out Xilisoft. Its products aren't cheap, but I've had good luck with them. Free trial versions are generally available from shareware sites like www.tucows.com.

Windows Movie Maker and Windows DVD Maker operate completely independently — it's like they're from two different planets. For example, Windows DVD Maker lets you save your "project," which is a collection of movies and pictures. Windows Movie Maker lets you save projects, too. Predictably a Windows DVD Maker project (MSDVD file) isn't anything like a Windows Movie Maker project (MSWMM file). So if you're in Windows DVD Maker and you choose File➪Open Project File, don't expect to see your Windows Movie Maker project. You can't open a Windows Movie Maker project in Windows DVD Maker. (Or vice versa, for that matter.)

If you create a movie in WMV format with Windows Movie Maker, you can play it only with Windows Media Player (WMP) version 9 or later. The original version of Windows XP came with WMP version 8 — and earlier incarnations of Windows ran positively ancient versions. If you have WMP version 8, 9, or 10, you can download version 11 from www.microsoft.com/windows/windowsmedia/download/default.asp — but be aware that it will take a long, long time if you have a dialup connection. So don't wait until Christmas morning to make sure that your WMV file can play on another computer, okay?

Book VIII

Vista Video

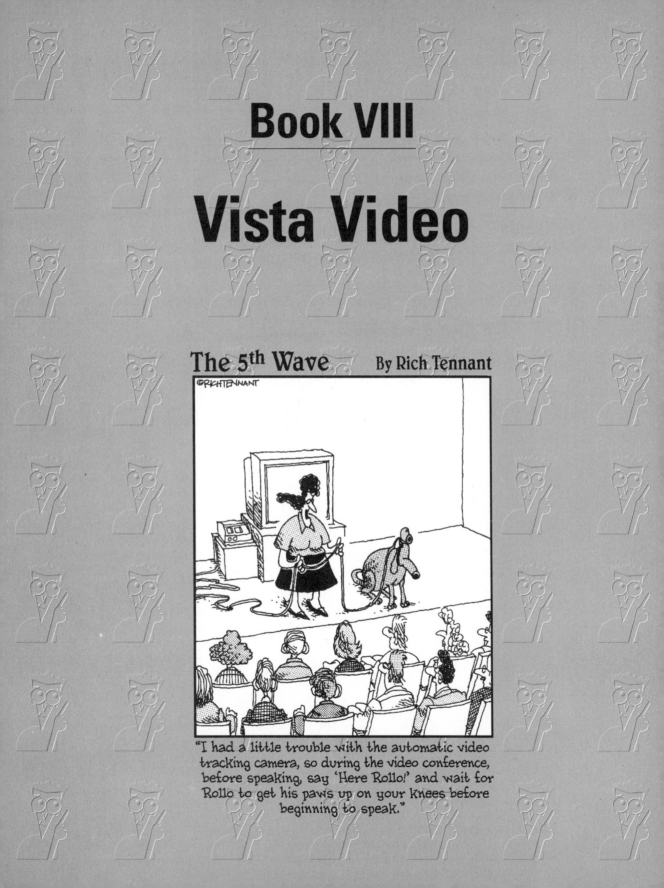

The 5th Wave   By Rich Tennant

"I had a little trouble with the automatic video tracking camera, so during the video conference, before speaking, say 'Here Rollo!' and wait for Rollo to get his paws up on your knees before beginning to speak."

Contents at a Glance

Chapter 1: Preparing a Media Center PC...619

Chapter 2: Starting Media Center..631

Chapter 3: Turning On the Tube 641

Chapter 4: Beyond the Media Center Basics 651

Chapter 1: Preparing a Media Center PC

In This Chapter

✔ **Figuring out where all those %$#@! wires go**

✔ **Connecting your TV**

✔ **Surrounded by sounds**

By the time you finish putting together your first Windows Media Center (MC) system, you may swear off assembling PCs ever again. If you can get it all in one box, you have it made. But the minute you start mixing and matching, adding home theater sound here, slapping around a set-top TV box there, and wedging that 120-inch LCD screen somewhere in the middle, you're going to find out a lot more than you ever wanted to know about Dolby 7.1, IR blasters and DVI connectors. In fact, one of the very best reasons for buying an MC component system from a local store is that you can hire the company that sold you the unit to put it together for you.

Not long ago, a friend of mine told me that he was getting out of the computer business because it's just gotten too complicated. He made that announcement — you guessed it — immediately after assembling a Windows Media Center PC. Of course, he built it from scratch. Definitely a fool's task.

Media Center PCs combine all the frustrations of assembling a complicated PC with the joys of figuring out how to attach your satellite box, where to hook up the speakers, which stack of books to stick under the TV, how to keep all the wires from pulling each other out, and what to do with the subwoofer. The only saving grace? You don't have to worry about a VCR. Probably.

Do You Need Media Center?

If you have to ask the question, you don't. Media Center ships in Windows Vista Home Premium and Ultimate editions. If you have Home Basic or either of the Business editions, you might wonder whether it's worth the bucks to upgrade.

Media Center draws people in with its incredible interface; its power; its seductive, immersive multimedia capabilities; its position as the physical and logistical center of all your audio and visual equipment — and the ability to control all that and more with a remote from across the room. With the Xbox Media Center extender, your game machine can tap into the full Vista Media Center as well. And do it, uh, well.

Here's what Media Center offers that most people want:

✦ The ability to record TV shows with instant-action replay (yes, it keeps recording the halftime show while you watch Justin Timberlake again), easy recording setup via a program guide, and a tiny TV mini-screen that appears just about everywhere you might want it. Best of all, you can copy the recorded TV shows (at least, the ones that aren't protected, like HBO broadcasts) to DVD.

✦ The full spectrum of Windows Media Player capabilities (they're extensive — see Book VII, Chapter 1), with a gorgeous user interface, all wide-screen friendly, all accessible via remote.

✦ A window into Vista's Photo Gallery (see Book VII, Chapter 4): one central location for all your photo stuff — transferring pics and videos from a camera, playing videos, ripping and burning CDs and DVDs, leafing through photos, running slide shows, and making prints.

✦ Internet Explorer, sorta, on a big screen, controlled by remote.

✦ All the bells and whistles you would expect from a souped-up PC that's wired for sound. And video. If you have good audio or video equipment, you'll want to control it through Media Center.

That said, Media Center isn't for everybody. In particular, it has these drawbacks:

✦ **Bugs:** Media Center has gone through more than its fair share of bugs over the years. With deep hooks into Vista, Windows Media Player, Photo Gallery, Internet Explorer, and a half-dozen lesser luminaries in the Windows pantheon, Media Center falls prey to bugs in many of the major Windows applications — and it adds another layer, all by itself. If swatting bugs and rebooting your computer gives you the willies, give Media Center a pass.

✦ **Limitations:** Limitations are legion. As of this writing, you can drive a TV screen from your Media Center system, but you can't control another PC. An hour of recorded TV takes up more than a DVD's-worth of space, unless you use the "Fair" quality setting.

Of course, the biggest limitations center around Digital Rights Management, and they aren't all exclusive to Media Center. If you record your favorite TV show on your Media Center system (in "Fair" quality, of course), can you burn it to DVD and then watch the DVD on a neighbor's DVD player? On another PC? The answers aren't cut-and-dried. If you rip a CD that you bought on your Media Center computer, can you play the tracks on your iPod? Can you play them on the computer in the bedroom? Can your son take them to school on his portable? Sure, you can use Media Center (with its direct link to Media Player) to buy music from URGE and other companies that give Microsoft a cut, but if you buy a song from iTunes, can you play it on your Media Center PC? Tough questions. If they concern you, ask people who own and use Media Center (at, for example, `http://channels.lockergnome.com/media`) before you buy.

Windows Media Center remains the 800-pound gorilla of the genre: When Comedy Central thinks online, it thinks Media Center, with content that's specifically WMC friendly and adapted to Media Center through-and-through (see Figure 1-1.) The same with NBC and ESPN. Time Warner may be another story, but . . . if you want to stay near the bleeding edge of computerized home entertainment content, Media Center's the product of choice.

Figure 1-1:
Comedy Central thinks Media Center, appearing front and center on the Media Center Showcase.

Organizing the Normandy Invasion

So you have eight big boxes sitting on your living room (or dorm room or office) floor, and the first debilitating pangs of buyer's remorse have set in.

That's normal. Not to worry. The following sections offer a handful of tips that can help you through the assembly process. Go ahead and benefit from others' experience.

Gathering the tools for an easier setup

The folks at the computer store sold you everything that you need. But I can *guarantee* they forgot a couple of items that you will surely want. Before you assemble the beast, you need to run out and pick up what they forgot.

In particular, you need the following items:

✦ **A UPS (uninterruptible power supply):** If the sales droid let you walk out of the shop without a UPS, he should be lashed. No, a surge protector isn't good enough. You need a UPS big enough to handle your computer and any other sensitive hardware that's hanging around: TV, network hub, DSL or cable modem, scanner, external drives, or USB hubs — the whole nine yards.

No, you don't need to plug your printer into a UPS — and you should *never* plug a laser printer into a UPS. Laser printers draw a tremendous amount of power; a laser printer will probably blow out your UPS when it starts, and even if your UPS doesn't end up a heap of smoldering goo, if the power goes out, the UPS will die in seconds from the laser printer's power drain.

✦ **Lots of power strips:** The ones that plug into the UPS don't need surge protection, but any that plug straight into the wall should have surge protectors.

Anything with a "brick" that converts AC current to DC (which you commonly find with laptop computers, telephones, modems, and so on) doesn't require a surge protector. But any brick located at the end of a power cord will invariably take up two (or even three) slots on a power strip.

✦ **A roll of masking tape and a fine-point permanent-ink marker:** You should mark the end of every cable as you connect it: Wrap a piece of tape around the wire and write down where it's going. That way, when you look at a power strip with five plugs in it, you can tell which one goes to your PC and which one goes to your TV. You'll also be able to tell your left-front speaker from the right-side and center-rear without pulling the speaker cable out from under the rug.

If you save a snapshot of the final array of cables — even if you only use your Webcam — you'll have a good record of which cable went where, in case your three-year-old nephew decides to pull a few cables off the back of the TV.

✦ **Those little plastic gizmos that bundle cables together:** They're cheap, and they'll keep you from going nuts. By the time you're done, the back of your PC is going to look like a wiring bundle down the fuselage of a 747.

✦ **Video cables that are long enough to go where they need to go:** Before you assemble the beast, block out precisely where the PC will go, where the monitor will go, and where the TV (if you have one) will go. Then figure out how long the video cables must be. Then dig into the box and see whether the cables you have are long enough. I bet they aren't, particularly if you're connecting a TV. When you go out shopping, make sure that you get the right kind of cables.

You can try to figure out whether you need a composite RCA cable, an S-VHS cable, a DVI cable, or a reversible 3-plug mini-DIN with imploded wombat RJ-945 cable, but why sweat the hard stuff? If you have any doubt about what kind of cable you need, haul out your digital camera and take close-up shots of the connectors on the back of your computer and on the back of your TV. Then schlep the camera to the shop, and ask the salesperson to figure it out. Hey, that's what he's paid to do.

✦ **Speaker cables that are long enough to go . . . well, you get the idea:** I swear, the speaker cables that ship with Media Center PCs are never long enough. Make sure that you get the right kind of connectors on the ends. No, I never pay extra for ultra-fancy cables, but you might want to.

✦ **Remote hardware:** Some Media Center PC systems don't have keyboards or mice. I think that's a huge mistake. At least until Microsoft brings more functions into the Media Center umbrella, occasional trips out to Windows itself are inevitable — and for those, you're going to want a keyboard and mouse. If your Media Center PC sits in a cramped dorm room, running for the keyboard is no big deal, but if you have to get up off the couch and find a chair to put in front of the computer, it's a pain in the neck.

✦ **A nice bottle of wine:** Need I explain what this is for? Beer does in a pinch.

Working with Media Center's shortcomings

Every Media Center PC goes together a bit differently, and the instructions (for most systems, anyway) cover the details pretty well. In my School of Hard Knocks surveys, several readers have offered a few key assembly tips that overcome several of Media Center's shortcomings:

✦ **Media Center (as of this writing) doesn't allow you to watch one TV show while recording another one.** If you ever find yourself in a position where it'd be worthwhile to watch one show while recording another, consider using an old trick: Split the input line. Run one set of cables from the cable box to the Media Center PC. But run a second set of cables from the cable box straight to the TV and attach the cables to the Video 1 or AUX input. To watch live TV, just switch the TV over to Video 1, ignoring the Media Center PC.

✦ **Media Center doesn't work with VCRs.** You can think of it as benign neglect. I think of it as a failure to accept ubiquitous legacy hardware. Potato/potahtoe, you know. At any rate, you can still hook up your VCR, and Media Center can be, uh, coaxed into recording directly from your old videotapes. The process is not for the timid, but it's covered in depth in *Windows XP Media Center Edition 2004 PC For Dummies*, by Danny Briere and Pat Hurley (published by Wiley), where you might find some good tips that pertain to Windows Vista as well. Good book, that.

✦ **Don't hesitate to use your current sound system.** If you have a better sound system than the one that ships with your Media Center PC, your old sound system accepts digital optical cable input, and your Media Center PC has a digital optical output on the sound card or the motherboard, go right ahead and hook it up.

Also remember that you're under no obligation to attach everything. If you don't want to run your television through the Media Center PC, you don't have to.

Getting Windows in Gear

The first time you start your new Media Center computer, almost anything could happen. Why? Each manufacturer seems to have a different way of introducing you to the experience.

Making your video card acquiesce

If your Media Center PC came with its own TV set, if you're running videos on your computer monitor, or if you already have things set up so that video stuff shows up on your TV and computer stuff shows up on your monitor, breathe a sigh of relief and move on to the next section in this chapter to verify that your sound card is working right.

But if you want to connect both a TV and a computer monitor to your PC, and haven't yet figured out how to get movies to play on the TV instead of in a window on your PC's monitor, you have a bit of work to do.

Here's how things work with an NVIDIA video card. Your graphics card may be a little different. Each video card manufacturer does things differently, but the problems and their solutions are roughly the same.

Here's the core of the problem: Your video card probably has three connectors on the back. In the normal course of events, only two of the connectors work at the same time: One handles computer stuff (which appears on your computer monitor) and the other handles video stuff (which appears on your TV). You have to tell your video card which connector has the computer monitor and which has the TV. Here's how:

1. **Connect the cables.**

   Each board is a little different, and each TV is a little different. But you need to attach your computer monitor to the video card (probably with a VGA cable, or a DVI cable if you have a newer monitor) and your TV to the video card (probably with an SVHS cable or the three-cable red/green/blue "made for DVD" connectors, but possibly with a DVI cable or some other combination).

2. **Identify your video card.**

   Video companies change drivers like Paris Hilton changes traveling companions. To make things worse, Microsoft Update may not even advise you when a new video driver becomes available. To make sure that you get the latest, click the Start button, right-click Computer, and choose Properties➪Device Manager from the context menu that appears. Click the Continue button to get through the User Account Control dialog box, and then double-click Display Adapters. You should see your display adapter listed, as shown in Figure 1-2.

3. **Update your video driver.**

   To do so, double-click your display adapter, click Continue to get through the User Access Control box, click the Driver tab, and then click the Update Driver button. When Vista asks, click the Search Automatically for Updated Software link. Vista goes out to the Microsoft Web site to see whether a new video driver is available. If it is, the driver may be updated automatically (and your screen may go black for a moment — don't panic). You may have to follow some other instructions to install the new driver. Click OK to exit the Driver dialog box, and then click the red *X* to exit Device Manager.

4. **Reboot the computer.**

   Make sure that the TV is turned on and tuned to the correct input so that it can receive signals from your computer.

   Rebooting probably isn't necessary in all cases, technically, but it's a good idea.

Book VIII
Chapter 1

Preparing a Media
Center PC

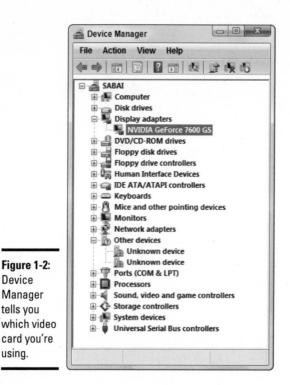

Figure 1-2:
Device
Manager
tells you
which video
card you're
using.

5. **Bring up the video driver manufacturer's control panel.**

Unfortunately, this can be a bit tricky; you may need to consult your
video card (or PC) user's manual to see how to do this. To bring up the
NVIDIA control panel, choose Start➪Control Panel, click the Classic View
link, and then double-click the NVIDIA Control Panel icon. Ultimately,
you see a dialog box like the one shown in Figure 1-3.

6. **Click through to the dialog box that lets you choose which connectors
to use.**

The NVIDIA Control Panel requires you to click the Display icon and then
another button to set preferences, finally arriving at the dialog box
shown in Figure 1-4.

7. **Set your display adapter to use the two displays independently.**

NVIDIA calls it "Dualview," but regardless of the terminology, the idea is
that you have two, independent pictures on the two monitors. One may
be an "extended desktop" for the other. But you have to use the two separately so that computer stuff shows up on the monitor and video stuff
shows up on the TV.

Figure 1-3:
The NVIDIA
Control
Panel.

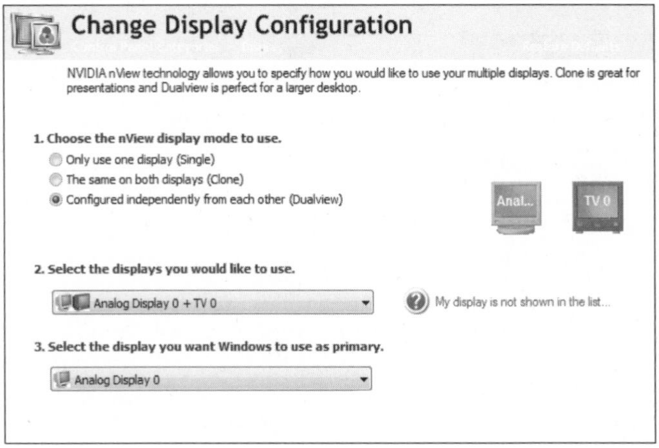

Figure 1-4:
Tell the
display
adapter
which
connectors
to use.

8. **Click OK as many times as necessary to exit the Control Panel, and then reboot your computer.**

Again, a reboot may not be absolutely necessary, but it wouldn't hurt.

Congratulations! Your Media Center PC can now see double.

Setting sound straight

Modern audio cards produce phenomenal sound. If you have a home theater (that is, audio) system to provide the oomph, Media Center can rock your house off its foundation. Kinda adds a new dimension to the old adage "if the house is a-rockin'" . . .

Setting up a sound system usually entails matching up the audio card's outputs (pink, blue, lime green, black, orange, tutti-frutti) to the audio amp's inputs, and then snaking a lot of wires over, under, around, and through the room. When you're done, the $64,000 question arises: Did you get the speakers hooked up right? Easy to ask. Not so easy to answer.

Every sound card works differently, but most of them can help you verify that the right plug on the back of the card is connected to the left, er, right speaker. For example, the Realtek AC'97 Audio chip (which ships on many AMD motherboards) can be tested in this way:

1. **Choose Start⇨Control Panel⇨Hardware and Sound⇨Sound.**

Vista opens the Sound dialog box, like the one shown in Figure 1-5.

Figure 1-5:
The Sound dialog box for the Realtek AC'97 Audio chip.

2. **Click the Speakers icon, and then click the Configure button.**

The Speaker Setup wizard appears, as shown in Figure 1-6.

3. **Choose the kind of speaker setup you have.**

The diagram changes based on your selection. For example, 5.1 Surround uses two front speakers, two back speakers, a center speaker, and a subwoofer. If you click 5.1 Surround, the diagram on the right shows five speakers plus a subwoofer.

4. Click the Test button to test each speaker, in turn, or click an individual speaker to make sure that it's properly identified.

If the wrong speaker sounds off, you probably messed up one of the color-coded connections on the back of the audio card. Rearrange the cables and try, try again.

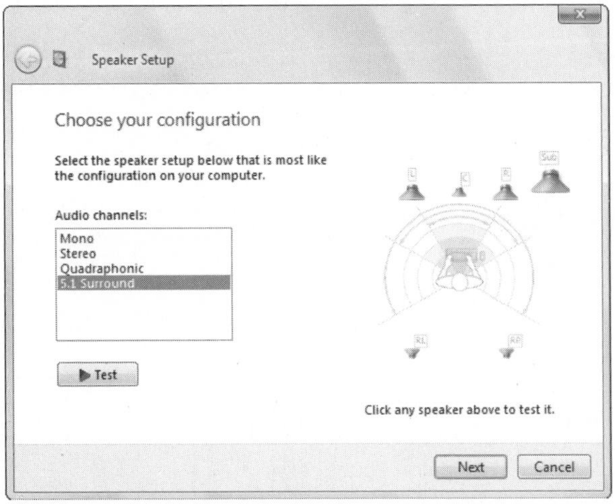

Figure 1-6:
Test your speakers to make sure that they're hooked up properly.

5. When you're done with a sound check, you can further customize the speaker layout by clicking Next, and work with the speaker configuration dialog shown in Figure 1-7.

Figure 1-7:
Vista gives you a great deal of control over your sound.

Or, you can click Cancel to exit the Sound dialog box; then click the red *X* to exit the Control Panel.

You're now ready to faithfully reproduce the sound of point-one hand clapping, in full 5.1 (or 7.1 or, heck, 149.1) surround sound.

Chapter 2: Starting Media Center

In This Chapter

✔ **Getting Media Center adjusted**

✔ **Making Windows safe for Media Center**

The first time you start your new Media Center computer, almost anything could happen. Why? Each hardware manufacturer seems to have a different way of introducing you to the experience.

Most people start with the Media Center setup routine, and that's the subject of this chapter. Perhaps surprisingly, if you make a few changes to Vista itself before you run Media Center setup, you may make things easier (and better) in the long run.

Also surprisingly, I *don't* recommend that you use Media Center's Express Setup. And therein lies a tale of woe. . . .

Altering Vista

Before you run the Media Center setup routine, you can make your Media, uh, Centering much more enjoyable if you spend a few minutes making Vista a much friendlier, more secure place.

If you've already gone through Media Center's setup, not to worry. You can run it again. I show you how at the end of this chapter.

Even if you've been using Media Center for years, it would behoove you to run through these steps quickly:

1. **Set up your users.**

    Vista lets you set up multiple users, and Media Center follows right in step. Each user can choose his or her own playlists, transitions, colors, notification sounds, and so on.

    To set up a new user, follow the instructions (and heed the warnings about administrator accounts!) in Book II, Chapter 2.

2. Make Windows show you filename extensions.

You'll save yourself all sorts of headaches (in Photo Gallery and Media Player, if nothing else) if you get this one out of the way. See Book II, Chapter 1 for details.

3. Download, install, and run antivirus software, antiscumware software, and a Registry protection program.

Yes, you need to set up a full line of defenses, even if you only use that PC with Media Center to drive a TV set. Scum is everywhere, and it'll creep in through Media Center, too. I recommend AVG Free (which is free), Microsoft Window's Defender (which is also free and built into Vista) and if you're willing to pay the money, Webroot Spysweeper. See Book III, Chapter 5 for details.

4. Create a System Restore point.

Right now, when everything is working fine, crank up Windows System Restore and create a restore point. See Book II, Chapter 3 for details on how to do it. Someday, you may thank me for that.

That should put Windows in a minimally functional state.

Setting Up Media Player

Lots of people get confused about the difference between Media Center and Windows Media Player (WMP). Don't let the similarity in names cause any heartburn. In fact, Media Player (see Book VII, Chapter 1) is just one component of Media Center — it's the part of Media Center that plays music, movies, and recorded TV shows. Media Center doesn't look anything at all like Media Player (well, okay, you can show the WMP "visualizations" in Media Center), but every time you play a song or view a movie, WMP is running in the background.

Although you can get at some Windows Media Player settings from inside Windows Media Center, using Media Center to change WMP is a bit like trying to drive a Volkswagen with a bazooka.

Unless you've gone through the motions, Windows Media Player has no idea what audio or video tracks are on your computer or on your network, other than those in your Music folder — it doesn't know whether you *have* other songs or videos, or where they might be located. And if Windows Media Player doesn't know about them, Windows Media Center doesn't know about them, either. Windows Media Center lets you add high-level folders to the WMP "watch" list (so that it knows to watch for new movies or songs in those folders), but if you want to put a lower-level folder on the list, you have to work with WMP itself.

I have full details about scanning for tracks for Windows Media Player in Book VII, Chapter 1 — particularly important details about ripping MP3 tracks from CDs, if you're going to use Media Center to rip music from CDs that you've bought. But if you just want to get Windows Media Player to scan for all the audio and video tracks that are already on your drive and on your network, follow these steps:

1. **Start Windows Media Player.**

   If you haven't used WMP before, you would most likely choose Start⇨ All Programs⇨Windows Media Player. If you've already used WMP, you can just click the WMP icon in the Quick Start toolbar.

2. **If this is your first time with WMP, follow the instructions in Book VII, Chapter 1 to go through the Windows Media Player setup.**

   You probably don't want to use Microsoft's default privacy settings, and I bet you could go a lifetime or two or three without setting up URGE as your music store of choice.

3. **Click the little down arrow below the Library tab and choose Add to Library.**

   You get the Add to Library dialog box that I discuss in Book VII, Chapter 1.

4. **If you have music stored on your computer (or on your network) in any location other than your Music folder or your Public Music folder, click the Advanced Options button and tell WMP where to look for additional music. Click OK.**

   Searching for tracks can take an enormous amount of time. Consider picking up where you left off in *War and Peace.*

   When you're done with *War and Peace,* consider cataloging your CD collection.

5. **After Windows Media Player is well and truly done, click the red *X* to exit WMP.**

After you've chosen the folders for Media Player to monitor, Media Center "inherits" them.

Microsoft tries to discourage you from sharing audio CDs. The Official Party Line states that "Audio CDs inserted into your computer can't be shared." That's literally true, I suppose, but don't let it deter you: You can *share the CD (or DVD) drive.* Two PCs can play the same CD at the same time, although the drive may have a hard time keeping up with two PCs playing a fast-action movie. Just choose Start⇨Computer, right-click the drive, and choose Share. If the Share button is grayed out, click the Advanced Sharing button, select the Share This Folder check box (the drive's a folder, eh?), and click OK twice to get back out.

Book VIII
Chapter 2

Starting Media Center

Setting Up Photo Gallery

Much the same as Media Player (see the preceding section), Vista's Media Center relies on the Photo Gallery to show pictures: Media Center uses the Photo Gallery as the "engine" to serve up pictures on your TV.

Media Player only has very coarse tools for controlling the Photo Gallery — again, it's very similar to the difference between Media Center and Media Player. In particular, you can go into Photo Gallery and choose precisely which folders you want to include in your photo collection; Media Player doesn't give you anywhere near as much fine control.

I know people who only use Media Center for its slide-show capability: The slide show in Media Center runs rings around the one in Photo Gallery.

To set up Photo Gallery in a Media Center–savvy way, follow these steps:

1. **Start Photo Gallery.**

   Usually you would choose Start⇨All Programs⇨Windows Photo Gallery.

2. **Click the small down arrow to the right of the File button and choose Add Folder to Gallery.**

   Vista opens the Add Folder to Gallery dialog box.

3. **Navigate to any folder that you want to add to Photo Gallery — and, thus, to Media Center. When you find the folder you want, click OK.**

   Photo Gallery can take a year or two to process your entire photo collection, so go grab a latte.

4. **To add another folder, click the down arrow next to the File button and have at it again.**

   Repeat the process until you have all the folders lassoed.

5. **Click the red *X* to exit the Photo Gallery.**

   You're ready to set up Media Center.

Setting Up Media Center — At Last

With Vista finally cowed into subservience, at last you're ready to set up Windows Media Center. Here's how:

1. **Click the Start button on your remote (if your TV is set up) or choose Start⇨All Programs⇨Windows Media Center.**

   If this is your first time in the Media Center, you immediately go into the setup program (see Figure 2-1).

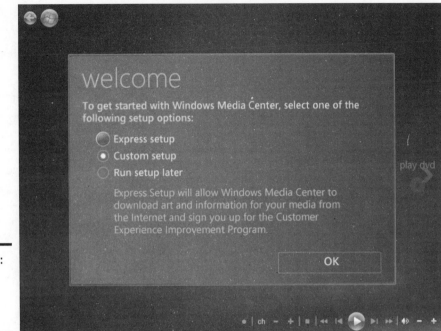

Figure 2-1:
Media
Center's
custom
setup.

To rerun setup at any time, flip to Media Center's Tasks menu, choose Settings⇨General⇨Windows Media Center Setup⇨Run Setup Again. (Yep, that's where they hid it.) Media Center warns you that rerunning setup will overwrite all current preferences and settings. Click Yes, and you find yourself at the beginning of a new custom setup.

2. **Select the Custom Setup option and press Enter (on the remote) or click OK.**

I strongly advise you to take the custom setup route. Why? If you choose Express Setup, Microsoft signs you up for the Customer Experience Improvement Program (see Step 5). You find only three additional steps in the custom setup — and two of them are directly related to your privacy.

3. **Media Center tells you that there are two parts to setup: a required part and an optional part. Click Next.**

4. **Setup asks whether you have an "always on" Internet connection. Choose Yes or No and click Next.**

5. **Microsoft then asks whether you want to sign up for the Customer Experience Improvement Program (see Figure 2-2). Click the No, Buzz Off Turkey, er, No Thank You button, and then click Next.**

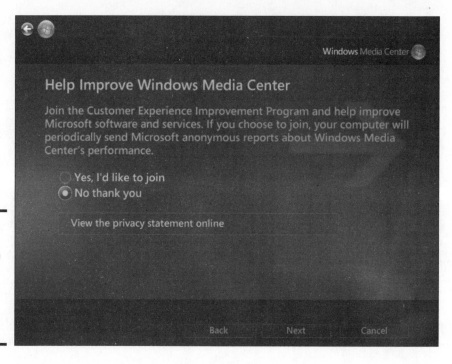

Figure 2-2:
Customer
Experience
Improve-
ment?
Who's
kidding
whom?

Like so many other offers from Microsoft, the Customer Experience Improvement Program claims to maintain your confidentiality, not collect personally identifiable information, and so on. Like so many other offers from Microsoft, you have to ask yourself whether you trust the company and everyone in it. If you have an "always on" Internet connection, Microsoft can (and probably does) collect your Internet Protocol (IP) address, along with detailed information about the movies you watch, your music preferences, buying patterns, TV, and so on. I bet the remote even checks to see whether you pick your nose. It's none of Microsoft's business. Just say NO.

6. **Media Center then asks whether you want to hit the Web to retrieve cover art for albums and DVDs, TV program listings, and "Internet Services" (which aren't explicitly listed, but appear to include things like the "What's New" links). You may disagree — given Microsoft's track record, I wouldn't blame you — but I figure the additional benefits are worth giving up some of my privacy, so I choose Yes (see Figure 2-3). Click Next.**

7. **Setup tells you that the required components are set up. Click the Next button.**

The Optional Setup dialog box appears (see Figure 2-4), kicking off a series of options that can make Media Center work better.

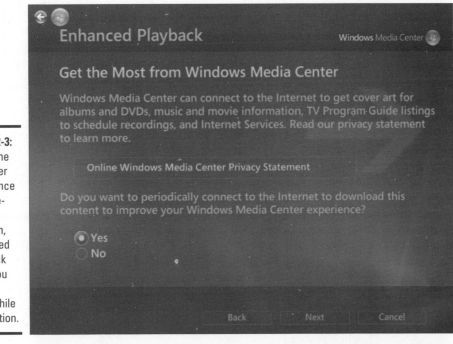

Figure 2-3:
Unlike the
Customer
Experience
Improve-
ment
Program,
Enhanced
Playback
gives you
some
worthwhile
information.

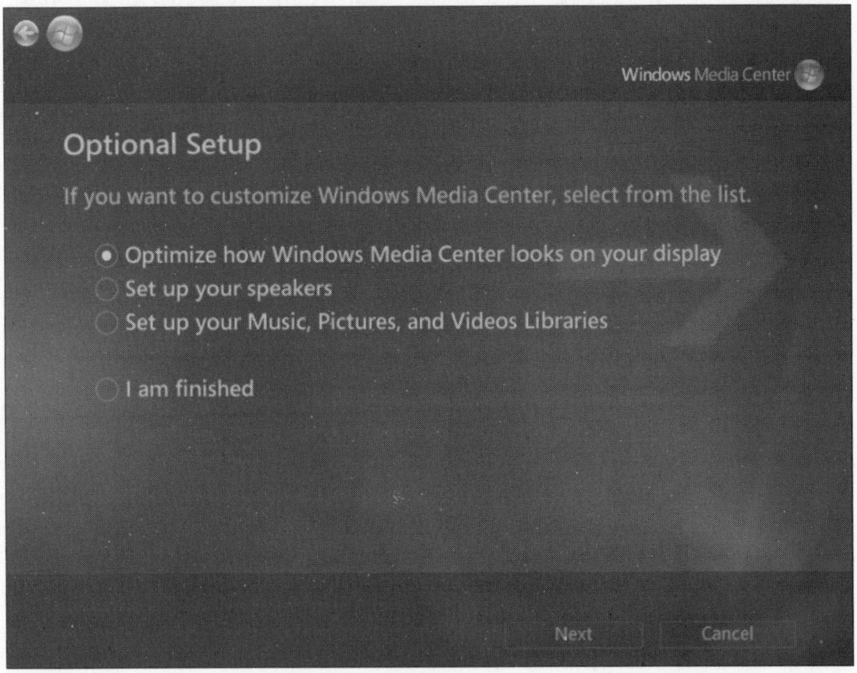

Figure 2-4:
The real
setup
options.

Book VIII
Chapter 2

Starting Media
Center

8. **Select the Optimize How Windows Media Center Looks on Your Display option and click Next.**

   Setup steps you through settings for your display — the display type (TV, monitor, projector, and so on); whether it's connected by S-Video, DVI, or component cable; the display width in pixels; and so on. When setup finishes, you return to the dialog box shown in Figure 2-4.

9. **Select the Set Up Your Speakers option and click Next.**

   If you followed the instructions in Book VIII, Chapter 1 and verified that your speakers are connected correctly, the subsequent series of steps should be a straightforward confirmation that Media Center is talking to your speakers properly. When setup finishes with your speakers, you are again returned to the dialog box shown in Figure 2-4.

   The final Optional Setup choice, Set Up Your Music, Pictures, and Videos Libraries, gives you very limited choices for adding folders to Photo Gallery and Media Player. Because you were smart and followed the instructions in the first three sections of this chapter, you don't need (or want!) to change the folders.

10. **Select the I Am Finished option and click the Next button.**

    Media Player shows you a You Are Done! screen.

11. **Click Finish.**

    If you ever want to run setup again, see Step 1 earlier in this section.

The key "required" settings — your privacy settings — can be accessed directly, without going through setup. Just scroll to the Tasks menu and choose Settings⇨General⇨Privacy⇨Privacy Settings. From the dialog box shown in Figure 2-5, you can turn on or off the two privacy settings.

Here's what the settings mean:

✦ **Use the Guide and Send Anonymous Information . . .** means that you get to use the Program Guide, but Microsoft collects information about your use of the Program Guide, including your IP address (which uniquely identifies your computer), customized TV listings, zip code, and television service provider. If you change a Guide entry, Microsoft notes that, too, and uses the information to make the Guide more accurate. Microsoft's privacy statement isn't clear, at least to me, about whether viewing information (such as which programs you watched and when) and Guide use information (such as which stations you flip to from the Guide) get sent to the mother database. Unless Microsoft comes out at some point in the future and denies that it's collecting such information, you should assume that checking this box gives Microsoft permission to track what you watch.

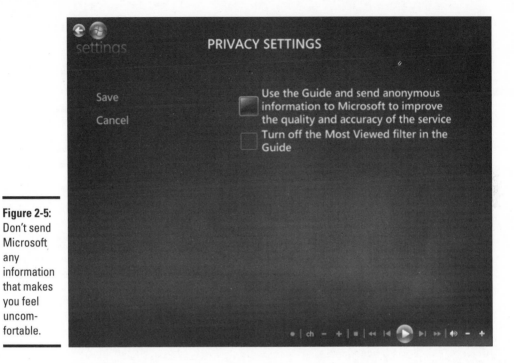

Figure 2-5: Don't send Microsoft any information that makes you feel uncomfortable.

✦ **Turn Off the Most Viewed Filter in the Guide:** Media Center keeps track of the shows you watch the most, so it can present the Most Viewed list as one of the categories in the Guide (see Figure 2-6), thereby narrowing down the list of TV stations displayed in the Guide. I can find no reference in Microsoft's privacy statement to the ways in which this information can be used. Unless Microsoft comes out at some point in the future and denies that it's collecting such information, you should assume that checking this box gives Microsoft permission to track what you watch. (Have you heard that one before?)

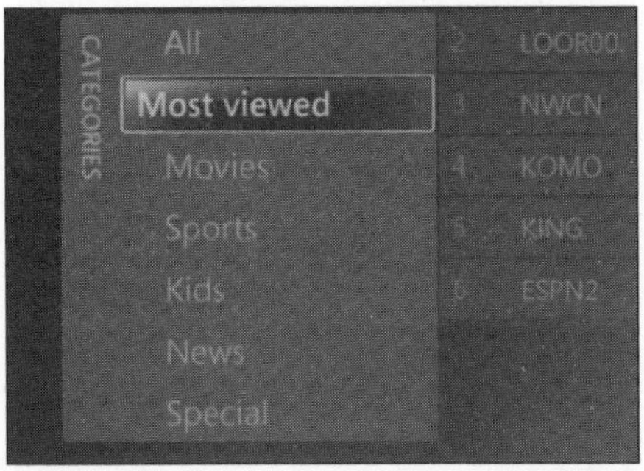

Figure 2-6: The Most Viewed list in the Program Guide.

Chapter 3: Turning On the Tube

In This Chapter

✔ **Getting your TV settings right**

✔ **Updating the Guide**

✔ **Tricking out the Guide**

So you bought a PC with Vista Home Premium because you wanted to get something better than a TiVo. Or you wanted to record TV without paying a monthly fee. Am I right or am I right?

Fair enough. When you get right down to it, Media Center's TV capabilities (see Figure 3-1) and the $20 (or is it $120?) remote are the two main capabilities that distinguish Vista Home Premium with Media Center from just plain ol' Vista Home Basic running Windows Media Player. Any version of Vista can play a DVD movie. Only Media Center — at least, in the Microsoft world — can deliver television.

I take you through a tour of your spankin'-new TV.

Setting Up Your TV

The first time you try to use your TV in Media Center — most likely by scrolling to the Movie + TV menu and choosing Live TV — Media Center puts you into the TV setup wizard.

Here's how to get Media Center to recognize your TV signal:

1. **Make sure that you have an approved Media Center–compatible TV input card.**

If you bought a PC that runs Media Center, you have a TV input card. If you're trying to put together a PC that can run Media Center, you need a card or some other piece of hardware with a fancy built-in computer called a *JPEG encoder.* A JPEG encoder takes a TV signal and turns it into a digital stream without burdening the main computer with the conversion.

Recorded shows by title   Description of the selected show

Figure 3-1:
Recorded
and live
TV —
Vista's
raison
d'être.

2. Plug the cable coming out of your cable TV or satellite box (a so-called *set-top box*) into your TV tuner card.

You may have a choice of different kinds of cables (S-VHS, composite, or maybe waxed string with two paper cups on the ends). If you have a choice, consult the tuner card's documentation and attach the card to the set-top box (STB) with the highest-quality connection available.

3. Set up your official Media Center–compatible remote.

You can't use just any PC remote control. Media Center doesn't let you go through the TV setup wizard — even if your set-top box is working fine — unless you have a specific kind of remote. Your remote must include a wire with a transmitter on it that's commonly called an *IR blaster*. One end of the IR blaster plugs into your remote control's sensor. The other attaches to the front of your set-top box, right over the STB's electronic "eye."

Here's how the IR blaster works. When you click the Media Center remote control, the signal goes into Media Center, as you would expect.

Media Center may then send a "click" to your STB, via the IR blaster, simulating a click on your cable TV or satellite TV remote.

You might think that Media Center would let you change channels any way you like — that it would be happy to accept any signal that gets fed to it via the TV input card. Ain't so. The simple fact is that the Media Center TV setup program doesn't let you go through setup unless you have a remote control with an IR blaster. I know it doesn't make sense, but it's true. Watch out.

4. **Follow the steps in Book VIII, Chapter 1 to make sure that your video card recognizes your TV as a valid "video out" device.**

5. **Start the TV Signal Setup Wizard.**

   Typically that happens when you scroll to the Movie + TV menu and choose Live TV, but you can also crank up the wizard by scrolling to the Tasks menu and choosing Settings➪TV➪Set Up TV Signal.

   Media Center shows you the TV Signal Setup Wizard, as shown in Figure 3-2.

6. **Click Next.**

   The TV Signal Setup Wizard asks you to choose a region (see Figure 3-3).

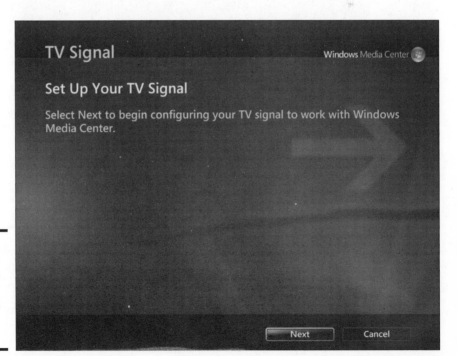

Figure 3-2: Make sure that Media Center recognizes your TV signal.

Book VIII
Chapter 3

Turning On
the Tube

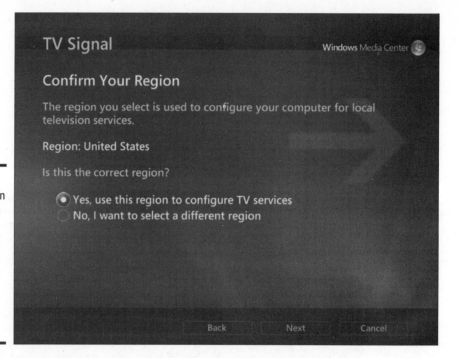

Figure 3-3:
The location
determines
both the
types of TV
guide to be
used and
the
television
services
available.

7. **Choose your region and click Next. Then follow along as Media Center downloads your TV setup options.**

The setup program then asks whether you want to configure your TV signal automatically (see Figure 3-4). Unless you have overwhelming reasons to try to configure the input signal manually, let Media Center take over.

8. **Select the Configure My TV Signal Automatically (Recommended) option and click Next.**

The wizard may take a minute to check the signal, and when it comes back, chances are very good that it'll identify your TV input signal correctly (see Figure 3-5).

9. **Select the Yes option and click Next. The wizard asks whether you're using cable TV or satellite. Choose appropriately, and click Next.**

A live picture from your TV set-top box appears (see Figure 3-6).

10. **From this point on, the wizard's quite simple. Follow along and your live TV feed will appear in no time.**

As long as TV is coming in, a preview screen appears in the lower-left corner of most Media Center windows.

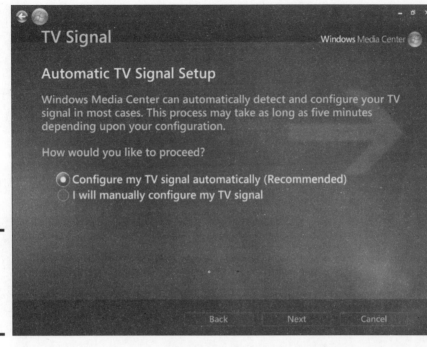

Figure 3-4:
Media Center can probably do the job for you.

Figure 3-5:
As long as you have a simple setup (which is to say, one set-top box), the wizard will undoubtedly identify it correctly.

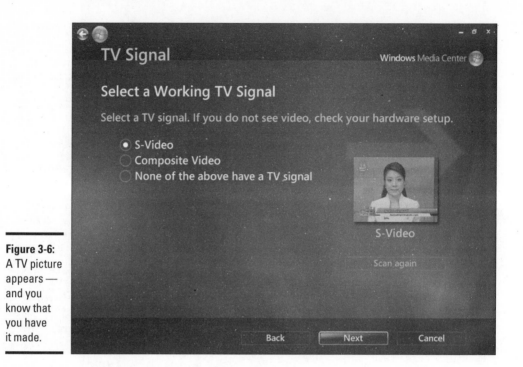

Figure 3-6:
A TV picture
appears —
and you
know that
you have
it made.

Getting the Guide

Your TV's heart resides in the Guide (see Figure 3-7).

To bring up the Guide, press the Guide button on your remote (D'oh!), or from the main screen, move to the TV + Movies menu and pick Guide. The currently playing TV show or movie continues to run, faded, in the background. Kind of like Regis and Kathy Lee, eh? What, you're too young to remember Regis and Kathy Lee? Gads.

When you find a show you want to watch, press the Enter button on your remote or click the appropriate listing with your mouse. Simple.

Under normal circumstances, Media Center downloads the latest Guide when you go through the TV Setup Wizard (see Step 7 in the preceding section). But if your computer has been disconnected from the Internet, or if the Guide isn't showing you what's really playing, you can do a manual update. Here's how:

1. **On the main menu, select the Tasks menu.**

2. **Choose Settings⇨TV⇨Guide.**

You see the Guide editing screen shown in Figure 3-8.

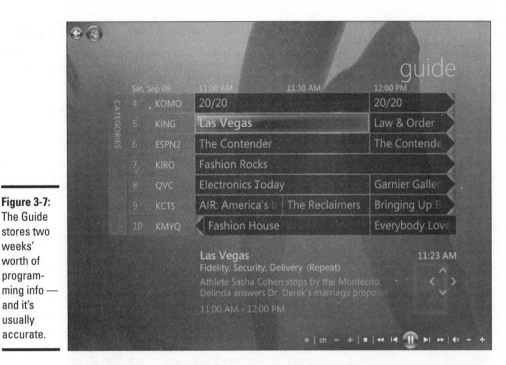

Figure 3-7:
The Guide stores two weeks' worth of programming info — and it's usually accurate.

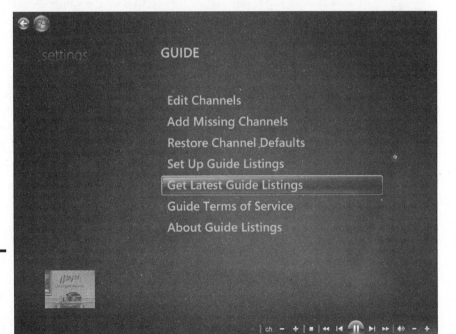

Figure 3-8:
Make changes to the Guide here.

Book VIII
Chapter 3

Turning On
the Tube

3. **Select the Get Latest Guide Listings option.**

Media Center goes out to Microsoft's servers and, based on the location that you specified during setup, retrieves the latest Guide. Downloading can take several minutes, particularly over a slow Internet connection.

4. **When Media Center comes back up for air, your new Guide is in place and ready to use.**

A few remote buttons can make your scrolling faster, as Table 3-1 describes.

Table 3-1	Remote Shortcuts in the Guide
Key on the Remote	*What It Does*
CH + or Channel Up	Moves up a page in the Guide (7 channels)
CH – or Channel Down	Moves down a page in the Guide
Fast Forward	Advances 3 hours in the Guide
Rewind	Jumps back 3 hours in the Guide
Skip	Advances 12 hours in the Guide
Replay	Jumps back 12 hours in the Guide

In addition, if you press the remote's Guide button twice, a panel appears at the bottom of the screen, allowing you to limit the Guide — called *filtering* — to certain kinds of programs: News, Sports, Movies, Kids, and Special.

Editing TV Stations in the Guide

You can add and remove stations from the Guide. When you remove a station, its listing simply doesn't appear when you bring up the Guide (the station's still there, though, and you can watch it). When you add a station, the Guide won't have any information about programming on the station, but you can use the Guide to record whatever is playing on the station.

Here's how to add and remove stations:

1. **From the main Media Center menu, choose Tasks⇨Settings⇨TV⇨Guide.**

Media Center shows you the Guide Settings screen (refer to Figure 3-8).

2. **To add a channel, select the Add Missing Channels option and then choose Add Channel.**

The screen shown in Figure 3-9 appears.

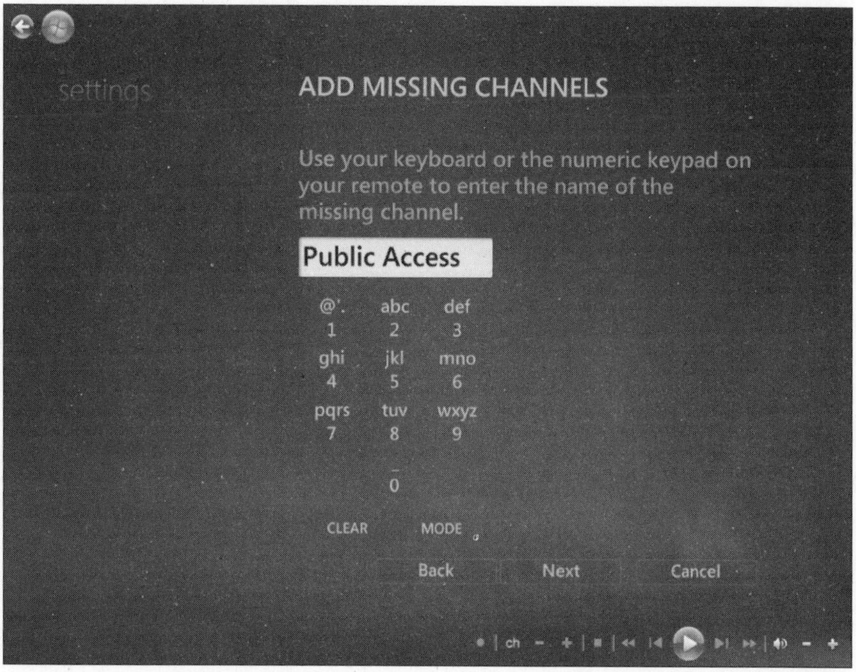

ADD MISSING CHANNELS

Use your keyboard or the numeric keypad on
your remote to enter the name of the
missing channel.

Public Access

@'.	abc	def
1	2	3
ghi	jkl	mno
4	5	6
pqrs	tuv	wxyz
7	8	9

0

CLEAR   MODE

Back   Next   Cancel

Figure 3-9:
You can add
your own
channels to
the Guide.

3. **Type a name, and click Next. Then type the channel number and click the Add button.**

The process can be rather time-consuming if you have to enter the channel name through the remote, but if you're a victim — er, veteran — of SMS (you know, typing a message on your mobile phone), you should pass through the ordeal unscathed.

You end up back at the Guide Settings screen (refer to Figure 3-8). If you've added a new channel, the best way to make sure that it "took" is to immediately go into the Edit Channel window — in other words, proceed with the next step.

4. **Select the Edit Channels option.**

Media Center shows you a list (see Figure 3-10) of all the stations that have either been identified automatically (based on the TV provider that you specified and/or your zip code) or that you have entered manually (using the preceding step).

5. **Make sure to select each station that you want to appear in the Guide and to deselect those stations that you want to exclude from the Guide.**

This setting only affects the station's inclusion in the Guide. You can still watch excluded stations: They just aren't as easy to find.

Book VIII
Chapter 3

Turning On
the Tube

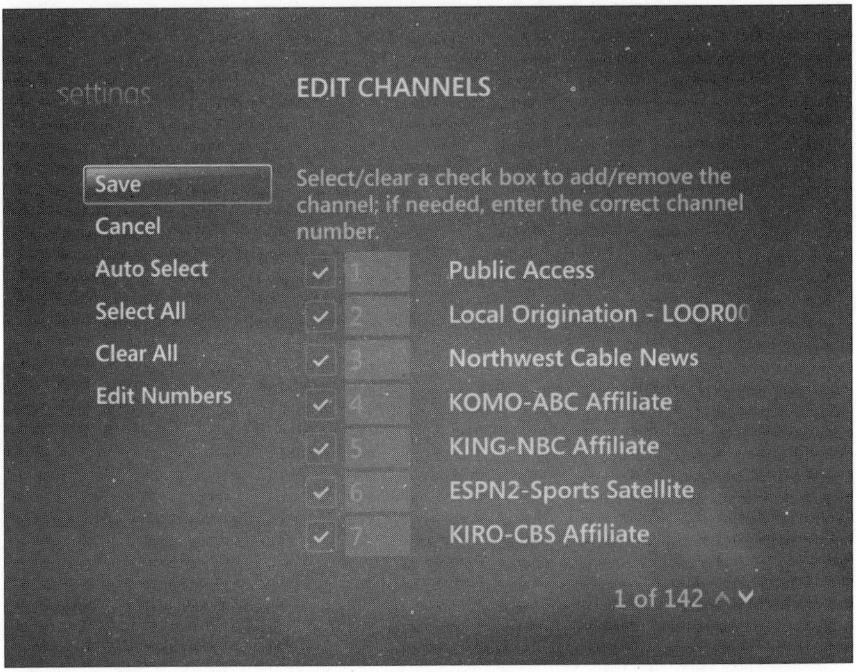

EDIT CHANNELS

Save

Cancel

Auto Select

Select All

Clear All

Edit Numbers

Select/clear a check box to add/remove the channel; if needed, enter the correct channel number.

✓ 1   Public Access

✓ 2   Local Origination - LOOR0C

✓ 3   Northwest Cable News

✓ 4   KOMO-ABC Affiliate

✓ 5   KING-NBC Affiliate

✓ 6   ESPN2-Sports Satellite

✓ 7   KIRO-CBS Affiliate

1 of 142 ∧ ∨

Figure 3-10: Ever wondered how to change the name of a channel, or to hide a channel?

If you manually added a station to the Guide list, that means Media Center wasn't able to find a schedule for that station. So even if you choose to have the channel listed in the Guide, no programming information will be available.

6. **When you're done, click the Save button.**

   You go back to the Guide Settings screen (refer to Figure 3-8).

7. **Now is a good time to update your Guide, if you haven't recently, so select the Get Latest Guide Listings option.**

   Follow the steps in the preceding section to have Media Center download the latest version of the Guide. If you go out to Windows itself, you'll see an icon in the system tray, down near the clock, that tells you a Guide update is in progress.

8. **Press the TV button on your remote or choose TV+Movies⇨Live TV.**

   Revert to your reclining position on the couch.

Chapter 4: Beyond the Media Center Basics

In This Chapter

✔ Recording TV

✔ Using the live TV mini guide

✔ Watching recorded TV shows on Media Center and plain-vanilla PCs

✔ Burning a DVD with a remote

✔ Tweaking and tricking

*A*fter you set it up, most of Media Center is, simply, self-explanatory. The parts that work right require very little digging beyond the normal scope of a couch potato with a remote — which describes me perfectly when I'm tired of working and just want to relax.

Tackling the parts that don't work right — say, trying to get two set-top boxes to coexist — takes an advanced degree in Cable Guy Engineering, a van stuffed with specialized electronic gizmos, and three martinis, in more or less that order.

(Okay, I exaggerated a bit. You *can* get two set-top boxes to work with one Media Center PC, sorta, but the solution's a kludge. You have to install a line splitter and switch manually between the two boxes — and only one of the boxes can be controlled by Media Center. Blech.)

Media Center can't — won't — do some things. Unless laws in the United States change drastically, Microsoft will never offer a program that rips DVDs. Recording FM and AM radio seems arcane enough to the 'Softies that it'll never happen. Some things remain, as of this writing, in the undefined future: support for Digital Cable Tuners (also known as OCUR units); coordinating between two (or more) Media Center PCs, beyond simple file sharing; video playlists; and more.

This chapter delves into the more-advanced Media Center topics that seem to crop up over and over again. In some cases, you can "discover" the features easily in couch potato mode. But in a surprising number of cases, it really helps to know where the bodies are buried.

Recording TV

Media Center is a great PVR. That's a *Personal Video Recorder* to the unwashed masses — a TiVo-like gizmo, to you and me. Before you start recording TV shows, take a few seconds to make sure that your settings reflect the way you want your TV, uh, experience to go. It's seamless.

Man, I hate the word *seamless*. What on earth does it mean? Whenever Microsoft uses the word *seamless,* you know that it's trying to sell you something. Hey, you guys in Redmond, listen up! Just give me something that works, okay? I don't care about the seams or lack thereof. Sheesh.

The following sections walk you through the settings and then explain how to record your favorite shows.

Setting the settings

Here's how to get your recording settings straight:

1. **On the main Media Center screen, navigate to the Tasks menu, and choose Settings➪TV.**

Media Center displays the TV Settings screen, as shown in Figure 4-1.

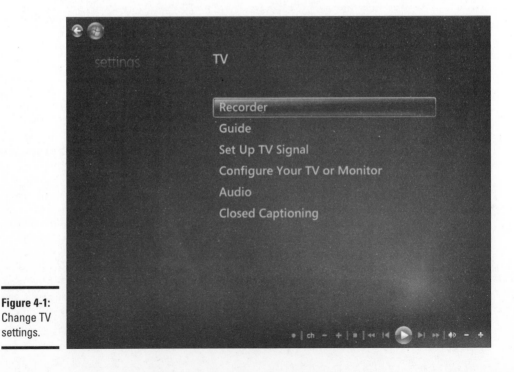

Figure 4-1:
Change TV settings.

2. Choose Recorder.

You see the Recorder Settings screen, per Figure 4-2.

3.Choose Recorder Storage.

You see the Storage screen, as shown in Figure 4-3.

4. Change the settings to allocate as much room for your recorded TV shows as you feel comfortable with.

If you have a second (or third or fourth) hard drive, use it.

When you get to the Recording Quality setting, the Best setting consumes about four times as much hard-drive space as the Fair setting, and about twice as much as Good. You can see the net effect on the Available Recording Space slider (at the bottom of the screen) as you change the Recording Quality setting.

5. Click the Save button on the left of the screen.

Your TV-recording destiny is sealed. Until you change it, of course. Media Center goes back to the Recorder Settings screen (refer to Figure 4-2).

6. Choose Recording Defaults.

Media Center's Recording Defaults screen appears, as shown in Figure 4-4.

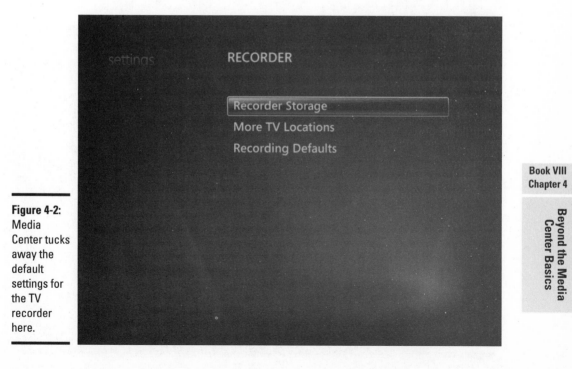

Figure 4-2:
Media Center tucks away the default settings for the TV recorder here.

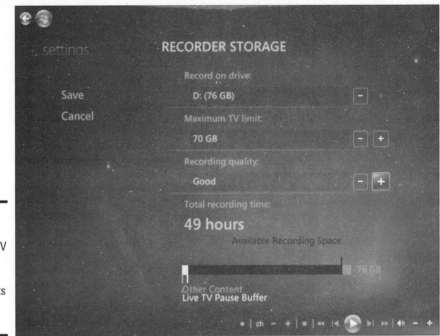

Figure 4-3:
Store
recorded TV
programs
on a drive
that has lots
of free
space.

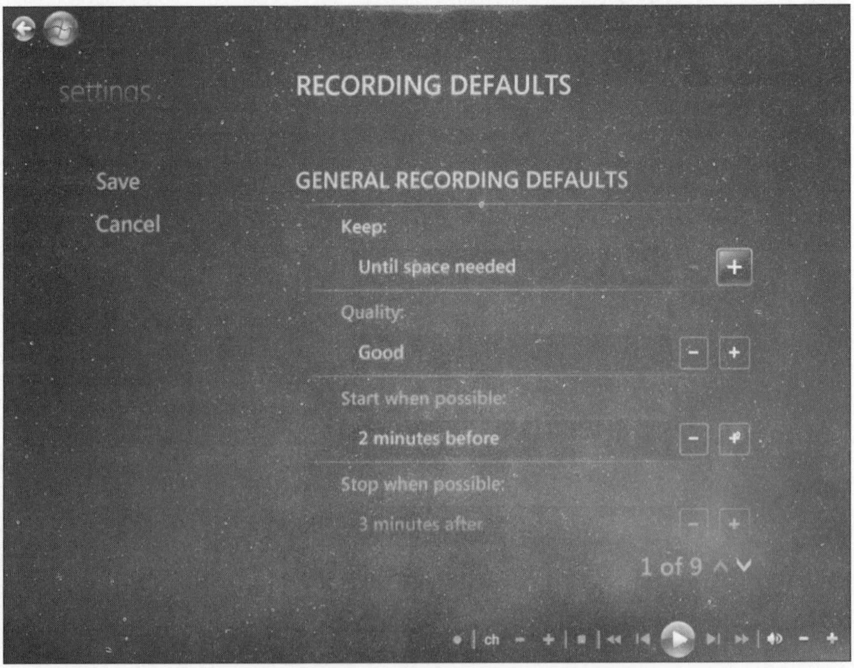

Figure 4-4:
Judicious
use of the
recording
defaults can
help you
record
precisely
what you
want, when
you want.

7. **Consider tweaking the start and stop times.**

Although the big networks almost always start shows precisely on time (except when, say, the news anchor decides to walk off) and your PC's clock should be accurate to the nearest tenth of a second or so, sometimes things go awry and a show starts a shade early or finishes a tad late. Give yourself a tiny bit of breathing room.

No, you can't set the recording default to "Turn off after the last over-time inning" or "Check out when the fat lady sings."

8. **If you do a lot of unattended recording, scroll down with the little up/down arrows and make sure that you like the settings for Airtime (how many times per day Media Center should record a specific show — watch out for** *The Prisoner* **marathons), as in Figure 4-5.**

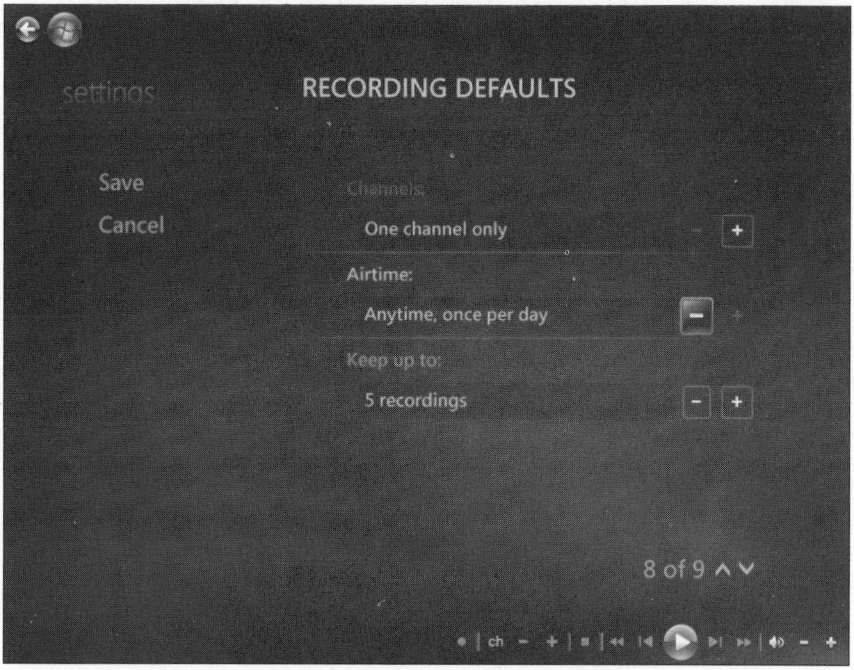

Figure 4-5:
Take care when recording multiple shows in a series, so you don't eat up all your hard disk space.

RECORDING DEFAULTS

settings

Save
Cancel

Channels:
One channel only   − +

Airtime:
Anytime, once per day   − +

Keep up to:
5 recordings   − +

8 of 9 ∧ ∨

If you commonly record multiple shows in the same series, click the + and − buttons next to the Keep Up To box (how many shows in a given series to keep on the hard drive), the Show Type box (don't record reruns), and the Channels box (which channels to monitor for a specific show).

9. **When you're done, click the Save button.**

Then either jump to your preferred Media Center app by pressing a key on the remote or click the back arrow three (yes, three) times.

Selecting a show to record

After your settings look good, recording a show takes less effort than opening a bag of corn chips. Follow these steps:

1. **Press the TV button on the remote.**

2. **Choose Recorded TV⇨Add Recording.**

3. **Select the Guide option.**

4. **Click the show you want to record.**

5. **Press the Record button on your remote (or click the Record button or the red button at the bottom of the screen).**

Sometimes, Media Center doesn't record a program correctly. ('Fess up. Your ancient VCR didn't always record correctly either, did it?) If you get a message saying that the recorder failed, your best bet is to restart Windows.

Yes, Media Center needs to be restarted from time to time. We're talkin' about Windows here. . . .

If you record a High-Definition (HD) show, you get an HD recording — even if your computer isn't currently hooked up to an HD TV. That's particularly cool if you record shows on your laptop and later lug the laptop over to a wide-screen TV.

Using the Mini Guide

You don't need to interrupt what you're viewing to scroll, scroll, scroll through Media Center's Guide (see Book VIII, Chapter 3). You can use the mini guide at any time — and you can see what's playing now, or in the future, without disturbing the current show one little bit. Here's how:

1. **While watching live TV or a recorded TV show, press the More Info button on the remote or right-click the TV screen and choose Mini Guide.**

Media Center's mini guide appears (see Figure 4-6).

2. **Use your remote's up- or down-arrow buttons (or the up- or down-arrow keys on your keyboard) to scroll through the mini guide, one channel at a time.**

3. **Press the right-arrow button (or click the right-arrow key) to move forward in time.**

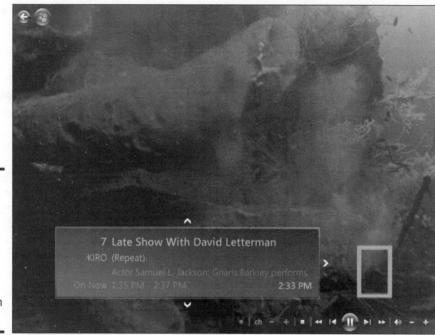

Figure 4-6:
The mini guide lets you see what's happenin' without interrupting the show on the screen.

7 Late Show With David Letterman
KIRO (Repeat)
Actor Samuel L. Jackson; Gnarls Barkley performs
On Now 1:35 PM 2:37 PM   2:33 PM

When you're in the future, you can use the left-arrow button/key to get back to where you once belonged, Loretta.

4. **If you find a show and want to change channels, press the Enter button on the remote (or press Enter on your keyboard).**

   You get whisked away.

   Clicking the back arrow, in the upper-left corner of the screen, moves you back to your original show.

If you've used the mini guide for any time at all, you probably have to retrain your fingers to use the remote's up- and down-arrow buttons in a bass-ackward way. Why? The mini guide works differently from the usual TV channel changer.

If you're currently on Channel 22, say, and you press the Up button on the remote, you go to Channel 23. But if you're in the mini guide, and the mini guide is showing the listing for Channel 22, if you press the Up button on the remote, you go to Channel 21.

Yeah, yeah. A foolish inconsistency is the hobgoblin of little minds like mine. I know. But if you have a keyboard and mouse attached to your Media Center PC, and don't mind running through the Registry, you can make the mini guide work the same way as the TV. Here's how:

1. **Log on with an administrator account (see Book II, Chapter 2).**

2. **If Media Center is running, click the red *X* to exit it.**

3. **Click the Start button, type** regedit, **and press Enter.**

   Click the Continue button on the User Account Control prompt.

4. **On the left, double-click to navigate to HKEY_LOCAL_MACHINE⇨ SOFTWARE⇨Microsoft⇨Windows⇨CurrentVersion⇨Media Center⇨ Settings⇨Video Settings.**

   Yes, I know your clicking finger is about ready to fall off.

5. **On the right, double-click the ChannelBrowserArrowUpMeansChannelUp line.**

   An Edit DWORD (32-bit) Value dialog box appears, as shown in Figure 4-7.

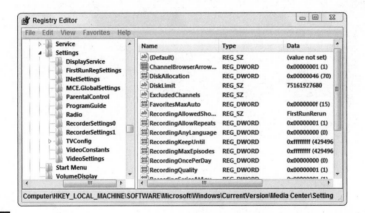

Figure 4-7:
The Registry setting that makes the mini guide work the right way.

6. **Type 1 in the Value Data box, and then click OK.**

7. **Choose File⇨Exit to exit the Registry Editor.**

8. **Start Media Center.**

   The mini guide works the way it should.

If you ever want to make the mini guide work the old way, follow the same steps, but in Step 6, type **0** and click OK.

Playing Recorded TV Shows

Playing a TV show on the Media Center PC that recorded it couldn't be simpler. On the Media Center main menu, select the TV + Movies option (or press the TV button on the remote) and then choose Recorded TV (Figure 4-8).

Figure 4-8:
Playing a TV show on the PC that recorded it is easy.

The shows listed on the screen are all those that you've recorded. To play a recorded show, just click it.

But playing a recorded TV show on a PC other than the PC that recorded it can be interesting. The key problem: Digital Rights Management.

Did you see my discussion of C.R.A.P. music in Book VII, Chapter 1? Every TV program that you record with Media Center is in Microsoft's proprietary, protected format — so recorded TV is C.R.A.P., any way you slice it.

Book VIII
Chapter 4

Beyond the Media
Center Basics

When Media Center records a TV show, it brands the recorded file with whatever restrictions the broadcaster imposes. For some shows, on some stations, it's no big deal. But for movie channels like HBO, the restrictions can be considerable. As of this writing, that may include a restriction that you can play the show back only on the PC on which it was recorded. Heaven only knows what kind of restrictions may come in the future — will it only allow you to play a program on alternate Thursdays or within a day of when it's recorded? Who knows. We ain't talkin' VHS videotape here.

You can move the recorded TV file (it's a `.dvr-ms` file, located in the Public Folder's Recorded TV folder) by any convenient method — burn it onto a DVD, copy it across a network, send it by e-mail, or etch it on papyrus. After you get the file on a new machine, if it's going to play, it'll play with Windows Media Player. In a pinch, you can also use Media Center or even Windows Movie Maker.

In Book VII, Chapter 5, I show you how to convert DVR-MS files *that aren't protected* into much, much smaller (but still Microsoft-proprietary format) WMV files.

If you're willing to walk on the wild side — keep in mind that cracking DVR-MS files may well be illegal, depending on what's inside the file — you might think about using Google to search for "convert dvr-ms." Never know what you might find.

Burning DVDs

Media Center uses the (truly underpowered) Windows DVD Maker to burn DVDs and CDs. Don't expect anything great, but you can burn a DVD with your Media Center remote.

To burn a data DVD, consider using Windows itself and drag the files you want to the DVD drive (see Book II, Chapter 1). To burn music — either as an audio CD or as a data CD with MP3 files — use Windows Media Player (see Book VII, Chapter 1). For pictures or videos, try Photo Gallery (see Book VII, Chapter 4). To burn recorded TV that isn't protected, use Windows Movie Maker to convert the DVR-MS files to WMVs and burn them to CD or DVD.

If you're stuck with protected DVR-MS files (recorded from, say, a movie channel) or if you can't get a mouse or keyboard hooked up to your PC, you can use Media Center to burn a DVD. Here's how:

1. Stick a blank DVD (or CD) in your DVD drive.

Media Center is going to want a blank DVD or CD, so you might as well insert it first. If Media Center is running full-screen, you see the Burn a CD or DVD message shown in Figure 4-9.

Figure 4-9:
Put a blank DVD in the drive.

2. Click the picture of the CD.

Media Player asks you to pick a disc format (see Figure 4-10).

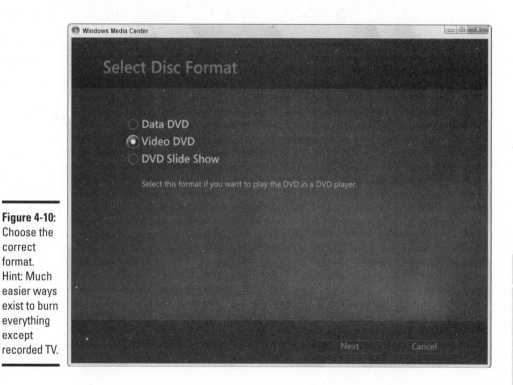

Figure 4-10:
Choose the correct format. Hint: Much easier ways exist to burn everything except recorded TV.

3. **To create a DVD that can be played on your TV (providing the files aren't protected), select the Video DVD option and click Next.**

   Media Center asks you to type in a name for the DVD (see Figure 4-11). Time to exercise those SMS skills, eh?

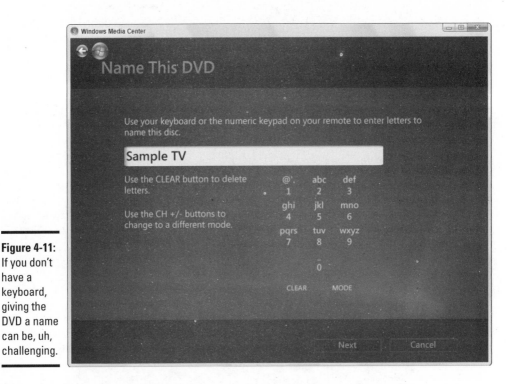

Figure 4-11: If you don't have a keyboard, giving the DVD a name can be, uh, challenging.

4. **Type a name for the DVD and click Next.**

   Media Center wants to know whether it should look in your Public/ Recorded TV or Public Videos folder (see Figure 4-12).

5. **Choose between recorded TV and videos, and click Next.**

   Media Center presents you with a list of all your recorded TV shows (or videos) that pass Digital Rights Management muster — you don't even see the recorded TV shows that are restricted. Media Center invites you to select the ones you want to burn.

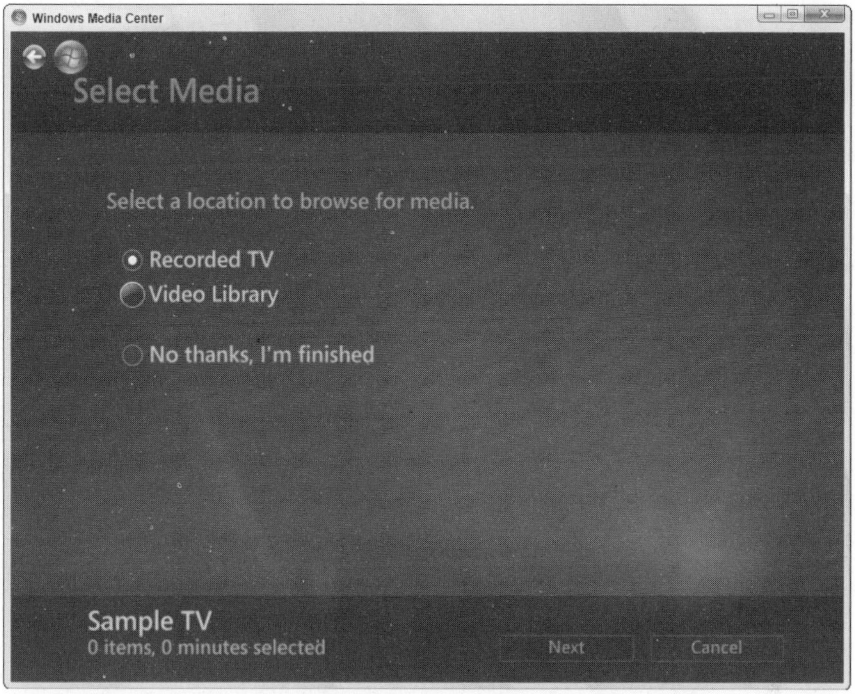

Figure 4-12:
You can
either burn
recorded TV
or you can
burn videos,
but not both.

6. **Check the box in the lower-right corner of each recorded TV program that you want to record, and then click Next.**

   You have a chance to review the list of selected programs and/or to change the order in which they will be recorded.

7. **Follow the instructions to pick the final form of your DVD and, when you're ready, click the Burn DVD button.**

   Media Center asks one last time whether you want to burn the chosen clips to DVD. Resist the temptation to click No, You Stupid Machine, I've Been Jumping through All These Hoops with a Lousy Remote Because I Needed the Practice.

8. **Click the Yes button and go grab a latte.**

   This is going to take a while. Better yet, go to your favorite restaurant, order a seven-course meal, and don't forget the cognac and cigars when you're done.

   When Media Center comes back, you'll have a fully functional DVD ready to pop into any DVD player.

Getting the Most out of Other Media

Most of the rest of Windows Media Center relies on the good services of Windows Media Player. (Little-known fact: Even the pictures that appear to come from Photo Gallery actually arrive by way of Media Player.) So if you know the quirks of Windows Media Player, you can usually bypass analogous problems in Windows Media Center. Take MP3 ripping, for example.

Unless you specifically change things, Windows Media Center allows you to rip CDs — copy music from an audio CD to your computer — but the songs get ripped in the WMA format.

When you insert an audio CD in your CD drive, if Media Center is running full-screen, it asks whether you want to play the CD. Click the picture of the CD, and you're given the option to copy the CD. Click that option, and Media Center gives you two choices (see Figure 4-13).

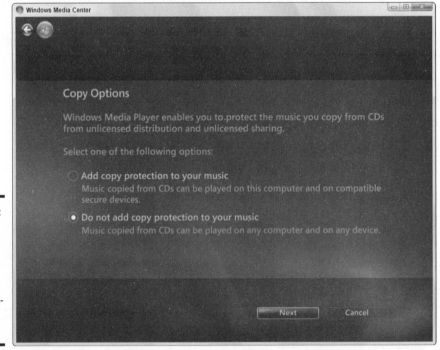

Figure 4-13:
Who would
voluntarily
put copy
restrictions
on his own
bought-and-
paid-for
music?

In some parallel universe, I suppose someone is gullible enough to voluntarily put copy restrictions on his ripped music, but anybody who knows about C.R.A.P. music (see Book VII, Chapter 1) should smell a, uh, rat.

If you have the temerity to tell Media Center that you don't want to encumber your music with Microsoft's proprietary copy protection, the next dialog box warns you that selling copies of CDs at flea markets is illegal, immoral, and fattening. In the next dialog box, Media Center offers to rip your music in one of two "new Windows Media Audio formats," variable speed and lossless. Of course, those "new" formats have been around for quite some time: The lossless format came out in 2003.

The only way to change Media Center so that it rips to MP3 format involves running back out to Windows itself and changing Windows Media Player so that it uses MP3. I talk about the process, the pros, and the (ahem) cons in Book VII, Chapter 1.

The Media Center tiara contains many, many more gems than what I've covered here. To explore more of Media Center's nooks and crannies, I strongly recommend reading *Windows XP Media Center Edition 2004 PC For Dummies,* by Danny Briere and Pat Hurley (published by Wiley). Although it's XP-centric, you may find many gems that still relate to Vista, and it steps you through the key capabilities of Media Center, with a special eye toward giving you the greatest amount of flexibility and getting your Media Center money's worth.

Tweaking Till the Cows Come Home

As this book went to press, the Media Center developers at Microsoft were working furiously on the latest version of TweakMC.

TweakMC, like its predecessors, is a Microsoft "skunk works" program that reaches into Media Center and makes changes that would be difficult to accomplish manually. Microsoft employees build the program. Microsoft distributes the program. But Microsoft swears it doesn't support the program. Of course, TweakMC will no doubt end up in dozens, if not hundreds, of Microsoft Knowledge Base articles.

Exact details aren't set as of this writing, but if you're interested in twiddling with Media Center, use Google to look for "TweakMC Vista" or "TweakMCE" (which is the name of the older Windows XP Media Center Edition version).

Book IX

Setting Up a Vista Network

The 5th Wave   By Rich Tennant

"That's it! We're getting a wireless network for the house."

Contents at a Glance

Chapter 1: Those Pesky Network Things You Need to Know..669

Chapter 2: Building Your Network 683

Chapter 3: Putting the Why in Wi-Fi 705

Chapter 1: Those Pesky Network Things You Need to Know

In This Chapter

✔ Finding out why you really *do* want a network, at the office and at home

✔ Comparing client/server (domain) and peer-to-peer (workgroup) networking

✔ Gathering the stuff you need to get started

✔ Networking for Neanderthals

*W*hen business people talk to each other, it's called networking. When computers talk to each other, it's called pandemonium.

This chapter tries to distill 30 years of advances in computer pandemonium, er, networking, into a succinct, digestible, understandable synopsis. I think you'll be pleasantly surprised to discover that even the most obnoxiously inscrutable networking jargon — much of which has made its way into Windows Vista — has its roots in simple concepts that everyone can understand.

Understanding Networks

Not long ago, networks were considered esoteric and intimidating, the province of guys in white lab coats, whose sole purpose in life was to allow you to print on the company's fancy laser printer or share that super-fast Internet connection but keep you from seeing your boss's personnel file or the company's budget. Those same guys (and they were always guys, it seems) often took it upon themselves to tell you what you could and couldn't do with your PC — what software you could use, how you could use it, where you could put your data, and so much more. They hid behind a cloak of mumbo-jumbo, initiates in the priesthood of "systems administration."

That's changed a lot. With Windows Vista, a network is something that your 13-year-old can throw together in ten minutes. Mine did. (Your results may vary!)

The terminology doesn't help. Ask a network geek — or computer store salesperson — about the difference between a LAN and a WAN, and you'll provoke a tirade of inscrutable acronyms so thick that you need a periscope to see out.

In the following sections, I cut through the bafflegab.

What a network can do for you

Do you need a network? The short answer: Yes. If you have two or more computers, with one running Windows Vista and the other running Windows 98 or later, a network is well worth the hassle. You don't need a fancy one. But you do need one. Consider these facts:

✦ **If you have a network, just about any piece of hardware attached to one computer can be used by the other.** That dual-scan DVD recorder on your desktop, for example, can be used by your portable, the same way as if it were connected directly. A printer or (in some cases) a scanner attached to one computer can be shared by all computers.

✦ **All your computers can use a single Internet connection.** When all your computers are connected to a hub or a router, you don't need to pay for two Internet accounts or run two connections (over the phone, or via DSL or cable modem) at the same time. If every computer on the network is downloading huge files at the same time, you'll feel the performance hit, of course, but in most normal circumstances, you won't notice any performance change.

✦ **You can use Vista's features on data from other machines, regardless of whether they're running Vista.** For example, with Vista's Explorer, you can view pictures stored on a networked computer as a slide show, even if the pictures are stored on a computer running Windows 98. You can burn a DVD with Windows Vista's built-in DVD burning support, using data from any computer on your network. Even the Windows Media Player and Media Center can work with sound and video clips from other machines.

✦ **You have an easy way to make backups.** The easiest, fastest, most reliable way to back up data is to copy it from the hard drive in one machine to the hard drive in another machine on the network.

✦ **You can share documents, pictures, music — just about anything — between the networked computers, with practically no effort.** Although very few applications allow you to share individual files simultaneously — Word doesn't let two people on two different machines edit the same document at the same time, for example — sharing data on networked machines is still much simpler. If you get Windows Meeting Space cranked up (see Book IX, Chapter 2), sharing stuff among Vista PCs is like falling off a log.

How a network networks

All you really need to know about networks you learned in kindergarten. Here's the lowdown:

✦ Good computers talk to each other over a network. If your computer is on a network, it can play with other computers on the same network. If your computer is not on a network, it can only sit in the corner and play by itself.

✦ You can see all the computers on your network by looking at Mister Rogers' . . . uh, by choosing Start➪Network.

✦ Every computer in a network has its own name — actually, it's a number called an *IP address* — and all the names (er, numbers) are different. That's how computers keep track of each other.

✦ You can share stuff on your computer. You have two different ways to share. The way you share depends on how the network — uh, kindergarten class — is organized:

   • If you have a really mean teacher (called a *network administrator*), she decides what can be shared. When other kids want to borrow your stuff, they usually have to ask the teacher. I don't talk about this kind of network very much because the teacher makes most of the decisions. Details are in the next section of this chapter.

   • On the other hand, if the kids are in charge of sharing, each kid can share his stuff in one of two ways. He can put the stuff that he wants to share in a special place that's called Public (that's a Public folder) and tell Vista that he wants to share it (see Book II, Chapter 1), or he can tell the computer to just go ahead and share the stuff (using a shared folder, shared drive, or a shared printer).

✦ Your network can share with other networks, just like kids in your class can share with kids in other classes. The Internet is the biggest class of all. Yippie!

✦ Unfortunately, some creeps are in other classes, and they may want to take things from you or share something that can hurt you. You have to protect yourself.

✦ When you run into trouble, the advice you hear over and over again (especially in the Vista Help and Support Center) is "talk to your teacher," uh, "contact your system administrator." That advice is every bit as useless now as it was when you were five.

When networks work right — which they do about 90 percent of the time in Vista — they really are simple.

Organizing Networks

To understand an abstract computer concept, nothing works better than a solid analogy. I use lots of them in this book: A document is like a sheet of paper; a CPU is like a car engine; a modem is like a high-tech hearing aid with a pronounced stutter set to "max" at a Nine Inch Nails concert. You know what I mean.

That's the problem with configuring networks. No really good analogies exist for all the bits and pieces. Yes, you can say that a server is like a gatekeeper, or a hub is like a collection of tap-dancing monkeys at a hyperactive organ-grinder's convention, but all the analogies fall flat in short order. Why? Because networks are different from what you experience day to day. So without benefit of a good analogy, I shall forge ahead anyway.

Understanding servers and serfs

Two fundamentally different kinds of networks exist. They both use the same basic kind of hardware — cables, boxes, interface cards, and so on. They both talk the same basic kind of language — Ethernet and something called TCP/IP, usually, but a few renegades speak in tongues. They differ primarily on a single, crucial philosophical point.

In one kind of network, a leader, a top-dog PC, controls things. The leader is called (you guessed it) a *server*. I still get shivers down my spine at the Orwellian logic of it all. In this kind of network, the lowly serf PCs are called *clients*. Thus, this type of network gets the moniker *client/server*. Microsoft calls this kind of network a *domain*. If you've ever wondered how in the realm of the English language a "client" could be all that much different from a "server," now you know: In the topsy-turvy world of PC networking terminology, a server is really a master.

Client/server networks abound in large companies, where central control is crucial. Network administrators set up security rules, grant access where needed, allow new users to operate client PCs, and generally ride herd on the entire network. Usually the server(s) hold important corporate files and backup copies of key files on the client computers. Usually the major

Organizing Networks **673**

Book IX
Chapter 1

Those Pesky
Network Things
You Need to Know

networked printers hang off of the server(s). Usually all Internet access goes through the server(s). Usually.

In the other kind of network, all the pigs, er, PCs are created equal. No single PC dominates — perhaps I should say *serves* — all the others. Rather, the PCs maintain an equal footing. This kind of network is called, rather appropriately, *peer-to-peer,* which sounds veddy British to me. Eh, wot? Microsoft calls them *workgroups,* which isn't nearly as classy.

Peer-to-peer networking doesn't get hung up in the kind of security and central administration that client/server networks take for granted. For example, a typical user on a peer-to-peer network can share a disk drive so that anybody on the network can see it. On a client/server network, you'd have to call in the network administrator.

At the risk of oversimplifying, peer-to-peer networking works best in homes and small offices where security isn't a major concern. Client/server networking works best in larger companies with significant security needs — and a budget to match. Network administrators don't come cheap. So much for the overview. I now take a look at the details.

Introducing client/server networks

Client/server networks have one PC, called a server, that's figuratively "on top" of all the others. Figure 1-1 shows a logical diagram of a client/server network. It's important that you not take the diagram too seriously: It only shows the way client PCs are subservient to the server. It doesn't show you how to hook up a network.

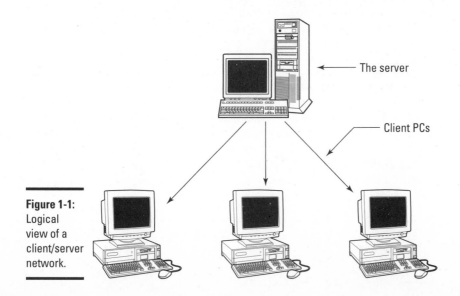

The server

Client PCs

Figure 1-1:
Logical
view of a
client/server
network.

Client PCs have some autonomy in a client/server network, but not a whole lot. And a bit of leeway exists in how much security a specific network or server enforces — some less-secure networks may allow guest accounts, for example, that don't require passwords. But by and large, client/server networks are set up to be secure. They exist to allow computers (and users and peripherals) to talk to each other. But strict limits are rigorously enforced on what individual users can do, where they can go, and what they can see.

Microsoft introduced a new umbrella security system in Windows 2000 Server called Active Directory. It's designed to put control of all client/server security activities in one place. Active Directory is a very complex program — a world unto its own. If you have trouble talking to your network administrator in simple English, you may take some solace in the fact that he has to talk to Active Directory, and the translation can be challenging. The African "click" languages pale in comparison.

In general, you want to use Windows Vista Enterprise Edition (or possibly Ultimate) if you're on a client/server network. Yes, you can set up Vista Business Edition to work on a client/server network. No, it isn't worth the effort — or added expense.

In this book, I don't talk about client/server networks (er, *domains*) very much, simply because you don't have much control over them. If you use a client/server network, chances are good that somebody else in your company made the decision to go with client/server. He or she probably installed your copy of Vista — most likely Vista Enterprise — or bought a new machine rigged to his specifications and configured it to work with your company's network. He also gets to fix things when your network connection goes bump in the night. Poetic justice, sez I.

I have to talk about client/server from time to time, though, for three big reasons:

✦ **You may have an existing client/server network that you want to convert to a peer-to-peer network.** Many Dummies (I'll raise my hand here) installed Windows NT, Windows 2000, or Windows 2003 client/server networks in their homes or offices, and they're tired of the constant hassles. They need to understand enough about client/server to get rid of it.

✦ **You may actually need some of the features that client/server offers and not know it.** In that case, you are better off to bite the bullet now and get client/server going, instead of struggling with peer-to-peer as an unintentional stopgap.

✦ **Client/server is the original form of networking** (at least in the business environment; you can argue about academia some other time). As such, many networking concepts — and much of the obscure terminology — originated in the client/server cauldron.

Administrator accounts on client computers can make major changes to the client PC in question, but the real action is on the server. If you really want to change things around, you need an administrator account on the server. That's the seat of power in the client/server milieu.

In a client/server network, the network's Internet connection is (almost) always controlled through the server, using the following:

✦ **Windows Proxy Server:** A *proxy server* is a program that allows all the people on a network to share one Internet connection and, at the same time, almost always acts as a *firewall*. A server firewall monitors data as it passes between your network and the Internet, acting as a security barrier.

✦ **Microsoft Internet Security and Acceleration Server:** This is a souped-up, extra-charge proxy server.

✦ **Other proxy servers:** Many proxy servers are made by companies other than Microsoft. Ositis Software's WinProxy, for example, is used in many companies to protect their client/server networks. (See `www.winproxy.com`. WinProxy works on peer-to-peer networks, too.)

Introducing peer-to-peer networks

On the other side of the networking fence sits the undisciplined, rag-tag, scruffy lot involved in peer-to-peer computing. In a peer-to-peer environment, all computers are created equal, and security takes a backseat to flexibility. I like peer-to-peer networks (see Figure 1-2). Could you tell?

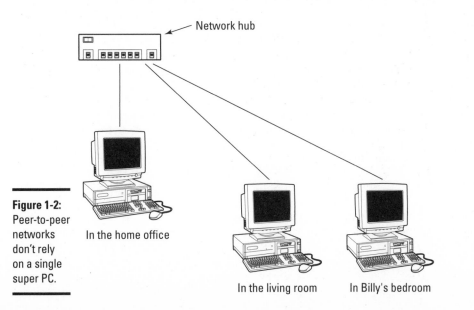

Network hub

Figure 1-2: Peer-to-peer networks don't rely on a single super PC.

In the home office

In the living room

In Billy's bedroom

At different times, in different places, Microsoft calls peer-to-peer networks by the following names:

✦ Workgroups and/or workgroup networks

✦ Small-office networks and/or small-business networks

✦ Home networks

The Windows Vista Help and Support Center also, on occasion, refers to peer-to-peer networks as, uh, peer-to-peer networks. They all mean the same thing.

Traditionally, client/server networks (see the preceding section) dangled all the shared peripherals off the server. Fifteen years ago, your office's big laser printer was probably connected directly to the server. The massive bank of 2GB hard drives no doubt lived on the server, too. Even today, you hear reference to *print servers* and *file servers* in hushed tones, as if only the server itself were capable of handling such massive processing demands.

Nowadays, you can buy a laser printer out of petty cash — although you better have a line in the budget for toner and paper — and 500GB hard drives fit on the head of a pin. Well, almost.

Peer-to-peer networks dispense with the formality of centralized control. Every authorized administrator on a particular PC — find out more about administrators in Book II, Chapter 2 — can designate any drive, folder, or piece of hardware on that PC as shared, and thus make it accessible to anyone else on the network.

In a peer-to-peer network (a *workgroup*), any administrator on a given PC can share anything on that PC. If you're the least bit concerned about security, that fact should give you pause, high blood pressure, and intense anxiety attacks. Not to mention apoplexy. Say you set up a home office network using the standard Vista Home Basic settings. The network that is installed is a peer-to-peer network, quite frequently with no passwords. That means anyone can walk up to a Welcome sign-on screen, click one of the usernames, and immediately designate every drive as shared. The entire process would take less than 30 seconds. From that point on, anybody who can get to any of the computers on the network would have full control over all the files on the shared drive — anybody can read, change, and even delete them permanently, without the benefit of the Recycle Bin.

The primary distinguishing factor among PCs in a peer-to-peer network lies in the shared hardware hanging off an individual PC. Refer to Figure 1-2, for example, and you see that only one PC has a scanner attached to it. Although you may be tempted to call this machine "The PC with the Scanner Hanging off of It," in general parlance, you hear the PC referred to as the scanner's *host*.

Peer-to-peer networks are far more adaptable (computer nerds would say "more robust") than their client/server cousins because they don't rely on a single PC to keep the network running. In a peer-to-peer network, if the laser printer's host PC breaks down, you only need to schlep the printer over to a different PC and install it. You can immediately begin using the printer from any PC in the network. (If auto-detect kicks in properly, it's particularly simple: You only need to change the printer in the File⇨Print dialog box.) In a client/server network, if the server PC breaks down, you can probably kiss your weekend good-bye.

To the outside world, your peer-to-peer network appears as if you have just one PC connected to the Internet — and it sits behind a big, scary firewall to fend off would-be attackers. To little Johnny, who's using the PC in his bedroom to download massive full-color pictures of anatomically correct Pokemon figures, his Internet connection works just like it always did: slow and cantankerous, with frequent dropped connections and unexplained outages. But at least everybody in the family gets bumped off the Internet at the same time.

Comparing the p-pros and c-cons

If you need to decide between installing a client/server network (Microsoft calls it a *domain*) and a peer-to-peer network (*workgroup* in MS-speak), you should read the two preceding sections for an overview of how each works, and then weigh each of these factors:

✦ **The *C* in client/server stands for complicated, cumbersome, and costly.** You, or someone you hire, will spend a lot of time setting up a client/server network. If you have a small network with few employees and one or two applications, you know precisely what machines will be performing which tasks, and you know who needs access to what information and where it's stored, a real pro with extensive Active Directory experience can probably set up your client/server network using Windows Small Business Server in half a day. Beyond that, the sky's the limit — and plan on getting your network consultant's home telephone number, because you're going to need it every time you get a new employee, install a new computer, or maybe even begin using a new application.

✦ **Client/server networks can handle enormous volumes of data.** High-end servers can juggle hundreds (or even thousands or tens of thousands) of client PCs, with data transmission speeds that would bring tears to a lowly peer-to-peer network's eyes. The server can take on additional functions, such as handling e-mail for the entire network (most likely using Exchange Server, another cantankerous Microsoft product that's chock full of features). Data backup and other maintenance tasks that would be a nightmare to coordinate over a peer-to-peer network are all localized (that is, wrapped up into a server).

✦ **The *P* in peer-to-peer stands for powerful, painless, and potentially embarrassing.** If you get your Internet company to install a wireless network, you can have your network up and running in hours — and most of that time will be sweating over sharing printers and Public folders (see Book II, Chapter 1). When it's up, the network will be reliable and easy to use — and as exposed as a lobster in a glass tank. Unless you go to the trouble of setting up and rigorously using passwords (see Book II, Chapter 2), anybody who can sit down at a PC can make all the PC's contents available to anyone on the network, at any time. Except in extreme situations, not even Windows Firewall can help.

If you try to install and maintain a client/server network yourself — even with helper tools such as Microsoft's Small Business Server — be aware that it's not nearly as simple as the marketing brochures would have you believe. Many Dummies, this one included, feel that installing and maintaining your own client/server network rates as a low-benefit, high-commitment time sink of the first degree.

Someday, secure networks will be easy to set up and use. That day hasn't arrived yet. Although peer-to-peer networking in Windows Vista has made simple networking a reality, truly secure networks — and really big networks — are still the province of guys in white lab coats.

Cutting through the Terminology

Peer-to-peer networks work great over wireless connections. If the people who sell you an Internet connection have a wireless box, get it. The installation folks plug the *wireless router* into the phone line or cable TV outlet, and every machine that has a wireless card gets on the Internet with a minimum of fuss.

Confused by the terminology? Don't be. Here's a quick reference:

✦ A *wireless router* combines the functions of a *wireless access point,* a *DSL or cable "modem,"* and (usually) a *hub.* If you buy or rent a wireless router from your Internet company, you don't have to futz with any of the details — or any of the other terms in this list.

✦ A *wireless access point* is a box with a pair of rabbit ears on top. PCs with wireless cards talk to the wireless access point.

✦ A *DSL "modem"* is a box that connects to your phone line and (usually) delivers always-on, fast Internet, most commonly using a technology called asymmetric digital subscriber line (ADSL).

✦ A *cable "modem"* is a box that does the same thing, but it connects to your cable TV cable.

✦ A *hub* is a box with a bunch of slots on the back that take local-area network (LAN) cables. The hub connects all the PCs and other boxes that are plugged into it.

✦ A *LAN cable* looks like an extra-wide phone cable. It's used to connect PCs (usually ones without wireless cards) and other boxes.

If the people who sell you your Internet connection don't have a wireless router, you can use all sorts of combinations to accomplish the same thing. Vista works well with the following:

✦ **A cable or DSL "modem" attached to the Internet and plugged into a Vista (or Windows XP) PC:** If you only have one PC, that's all you need. If you want to share the Internet connection with more than one PC, you plug a hub into the back of the PC with the Internet connection and plug other computers into the hub. Vista (or Windows XP) can run a program called *Internet Connection Sharing,* which shares the single Internet connection among all the attached computers.

✦ **A cable or DSL "modem" attached to the Internet and plugged into a hub:** You don't get wireless that way, but any computer close enough to the hub can simply be plugged in, and you all share the Internet connection. This is also a good solution if wireless reception isn't too wonderful and you already have LAN cable pulled through your house or office.

✦ **A cable or DSL "modem" attached to the Internet and connected in some way to other computers:** Alternatives include using the power lines or using an existing telephone line (HPNA — a de facto home networking standard developed by the Home Phoneline Networking Alliance). You'll need specialized hardware for each computer.

Wired and wireless connections aren't mutually exclusive. Almost every wireless network has the capability for attaching wired computers. In fact, most wireless networks you bump into every day have one or more computers running on wires. They all meet together at the router.

Making Computers Talk

Getting computers to talk to each other can be as simple as buying a box and some cables and plugging it all together like you do with telephones — or as painful, expensive, and hair-challenging (as in pulling it out by the roots) as any computer pursuit you've ever encountered.

In the following sections, I step you through the details of setting up a simple, traditional peer-to-peer network with interface cards in each PC, a *hub* (which is an incredibly dumb switch), and a bunch of cable.

After you see the basics, I step you through the same territory, using wireless technology. If you want to set up a wireless network, I suggest you read about setting up a wired network first (in the next chapter). Walk before you run, ya know?

For details on actually assembling a network — choosing hardware components, installing and testing them, and then getting Windows Vista to recognize the network — see Book IX, Chapter 2.

If you're setting up a new network, chances are very good that you're looking at a wireless peer-to-peer ("workgroup") network. That's a great choice. For the advanced course on wireless networks — surely the simplest kind of network to install — see Book IX, Chapter 3.

Understanding Ethernet

The easiest, fastest, cheapest, most reliable, and most secure way to hook up a peer-to-peer network is also the oldest, least flexible, and most boring. If you want sexy, look somewhere else. If you want an old workhorse, hey, do I have a horse for you: It's called *Ethernet* (see Figure 1-3), and it works like a champ.

Ethernet really isn't that complicated. In the early 1970s, Bob Metcalfe came up with an interesting new way to connect Xerox Alto computers. He called the technique *EtherNet*. The name stuck, give or take a capital *N*. So did the technology. By modern standards, Ethernet isn't very sophisticated. Here's how it works:

✦ All the PCs on a network watch messages going over a wire.

✦ When PC *A* wants to talk to PC *B*, *A* shoots a message out on the wire, saying something like, "Hey *B*, this is *A*," followed by the message.

✦ PC *B* sees the message on the wire and retrieves it.

It's hard to believe, but with a few minor tweaks — like what happens when two PCs try to send messages at the same time so that they're talking over the top of each other — that's really all there is to Ethernet.

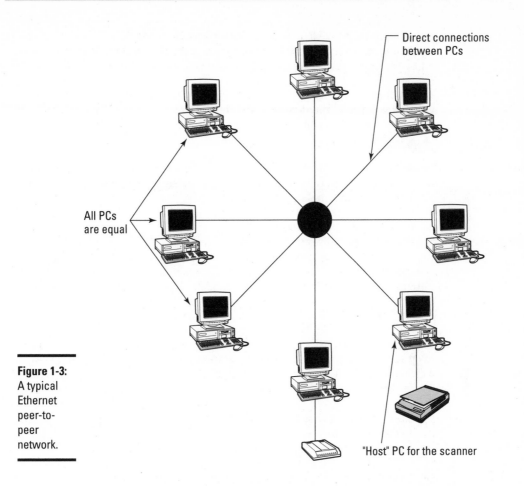

Direct connections
between PCs

All PCs
are equal

"Host" PC for the scanner

Figure 1-3:
A typical
Ethernet
peer-to-
peer
network.

Here's what's even harder to believe: PCs using plain old Ethernet can send and receive messages at the rate of 10 Gbps, or 10,000,000,000 bits per second. Even garden-variety Ethernet systems work at 100 Mbps, or 100,000,000 bits per second. (By comparison, a 56K modem, under the best possible circumstances, receives data at slightly more than 50,000 bits per second.) Things get slow if many PCs are trying to talk to each other at the same time — they start talking over the top of each other — but for a typical peer-to-peer network, 100 Mbps (also called 100Base-T) works great.

Ethernet relies on a *hub* — a box — and cables running from the hub to each PC. The PCs need network cards so that you have a place to stick the cables. The PCs can be using any flavor of Windows since Windows 98. Plug it all together, run the Set Up a Network Wizard on your Windows Vista machine(s), run a special program that Vista sticks on a key disk on the other machines, and your network is ready to use.

That's the theory, anyway. Surprisingly, at least 90 percent of the time, it works. I go into all the details in the next chapter.

Adding wireless

What's the biggest problem with Ethernet? The cables. Unless your office or home has been wired with those big eight-wire Ethernet cables, you have to string them across the floor or under the rug, run them up and down staircases, or hang them out the window and pray they don't blow away. Don't laugh. I've done all that and more.

Wireless networking relies on radio transmitters and receivers in place of Ethernet's cables. You need a wireless access point (which goes by a lot of different names, most commonly WAP, as in, uh, *Whap!*), wireless receivers plugged into each PC (possibly by a card or connected via a USB adapter), or wireless built into the computer (common with laptops).

Wireless networks use the same kind of technology as everyday wireless telephones: The part that moves (the telephone handset) communicates with a base that stays put (the phone cradle). Wireless connections suffer all the problems that you've no doubt encountered with portable telephones:

+ The signal gets weaker as you move farther away from the base station, and at some point it disappears.

+ If the base gets unplugged, everything goes bananas.

+ Other people can eavesdrop on your conversations, unless you're cautious. Ain't no such thing as a free lunch.

I go into detail about wireless networking in Book IX, Chapter 3.

Chapter 2: Building Your Network

In This Chapter

✔ **Getting everything you need to get your network going**

✔ **Making a list of what to buy**

✔ **Hooking it together**

✔ **Convincing Vista that your network works**

✔ **Using one Internet connection for the whole network**

Sharing a printer. Transferring files. Freeing a phone line. Saving money. Those are great reasons for setting up a network. Snooooooooore.

I know you really want to get your office or house computers networked so that you can blister your coworkers or friends at Half-Life 2 or Warcraft III. Maybe you want to spend some quality time with your son one Sunday afternoon spraying demons in Doom III. Splat! Don't worry. I won't tell anybody.

So you read Book IX, Chapter 1, and you're convinced that you want to assemble your own network. Good. About 90 percent of the time, in my experience anyway, it's pretty easy to put it all together if you know the tricks. Vista really does make networking simple. In this chapter, I show you how.

Although this chapter deals with wired networks (see Book IX, Chapter 3 for the lowdown on wireless), you should check out this chapter even if you're going wireless. Why? Two reasons. First, the concepts and terms introduced in this chapter apply to wireless, too. Second, almost every wireless network uses at least one wired connection. So you're gonna get wired whether you want to or not. Can't win for losin', eh?

Planning Your Network

Yeah, you have to plan your network. Sorry.

You have a choice of lots and lots of ways to put together networks. The way I show you in this chapter is the way I recommend for first-time networkers who don't want to spend the money to go wireless. It ain't cool. It ain't sexy. It ain't state of the art. But it works.

Using a wired network

You have four good reasons for going with a wired network:

✦ **It's cheap.** You probably have all the hardware you need already, plus or minus a cable and a (very cheap) router.

✦ **It's fast.** Wired connections work much faster than wireless. You won't see any difference if you're checking your Gmail or surfing a news site. But the minute you start slinging around big files, man, you can tell the difference.

✦ **It's reliable.** When you're hooked into a network cable, you're on. When you rely on wireless, you may be on, off, or somewhere in between. The weather, your physical location, the interference emanating from a copy machine or a coffee machine — even sun spots, for heaven's sake — can clobber the connection.

✦ **It's secure.** Just about anybody with a nodding interest can listen in on a wireless connection. (Yet another reason why you should only use secure Web sites — it's hard to unscramble what's being sent.) And unless you lock down your wireless network (see Book IX, Chapter 3), even your next-door neighbor can go banging around your network. Tapping into a wired network is considerably more difficult.

If you're willing to take the wireless plunge, you should read through this chapter to understand the basic technology and terminology, and how things hang together. Then in the next chapter, I show you how to do the wireless thang — whether you tie your wireless network into a wired network or not.

In case you haven't had enough of the arcane terminology yet, this chapter shows you how to put together a *100Base-T Ethernet peer-to-peer network*. There. Now you can impress your friends and neighbors. Harrumph.

Follow the next sections in order, and you'll have your network up and networking in no time.

Blocking out the major parts

To set up a wired network, you need only a handful of parts: a network adapter; a hub, switch, or router; and cables. The exact parts and quantities you need to get depend on how many computers you plan to network and what your existing system already has. The following sections help you begin with a basic understanding of these parts.

A few tricks lurk in the dark corners, as you may imagine, but all in all, if you stick to the simple, old-fashioned (cheap!) equipment, you'll be fine.

A network adapter

Each PC needs a network adapter (also called a *LAN* or *local-area network* adapter). Most PCs have network adapters built in. See the nearby sidebar if you need to buy one.

How can you tell whether your computer has a network adapter? The easiest way is to look at the back of the computer. If you see a place to plug in a cable with a receptacle that's about 50% wider than a telephone cable — it's for a *LAN cable* or an *RJ-45 cable* (see the section "Selecting cables," later in this chapter, for details) — you almost undoubtedly have a network adapter.

To confirm, crank up Vista, click the Start button, right-click Computer, choose Properties, and in the View Basic Information about Your Computer dialog box, click the Device Manager button. Under the Network Adapters heading (see Figure 2-1), you should have an entry for your network adapter. Almost every entry for a network adapter says "10," "100," "1000," or some combination thereof — indicating the speed of the adapter, in Mbps (millions of bits per second).

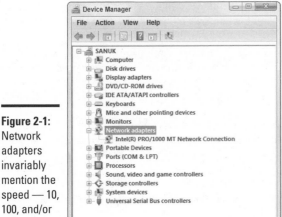

Figure 2-1:
Network
adapters
invariably
mention the
speed — 10,
100, and/or
1000.

Unfortunately, very rarely, some PCs have "dead" RJ-45 jacks. (Don't believe it? I'll introduce you to my IBM ThinkPad someday.) Some manufacturers put jacks in all their machines — presumably that cuts costs — but don't hook up a network adapter unless you pay for one. The only way to tell for sure whether a suspect RJ-45 jack is dead or alive is to plug it into a hub and turn on both the hub and the PC. If the light on the hub shows that the PC is online, the RJ-45 jack is alive. No light, no adapter.

Buying a network adapter

If you need to buy a network adapter for your PC, your first choice should be a USB network adapter. They're fast and easy, and they work like champs.

Sometimes, USB network adapters interfere with other USB devices. I have a portable, for example, that works fine with a USB network adapter and works fine with a USB mouse, but starts acting like a jilted lover when I put the two together. The only solution I've found is to use the network or use the mouse, but not to use both at the same time.

If USB isn't an option, for whatever reason, you can live with a PCMCIA Ethernet adapter for a laptop, or an old-fashioned Network Interface Card (NIC, pronounced "nick") for a desktop. The PCMCIA card should slide into its slot and just start working. The NIC requires a screwdriver and a bit of patience. If you don't feel comfortable installing the NIC yourself — and I don't blame you; it's easy to mess up a card if you've never installed one before — have the shop where you bought the card install it. You may have to spend a few extra bucks, but you'll save yourself a lot of grief in the process — and when it's all done, the card should work right, the first time.

All the network adapters on your network must run Fast Ethernet (or 100 Mbps or 100Base-T). If you have just one adapter card on the entire network that's only capable of the old, slow Ethernet speeds (10 Mbps or 10Base-T), the whole network will run at the lower speed, unless you sink a lot of money into a hub or switch that sidesteps the differences. Fast Ethernet adapters are cheap. Use 'em. And if you can afford Gigabit cards and switches (1 Gbps or 1000Base-T), go for them.

A hub, switch, or router

If you're going to have three or more computers in your network, you need a box called a network *hub* or a *switch.* Or, check whether your cable modem and/or DSL modem (if you have one) comes with a *broadband router.*

A *hub* is nothing more than a box that connects together all the wires in all the cables that are plugged into it. A *router* is a hub with an attitude. A *switch* is a hub that's stuck in its ways.

Before you get bogged down in semantic differences, you need to realize that when most computer geeks talk about hubs and routers and switches, they use the terms interchangeably: Geek A may call a particular box a "hub," Geek B may insist on calling it a "router," Geek C could call the same box a "switch," and Microsoft might call it a "residential gateway." (A similar box in the wireless world could also be called a "wireless access point," "wireless hub," "wireless router," "wireless switch," or "hairless schnauzer.") In fact, differences exist between hubs, switches, and routers.

Give or take a dotted *i,* switches and hubs perform the same job, and you can think of them interchangeably. Routers, on the other hand, have a bit of smarts inside their drab boxes. A *broadband router* is smart enough to handle a fast Internet connection on one end and your network on the other. Plug a cable or DSL modem into a special slot in the router, plug all your network cables into the other slots, turn on the router, and you're off to the races. The best technical description of broadband routers I've read is at www. duxcw.com/faq/ics/diffrout.htm.

Both hubs and switches are commonly identified by the speed of the connection: a 10/100 Ethernet switch, for example, handles both 10 Mbps and 100 Mbps network connections.

If you have a broadband router, you don't need a hub or switch: The router has slots for network cables. Similarly, most wireless routers (or wireless access points) have built-in hubs. Look on the back of the box with rabbit ears to see whether you can find places to plug in network cables.

Before you run out to buy a hub, switch, or router, it's helpful to know how you plan to set up your Internet connection. You find out more in the sections "Hooking up to the Internet" and "Selecting a hub/router," later in this chapter.

If you want to network only two computers, you don't need a hub (or a switch).

Cables

The cabling you get depends on how many computers you want to connect to your network, as I describe in the following list:

✦ **If you're networking three or more computers to your wired network, you need cables to connect each PC to the hub or switch or router.** Take a cable. Plug one end of the cable into the PC's network adapter and the other end into an open slot on the hub. Repeat for each PC. Sounds like the instructions on a shampoo bottle, eh?

✦ **If you are connecting only two computers on your network, all you need is a special kind of cable called a *crossover cable.*** You can buy one — and you only need one — at any store that sells networking cables; just tell the salesperson that you want an RJ-45 crossover cable to network two PCs. Plug one end of the cable into the network adapter on one PC and the other end of the cable into the network adapter on the other PC, and you're ready to run the Set Up a Network Wizard. It's that easy.

Before you run out to buy cables, you need to think about how your installation will work. See the sections "Hooking up to the Internet" and "Selecting cables," later in this chapter, for more details.

Knowing what you (probably) can't network

Don't bother trying to connect an old machine — one running Windows 95 or NT 4 or earlier — to your network. With rare exceptions, you spend more time and money getting a new network adapter to work on an old Windows 95 machine than you would pay to throw the slacker PC away (or donate it to a worthwhile charity) and buy a cheap, new machine. Why is it so hard to get network adapters to run properly on Windows 95 and NT 4 machines? Millions of analyst hours have been spent pondering that question (both computer analyst and psychiatric analyst, I assure you).

It all boils down to a fundamental difficulty in making the network adapter cooperate with the PC. Network adapters make two big demands on PCs: something called an *interrupt request line (IRQ)* (an internal line for sending information into and out of the PC) and a *base address* (a location inside the PC for the network adapter to stick the information that's coming and going). Both the IRQ and the base address must be unique; the network adapter can't share either with any other part of your computer. If you find yourself in the disastrously unenviable position of trying to get a network adapter card to work in an older PC, do yourself a favor and give up. Life's too short. Have to make it work? Hire an old geezer at a computer shop to wrestle with the problems. I'm an old geezer. I know whereof I speak.

Some folks would have you believe that Macs and Linux PCs can participate in a Windows network, with nary a hitch. Sorry, but I don't buy it. Some Macs seem to work well on a Windows network, but others can curl your hair. I don't claim to know why. And Linux is . . . well, Linux, if you know what I mean. If you can get a Linux machine to run on a Windows network, I salute you.

Hooking up to the Internet

When you work with home networks, the crucial decision you have to make is how to hook up the Internet. You can choose between two general approaches:

✦ You can connect the Internet to one computer, and then have that computer share its Internet connection with all the other computers on the network (see Figure 2-2).

✦ You can connect the Internet to the network box (typically a router) so that all the computers on the network go through the network box to get to the Internet (see Figure 2-3). Many DSL and cable modems have built-in broadband routers, so a single box — a *residential gateway* — takes care of all the details.

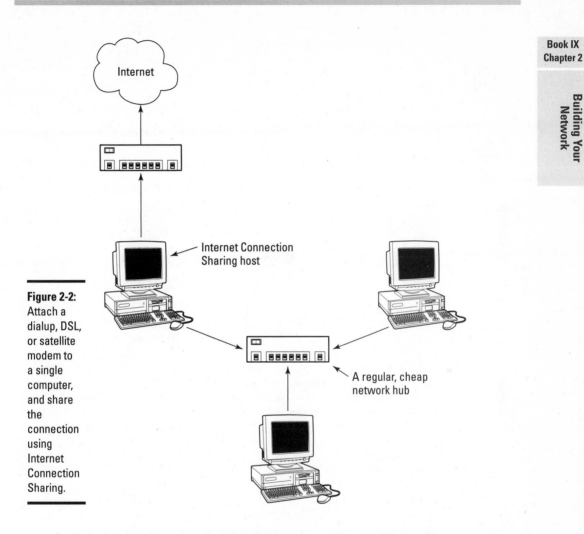

Figure 2-2:
Attach a
dialup, DSL,
or satellite
modem to
a single
computer,
and share
the
connection
using
Internet
Connection
Sharing.

Sometimes you can choose which approach you want to take. But you may be stuck with the first approach if any of the following occur:

✦ You use a dialup modem. Almost all dialup modems connect to a computer, not a network box, and you can't do much about it.

✦ You have a DSL or cable modem, you don't want to buy a different one, and it can only connect to a computer (typically through a USB port).

✦ The folks who put together your Internet connection supply a DSL or cable modem, you can't change the modem (or don't want to go to the hassle of changing it), and it can only connect to a computer (typically through a USB port).

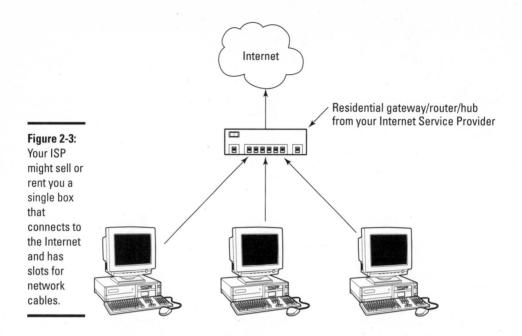

Residential gateway/router/hub
from your Internet Service Provider

Figure 2-3:
Your ISP
might sell or
rent you a
single box
that
connects to
the Internet
and has
slots for
network
cables.

Vista includes a very solid program called *Internet Connection Sharing (ICS)* that makes it easy to share one computer's Internet connection among all the computers on the network. ICS turns that one PC into an Internet Mother Hen (that's a technical term). The anointed ICS PC interacts with the Internet. All the other PCs on the network interact with the ICS PC. To the outside world, you have only one connected PC. But all the other PCs in your network think they're on the Internet, too, thanks to the ICS Mother Hen. Clever — and effective.

On the other hand, if you connect the Internet to your network's router — typically by plugging a cable modem or DSL modem into a special slot on the back of the router — the Mother Hen functions may be taken over by the router, or by the cable or DSL modem. The net result: The computers on your network interact with the router, the router interacts with the cable or DSL modem, the modem talks to the Internet, and to the outside world, you have only one connected PC. All the PCs on your network think they're connected directly to the Internet, thanks to the hardware Mother Hen.

Things get really nasty when a network has two or more Mother Hens, and they both think they're in control: One fights for all the chicks, the other fights for all the chicks, and then they both start looking at *each other* as chicks, and . . . all hell breaks loose. You think a catfight looks bad, you should see what these Mother Hens do to each other. At least 90 percent of all the confusion I've seen in setting up a network has to do with two or more Mother Hens fighting for control.

(Okay, okay. Computer geeks don't call them Mother Hens. They're called *Dynamic Host Configuration Protocol [DHCP] servers.* But they sure act like Mother Hens — mean ones, at that. More about battling Mother Hens later in this chapter.)

If your DSL or cable Internet Service Provider offers a single box that combines the functions of a DSL modem and a router, you're in luck. Just plug the phone line or cable into the back of the box, and then plug in the network cables for all your PCs, and you're off and running. The main advantage? There's only one Mother Hen.

When you get a cable, DSL, or satellite connection, usually the company that sets up the connection can sell or lease you a modem that works with the line. If the modem seems reasonably priced (check with your Friendly Local Computer Shoppe) and it has a network connection (sometimes called a LAN connection, a network interface, a 100Base-T connection, a CAT-5 connection, and/or an RJ-45 jack) that can plug into a broadband router, go for it. On the other hand, if the modem only has a USB connection — and it can thus only plug into a single computer — consider carefully whether you want to funnel all your network's Internet activity through a single computer.

I have used the first approach (Internet Connection Sharing) for years, with very few problems. When you connect one computer to the Internet, and share that connection among all the other computers on your network, you have one big advantage: It's easy to reconfigure the Internet connection when something goes wrong. If your cable or DSL connection goes down, you can dial out on any handy modem and get the system reconfigured in minutes. I also found that ICS had far fewer problems with battling Mother Hens.

Increasingly, though, I've come to rely on the second approach (connecting the cable/DSL modem directly to a broadband router). With the Internet connection going directly through the router, I don't have to worry about one PC going down and taking all Internet access with it. Some technical advantages and a few security advantages exist to running off the router. Mostly, though, putting my cable/DSL modem on the broadband router shares my fast Internet connection with all the PCs in the network, without having them bog down the one dedicated to Internet Connection Sharing. Of course, the price I pay is constantly battling with all of those *prima donna* Mother Hens.

Sharing IP addresses

Every computer connected to a network — at least the kind of networks I'm talking about in this book — has to have a number. A lot of mumbo-jumbo is involved, but basically the number is called an *IP address,* and it uniquely identifies the computer. Every computer on a network has an IP address, and every IP address is different. Easy, right?

Well, not so easy, for a number of reasons, but I'd like to concentrate for the moment on the problem of getting an IP address when you're connected to the Internet. Your Internet Service Provider gives you an IP address. Depending on the kind of Internet connection you have, that IP address may be assigned to you permanently (commonly the case with DSL or cable modems), or you may be assigned a new IP address every time you connect to the Internet.

If you have a permanent Internet connection, you pay for one IP address. In the not-so-good old days, that generally meant you could connect exactly one computer to the Internet: one computer, one IP address, one Internet connection, one bill. If you and your daughter shared a dialup Internet account, chances are pretty good that both of you couldn't be online at the same time. Your daughter would dial up and get an IP address assigned, but if you dialed up and tried to get a second IP address assigned at the same time, the Internet Service Provider probably prohibited it. (Some ISPs would hand out more than one IP address to a particular account simultaneously, but they were pretty few and far between, and you paid for the privilege!)

Ultimately, the question of billing for Internet access hinges on IP addresses — who gets an address, and when, and how much the person has to pay for it.

That's why IP address sharing is so popular. If you have a router connected to the Internet, or if you use Vista's Internet Connection Sharing, all the PCs on your network share a single IP address. With cable, DSL, or satellite modems connected to broadband routers, all the PCs on your network share a single IP address, and a little computer inside the router takes care of keeping things coordinated. With Internet Connection Sharing, the PC that's running the ICS program takes care of all the details. As far as your Internet Service Provider knows, you have only one computer connected to the Internet — after all, the ISP has doled out only one IP address.

Although it's becoming less common, your DSL or cable Internet Service Provider (ISP) may get hot under the collar if it discovers that you've hooked up more than one computer to the Internet, to allow more than one person on your network to use the Internet at the same time. Such inappropriate behavior may circumvent their obscene, extortionate billing policies, and the ISP may demand that you ante up. Aside from the sheer audacity of it all — you should tell 'em to take a flying leap, as far as I'm concerned — technically, you only have one computer connected to the Internet. Whether it's a PC running Vista Internet Connection Sharing or the little computer inside an IP Address Sharing broadband router, only that one computer is talking to your Internet Service Provider's computer. That may provide little solace if the ISP has a monopoly in your area and you have to play by its rules. But it's a fact, nonetheless.

Selecting a hub/router

After you decide how to connect to the Internet, you're ready to choose a switch or a router. You need to choose whether you connect a computer to the Internet and then hang the other computers off the connected one, or simply connect all your computers to one central point. Specifically:

✦ If you're going to connect the Internet to one computer and use Internet Connection Sharing, and you won't ever need wireless access, go for the cheapest, plain 10/100 Ethernet switch you can find. Make sure that it has enough slots for all the network cables that connect to your network's PCs, now and in the future — if in doubt, multiply the current number of cables by two.

✦ If the company that provides an Internet line to you — typically a cable TV company or a phone company — has a single box that connects to the cable or phone line and lets you plug network cables from all your PCs into the back, get it. You'll save so much hassle fighting with Mother Hens that the unit will pay for itself in no time. (Some locations are fortunate enough to have retailers who sell these boxes, too, but be careful to get one that works with your specific Internet line.)

In either case, if you ever decide in the future to add wireless networking, it's comparatively easy to plug a dumb wireless access point into the hub.

In all other cases, I strongly recommend that you get a *wireless broadband router* (also known as a *wireless Internet gateway*). These network boxes have slots to plug in network cables, a unique slot to plug in your cable or DSL modem, and a wireless (radio frequency) access point — a box with rabbit ears — that functions similarly to the one in your cordless telephone. Even if you don't anticipate ever running wireless, or the prospect of getting broadband lies clouded in the future, the added cost of getting everything in one box is minuscule. You can save a few pennies by cutting back on features, but it just isn't worth the bother. Go for the whole enchilada.

At the of this writing, I was using three different "802.11g" wireless broadband routers, for three different networks, connected to three different Internet lines, and they all work like a-ringin' a bell. Each broadband router has four RJ-45 slots for network cables, one slot for a cable or DSL modem, and rabbit ears to handle wireless access. Sweet. Cheap, too. My kind of hardware.

Selecting cables

To get your network running, you have to connect each PC to the hub with cables. (Again, I talk about wireless connections in Book IX, Chapter 3, but when you first set up a wireless network, you almost always start with a plugged-in, wired connection on the first computer.) Ethernet — the kind of network that you're building — can run over many different kinds of cables. I don't tell you about all the different options because I want you to get one, specific kind of cable.

A problem exists, though, and it all comes down to networking's lousy terminology. This specific kind of cable goes by five (or six or seven) different names. It looks a bit like a telephone cable. Telephone cable has four wires in it, but this particular kind of Ethernet cable has eight wires inside.

The ends of the cable have little plastic snap-in connectors, much like telephone wire connectors, except they're wider (they have to hold eight wires instead of four, eh?). The connectors on the end are called RJ-45 connectors, and that's the easiest way to reliably talk about the kind of cable you want — tell anyone trying to sell you cable that you want good-quality network cable with RJ-45 connectors.

The cable itself is frequently called "RJ-45 cable" (in honor of the connectors at the ends), but you may also find that it's called LAN cable, network cable, 10Base-T cable (or 100Base-T, 10/100Base-T, or 10/100/1000Base-T cable), twisted-pair Ethernet cable (*twisted-pair* being old-fashioned telephone lingo for the innards of a common phone line, although it sounds considerably more interesting), TPE cable, unshielded twisted-pair (UTP) 10Base-T cable, IEEE 802.3 UTP cable, Category 5 cable, and heaven only knows what else. I tend to call the stuff "Cat-5" or "Cat-5e" cable.

Category 5 refers to the quality of the cable. If you're offered Category 3 cable, don't buy it. It costs about as much as Category 5, but it may not be able to handle the blazing speeds that you want to install. Category 6 cable is okay, but I wouldn't pay extra money for it, unless you need to put a wired computer in your dining room and stick the hub 500 feet away in your neighbor's attic. Don't ask.

You need one piece of Cat-5 cable for each PC in your network. (If you're going to connect your cable/DSL modem directly to the hub, you need a piece of Cat-5 cable for the modem, too.) The cable has to be long enough to stretch from the PC to the hub. When in doubt, overshoot: A cable that's too long can be coiled up and stuffed behind a desk; a cable that's too short can be painted black and studded with sharp steel spikes to make a stylish necklace. Or so I'm told.

Scoping out the installation

Measure twice, cut once. That's awfully good advice, even in the electronic era.

If you've been following along so far in this chapter, you should be armed with a concrete idea of what pieces you need to make your network network. Now it's time to figure out exactly where those pieces go. Physically. In meatspace. Keep these tips in mind:

✦ If you're going to connect the Internet to a single PC and share that connection across the network, the PC that's connected to the Internet must be running Vista or Windows XP Service Pack 2 or later. In meatspace terms, that means you need to have a pretty hefty machine located next to a telephone jack, your DSL connection, or your cable modem.

✦ On the other hand, if you're going to connect your cable, DSL, or satellite modem directly to a broadband router, the router *doesn't* have to be close to the cable/DSL/satellite modem. You just run a regular Cat-5 network cable between the modem and the router.

✦ The switch or router can go anywhere. Once in a blue moon, you may want to watch the lights on the panel blinking, just to make sure that all your machines are talking to each other, but you really don't need to put the hub on your desk. If you want a light show, get a flashlight. It's cheaper and marginally more interesting.

I've found no particular reason to stick a specific peripheral on a specific PC. A networked printer, for example, works fine whether it's attached to a Vista machine or a Windows 98 machine.

There's a theoretical limit to the length of the Cat-5 cable connecting the hub, switch, or router to a networked PC: 100 meters, or about 330 feet. (Cat-6 can, in theory, go farther.) If you go much farther than that, you may have problems with the network crashing. When you figure out where your hub is located, keep that in mind — and the fact that I'm talking about the length of the cable itself, not distances "as the crow flies." If you get stuck, talk to your friendly local hardware purveyor about connecting a switch through an "uplink port." It's an easy, cheap way to set up a second switch that's connected to the main hub/switch/router, and cables can go another 100 meters from the satellite switch.

Installing Your Network

You have your PCs ready to go — network adapters installed and waiting. The hub's sitting in a box on the floor. All that cable makes quite a mess, and your spouse is starting to wonder, out loud, just what in the Sam Hill you expect to do with all of it. Yep. You're ready.

If you are trying to convert an existing network to a Vista-style peer-to-peer network, beware of a few additional wrinkles. Follow the instructions in the "Troubleshooting" section near the end of this chapter.

If you are going to set up a wireless network (see the next chapter), you need to start with this procedure to get your router going, typically by plugging just one computer into the router with a Cat-5 cable. When the router's working and you can connect that hardwired computer to the Internet, you'll be ready to start adding wireless computers.

Here's a simple, 15-step process for getting your new network up and running with a minimum of fuss and hassle:

1. **Set up each of the PCs.**

Get the network adapters installed, but don't plug in the network cables (the Cat-5 cables) just yet. Connect the peripherals. Test each machine to make sure that that it's working.

If you're going to be sharing an Internet connection through one PC, get that PC connected to the Internet, and make sure that everything is working fine.

2. **Turn off all the PCs, unplug the modems — both from the power outlet and from the phone line/cable/satellite feed — and let everything sit for at least 30 seconds.**

Yeah, that sounds weird, but do it.

3. **With all the power off, put the hub, switch, or router where it's going to go, and connect all the Cat-5 cables, both at the hub and at each individual PC.**

If you have a cable, DSL, or satellite modem, make sure that it's connected to the phone line or cable TV line and make sure that it's plugged into the PC (if the Internet connection is going to be shared from a single PC) or the broadband router (if you're connecting it to a router).

Broadband routers have only one, specific place where you can plug in a cable/DSL modem. That location frequently sits next to the "normal" slots, so read the documentation (or at least squint at the back of the hub!) to make sure that you plug your cable/DSL modem into the right slot.

If you have a dialup modem, make sure that the phone line is plugged in.

4. **If you have a cable/DSL/satellite modem, stick the modem's power plug in the wall, turn the modem on, and wait for the lights to stop flashing.**

   That establishes the DSL/cable/satellite modem as the Mother of all Mother Hens. It also gives the modem a chance to run out to the Internet and gather anything it needs.

5. **Plug in the hub, switch, or router, and wait for the lights to stop blinking.**

   If your router wants to be a Mother Hen, it should work out its differences with the modem at this point.

6. **Pick a PC and turn it on.**

   If you're going to use Internet Connection Sharing, turn on the Internet-connected computer first.

   Verify that the light on the hub for that PC comes on — in other words, make sure that the network adapter and cable for that PC are working okay. Now's the time to sort out connection problems: If the light doesn't go on, a cable is probably loose or an adapter card isn't installed correctly. Fix the problem now. When the light comes on at the hub, this PC's ready to set up.

7. **If you're going to use Internet Connection Sharing, and you just turned it on, get it connected to the Internet (turn on the modem if necessary, log on, do whatever you need to do). Then follow these steps:**

   a. Choose Start⇨Control Panel⇨Network and Internet⇨Network and Sharing Center.

   b. In the Network and Sharing Center, on the left, click the Manage Network Connections link.

   c. Right-click the Internet connection and choose Properties; then click the Sharing tab.

   d. Select the Allow Other Network Users to Connect through This Computer's Internet Connection check box. Then click the OK button twice, and click the red X in the upper-right corner to leave the Manage Network Connections dialog box.

   When Step 7d. is done, the PC you've chosen becomes the designated ICS computer. You should continue to set it up just like any other computer.

8. **Choose Start⇨Control Panel⇨Network and Internet⇨Network and Sharing Center.**

   You see the Network and Sharing Center, as shown in Figure 2-4.

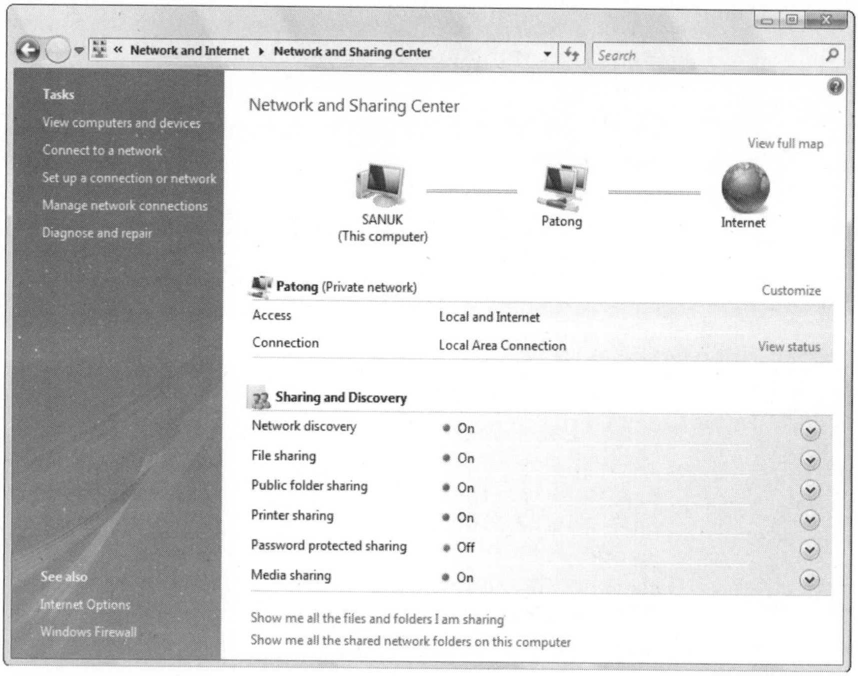

Figure 2-4:
See
whether
Vista found
your
network.

Usually Vista does a very good job of identifying an existing network, or automatically setting up a new network if one doesn't already exist. If you see that your computer is connected to the Internet, you're in very good shape. If you don't, try the troubleshooting steps at the end of this chapter.

9. **To the right of the Network icon, click the Customize link.**

Vista shows you the Set Network Location dialog box shown in Figure 2-5.

10. **Because this is your home network, make sure that the Private option is selected, and type in the name you would like to use for your network in the Network Name box. Then click the Next button.**

In Figure 2-5, I tell Vista to hook me up to the network called Patong.

You need to enter the same network name for every computer on the network. Keep it short and simple, and don't use any weird characters like dollar signs or slashes.

When you click the Next button, Vista comes back with the Set Network Location dialog box (see Figure 2-6) that confirms your network settings.

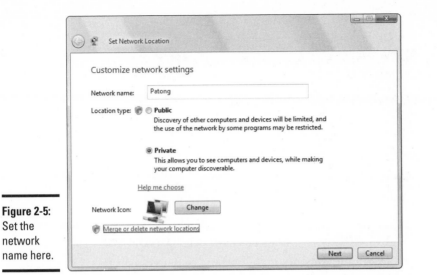

Figure 2-5:
Set the
network
name here.

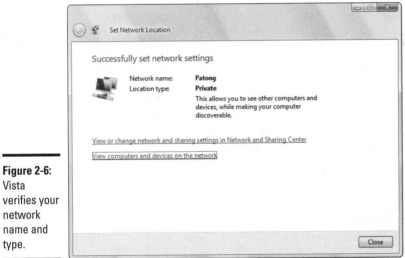

Figure 2-6:
Vista
verifies your
network
name and
type.

11. **At the bottom of the Set Network Location dialog box, click the View
Computer and Devices on the Network link.**

Vista shows you any other computers that are currently hooked up to
the network. If this is the first computer you've set up on the network,
you won't see any others. But as you add computers, they appear in the
Network dialog box shown in Figure 2-7.

Figure 2-7:
List of all the computers on your network.

12. **Click the Close button to exit the Set Network Location dialog box.**

13. **Back in the Network and Sharing Center, go over the Sharing and Discovery settings for this computer.**

    The settings I use for my home office are shown in Figure 2-4. They're very permissive — I assume that anybody connected to my network should be able to get at all my Public folders and do with them what they will.

    I provide a detailed discussion of the settings, and their effects, in Book II, Chapter 1.

14. **When you're happy with your Sharing and Discovery settings, click the red *X* to exit the Network and Sharing Center.**

    Congratulations! The network is now ready — on this computer.

15. **Pick the next computer on your new network, and repeat Steps 6 through 15 for each computer.**

If you are adding Windows XP computers to your network, make sure that you have installed Windows XP Service Pack 2 or later, and then run the Network Setup Wizard. To get to the wizard on a WinXP computer, choose Start➪All Programs➪Accessories➪Communications➪Network Setup Wizard. Be braced for some of the most confusing questions that any version of Windows has ever asked. I go into detail in my earlier book, *Windows XP All-in-One Desk Reference For Dummies, 2nd Edition* (published by Wiley).

When you're done, you're, uh, done. The network should be networking. Try choosing Start➪Network on any of the Vista PCs and make yourself at home. Try printing on a networked printer. Betcha bucks to buckaroos that it sets itself up just that easily.

Troubleshooting

I've encountered three general types of problems — or should I say opportunities? — while working with Vista and Windows XP peer-to-peer networks. I describe them in the following sections.

Two Mother Hens fighting

Man, you ain't seen nothin' till you've seen two fighting Mother Hens.

Many modern cable/DSL/satellite modems get attached directly to broadband routers. In fact, that may be the most common configuration: It's cheap, effective, flexible . . . and sometimes infuriating.

Many cable/DSL/satellite modems are set up as DHCP servers — Mother Hens — that expect to dole out IP addresses to each computer on the network. Many cable/DSL/satellite modems assign themselves an IP address of 192.168.1.1 and then hand out IP addresses starting in that range. (See the sidebar "Sharing IP addresses," earlier in this chapter, for a quick introduction to IP addresses.)

Unfortunately, many broadband routers are also set up as Mother Hens. They, too, expect to hand out IP addresses. Many of them assign themselves an IP address of 192.168.1.1 and expect to hand out IP addresses starting in that range.

What's wrong with this picture? Well, if you power up your modem and it assigns itself an address of 192.168.1.1, and then you power up your broadband router and it assigns *itself* an address of 192.168.1.1, you suddenly have an enormously unstable situation. It's as if two different clones of Paula Zahn were forced to sit down and talk to each other. And when the unsuspecting PCs come up for air, seeking a Mother Hen to assign them an IP address, the feathers start flying.

Here's my favorite solution. Don't start your DSL/cable/satellite modem. Instead, start your router and then start a PC attached to the router. Follow the manufacturer's instructions to get into the router from the PC (usually you crank up Internet Explorer and type **http://192.168.1.1**). Then change the router's starting IP address to, say, 192.168.2.1. Make sure that you update and reboot the router.

Although it's possible to go diving into the DHCP server settings on the router or on the modem, you don't need to. By setting the starting IP address on the router to something different from the starting IP address on the modem, you move each of the Mother Hens into her own, separate hen house. End of fighting. All is right in the world.

Internet Explorer doesn't work with Internet Connection Sharing

I don't know why, but sometimes Internet Explorer (IE) doesn't connect when I'm using a peer-to-peer network with Internet Connection Sharing.

The solution is pretty easy. You have to tell IE to go straight to the network. Here's how:

1. **Start Internet Explorer.**

2. **On the right, click the Tools icon and choose Internet Options. Click the Connections tab.**

You see the dialog box shown in Figure 2-8.

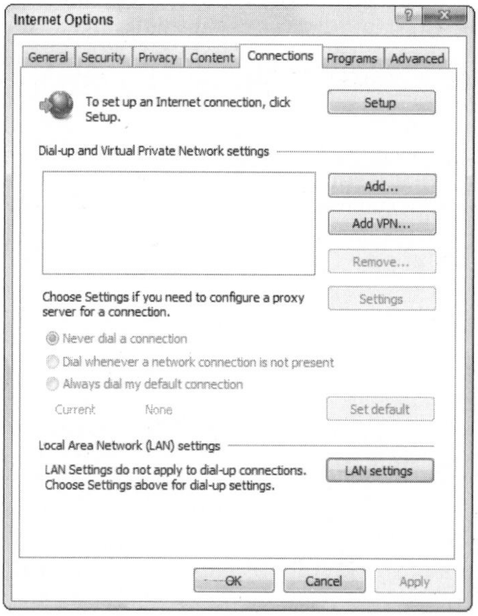

Figure 2-8: Make sure that IE doesn't try to dial out.

3. **Make sure that the Never Dial a Connection option is selected, and then click the LAN Settings button at the bottom.**

IE shows you the LAN Settings dialog box shown in Figure 2-9.

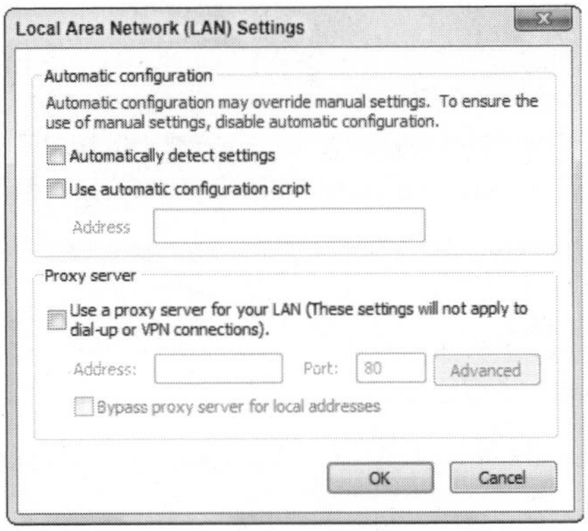

Figure 2-9:
Force
Internet
Explorer to
use all the
default
settings.

> **Local Area Network (LAN) Settings**
>
> **Automatic configuration**
> Automatic configuration may override manual settings. To ensure the
> use of manual settings, disable automatic configuration.
>
> ☐ Automatically detect settings
>
> ☐ Use automatic configuration script
>   Address   [   ]
>
> **Proxy server**
>
> ☐ Use a proxy server for your LAN (These settings will not apply to
> dial-up or VPN connections).
>
>   Address: [   ]   Port: [80]   [Advanced]
>
>   ☐ Bypass proxy server for local addresses
>
>   [OK]   [Cancel]

4. **Deselect all the check boxes.**

5. **Click the OK button twice to go back to Internet Explorer.**

Type in a new address and press Enter. IE should connect.

Networking on the road

Most of the time when I travel, I need to connect two PCs. Guess it's the
writer in me, but I've spent hours — days, weeks — trying to get PCs paired
up in the field. Direct cable connect. Laplink. USB-to-USB adapters. A dozen
other hardware and software kludges. I've resorted to e-mailing files to
myself more times than I care to admit.

Suddenly, with Vista and Windows XP peer-to-peer networking, it's easy. I
mean, really easy.

If you're on the road and you need to plug your PC into a "foreign" network,
there's nothing to it, as long as your portable and the foreign network are
running Vista or Windows XP peer-to-peer networks. Plug an RJ-45 cable into
the portable's network adapter, plug the other end into an available slot on
the hub, turn on the portable, and ba-da-boom-ba-da-bing, the whole operation takes maybe 30 seconds.

More than that, though, if I'm carrying two portables that I need to network,
all it takes is a crossover cable. (For a discussion of crossover cables —
basically, an RJ-45 cable with one pair of wires crossed — see the section
"Blocking out the major parts," earlier in this chapter.)

Whenever I pack two portables, I carry a little 1-meter-long crossover cable. If I need to network the portables, I plug one end of the cable into the network adapter on one portable and the other end into the other portable, and suddenly my Vista peer-to-peer network is right there with me. Everything I can do on the "big" network in my office works precisely the same way on the road. Absolutely phenomenal.

Chapter 3: Putting the Why in Wi-Fi

In This Chapter

- ✓ Finding out why wireless may be right for you
- ✓ Setting up a wireless network
- ✓ Connecting to a wireless network — anywhere, anytime
- ✓ Understanding wireless (in)security

I remember the first time I tried to install a wireless network in my home office.

It was an unmitigated disaster. I live in a three-story concrete townhouse. I put the *wireless access point (WAP)* (the base station — the thing with rabbit ears on top) on the middle floor. As long as my laptop sat right next to the WAP, everything worked great. The minute I moved it downstairs or upstairs — or even walked into the stairwell — it died. Completely, totally, utterly gone. No amount of futzing with the rabbit ears helped. It's like the bunny turned belly up, and that's all she wrote.

That was more than five years ago. Times change. The minute that 802.11g equipment became available in my neck of the woods, I ran out and bought another wireless base station, er, WAP. And therein lies a story. . . .

802.11g

I bought an 802.11g wireless broadband router and a PC plug-in card for the laptop. I paid less than $150 for the whole shootin' match. Installation was a breeze. I shut down every PC on my network, unpacked the router, unplugged my (very) old hub, plugged in the new hardware, brought up the PCs — and all my hardwired network cable connections worked. Fair enough, but that's not much of a big deal: I expected any replacement for the old hub to work right the first time.

So what about Bluetooth?

Bluetooth is a horse of a different color. The wireless networks I talk about in this chapter are designed to replace wired *local-area networks (LANs)*. They need to haul a lot of data over a fairly long distance — say, across a building or even many buildings.

Bluetooth, on the other hand, deals with relatively small amounts of data traveling over a short distance — perhaps 10 meters. It's built for connecting headphones to telephones,

speakers to sound systems, or Palm computers to notebooks.

To put it another way, if you want to transmit data from a dialup modem — perhaps a General Packet Radio Service (GPRS) modem in a mobile phone — to a nearby computer, Bluetooth works great. But if you need to send broadband across the room, you need to haul out the bigger Wi-Fi guns.

So I plugged the wireless card into the laptop and powered it up. Windows XP Pro recognized it, installed the driver, told me the card was available . . . and it worked. I mean, right then and there, not having done a thing, Internet Explorer picked up the network connection, reached out across my peer-to-peer network, through my DSL modem, and started pulling pages off the Web — much to my amazement.

I took the portable up and down the stairs and ran McAfee's Speedometer (http://us.mcafee.com/root/speedometer.asp) to judge how fast my Internet connection was running. Depending on my location, the speed was within 25 percent of the speed of the hard-linked connections. I couldn't believe it.

So what is 802.11g? It's a wireless access method that's been around for a long time, and it's by far the most popular method of getting computers to network without wires, as of this writing. Other than that, all you really need to know is that it works on the same 2.4-GHz bandwidth as many telephones and other wireless devices; that it blasts through concrete walls considerably better than its predecessor, 802.11b (see Table 3-1); and that it runs about five times as fast as 802.11b — more than fast enough to keep up with a good cable modem or DSL connection. Oh, and it has a horrible name that's just as senseless as 99 percent of the names in the computer business.

But ho! The 802.11g standard is growing a bit long in the tooth. The 802.11a standard stands poised to become the new local network connection method of choice, as soon as the prices come down. Yes, I know that *a* comes before *g* — it's a long story — but if you're buying new wireless equipment, and

Book IX
Chapter 3

Putting the Why
in Wi-Fi

802.11a/b/g compatibility doesn't cost two arms and two legs, you should consider splurging.

Wi-Fi (pronounced *why-fie*) is a term that encompasses all the 802.11 protocols. Usually, when you hear the term *Wi-Fi,* it specifically refers to 802.11b or g networks.

Table 3-1			Those 802 Numbers
Standard	*Rated (Theoretical) Speed (Mbps*)*	*Realistic Speed (Mbps)*	*My Recommendation*
802.11b	10	4	Don't bother. The signal doesn't reach as far as 802.11g, and it's slower.
802.11g	50	20	The sweet spot. Backward compatible with 802.11b, so if you have an old wireless card, it'll work with your 802.11g base station. But it uses the same frequency range as many cordless phones.
802.11a	50	30	Not as popular as 802.11g (at least this week), thus more expensive. Not compatible with 802.11b or 802.11g, so that notebook adapter that you buy for your 802.11a network at home probably won't work when you go to Starbucks, unless it's specifically 802.11a/b/g. Uses a much higher frequency than cordless phones, but it doesn't poke through walls as well as 802.11g.

*Million bits per second

Installing a Wireless System

If you've never dealt with a network before, read Book IX, Chapter 2 to make sure that you understand the basics. If you think of a wireless network as being very similar to a "regular" wired network, with radio waves in place of network cables, you're pretty close to the mark.

Here we go with the stupid terminology again.

Wireless cards

Every computer in a wireless network must have a wireless adapter. A *wireless adapter* is just a radio receiver/transmitter, similar to the kind in cordless telephones. Most commonly, wireless adapters plug into USB ports,

PCMCIA notebook ports (the flat ones about the size of a pack of playing cards), or local-area network ports (RJ-45 slots, the kind you normally plug network cables into), or they go inside the computer, either built into the motherboard or screwed down as a PCI card.

Many hand-held computers (such as Pocket PCs) either have built-in wireless or they support wireless adapters that plug into the slot used for Compact Flash memory cards.

Wireless networks use a *wireless access point* — a WAP — that acts much like a base station for a cordless telephone. A WAP isn't technically necessary because you can instruct wireless adapters to talk to each other, much as you would use walkie-talkies. (See Vista's Windows Help and Support topic on Ad Hoc Wireless Networks.) But if you plan to run much data over your wireless network, it's far better to run everything through a WAP.

If you already have a wired network set up, adding a wireless base station, er, WAP is as simple as plugging one into your existing hub (router, switch, whatever) and adjusting the bunny ears. If you don't have a wired network already, I urge you to follow the advice in Book IX, Chapter 2, and start with a *wireless broadband router* (also known as a *wireless Internet gateway* or just a *wireless router*).

The wireless broadband router acts as a wireless base station, but it also has slots for regular wired network cables and a special slot to connect your cable/DSL/satellite modem. Almost every wireless network starts out with a PC plugged into the back of the wireless router or access point — that's how you set up the WAP.

Location, location, location

The location of the wireless access point matters — the stronger the signal, the faster the data travels over the waves. Here are my suggestions:

✦ If you know which computers will use wireless the most, put the WAP as close as you can to them. If you don't know which computers will drive the largest volume (or you don't know where the high-volume computers will be located), put the WAP as close to the physical center of the coverage area as you can.

✦ Do not put the WAP right next to a wall. Move it away from the wall by at least 6 inches. Don't put one on the floor or directly attached to the ceiling, either.

✦ Remember that metal, water (read: fish tanks), and concrete affect signal strength. Wood and drywall don't matter much. Glass, brick, and stone sit somewhere in between.

✦ Try hard to connect your cable/DSL/satellite modem to the WAP by a regular network cable. Although it may be technically possible to go wireless, there's no reason to bog down the wireless system with the highest-volume link in your network.

That said, remember that your wireless broadband router (er, wireless Internet gateway, uh, wireless router) doesn't need to be located right next to the cable/DSL/satellite modem. As long as you can stretch a cable between them (up to 100 meters — 300 feet or so), you're fine.

✦ WAPs and cordless phones can have problems coexisting. I've heard that microwave ovens can cause interference, too, although I've never had the problem. If you have something that operates on the 2.4-GHz frequency — and many cordless phones do — it may give your wireless network heart flutters. I minimized the problem in my office by moving to 5.8-GHz telephones.

To plug a wireless broadband router into a network, follow the detailed instructions in Book IX, Chapter 2. If you follow those instructions and the ones in the user's manual, and you can't get anything to work right (particularly, if you reboot a computer or two and it doesn't work right), see my discussion of fighting Mother Hens in the "Troubleshooting" section of that chapter. Ninety percent of the time, the cable/DSL modem thinks it's a Mother Hen and the broadband router also thinks it's a Mother Hen. Feathers fly.

Setting Up a Secure Wireless Network

Ya gotcher ears on, good buddy? 10-4 that. Truckers do the wireless thang. You should too.

Microsoft has developed a program and set of de facto standards that fall under the sobriquet *Wireless Zero Configuration*, or *WZC*. Almost all modern network adapters can use WZC — and many of them, surprisingly, work.

In the following 20-step process (the last and longest in this book!), I take you through the process of getting a PC connected to your wireless network and then securing the network.

Why? The first law of wireless networks pertains: Any default installation of a wireless network is absolutely wide open and vulnerable to the most casual eavesdropping. If you don't lock your wireless network down, somebody's going to blow it away.

If all goes well, here's how you connect the first PC to your new wireless network, and then harden the network so that it doesn't quack like a sitting duck:

1. **Make sure that your WAP is installed and all the lights are blinking.**

2. **If you have a wireless adapter that goes inside your PC, put it in. Start your PC. If you have a wireless adapter that plugs into a USB port or PCMCIA slot, stick it in.**

The instructions that come with your plug-in wireless adapter undoubtedly tell you to run the CD that came with the adapter before you plug it in. Bah, humbug. Most of the time, Vista installs everything just fine, and the installation CD puts all sorts of useless junk on your machine. I only use the installation CD if absolutely nothing else works.

The Found New Hardware Wizard should appear (see Figure 3-1).

Figure 3-1:
Vista finds
a newly
inserted
USB 802.11g
wireless
network
adapter.

3. **Click the Locate and Install Driver Software (Recommended) icon.**

You have to click through a User Account Control box, and when you do, Vista should come up with the Found New Hardware dialog box shown in Figure 3-2.

4. **Put the installation CD in your CD drive.**

If you don't have the installation CD, select the I Don't Have the Disc. Show Me Other Options icon — and immediately head out to the Internet and download the latest driver from the hardware manufacturer.

When you insert the CD in your drive, Vista immediately scans it and searches for the driver. If it finds the driver, you see the progress bar shown in Figure 3-3.

When Vista finishes installing the driver, it tells you (see Figure 3-4).

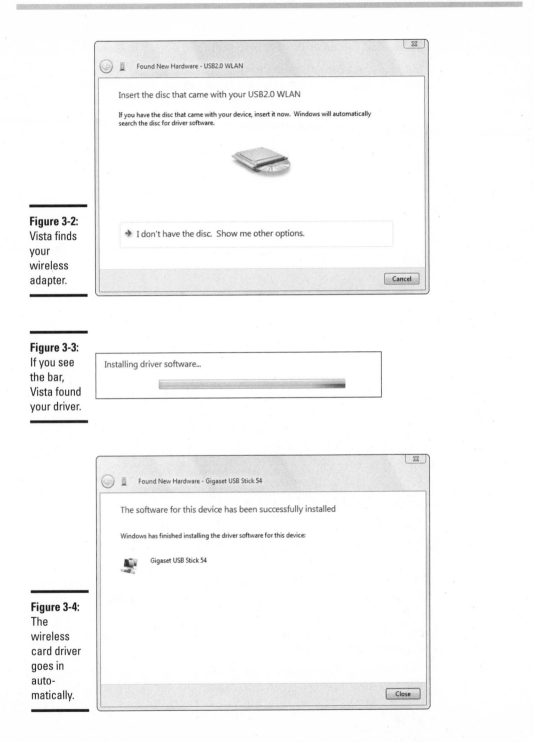

Figure 3-2:
Vista finds
your
wireless
adapter.

Figure 3-3:
If you see
the bar,
Vista found
your driver.

Figure 3-4:
The
wireless
card driver
goes in
auto-
matically.

5. Verify that the driver's installed, and then click the Close button.

In the notification area, next to the clock, a network "power bar" starts throbbing or a red *X* appears on the connectivity icon. Hover your mouse over the icon, and you see a balloon that tells you that you're not connected — but wireless networks are available.

6. Click the balloon.

Vista brings up the Connect to a Network dialog box, as shown in Figure 3-5. Because you just set up your network, it's unsecured.

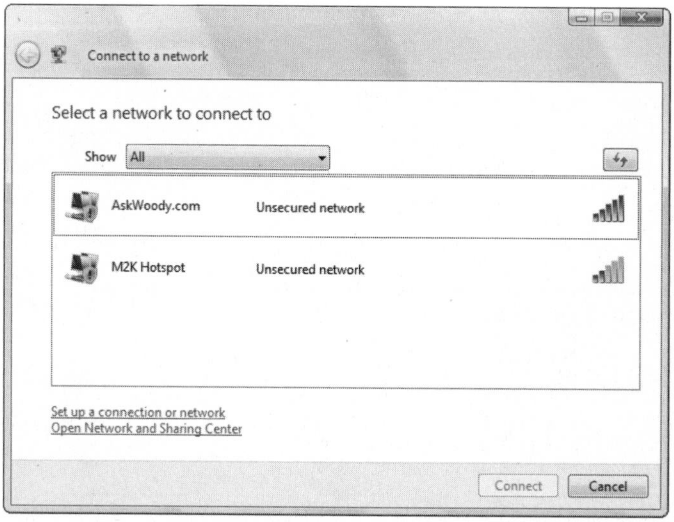

Figure 3-5:
Two unsecured networks are currently available.

7. Double-click the network you want to connect to.

Vista goes out to the WAP, retrieves the information it needs to get hooked up, and then shows you the Successfully Connected dialog box shown in Figure 3-6.

8. Click the Close button.

You're connected to your wireless network. But you aren't done yet. The most important parts lie ahead.

9. Choose Start⇨Control Panel⇨Network and Internet⇨Network and Sharing Center.

Vista shows you the Network and Sharing Center. In Figure 3-7, the Network and Sharing Center reports that the computer is connected to the Patong wireless network, but that the network isn't connected to the Internet.

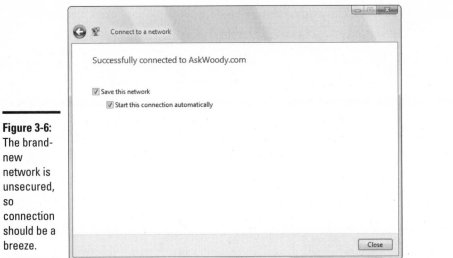

Figure 3-6:
The brand-
new
network is
unsecured,
so
connection
should be a
breeze.

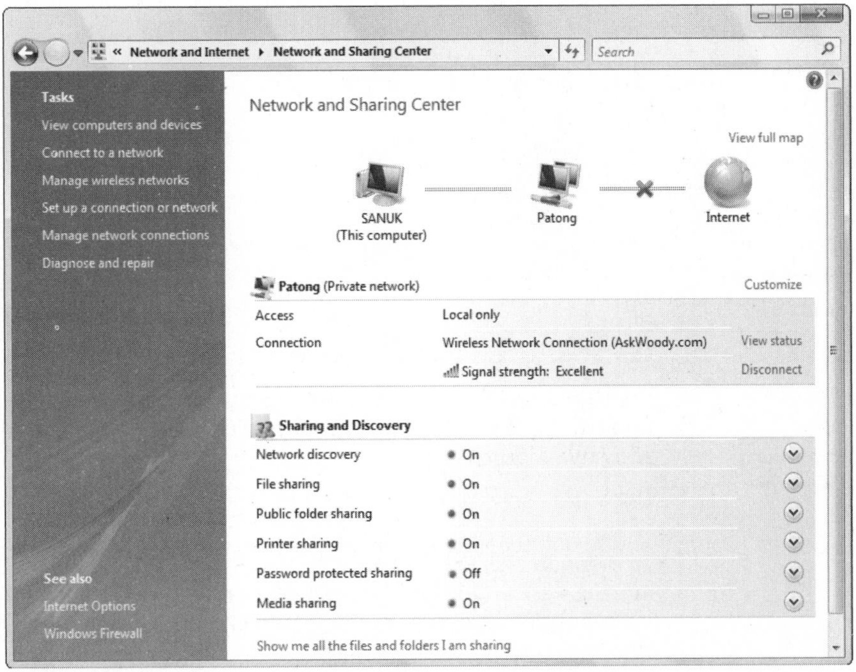

Figure 3-7:
The
wireless
connection
is working,
but the
Patong
network is
not getting
through to
the Internet.

10. **If you see anything unexpected, double-click it.**

For example, in Figure 3-7, I click the red *X* connecting the Patong network and the Internet.

If you click any part of the Network and Sharing Center diagram, Vista runs its diagnostic routines to see whether a problem exists and presents you with a list of possible solutions. There are many possible problems, so if you find that something isn't working right, follow the instructions to see whether you can narrow the source (and the solution!).

Ultimately, the Network and Sharing Center reports that all is well with the world, as shown in Figure 3-8.

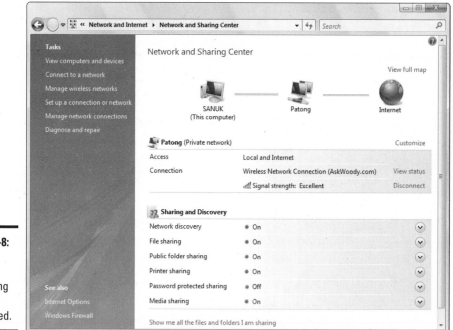

Figure 3-8:
Sooner
or later,
everything
gets
connected.

11. **Go through the Sharing and Discovery part of the Network and Sharing Center, and make sure that you get the settings the way you want them.**

The settings I use for my home office are shown in Figure 3-8. They're very permissive — I assume that anybody connected to my network should be able to get at all my Public folders and do with them what they will.

I provide a detailed discussion of the settings, and their effects, in Book II, Chapter 1.

12. **On the left side of the Network and Sharing Center, click the Set Up a Connection or Network link.**

Vista shows you the Set Up a Connection or Network dialog box, as shown in Figure 3-9.

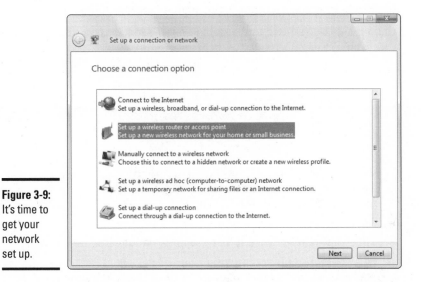

Figure 3-9:
It's time to get your network set up.

13. **Click the Set Up a New Wireless Network for Your Home or Small Business icon and click the Next button.**

Vista shows you a splash screen.

14. **Click the Next button.**

Vista reaches out to your wireless router (or wireless access point) and, if it determines that it can't configure the router automatically, presents you with the Cannot Configure dialog box shown in Figure 3-10.

15. **Click the Configure This Device Manually icon.**

The setup wizard opens the main page on your wireless router. Every router has a slightly different setup procedure, but they all share a few items in common. You need to dig out your router's instruction manual, or hunt and peck through the interface, and change these four things:

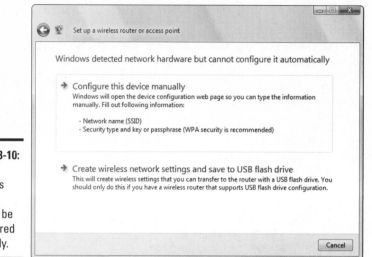

Figure 3-10:
Most
wireless
routers
have to be
configured
manually.

- **Make your own service set identifier (SSID).** Your router probably has an SSID of "linksys," "Default," "3Com," "NETGEAR," "WLAN," or "wireless." You should change it to something that isn't so easy to guess.

  This isn't high security. It just keeps the kiddie crackers away.

- **Don't broadcast the SSID.** That way, people will need to know the SSID of your network (or they have to crack it) before they can connect.

  Again, this ain't high security — it's easy to figure out an SSID even if it isn't broadcast. But it'll keep the hoi polloi from gumming up your network.

- **Enable WPA encryption.** If your router and all your wireless cards can support WPA encryption, use it. WPA's the only form of security on a wireless connection that works. See Figure 3-11 for an example of how one router asks for the WPA *passphrase*. In this case, the router manufacturer calls it a *Pre-Shared Key* (which I suppose is better than a Post-Shared Key, eh?).

  The details of WPA encryption are beyond the scope of this book, but you can find an excellent overview in *Wireless Home Networking For Dummies, 2nd Edition,* by Danny Briere, Pat Hurley, and Edward Ferris (published by Wiley).

- **Change your router's password.** It amazes me how many people get their security settings straight — WPA and all — and then forget to set a password for the router. If you're still using the default password, it'll take about 10 seconds for somebody to come in and erase all that protection you've instituted.

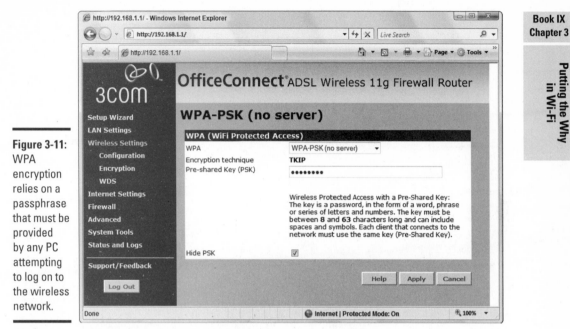

Figure 3-11:
WPA
encryption
relies on a
passphrase
that must be
provided
by any PC
attempting
to log on to
the wireless
network.

16. **You must click the Apply button, or do whatever the router requires, to make the new settings "stick."**

Routers aren't terribly sophisticated: You have to tell them to remember the new settings, and when you do, they reboot — a process that can take many minutes.

When you tell the router to remember its settings, you see a message saying that the data is being updated, and then Internet Explorer keels over with a Cannot Display the Web Page warning. Don't worry. That's normal. It's exactly how things are supposed to work.

17. **Click the red *X* to exit Internet Explorer, and then cancel the Cannot Configure dialog box (refer to Figure 3-10).**

Down in the notification area, next to the clock, you should see that your network has been disconnected — either a red *X* will appear over the connection icon or the signal strength bar will start pulsing.

18. **Double-click the red *X* connection icon or the throbbing signal strength bar.**

Vista tells you that the settings you have for your old connection don't work anymore (see Figure 3-12).

Figure 3-12:
Your old
connection
is hidden
and
encrypted —
Vista can't
connect.

19. **Double-click your old connection.**

If you can't see the old connection, click the Set Up a Connection or
Network link, choose Manually Connect to a Wireless Network, and click
the Next button.

You see the Manually Connect to a Wireless Network dialog shown in
Figure 3-13.

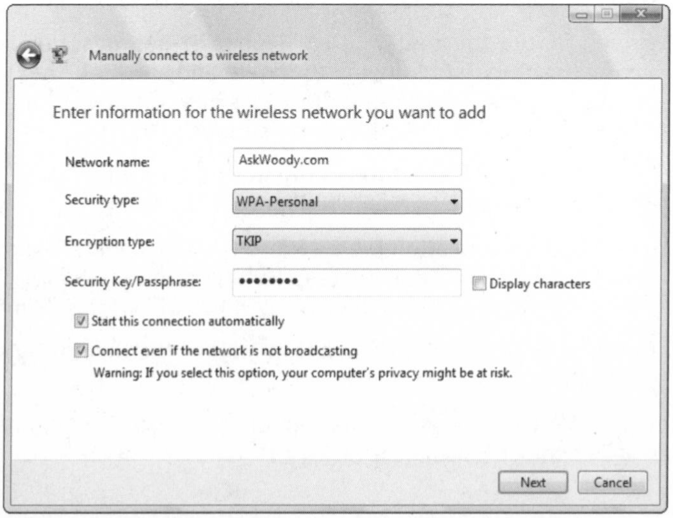

Figure 3-13:
You need to
know all the
details to
connect
to your
protected
network.

20. **Fill in the SSID (Microsoft calls it a "network name" for reasons known only to Redmond), the security type, and the passphrase, and select the Connect Even if the Network Is Not Broadcasting check box to make Vista connect. Click the Next button.**

At long, long last, you're set up and secure.

Windows keeps constant watch for new networks that broadcast their system IDs. If you walk into a Starbucks and you suddenly see a notification that another system is available, hooking into the system is as simple as clicking the icon in the notification area, clicking the new network, and clicking the Connect button.

Index

Numerics

0day exploits, 195–196, 266, 268
4:3 aspect ratio, 446, 447
12:5 aspect ratio, 448
16:9 aspect ratio, 446–447, 449
100Base-T connection, 691
802.11a, 707
802.11b, 707
802.11g
  compatibility, 706–707
  defined, 707
  speed, 707
  wireless broadband routers, 693
1394 slots, 443

A

AAC (Advanced Audio Coding) files
  defined, 150
  MP3 files instead of, 471
Accelerated Graphics Port (AGP)
    interface, 441
Active@Undelete, 80
adapter cards
  AGP interface, 441
  defined, 440
  interfaces, 440–442
  ISA interface, 442
  PCI Express interface, 441
  PCI interface, 441
  PCI-X interface, 441
Add a Favorite dialog box, 383–384
Add a Port dialog box, 241
Add Files to Restore dialog box, 128
Add or Remove Snap-ins dialog box, 244
Add to Library dialog box, 528–529
Address bar (IE)
  defined, 368
  illustrated, 369

administrative actions, 101
administrator accounts
  changing user accounts with, 107–111
  defined, 100
  scope of power, 100–101
  using, 100–101
  when to use, 102
Advanced Audio Coding (AAC) files
  defined, 150
  MP3 files instead of, 471
Advanced Options dialog box, 327
Advanced Research Project Agency
    (ARPA), 348
Advanced Tag Editor, 532
adware, 25
Aero Glass
  benefits, 28
  computer requirements, 44
  defined, 27
  illustrated, 28
  Sidebar, 29–30
  upgrading to, 32
AGP (Accelerated Graphics Port)
    interface, 441
AIM (AOL Instant Messenger), 414
All Programs menu. *See also* Start menu
  changing, 311–314
  folders, 311
  programs, accessible to everyone, 313
  relocating in, 312
  removing from, 312
  renaming in, 312
  shortcut, 314
anonymizer toolbar, 203
antispyware protection, 199
antivirus software. *See also* AVG Free
  caring for, 270–272
  challenges, 265
  false positives, 266–267
  on the fly method, 264

antivirus software *(continued)*
  full scans, 264, 271
  heuristic analysis, 264, 265
  infection watch methods, 264–265
  lurking method, 265
  manufacturers, 265, 272
  methods, 264
  obtaining, 272
  signature files, 270
  signature matching, 264
  understanding, 263–267
  Windows activation, 274–275
  0day attack protection, 266
AOL Instant Messenger (AIM), 414
Appearance and Personalization option
  (Control Panel), 115
Appearance Settings dialog box, 288
archived Web pages, 360
ARPA (Advanced Research Project
  Agency), 348
Ask.com. *See also* search engines
  defined, 428
  illustrated, 429
AskWoody.com
  defined, 186
  search engine information, 425
  uses, 175
aspect ratio. *See also* monitors
  defined, 445
  4:3, 446
  12:5, 448
  16:9, 447–448, 449
attachments. *See also* e-mail
  blocked, 406
  blocked, receiving, 407–409
  creating, 411–412
  defined, 402
  paperclip, 405
  receiving, 405–409
  security, 408–409
  unzipping, 406

attacks. *See also* malware protection
  DDoS, 192
  recovering from, 209
  0day, 195–196, 266, 268
Audacity
  background music, 560
  defined, 559
  illustrated, 560
  recording in, 560–561
  starting, 559
  tutorial/reference, 561
audio cards, 627, 628
audio tracks
  burn cost, 150
  burning, 149, 150, 541–544
  defined, 149
  ripping, 150
Auto-Hide, 91
Automatic Updates, 219
AutoPlay dialog box, 153
AVG Free. *See also* antivirus software
  benefits, 272
  defined, 263
  downloading, 272, 273
  First Run Wizard, 274
  illustrated, 273
  installing, 272–274
  Windows identification, 274

B

backbone, Internet, 350
backdoors
  defined, 191
  PC acquisition, 191–192
  worm, 192
background, desktop
  changing, 64
  defined, 285
  picking, 288–289
  pictures, 288–289
  wallpaper, choosing, 289

BackRub, 425
Backup and Restore Center, 123–124, 128
Backup and Restore Wizard,
    127, 128, 129, 130
backups
  automatic, 38
  before clean installs, 47
  Box.Net, 119
  categories, 119
  complete, 119
  CompletePC, 130–131
  creating, 118–131
  data, 119, 122–130
  GDrive, 119
  incremental, 123
  list, 129
  Live Drive, 119
  manual, 123–124
  off-site storage, 118
  options, 120
  shadow copies, 119, 120–122
  system restore points, 119
banner printers, 495
BIOS locking, 54
BitLocker
  defined, 39
  Encrypting File System (EFS) and, 40
Blogger, 394–395
blogs
  defined, 393
  with Internet Explorer, 393–395
  starting out with, 394
  types of, 394
Bluetooth, 706
Blu-Ray, 20
botnets
  defined, 25, 192
  keyloggers, 192
  as rootkits, 192
  white paper, 192
Bove, Tony (*iPod & iTunes For Dummies*),
    483

Box.Net, 119
Briere, Danny
  Windows XP Media Center Edition 2004
    PC For Dummies, 666
  Wireless Home Networking For
    Dummies, 2nd Edition, 716
broadband connections. *See also*
    Internet connections
  defined, 25, 353
  excuses for, 355–356
  last mile, 354–355
broadband routers. *See also* networks;
    routers
  cable modems, 688, 691
  defined, 686
  DSL modem, 691
  function, 687
  wireless, 693, 708
buffer overflows, 191, 192
bugs, 25, 193
Burn List
  defined, 542
  populating, 542
  saving, 543
burning
  CDs, 540–544
  characteristics, 543
  data files, 152
  defined, 541
  Live File System formatting, 151–158
  Mastered formatting, 150–151, 152–158
  movies, 615
  song costs, 150
  steps, 152–157
  support, 147
  with Vista, 152–158
  volume level, 544
  in Windows Media Player, 540–544
burning DVDs
  disc format, 662
  with Media Center, 661–664
  naming, 662–663

burning DVDs *(continued)*
  recorded show selection, 663–664
  with Windows, 660

C

cable modems. *See also* Internet
    connections; modems
  broadband routers, 688, 691
  defined, 679
  as DHCP servers, 701
  installation, 459
cables
  bundling, 623
  Cat-5, 691, 694, 695
  Cat-6, 695
  crossover, 687, 703, 704
  LAN, 20, 679, 685, 694
  network, 687–688
  RJ-45, 20, 685, 691
  selecting, 694
  speaker, 623
  USB, 20, 53
  video, 623
cache, clearing, 203
Calculator
  defined, 165
  Scientific, 165–166
  tricks, 165
camcorders. *See also* digital cameras
  batteries, 571
  considerations, 571
  defined, 565
  dropouts, 572
  illustrated, 565
  manufacturer Web sites, 575
  media, 572
  popularity, 571
  purchasing, 572–574
  tips, 572
Canon, 575
card slots, 17

Casio, 575
Cat-5 cables. *See also* cables
  connection, 691
  defined, 694
  theoretical limit, 695
Cat-6 cables, 695
cathode ray tubes (CRT) monitors, 444
CD drives, 19
CD-R
  defined, 148
  discs, burning, 541
  discs, cost, 149
  drives, 151
  information, 148
CD-R FAQ, 148
CD-RW, 148
CDs
  for all current used software, 47
  audio, burning, 541–544
  audio tracks, 149
  bits, 149
  burn steps, 152–157
  burning, 147–158, 540–545
  data, burning, 544
  data files, 149
  playing, WMP, 522–524
  from playlists, 536
  printer, 499
  ripping, 524–527
  sharing, 633
  USB hardware, 463
CF (Compact Flash) cards, 454
Character Map
  defined, 164
  illustrated, 164
  opening, 164
  uses, 165
Check Disk, 133
checkpoints
  creating, 143–144
  defined, 143
  naming, 144

Chess Titans, 343
Choose an Antivirus Option
    dialog box, 275
clean install
  caution, 48
  defined, 46
  performing, 46–48
cleanups, scheduling, 134
ClickLock, 66
client/server networks. *See also*
    networks
  clients, 674
  conversion to peer-to-peer, 674
  defined, 672
  illustrated, 673
  Internet connection, 675
  introduction to, 673–675
  lack of control, 674
  as original networking form, 674
  pros/cons comparison, 677–678
  servers, 673, 676, 691
  use of, 672–673
clips. *See also* movies; Windows Movie
    Maker
  combining, 605–606
  deleting, from workspace, 600
  dragging, to storyboard, 600
  effects, applying, 605
  formats, 611
  gathering, 598
  importing, 610–611
  locating, 600
  moving, to workspace, 600
  playing, 601–602
  selecting, 599
  sound, 608–609
  sources, 598
  splitting, 605–606
  trimming, 603–604
Clock, Language, and Region option
    (Control Panel), 115

collections (WMM). *See also* Windows
    Movie Maker
  collections inside, 597
  combining clips in, 606
  defined, 597
  splitting clips in, 606
Color and Appearance dialog box, 286
color laser printers, 494
colors
  desktop base, 284
  layman's guide, 593
  schemes, 287
  setting, 286–288
combining clips, 606
Command bar (IE)
  defined, 368
  illustrated, 368
  options, 369
commercial firewalls, 248
Compact Flash (CF) cards, 454
complete backups, 119
CompletePC backups. *See also* backups
  defined, 130
  ghosting with, 130–131
compressed files
  blocked attachments, 405–406
  with .zip filename extension, 407
Compressed (zipped) Folders Extraction
    Wizard, 142, 143
compression
  defined, 139
  functioning, 139
  Huffman encoding, 139
  NTFS, 139, 141–142
  techniques, 139
  techniques comparison, 140
  zipped, 139, 142–143
computers. *See also* monitors
  big box, 15–17
  buying, 14–22
  card slots, 17

computers *(continued)*
  communication with computers, 678–682
  connections, 20–21
  copying songs to, 481–482
  deauthorizing (iTunes), 474
  drives, 18–19
  host, 503
  list on network, 700
  memory, 16
  minimum requirements, 15
  moving images to, 574–578
  operating systems, 14
  performance details, 50
  processors, 16
  requirements for Aero Glass, 44
  requirements for Windows Vista, 43–45
  restarting, 95
  restoring, 145
  sleep, 94–95
  sound, 22
  turning off, 96
  turning off at night, 95
  upgrade dos/don'ts, 17
ConceptA virus, 190
Confirmation ID. *See also* Installation ID
  defined, 55
  new, contacting Microsoft for, 56
  storage, 55
Connect to a Network Wizard, 82
Connect to the Internet Wizard, 357
Content Restriction, Annulment, and Protection (C.R.A.P.)
  defined, 514
  music versions, 514
  restrictions, 515
Control Panel
  Appearance and Personalization pane, 115
  Clock, Language, and Region option, 115
  Ease of Access option, 115
  Get Started with Windows option, 64
  Hardware and Sound option, 115, 504, 628

  illustrated, 114
  maintenance with, 113–116
  Mouse option, 66
  Network and Internet option, 114–115, 233
  Network and Sharing Center option, 73, 697, 712
  NVIDIA, 626, 627
  Personalization pane, 64
  Programs option, 115, 116, 118
  Security option, 114, 237
  settings duplication, 115
  System and Maintenance option, 114, 123, 158, 177
  Uninstall a Program option, 65
  User Accounts and Family Safety option, 110, 115, 212
conventions, this book, 3
cookies. *See also* protection
  defined, 203, 393
  deleting, 393
  doubleclick reality, 205
  existence, 204
  functioning of, 204–205
  information collection, 206
  information update, 207
  planting of, 205
  retrieval, 206
CoolSwitch, 169–170
CPU
  card slots, 17
  defined, 15
  memory, 16
  processor, 16
  upgrade dos/don'ts, 17
C.R.A.P. (Content Restriction, Annulment, and Protection)
  defined, 514
  music versions, 514
  restrictions, 515
credit card fraud. *See also* protection
  identity theft and, 202
  non-U.S. companies, 202
  ordering safety, 200
  precautions, 201–202

critical security holes, 262
crossover cables, 687, 703
CRT (cathode ray tube) monitors, 444
currency converter gadget, 291
Customer Experience Improvement
    Program, 636
Customize Start Menu dialog box,
    83, 84, 315–316

D

data backups. *See also* backups
  creating, 122–127
  defined, 119
  drives on networks, 125
  frequency, 126–127
  incremental, 123
  list, 129
  location, 125
  media, 124
  restoring, 127–130
data CDs/DVDs, burning, 544
DDoS (Distributed Denial of Service)
    attacks, 192
defragmenting, disk, 134
del.icio.us, 430
desktop
  background, 64–65, 285, 288–289
  base color, 284
  defined, 62, 283
  icons, 285, 292–293
  icons, cleaning up, 65
  illustrated, 62, 284
  levels, 283–285
  mouse, 285, 294–295
  personalizing, 283–302
  screen saver, 285, 295–301
  search, 322–323
  Sidebar, 65, 285, 289–292
  taskbar, 66
Desktop Themes
  availability, 302
  defined, 301

mouse pointers, 294
  selecting, 302
  using, 301–302
Desktop Windows Manager, 28–29
Device Manager window, 460–461, 626
Device Properties dialog box, 461
DHCP (Dynamic Host Configuration
    Protocol) servers, 691, 701
dialup connections. *See also* Internet
    connections
  defined, 25
  last mile, 354–355
  no dial tone, troubleshooting, 358
  options, changing, 358
  setting up, 357–359
  shortcuts, 93
  tech support, 359
dialup modems, 689
Digg, 430
Digital Cable Tuners, 651
digital cameras
  batteries, 574
  categories, 565
  choosing, 564–572
  compatibility, 569
  defined, 564
  digital zoom, 567
  exposure control, 568
  external flash, 568
  flash, 568
  focusing, 567
  hot shoe, 568
  illustrated, 564
  image, moving to computer, 574–578
  image storage/transfer, 568–569
  image transfer application, 577
  look and feel, 569
  manufacturer Web sites, 575
  memory cards, 568–569
  optical zoom, 567
  pixels, 566
  point-and-shoot, 565
  print size, 566

digital cameras *(continued)*
  purchasing, 572–574
  resolution, 566
  SLRs, 565
  stabilizing, 568
  understanding, 566–569
  USB interface, 569
  Vista not recognizing, 577
  Web comments, 573
  Web prices, 573
  webcam, 565, 570–571
  zoom lens, 566–567
Digital Photography For Dummies,
    5th Edition (King), 579
digital rights management
  defined, 513
  iTunes songs, 466, 467
Digital Visual Interface (DVI), 445
digital zoom, 567
Disk Cleanup. *See also* Task Scheduler
  defined, 134, 135
  parameters, 135–136
  running, 134, 138
  use steps, 136–138
Disk Cleanup Settings dialog box,
    135–136
Disk Defragmenter, 134
display adapters
  connectors, 627
  Media Center and, 626
Display Settings dialog box, 449–450
Distributed Denial of Service (DDoS)
    attacks, 192
DNSStuff, 359–360
documents
  canceling, 506–507
  pausing, 506
  restarting, 506
  resuming, 506
Documents folder. *See also* folders
  illustrated, 68
  opening, 69, 324

Dogpile
  defined, 427
  Firefox with, 431–433
  illustrated, 427
  Images link, 434
domain networks, 231
domains, 97, 672
downloading, 25
drafting printers, 495
drivers. *See also* hardware
  data, checking, 460–461
  dealing with, 444
  defined, 23
  printer, 497–498, 500
  SATA drive, 489
  versions, checking, 460–461
  video card, 451, 625
  wireless adapter, 710–711
drives. *See also* computers; hard drives
  CD, 19
  CD-R, 151
  cleanups, scheduling, 134
  defined, 131
  DVD, 19
  flash, 19
  floppy disk, 18
  formatting, 132
  key, 455
  maintaining, 131–134
  prevention, 131
  shortcuts, 93
  U3, 455
  USB flash, 19
dropouts, 572
DSL
  as broadband connection, 353
  broadband router and, 691
  last mile, 354–355
DSL modems. *See also* modems
  defined, 679
  as DHCP servers, 701
DSLReports, 359

duplex printing, 495
DV-AVI files, 614
DVD drives, 19
DVD-R (DVD+R), 148
DVD-RW (DVD+RW), 149
DVDs
  bits, 149
  burn steps, 152–157
  burning, 147–158
  burning, in Media Center, 660–664
  data, burning, 544
  data files, 150
  legalities, 615
  publishing movies on, 611, 612
  sharing, 633
  video tracks, 149
DVI (Digital Visual Interface), 445
DVR-MS format, 531
dye sublimation printers, 494
Dynamic Host Configuration Protocol
      (DHCP) servers, 691, 701

E

Ease of Access option (Control Panel),
      115
Easy Transfer
  advantages, 52
  Alohabob, 52
  defined, 51
  illustrated, 53
  limitations, 51–52
  starting, 53
  steps for using, 52–53
  transfer contents, 52
EFS (Encrypting File System), 40
EIDE (Enhanced Integrated Drive
      Electronics) interface, 487, 488
802.11a, 707
802.11b, 707
802.11g
  compatibility, 706–707

defined, 707
speed, 707
wireless broadband routers, 693
e-mail
  addresses, 402
  anonymous, sending, 203
  attachments, 199, 406, 407–409, 411–412
  automatic downloading of pictures, 208
  creating, 409–412
  receiving, 405–409
  saving, 412
  sending, 412
  signatures, 410
  spam, 206, 207–209
  spelling, checking, 410–411
  trusting, 200
e-mail programs
  Outlook, 400
  selecting, 399–402
  Windows Live Mail, 400–401
  Windows Live Mail Desktop, 401
  Windows Mail, 399, 400–412
Encrypting File System (EFS), 40
encryption, WPA, 716, 717
End User License Agreement (EULA),
      12, 13
Enhanced Integrated Drive Electronics
      (EIDE) interface, 487, 488
ePodcast Producer, 562
ergonomic keyboards, 451
Ethernet. *See also* wired networks
  defined, 680
  functioning of, 680
  history, 680
  hubs, 681
  100Base-T peer-to-peer network, 684
  peer-to-peer network illustration, 681
  rate, 681
EULA (End User License Agreement),
      12, 13
Experience Index, 158–160
exposure control, digital cameras, 568

Extensible Markup Language (XML) files, 330
external devices
  advantages, 440
  defined, 440
  interfaces, 442–443
external flash, digital cameras, 568

F

Fair Credit Billing Act, 200
false positives, 266–267
Fast User Switching, 111
Favorites (IE). *See also* Internet Explorer
  adding, 383–384
  defined, 382
  deleting, 385
  exploring, 383
  moving, 385
  organizing, 384–385
  renaming, 385
Favorites menu (Start menu), 316
feed readers, 396
FeedBurner, 562
Ferris, Edward (*Wireless Home Networking For Dummies, 2nd Edition*), 716
File and Folder Backup Wizard, 122, 123, 126
File and Folder Restore Wizard, 127–130
file servers, 676
File Sharing
  dialog box, 77
  turning on, 74
file transfers
  data files, 52
  with Easy Transfer, 51–53
  Microsoft Office settings, 52
  Windows settings, 52
filenames
  in data backups, 126
  extensions, 68

extensions, showing, 69–71, 297
  prohibited characters, 67
files
  attaching, 411–412
  compression, 139–142
  copying/moving, 88
  creating, 87–88
  data, on CDs/DVDs, 150
  defined, 67
  deleting, 79–80
  in Public folder, 72–76
  restoring, 80, 128
  saving Web pages to, 380
  shared, viewing, 78–79
  sharing, 71–76
  sharing, with Windows Live Messenger, 423–424
  uncompressing, 142
  versions, previous, 89–90
  versions, restoring, 89–90
  in Windows Explorer, 86
  working with, 67–80
  Zip, 140, 142–143
film cameras, 564, 570
Firefox. *See also* Internet Explorer
  Add-Ons page, 431–432
  addresses, typing, 388
  anti-phishing consequences, 375
  anti-phishing tools, 374, 378–379
  Bookmarks, 382–385
  coexistence with Internet Explorer, 351, 365
  connecting with, 348
  cookies, deleting, 393
  as default browser, 365
  defined, 348, 364
  Dogpile with, 431–433
  Full Screen view, 388
  graphics, turning off, 389
  home page, 365, 367
  illustrated, 364
  Links toolbar, 391

Live Bookmarks feature, 395
  obtaining, 365
  phishing settings, changing, 378
  pop-up filter, 378
  Rollyo, 433
  RSS feeds, 395, 396–397
  search engine, changing, 431
  tabs, 371–372
firewalls. *See also* Windows Firewall (WF)
  checking, 237
  commercial, 248
  comparing, 225–227
  competitive, 226
  defined, 219, 225
  hardware, 226
  inbound, 219, 225
  opening ports, 238
  outbound, 31, 219, 225
  proxy server, 675
  public, settings, 236
  Remote Assistance interference, 178
  stateful, 229
  terminology, 229–230
  third-party, 238
  use of, 198
FireWire slots, 443
firmware, 467
flash, digital cameras, 568
flash drives, 19
flash memory
  defined, 454
  packaging, 454
  purchasing, 455
  types of, 454
  USB connector, 454
Flickr, 579
floppy disk drives, 18
focusing, digital cameras, 567
Folder Options dialog box, 298, 328–329
Folder View Advanced Settings
      dialog box, 70

folders
  All Programs menu, 311
  built-in permissions, 76
  creating, 87–88
  defined, 67
  deleting, 79–80
  Documents, 68, 69, 324
  Music, 530–531
  names, 67
  organization, 68
  Other Media, 531
  Personal, 316
  Picture, 531, 584
  predefined, shortcuts, 82
  Programs, 313, 314
  Public, 71–76
  Recorded TV, 531
  restoring, 80, 128
  shared, viewing, 78–79
  sharing, 71–79
  sharing, with Windows Live Messenger,
      423–424
  shortcuts, 93
  uncompressing, 142
  Video, 531
  in Windows Explorer, 86
  WMP Library, 530
  working with, 67–80
fonts
  formats, 81
  Notepad, changing, 161
  understanding, 81
  Windows, 164
Forgotten Password Wizard, 110
formatting
  drives, 132
  Live File System, 151–158
  Mastered, 150–151, 152–158
  NTFS, 491
  SATA drives, 491
  WordPad, 163

Fotki, 579
Found New Hardware Wizard, 498–499, 710
4:3 aspect ratio, 446, 447
FreeCell. *See also* games
  defined, 338
  hands, replaying, 338
  hands numbering, 338
  illustrated, 337
  opening, 337
  rules, 338
  score storage, 339
  scoring, 338
  Solitaire resemblance, 338
  winning statistics, 338–339
Frisk F-PROT, 271
F-Secure, 271
Fuji, 575

G

gadgets. *See also* Sidebar
  adding, 291
  behavior, changing, 291
  creation, 30
  currency converter, 291
  defined, 29, 289
  playing with, 291–292
games
  Chess Titans, 343
  FreeCell, 337–339
  InkBall, 343
  Mahjong Titans, 343
  Minesweeper, 340–343
  parental control, 214
  Purble Place, 343
  Solitaire, 334–337
  Spider Solitaire, 339–340
  viewing, 333
Games option, 67
GDrive, 119

ghosting, 130–131
gigabytes, 485
Gmail, 402
GoDaddy, 561
Goodervideo, 599
Google. *See also* search engines
  calculator, 435
  conversions, 435
  as default search service, 367–368
  Desktop Search, 323
  Google Earth, 355–356
  Google Images, 433–434
  Google News, 435
  Google Talk, 415
  history, 425–426
  newsgroups, 435
  package shipping status, 435
  PageRank system, 425
  as podcast source, 555, 557
  services, 435
  spiders, 426
  statistics, 426
  stock ticker, 435
  tricks, 433–435
  Windows Help, 186
graphics processors (GPUs), 18
graphics tablets, 453
Guest accounts, 107
Guide, TV
  bringing up, 646
  manual update, 646–648
  Media Center download, 646
  Most Viewed list, 639
  program storage, 647
  remote shortcuts, 648
  station name, changing, 650
  stations, adding, 648–649
  stations, deleting, 649
  stations, list, 649
  use information, 638

H

hard drives. *See also* drives
  capacity, 485
  defragmenting, 134
  EIDE, 487, 488
  error check, 132–133
  external, 19, 486
  formatting, 132
  gigabytes, 485
  hot-swappable, 485
  IDE, 487, 488
  installation, 19, 488–491
  interfaces, 486–488
  maintaining, 131–134
  pending crash symptoms, 131
  prevention, 131
  purchasing, 18–19
  reliability, 18
  SATA, 19, 487, 488–491
  SCSI, 488
  second, adding, 485–488
  speed, 19
  surface scan, 133
  "sweet spot," 486
  utilities, 132
hardware. *See also* drivers
  adapter cards, 441–443
  defined, 12
  external devices, 440
  firewalls, 226
  flash memory, 454–455
  graphics tablets, 453
  installation, 458–463
  installation guidelines, 458–459
  installation troubleshooting, 462
  internal devices, 440
  key drives, 455, 457
  keyboards, 451–452
  monitors, 444–450
  mouse, 452–453

  printers, 493–503
  store installation, 458–459
  trackballs, 453
  types, 439–443
  upgrading, 443–454
  video adapters, 450–451
Hardware and Sound option (Control
    Panel), 115, 504, 628
HD-DVD
  Blu-ray versus, 20
  discs, 149
Help
  AskWoody.com, 175, 186, 425
  getting most from, 184–186
  Google, 186
  Help and Support, 171–174
  index, 185–186
  keywords, 185
  Microsoft Knowledge Base, 186
  Microsoft Online Assisted Support, 175
  newsgroups, 174, 186
  Remote Assistance, 176–184
  Web, 186
Help and Support
  best use, 174
  categories, 172
  existence, 173
  gotchas, 173–174
  illustrated, 172
  opening, 171
  options, 184–185
  overviews, articles, tutorials, 172
  tasks, 172
  troubleshooters, 172, 173
  walk-throughs, 172
heuristic analysis, 264, 265
heuristic detection, 196
home networks. *See* peer-to-peer
    networks
home page
  changing, 366–367
  defined, 365

host computers, 503
hot shoe, digital cameras, 568
Hotmail
  defined, 400
  history, 401
  Windows Live Mail, 400–401
HTML (HyperText Markup Language),
  350
hubs. *See also* routers; switches
  defined, 25, 679, 686
  Ethernet, 681
  function, 687
  identification, 687
  placing, 696–697
  selecting, 693
  wireless router, 687
Hurley, Pat
  *Windows XP Media Center Edition 2004
    PC For Dummies*, 666
  *Wireless Home Networking For
    Dummies, 2nd Edition,* 716
HyperText Markup Language (HTML),
  350

1

icons
  arranging, 292–293
  controlling, 292–293
  deleting, 292, 293
  desktop, 285
  desktop, cleanup, 65
  hard-wired, 293
  hiding, 293
  looking for, 293
  Quick Launch toolbar, 317–318
  shortcut, 293
  this book, 6–7
ICQ, 414
ICS. *See* Internet Connection Sharing

IDE (Integrated Drive Electronics)
  interface, 487, 488
iDefense, 195
identity theft, 202
IM. *See* instant messaging
image backups. *See* CompletePC
  backups
image stabilizers, digital cameras, 568
images
  adding to Photo Gallery, 583–586
  copying, 591
  e-mail blocking of, 407
  erasing after importing, 577
  file-hosting, 578
  moving, to computer, 574–578
  picture-sharing sites, 579
  searching for, 433–434
  sharing on the Web, 578–579
  tagging, 576–577, 581
  touching up, 590–593
  viewing by folder, 586–587
  viewing by tags, 587–590
  Web page, saving, 380–381
important security holes, 262
importing
  clips, 610–611
  erasing images after, 577
inbound firewalls. *See also* firewalls
  adding ports, 241–243
  adding programs, 240–241
  defined, 219, 225
  need for, 225
  predefined services, 239
incremental backups, 123
indexing
  defined, 322
  in practice, 322
  rebuilding, 327
  results, 328
Indexing Options dialog box, 326–327
Initialize Disk dialog box, 489

InkBall, 343
inkjet printers. *See also* printers
  choosing, 496
  defined, 493
installation
  cable modem, 459
  clean, 46–48
  hard drive, 19, 488–491
  hardware, 459–463
  network, 695–700
  network printer, 502–503
  patch, 250, 258, 261
  printer, 496–503
  product activation, 54–57
  router, 696–697
  switch, 696–697
  update, 258
  USB hardware, 463
  Windows Live Messenger, 416–417
  Windows Vista disc, 48
  wireless adapter driver, 711–712
  wireless network, 707–709
Installation ID. *See also* Confirmation ID
  defined, 54
  storage, 55
instant messaging (IM)
  alternatives, 413–416
  AOL Instant Messenger, 414
  Google Talk, 415
  ICQ, 414
  in Microsoft, 413
  MSN Messenger, 414, 415
  recommendations, 415–416
  Trillian, 415
  Windows Live Messenger, 413, 416–424
  Yahoo! Messenger with Voice, 415
Instant Messenger, 179
Integrated Drive Electronics (IDE),
    487, 488
interfaces. *See also* hardware
  adapter card, 440–441
  Aero Glass, 27–30, 32, 44

AGP, 441
  choosing, 440
  defined, 440
  disk drive, 486–488
  EIDE, 487, 488
  external, 442–443
  FireWire, 443
  IDE, 487, 488
  internal, 440–442
  ISA, 442
  parallel, 443
  PCI, 441
  PCIe (PCI-2), 441
  PCI-X, 441
  SATA, 487
  SCSI, 488
  serial, 443
  USB, 442
internal devices
  advantages, 440
  defined, 440
  interfaces, 440–442
Internet
  backbone, 350
  beginnings, 348
  computer equality, 349
  defined, 348–349
  fixed-sized packets, 349
  as free, 351
  inside, 349–350
  newsgroups, 435
  packet delivery, 349
  reference tools, 359–361
  searching, 425–435
Internet Accounts dialog box, 404
Internet Connection Sharing (ICS)
  advantage, 691
  defined, 688
  illustrated, 689
  installation with, 697
  Internet Explorer functioning with,
    702–703

Internet connections
  broadband, 25, 353, 353–356
  client/server networks, 675
  details, changing, 357–358
  dialup, 25, 354–355, 357–359
  last mile, 354–355
  methods, 353–356
  setting up, 357–359
Internet Explorer. *See also* Firefox
  Address bar, 368, 369
  addresses, typing, 387
  alternatives, 363–365
  animations, turning off, 389
  anti-phishing consequences, 375
  anti-phishing tools, 374
  blogging with, 393–395
  coexistence with Firefox, 351
  Command bar, 368, 369
  connecting with, 348
  cookies, deleting, 393
  default search service, changing,
    367–368
  defined, 347
  faster running, 389–391
  Favorites, 382
  Full Screen view, 388
  graphics, turning off, 389
  history, 370–371
  home page, 365
  home page, changing, 366–367
  Internet Connection Sharing
    functioning with, 702–703
  launching, 365
  Links toolbar, 391
  Phishing Filter, 374, 375–377
  pop-up filter, 378
  RSS feeds in, 398
  Search box, 368, 369
  search engine, changing, 430
  sounds, turning off, 390
  Status bar, 368, 369
  storage space, boosting, 390–391
  tabs, 371–372
  Temporary Internet Files, 371
  text size, 388
  using, 387–389
  window, 368–370
  window illustration, 369
  Windows Live Search use, 430
Internet Service Providers (ISPs)
  e-mail account setup information, 404
  networking response, 692–693
  Web servers, 578
interrupt request line (IRQ), 688
IP addresses
  defined, 230, 692
  sharing, 692
iPod & iTunes For Dummies (Bove and
    Rhodes), 483
iPods
  automatic updating, 476, 478
  database, 482
  disconnection, 477
  ecosystem, 483
  firmware, 467
  first time setup, 477
  identifying, 468
  limitations, 466–467
  listing in iTunes, 477
  manual management, 480
  models, 468
  moving music to, 476–479
  naming, 476
  plugging in, 469, 476
  registering, 476
  setting up, 469
  songs, copying to PC, 481–482
  synching, 479–481
  too much music for, 478
  Updater, 469
  updating, 467–470, 476
  Web site information, 483
IPv4, 348
IR blaster, 642, 643

IRQ (interrupt request line), 688
ISA interface, 442
ISO. *See* Mastered formatting
ISPs. *See* Internet Service Providers
iTunes
  burning to CD, 475
  deauthorizing computers, 474
  dragging albums into, 473
  illustrated, 472
  iPod list, 477
  PC limit, 474
  playlists, overflow, 478
  podcast collection, 555–556
  setting up, 470–471
  Setup Assistant, 470–471
  song format, 473
  status bar, 475
  submission to, 562
  synching control, 479–481
  working with, 470–479
iTunes Music Store
  accounts, 476
  five-PC limit, 474
  song restrictions, 475

J

jacks
  computer sound, 22
  line in, 22
  line out, 22
  mike in, 22
  RJ-45, 20, 691, 694
  speaker out, 22
JPEG encoders, 641
JPG format, 567

K

key drives, 455, 457
keyboards. *See also* hardware
  ergonomic, 451
  guidelines, 451

upgrading, 451–452
  wireless, 23, 452
keyloggers, 192
King, Julie Adair (*Digital Photography For
    Dummies, 5th Edition*), 579
Kodak, 575
Konfabulator, 292

L

label printers, 495
LAN adapter, 685
LAN cables
  defined, 20, 679, 694
  RJ-45 jacks, 694
LAN Settings dialog box, 702–703
laser printers. *See also* printers
  choosing, 496
  color, 494
  defined, 493–494
last mile, 354–355
LCD (liquid crystal display) monitors.
    See also monitors
  considerations, 444–445
  dead pixels, 445
  Digital Visual Interface (DVI), 445
  reading angles, 445
  refresh rate, 444
Leonhard, Woody
  *Windows Vista Timesaving Techniques
      For Dummies*, 82, 435
  *Windows XP All-in-One Desk Reference
      For Dummies, 2nd Edition*, 700
Liberated Syndication, 561
Library. *See also* Windows Media Player
    (WMP)
  adding to, 528–529
  defined, 528
  deleting from, 530
  folders, 530–531
  leafing through, 530–531
  Music folder, 530–531
  options, 551

Library *(continued)*
  organizing, 527–540
  Other Media folder, 531
  Pictures folder, 531
  playlists, 536–539
  Recorded TV folder, 531
  references, 529–530
  tracks, deleting, 539–540
  tracks, finding, 531–534
  tracks, playing, 534–535
  "Unknown" album data, 535–536
  Video folder, 531
line in jack, 22
line out jack, 22
links
  changing/deleting, 392
  defined, 351
  using, 391–392
Links toolbar
  defined, 391
  displaying, 391–392
  links, changing/deleting, 392
  shortcuts, placing, 392
Linux, 14
liquid crystal display. *See* LCD monitors
lithium-ion (Li-Ion) batteries, 574
Live Bookmarks feature (Firefox), 395
Live Drive, 119
Live File System formatting. *See also*
    burning
  CDs/DVDs, removing, 156
  choosing, 154
  copying with, 155
  defined, 151
  selection, 152
local area networks
  LAN adapter, 685
  LAN cables, 20, 679, 694
local loop, 355
local printers, 497–501
Local Security Setting dialog box,
    104–105

logging on, 98–99
Logitech, 575
LogMeIn, 40
"Logon screen". *See* Welcome screen
low security holes, 262

M

McAfee, 271, 706
Magellan, 323
Mahjong Titans, 343
maintenance
  backups, 118–131
  checkpoints, 143–145
  with Control Panel, 113–116
  drive, 131–134
  program change/removal, 116–118
  scheduling, 134–138
  Windows patches removal, 118
  zipping/compressing, 139–143
malware outbreaks, checking for, 270
malware protection. *See also* protection
  rootkit, 220–223
  spyware, 219
  virus, 219
Manage Accounts window, 105–106
Manually Connect to a Wireless Network
    dialog box, 718–719
Master Boot Record viruses, 190
Mastered formatting. *See also* burning
  CD (DVD) burning, 155–156
  choosing, 154
  copying with, 154
  defined, 150–151
  files, adding, 158
  selection, 152
Media Center
  bugs, 620
  burning DVDs, 660–664
  cable connection, 625
  copy restrictions, 665–666
  custom setup, 635

Customer Experience Improvement
    Program, 636
display adapter settings, 626
features, 620
illustrated, 621
interface, 620
limitations, 620–621
mini guide, 656–659
most viewed shows, 639
need for, 619–621
obtaining, 30
Photo Gallery setup, 634
power strips, 622
preparing, 619–630
Program Guide, 638
as PVR, 652
recorded shows, playing, 659–660
Recorded TV folder, 660
Recorder Settings screen, 653
Recorder Storage screen, 653, 654
Recording Defaults screen, 653, 654, 655
remote hardware, 623
remote setup, 642–643
ripping CDs, 665–666
setting up, 632–633, 634–639
setup options, 636–638
setup tools, 622–623
shortcomings, working with, 623–624
sound system setup, 628–630
starting, 624, 634
Tasks menu, 635
TV input card, 641
TV recording, 652–656
TV Settings screen, 652
TV signal recognition, 641–646
TweakMC, 666
UPS, 622
user setup, 631
VCR not working with, 624
video card identification, 625
Vista versions, 619
Windows Media Player setup, 632–633
Xbox extender, 620

memory
  CPU, 16
  flash, 454–455
  measurement, 16
  SD/xD/CF card, 18
  suggested, 16
memory card readers, 577
Messenger Plus! Live site, 422
metadata, 323
mice
  buttons, interchanging, 66
  desktop level, 285
  mickeys, 67
  optical, 452
  pointers, changing, 294–295
  selecting, 452–453
  trackballs versus, 453
  wireless, 23
mickeys, 67
Microsoft Internet Security and
    Acceleration Server, 675
Microsoft Knowledge Base, 186
Microsoft Management Console, 243
Microsoft office, settings transfer, 52
Microsoft Online Assisted Support, 175
Microsoft Security Response Center
    (MSRC) blog, 197, 259
Microsoft SpyNet, 278
Microsoft Word
  Notepad/WordPad versus, 160
  in printing from Web pages, 381
mike in jack, 22
MillerSmiles, 195
MIME (Multipurpose Internet Mail
    Extensions), 402
Minesweeper. *See also* games
  cheats, 342
  clock, stopping, 342
  customizing, 341
  defined, 340
  flags, 341

Minesweeper *(continued)*
  illustrated, 341
  options, 341
  playing levels, 341
  statistics, 341
  top scores, 343
mini guide. *See also* Media Center
  defined, 656
  future times, 656–657
  Registry setting, 657–658
  scrolling through, 656
  using, 656–659
  working same as remote, 657–658
minibooks, this book, 5–6
mini-DIN connectors, 21
modems
  cable, 459, 679
  defined, 25
  dialup, 689
  DSL, 679
  sales/lease, 691
  satellite, 701
moderate security holes, 262
monitors
  aspect ratio, 445–447
  choosing, 444–450
  CRT, 444
  defined, 17
  DVI interface, 445
  LCD, 17, 444–445
  native resolution, 447
  pixels, 17, 18, 445
  reviews, 444
  screen resolutions, 447–450
most recently used programs
  clearing, 310–311
  counter, 310
  at first startup, 309
  location, 309
  program removal, 311
motherboards, 16

movies. *See also* clips; Windows Movie
  Maker
  assembling, 599–611
  burning, 615
  converting, 615
  creation steps, 599–600
  effects, 604–605
  narration, 608–610
  playing, 601–602
  publishing, 611–615
  ripping, 615
  saving, 600
  sound clips, 608–610
  titles, 606–608
  transitions, 604–605
MP3 format
  AAC format versus, 471
  burn cost per song, 150
  iPod use of, 472, 473
  music files, 467
  players, 514
  ripping to, 666
MS-DEFCON, 258–259
MSN Messenger, 414, 415
MSN Search Toolbar with Windows
  Desktop Search, 323
MSRC (Microsoft Security Response
  Center) blog, 197, 259
multifunction card readers, 18
multifunction devices, 494
Multipurpose Internet Mail Extensions
  (MIME), 402
music
  converting to MP3 format, 472–473
  copying from iPod to PC, 481–482
  C.R.A.P., 514
  formats, 514
  moving to iPod, 476–479
  "Plays for Sure," 466
  renting, 520
  searches, 330
Music folder, 530–531

N

narration
  recording, 608–609
  synchronizing, 610
navigation, with Windows Explorer, 85–86
network adapters
  buying, 686
  confirming, 685
  defined, 685
  speed, 685
  USB, 686
Network and Internet option (Control Panel)
  defined, 114–115
  View Network Status and Tasks link, 233, 235
Network and Sharing Center
  diagnostic routines, 714
  illustrated, 233, 698
  network type, changing, 234
  opening, 73, 233, 697, 712
  public firewall settings, 235
  Set Up a Connection or Network link, 715
  Sharing and Discovery settings, 700
  wireless networks, 712–715
Network Discovery, 74
Network Interface Cards (NICs), 20
network printers. *See also* printers
  connecting, 501–503
  manual installation, 502–503
  Vista identification, 501–502
networks
  benefits, 670–671
  building, 683–704
  cables, 687–688
  client/server, 672–675
  computer communication, 679–682
  computer list on, 700
  computer names, 671
  domain, 231
  Ethernet, 680–682
  existing, converting, 696
  functioning, 671–672
  hubs, 686–687, 696–697
  installing, 695–700
  Internet connection, 688–693
  ISPs response to, 692–693
  naming, 699
  network adapters, 685
  organizing, 672–678
  parts, blocking out, 684–688
  peer-to-peer, 673, 675–678
  planning, 683–695
  portables, 703–704
  private, 231
  public, 231
  on the road, 703–704
  routers, 686–687, 693, 696–697
  settings, changing, 235–236
  sharing, 670, 671
  switches, 687
  terminology, 678–679
  troubleshooting, 701–704
  type, changing, 233–235
  type, establishing, 232–233
  understanding, 669–672
  username/password logon, 75
  uses, 670–671
  Vista identification, 698
  Windows Firewall settings, 233
  Windows XP computers on, 700
  wired, 684
  wireless, 682, 707–719
newsgroups, 174, 186, 435
Nickel-cadmium (NiCad) batteries, 574
Nickel-Metal Hydride (NiMH) batteries, 574
NICs (Network Interface Cards), 20
Nikon, 575

Notepad
  benefits, 161
  defined, 160
  file size, 161
  fonts, changing, 161
  running, 160–162
  starting, 161
  text wrapping, 162
  timestamp feature, 162
notification area, 62
NT Compatibility Web site, 45
NTFS compression
  availability, 141
  defined, 139
  using, 141–142
NTFS (NT File System) formatting, 491
NVIDIA Control Panel, 626, 627

O

OCUR units, 651
Odeo, 562
Office 2007 Setup dialog box, 117
OGG, 150
Olympus, 575
100Base-T connection, 691
operating systems, 14
optical mice, 452
optical zoom, 567
Options dialog box (WMP), 551–552
organization, this book, 4–6
Organize Favorites dialog box, 384–385
Other Media folder, 531
outbound firewalls. *See also* firewalls
  changing, 243
  default settings, 226
  defined, 31, 219, 225
  disabling, 226
  user interface, 31
  Vista, 243–248
Outlook, 400
Outlook Express. *See* Windows Mail

P

packets
  allowing, 231
  delivery, 349
  fixed-size, 349
  inbound, 230, 231
  inbound, exceptions, 238–243
  outgoing, tracking, 230
Paint
  defined, 166
  opening, 166
  using, 167
Panasonic, 575
parallel interface. *See also* interfaces
  defined, 443
  printer, 497, 498
parallel ports, 21
parental controls
  account selection, 212
  game access, 214
  holes in, 215
  information tracking, 213
  programs, 214
  reports, 214
  setting, 109, 212–214
  time limits, 214, 215
  white lists, 213
passwords
  administrator, 102
  router, 716
  user account, 110
  user, creating/changing/removing, 108
  Web site, 389
patches
  applying, 256–258
  available, 256
  bad, 251, 253
  blindly applying, 249
  downloading, 250
  getting, through Security Bulletin, 261

installing, manually, 250, 261
Knowledge Base article reference, 261
list of, 197
MS04-014, 251
MS06-015, 250
problems, 250–253, 257
removing, 118
security, 197
Security Bulletins, 259–261
selective use, 255–262
UPnP, 250
when safe to install, 258
pausing
documents, 506
print queue, 505
PCI Express interface, 441
PCI (Peripheral Component
Interconnect) interface, 441
PCI-X interface, 441
PCs. *See* computers
peer-to-peer networks. *See also* networks
adaptability, 677
defined, 673
Ethernet, 680–681
illustrated, 675
100Base-T Ethernet, 684
principle, 676
pros/cons comparison, 677–678
uses, 673
Performance Information and Tools
dialog box, 158, 160
Peripheral Component Interconnect
(PCI) interface, 441
permissions
built-in, 76
defined, 76
level, increasing, 78
as minefield, 77
Reader, 78
setting, 77–78
sharing, 76–79
sharing process, 77–79

Personal folder, 316
Personal Video Recorder (PVR), 652
Personalize Appearance and Sounds
dialog box, 286
Personalize Settings for Network dialog
box, 234
phishing
anti-phishing consequences, 375
defined, 193, 372
example, 194
fight against, 195, 372–379
functioning, 194
message example, 372–373
popularity, 194
Phishing Filter. *See also* Internet Explorer
functioning, 375–376
page examination, 375–376
settings, 377
site reporting, 376–377
turning on, 374
warning, 376
Photo Gallery. *See also* images
Add Tags icon, 588
Crop Picture icon, 591
defined, 563
file support, 563
Fix icon, 591
Fix Red Eye icon, 592
fix tools, 590
illustrated, 578, 582, 583, 585
index, 587
indexing methods, 581
limitations, 583
Media Center setup, 634
with multiple pictures, 585
opening, 585
for photo searches, 330
with single picture, 583
tag management, 589–590
tagged photos, 588–590
tagging, 588–590
tools, 581

Photo Gallery *(continued)*
  views, 582
  working in, 581–593
photos
  adding, 583–586
  adding from different folders, 585–586
  cropping, 591–592
  deleting, 586
  finding, 586–590
  manually adjusting, 591
  tagged, creating, 588
  tagged, finding, 588–589
  tagged, rearranging, 589–590
  touching up, 590–593
  viewing by folder, 586–587
  viewing by tags, 587–590
Picture folder, 531, 584
pictures. *See* images
pinned programs
  arranging, 307
  Internet/e-mail, changing, 308–309
  naming, 307
  removing, 307–308
pinning. *See also* Start menu
  defined, 305
  from location, 306
  program search, 306
  tips, 306–307
pixels, monitor
  colors, 17
  dead, 445
  defined, 17
  digital camera, 566
  in screen resolution, 18
playlists. *See also* iPods; iTunes
  adding tracks to, 538
  Burn List as, 542–543
  CDs as, 523
  contents, managing, 539
  creating, 536–538
  defined, 528
  deleting, 538–539

  in making CDs, 536
  managing, 536–539
  manually managing, 480
  naming, 537, 543
  overflow, 478
  renaming, 538
  saving, 537, 543
  song ratings, 532
  Sync List as, 545–546
  synching, 480
Podcast Alley, 558, 562
podcasts. *See also* podcasts (iTunes)
  background music, 560
  benefits, 554
  defined, 553
  finding, 555–556
  four-step process, 554
  Google, 555, 557
  identification, 561
  listing services, 562
  playing, 557
  Podcast Alley, 558
  Podscope, 558
  Podzinger, 558
  publishing, 559–562
  RSS feed files, 562
  Singing Fish, 557–558
  software, 562
  sources, 557–558
  understanding, 553–554
  uploading, 561
  Yahoo! Podcasts, 558
podcasts (iTunes)
  episodes, getting, 557
  main page, 555
  Top Podcasts list, 556
Podscope, 558
Podzinger, 558
pointers, mouse, 294–295
polymorphic viruses, 265
POP3 (Post Office Protocol 3) servers,
    402

pop-ups, 378
portable players. *See also* iPods
  deleting tracks from, 548–549
  moving tracks from, 547–548
  moving tracks to, 545–546
  syncing with, 545–549
ports
  adding, to firewall exceptions list,
    241–243
  file and printer sharing, 240
  number, opening, 242
  opening, 242–243
  parallel, 21
  serial, 21
  USB, 53, 458
  when to open, 238
Post Office Protocol 3 (POP3) servers,
  402
power strips, 622
prefetching data, 454
Previous Versions dialog box, 121
print queues
  automatic use, 504
  defined, 503
  displaying, 504
  documents, canceling, 506–507
  documents,
    pausing/resuming/restarting, 506
  on host PC, 504
  illustrated, 505
  information, 504
  pausing, 505
  resuming, 505
print servers, 676
printers. *See also* hardware
  availability methods, 496
  banner, 495
  CD, 499
  changing, temporarily, 504
  choosing, 496
  color laser, 494

drafting, 495
driver sites, 497–498
drivers, 500
duplex printing, 495
dye sublimation, 494
evaluating, 493–496
features, 495–496
inkjet, 493
installing, 496–503
label, 495
laser, 493–494
list, 498, 502
local, attaching, 497
in multifunction devices, 494
network, 501–503
non-detection, 507
page protection, 509–510
photo, 494
Properties dialog box, 509
renaming, 499
Reset control, 509
serial/parallel connectors, 497
sharing, 500–501
shortcuts, 93, 94
troubleshooting, 507–510
USB connectors, 497
Vista sensing, 499
printing
  duplex, 495
  networked computer, 700
  no document problem, 508–509
  photos, 494
  with Print Preview feature, 382
  "Printer Overrun" error message, 509
  troubleshooting, 507–510
  Web pages, 381–382
privacy. *See also* protection
  attitude towards, 202
  convenience versus, 202
  defense, 202–203
  guidelines, 203

private networks. *See also* networks
  defined, 231
  using, 231–236
processors, 16
product activation
  bypass, 57
  Confirmation ID, 55, 56
  Installation ID, 54
  as mandatory, 57
  registration versus, 56
  time period, 56
  25-character code, 54, 55
  25-character code recalculation, 55, 56
  with Windows Product Activation
    (WPA), 54–56
product support options, 186
programs
  adding, to firewall exceptions list,
    240–241
  backdoor, 191
  changing, 116–118
  defined, 12, 23
  desktop, cleaning up, 65
  dragging/dropping, 307
  g, avoiding, 199
  installing, 23
  launching (running), 24
  most recently used, 309–311
  new installation boxes, turning off, 316
  parental control, 214
  pinning, 306–307
  playing at startup, 318–319
  removing, 116–118
  searching for, 306
  shortcuts, 93
  Start menu, adding/removing, 81
  startup, 278–279
  switching between, 29
  thumbnails, 29
  unpinning, 307–308
  virus protection, 198
Programs folder, 313, 314

Programs option (Control Panel), 115,
  116, 118
protection
  antispyware, 199
  antivirus software, 199
  cookies, 203–207
  credit card fraud, 200–202
  identity theft, 202
  malware, 219–220
  parental controls, 211–215
  privacy, 202–203
  spam, 207–209
  spyware, 220
  virus, 198–200, 263–280
proxy servers, 675
proxy settings, 552
PS/2 connectors, 21, 453
Public folder. *See also* folders
  access, considering, 74
  access, restricting, 75
  defined, 71
  making public, 71–76
  Password Protected Sharing setting,
    75–76
  username/password logon, 75–76
public networks. *See also* networks
  defined, 231
  using, 231–236
Publish Movie dialog box, 613
publishing movies. *See also* movies;
    Windows Movie Maker
  on computer, 612
  digital video camera, 612
  DV-AVI file caution, 614
  DVD, 611, 612
  e-mail, 612
  file qualities, 614
  methods, 612
  recordable CD, 612
  steps, 613–614
Purble Place, 343
PVR (Personal Video Recorder), 652

Q

Quick Launch toolbar
  defined, 92, 317
  icons, adding, 317–318
  illustrated, 90, 317
  opening, 317
  resizing drag handles, 318
  using, 317–318

R

RAW file format, 567
ReadyBoost
  as AutoPlay option, 456
  data storage format, 457
  defined, 456
  setting up, 456–457
Really Simple Syndication. *See* RSS
RealNetworks, 417
Recent Items list. *See also* Start menu
  clearing, 314–315
  defined, 314
  love/hate relationship, 314
Recorded TV folder, 531
recording TV. *See also* Media Center; TV
  defaults, 653–655
  failure, 656
  hard drive storage, 653, 654
  High-Definition (HD), 656
  recorded shows, playing, 659–660
  settings, 652–655
  show selection, 656
  start/stop times, 655
  unattended, 655
Recycle Bin
  defined, 79
  emptying, 80
  illustrated, 62
  restoring from, 80
  using, 79–80

red eye. *See also* photos
  defined, 593
  fixing, 592
refreshing pages, 371
registration
  database, 207
  as optional, 57
  Windows Live ID, 56
Remote Assistance
  assistant notification, 180
  bar, 182
  connecting to, 176–184
  connection setup steps, 178–183
  defined, 176
  Expert, 182, 183
  firewalls interference, 178
  invitation, creating, 180
  invitation, limiting, 177
  invitation, sending, 181
  permission, 181–182, 183
  problems, 173
  sessions, 183
  troubleshooting, 178
  Windows Firewall functioning with, 231
  Wizard, 179–180
Remote Desktop
  defined, 38
  LogMeIn alternative, 40
  using, 40
remote, TV. *See also* Media Center; TV
  Guide button, 646
  Guide shortcuts, 648
  setting up, 642–643
  up/down arrow buttons, 656, 657
removing programs, 116–118
residential gateways, 688
resolution
  monitor, 447–450
  native, 447
  screen, 447–450
  webcams, 570
  Windows Vista, 17

restore
 backed-up data, 127–130
 computer, 145
 file/folder selection, 128
 location, 129–130
restore points
 creating, 143–144, 632
 defined, 143
 selecting, 145
 system, 119, 632
resuming
 documents, 506
 print queues, 505
Revelation software, 46, 47
Rhapsody, 417
Rhodes, Cheryl (*iPod & iTunes For
  Dummies*), 483
Rich Text Format (RTF), 163
ripping
 album information, 526
 all tracks, 526
 audio tracks, 150
 copy restrictions, 665
 defined, 149
 list, 525
 in Media Center, 665–666
 movies, 615
 options, 551
 selected songs, 526
 in WMP, 524–527
RJ-45 jacks
 defined, 20, 691
 illustrated, 20
Roboform, 46, 389
Rollyo, 433
rootkits
 defined, 192
 free detection, 221
 scanning for, 220–223
 Sophos Anti-Rootkit, 221–223

routers
 broadband, 686, 687
 defined, 25, 686
 installing, 696–697
 passwords, 716
 selecting, 693
 wireless, 25, 678, 679
RSS (Really Simple Syndication) feeds
 accessing, 397
 benefits, 398
 content, 397
 defined, 395
 feed reader, 396
 files, building, 562
 in Firefox, 395, 396–397
 in Internet Explorer, 398
 working with, 395–398
RTF (Rich Text Format), 163
Run dialog box, 84

S

SafeDocs, 38
SANS Internet Storm Center (ISC), 197
SATA drives. *See also* drives
 comparison, 488
 connecting, 488–489
 defined, 487
 drivers, 489
 formatting, 491
 initializing, 489–490
 installing, 488–491
 New Simple Volume Wizard, 490–491
 partitioning, 489
 SATA I, 487
 SATA II, 19, 487
 standards, 487
 versions, 487
satellite modems, 701
Save As dialog box, 331

Save Webpage dialog box, 380
saved searches. *See also* searches
  creating, 330–331
  finding, 331
  history, 330
Scalable Links Interface (SLI), 441
scanning, 322
Scientific Calculator, 165–166
screen resolution. *See also* monitors
  change effects, 448
  changing, 449–450
  4:3 aspect ratio, 447
  selecting, 447–448
  16:9 aspect ratio, 448–449
  types of, 448
Screen Saver Settings dialog box, 299
screen savers
  caution, 297
  changing, 296–297
  as desktop level, 285
  program files, 301
  purpose, 295
  scr files, 299
  selecting, 295–301
  for Super Boss Key, 297–300
screens. *See* monitors
SCSI (Small Computer System Interface)
    interface, 488
scumware, 25
SD (Secure Digital) cards, 454
Search box (IE), 368, 369
search engines
  Ask.com, 428–429
  audience participation, 430
  BackRub, 425
  changing, 430–433
  choosing, 425–430
  default, changing, 367–368
  del.icio.us, 430
  Digg, 430
  Dogpile, 427
  Google, 367–368, 425–427

  info at AskWoody.com, 425
  Rollyo, 433
  Technorati, 430
  Windows Live Search, 427–428
  Yahoo! Search, 428, 429
Search pane, 325
searches
  advanced, 325, 326–329
  basics, 324–330
  desktop, 321–323
  example, 324–329
  expanding, 326
  history, 321–323
  indexing, 322, 327–328
  Internet, 425–430
  music, 330
  narrowing, 325
  options, 329
  options settings, 330
  picture, 330, 433–434
  quick access, 82
  results, manipulating, 329
  reusing, 330–331
  running, 324–329
  saving, 89, 330–331
  scanning, 322
  tips, 330
  Windows Media Player (WMP), 533–534
  Windows performance, 321
  WinFS, 323
Secure Digital (SD) cards, 454
security
  BitLocker, 39
  features, 31
  levels, 262
  outbound firewall, 31
Security Bulletins. *See also* patches;
    updates
  dating, 261
  decoding, 260–261
  defined, 197, 259
  getting patches through, 261

Security Bulletins *(continued)*
  illustrated, 260
  KB articles, 261
  latest, 259
  numbering, 197, 260
Security Center
  automatic updating settings, 219
  current status, 217–218
  defined, 217
  entering, 217–218
  firewall settings, 219
  illustrated, 218
  malware protection settings, 219–220
  opening, 218
  other security settings, 219
  shield color, 217–218
  shield location, 218
  software identification, 274
  working with, 219–220
security holes
  buffer-overrun, 191
  critical, 262
  important, 262
  low, 262
  moderate, 262
Security option (Control Panel)
  Allow a Program through Windows
    Firewall link, 240, 241
  Check Firewall Status link, 237
  defined, 114
  illustrated, 218
  Security Center icon, 274
  Windows Update icon, 253, 255
Select Computer dialog box, 244
Select Privacy Options dialog box,
    516–517
Serial Advanced Technology
    Attachment. *See* interfaces; SATA
    drives
serial interface. *See also* interfaces
  defined, 443
  printer, 497, 498
serial ports, 21

servers. *See also* client/server networks
  defined, 673
  DHCP, 691
  file, 676
  print, 676
  proxy, 675
Service Pack 1, 19, 36, 42, 56, 82, 134, 332
service set identifiers (SSIDs), 716, 719
Set Network Location dialog box,
    698–699
Set Up a Connection or Network dialog
    box, 715
set-top boxes. *See also* TV
  defined, 642
  multiple, 651
  picture from, 644, 646
shadow copies. *See also* backups
  automatic generation, 120–121
  data recovery, 121
  defined, 119
  in file deletion, 122
  using, 120–122
ShadowCopy, 39
Shared Folders. *See also* Windows Live
    Messenger
  defined, 423
  working with, 423–424
Shared Printers dialog box, 502–503
sharing folders. *See also* folders
  methods, 71
  with permissions, 71, 76–79
  with Public folder, 71–76
  with Windows Live Messenger, 423–424
sharing printers, 500–501
Shortcut Properties dialog box, 300
shortcuts
  All Programs list, 314
  creation methods, 93–94
  defined, 92
  functions, 93
  icon, 293
  items, 92–93
  Links toolbar, 392
  startup, 318–319

using, 93
Windows Media Player, 518
Sidebar
  closing, 290
  defined, 29
  enabling, 65
  gadgets, 29–30, 289, 291–292
  icon, 289
  illustrated, 62
  location, changing, 291
  opening, 289
  properties, 290–291
  settings, changing, 290–292
  stability problems, 290
  using, 289–292
signature matching
  database file, 270
  defined, 264
signing on, 98–99
"Sign-on screen". *See* Welcome screen
Simple Mail Transfer Protocol (SMTP)
    servers, 402
Singing Fish, 557–558
16:9 aspect ratio, 446–447, 449
skins. *See also* Windows Media Player
    (WMP)
  built-in, 550
  bundling, 551
  defined, 549
  downloaded, scanning, 551
  in full mode, 550–551
  illustrated, 550
  practical advantage, 549
  in skin mode, 549
Skype, 422
Slammer worm, 266
sleep, 94–95
SLI (Scalable Link Interface), 441
SM (Smart Media) cards, 454
Small Computer System Interface (SCSI)
    interface, 488
SMTP (Simple Mail Transfer Protocol)
    servers, 402

Smugmug, 579
SnadBoy Revelation software, 46, 47
software. *See* programs
Solitaire. *See also* games
  cards, double-clicking, 334
  cheating, 337
  defined, 334
  Draw One option, 336
  Draw Three option, 336, 337
  hints, 334
  illustrated, 335
  inventor, 336
  rules, 334
  standard scoring, 335
  timed games, 336
  Vegas scoring, 336–337
Sony, 575
Sophos Anti-Rootkit. *See also* rootkits
  defined, 221
  illustrated, 221
  obtaining, 222, 223
  rootkit display, 223
sound cards
  output, 22
  output matchup, 628
  plug verification, 628
  sound production, 627
sound clips. *See also* clips; movies;
    Windows Movie Maker
  adding, 610
  narration, 608–610
sound computer jacks, 22
Sound dialog box, 628–630
Sound Recorder, 559
spam. *See also* e-mail
  exposure, minimizing, 208
  filters, 206
  offerings, not buying, 208
  opting out of, 208
  reducing, 207–209
  scanners, 206
  Web beacons, 407
SP1, 19, 36, 42, 56, 82, 134, 332
SPAM act, 207

Speaker Setup wizard, 628
speakers
  configuring, 628–629
  out jack, 22
  testing, 629
spell-checking, e-mail messages, 410–411
Spider Solitaire. *See also* games
  defined, 339
  illustrated, 340
  re-dealing, 340
  scores, 340
spiders, 208
splitting clips, 605–606
sploits, 196
spyware
  antispyware protection, 199
  dealing with, 276–280
  defined, 25
  determination, 276
  protection, 220
  Webroot SpySweeper and, 280
  Windows Defender and, 276–280
SSIDs (service set identifiers), 716, 719
standard accounts. *See also* user
    accounts
  administrator credentials, 102
  defined, 100
  when to use, 102
Start button, 62, 81, 313
Start menu
  All Programs menu, 136, 145, 311–314
  author's, 304
  Computer option, 53, 89, 133, 141, 316
  Control Panel option, 64, 65, 66, 113,
    123, 316
  Customize button, 83
  customizing, 303–317
  Documents option, 68, 70,
    78, 85, 89, 316
  Favorites menu, 316
  features, enabling/disabling, 316
  Games option, 67, 316, 337

genesis, 304
  Help and Support option, 171, 175
  illustrated, 82
  most recently used programs, 309–311
  Music option, 85, 316
  Network Places option, 53
  options, 81
  Personal folder, 316
  Pictures option, 72, 85, 316
  pinned programs, 305–309
  pinning to, 305–309
  programs, adding, 81
  programs, removing, 81
  Recent Items list, 314–315
  right side, 82–83
  right side, modifying, 83
  right-click menu, 83
  tweaking, 315–316
  user pictures, 81
  Windows Easy Transfer option, 53
startup programs
  disabling, 279
  list, 278
  reigning in, 279
startup shortcuts. *See also* shortcuts
  creating, 318–319
  defined, 318
  removing, 319
stateful firewalls, 229
Status bar (IE)
  defined, 368
  illustrated, 369
SteadyHand, 599
storyboard (WMM). *See also* Windows
    Movie Maker
  defined, 597
  dragging clips to, 600
  illustrated, 602
  uses, 602
  viewing, 602–603
subscription model, 37

Super Boss Key
  defined, 297
  file, 300
  setting up, 297–300
  testing, 301
SuperFetch, 454
surfing. *See also* Internet;
      World Wide Web
  anonymously, 203
  history, 370–371
switches. *See also* hubs; routers
  defined, 686
  function, 687
  identification, 687
  installing, 696–697
switching users, 111
Symantec, 271
Sync List
  dragging tracks to, 545
  illustrated, 546
  opening, 545
  saving, 546
synching. *See also* iPods; iTunes
  control, 479–481
  defined, 479
  playlists, 480
  with portable players, 545–549
synchro-flash terminal, 568
System and Maintenance (Control Panel)
  Allow Remote Access link, 177
  Back Up Your Computer link, 123
  Check Your Computer's Windows
      Experience Index Base Score option,
      158
  defined, 114
system backups. *See* CompletePC
      backups
System Properties dialog box, 50, 144
System Restore
  checkpoint generation, 143–144
  points, 119
  Wizard, 145

T

tablet PCs, 453
tabs, Web browser, 371–372
tagged photos. *See also* images; Photo
      Gallery
  creating, 588
  finding, 588–589
  list, rearranging, 589–590
  tag combinations, 589
Task Manager
  Applications tab, 168
  functions, 168
  opening, 167
  Performance tab, 168, 169
Task Scheduler
  defined, 134
  Disk Cleanup, 134, 135–138
  hibernating PCs with, 135
  illustrated, 137
  scheduling, 134–138
  task naming, 137
  uses, 134–135
Task Scheduler Wizard, 136
taskbar
  Auto-Hide, 91
  illustrated, 62, 90
  making taller, 66
  Quick Launch toolbar, 90, 92
  sizing, 66
  working with, 90–92
Taskbar and Start Menu Properties
      dialog box, 83
tasks (WMM), 596
TCP (Transmission Control Protocol)
  defined, 229
  packets, allowing, 239
Technorati, 430
Temporary Internet Files, 371
Temporary Internet Files and History
      Settings dialog box, 391
terminators, 20
terminology, 23–25

1394 slots, 443

thumbnails, of running programs, 29

timeline (WMM). *See also* Windows
    Movie Maker
  defined, 597
  illustrated, 602
  uses, 602
  viewing, 602–603

titles (WMM)
  adding, 607
  illustrated, 607, 608
  text types, 607
  typing, 606–608

touchpads, 453

trackballs, 453

tracks. *See also* Windows Media Player
    (WMP)
  adding to playlists, 537, 538
  deleting, 539–540
  deleting from playlist, 539
  deleting from portable player, 548–549
  dragging to Burn List, 542
  finding, 531–534
  moving from portable player, 547–548
  moving to portable player, 545–546
  playing, 534–535
  position in playlist, 539
  sorting, 532–533

transitions (WMM), 604–605

Transmission Control Protocol (TCP)
  defined, 229
  packets, allowing, 239

Trillian, 415

trimming clips, 603–604

Trojans, 25

troubleshooters, 172, 173

TV
  Guide, 638, 639, 646–648
  input card, 641, 642
  most viewed shows, 639
  recorded shows, playing, 659–660
  recording, 652–656
  remote setup, 642–643
  setting up, 641–646
  set-top box, 642, 644, 651
  shows, burning, 660–664

TV signal
  automatic configuration, 644, 645
  confirmation, 645
  recognition, 641–646
  region confirmation, 644

TV Signal Setup Wizard, 643–646

TweakMC, 666

12:5 aspect ratio, 448

U

U3 drives, 455

UDF. *See* Live File System formatting

UDP (User Datagram Protocol)
  defined, 229
  packets, allowing, 239

Uninstall or Change a Program dialog
    box, 117, 118

uninterruptible power supply (UPS), 622

Universal Serial Bus. *See* USB

Updater (iPod), 469

updates. *See also* Windows Update
  applied, viewing, 255
  available, viewing, 257
  checking, 257
  critical, 262
  installing, 258
  level, choosing, 252–253
  level, setting, 253–255
  ready to download, 256

upgrades
  compatibility problems list, 45
  minimum computer requirements,
    43–44
  video cards, checking, 44

uploading, 25

UPS (uninterruptible power supply), 622
URGE, 417, 515, 516
USB hubs
  daisy-chaining, 458
  defined, 457
  powered, 458
USB (Universal Serial Bus)
  cable length, 458
  cables, 20, 53
  connectors, 21
  digital camera interface, 569
  flash drives, 19
  flash memory, 454–455
  hardware installation, 463
  interface, 442–443
  key drives, 455, 457
  network adapters, 686
  ports, 53, 458
  Webcam interface, 570
User Account Control
  defined, 61
  disabling, 104–105
  origin, 103
  problems with, 103
  working with, 101–103
user accounts
  administrator, 100–101
  changing, 107–111
  deleting, 109
  Guest, 107
  managing, 105–106
  names, changing, 108
  naming, 106
  other, maintaining, 108
  own, deleting, 109
  parental controls, 109, 211–215
  passwords, 110
  standard, 100
  type, 99–100
  type, changing, 109
  Welcome screen, 99

User Accounts and Family Safety option
    (Control Panel), 110, 115, 212
User Controls dialog box, 212
User Datagram protocol (UDP)
  defined, 229
  packets, allowing, 239
user experience, 84
users
  adding, 105–107
  other settings, changing, 108–109
  own settings, changing, 110–111
  switching, 111

V

versions. *See also specific versions*
  to ignore, 37–38
  key features, 38
  selecting, 35–42
  types of, 35–36
video adapters. *See also* hardware
  cooler, 451
  drivers, 451
  guidelines, 450
  heat problem, 451
  importance, 450
  selecting, 450–451
video cards
  drivers, 625
  identifying, 625
  manufacturers' sites, 33
  Media Center functioning with, 625
  minimum requirements, 33
  on-board, 44
Video folder, 531
video tracks, 149
viruses
  antispyware protection, 199
  checking for, 270
  ConceptA, 190
  e-mail attachment, 408

viruses *(continued)*
 hoaxes, 210
 Master Boot Record, 190
 polymorphic, 265
 protection, 198–200, 219, 263–280
 real, response to, 211
 recovery, 209
 reporting, 271
 solution, being part of, 209–211
 Winword ConceptA, 190
Vista. *See* Windows Vista
Vista Business Edition
 backup options, 120
 defined, 36
 key features, 38
 reasons for choosing, 39–40
 Windows Rights Management
  (WRM), 40
Vista Business N. *See also* versions
 defined, 36
 ignoring, 37
Vista Enterprise Edition. *See also*
  versions
 backup options, 120
 defined, 36
 ignoring, 37–38
Vista Home Basic Edition. *See also*
  versions
 backup options, 120
 defined, 36
 key features, 38
 reasons for, 39
 thumbs down, 39
 upgrading to, 32, 39
Vista Home N. *See also* versions
 defined, 36
 ignoring, 37
Vista Home Premium Edition. *See also*
  versions
 backup options, 120
 defined, 36
 key features, 38

 missing features, 41
 as sweet spot, 41
Vista Ultimate. *See also* versions
 backup options, 120
 defined, 36
 previous file versions, 90
 reasons for getting, 41

W

wallpaper. *See also* background, desktop
 changing, 64–65
 defined, 64
 picture, positioning, 65
 solid-color, 65
WAPs (wireless access points). *See*
  wireless routers
Wayback Machine, 360–361
Web beacons, 407
Web browsers. *See also* Firefox; Internet
  Explorer
 buttons, 370
 cookies, deleting, 393
 default search service, changing,
  367–368
 defined, 350
 graphics, turning off, 389–390
 home page, 365
 pop-up filters, 378
 tabs, 371–372
Web pages
 addresses, 350
 archived, 360
 history, 371
 home, 365
 hot links, 351
 HTML, 350
 images, saving, 380–381
 printing, 381–382
 reading, 350
 refreshing, 371
 saving, 379–382

saving, to files, 380
text size, 388
using, 379–382
Web servers, 578
Web sites
  benefits, 351–352
  entrance fees, 352
  passwords, 389
  payment, 351–352
webcams
  defined, 565
  resolution, 570
  USB interfaces, 570
  uses, 570, 571
Webroot SpySweeper, 280
Welcome Center
  Add New Users option, 49, 105
  Change Settings option, 50
  disabling, 63–64
  enabling, 64
  illustrated, 48, 63
  Run at Startup check box, 63
  Set Up Devices option, 49
  View Computer Details option, 49–50
  working through, 48–51
Welcome screen
  defined, 11, 98
  illustrated, 99
  user accounts, 99
WF. *See* Windows Firewall
WFWAS. *See* Windows Firewall with
    Advanced Security
white lists, 213
Wi-Fi, 707
Winamp, 516
Windows
  End User License Agreement (EULA),
    12, 13
  PCs running, 14
  Windows XP, 27–33, 700
Windows Anytime Upgrade, 36

Windows Automatic Update
  Download, Don't Install option, 252
  levels, 252–255
  levels, choosing, 252–253
  levels, setting, 253–255
  Never Check for Updates option, 252
  not trusting, 251
  Notify, Don't Download option, 252
  suggested level, 252
  Update Automatically option, 252, 254
Windows Defender. *See also* spyware
  "always allow" items, 278
  defined, 263, 276
  History icon, 276
  home page, 277
  opening, 276
  program information, 279
  Scan icon, 276
  scan results, 276, 277
  Software Explorer link, 278
  spyware criteria, 276
  Tools and Settings pane, 278
  Tools icon, 278
  use steps, 276–279
Windows DVD Maker
  defined, 612
  MSDVD files, 615
  operation, 615
  starting, 612
  Vista versions, 611
Windows Explorer
  command bar, 86
  copies, opening, 86
  defined, 68
  Details view, 87
  Extra Large Icons view, 86
  files/folders, clicking, 86
  files/folders, creating, 87–88
  files/folders, modifying, 88
  illustrated, 85
  Large Icons view, 86

Windows Explorer *(continued)*
Medium Icons view, 86
navigating with, 85–86
navigation bar, 86
opening, 70
Small Icons view, 86
Tiles view, 86
in user experience, 84
using, 84–90
for viewing, 86–87
Windows Firewall (WF)
adding ports, 241–243
adding programs, 240–241
Block All Incoming Connections setting, 228, 237
characteristics, 227
defined, 227
duties, 230–231
features, 227–228
general settings, 237
inbound exceptions, 238–243
inbound "lockdown" mode, 227
inbound settings, 227
network settings, 233
On setting, 237
Remote Assistance functioning with, 231
settings, modifying, 235–236
tracking outgoing packets, 230
Windows Firewall with Advanced Security (WFWAS)
defined, 244
illustrated, 245
New Outbound Rule Wizard, 246
opening, 244
predefined rules, 245
program selection, 247
rule blocking, 247–248
Windows Flip
activating, 29
defined, 29, 91

illustrated, 30
3D, 91–92, 170
using, 91
Windows Genuine Advantage program, 251
Windows Help and Support center, 13
Windows Live ID
defined, 56
signing up for, 416
Windows Live Mail, 400–401
Windows Live Mail Desktop, 401
Windows Live Messenger. *See also* instant messaging (IM)
closing, 421
Contact list, 420
contacts, 418–419, 420
conversations, starting, 420–421
customizing, 422
downloading, 416
extensions, 422
history behind, 414
illustrated, 419
installing, 416–417
message length, 421
settings, changing, 421–422
Shared Folders, 422–424
sign-in screen, 418
typing in, 421
working with, 416–421
Windows Live OneCare
antispyware program, 41
antivirus program, 41
backup program, 41
as conflict of interest, 267
defined, 268
elements, 41
illustrated, 267
need for, 222
price, 222, 268
safety scanner, 269, 270
Windows Live Safety Center, 269

Windows Live Search. *See also* search
 engines
 defined, 427
 illustrated, 428
 Internet Explorer use, 430
Windows Mail
 attachment retrieval, 405–409
 blocked attachments, receiving,
  407–409
 blocked "unsafe" attachments, 406
 defined, 400
 Drafts folder, 412
 mail accounts, setting up, 404–405
 messages, creating, 409–412
 messages, entering, 409–410
 messages, retrieving, 405
 messages, saving, 412
 messages, sending, 412
 New Message window, 409
 options, 408
 panels, 403
 paperclip, 405
 picture blocking, 407
 signatures, 410
 spelling, checking, 410–411
 starting with, 402–404
 tools, 403–404
 in Vista, 399
 window, 402–403
Windows Media Audio (WMA)
 audio conversion, 466, 472–473
 defined, 150
 as Microsoft proprietary format, 150
Windows Media Player (WMP)
 Advanced Tag Editor, 532
 album identification, 524
 artist folders, 527
 audio CDs, 541–544
 behavior, controlling, 551
 Burn List, 542–543
 CDs, as playlists, 523
 CDs, burning, 540–544

CDs, inserting, 523
CDs, playing, 522–524
CDs, ripping, 524–527
clock option, 520
competition, 516
control buttons, 521
Copy from Device button, 547, 548
customizing, 551–552
data CDs/DVDs, burning, 544
as default player, 518
devices, 551
download, 516
files, burning, 152
functions, 513
install options, 516–519
Library, 527–540
as Media Center component, 632
Music folder scan, 519
for music searches, 330
Now Playing window, 521–522
options, 551–552
options after installation, 519–520
playback buttons, 522
playlists, 528
playlists, managing, 536–539
privacy settings, 515–520, 551
privacy settings control, 520
proxy settings, 552
Rip button, 525
ripping options, 551
searching, 533–534
setting up in Media Center, 632–633
shortcuts, 518
skin mode, 549
skins, 549–551
song ratings, 532
starting, 521
streaming media control, 551
Sync button, 545, 547
Sync List, 545–546
syncing with portable player, 545–549
tracks, finding, 531–534

Windows Media Player (WMP) *(continued)*
  tracks, playing, 534–535
  usage, 506
  video DVDs, 541
  in Vista, 540
Windows Movie Maker. *See also* clips;
    movies
  collections pane, 596
  defined, 563, 595
  effects, 604–605
  functions, 595
  illustrated, 596
  Import Media button, 598
  interface, 575
  movies, assembling, 599–611
  MSWMM files, 615
  narration, 608–610
  preview pane, 597
  publishing in, 611–615
  slider, 601, 603
  sound clips, 608–610
  Start/Stop Narration buttons, 609
  storyboard, 597, 602–603
  tasks pane, 596
  timeline, 597, 602–603
  titles, 606–608
  transitions, 604–605
  workspace, 597
Windows Photo Gallery. *See* Photo
    Gallery
Windows Picture and Video Import
  adding photos with, 584
  defined, 563
  image tagging, 576–577
  in image transfer, 575–577
  opening, 576
Windows Product Activation (WPA)
  bypass, 57
  Confirmation ID, 55, 56
  defined, 54
  encryption, 716, 717
  functioning, 54–56

Installation ID, 54, 55
  25-character code, 54, 55
  25-character code recalculation, 55, 56
  window, 55
Windows Rights Management (WRM), 40
Windows Secrets newsletter, 197
Windows Sidebar Properties dialog box,
  290
Windows Starter 2007. *See also* versions
  defined, 36
  ignoring, 37
Windows Update
  applying patches from, 256–258
  defined, 255
  status report, 253
Windows Vista
  Aero Glass interface, 27–30, 32, 44
  author Web site, 7
  CD 25-character code, 55
  compatibility problems, 45
  computer requirements, 43–45
  dead, troubleshooting, 58
  features, 30–31
  need for, 32–33
  resolution, 17
  running, 61–96
  size and expense, 11
  as software, 12
  starting with last know good
    configuration, 462–463
  subscription model, 37
  upgrading to, 32
  versions, selecting, 35–42
  Windows XP versus, 27–33
*Windows Vista Timesaving Techniques
  For Dummies* (Leonhard), 82, 435
Windows Vista Upgrade Advisor
  defined, 44
  downloading, 44
  running, 44–45
  warnings, 45

Windows XP All-in-One Desk Reference For Dummies, 2nd Edition (Leonhard), 700
Windows XP Media Center Edition 2004 PC For Dummies (Briere and Hurley), 666
WinFS, 323
Winword ConceptA virus, 190
wired networks. *See also* networks
  benefits, 684
  cables, 687
  Ethernet, 680–682
  PC setup, 696
  troubleshooting, 701–704
wireless
  defined, 25
  keyboards, 23, 452
  mice, 23
wireless access points (WAPs). *See* wireless routers
wireless adapters
  built-in, 708
  CD, running, 710
  defined, 707
  driver, 710–711
  driver installation, 711–712
wireless broadband routers
  cordless phones problem, 709
  connecting to the Internet, 693
  location, 709
  network cable connection, 709
  plugging into network, 709
  as wireless base station, 708
Wireless Home Networking For Dummies, 2nd Edition (Briere, Hurley and Ferris), 716
wireless Internet gateway, 693
wireless networks. *See also* Ethernet
  access point, 682, 708–709
  defined, 682
  diagnostic routines, 714
  installing, 707–709
problems, 682
setting up, 709–719
technology, 682
wireless adapters, 707–708
WZC, 709
wireless routers. *See also* routers
  configuring, 715–716
  defined, 25, 678
  hubs, 687
  location, 708–709
  makeshift, 679
  need for, 708
  passwords, 716
  SSIDs, 716, 719
Wireless Zero Configuration (WZC), 709
wizards. *See specific wizards*
WMA. *See* Windows Media Audio
WMP. *See* Windows Media Player
WordPad
  defined, 162
  formatting capability, 163
  writing with, 162–164
workgroups, 97, 676
workspace (WMM)
  combining clips in, 605
  defined, 597
  moving clips to, 600
  splitting clips in, 605–606
World Wide Web. *See also* Internet
  defined, 350
  ground rules, 350–351
  surfing, 370–371
worms
  backdoors, 192
  buffer-overrun security holes, 191
  defined, 25
  Mydoom, 192
  recovery from, 209
  Slammer, 266
  Sobig, 192
  0day, 266
WPA. *See* Windows Product Activation

WRM (Windows Rights Management), 40
WZC (Wireless Zero Configuration), 709

X

Xilisoft Corporation, 615
XML (Extensible Markup Language) files, 330

Y

Yahoo! Mail, 402
Yahoo! Messenger with Voice, 415
Yahoo! Podcasts, 558
Yahoo! Search. *See also* search engines
  defined, 428
  illustrated, 429
Yahoo! Widget Engine, 292

Z

0day exploits, 195–196, 266, 268
Zip files. *See also* compression
  adding files to, 142
  contents, 140
  copying files from, 142–143
  creating, 142–143
zoom lenses. *See also* digital cameras
  defined, 566
  digital, 567
  optical, 567

Notes

Notes

BUSINESS, CAREERS & PERSONAL FINANCE

0-7645-9847-3   0-7645-2431-3

Also available:
- Business Plans Kit For Dummies
  0-7645-9794-9
- Economics For Dummies
  0-7645-5726-2
- Grant Writing For Dummies
  0-7645-8416-2
- Home Buying For Dummies
  0-7645-5331-3
- Managing For Dummies
  0-7645-1771-6
- Marketing For Dummies
  0-7645-5600-2

- Personal Finance For Dummies
  0-7645-2590-5*
- Resumes For Dummies
  0-7645-5471-9
- Selling For Dummies
  0-7645-5363-1
- Six Sigma For Dummies
  0-7645-6798-5
- Small Business Kit For Dummies
  0-7645-5984-2
- Starting an eBay Business For Dummies
  0-7645-6924-4
- Your Dream Career For Dummies
  0-7645-9795-7

HOME & BUSINESS COMPUTER BASICS

0-470-05432-8   0-471-75421-8

Also available:
- Cleaning Windows Vista For Dummies
  0-471-78293-9
- Excel 2007 For Dummies
  0-470-03737-7
- Mac OS X Tiger For Dummies
  0-7645-7675-5
- MacBook For Dummies
  0-470-04859-X
- Macs For Dummies
  0-470-04849-2
- Office 2007 For Dummies
  0-470-00923-3

- Outlook 2007 For Dummies
  0-470-03830-6
- PCs For Dummies
  0-7645-8958-X
- Salesforce.com For Dummies
  0-470-04893-X
- Upgrading & Fixing Laptops For Dummies
  0-7645-8959-8
- Word 2007 For Dummies
  0-470-03658-3
- Quicken 2007 For Dummies
  0-470-04600-7

FOOD, HOME, GARDEN, HOBBIES, MUSIC & PETS

0-7645-8404-9   0-7645-9904-6

Also available:
- Candy Making For Dummies
  0-7645-9734-5
- Card Games For Dummies
  0-7645-9910-0
- Crocheting For Dummies
  0-7645-4151-X
- Dog Training For Dummies
  0-7645-8418-9
- Healthy Carb Cookbook For Dummies
  0-7645-8476-6
- Home Maintenance For Dummies
  0-7645-5215-5

- Horses For Dummies
  0-7645-9797-3
- Jewelry Making & Beading For Dummies
  0-7645-2571-9
- Orchids For Dummies
  0-7645-6759-4
- Puppies For Dummies
  0-7645-5255-4
- Rock Guitar For Dummies
  0-7645-5356-9
- Sewing For Dummies
  0-7645-6847-7
- Singing For Dummies
  0-7645-2475-5

INTERNET & DIGITAL MEDIA

0-470-04529-9   0-470-04894-8

Also available:
- Blogging For Dummies
  0-471-77084-1
- Digital Photography For Dummies
  0-7645-9802-3
- Digital Photography All-in-One Desk Reference For Dummies
  0-470-03743-1
- Digital SLR Cameras and Photography For Dummies
  0-7645-9803-1
- eBay Business All-in-One Desk Reference For Dummies
  0-7645-8438-3
- HDTV For Dummies
  0-470-09673-X

- Home Entertainment PCs For Dummies
  0-470-05523-5
- MySpace For Dummies
  0-470-09529-6
- Search Engine Optimization For Dummies
  0-471-97998-8
- Skype For Dummies
  0-470-04891-3
- The Internet For Dummies
  0-7645-8996-2
- Wiring Your Digital Home For Dummies
  0-471-91830-X

* Separate Canadian edition also available
† Separate U.K. edition also available

SPORTS, FITNESS, PARENTING, RELIGION & SPIRITUALITY

0-471-76871-5

0-7645-7841-3

Also available:

- Catholicism For Dummies
  0-7645-5391-7
- Exercise Balls For Dummies
  0-7645-5623-1
- Fitness For Dummies
  0-7645-7851-0
- Football For Dummies
  0-7645-3936-1
- Judaism For Dummies
  0-7645-5299-6
- Potty Training For Dummies
  0-7645-5417-4
- Buddhism For Dummies
  0-7645-5359-3

- Pregnancy For Dummies
  0-7645-4483-7 †
- Ten Minute Tone-Ups For Dummies
  0-7645-7207-5
- NASCAR For Dummies
  0-7645-7681-X
- Religion For Dummies
  0-7645-5264-3
- Soccer For Dummies
  0-7645-5229-5
- Women in the Bible For Dummies
  0-7645-8475-8

TRAVEL

0-7645-7749-2

0-7645-6945-7

Also available:

- Alaska For Dummies
  0-7645-7746-8
- Cruise Vacations For Dummies
  0-7645-6941-4
- England For Dummies
  0-7645-4276-1
- Europe For Dummies
  0-7645-7529-5
- Germany For Dummies
  0-7645-7823-5
- Hawaii For Dummies
  0-7645-7402-7

- Italy For Dummies
  0-7645-7386-1
- Las Vegas For Dummies
  0-7645-7382-9
- London For Dummies
  0-7645-4277-X
- Paris For Dummies
  0-7645-7630-5
- RV Vacations For Dummies
  0-7645-4442-X
- Walt Disney World & Orlando
  For Dummies
  0-7645-9660-8

GRAPHICS, DESIGN & WEB DEVELOPMENT

0-7645-8815-X

0-7645-9571-7

Also available:

- 3D Game Animation For Dummies
  0-7645-8789-7
- AutoCAD 2006 For Dummies
  0-7645-8925-3
- Building a Web Site For Dummies
  0-7645-7144-3
- Creating Web Pages For Dummies
  0-470-08030-2
- Creating Web Pages All-in-One Desk
  Reference For Dummies
  0-7645-4345-8
- Dreamweaver 8 For Dummies
  0-7645-9649-7

- InDesign CS2 For Dummies
  0-7645-9572-5
- Macromedia Flash 8 For Dummies
  0-7645-9691-8
- Photoshop CS2 and Digital
  Photography For Dummies
  0-7645-9580-6
- Photoshop Elements 4 For Dummies
  0-471-77483-9
- Syndicating Web Sites with RSS Feeds
  For Dummies
  0-7645-8848-6
- Yahoo! SiteBuilder For Dummies
  0-7645-9800-7

NETWORKING, SECURITY, PROGRAMMING & DATABASES

0-7645-7728-X

0-471-74940-0

Also available:

- Access 2007 For Dummies
  0-470-04612-0
- ASP.NET 2 For Dummies
  0-7645-7907-X
- C# 2005 For Dummies
  0-7645-9704-3
- Hacking For Dummies
  0-470-05235-X
- Hacking Wireless Networks
  For Dummies
  0-7645-9730-2
- Java For Dummies
  0-470-08716-1

- Microsoft SQL Server 2005 For Dummies
  0-7645-7755-7
- Networking All-in-One Desk Reference
  For Dummies
  0-7645-9939-9
- Preventing Identity Theft For Dummies
  0-7645-7336-5
- Telecom For Dummies
  0-471-77085-X
- Visual Studio 2005 All-in-One Desk
  Reference For Dummies
  0-7645-9775-2
- XML For Dummies
  0-7645-8845-1

HEALTH & SELF-HELP

0-7645-8450-2

0-7645-4149-8

Also available:
- Bipolar Disorder For Dummies
  0-7645-8451-0
- Chemotherapy and Radiation For Dummies
  0-7645-7832-4
- Controlling Cholesterol For Dummies
  0-7645-5440-9
- Diabetes For Dummies
  0-7645-6820-5* †
- Divorce For Dummies
  0-7645-8417-0 †

- Fibromyalgia For Dummies
  0-7645-5441-7
- Low-Calorie Dieting For Dummies
  0-7645-9905-4
- Meditation For Dummies
  0-471-77774-9
- Osteoporosis For Dummies
  0-7645-7621-6
- Overcoming Anxiety For Dummies
  0-7645-5447-6
- Reiki For Dummies
  0-7645-9907-0
- Stress Management For Dummies
  0-7645-5144-2

EDUCATION, HISTORY, REFERENCE & TEST PREPARATION

0-7645-8381-6

0-7645-9554-7

Also available:
- The ACT For Dummies
  0-7645-9652-7
- Algebra For Dummies
  0-7645-5325-9
- Algebra Workbook For Dummies
  0-7645-8467-7
- Astronomy For Dummies
  0-7645-8465-0
- Calculus For Dummies
  0-7645-2498-4
- Chemistry For Dummies
  0-7645-5430-1
- Forensics For Dummies
  0-7645-5580-4

- Freemasons For Dummies
  0-7645-9796-5
- French For Dummies
  0-7645-5193-0
- Geometry For Dummies
  0-7645-5324-0
- Organic Chemistry I For Dummies
  0-7645-6902-3
- The SAT I For Dummies
  0-7645-7193-1
- Spanish For Dummies
  0-7645-5194-9
- Statistics For Dummies
  0-7645-5423-9

Get smart @ dummies.com®
- **Find a full list of Dummies titles**
- **Look into loads of FREE on-site articles**
- **Sign up for FREE eTips e-mailed to you weekly**
- **See what other products carry the Dummies name**
- **Shop directly from the Dummies bookstore**
- **Enter to win new prizes every month!**

* Separate Canadian edition also available
† Separate U.K. edition also available

Available wherever books are sold. For more information or to order direct: U.S. customers visit www.dummies.com or call 1-877-762-2974.
U.K. customers visit www.wileyeurope.com or call 0800 243407. Canadian customers visit www.wiley.ca or call 1-800-567-4797.